AZ SUPER SCA
GREAT BRITAIN
NORTHERN IRELAND

Journey Route Planning maps

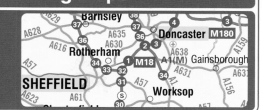

Airport plans

Access maps to principal Airports in Britain........205

Britain & Northern Ireland Road maps

Over 32,000 Index References

A

Abbas Combe. *Som* 4C 22
Abberley. *Worc* 4B 60
Abberley Common. *Worc* ..4B 60
Abberton. *Essx* 4D 54
Abberton. *Worc* 5D 61
Abberwick. *Nmbd* 3F 121
Abbess Roding. *Essx* 4F 53
Abbey. *Devn* 1E 13

Abersoch. *Gwyn* 3C
Abersychan. *Torf* 5F
Abertawe. *Swan*
......3F **31** & Swansea 2
Aberteifi. *Cdgn* 1B
Aberthin. *V Glam* 4D
Abertillery. *Blae* 5F
Abertridwr. *Cphy* 3E
Abertridwr. *Powy* 4C
Abertyleri. *Blae* 5F
Abertysswg. *Cphy* 5F

Including cities, towns, villages, hamlets and locations................206-232

Detailed Main Route maps

Index to Places of Interest

L

Lacock Abbey (SN15 2LG) 5E 35
Lady Lever Art Gallery (CH62 5EQ) 2F 83
Lady of the North (NE23 8AU) 2F 115
Laing Art Gallery (NE1 8AG) ...**Newcastle 197**
Lake District Nat. Pk. (LA9 7RL) 3E 103
Lakeside & Haverthwaite Railway (LA12 8AL) ...1C 96
Lamb House (TN31 7ES) 3D 28

Marwood
Mary Ard
Mary, Qu
Mary Ros
Max Gate
Megginch
Melbourn
Melford H
Mellersta
Melrose A

Full postcodes to easily locate popular places of interest on your SatNav 233-235

City and Town centre maps

Motorway Junctions

Junction	M1	
2	Northbound	No exit, access from A1 only
	Southbound	No access, exit to A1 only
4	Northbound	No exit, access from A41 only
	Southbound	No access, exit to A41 only
6a	Northbound	No exit, access from M25 only
	Southbound	No access, exit to M25 only

Details of motorway junctions with limited interchange......236

Sea Port & Channel Tunnel plans

Safety Camera Information

Details of Safety Camera symbols used on the maps, and the responsible use of Camera information ......Inside back cover

EDITION 24 2015
Copyright © Geographers' A-Z Map Company Ltd.
Telephone: 01732 781000 (Enquiries & Trade Sales)
01732 783422 (Retail Sales)

A-Z AZ AtoZ
registered trade marks of
Geographers' A-Z Map Company Ltd

www./az.co.uk

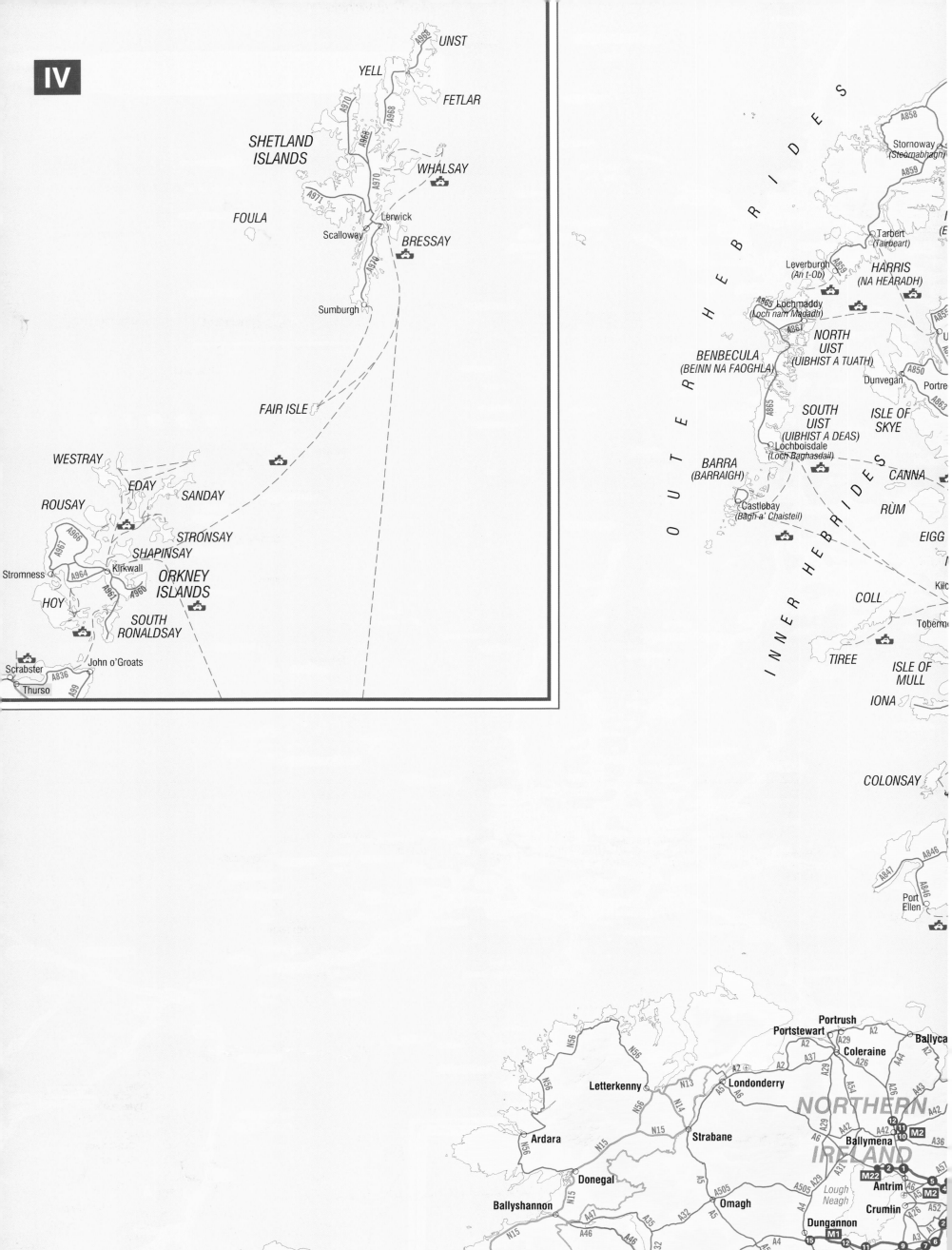

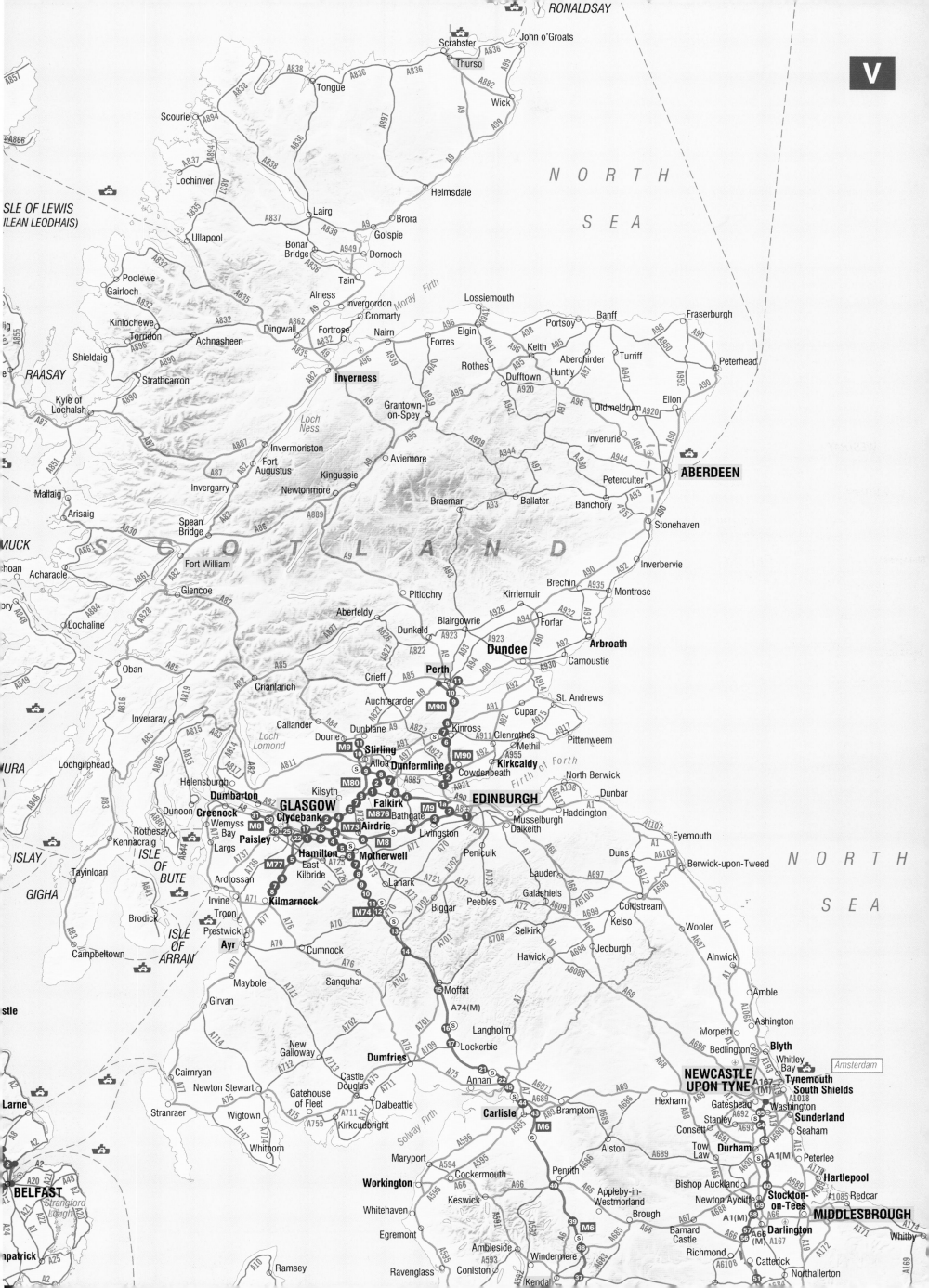

This chart shows the distance in miles and journey time between two cities or towns in Great Britain. Each route has been calculated using a combination of motorways, primary routes and other major roads. This is normally the quickest, though not always the shortest route.

Average journey times are calculated whilst driving at the maximum speed limit. These times are approximate and do not include traffic congestion or convenience breaks.

To find the distance and journey time between two cities or towns, follow a horizontal line and vertical column until they meet each other.

For example, the 285 mile journey from London to Penzance is approximately 4 hours and 59 minutes.

Northern Ireland

Journey times

	1:01	0:53	1:41	1:14	1:07	1:13	0:30
Antrim		1:32	1:06	1:39	0:31	0:46	0:57
	Armagh		2:09	0:52	2:00	1:43	1:11
43		Coleraine		1:29	1:37	0:39	1:38
40	61		Enniskillen		2:09	0:54	1:33
86	49	94		Londonderry		1:15	0:51
55	69	31	60		Newry		1:16
53	19	92	69	88		Omagh	
54	35	65	27	34	54		Belfast
22	41	56	84	72	37	68	

Distance in miles

Belfast to London = 440m / 9:46h (excluding ferry)
Belfast to Glasgow = 104m / 4:46h (excluding ferry)

Britain

Journey times

Distance in miles

Scale to Map Pages

1:158,400 = 2.5 miles to 1 inch (2.54 cm) **/ 1.6 km to 1 cm**

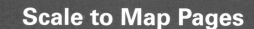

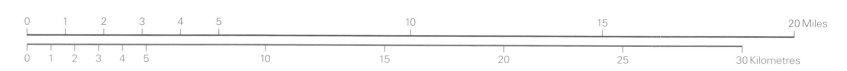

Reference

Motorway
Autoroute
Autobahn
`M1`

Motorway Under Construction
Autoroute en construction
Autobahn im Bau

Motorway Proposed
Autoroute prévue
Geplante Autobahn

Motorway Junctions with Numbers
Unlimited Interchange `4`
Limited Interchange `5`

Autoroute échangeur numéroté
Echangeur complet
Echangeur partiel

Autobahnanschlußstelle mit Nummer
Unbeschränkter Fahrtrichtungswechsel
Beschränkter Fahrtrichtungswechsel

Motorway Service Area (with fuel station)
with access from one carriageway only
(S)
(S)

Aire de services d'autoroute (avec station service)
accessible d'un seul côté

Rastplatz oder Raststätte (mit tankstelle)
Einbahn

Major Road Service Areas (with fuel station) with 24 hour facilities
Primary Route (S)   Class A Road (S)

Aire de services sur route prioriataire (avec station service) Ouverte 24h sur 24
Route à grande circulation   Route de type A

Raststätte (mit tankstelle) Durchgehend geöffnet
Hauptverkehrsstraße   A- Straße

Truckstop (selection of)
Sélection d'aire pour poids lourds
Auswahl von Fernfahrerrastplatz
(T)

Primary Route
Route à grande circulation
Hauptverkehrsstraße
`A41`

Primary Route Junction with Number
Echangeur numéroté
Hauptverkehrsstraßenkreuzung mit Nummer
`5`

Primary Route Destination
Route prioritaire, direction
Hauptverkehrsstraße Richtung
DOVER

Dual Carriageways (A & B roads)
Route à double chaussées séparées (route A & B)
Zweispurige Schnellstraße (A- und B- Straßen)

Class A Road
Route de type A
A-Straße
`A129`

Class B Road
Route de type B
B-Straße
`B177`

Narrow Major Road (passing places)
Route prioritaire étroite (possibilité de dépassement)
Schmale Hauptverkehrsstraße (mit Überholmöglichkeit)

Major Roads Under Construction
Route prioritaire en construction
Hauptverkehrsstaße im Bau

Major Roads Proposed
Route prioritaire prévue
Geplante Hauptverkehrsstraße

Safety Cameras with Speed Limits
Single Camera `30`
Multiple Cameras located along road `50`
Single & Multiple Variable Speed Cameras (V) (V)

Radars de contrôle de vitesse
Radar simple
Radars multiples situés le long de la route
Radars simples et multiples de contrôle de vitesse variable

Sicherheitskameras mit Tempolimit
Einzelne Kamera
Mehrere Kameras entlang der Straße
Einzelne und mehrere Kameras für variables Tempolimit

Fuel Station
Station service
Tankstelle

Gradient 1:5 (20%) **& steeper**
(ascent in direction of arrow)
Pente égale ou supérieure à 20% (dans le sens de la montée)
20% Steigung und steiler (in Pfeilrichtung)

Toll
Barrière de péage
Gebührenpflichtig
`TOLL`

Mileage between markers
Distence en miles entre les flèches
Strecke zwischen Markierungen in Meilen
`8`

Railway and Station
Voie ferrée et gare
Eisenbahnlinie und Bahnhof

Level Crossing and Tunnel
Passage à niveau et tunnel
Bahnübergang und Tunnel

River or Canal
Rivière ou canal
Fluß oder Kanal

County or Unitary Authority Boundary
Limite de comté ou de division administrative
Grafschafts- oder Verwaltungsbezirksgrenze

National Boundary
Frontière nationale
Landesgrenze

Built-up Area
Agglomération
Geschlossene Ortschaft

Village or Hamlet
Village ou hameau
Dorf oder Weiler

Wooded Area
Zone boisée
Waldgebiet

Spot Height in Feet
Altitude (en pieds)
Höhe in Fuß
• 813

Relief above 400' (122m)
Relief par estompage au-dessus de 400' (122m)
Reliefschattierung über 400' (122m)

National Grid Reference (kilometres)
Coordonnées géographiques nationales (Kilomètres)
Nationale geographische Koordinaten (Kilometer)
100

Page Continuation
Suite à la page indiquée
Seitenfortsetzung
`48`

Area covered by Main Route map
Répartition des cartes des principaux axes routiers
Von Karten mit Hauptverkehrsstrecken
MAIN ROUTE 180

Area covered by Town Plan
Ville ayant un plan à la page indiquée
Von Karten mit Stadtplänen erfaßter Bereich
SEE PAGE 194

Tourist Information Information Touristeninformationen i

Airport
Aéroport
Flughafen

Airfield
Terrain d'aviation
Flugplatz

Heliport
Héliport
Hubschrauberlandeplatz

Battle Site and Date
Champ de bataille et date
Schlachtfeld und Datum
1066

Castle (open to public)
Château (ouvert au public)
Schloß / Burg (für die Öffentlichkeit zugänglich)

Castle with Garden (open to public)
Château avec parc (ouvert au public)
Schloß mit Garten (für die Öffentlichkeit zugänglich)

Cathedral, Abbey, Church, Friary, Priory
Cathédrale, abbaye, église, monastère, prieuré
Kathedrale, Abtei, Kirche, Mönchskloster, Kloster

Country Park
Parc régional
Landschaftspark

Ferry (vehicular, sea)
      (vehicular, river)
      (foot only)

Bac (véhicules, mer)
      (véhicules, rivière)
      (piétons)

Fähre (auto, meer)
      (auto, fluß)
      (nur für Personen)

Garden (open to public)
Jardin (ouvert au public)
Garten (für die Offentlichkeit zugänglich)

Golf Course (9 hole) `9`   (18 hole) `18`
Terrain de golf (9 trous)   (18 trous)
Golfplatz (9 Löcher)   (18 Löcher)

Historic Building (open to public)
Monument historique (ouvert au public)
Historisches Gebäude (für die Öffentlichkeit zugänglich)

Historic Building with Garden (open to public)
Monument historique avec jardin (ouvert au public)
Historisches Gebäude mit Garten (für die Öffentlichkeit zugänglich)

Horse Racecourse
Hippodrome
Pferderennbahn

Lighthouse
Phare
Leuchtturm

Motor Racing Circuit
Circuit Automobile
Automobilrennbahn

Museum, Art Gallery
Musée
Museum, Galerie

National Park
Parc national
Nationalpark

National Trust Property
      (open) `NT`
      (restricted opening) `NT`
      (National Trust for Scotland) `NTS` `NTS`

National Trust Property
      (ouvert)
      (heures d'ouverture)
      (National Trust for Scotland)

National Trust- Eigentum
      (geöffnet)
      (beschränkte Öffnungszeit)
      (National Trust for Scotland)

Nature Reserve or Bird Sanctuary
Réserve naturelle botanique ou ornithologique
Natur- oder Vogelschutzgebiet

Nature Trail or Forest Walk
Chemin forestier, piste verte
Naturpfad oder Waldweg

Place of Interest   *Monument* •
Site, curiosité
Sehenswürdigkeit

Picnic Site
Lieu pour pique-nique
Picknickplatz

Railway, Steam or Narrow Gauge
Chemin de fer, à vapeur ou à voie étroite
Eisenbahn, Dampf- oder Schmalspurbahn

Theme Park
Centre de loisirs
Vergnügungspark

Tourist Information Centre
Syndicat d'initiative
Information

Viewpoint (360 degrees)   (180 degrees)
Vue panoramique (360 degrés)   (180 degrés)
Aussichtspunkt (360 Grade)   (180 Grade)

Visitor Information Centre
Centre d'information touristique
Besucherzentrum
`V`

Wildlife Park
Réserve de faune
Wildpark

Windmill
Moulin à vent
Windmühle

Zoo or Safari Park
Parc ou réserve zoologique
Zoo oder Safari-Park

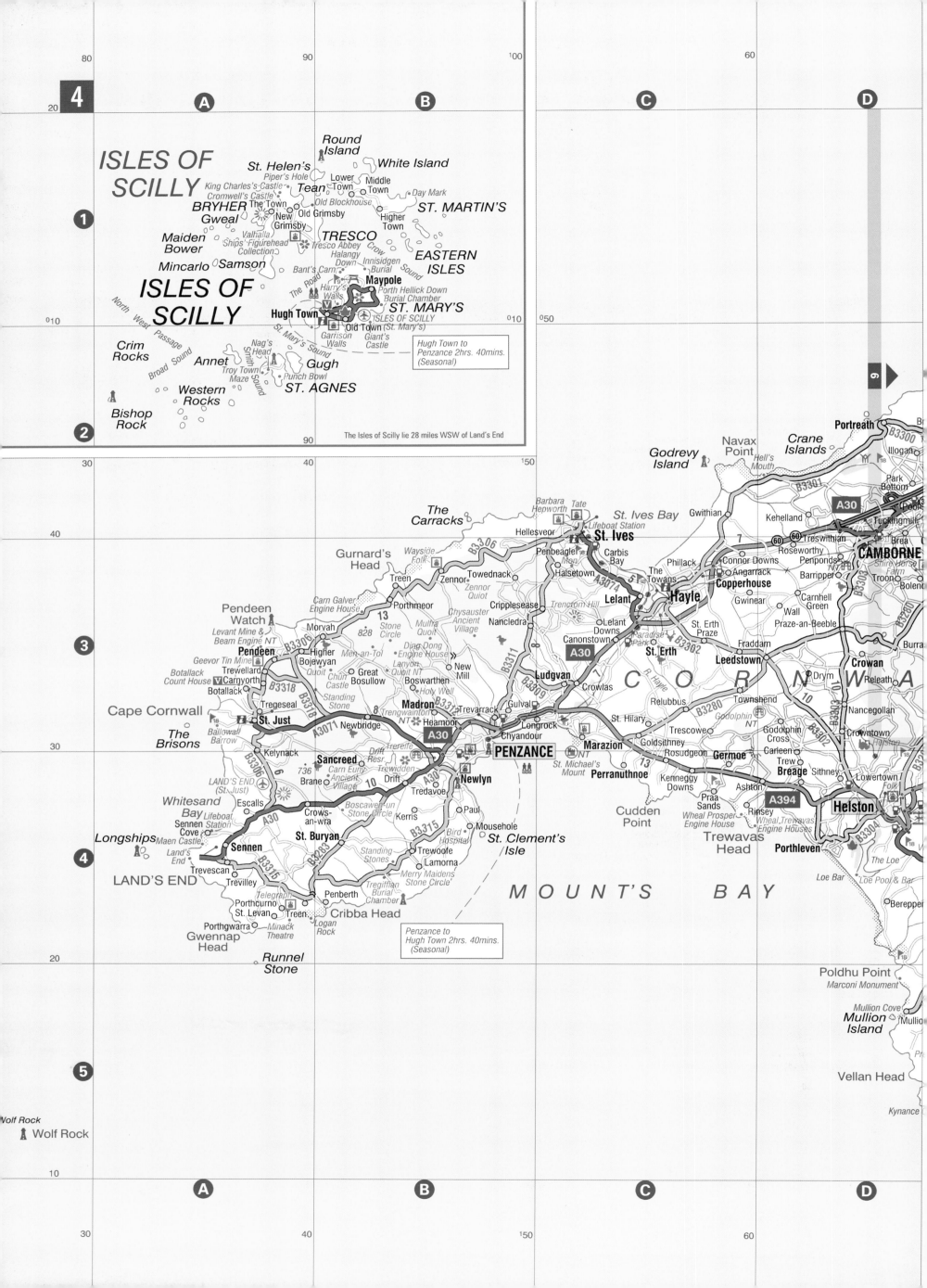

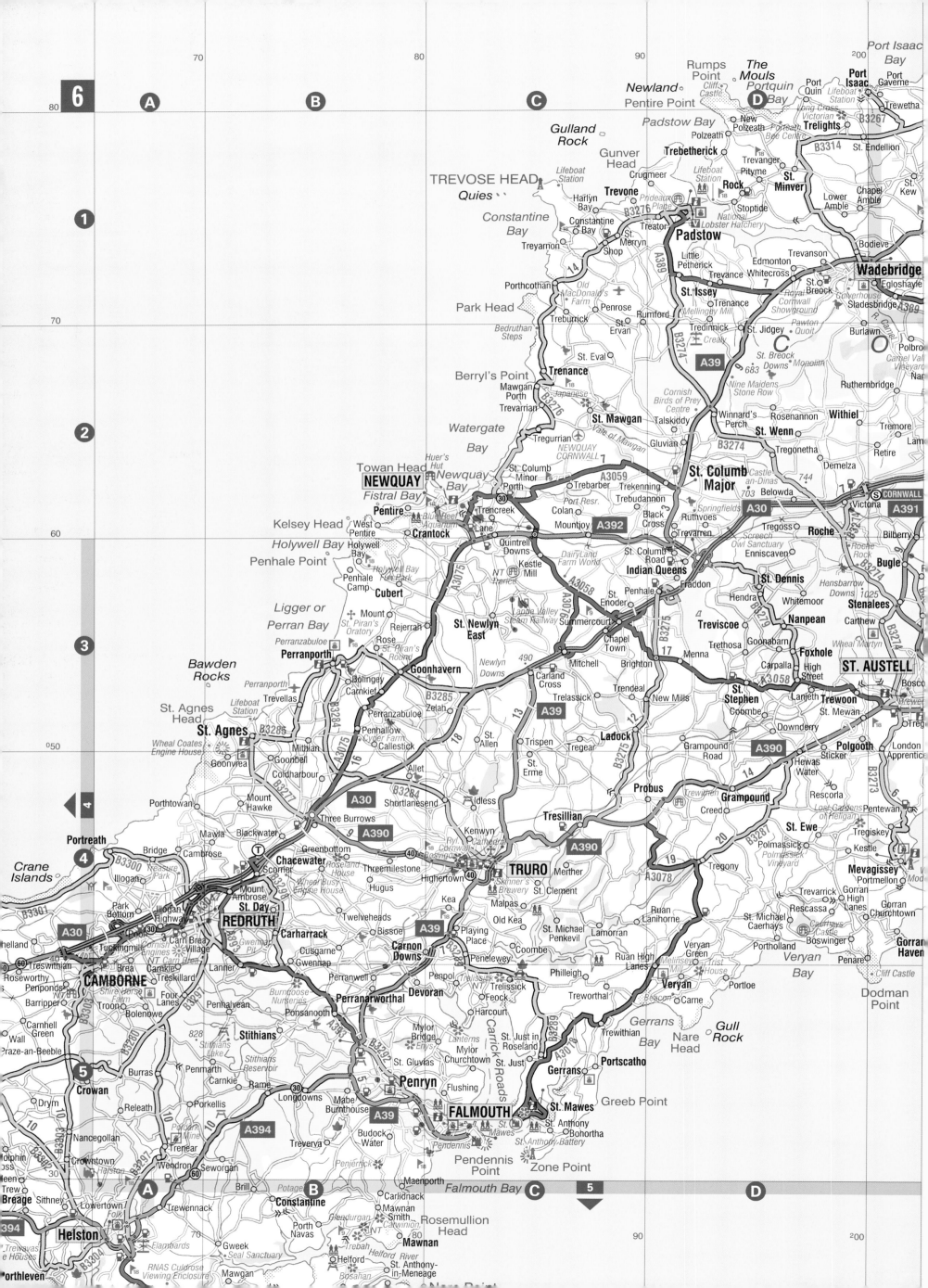

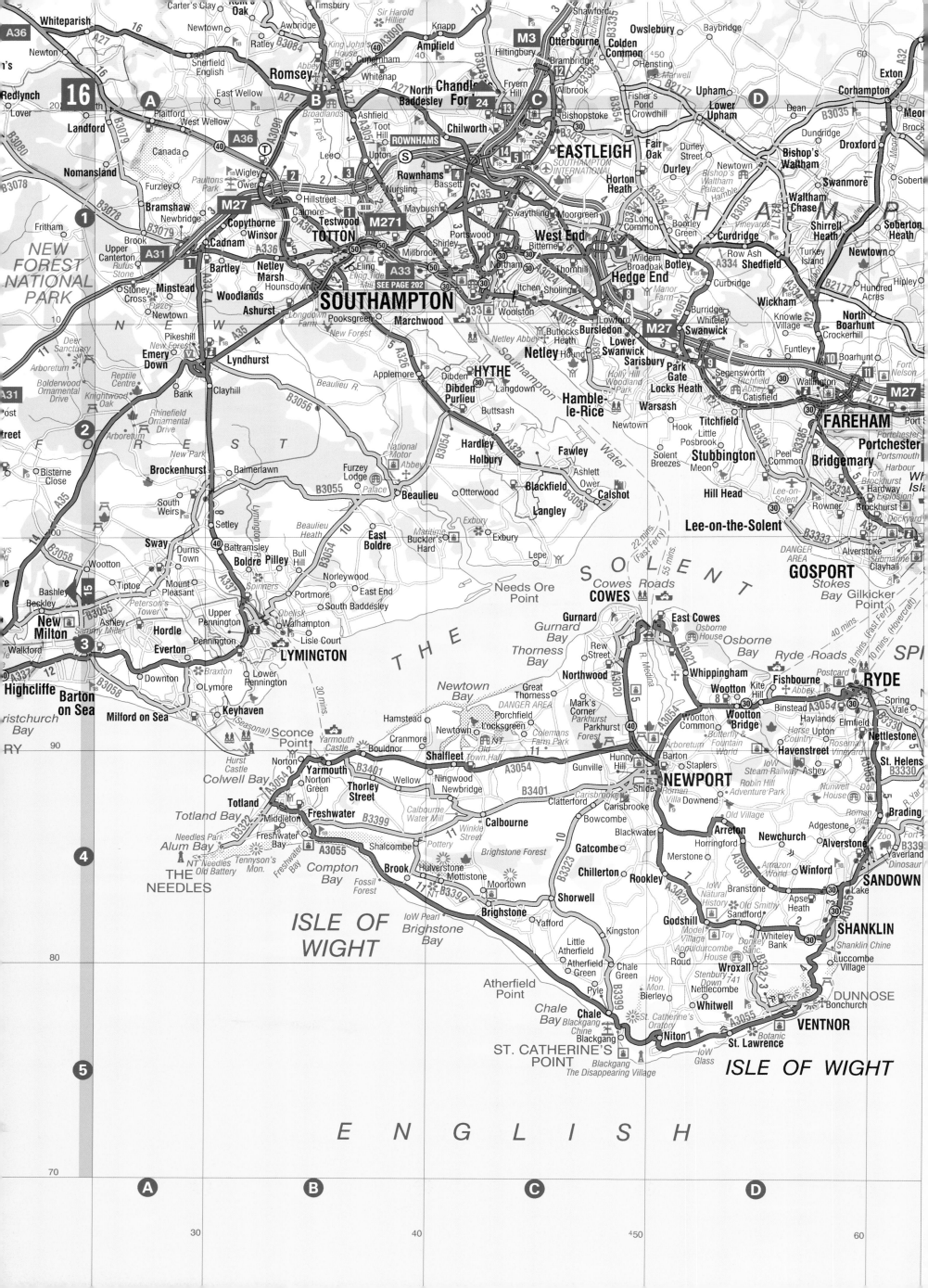

200

10

20

30

60

1

B R I S T O L

¹50

North West
Point
LUNDY

*Lundy
Marine
Conservation
Zone*

2

Lundy to:
Bideford 2hrs. (Seasonal)
Ilfracombe 2hrs.
(Seasonal)

South West
Point

Rat Island

40

3

BARNSTAPLE

OR

30

4 HARTLAND POINT Windbury BIDEFORD BAY
Point

Titchberry
Hartland Clovelly
Abbey Cheristow *Court* **Clovelly**
Lavender *Clovelly
Hartland Velly Donkeys
Hartland **Hartland** Higher
Quay Clovelly **Buck's Mills**
Stoke Natcott 710
B3248 24 Milky Way
Docton Mill Adventure Park Buck's
Milford Philham Cross
A39 Pa
Elmscott Edistone Welsford
Woolfardisworthy
or Woolsery
Alminstone Parkham
Cross Ash

20 South Hole
10 18 R. Torridge Ashmansworthy
Knaps Welcombe 771 East
Longpeak Meddon Putford
Mead West Putford
Gooseham Woolley East
Youlstone
Morwenstow Shop Eastcott West Dinworthy Gnome Reserve &
5 *Hawker's Hut* Youlstone Wild Flower Garden
Higher Sharpnose Woodford **CORNWALL** Colso
Point *Upper* **Bradworthy**
Tamar
Lower Sharpnose *Tamar* *Tamar Lake*
Point *Lakes* Alfardisworthy R. **Sutcombe** Venngre
Coombe **Kilkhampton** Thurdon *Lower* Waldon
Stibb B3254 *Tamar Lake* Soldon
10 A39 Cross

A **B** **10** **C** **D**
A388
Bude Poughill Dexbeer
200 Bush Lana
10 *Stratton* Hersham Holsworthy
1643 Grimscott Beacon Wood
Flexbury **Stratton** 30
Bude Bay Launcells Pancrasweek Chilsworthy
Lynstone 8
Holsworthy

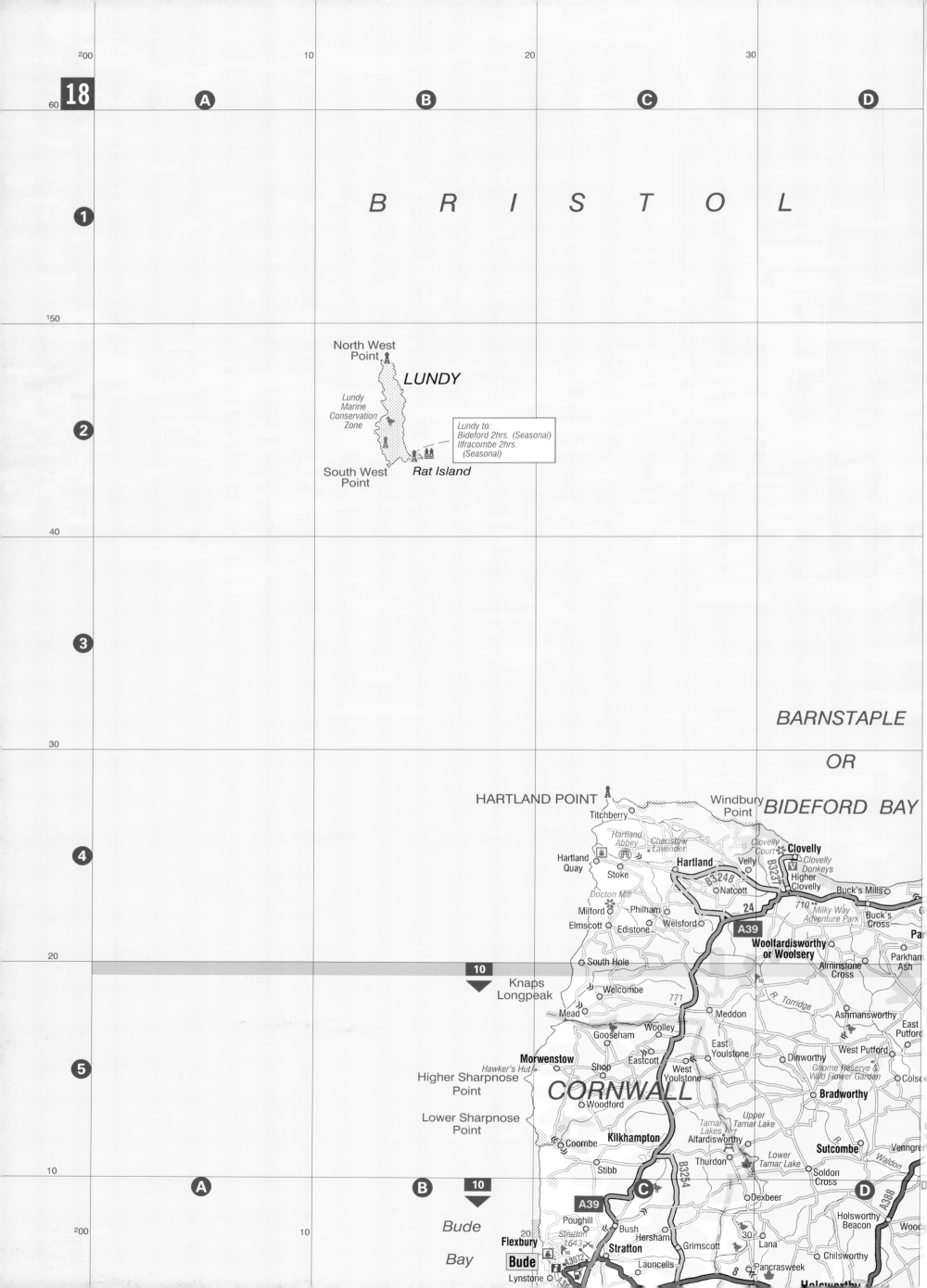

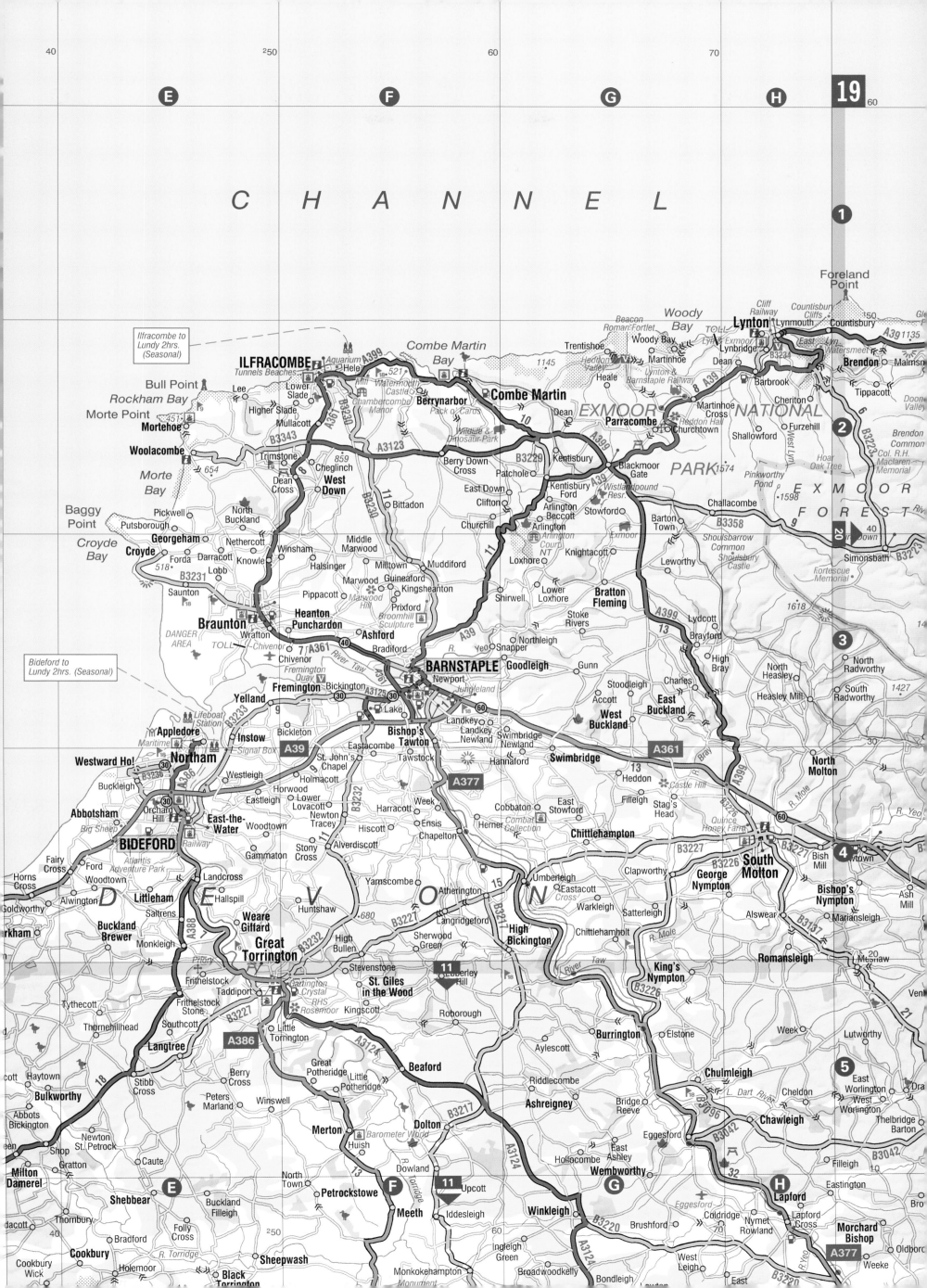

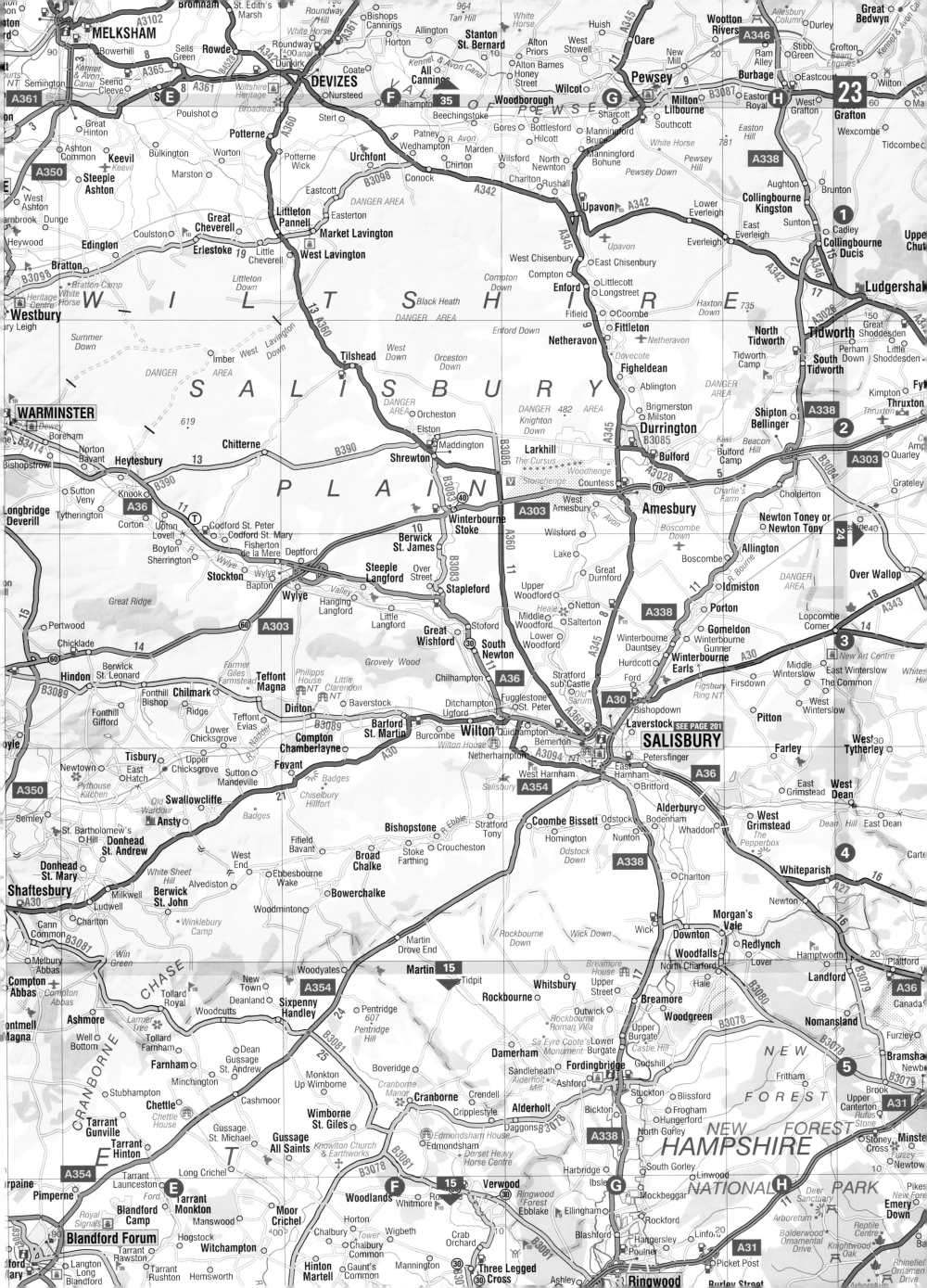

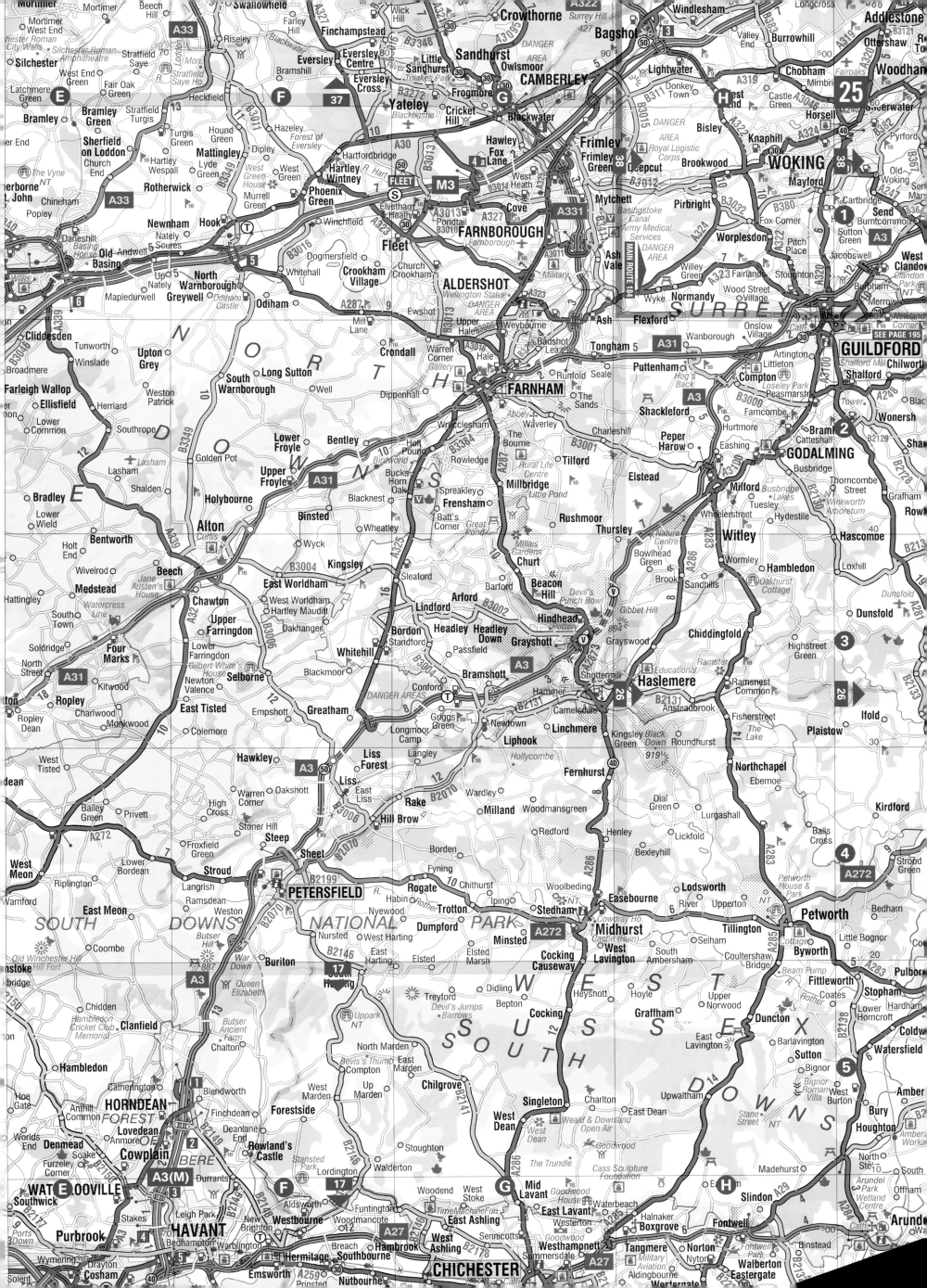

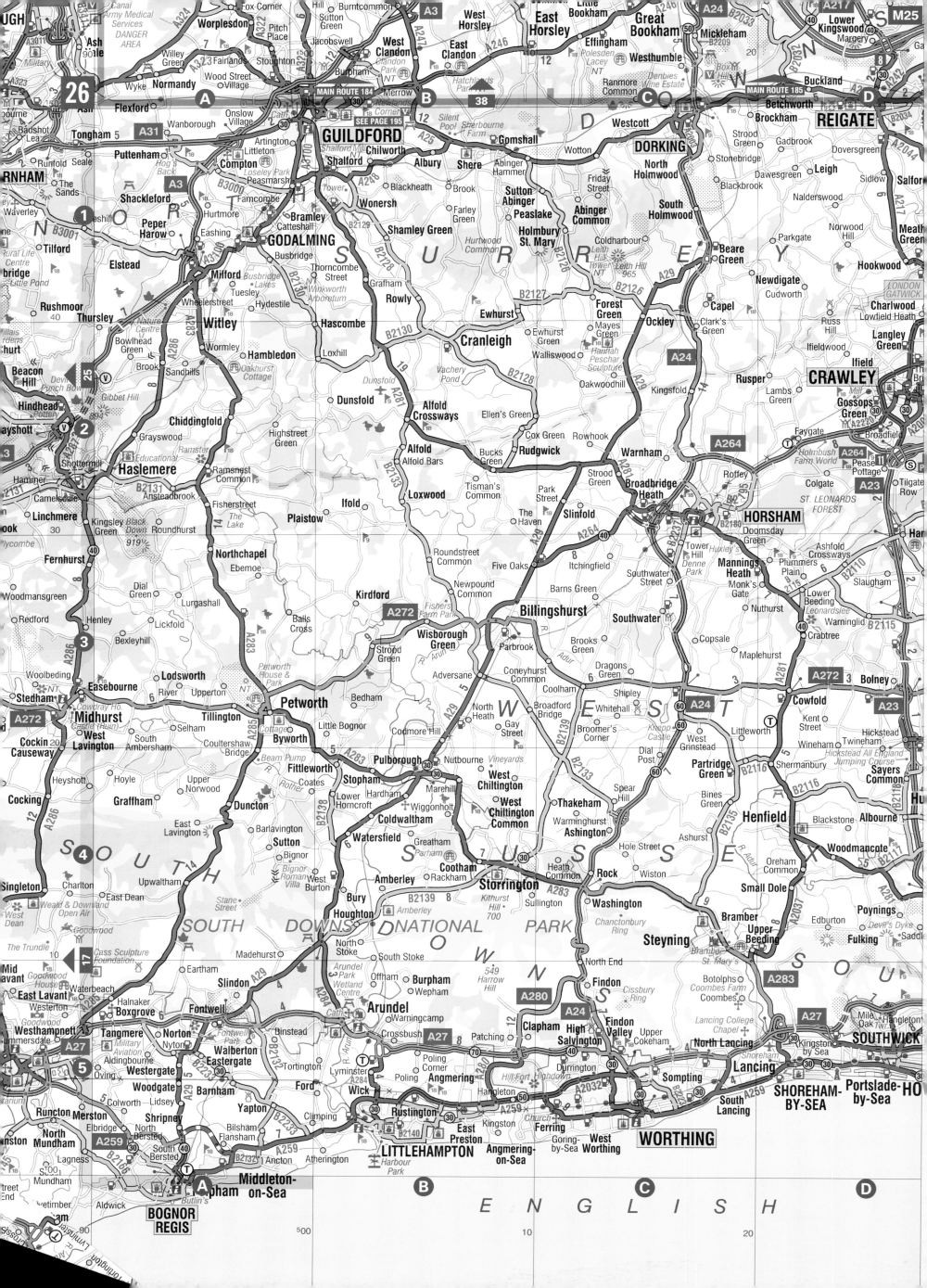

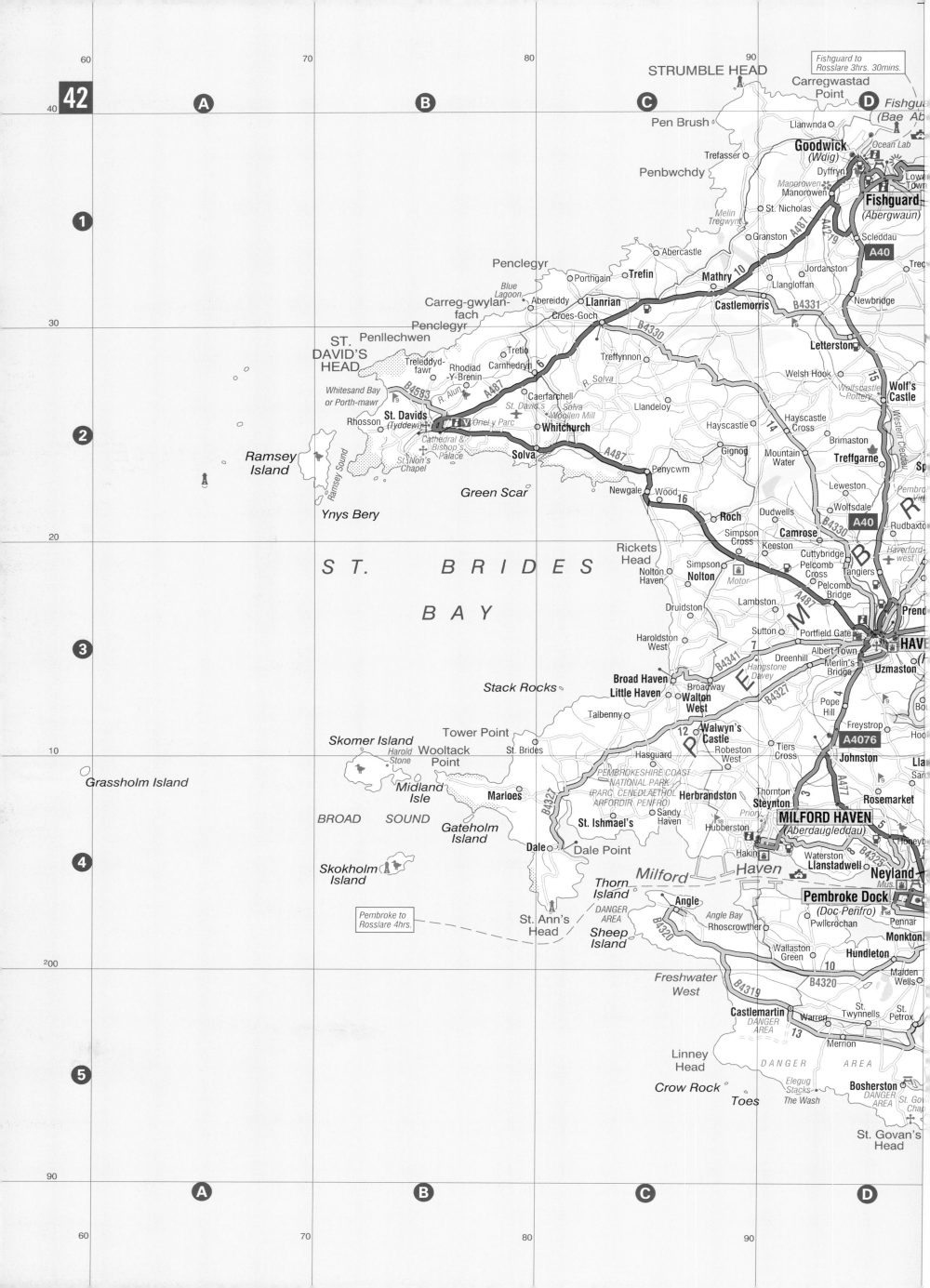

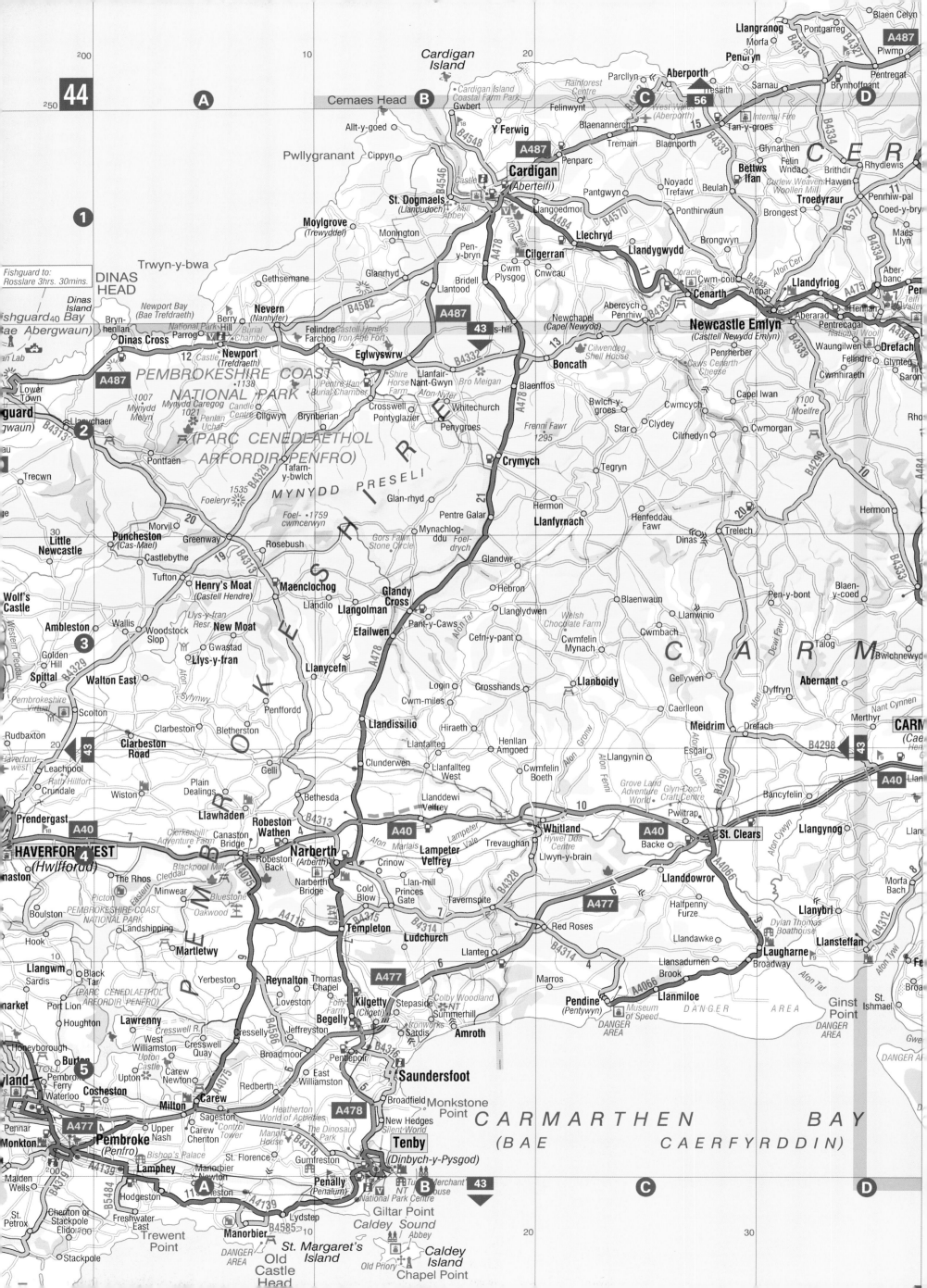

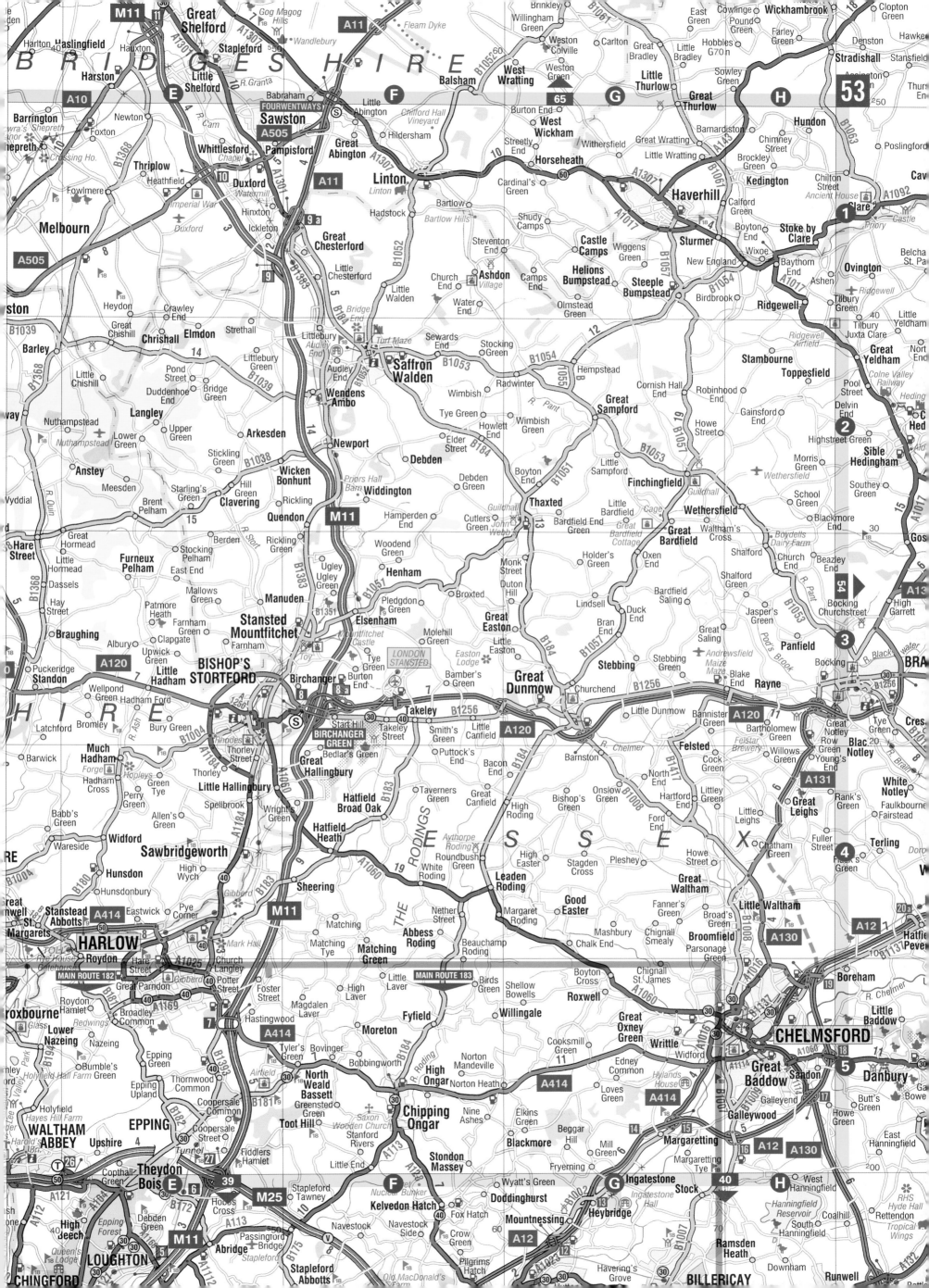

C A R D I G A N   B A Y

(B A E   C E R E D I G I O N)

Aberaeron

New Quay
(Ceinewydd)
Marine Wildlife Centre

Ffos-y-ffin

Llwyncelyn

Maen-y-
groes

Gilfachreda

Oakford
(Derwen Gam)

Cwmtudu

Cross Inn

New Quay
Honey Farm

Llanarth

Geneva

Nanternis

Caerwedros

Pen-cae

Ynys-Lochtyn

Llwyndafydd

Blaen Celyn

Synod Inn
(Post-Mawr)

Mydroilyn

Llangranog

Morfa

Pontgarreg

Plwmp

Penbryn

Pentregat

A487

Parcllyn

Aberporth

Tresaith

Sarnau

Brynhoffnant

Talgarreg

C

Cardigan
Island

Cemaes Head

Cardigan Island
Coastal Farm Park

Rainforest
Centre

West Wales
Aberporth

Internal Fire

Gwbert

Felinwynt

Allt-y-goed

A

Y Ferwig

44
Blaenannerch

B

15

Tan-y-groes

C

Capel
Cynon

Bwlch-y-fadfa

D

Pwllvgranant

Cippyn

B4548

A487

Penparc

Tremain

Blaenporth

B4333

Glynarthen

Cardw Weavers
Woollen Mill

Cardigan
(Aberteifi)

Castle

Noyadd
Trefawr

Beulah

Bettws
Ifan

Felin
Hawen

Brithdir

Rhydlewis

Ffostrasol

Pont-sian

St. Dogmaels
(Llandudoch)

Mill
Abbey

Langoedmor

Pantgwyn

Ponthirwaun

Troedyraur

Penrhiw-pal

Coed-y-bryn

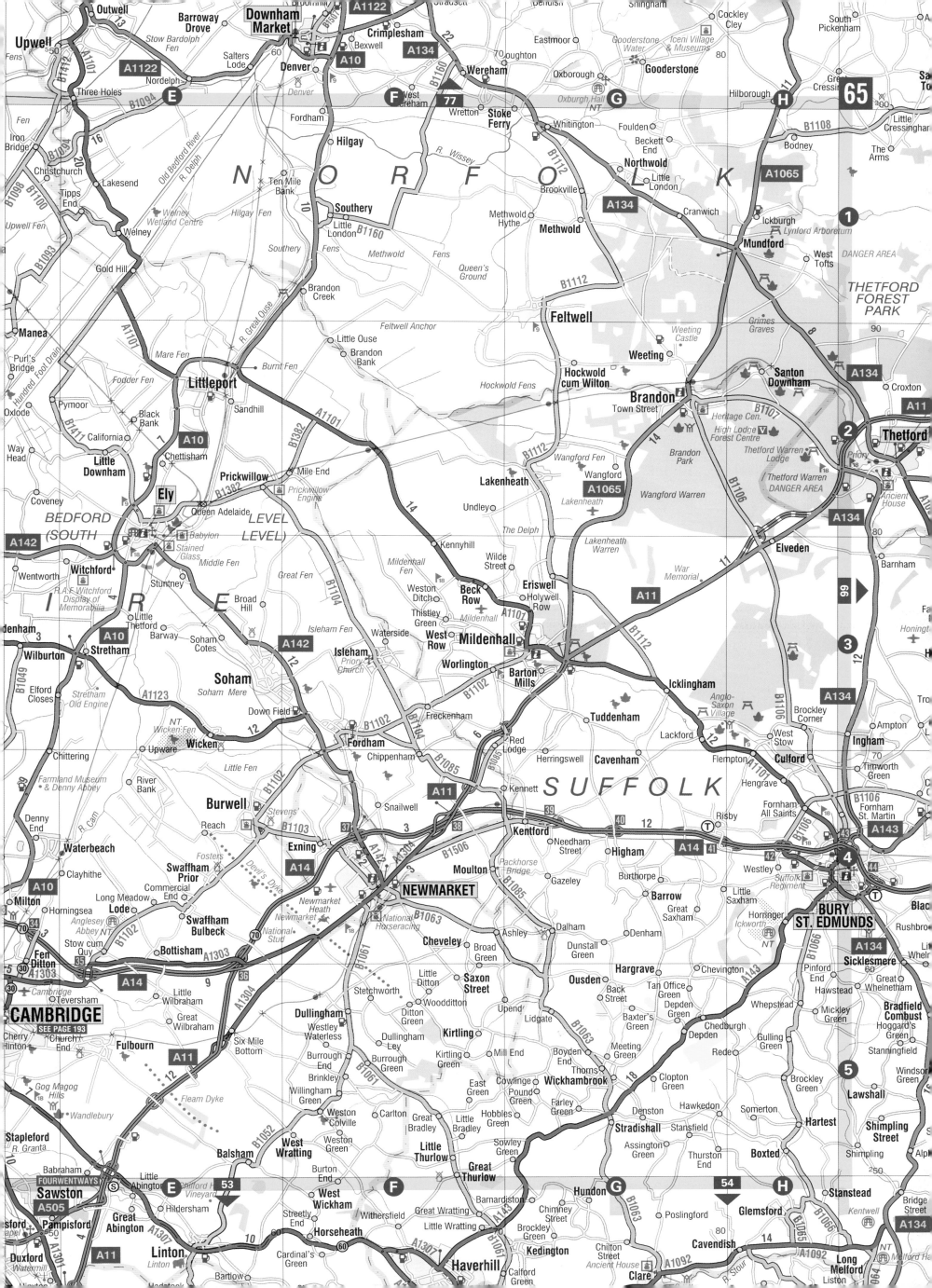

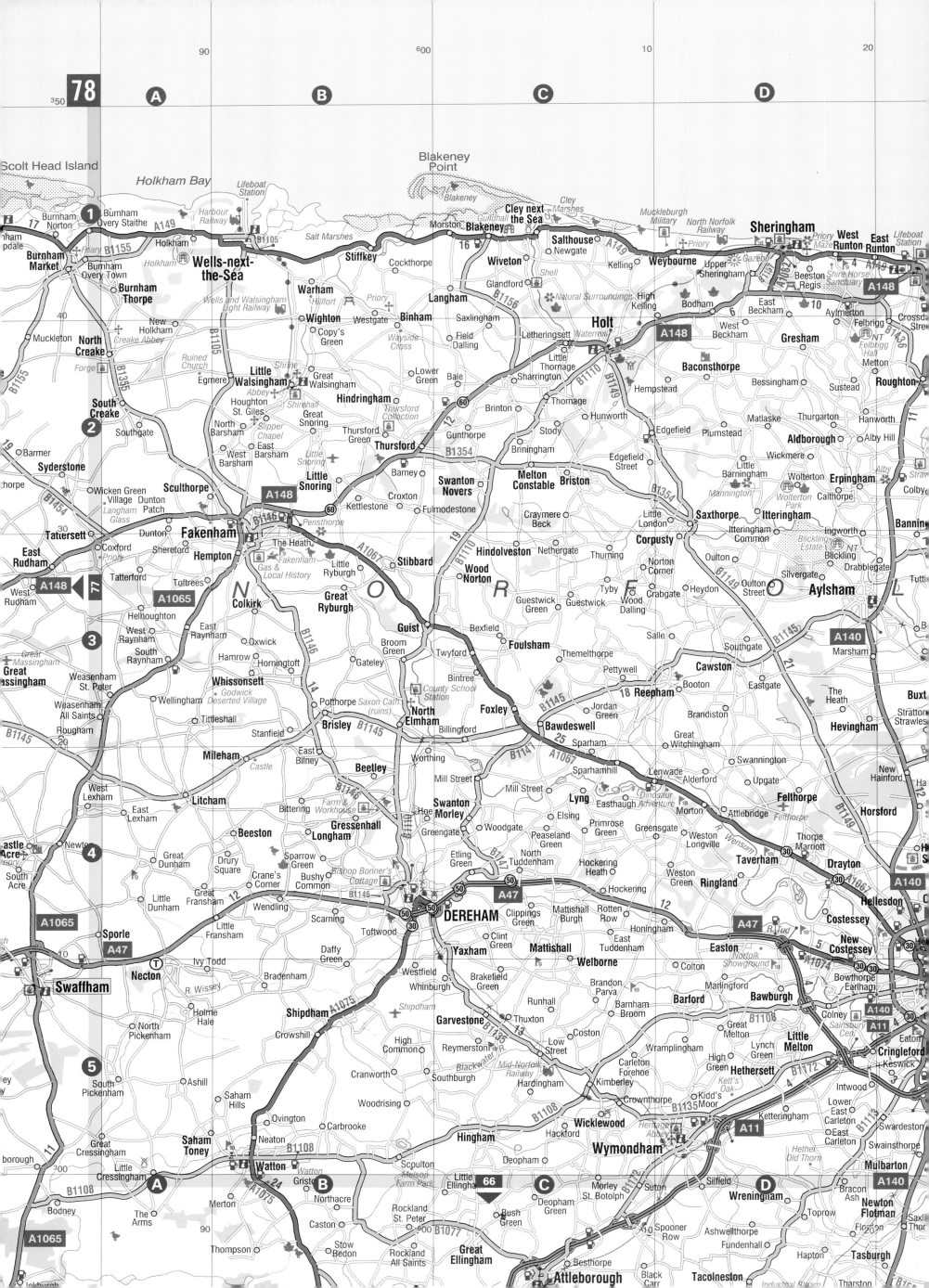

NORTH

SEA

CROMER
Foulness
A149
Overstrand
Northrepps Sidestrand
Frogshall Trimingham
Gimingham Cliftonville
Thorpe Mundesley
Market Stow
Southrepps Lower Paston
Street
Trunch Knapton Bacton
Bradfield Broomholm Green
Antingham Edingthorpe Bacton Keswick
Suffield Swafield Old Hall Pollard Walcott
Street Street Ostend
Lyngate Little Witton
London Bridge Ridlington Happisburgh
Felmingham Spa Happisburgh Whimpwell Lifeboat
Common Green Station
North Walsham Crostwight Eccles on Sea
Tungate White Horse Happisburgh Hempstead
Common Meeting Common
Norfolk House Hill Honing Ingham Sea Palling
Motorcycle East Corner
Skeyton Withergate Ruston Ingham Waxham
Corner Bengate Briggate
Westwick Lyngate Calthorpe
Skeyton Worstead Dilham Street
Swanton Sloley Smallburgh Stalham Hickling
Abbott Frankfort Anchor Stalham Horsey
RAF Coltishall Street Green
Lamas Pennygate Sutton Horsey
Scottow Barton Hickling NT
Tunstead Turf Wood Hickling Horsey
Bure Valley Ashmanhaugh Neatishead Street Heath Broad Mere
Railway Threehammer Irstead Catfield Hickling
Little Common Catfield Common
Hautbois Wroxham Sharp East
The Barns Cangate Street Somerton
Heath Hoveton How Hill Ludham West
Coltishall Hall Upper Potter Somerton Winterton-
Horstead Broads Street Ludham Heigham Damgate on-Sea
Waterloo Belaugh BeWILDerwood Bastwick West Martham
Frettenham Hoveton Toad Hole Johnson Thorne Cess Somerton Hemsby Hole
Wroxham Horning Cott. Street St. Benet's 13 Newport
Spixworth Upper Abbey Repps Hemsby
Crostwick Street Thurne Rollesby Ormesby
Woodbastwick Fleggburgh St. Margaret Scratby
Rackheath Salhouse Ranworth (Burgh California
New Pilson St. Margaret) Ormesby
NORWICH Rackheath Fairhaven Green Clippesby St. Michael Caister
INTERNATIONAL Cargate Roman
Catton Panxworth Green Billockby Filby Caister-
SEE PAGE 200 South Thrigby on-Sea
NORWICH Little Blofield Walsham Upton Mautby
Sprowston Plumstead Heath Pedham Fishley West West
Thorpe Great North End Caister
End Plumstead Hemblington Burlingham Acle Stokesby Runham Great
Thorpe Witton Damgate Yarmouth
St. Andrew Blofield Moulton GREAT
Thorpe Strumpshaw Beighton St. Mary Stracey YARMOUTH
Hamlet Brundall Lingwood Tunstall Arms Halvergate THE Sea
Trowse Postwick South Marshes Life
Newton Burlingham Halvergate BROADS Southtown Model
Kirby Surlingham Buckenham Wickhampton Burgh Village
Bedon Bramerton Berney Castle
Rockland Hassingham Southwood Arms Bradwell
Arminghall St. Mary Freethorpe Burgh Gorleston-
Caister Helfington Castle on-Sea
St. Edmund Claxton Cantley Limpenhoe Belton Browston
Dunston Ashby Langley Green
Upper Framingham St. Mary Green Langley Redwings Hopton
Stoke Pigot Carleton Street Horse Sanctuary on Sea
Poringland Framingham St. Peter Hardley Fritton Bunker's
Stoke Earl Yelverton Thurlton Street Reedham Fritton Hill The
Holy Cross Bergh Nogdam Lake Dell
West Apton End Lound
Poringland Alpington Herringfleet
Howe Chedgrave Norton Lower Blundeston
Brooke The Loddon Subcourse Thurlton Corton
Ling Thurlton Pleasurewood
Shotesham Sisland Thorpe Somerleyton Hills
Saxlingham Mundham Hales B1136 Haddiscoe
Nethergate Seething Stubbs Maypole
Saxlingham Kirstead Green Green
Green Green Raveningham
Seething Station A1117
Control Tower LOWESTOFT

NORTH

SEA

Theddlethorpe
St. Helen

Seal Sanctuary &
Wildlife Centre

Mablethorpe
Lifeboat Station
Ye Olde
Curiosity

Trusthorpe

Sutton on Sea

Sandilands

Thorpe

altby
Marsh

A1111 Hannah

Markby

R   E

Thurlby   Huttoft   Anderby
Creek
Drainage
Anderby

arlesthorpe   Mumby   Authorpe
Cumberworth   Row

Helsey   Chapel
St. Leonards

Bonthorpe

Hogsthorpe

Willoughby

Slackholme
Sloothby   End   Hardys
Animal
Hasthorpe   Farm

Addlethorpe   Ingoldmells

Ingoldmells
Point

elton
Marsh

Orby   Orby   Marsh   Skegness
(Ingoldmells)
Water
Leisure Park
Winthorpe

Seathorne

Burgh
le Marsh   A158   Church
Farm   Natureland
Seal Sanctuary

Bottoms
Model Village   Pleasure Beach

SKEGNESS

Thorpe   Croft
St. Peter

Seacroft

Croft Marsh

Bateman's
Brewery   Magdalen   Gibraltar Point

Wainfleet
All Saints   Gibraltar

St. Mary
ey's Toft

A52

DANGER AREA

Deeps

Boston

Scolt Head
Island

Brancaster Bay

Holme
Dunes

Holkham B

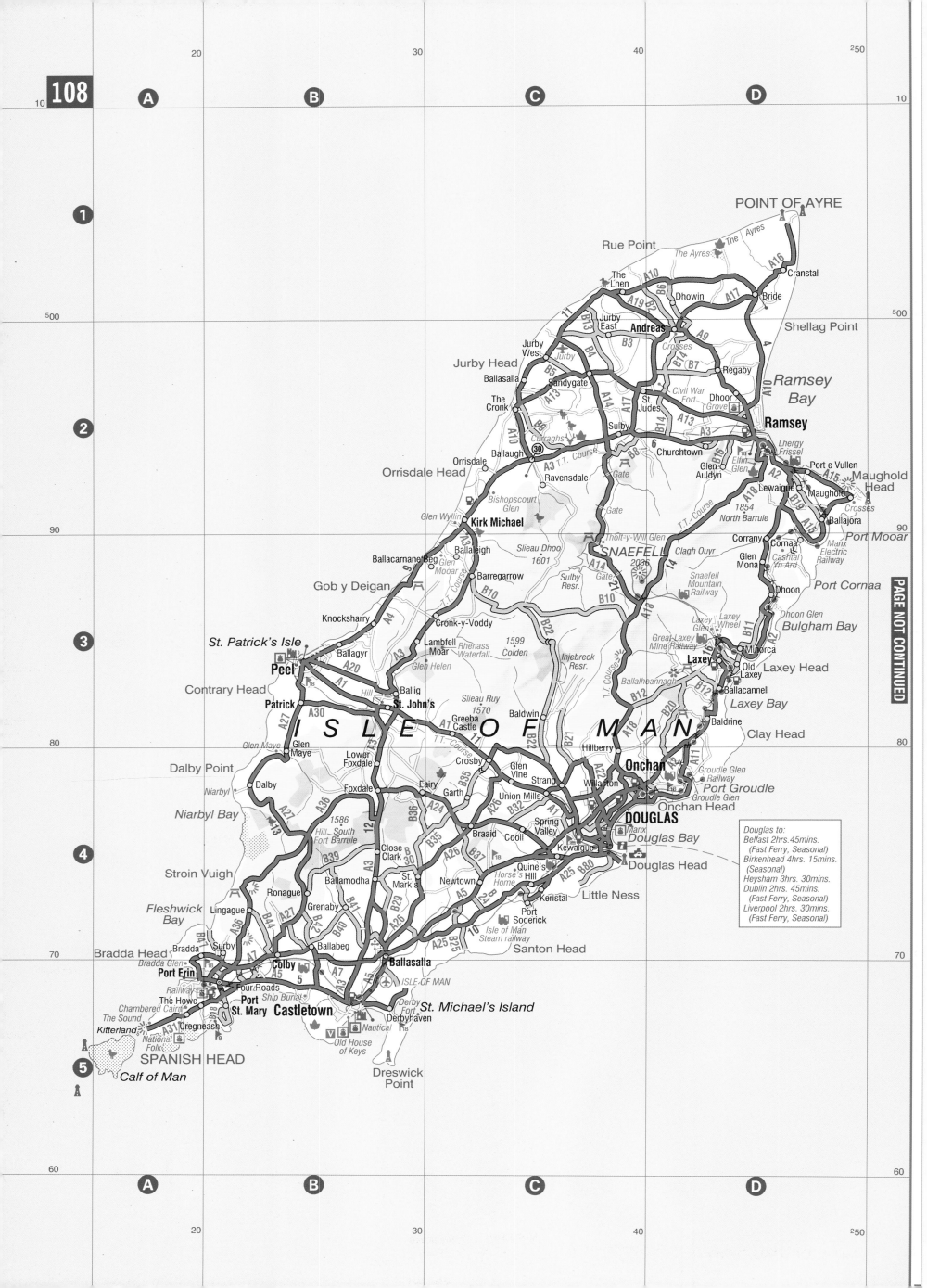

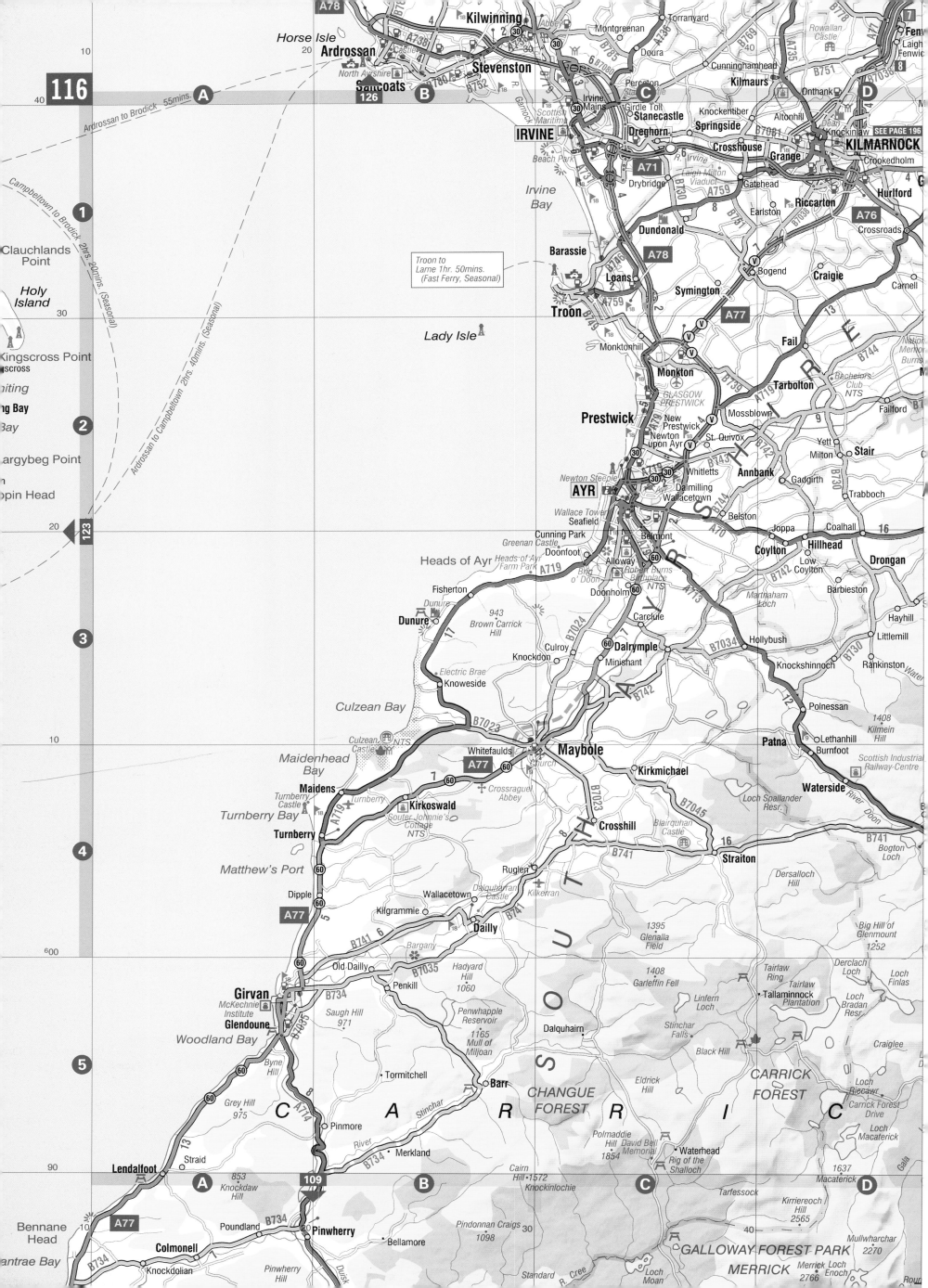

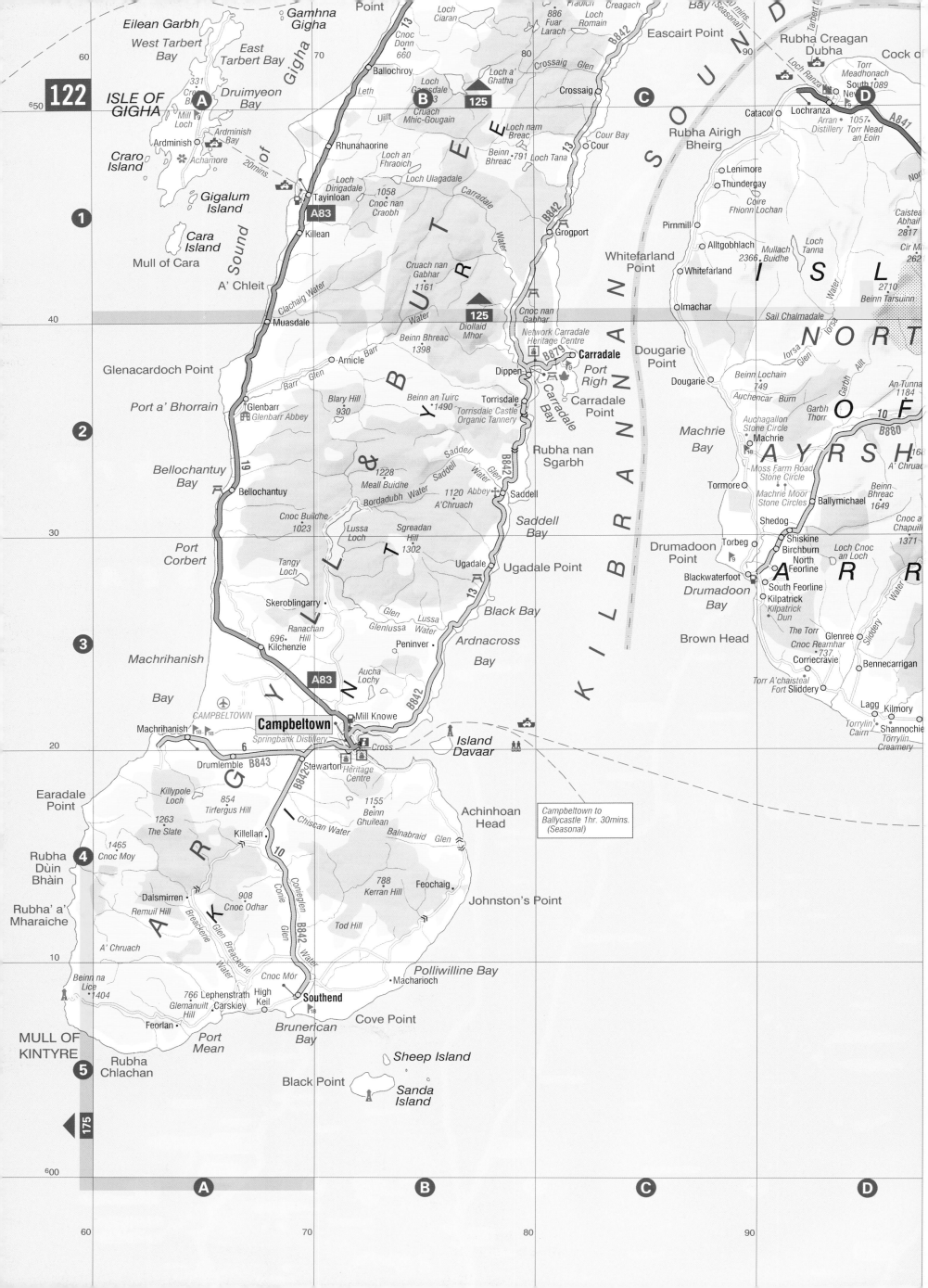

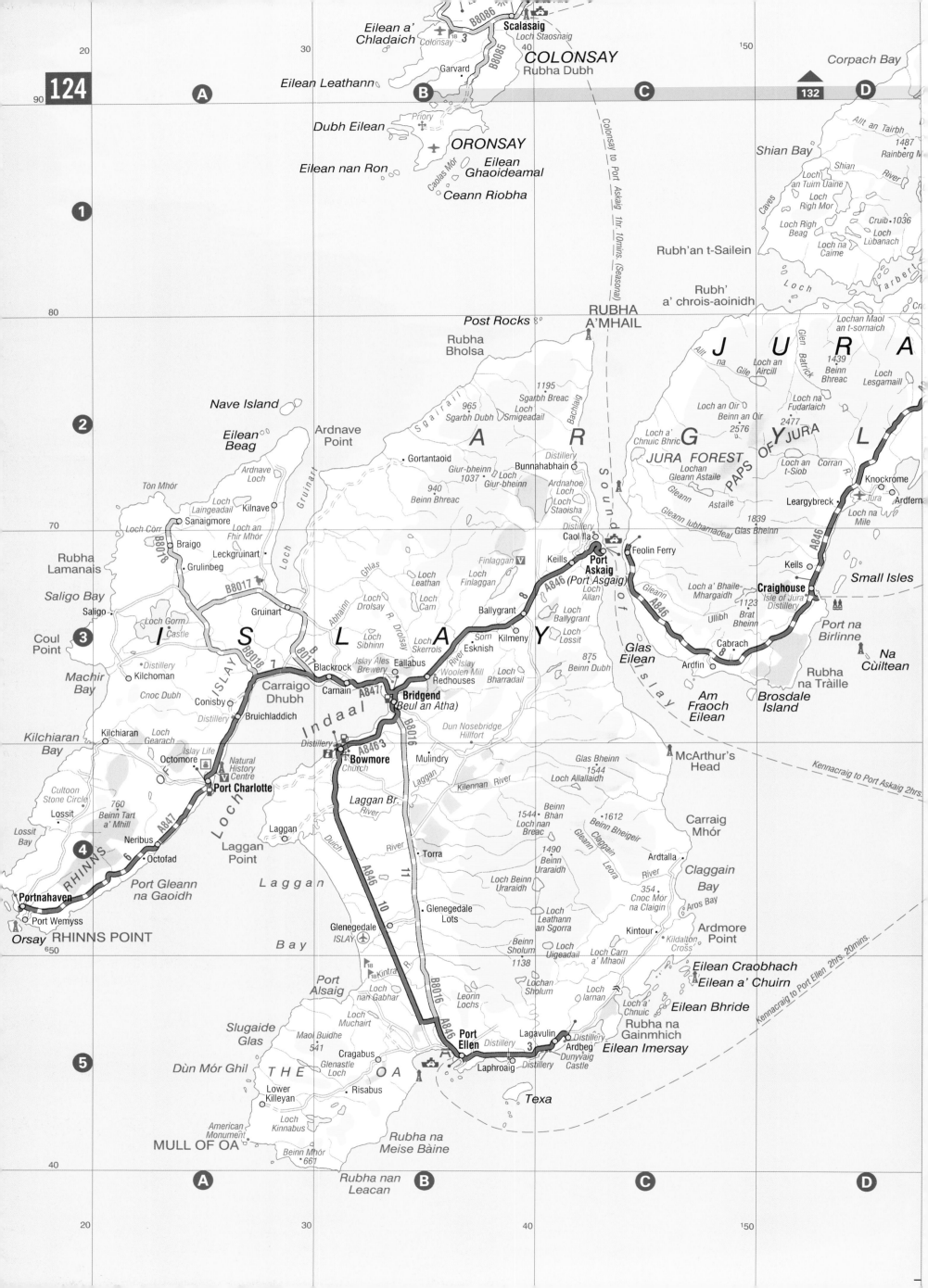

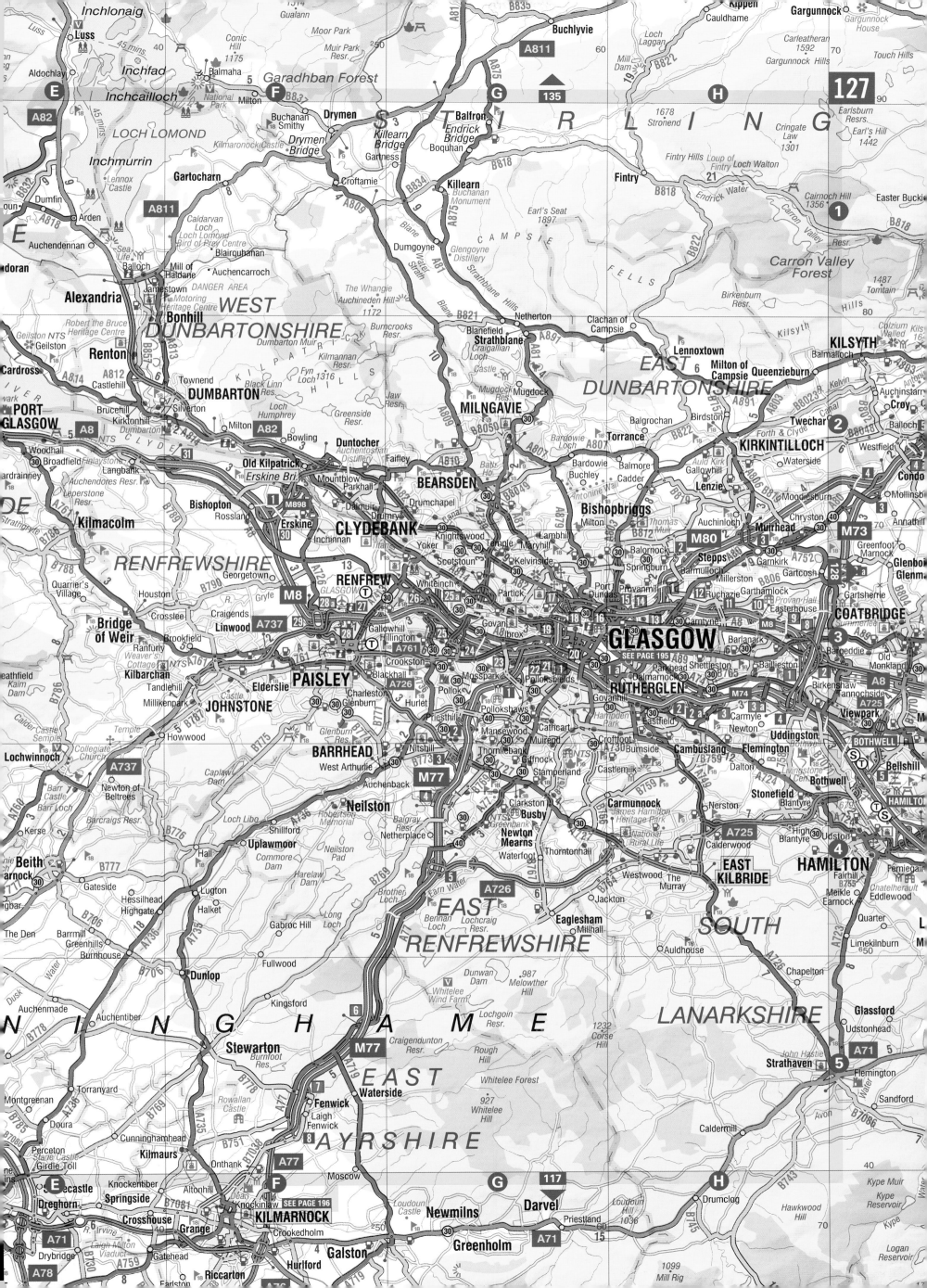

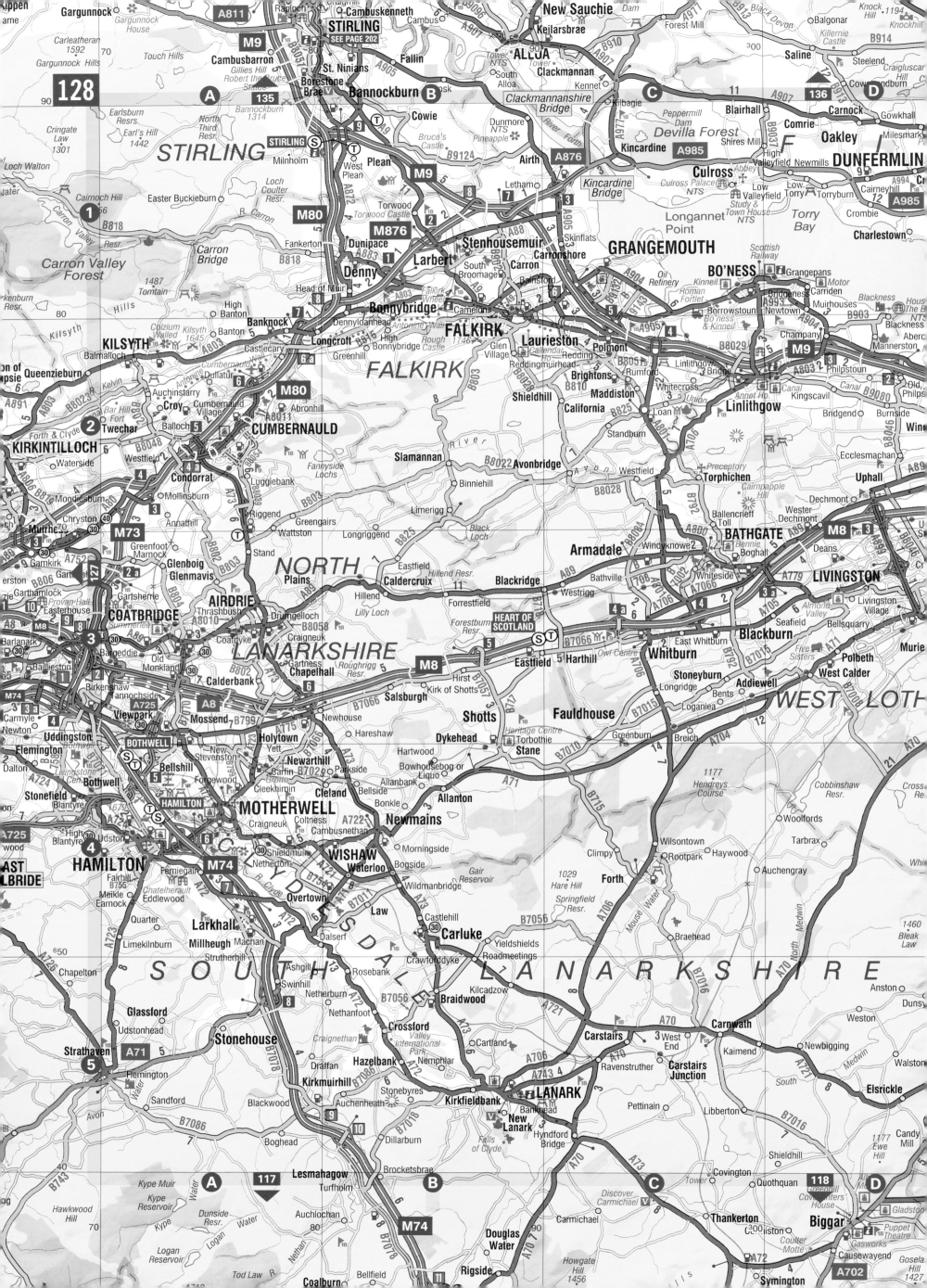

NORTH SEA

Fast Castle Head
Point
Fast Castle
Telegraph Hill
Lumsdaine
Cross Law •744
Coldingham Moor
ST. ABB'S HEAD
St. Abbs
Lifeboat Station
Coldingham Bay
Coldingham
Priory
Lifeboat Station
Houndwood
Eyemouth
Gunsgreenhill
Eye Water
859 Horseley Hill
Reston
Burnmouth
Auchencrow
Ayton
Ross
Chirnside
Lamberton
Marshall Meadows
Edrom
Chirnside-bridge
Tithe Barn
Clappers
Conundrum Farm
Foulden
Halidon Hill 1333
Bell Tower
Allanton
Hutton
Whiteadder Water
BERWICK-UPON-TWEED
Paxton
Castle
Whitsome
Paxton Ho.
R. Tweed
Union Bridge
Loanend
Tweedmouth
Lifeboat Station
Spittal
Fishwick
Chain Bridge Honey Farm
East Ord
Pot-a-Doodle Do
Redshin Cove
Horncliffe
Horndean
Murton
Thornton
Scremerston
Ladykirk
Norham
West Allerdean
Cheswick
Swinton
Norham Station
Shoreswood
Goswick
Simprim
Upsettlington
Shoresdean
HOLY ISLAND
Keel Head
Grindon
Ancroft
Berrington Law
Berrington
Haggerston
LINDISFARNE
Holy Island
Twizel Bridge
Felkington
Beal
Lindisfarne Centre
NT Lindisfarne
Stone Circle
Bowsden
Priory
Castle Point
Duddo
Castle Heaton
NORTHUMBERLAND
Burrows Hole
Lennel
Melkington
Barmoor
West Kyloe
Fenham
Cornhill-on-Tweed
Heatherslaw Light Railway
Etal
Lowick
East Kyloe
Coldstream
Waterford Hall
Mill
Kyloe Hills
Fenwick
FARNE ISLANDS
Staple Sound
West Learmouth
Barelees
Crookham
Ford
Buckton
East Learmouth
Branxton
Elwick
Ross
Chapel NT
Flodden Field Monument 1513
Flodden Field
Holburn
Detchant
Budle Bay
Pressen
Flodden
St. Cuthbert's Cave
Bamburgh
Hetton
Middleton
Inner Sound

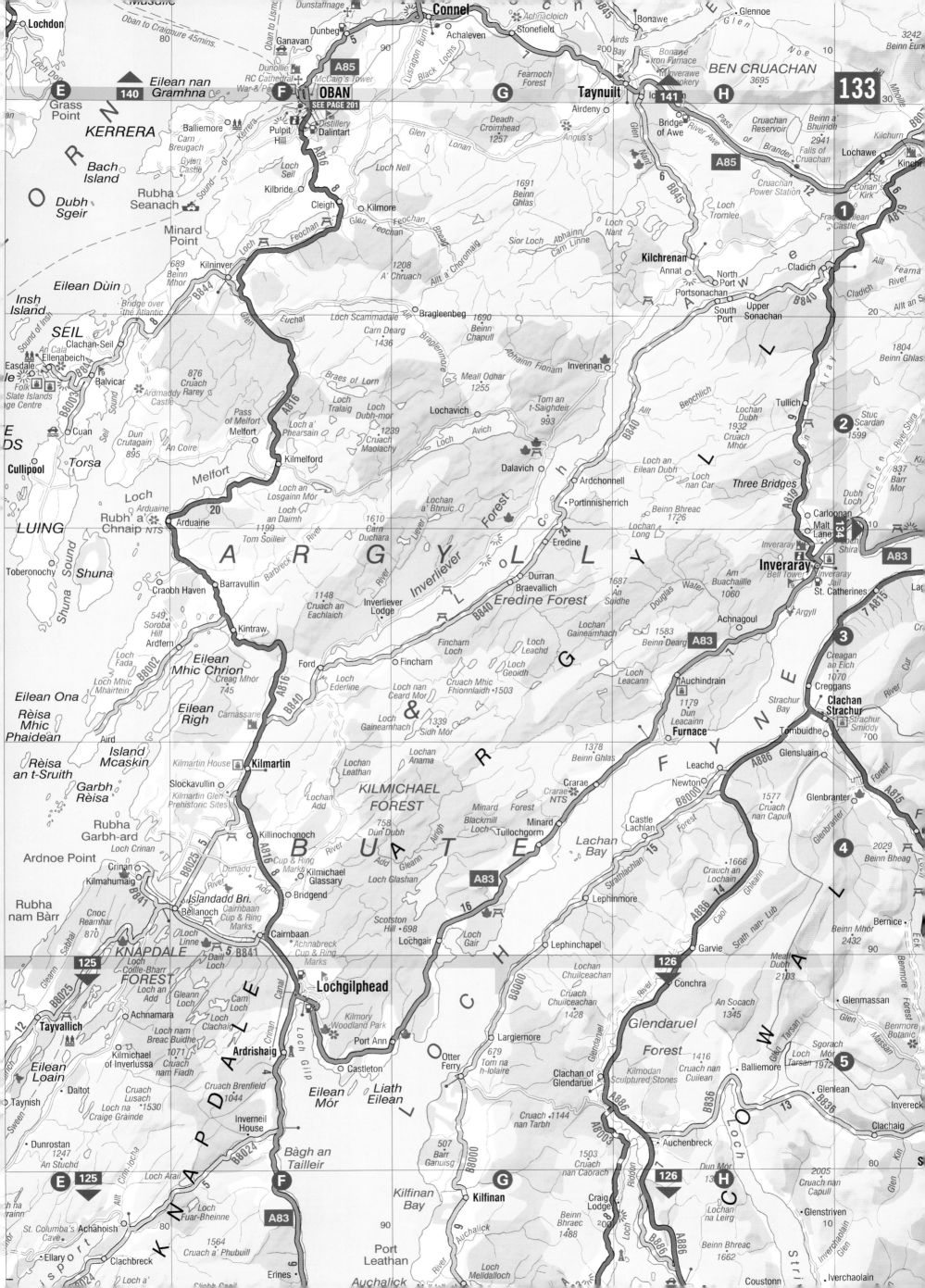

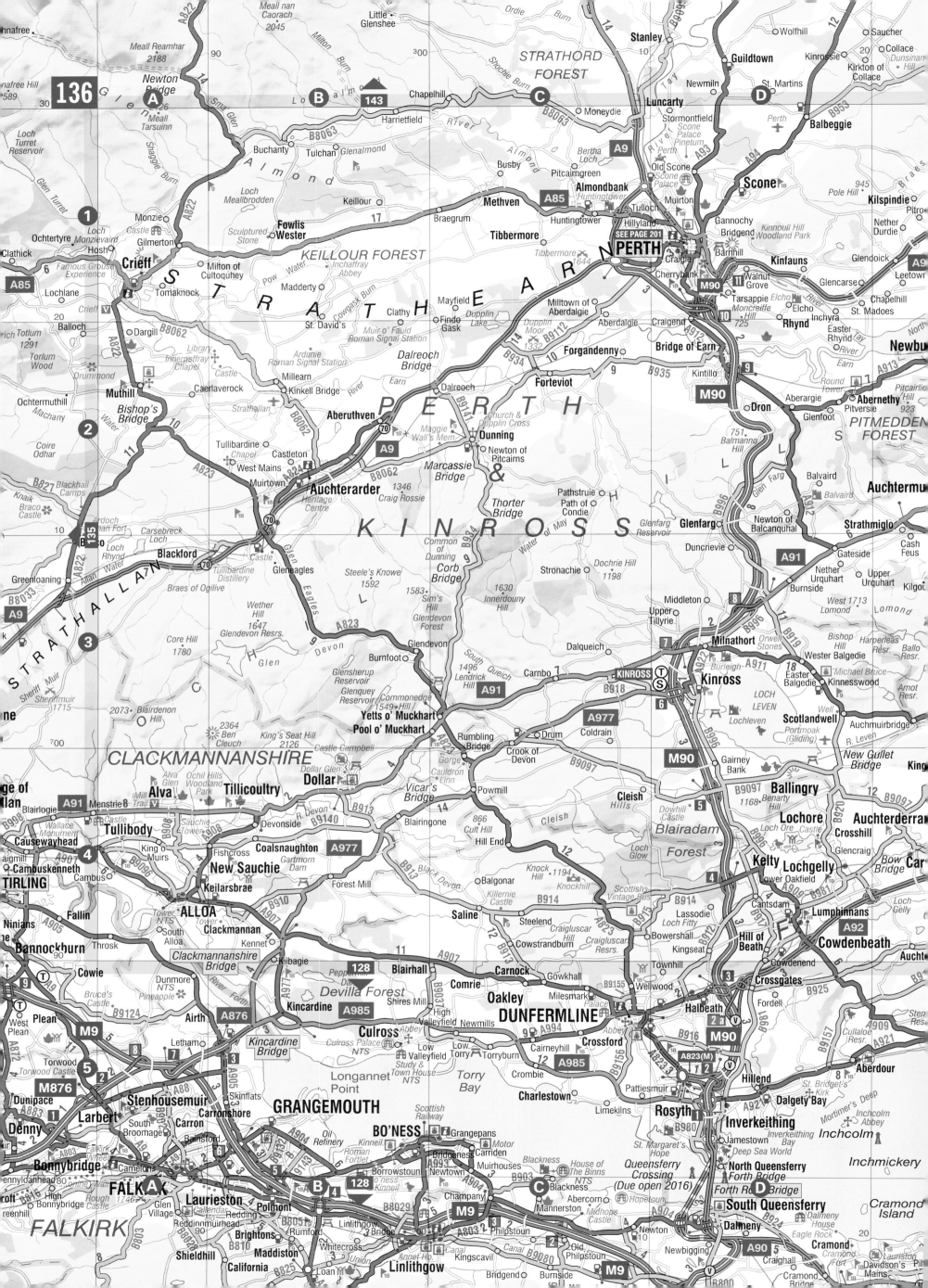

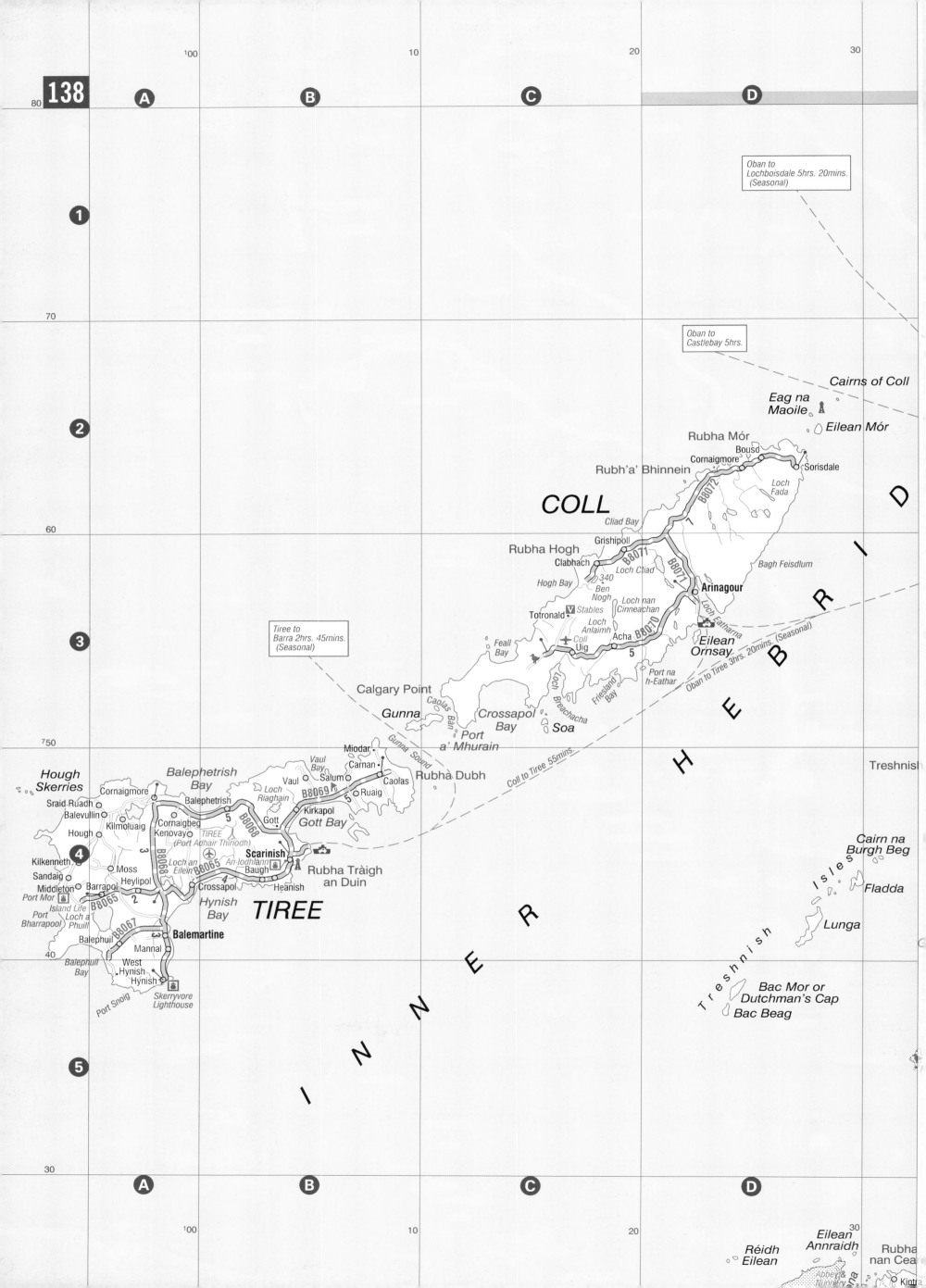

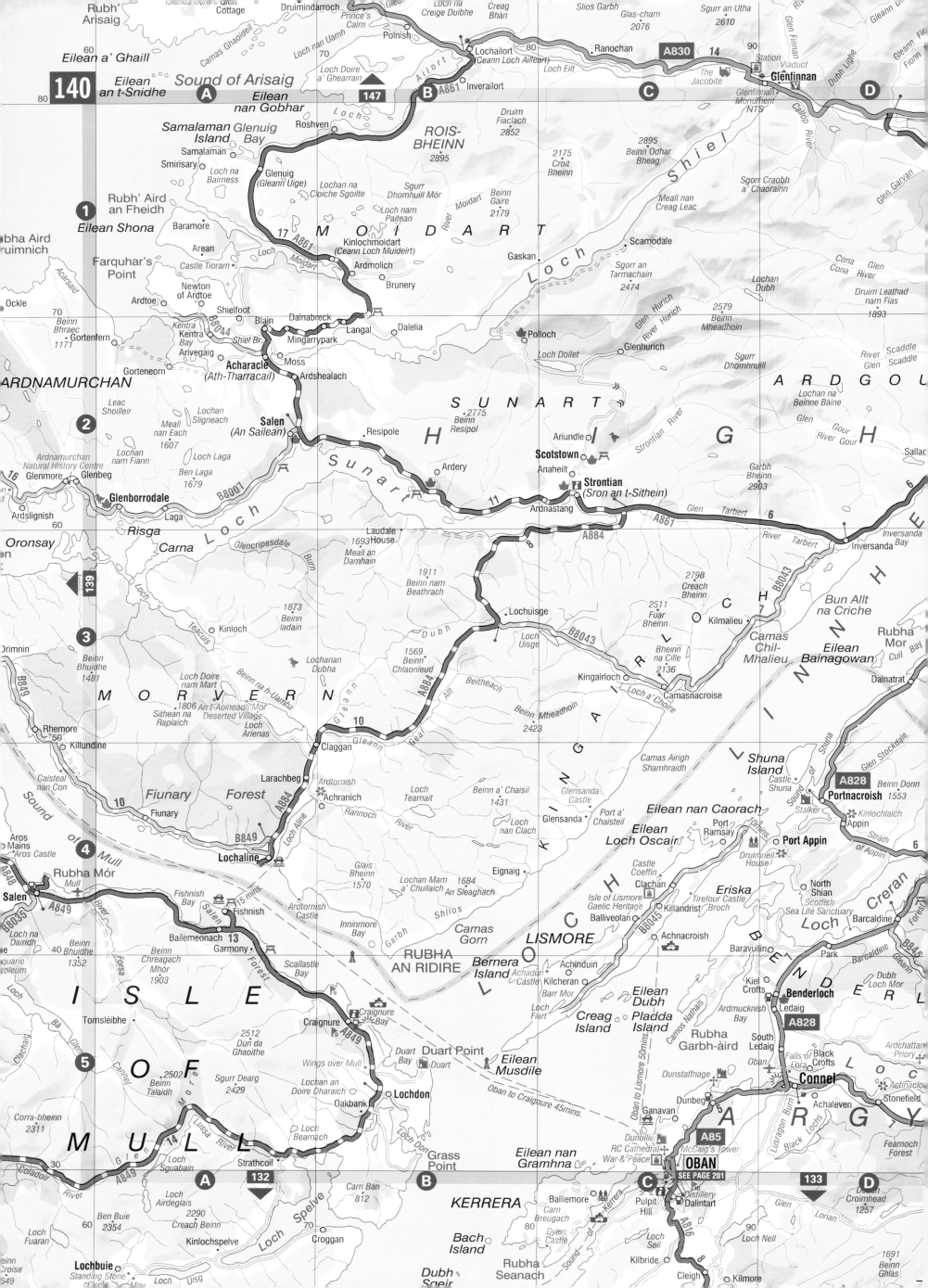

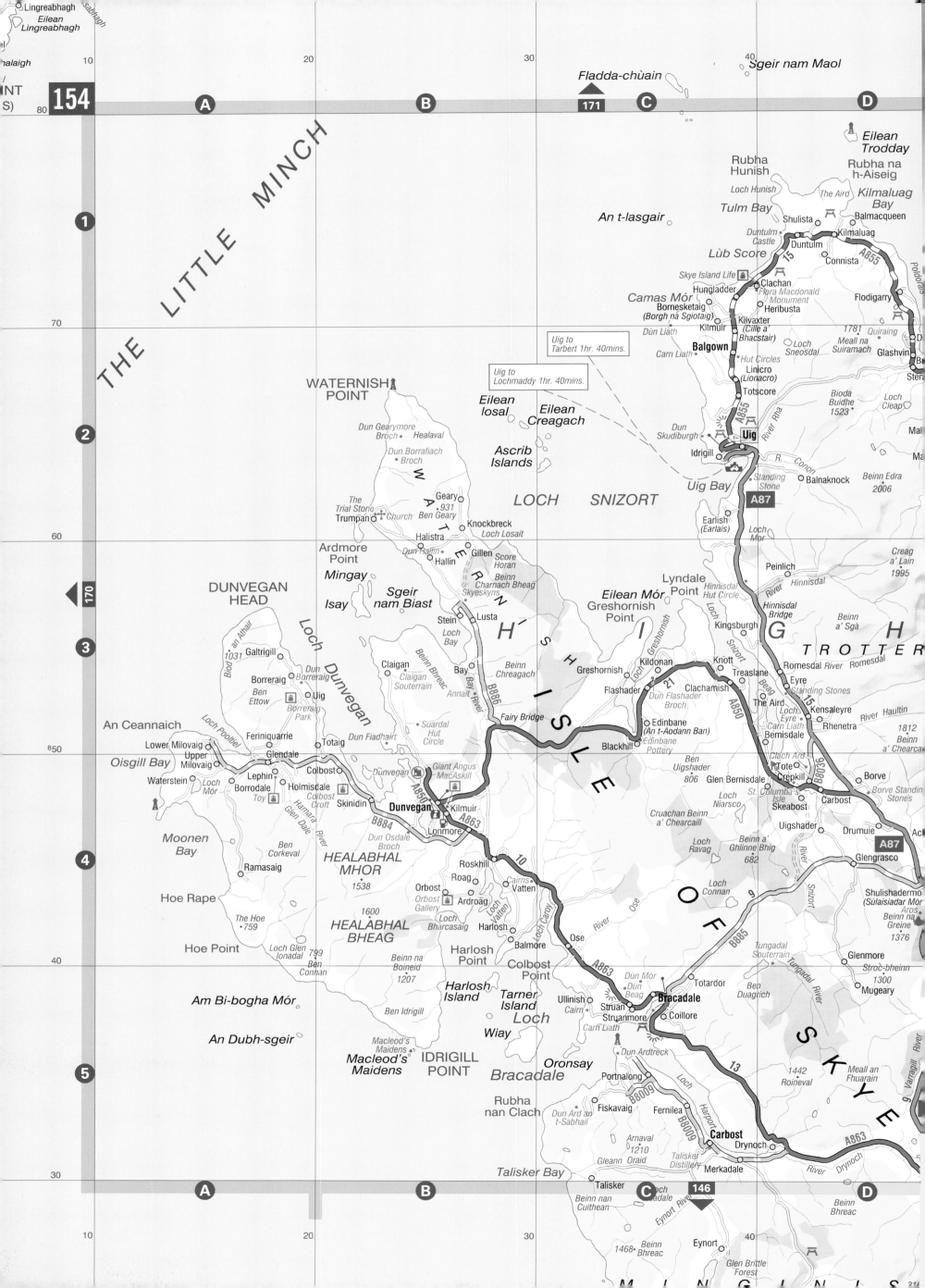

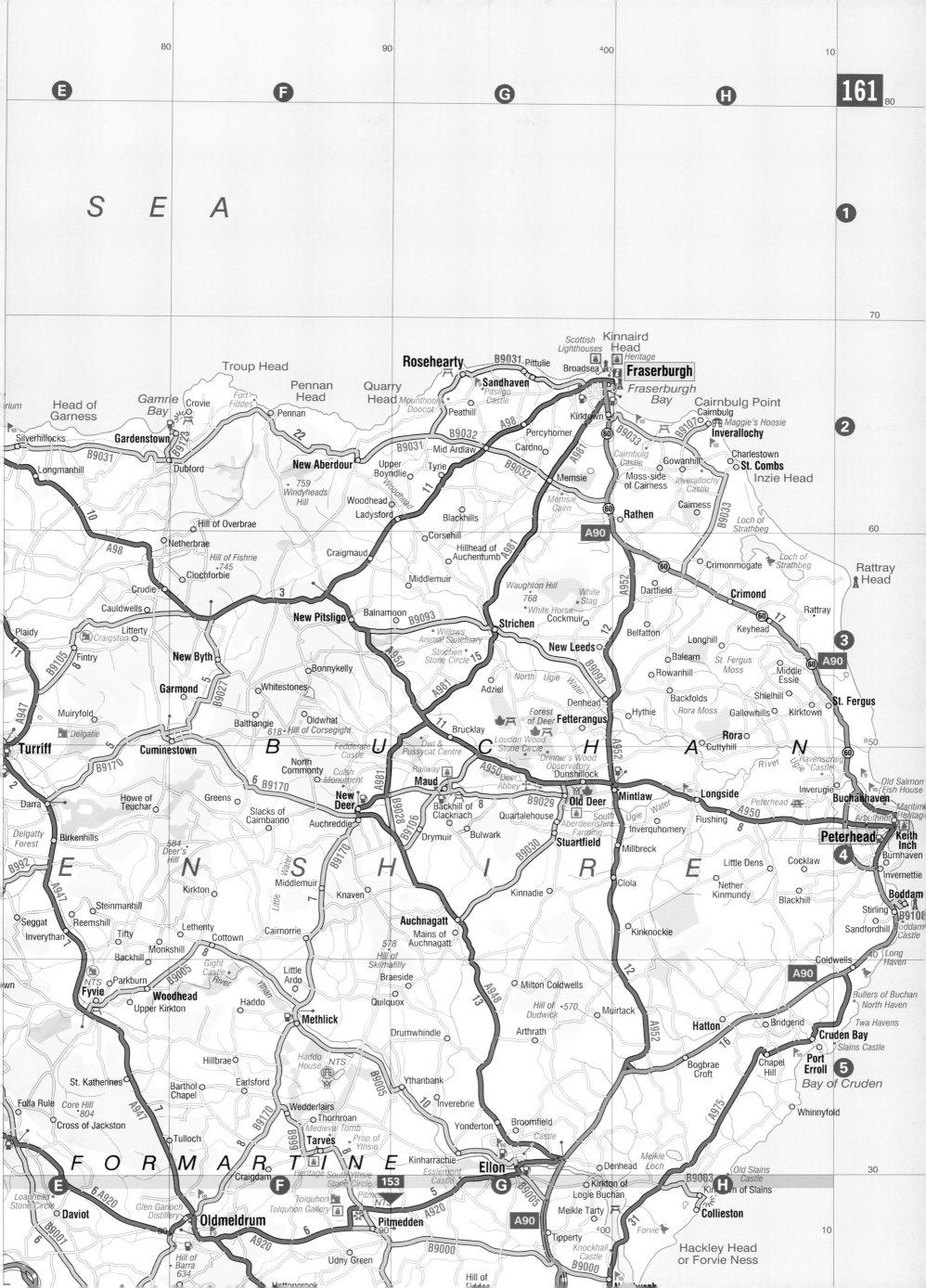

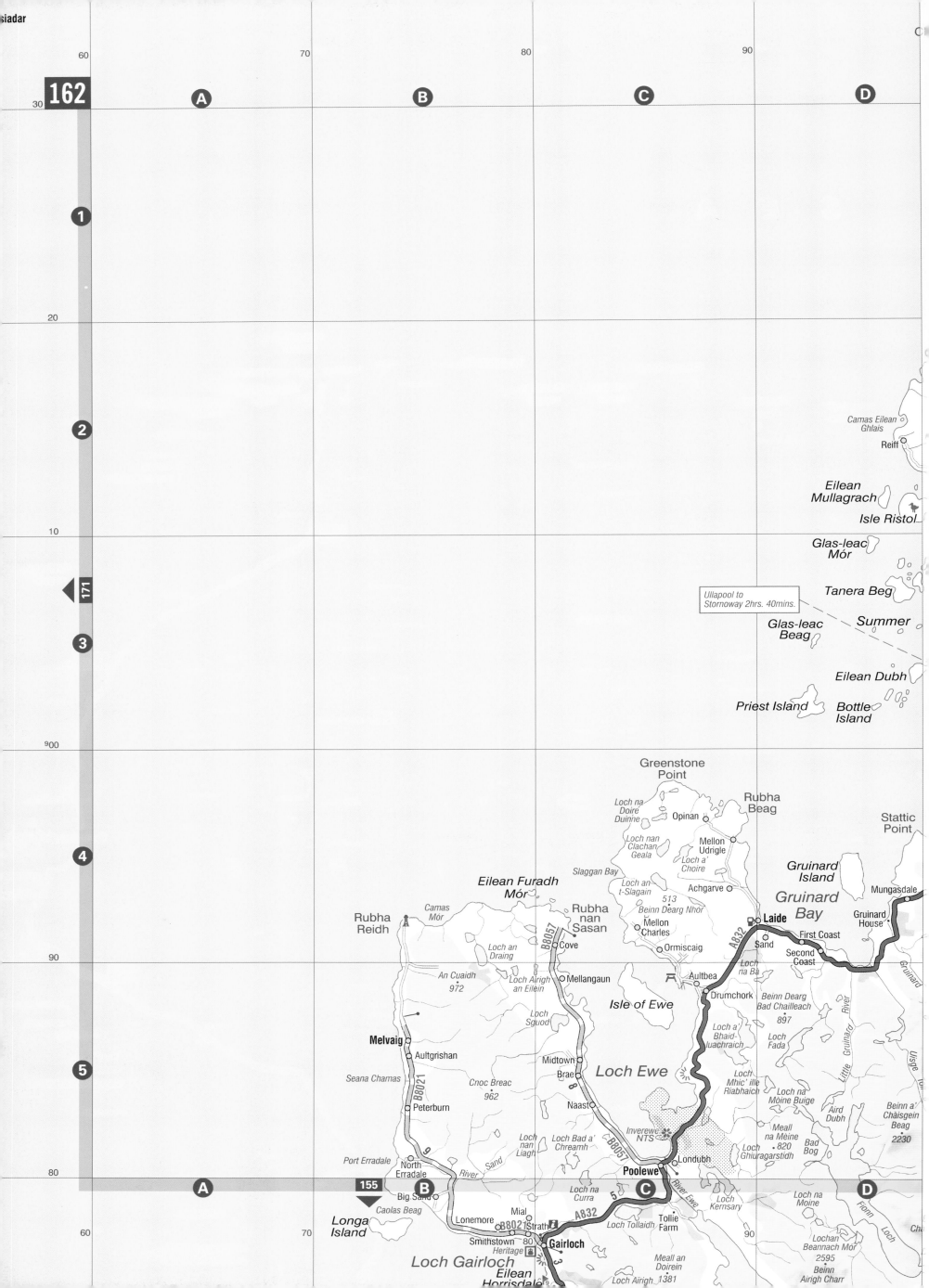

A **B** **C** **D**

1

2

3

171

4

5

Camas Eilean
Ghlais

Reiff

Eilean
Mullagrach

Isle Ristol

Glas-leac
Mór

Tanera Beg

Ullapool to
Stornoway 2hrs. 40mins.

Summer

Glas-leac
Beag

Eilean Dubh

Priest Island

Bottle
Island

Greenstone
Point

Loch na
Doire
Duinne

Opinan

Rubha
Beag

Stattic
Point

Loch nan
Clachan
Geala

Mellon
Udrigle

Loch a'
Choire

Achgarve

Gruinard
Island

Mungasdale

Slaggan Bay

Loch an-
t-Slagain

Eilean Furadh
Mór

513

Beinn Dearg Nhor

Gruinard
Bay

Gruinard House

Rubha
Reidh

Camas
Mór

Rubha
nan
Sasan

B8057

Cove

Mellon
Charles

Ormiscaig

Laide

A832

Sand

First Coast

Second
Coast

Loch an
Draing

Loch
na Ba

An Cuaidh
972

Loch Airigh
an Eilein

Mellangaun

Aultbea

Drumchork

Beinn Dearg
Bad Chailleach
897

Loch
Fada

Little Gruinard River

Melvaig

Loch
Sguod

Isle of Ewe

Loch a'
Bhaid-
luachraich

Aultgrishan

Midtown

Loch Ewe

Loch
Mhic' ille
Riabhaich

Loch na
Mòine Buige

Aird
Dubh

Beinn a'
Chàisgein
Beag
2230

Seana Chamas

B8021

Cnoc Breac
962

Brae

Naast

Peterburn

Loch
nan
Liagh

Loch Bad a'
Chreamh

Inverewe
NTS

Meall
na Mèine
820

Loch
Ghiuragarstidh

Bad
Bog

Port Erradale

North
Erradale

River
Sand

Londubh

Poolewe

Loch na
Curra

River Ewe

Loch
Kernsary

Loch na
Moine

Longa
Island

155

Caolas Beag

Big Sand

Lonemore

Mial

B8021

Strath

A832

Loch Tollaidh

Tollie
Farm

Lochan
Beannach Mór
2595

Smithstown

Heritage

Gairloch

Meall an
Doirein

Loch Airigh 1381

Beinn
Airigh Charr

Loch Gairloch

Eilean
Horrisdale

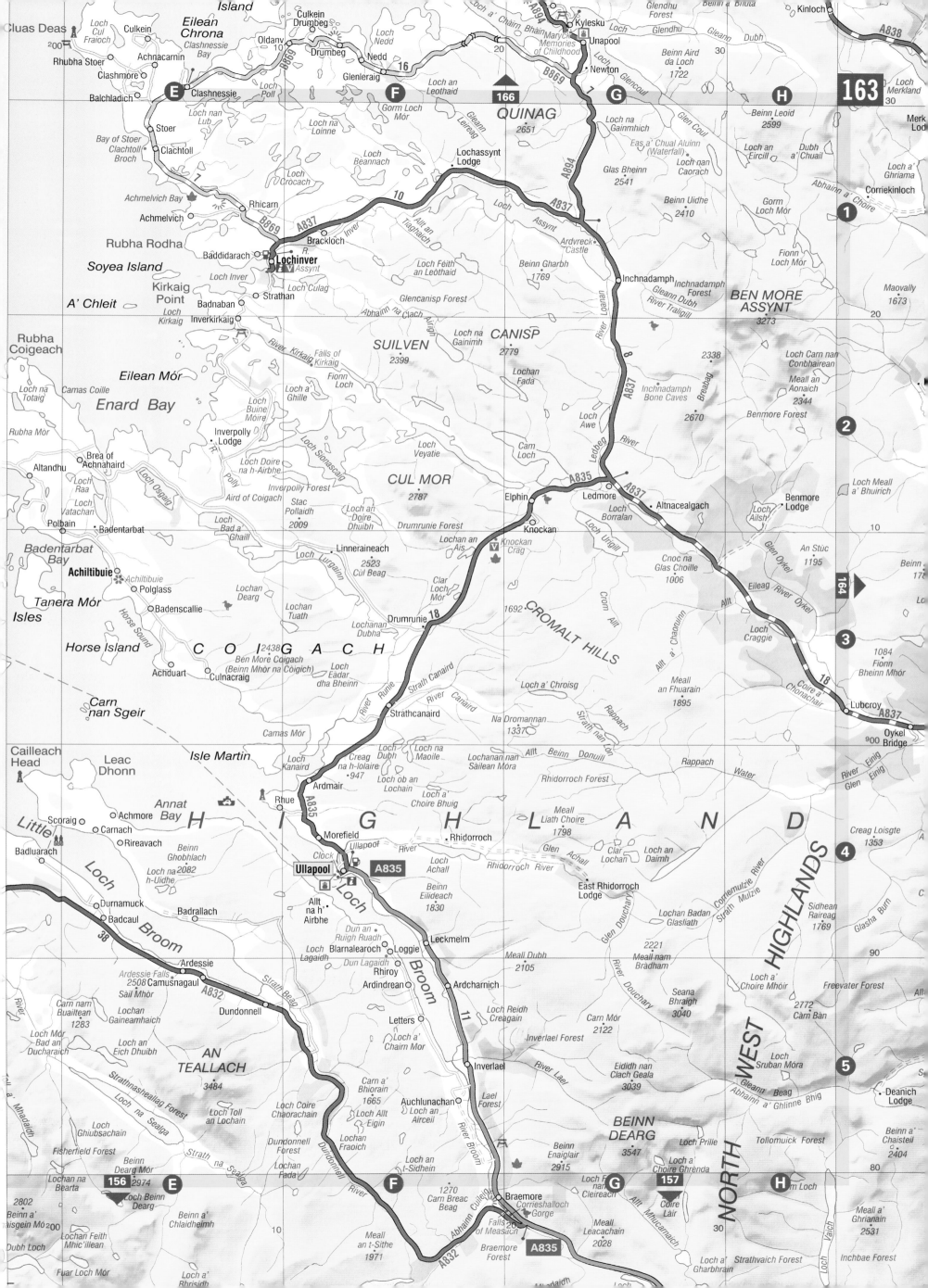

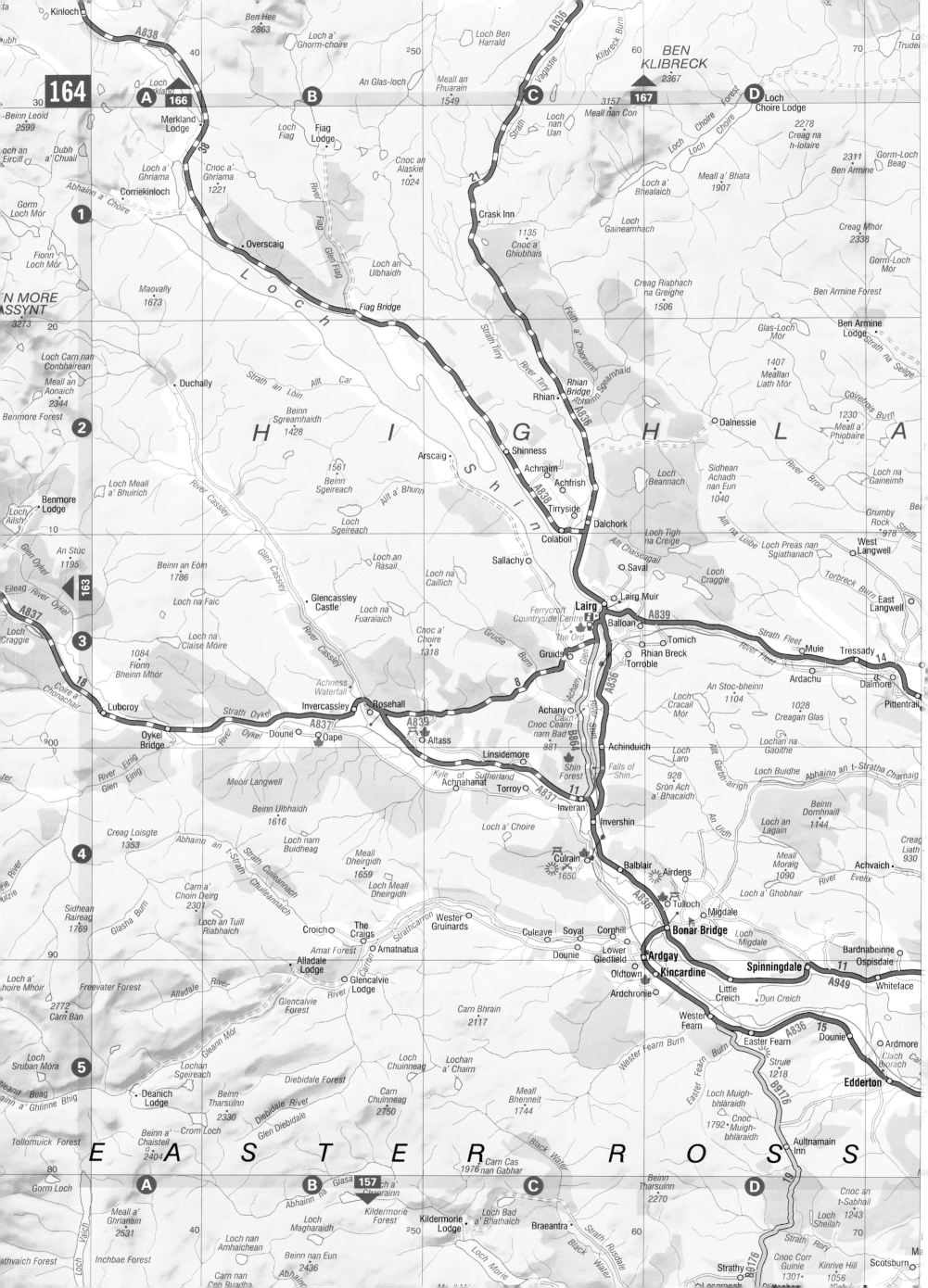

North Sea

Dornoch Firth

Tarbat Ness

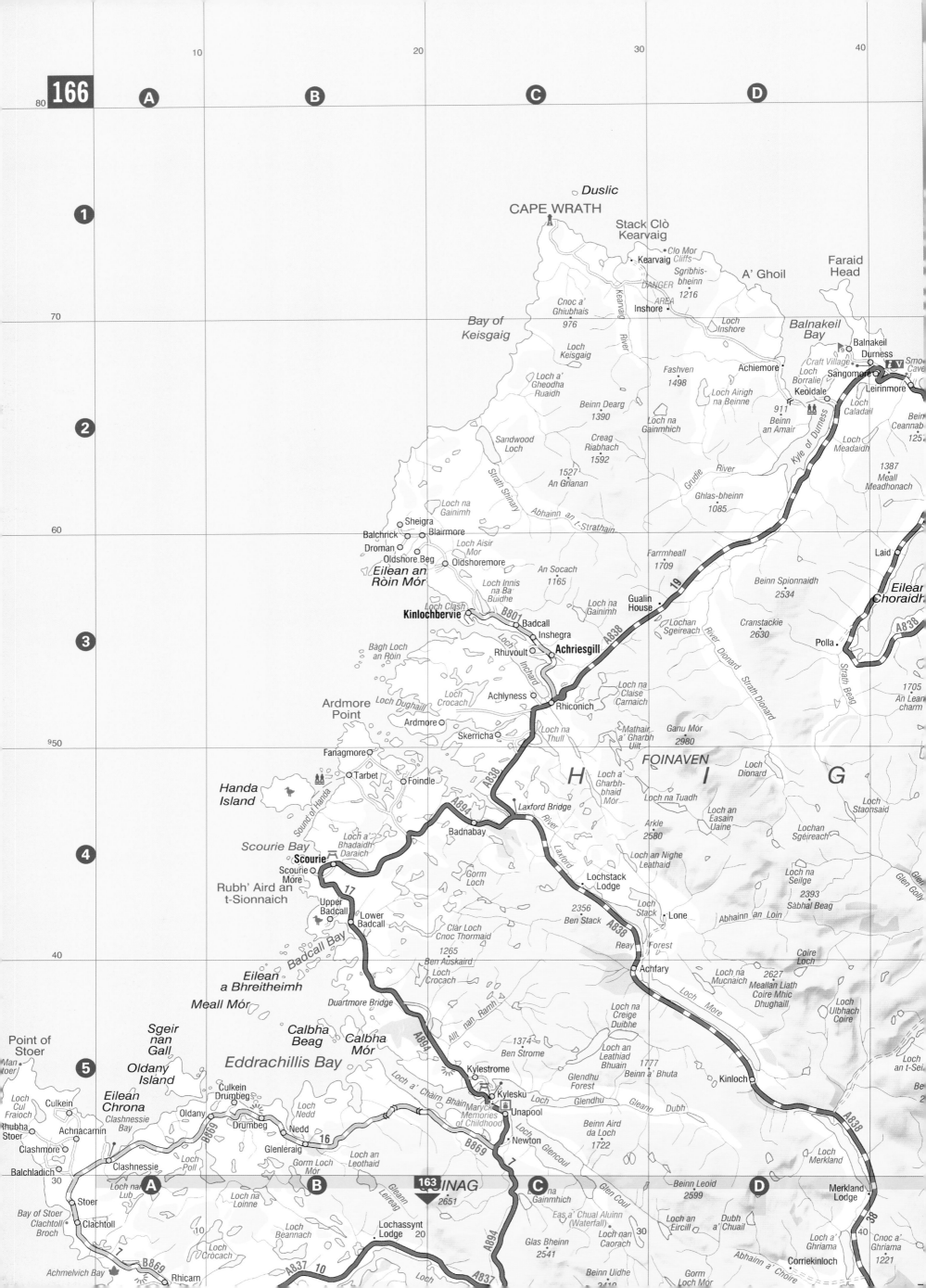

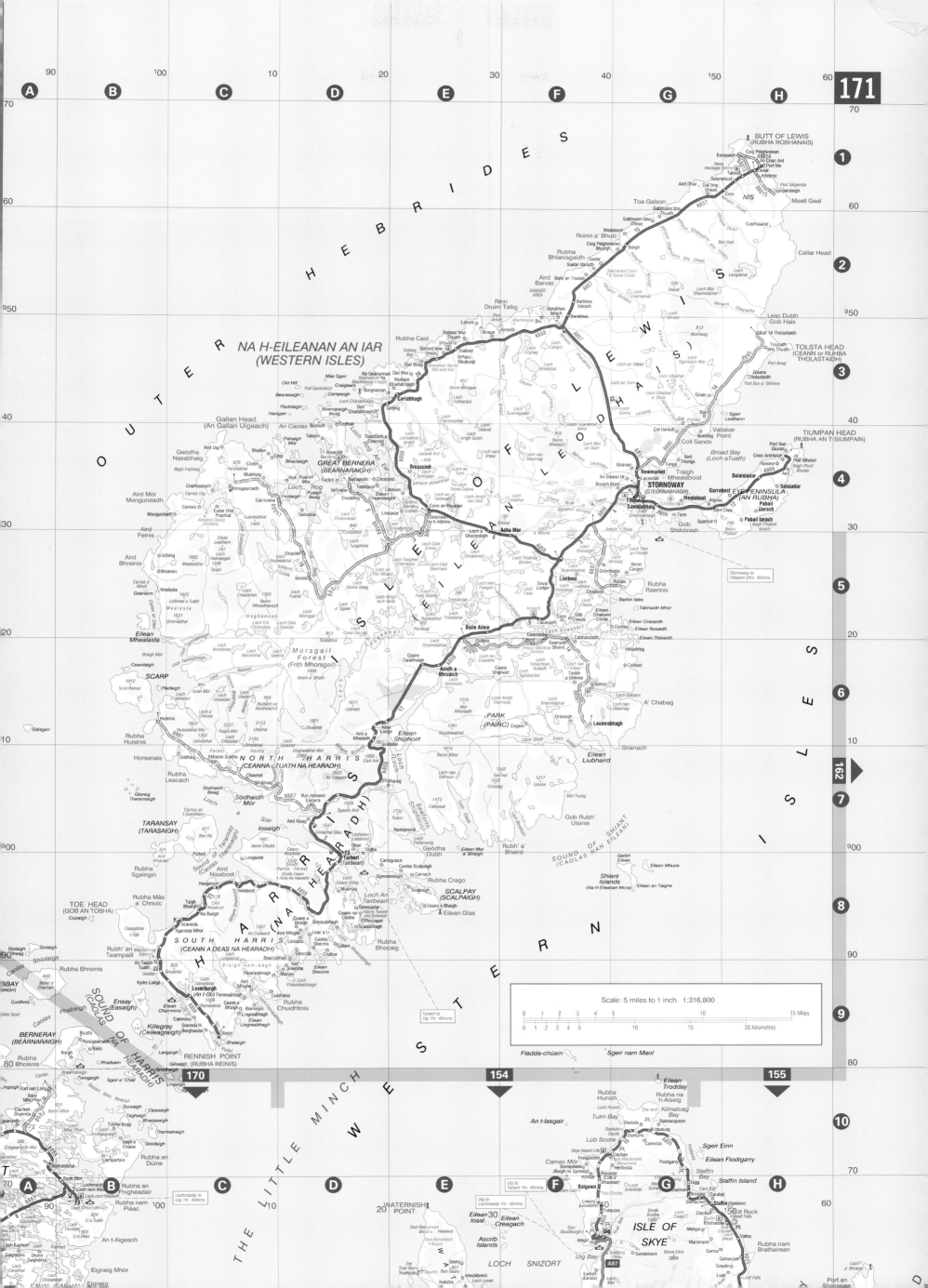

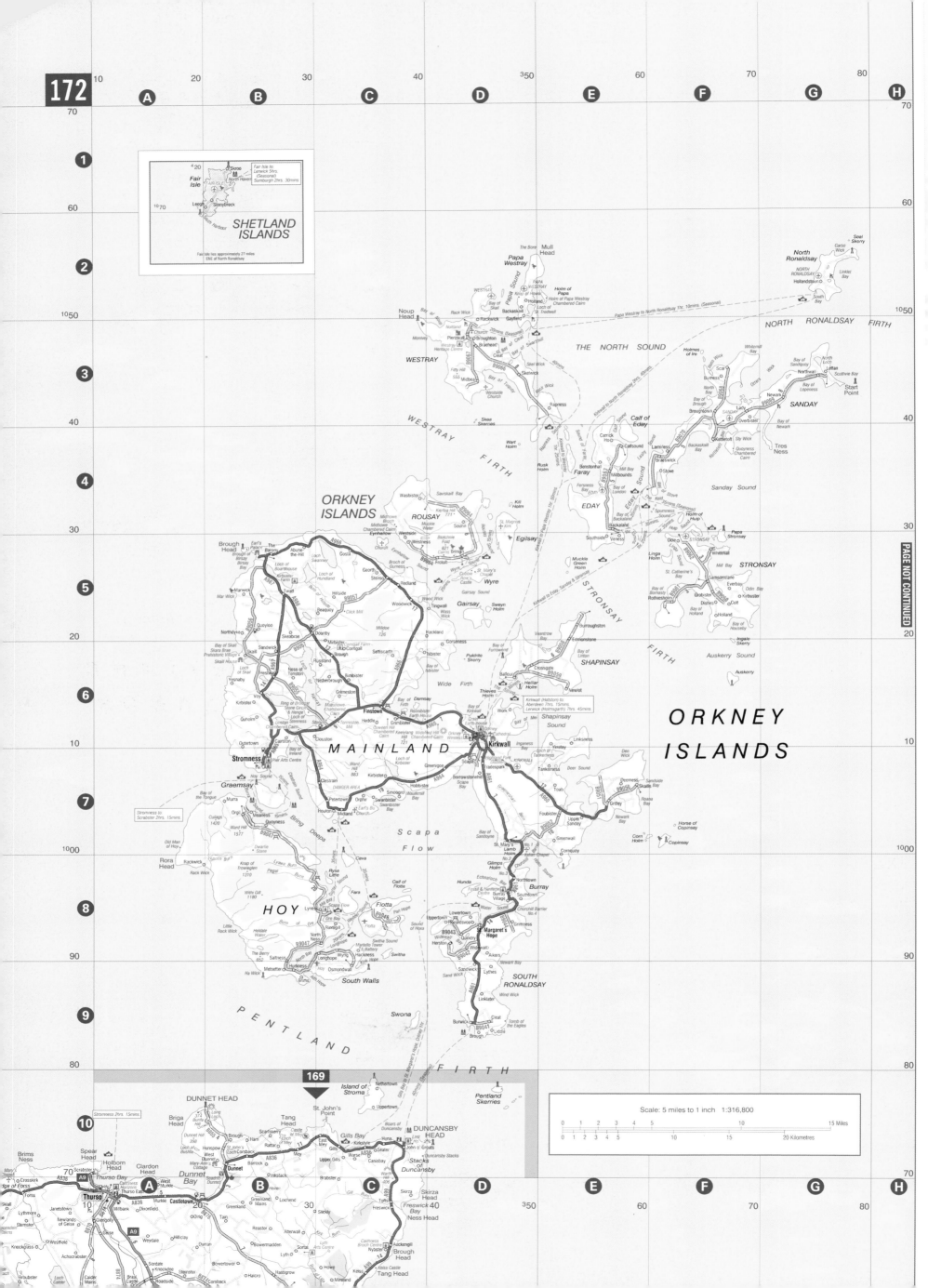

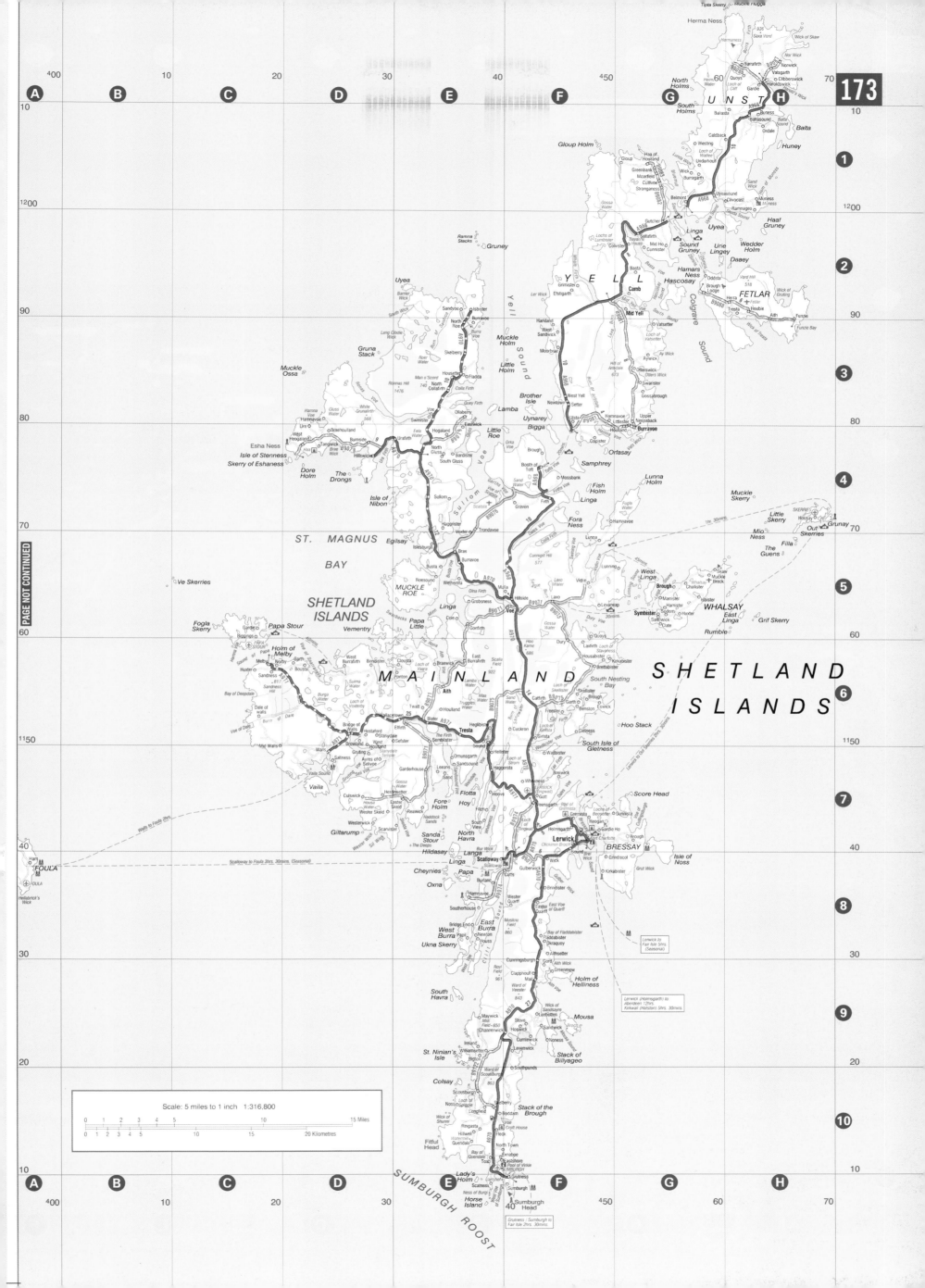

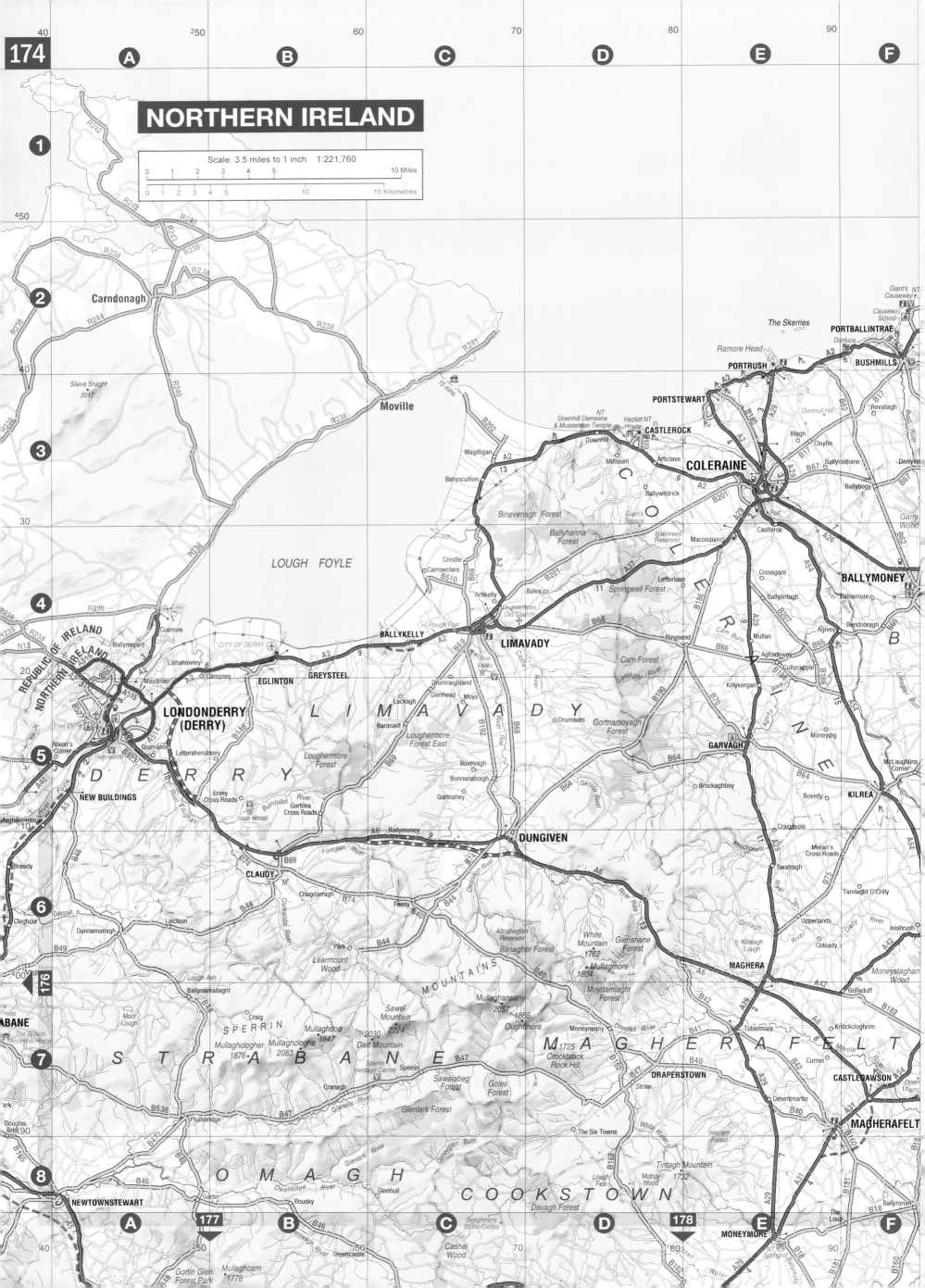

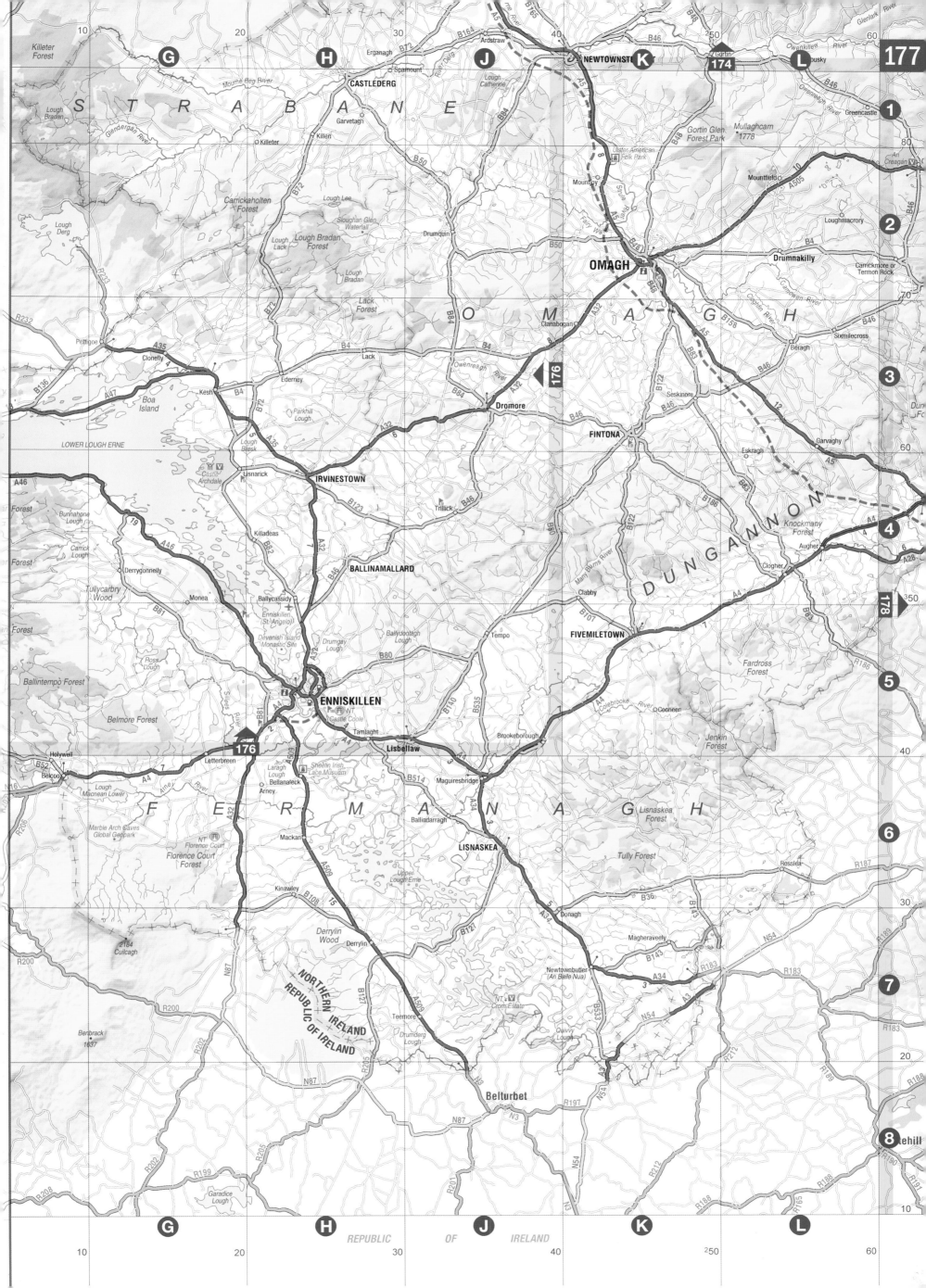

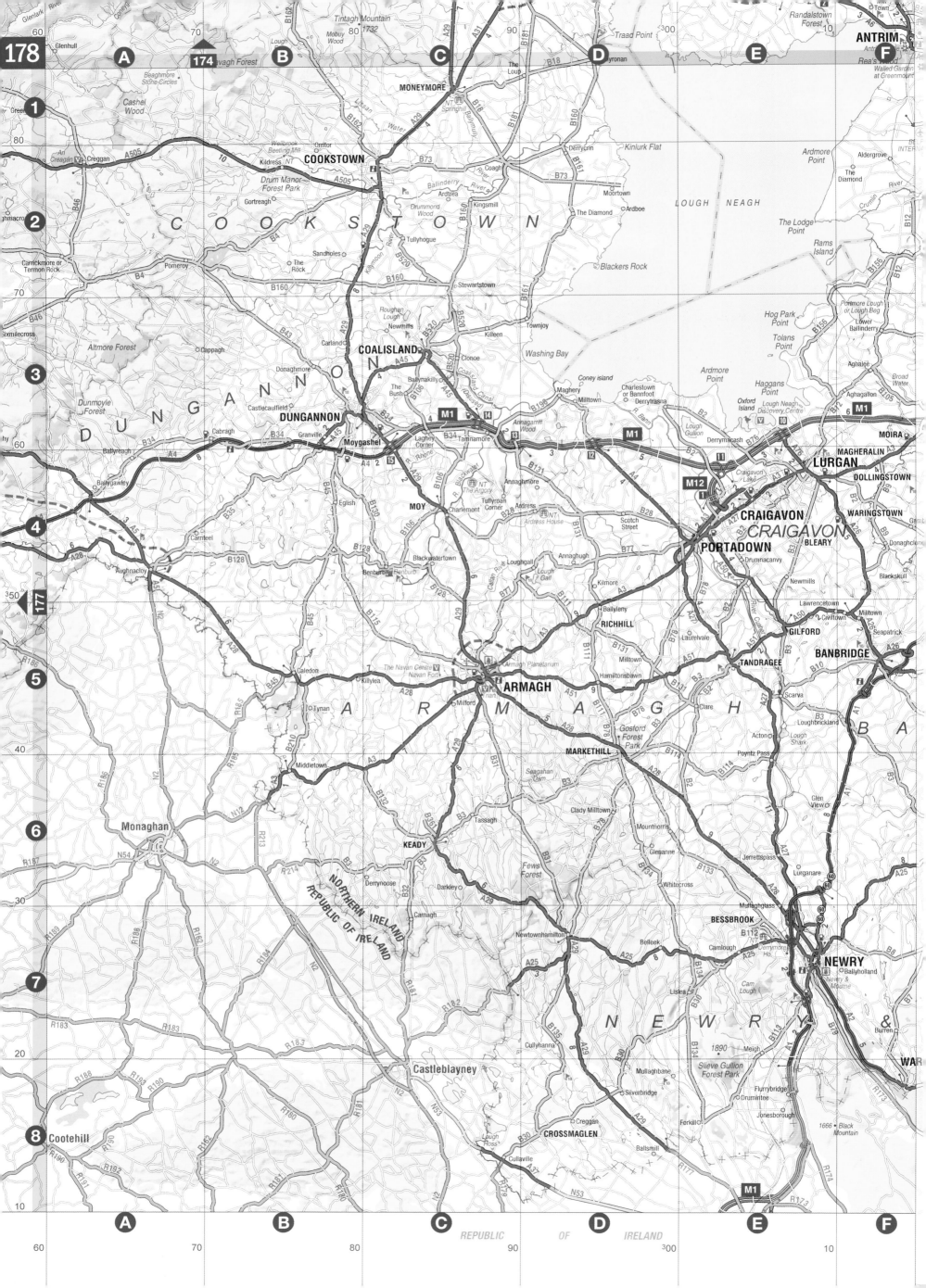

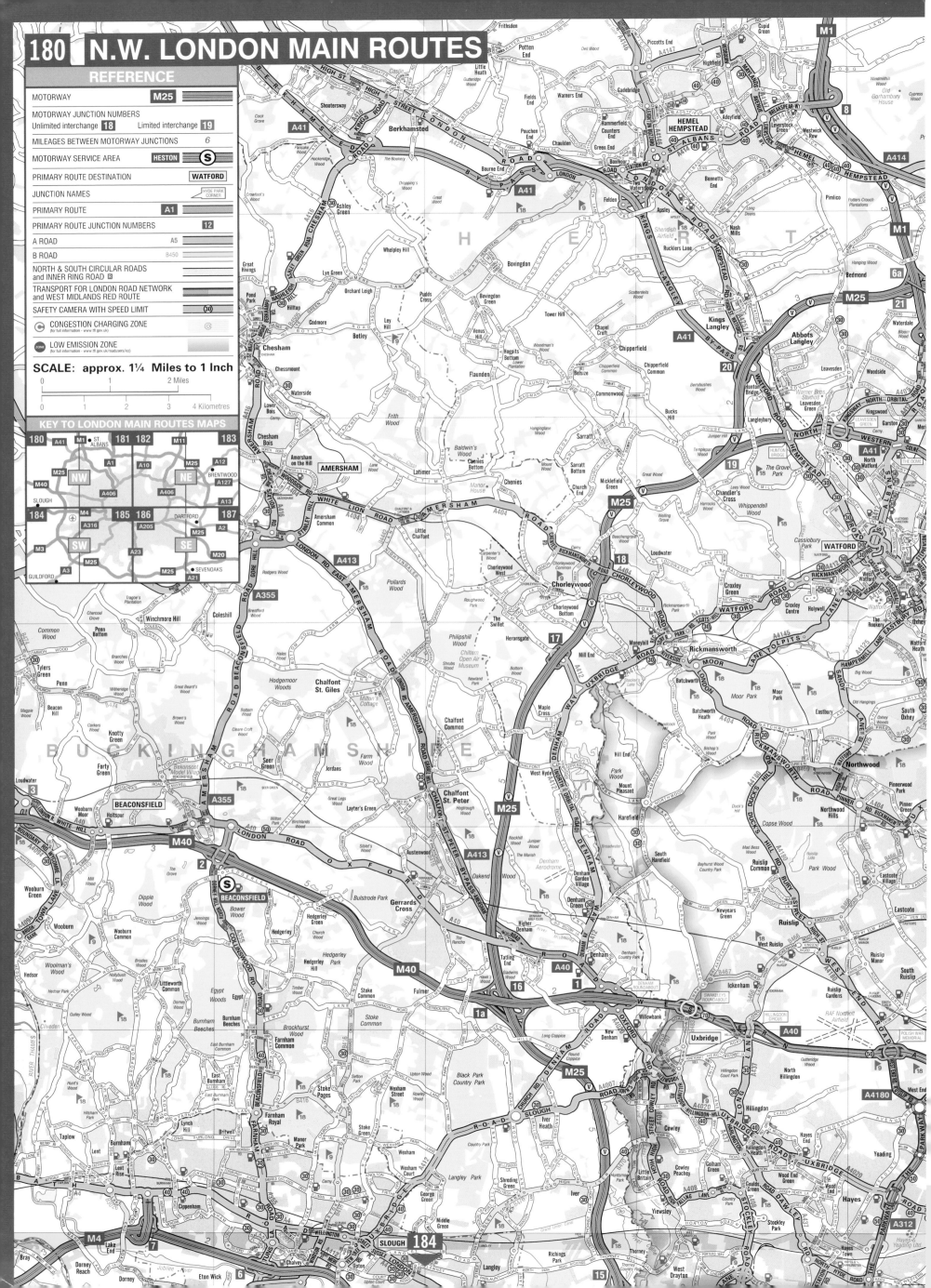

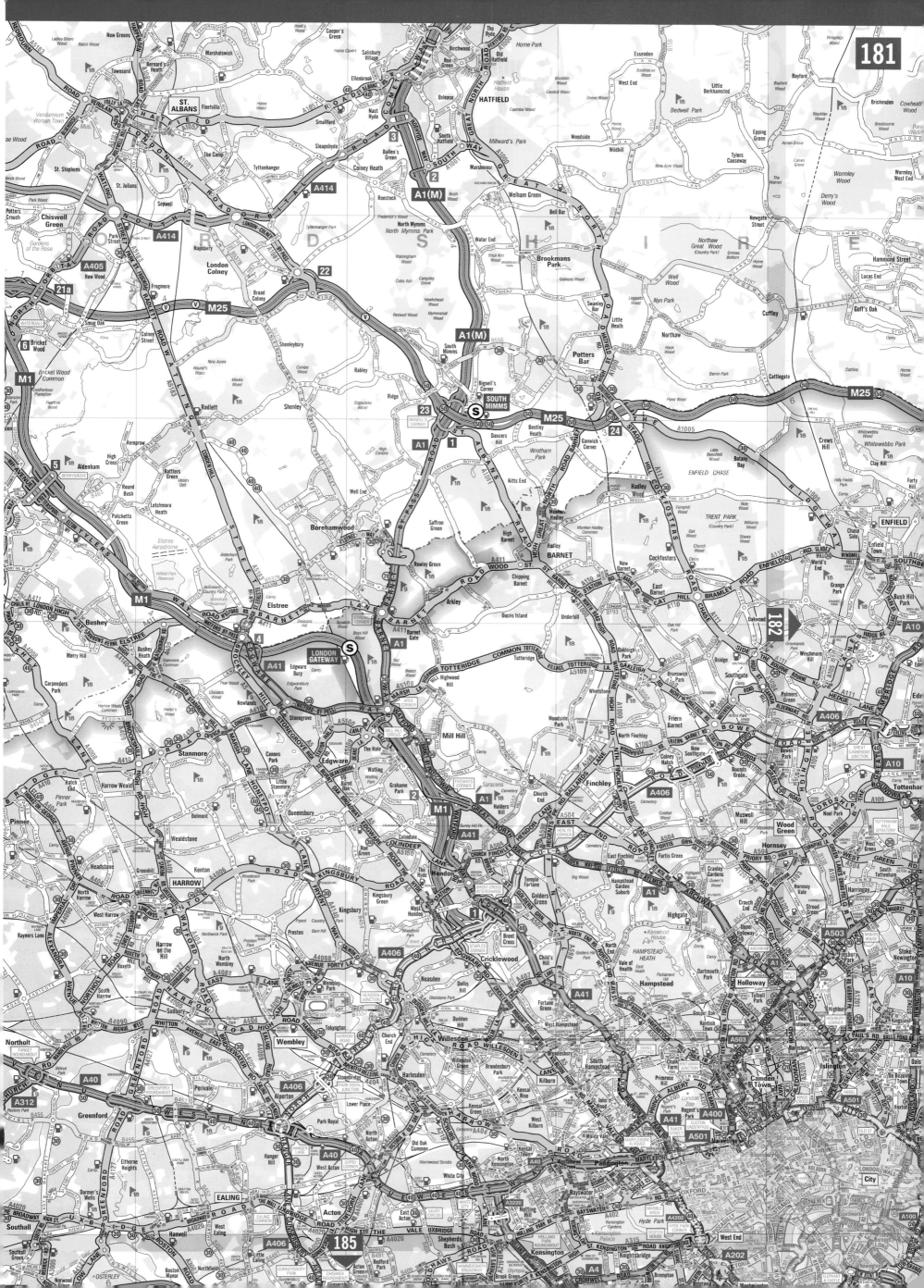

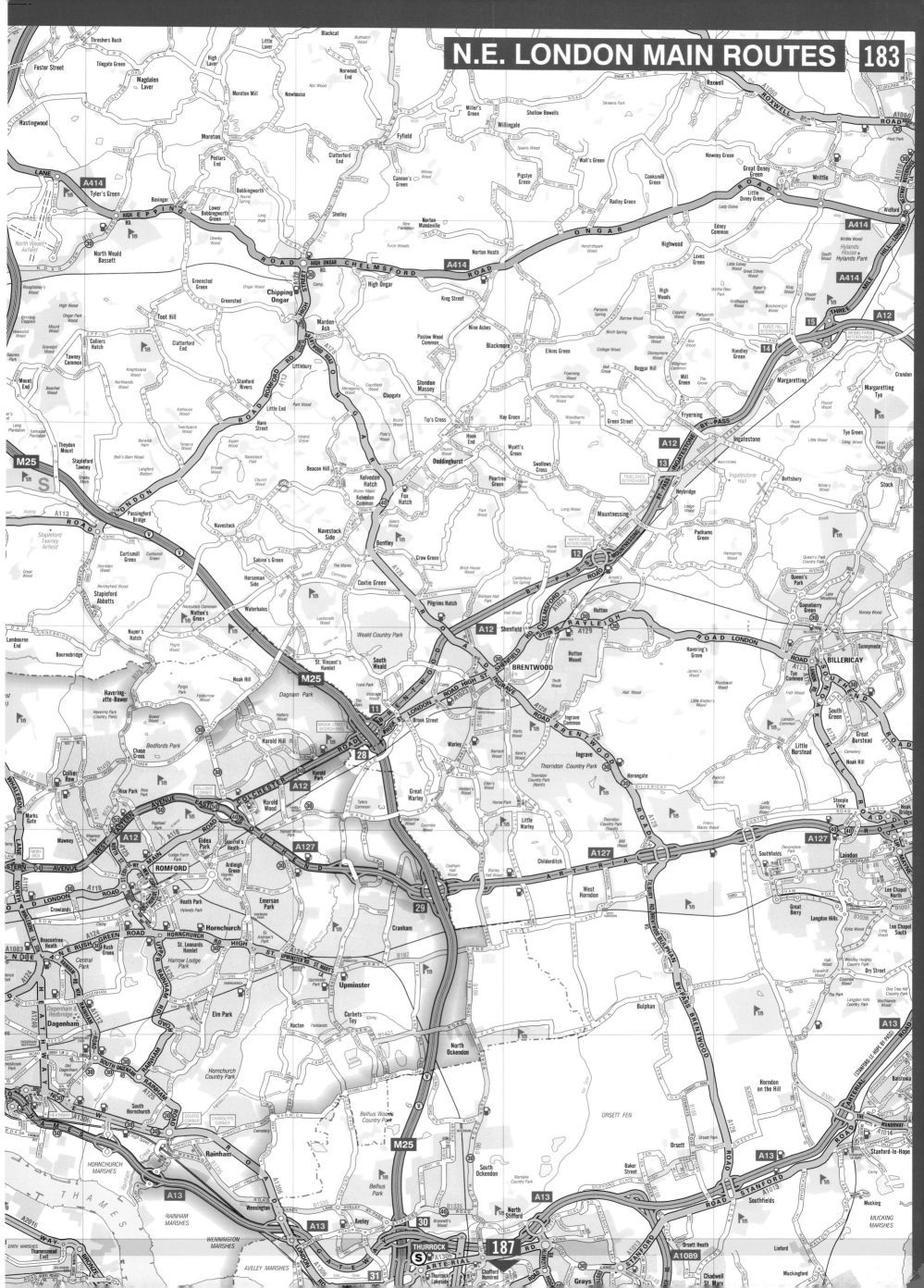

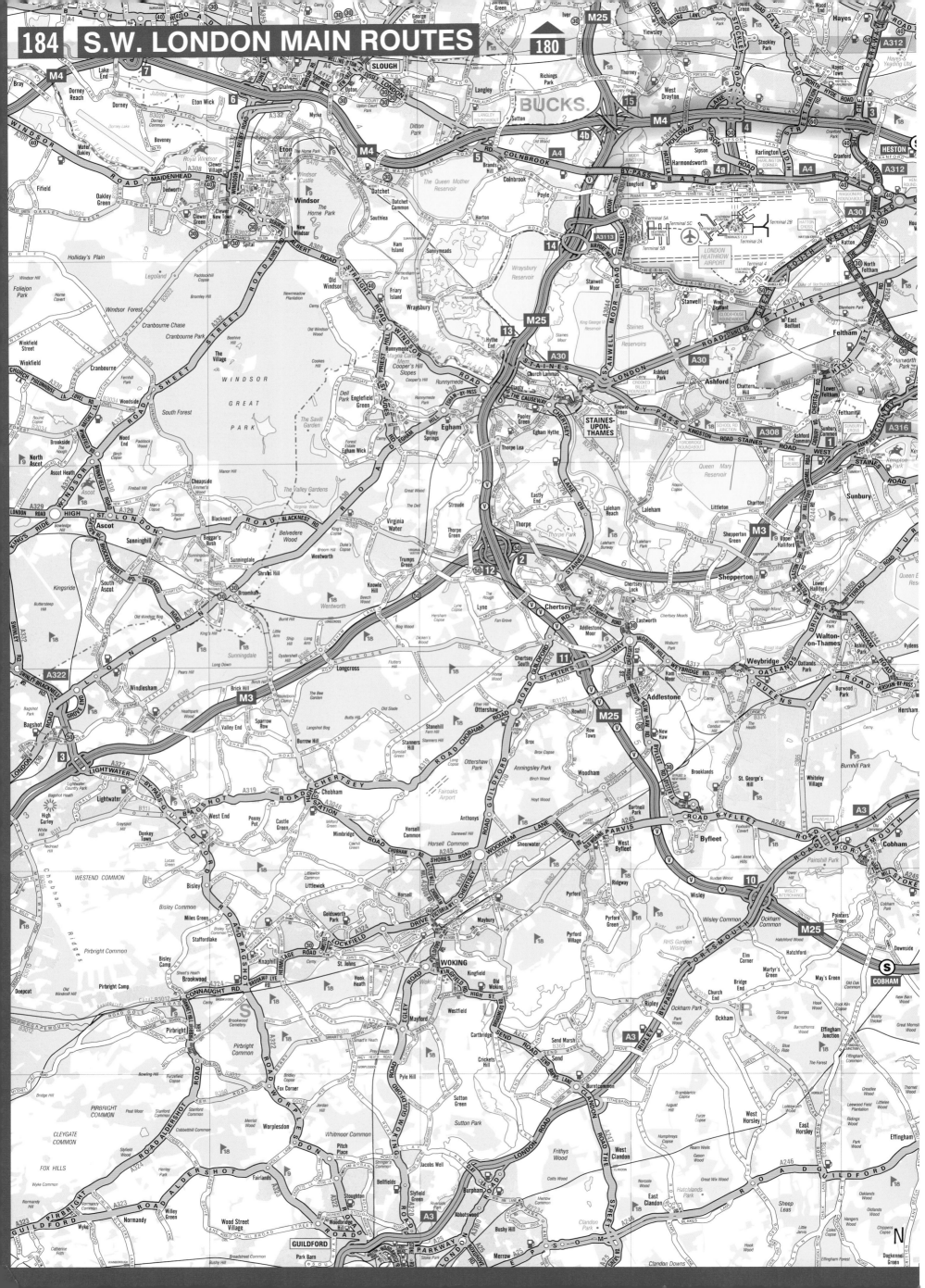

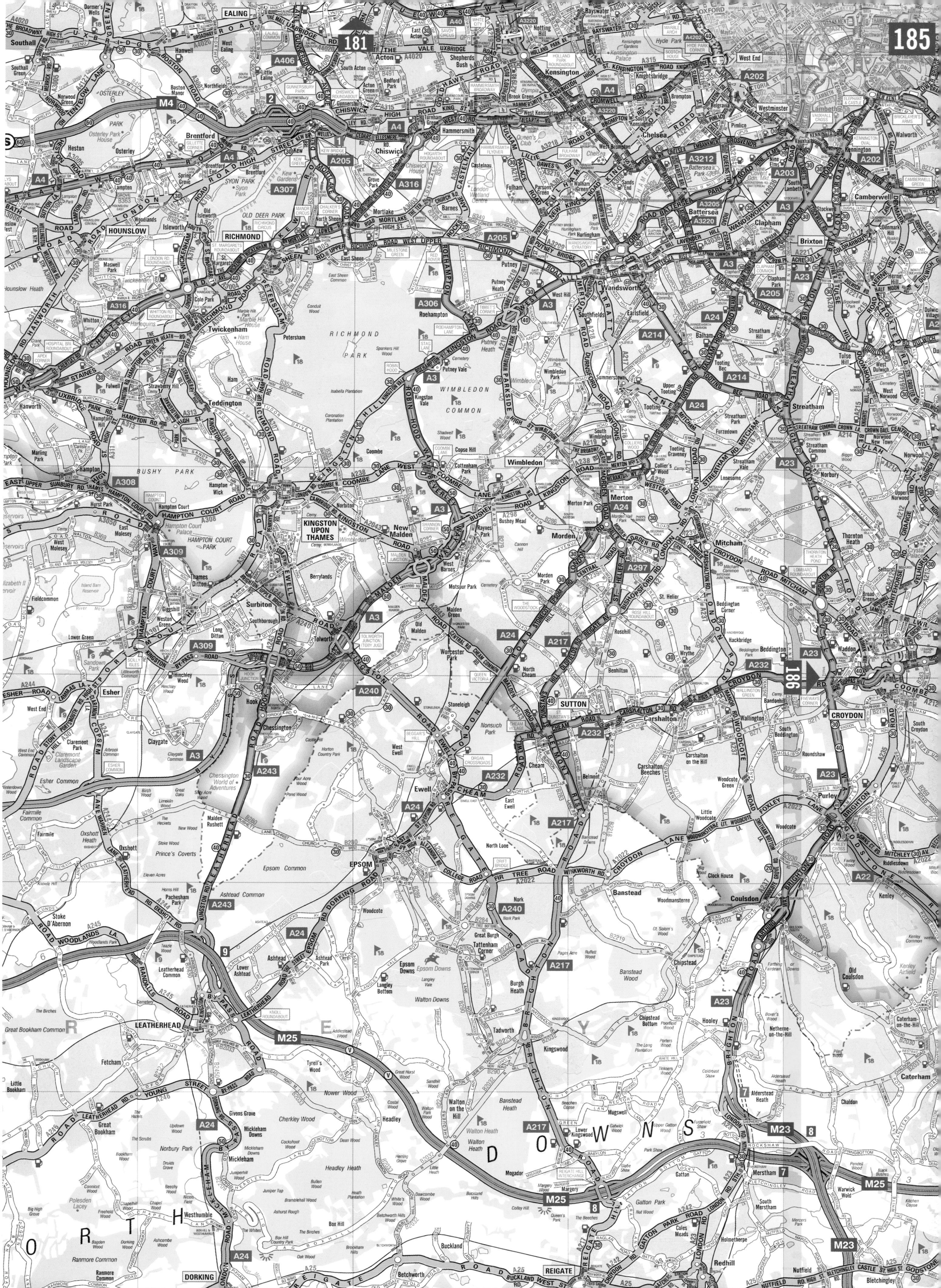
181
186
Southall
Ealing
Acton
Shepherds Bush
Notting Hill
Bayswater
Hyde Park
West End
Kensington
Knightsbridge
Hammersmith
Chiswick
Brentford
Osterley
Heston
Hounslow
Isleworth
Richmond
Kew
Mortlake
Barnes
Fulham
Chelsea
Westminster
Lambeth
Pimlico
Battersea
Clapham
Brixton
Camberwell
Walworth
Kennington
Putney
Wandsworth
Earlsfield
Southfields
Roehampton
Richmond Park
Twickenham
Teddington
Petersham
Ham
Hanworth
Hampton
Bushy Park
Hampton Court
Wimbledon Common
Wimbledon
Merton
Morden
Mitcham
Tooting
Balham
Streatham
Norbury
Thornton Heath
Kingston upon Thames
New Malden
Surbiton
Tolworth
Worcester Park
Esher
Claygate
Chessington
Ewell
Cheam
Sutton
Carshalton
Wallington
Croydon
Purley
Coulsdon
Epsom
Epsom Common
Ashtead
Oxshott
Leatherhead
Fetcham
Great Bookham
Banstead
Tadworth
Kingswood
Epsom Downs
Walton on the Hill
Headley
Box Hill
Mickleham
Dorking
Reigate
Redhill
Merstham
Caterham
Kenley
Chipstead
Hooley
Bletchingley
Nutfield
North Downs
M4
M25
M23
A3
A4
A23
A24
A217
A232
A240
A243

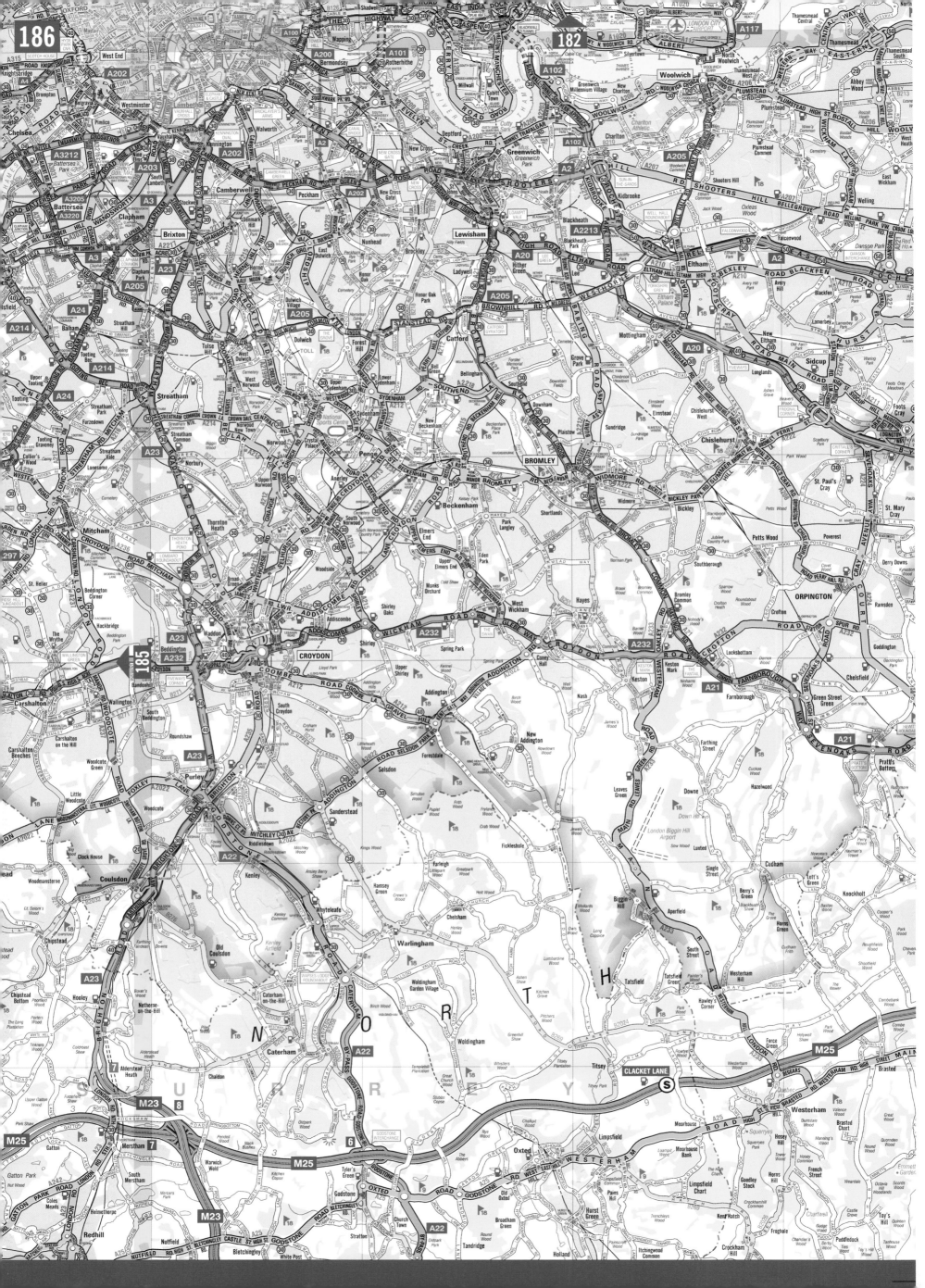

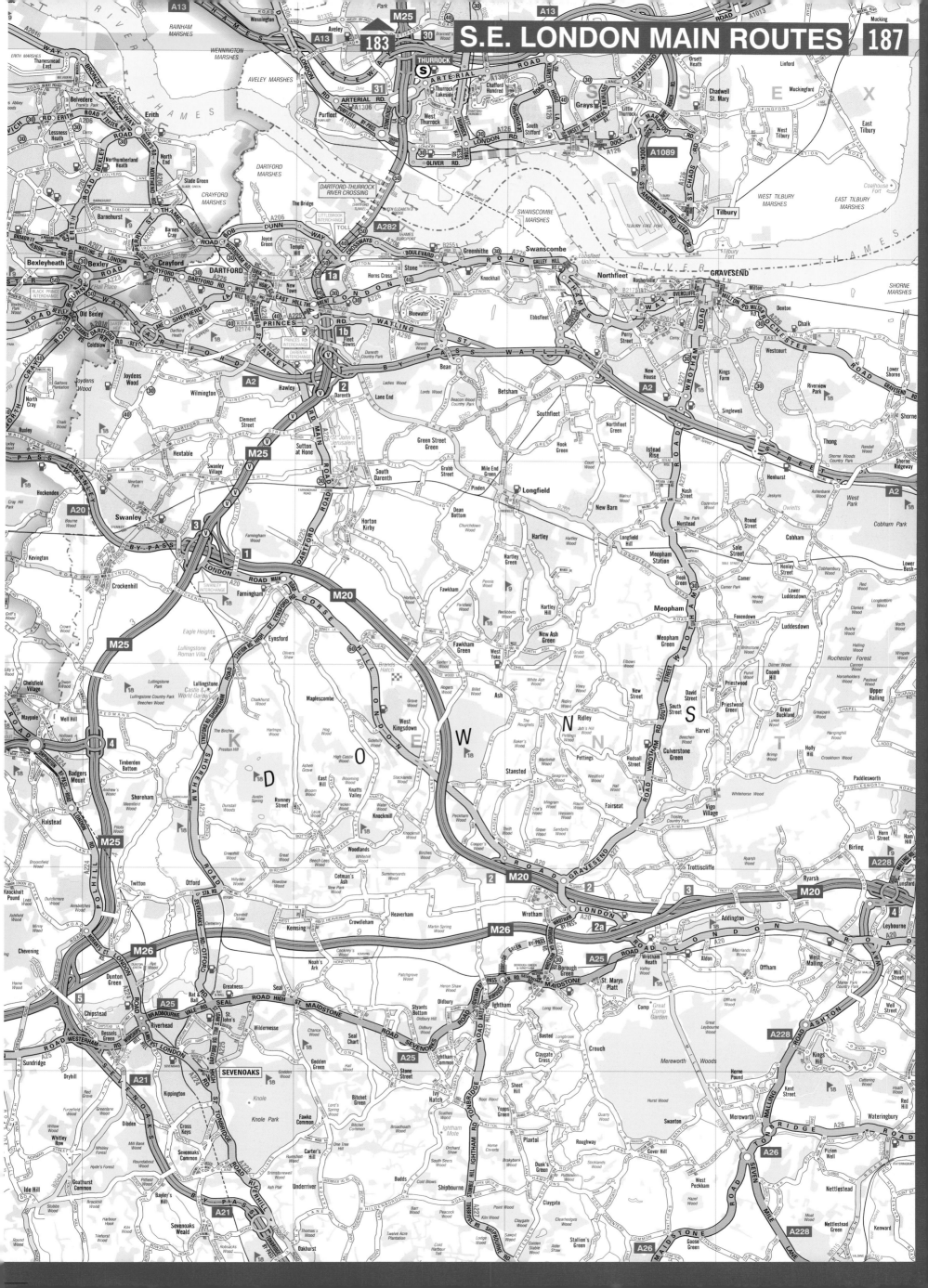

City & Town Centre Plans

Port Plans

Airport Plans

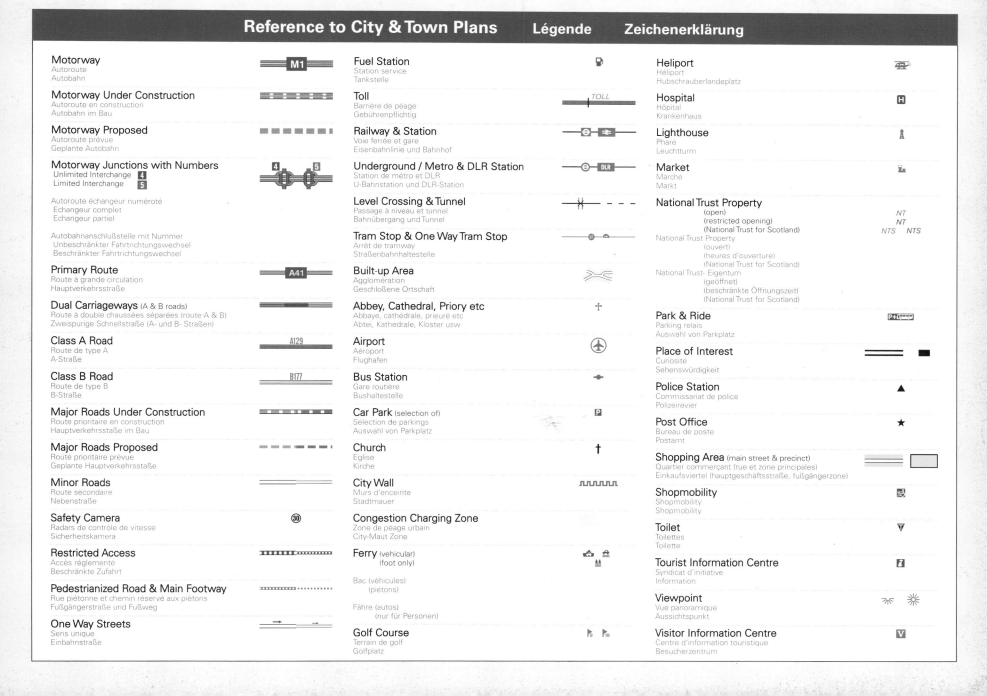

Reference to City & Town Plans   Légende   Zeichenerklärung

Motorway
Autoroute
Autobahn

Motorway Under Construction
Autoroute en construction
Autobahn im Bau

Motorway Proposed
Autoroute prévue
Geplante Autobahn

Motorway Junctions with Numbers
Unlimited Interchange 4
Limited Interchange 5
Autoroute échangeur numéroté
Echangeur complet
Echangeur partiel
Autobahnanschlußstelle mit Nummer
Unbeschränkter Fahrtrichtungswechsel
Beschränkter Fahrtrichtungswechsel

Primary Route
Route à grande circulation
Hauptverkehrsstraße

Dual Carriageways (A & B roads)
Route à double chaussées séparées (route A & B)
Zweispurige Schnellstraße (A- und B- Straßen)

Class A Road
Route de type A
A-Straße

Class B Road
Route de type B
B-Straße

Major Roads Under Construction
Route prioritaire en construction
Hauptverkehrsstraße im Bau

Major Roads Proposed
Route prioritaire prévue
Geplante Hauptverkehrsstraße

Minor Roads
Route secondaire
Nebenstraße

Safety Camera
Radars de contrôle de vitesse
Sicherheitskamera

Restricted Access
Accès réglementé
Beschränkte Zufahrt

Pedestrianized Road & Main Footway
Rue piétonne et chemin réservé aux piétons
Fußgängerstraße und Fußweg

One Way Streets
Sens unique
Einbahnstraße

Fuel Station
Station service
Tankstelle

Toll
Barrière de péage
Gebührenpflichtig

Railway & Station
Voie ferrée et gare
Eisenbahnlinie und Bahnhof

Underground / Metro & DLR Station
Station de métro et DLR
U-Bahnstation und DLR-Station

Level Crossing & Tunnel
Passage à niveau et tunnel
Bahnübergang und Tunnel

Tram Stop & One Way Tram Stop
Arrêt de tramway
Straßenbahnhaltestelle

Built-up Area
Agglomération
Geschlossene Ortschaft

Abbey, Cathedral, Priory etc
Abbaye, cathédrale, prieuré etc
Abtei, Kathedrale, Kloster usw

Airport
Aéroport
Flughafen

Bus Station
Gare routière
Bushaltestelle

Car Park (selection of)
Sélection de parkings
Auswahl von Parkplatz

Church
Eglise
Kirche

City Wall
Murs d'enceinte
Stadtmauer

Congestion Charging Zone
Zone de péage urbain
City-Maut Zone

Ferry (vehicular)
(foot only)
Bac (véhicules)
(piétons)
Fähre (autos)
(nur für Personen)

Golf Course
Terrain de golf
Golfplatz

Heliport
Héliport
Hubschrauberlandeplatz

Hospital
Hôpital
Krankenhaus

Lighthouse
Phare
Leuchtturm

Market
Marché
Markt

National Trust Property
(open)   NT
(restricted opening)   NT
(National Trust for Scotland) NTS   NTS
National Trust Property
(ouvert)
(heures d'ouverture)
(National Trust for Scotland)
National Trust- Eigentum
(geöffnet)
(beschränkte Öffnungszeit)
(National Trust for Scotland)

Park & Ride
Parking relais
Auswahl von Parkplatz

Place of Interest
Curiosité
Sehenswürdigkeit

Police Station
Commissariat de police
Polizeirevier

Post Office
Bureau de poste
Postamt

Shopping Area (main street & precinct)
Quartier commerçant (rue et zone principales)
Einkaufsviertel (hauptgeschäftsstraße, fußgängerzone)

Shopmobility
Shopmobility
Shopmobility

Toilet
Toilettes
Toilette

Tourist Information Centre
Syndicat d'initiative
Information

Viewpoint
Vue panoramique
Aussichtspunkt

Visitor Information Centre
Centre d'information touristique
Besucherzentrum

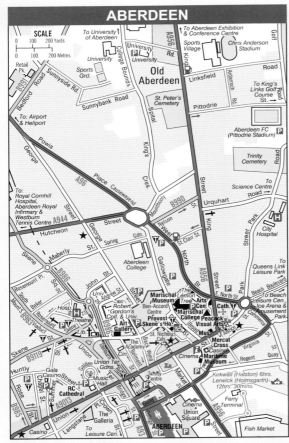

ABERDEEN

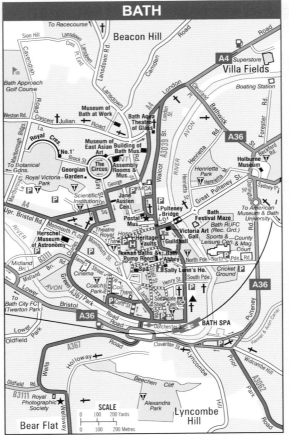

BATH

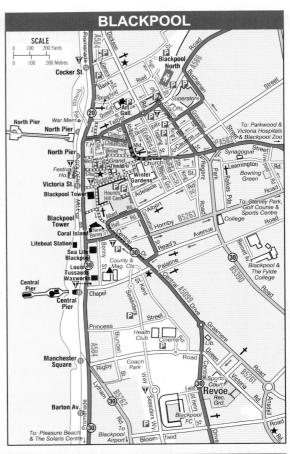

BLACKPOOL

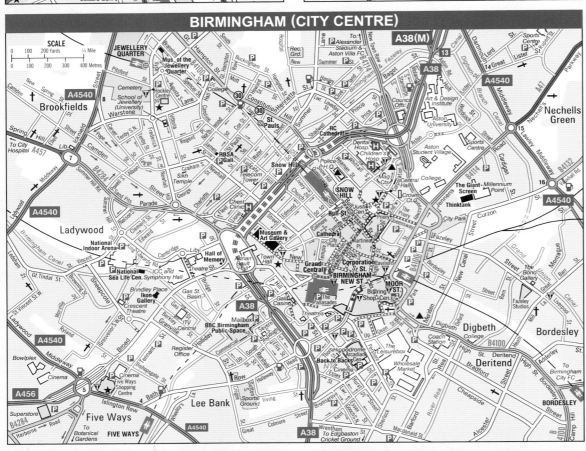

BIRMINGHAM (CITY CENTRE)

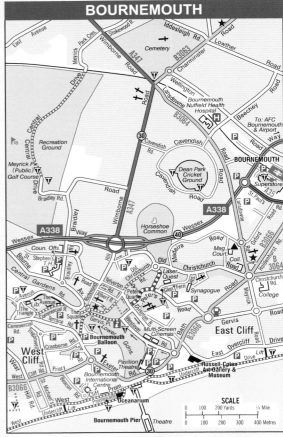

BOURNEMOUTH

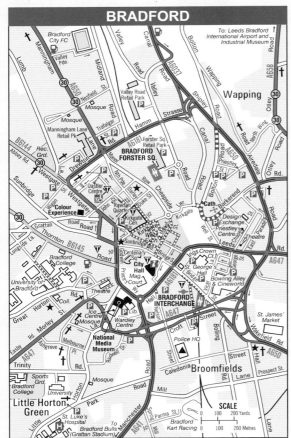

BRADFORD

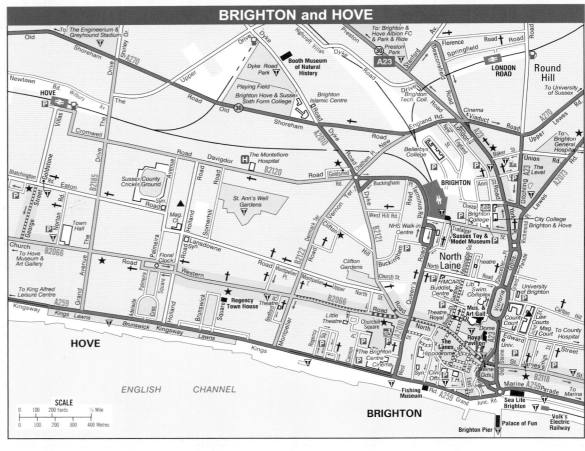

BRIGHTON and HOVE

BRISTOL

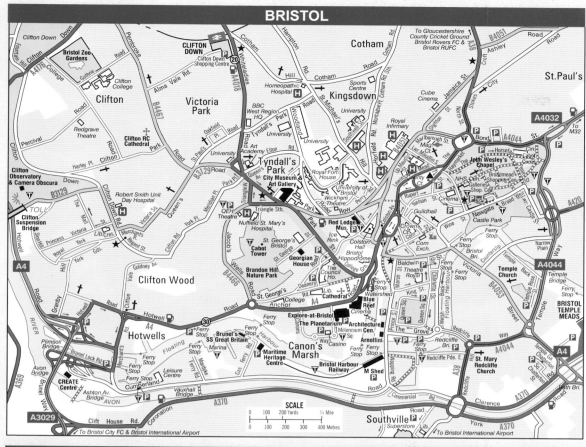

CANTERBURY

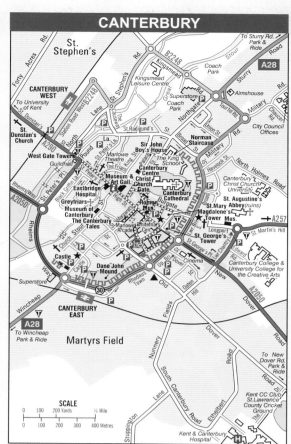

CAMBRIDGE

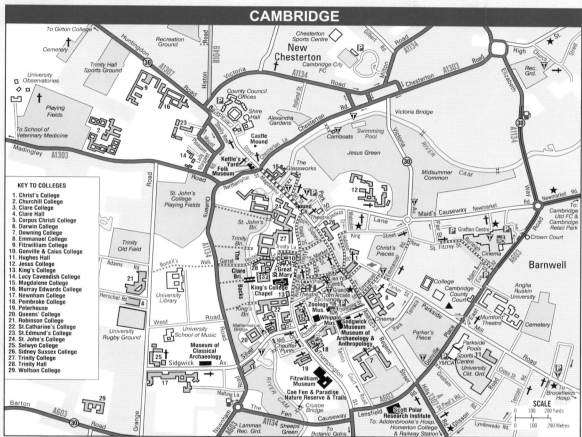

KEY TO COLLEGES
1. Christ's College
2. Churchill College
3. Clare College
4. Clare Hall
5. Corpus Christi College
6. Darwin College
7. Downing College
8. Emmanuel College
9. Fitzwilliam College
10. Gonville & Caius College
11. Hughes Hall
12. Jesus College
13. King's College
14. Lucy Cavendish College
15. Magdalene College
16. Murray Edwards College
17. Newnham College
18. Pembroke College
19. Peterhouse
20. Queens' College
21. Robinson College
22. St.Catharine's College
23. St.Edmund's College
24. St. John's College
25. Selwyn College
26. Sidney Sussex College
27. Trinity College
28. Trinity Hall
29. Wolfson College

CARLISLE

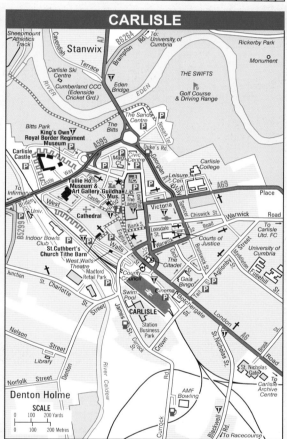

CARDIFF (CAERDYDD)

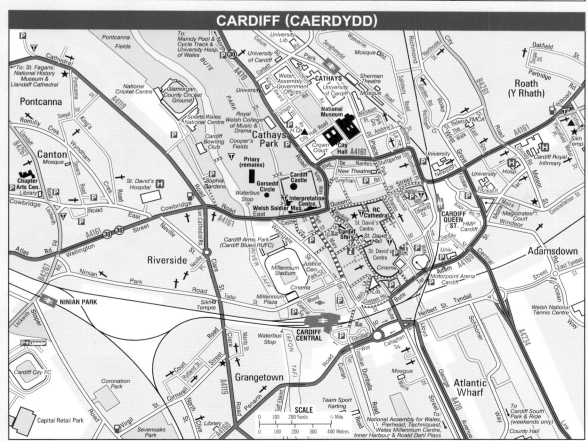

CHELTENHAM

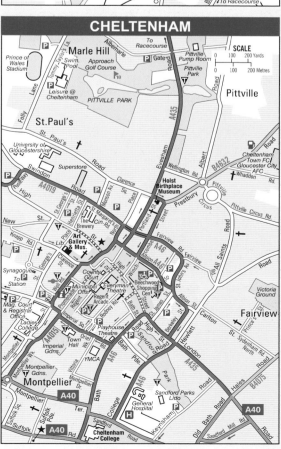

CHESTER

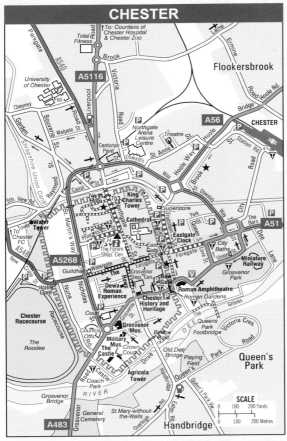

COVENTRY

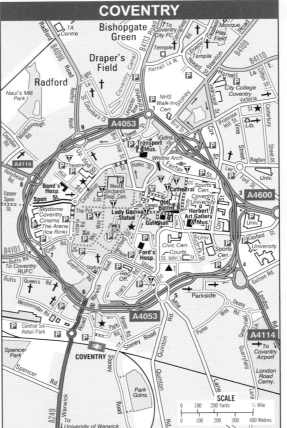

DERBY

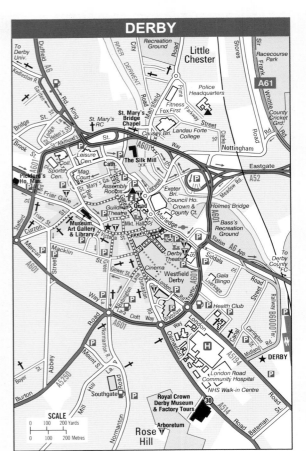

DOVER

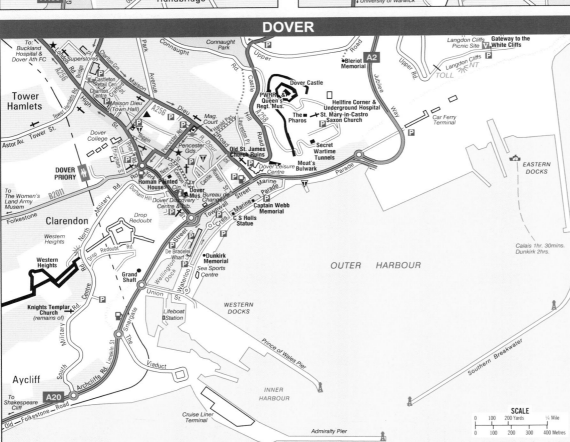

DUMFRIES

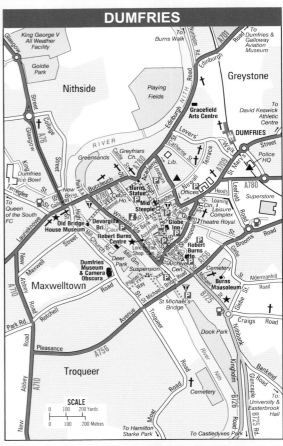

DUNDEE

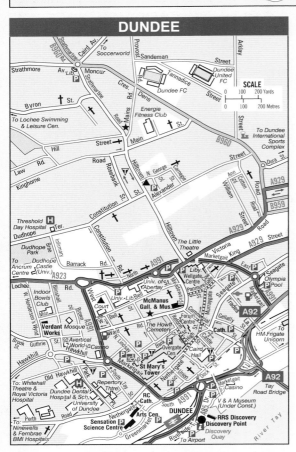

DURHAM

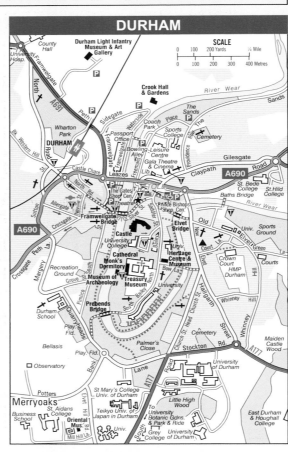

EASTBOURNE

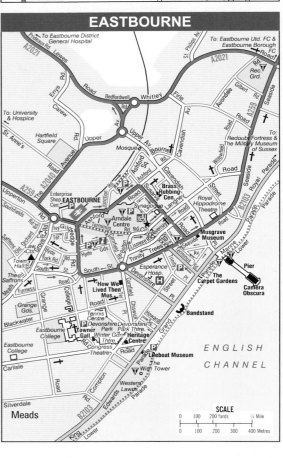

EDINBURGH
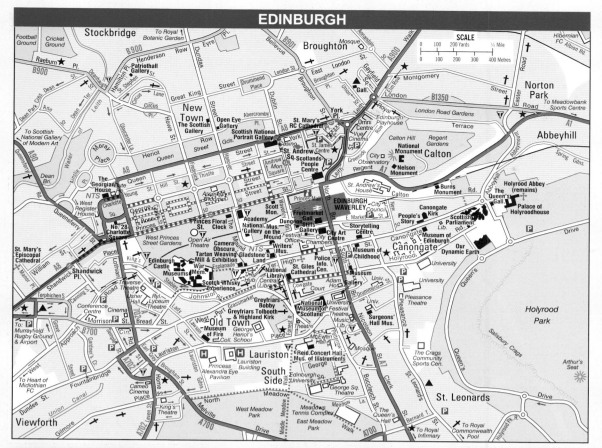

FOLKESTONE
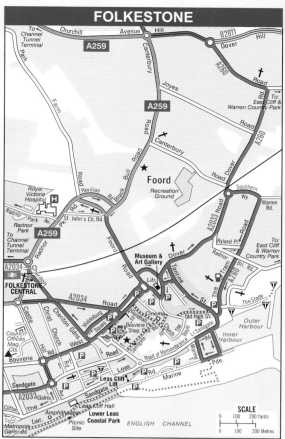

EXETER
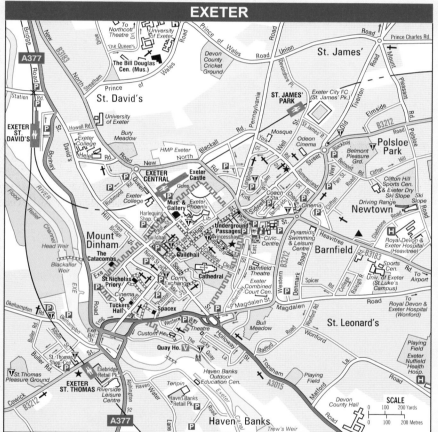

GUILDFORD
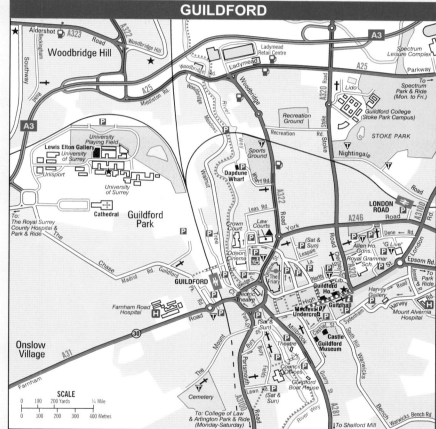

GLASGOW
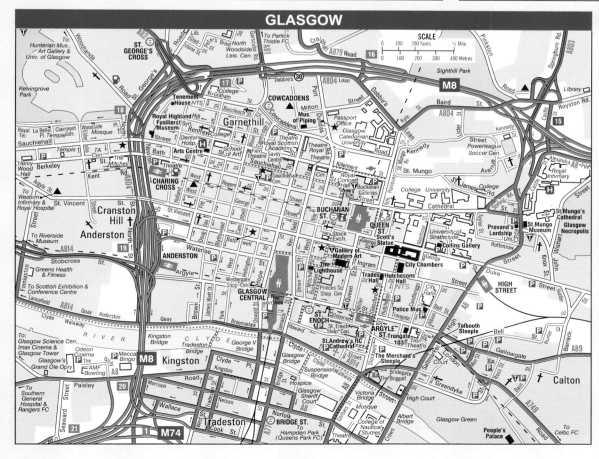

GLOUCESTER
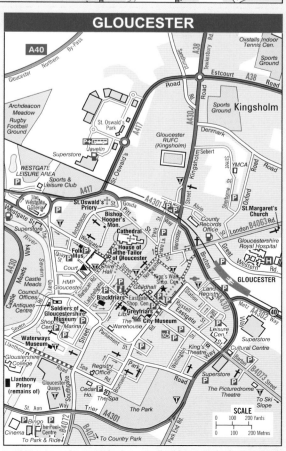

HARROGATE

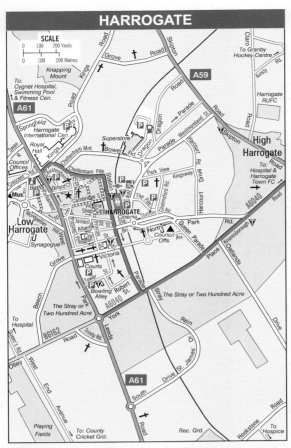

INVERNESS

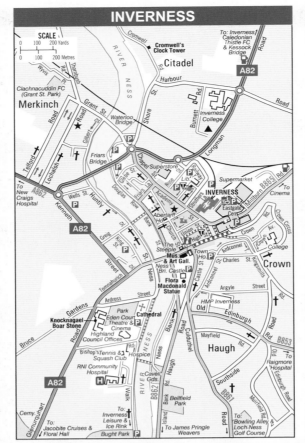

IPSWICH

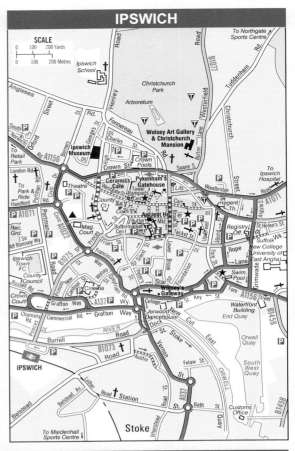

KILMARNOCK

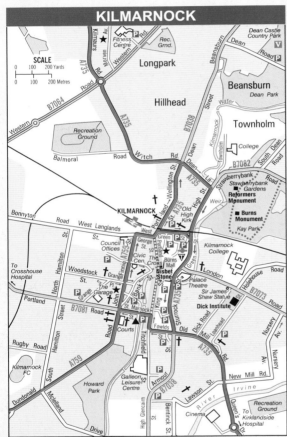

LEEDS

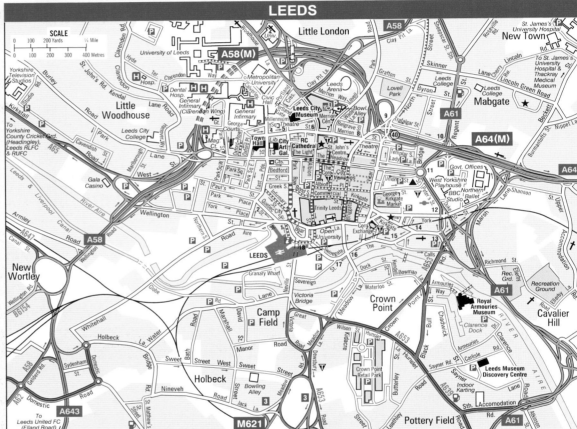

KINGSTON UPON HULL

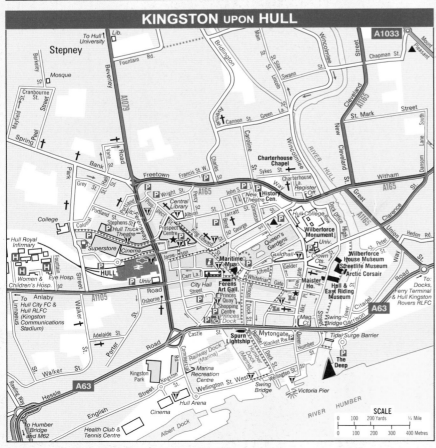

LEICESTER

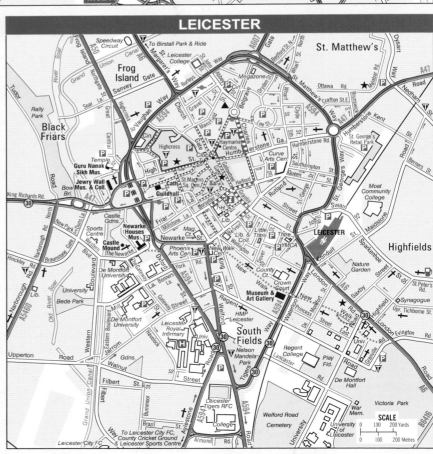

LINCOLN

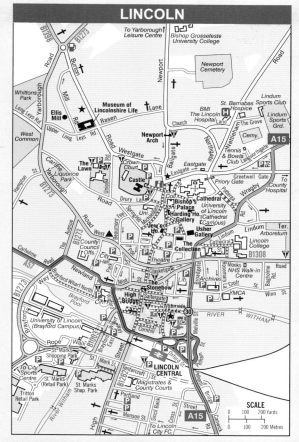

LIVERPOOL

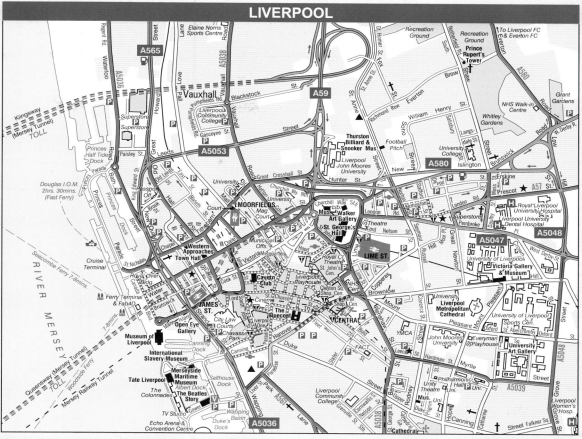

MANCHESTER (CITY CENTRE)

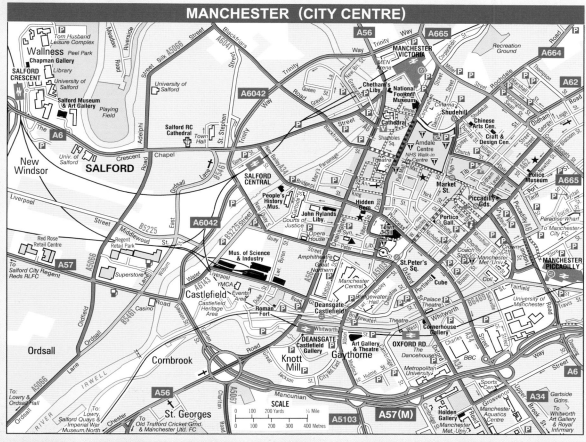

MIDDLESBROUGH

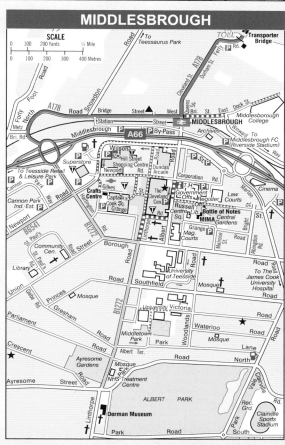

MEDWAY TOWNS

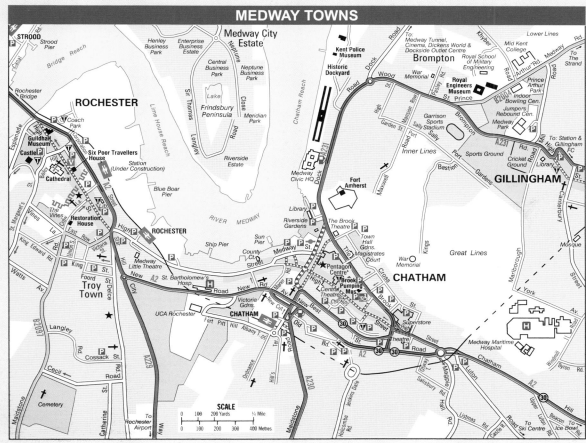

NEWCASTLE UPON TYNE

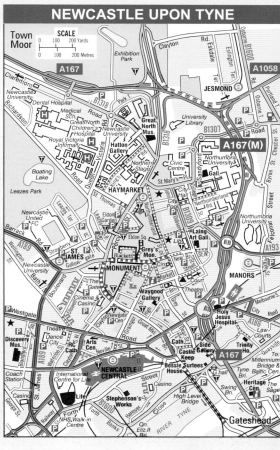

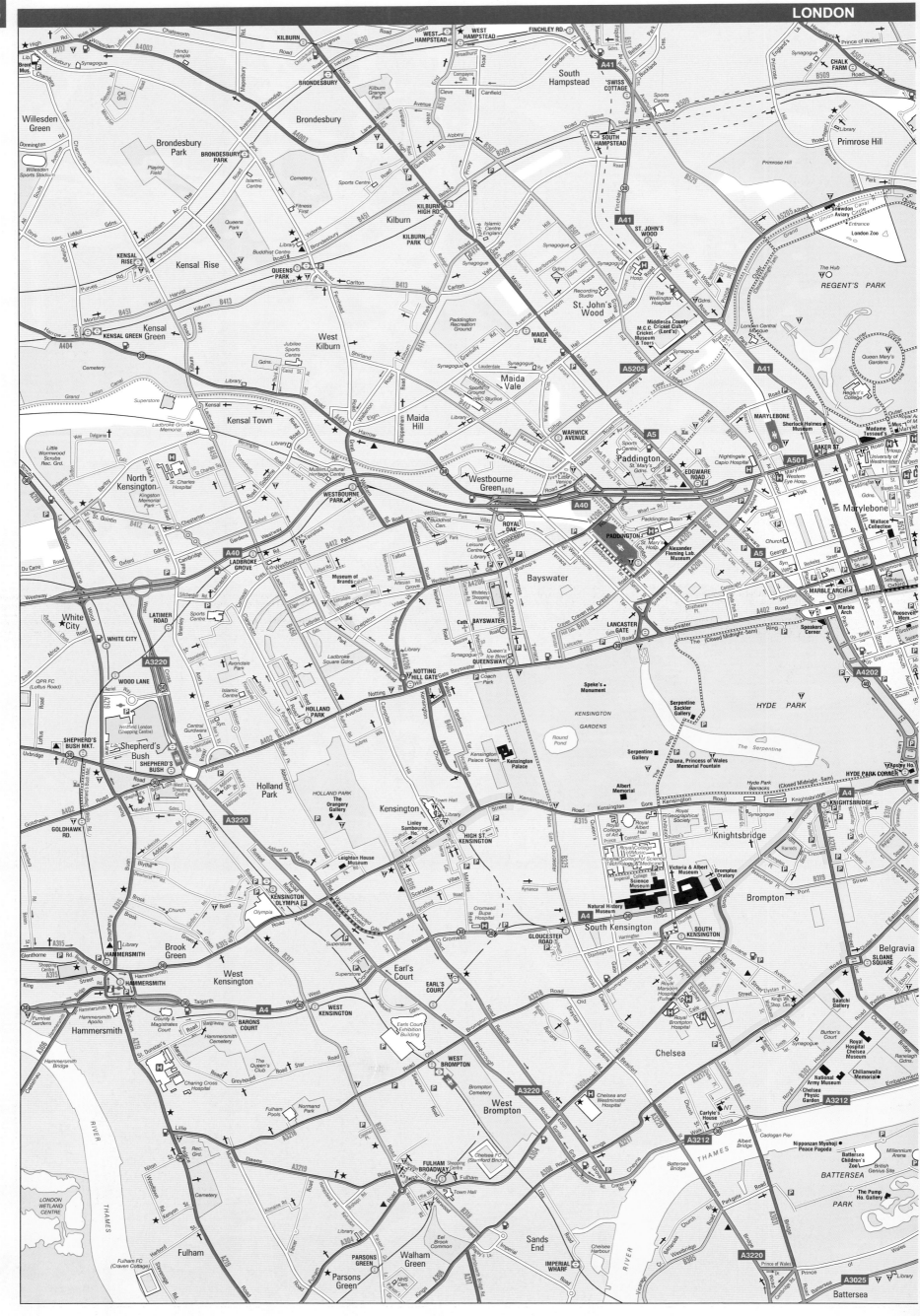

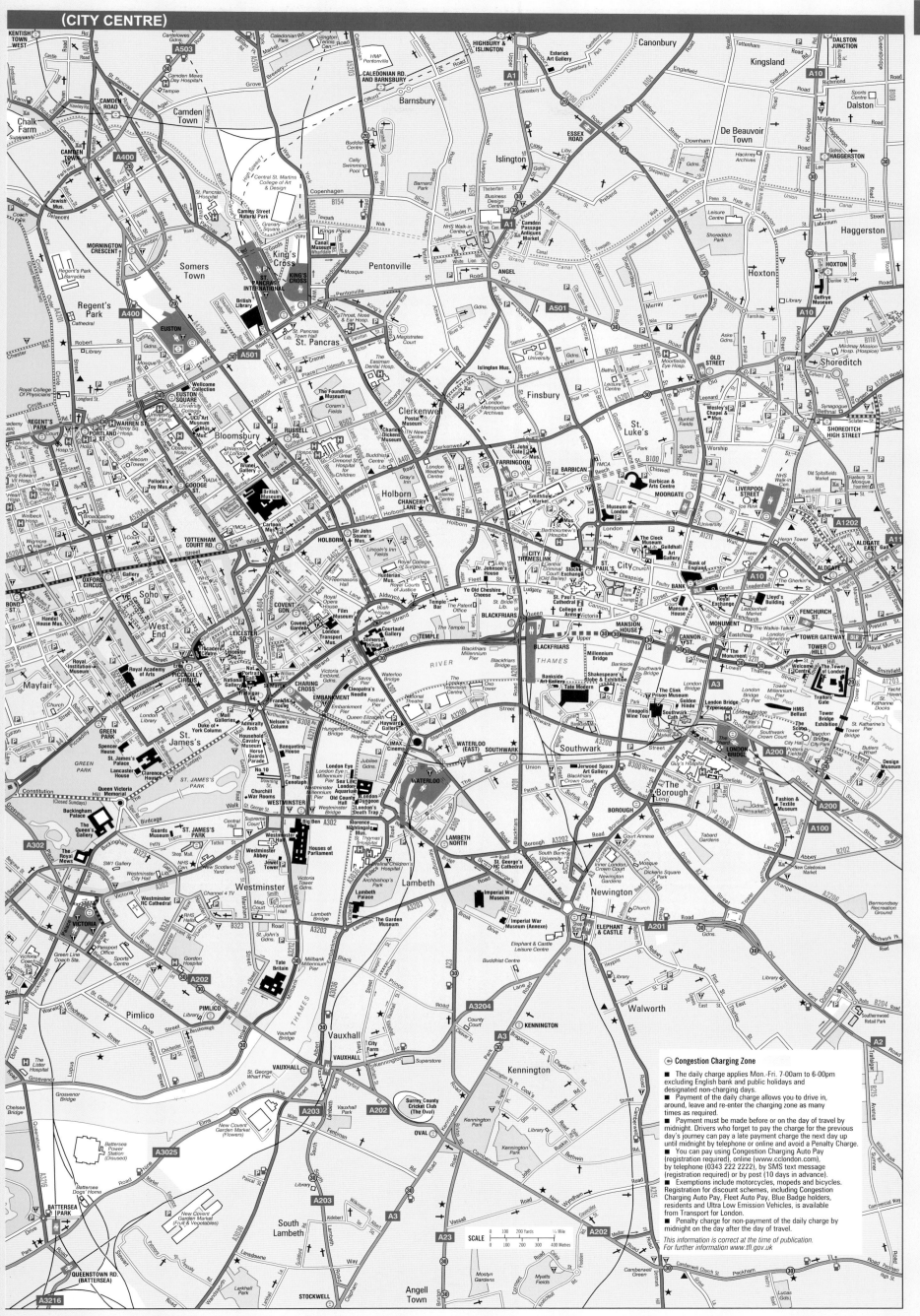

■ **Congestion Charging Zone**

■ The daily charge applies Mon.-Fri. 7-00am to 6-00pm excluding English bank and public holidays and designated non-charging days.

■ Payment of the daily charge allows you to drive in, around, leave and re-enter the charging zone as many times as required.

■ Payment must be made before or on the day of travel by midnight. Drivers who forget to pay the charge for the previous day's journey can pay a late payment charge the next day up until midnight by telephone or online and avoid a Penalty Charge.

■ You can pay using Congestion Charging Auto Pay (registration required), online (www.cclondon.com), by telephone (0343 222 2222), by SMS text message (registration required) or by post (10 days in advance).

■ Exemptions include motorcycles, mopeds and bicycles. Registration for discount schemes, including Congestion Charging Auto Pay, Fleet Auto Pay, Blue Badge holders, residents and Ultra Low Emission Vehicles, is available from Transport for London.

■ Penalty charge for non-payment of the daily charge by midnight on the day after the day of travel.

This information is correct at the time of publication. For further information www.tfl.gov.uk

SCALE
0   100   200 Yards   ¼ Mile
0   100   200   300   400 Metres

MILTON KEYNES

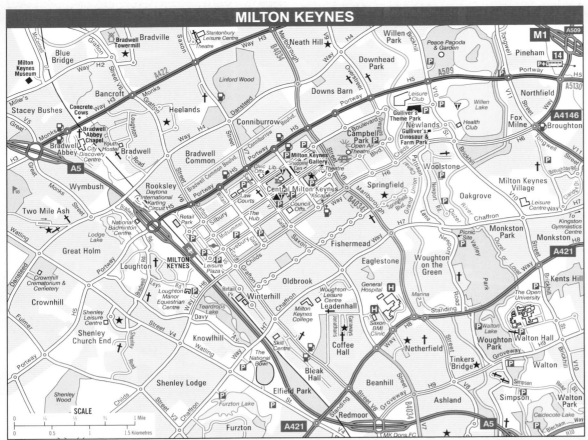

NEWPORT (CASNEWYDD)

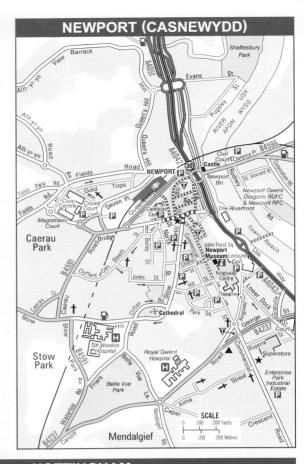

NORWICH

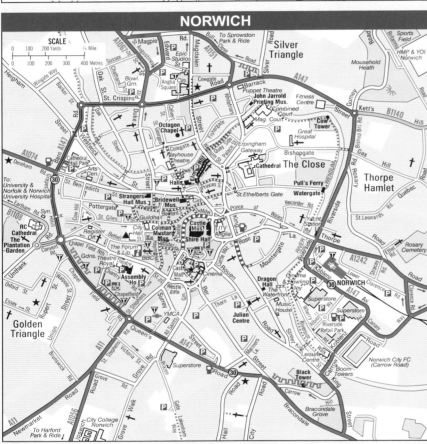

NOTTINGHAM

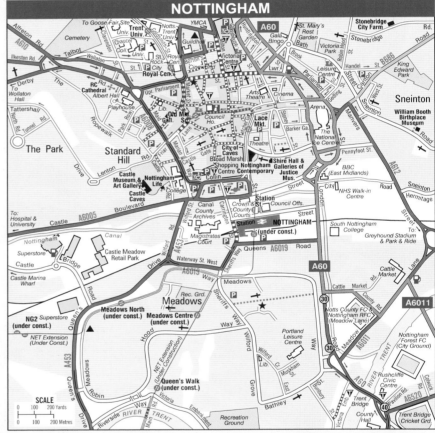

NORTHAMPTON

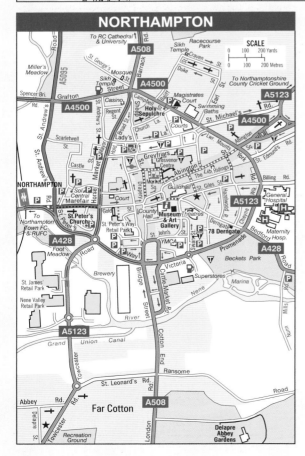

OXFORD

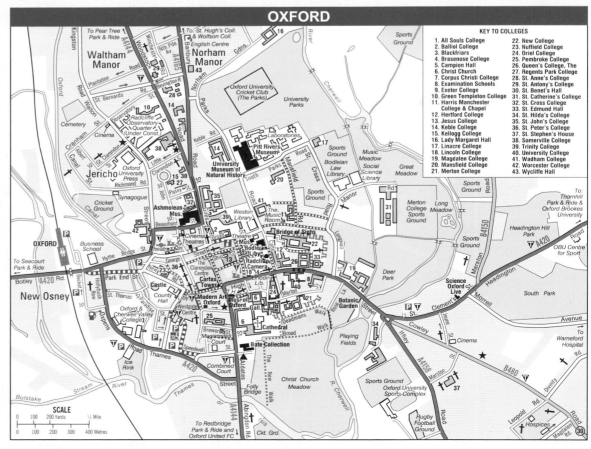

KEY TO COLLEGES

1. All Souls College
2. Balliol College
3. Blackfriars
4. Brasenose College
5. Campion Hall
6. Christ Church
7. Corpus Christi College
8. Examination Schools
9. Exeter College
10. Green Templeton College
11. Harris Manchester College & Chapel
12. Hertford College
13. Jesus College
14. Keble College
15. Kellogg College
16. Lady Margaret Hall
17. Linacre College
18. Lincoln College
19. Magdalen College
20. Mansfield College
21. Merton College
22. New College
23. Nuffield College
24. Oriel College
25. Pembroke College
26. Queen's College, The
27. Regents Park College
28. St. Anne's College
29. St. Antony's College
30. St. Benet's Hall
31. St. Catherine's College
32. St. Cross College
33. St. Edmund Hall
34. St. Hilda's College
35. St. John's College
36. St. Peter's College
37. St. Stephen's House
38. Somerville College
39. Trinity College
40. University College
41. Wadham College
42. Worcester College
43. Wycliffe Hall

OBAN
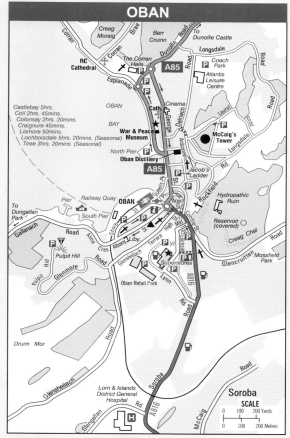

PERTH
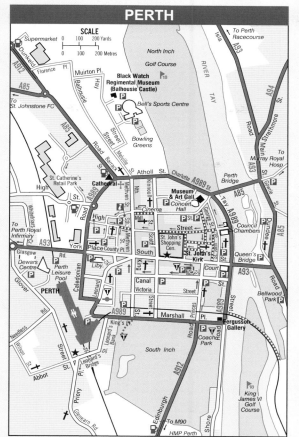

PETERBOROUGH
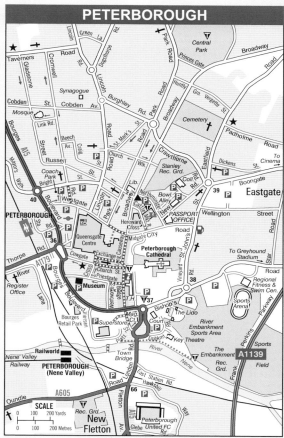

PLYMOUTH
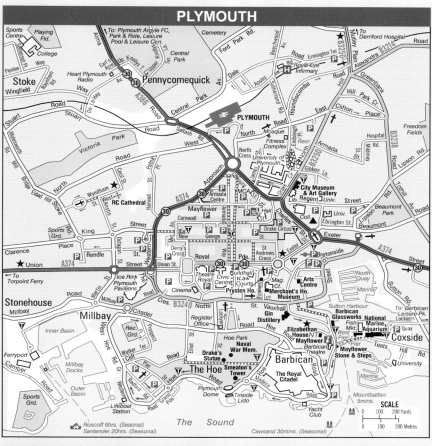

PORTSMOUTH
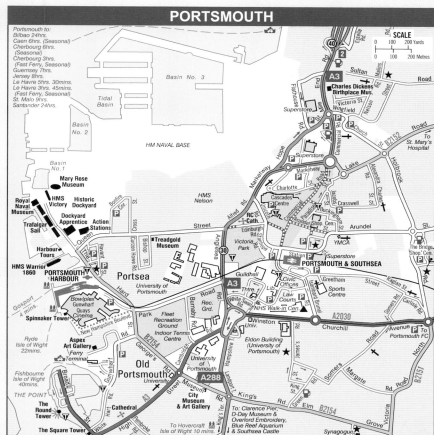

PRESTON
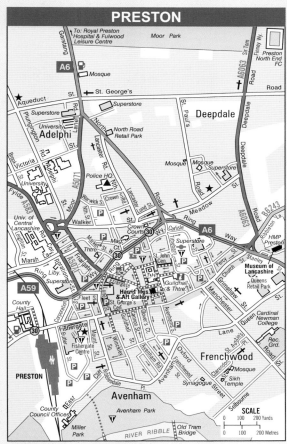

READING
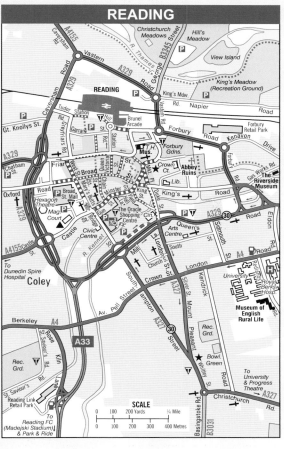

SALISBURY
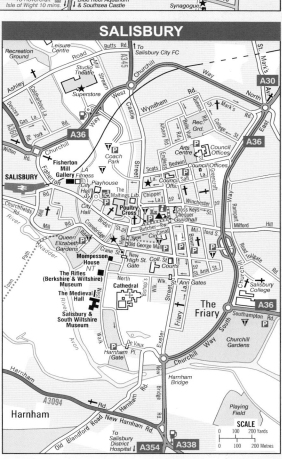

SHEFFIELD

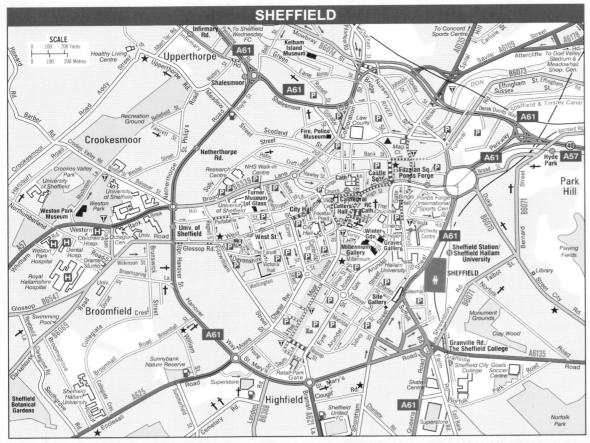

SHREWSBURY

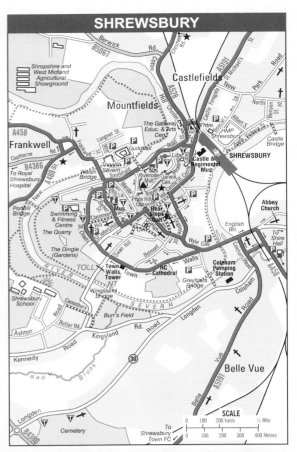

SOUTHAMPTON

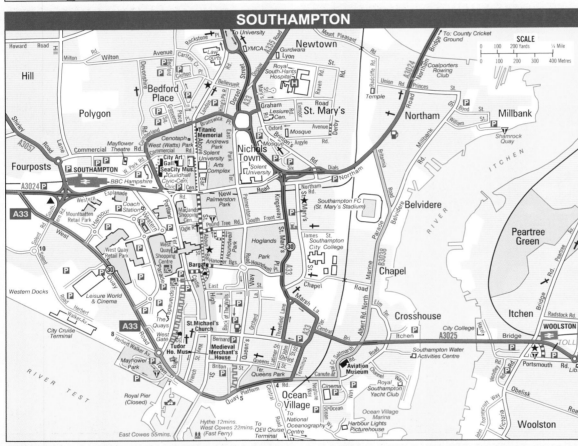

STIRLING

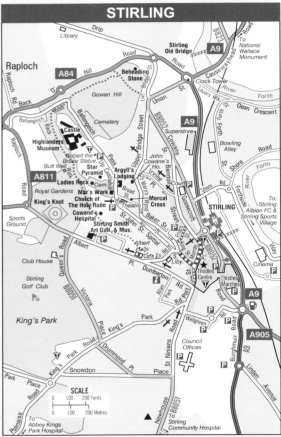

STOKE-ON-TRENT

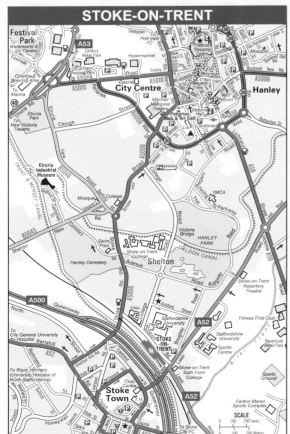

STRATFORD UPON AVON

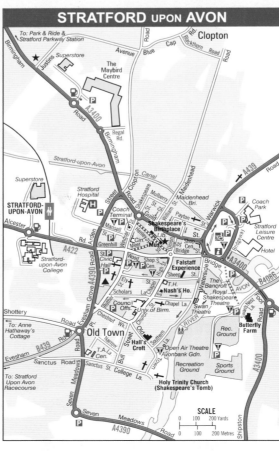

SUNDERLAND

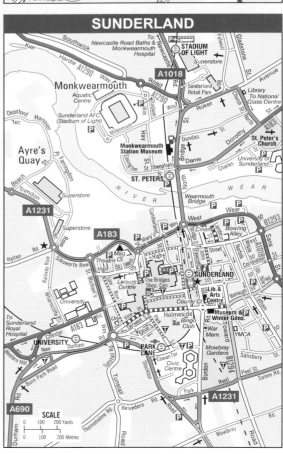

SWANSEA (ABERTAWE)
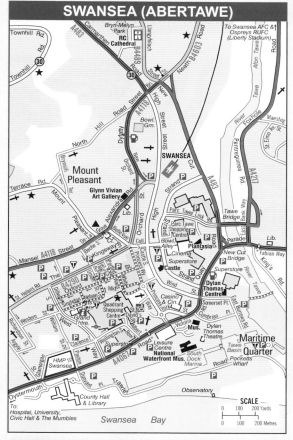

SWINDON
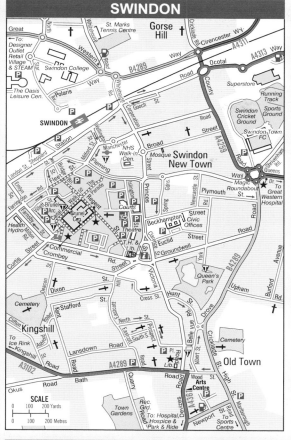

TAUNTON
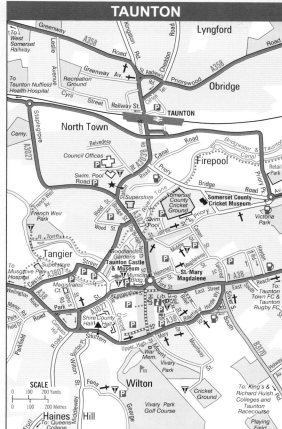

WINCHESTER
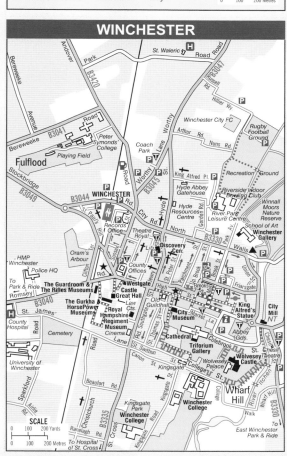

WINDSOR
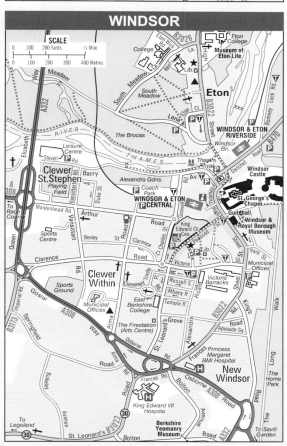

WOLVERHAMPTON
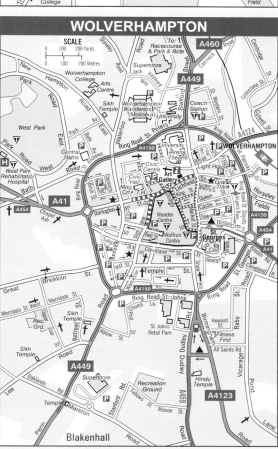

WORCESTER
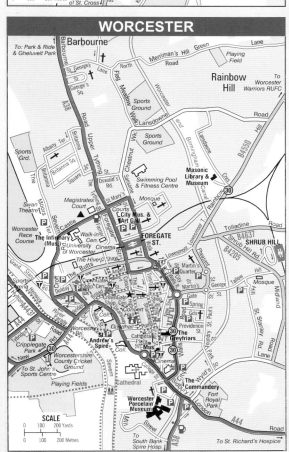

YORK
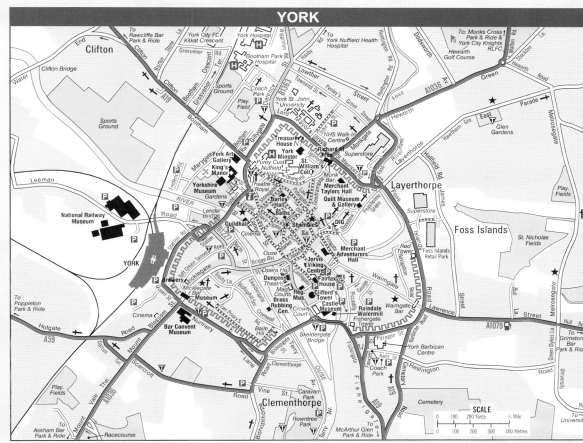

HARWICH

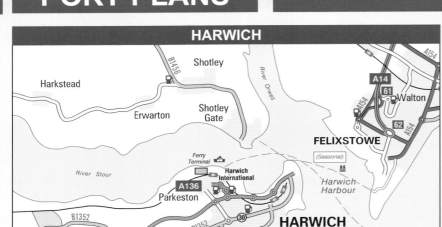

Harwich to:
Esbjerg 18hrs.
Hook of Holland 6hrs. 15mins.

KINGSTON UPON HULL

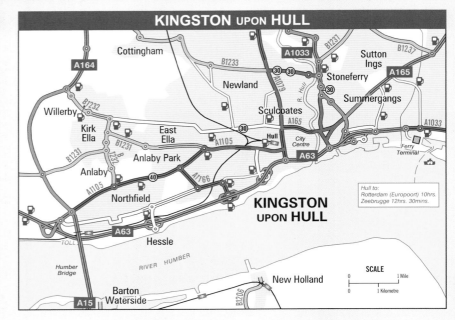

Hull to:
Rotterdam (Europoort) 10hrs.
Zeebrugge 12hrs. 30mins.

NEWCASTLE UPON TYNE

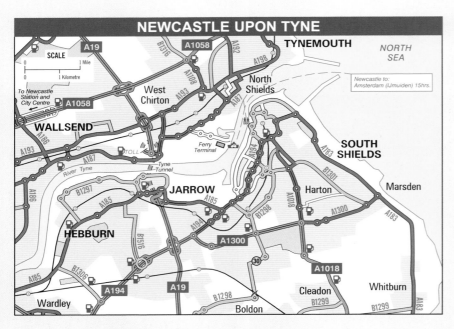

Newcastle to:
Amsterdam (IJmuiden) 15hrs.

NEWHAVEN

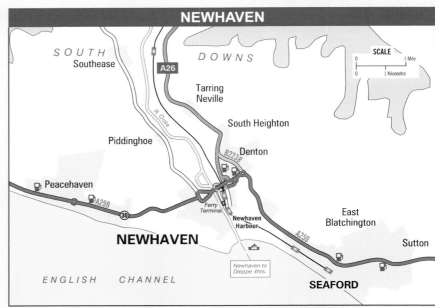

Newhaven to Dieppe 4hrs.

PEMBROKE DOCK (DOC PENFRO)

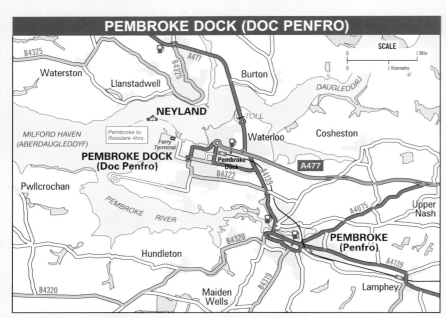

Pembroke to Rosslare 4hrs.

POOLE

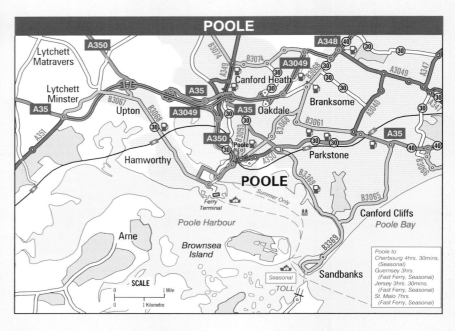

Poole to:
Cherbourg 4hrs. 30mins.
(Seasonal)
Guernsey 3hrs.
(Fast Ferry, Seasonal)
Jersey 3hrs. 30mins.
(Fast Ferry, Seasonal)
St. Malo 7hrs.
(Fast Ferry, Seasonal)

PORTSMOUTH

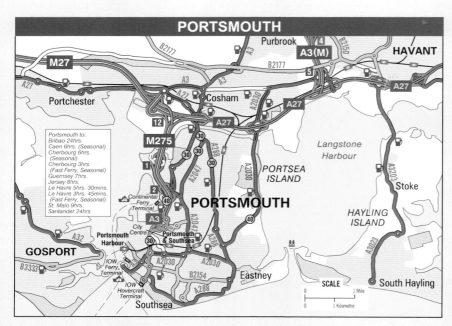

Portsmouth to:
Bilbao 24hrs. (Seasonal)
Caen 6hrs.
Cherbourg 6hrs.
(Seasonal)
Cherbourg 3hrs.
(Fast Ferry, Seasonal)
Guernsey 7hrs.
Jersey 8hrs.
Le Havre 5hrs. 30mins.
Le Havre 3hrs. 45mins.
(Fast Ferry, Seasonal)
St. Malo 9hrs.
Santander 24hrs.

WEYMOUTH

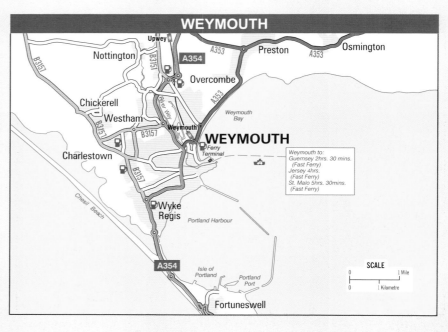

Weymouth to:
Guernsey 2hrs. 30 mins.
(Fast Ferry)
Jersey 4hrs.
(Fast Ferry)
St. Malo 5hrs. 30mins.
(Fast Ferry)

BIRMINGHAM

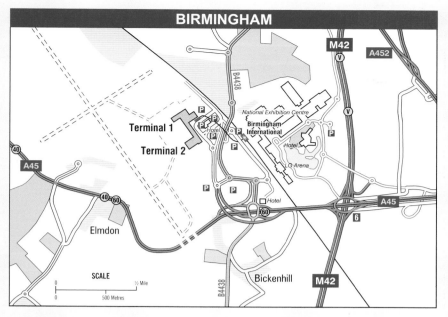

M42 · A452 · B4438 · V · National Exhibition Centre · Birmingham International · Terminal 1 · Terminal 2 · Hotel · V · Hotel · LG Arena · A45 · A45 · 6 · 60 · 40 · 60 · Elmdon · Hotel · B4438 · Bickenhill · M42

SCALE ½ Mile · 0 · 500 Metres

EAST MIDLANDS

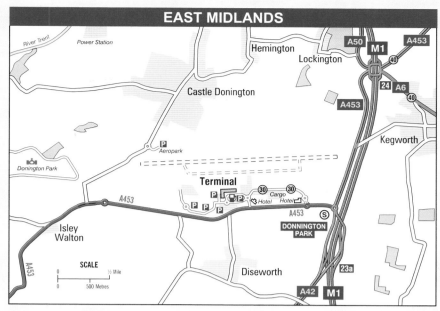

River Trent · Power Station · Hemington · Lockington · A50 · M1 · A453 · Castle Donington · A453 · 24 · A6 · Kegworth · Aeropark · P · Terminal · 30 · 30 · Cargo · Donington Park · P · P · Hotel · Hotel · A453 · S · A453 · Isley Walton · DONNINGTON PARK · A453 · Diseworth · 23a · A42 · M1

SCALE ½ Mile · 0 · 500 Metres

GLASGOW

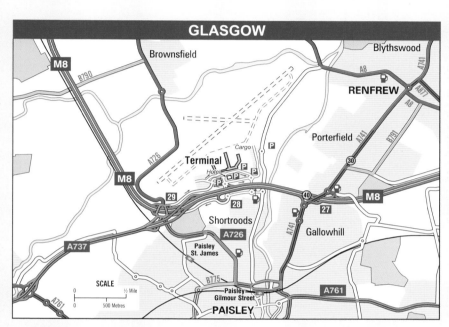

Brownsfield · Blythswood · M8 · B790 · A8 · A741 · RENFREW · A877 · Cargo · Porterfield · B789 · A741 · Terminal · P · Hotel · 30 · M8 · M8 · A726 · 40 · M8 · 29 · 28 · 27 · Shortroods · A741 · Gallowhill · A737 · A726 · Paisley St. James · B775 · Paisley Gilmour Street · A761 · A761 · PAISLEY

SCALE ½ Mile · 0 · 500 Metres

LONDON GATWICK

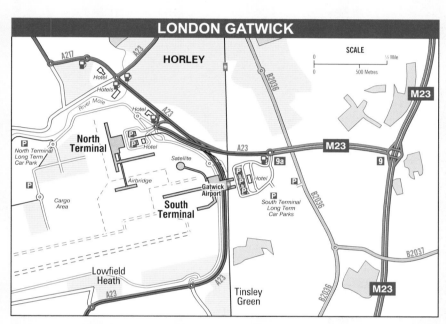

A217 · A23 · HORLEY · SCALE ½ Mile · 0 · 500 Metres · Hotels · B2036 · M23 · Hotels · River Mole · A23 · North Terminal · Hotel · A23 · M23 · 9a · North Terminal Long Term Car Park · P · P · Hotel · Satellite · 9 · B2036 · P · Airbridge · Gatwick Airport · Hotel · P · Cargo Area · South Terminal · South Terminal Long Term Car Parks · B2037 · Lowfield Heath · Tinsley Green · A23 · B2036 · M23

LONDON HEATHROW

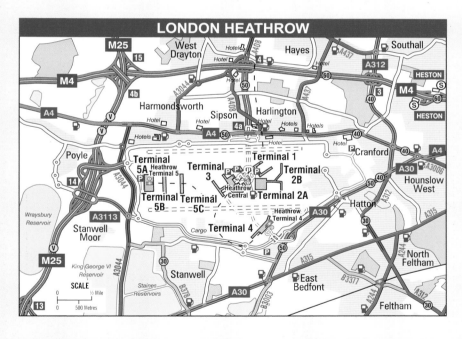

M25 · 15 · West Drayton · Hotel · Hayes · Southall · M4 · 4b · A312 · M4 · A4 · Harmondsworth · 50 · 60 · 3 · HESTON · Sipson · Harlington · Hotels · HESTON · Hotel · Hotels · Hotel · A4 · 50 · Cranford · A4 · Poyle · Hotels · Terminal 5A · Heathrow Terminal 5 · Terminal 1 · Terminal 3 · Terminal 2B · Terminal 2A · A30 · A3006 · 14 · Heathrow Central · Hounslow West · Terminal 5B · Terminal 5C · Heathrow Terminal 4 · Hatton · A30 · Wraysbury Reservoir · A3113 · Cargo · Terminal 4 · A315 · Stanwell Moor · 50 · 30 · M25 · King George VI Reservoir · A3044 · Stanwell · A30 · East Bedfont · B3377 · North Feltham · A244 · A312 · 13 · Staines Reservoirs · B378 · B3043 · Feltham

SCALE ½ Mile · 0 · 500 Metres

LONDON LUTON

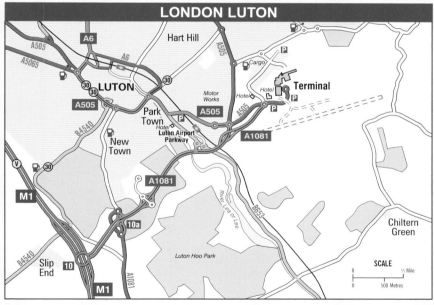

A505 · A6 · Hart Hill · A505 · A5065 · 30 · Cargo · Terminal · LUTON · Motor Works · Hotel · A505 · Park Town · Luton Airport Parkway · A1081 · New Town · A1081 · M1 · V · 30 · A1081 · 10a · B4540 · Luton Hoo Park · Chiltern Green · Slip End · 10 · A1081 · M1

SCALE ½ Mile · 0 · 500 Metres

LONDON STANSTED

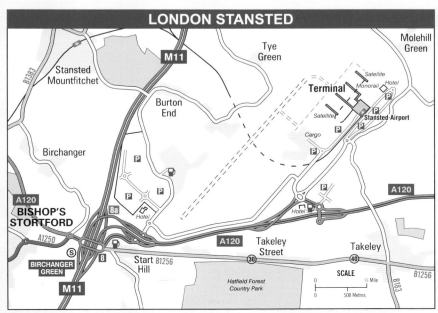

Tye Green · Molehill Green · M11 · Satellite · Hotel · Stansted Mountfitchet · B1383 · Burton End · Monorail · Terminal · Satellite · Stansted Airport · Birchanger · Cargo · P · P · A120 · A120 · A120 · Hotel · BISHOP'S STORTFORD · 8a · P · A1250 · P · A120 · Takeley Street · Takeley · BIRCHANGER GREEN · S · 8 · Start Hill · B1256 · 30 · 40 · B1256 · M11 · Hatfield Forest Country Park

SCALE ½ Mile · 0 · 500 Metres

MANCHESTER INTERNATIONAL

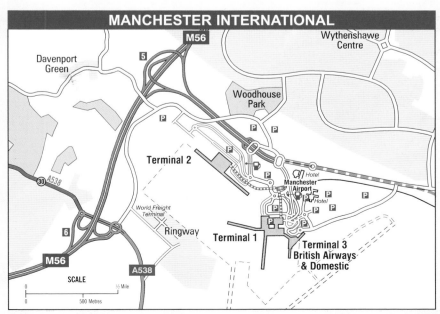

M56 · Wythenshawe Centre · Davenport Green · 5 · Woodhouse Park · Terminal 2 · Hotel · Manchester Airport · A538 · 30 · P · World Freight Terminal · 6 · Terminal 1 · Ringway · Terminal 3 British Airways & Domestic · M56 · A538

SCALE ½ Mile · 0 · 500 Metres

INDEX TO CITIES, TOWNS, VILLAGES, HAMLETS, LOCATIONS, AIRPORTS & PORTS

(1) A strict alphabetical order is used e.g. An Dùnan follows Andreas but precedes Andwell.

(2) The map reference given refers to the actual map square in which the town spot or built-up area is located and not to the place name.

(3) Major towns and destinations are shown in bold, i.e. **Aberdeen**. *Aber* . . . .3G 153 & 192
Where they appear on a Town Plan a second page reference is given.

(4) Where two or more places of the same name occur in the same County or Unitary Authority, the nearest large town is also given; e.g. Achiemore. *High* . . .2D 166 (nr. Durness) indicates that Achiemore is located in square 2D on page 166 and is situated near Durness in the Unitary Authority of Highland.

(5) Only one reference is given although due to page overlaps the place may appear on more than one page.

COUNTIES and UNITARY AUTHORITIES with the abbreviations used in this index

INDEX

Armadale—Beauly

Armadale. High 3E 147
(nr. Isleornsay)
Armadale. High 2H 167
(nr. Strathy)
Armadale. W Lot 3C 128
Armagh. Arm 5C 178
Armathwaite. Cumb 5G 113
Arminghall. Norf 5E 79
Armitage. Staf 4E 73
Armitage Bridge. W Yor 3B 92
Armley. W Yor 1C 92
Armoy. Moy 3G 175
Armscote. Warw 1H 49
Arms, The. Norf 1A 66
Armston. Nptn 2H 63
Armthorpe. S Yor 4G 93
Arncliffe. N Yor 2B 98
Arncliffe Cote. N Yor 2B 98
Arncroach. Fife 3H 137
Arne. Dors 4E 15
Arnesby. Leics 1D 62
Arnicle. Arg 2B 122
Arnisdale. High 2G 147
Arnish. High 4E 155
Arniston. Midl 3G 129
Arnol. W Isl 3F 171
Arnold. E Yor 5F 101
Arnold. Notts 1C 74
Arnprior. Stir 4F 135
Arnside. Cumb 2D 96
Aros Mains. Arg 4G 139
Arpafeelie. High 3A 158
Arrad Foot. Cumb 1C 96
Arram. E Yor 5E 101
Arras. E Yor 5D 100
Arrathorne. N Yor 5E 105
Arreton. IOW 4D 16
Arrington. Cambs 5C 64
Arrochar. Arg 3B 134
Arrow. Warw 5E 61
Arscaig. High 2C 164
Artafallie. High 4A 158
Arthington. W Yor 5E 99
Arthingworth. Nptn 2E 63
Arthog. Gwyn 4F 69
Arthrath. Abers 5G 161
Arthurstone. Per 4B 144
Articlave. Cole 3D 174
Artigarvan. Strab 2F 176
Artikelly. Lim 4C 174
Artington. Surr 1A 26
Arundel. W Sus 5B 26
Asby. Cumb 2B 102
Ascog. Arg 3C 126
Ascot. Wind 4A 38
Ascott-under-Wychwood.
Oxon 4B 50
Asenby. N Yor 2F 99
Asfordby. Leics 4E 74
Asfordby Hill. Leics 4E 74
Asgarby. Linc 4C 88
(nr. Horncastle)
Asgarby. Linc 1A 76
(nr. Sleaford)
Ash. Devn 4E 9
Ash. Dors 1D 14
Ash. Kent 5G 41
(nr. Sandwich)
Ash. Kent 4H 39
(nr. Swanley)
Ash. Som 4H 21
Ash. Surr 1G 25
Ashampstead. W Ber 4D 36
Ashbocking. Suff 5D 66
Ashbourne. Derbs 1F 73
Ashbrittle. Som 4D 20
Ashbrook. Shrp 1G 59
Ashburton. Devn 2D 8
Ashbury. Devn 3F 11
Ashbury. Oxon 3A 36
Ashby. N Lin 4B 94
Ashby by Partney. Linc 4D 88
Ashby cum Fenby.
NE Lin 4F 95
Ashby de la Launde.
Linc 5H 87
Ashby-de-la-Zouch.
Leics 4A 74
Ashby Folville. Leics 4E 74
Ashby Magna. Leics 1C 62
Ashby Parva. Leics 2C 62
Ashby Puerorum. Linc 3C 88
Ashby St Ledgers.
Nptn 4C 62
Ashby St Mary. Norf 5F 79
Ashchurch. Glos 2E 49
Ashcombe. Devn 5C 12
Ashcott. Som 3H 21
Ashdon. Essx 1F 53
Ashe. Hants 1D 24
Asheldham. Essx 5C 54
Ashen. Essx 1H 53
Ashendon. Buck 4F 51
Ashey. IOW 4D 16
Ashfield. Hants 1B 16
Ashfield. Here 3A 48
Ashfield. Shrp 2H 59
Ashfield. Stir 3G 135
Ashfield. Suff 4E 66
Ashfield Green. Suff 3E 67
Ashfold Crossways.
W Sus 3D 26
Ashford. Devn 3F 19
(nr. Barnstaple)
Ashford. Devn 4C 8
(nr. Kingsbridge)
Ashford. Hants 1G 15
Ashford. Kent 1E 28
Ashford. Surr 3B 38
Ashford Bowdler. Shrp 3H 59
Ashford Carbonel. Shrp 3H 59
Ashford Hill. Hants 5D 36
Ashford in the Water.
Derbs 4F 85
Ashgill. S Lan 5A 128
Ash Green. Warw 2H 61
Ashgrove. Mor 2G 159
Ashill. Devn 1D 12
Ashill. Norf 5A 78
Ashill. Som 1G 13
Ashingdon. Essx 1C 40
Ashington. Nmbd 1F 115
Ashington. W Sus 4C 26
Ashkirk. Bord 2G 119
Ashlett. Hants 2C 16
Ashleworth. Glos 3D 48
Ashley. Cambs 4F 65
Ashley. Ches E 2B 84
Ashley. Dors 2G 15
Ashley. Glos 2E 35
Ashley. Hants 3A 16
(nr. New Milton)
Ashley. Hants 3B 24
(nr. Winchester)
Ashley. Kent 1H 29
Ashley. Nptn 1E 63
Ashley. Staf 2B 72
Ashley. Wilts 5D 34
Ashley Green. Buck 5H 51
Ashley Heath. Dors 2G 15
Ashley Heath. Staf 2B 72
Ashley Moor. Here 4G 59
Ash Magna. Shrp 2H 71
Ashmanhaugh. Norf 3F 79
Ashmansworth. Hants 1C 24
Ashmansworthy. Devn 1D 10
Ashmead Green. Glos 2C 34
Ashmill. Devn 3D 11
(nr. Holsworthy)
Ash Mill. Devn 4A 20
(nr. South Molton)
Ashmore. Dors 1E 15
Ashmore Green. W Ber 5D 36
Ashorne. Warw 5H 61
Ashover. Derbs 4A 86
Ashow. Warw 3H 61
Ash Parva. Shrp 2H 71
Ashperton. Here 1B 48
Ashprington. Devn 3E 9
Ash Priors. Som 4E 21
Ashreigney. Devn 1G 11
Ash Street. Suff 1D 54
Ashtead. Surr 5C 38
Ash Thomas. Devn 1D 12
Ashton. Corn 4D 4
Ashton. Here 4H 59
Ashton. Inv 2D 126
Ashton. Nptn 2H 63
(nr. Oundle)
Ashton. Nptn 1F 51
(nr. Roade)
Ashton. Pet 5A 76
Ashton Common. Wilts 1E 23
Ashton Hayes. Ches W 4H 83
Ashton-in-Makerfield.
G Man 4D 90
Ashton Keynes. Wilts 2F 35
Ashton under Hill. Worc 2E 49
Ashton-under-Lyne.
G Man 1D 84
Ashton upon Mersey.
G Man 1B 84
Ashurst. Hants 1B 16
Ashurst. Kent 2G 27
Ashurst. Lanc 4C 90
Ashurst. W Sus 4C 26
Ashurst Wood. W Sus 2F 27
Ash Vale. Surr 1G 25
Ashwater. Devn 3D 11
Ashwell. Herts 2C 52
Ashwell. Rut 4F 75
Ashwellthorpe. Norf 1D 66
Ashwick. Som 2B 22
Ashwicken. Norf 4G 77
Ashwood. Staf 2C 60
Askam in Furness.
Cumb 2B 96
Askern. S Yor 3F 93
Askerswell. Dors 3A 14
Askett. Buck 5G 51
Askham. Cumb 2G 103
Askham. Notts 3E 87
Askham Bryan. York 5H 99
Askham Richard. York 5H 99
Askrigg. N Yor 5C 104
Askwith. N Yor 5D 98
Aslackby. Linc 2H 75
Aslacton. Norf 1D 66
Aslockton. Notts 1E 75
Aspatria. Cumb 5C 112
Aspenden. Herts 3D 52
Asperton. Linc 2B 76
Aspley Guise. C Beds 2H 51
Aspley Heath. C Beds 2H 51
Aspull. G Man 4E 90
Asselby. E Yor 2H 93
Assington. Suff 2C 54
Assington Green. Suff 5G 65
Astbury. Ches E 4C 84
Astcote. Nptn 5D 62
Asterby. Linc 3B 88
Asterley. Shrp 5F 71
Asterton. Shrp 1F 59
Asthall. Oxon 4A 50
Asthall Leigh. Oxon 4B 50
Astle. High 4E 165
Astley. G Man 4F 91
Astley. Shrp 4H 71
Astley. Warw 2H 61
Astley. Worc 4B 60
Astley Abbotts. Shrp 1B 60
Astley Bridge. G Man 3F 91
Astley Cross. Worc 4C 60
Aston. Ches E 1A 72
Aston. Ches W 3H 83
Aston. Derbs 2F 85
(nr. Hope)
Aston. Derbs 2F 73
(nr. Sudbury)
Aston. Flin 4F 83
Aston. Here 4G 59
Aston. Herts 3C 52
Aston. Oxon 5B 50
Aston. Shrp 1C 60
(nr. Bridgnorth)
Aston. Shrp 3H 71
(nr. Wem)
Aston. S Yor 2B 86
Aston. Staf 1B 72
Aston. Telf 5A 72
Aston. W Mid 1E 61
Aston. Wok 3F 37
Aston Abbotts. Buck 3G 51
Aston Botterell. Shrp 2A 60
Aston-by-Stone. Staf 2D 72
Aston Cantlow. Warw 5F 61
Aston Clinton. Buck 4G 51
Aston Crews. Here 3B 48
Aston Cross. Glos 2E 49
Aston End. Herts 3C 52
Aston Eyre. Shrp 1A 60
Aston Fields. Worc 4D 60
Aston Flamville. Leics 1B 62
Aston Ingham. Here 3B 48
Aston juxta Mondrum.
Ches E 5A 84
Astonlane. Shrp 1A 60
Aston le Walls. Nptn 5B 62
Aston Magna. Glos 2G 49
Aston Munslow. Shrp 2H 59
Aston on Carrant. Glos 2E 49
Aston on Clun. Shrp 2F 59
Aston-on-Trent. Derbs 3B 74
Aston Pigott. Shrp 5F 71
Aston Rogers. Shrp 5F 71
Aston Rowant. Oxon 2F 37
Aston Sandford. Buck 5F 51
Aston Somerville. Worc 2F 49
Aston Subedge. Glos 1G 49
Aston Tirrold. Oxon 3D 36
Aston Upthorpe. Oxon 3D 36
Astrop. Nptn 2D 50
Astwick. C Beds 2C 52
Astwood. Mil 1H 51
Astwood Bank. Worc 4E 61
Aswarby. Linc 2H 75
Aswardby. Linc 3C 88
Atcham. Shrp 5H 71
Atch Lench. Worc 5E 61
Athelhampton. Dors 3C 14
Athelington. Suff 3E 66
Athelney. Som 4G 21
Athelstaneford. E Lot 2B 130
Atherfield Green. IOW 5C 16
Atherington. Devn 4F 19
Atherington. W Sus 5B 26
Athersley. S Yor 4D 92
Atherstone. Warw 1H 61
Atherstone on Stour.
Warw 5G 61
Atherton. G Man 4E 91
Ath-Tharracail. High 2A 140
Atlow. Derbs 1G 73
Attadale. High 5B 156
Attenborough. Notts 2C 74
Atterby. Linc 1G 87
Atterley. Shrp 1A 60
Atterton. Leics 1A 62
Attical. New M 8G 179
Attleborough. Norf 1C 66
Attleborough. Warw 1A 62
Attlebridge. Norf 4D 78
Atwick. E Yor 4F 101
Atworth. Wilts 5D 34
Auberrow. Here 1H 47
Aubourn. Linc 4G 87
Aucharnie. Abers 4D 160
Auchattie. Abers 4D 152
Auchavan. Ang 2A 144
Auchbreck. Mor 1G 151
Auchenback. E Ren 4G 127
Auchenblae. Abers 1G 145
Auchenbrack. Dum 5G 117
Auchenbreck. Arg 1B 126
Auchencairn. Dum 4E 111
(nr. Dalbeattie)
Auchencairn. Dum 1A 112
(nr. Dumfries)
Auchencarroch. W Dun 1E 127
Auchencrow. Bord 3E 131
Auchendennan. W Dun 1E 127
Auchendinny. Midl 3F 129
Auchengray. S Lan 4C 128
Auchenhalrig. Mor 2A 160
Auchenheath. S Lan 5B 128
Auchenlochan. Arg 2A 126
Auchenmade. N Ayr 5E 127
Auchenmalg. Dum 4H 109
Auchentiber. N Ayr 5E 127
Auchenvennel. Arg 1D 126
Auchindrain. Arg 3H 133
Auchininna. Abers 4D 160
Auchinleck. Dum 2B 110
Auchinleck. E Ayr 2E 117
Auchinloch. N Lan 2H 127
Auchinstarry. N Lan 2A 128
Auchleven. Abers 1D 152
Auchlochan. S Lan 1H 117
Auchlunachan. High 5F 163
Auchmillan. E Ayr 2E 117
Auchmithie. Ang 4F 145
Auchmuirbridge. Per 3E 136
Auchmull. Ang 1E 145
Auchnacree. Ang 2D 144
Auchnafree. Per 5F 143
Auchnagallin. High 5E 159
Auchnagatt. Abers 4G 161
Aucholzie. Abers 4H 151
Auchreddie. Abers 4F 161
Auchterarder. Per 2B 136
Auchteraw. High 3F 149
Auchterderran. Fife 4E 136
Auchterhouse. Ang 5C 144
Auchtermuchty. Fife 2E 137
Auchterneed. High 3G 157
Auchtertool. Fife 4E 136
Auchtertyre. High 1G 147
Auchtubh. Stir 1E 135
Auckengill. High 2F 169
Auckley. S Yor 4G 93
Audenshaw. G Man 1D 84
Audlem. Ches E 1A 72
Audley. Staf 5B 84
Audley End. Essx 2F 53
Audmore. Staf 3C 72
Auds. Abers 2D 160
Augher. Dngn 4L 177
Aughertree. Cumb 1D 102
Aughnacloy. Dngn 4A 178
Aughton. E Yor 1H 93
Aughton. Lanc 3E 97
(nr. Lancaster)
Aughton. Lanc 4B 90
(nr. Ormskirk)
Aughton. S Yor 2B 86
Aughton. Wilts 1H 23
Aughton Park. Lanc 4C 90
Auldearn. High 3D 158
Aulden. Here 5G 59
Auldgirth. Dum 1G 111
Auldhouse. S Lan 4H 127
Ault a' chruinn. High 1B 148
Aultbea. High 5C 162
Aultdearg. High 2E 157
Aultgrishan. High 5B 162
Aultguish Inn. High 1F 157
Ault Hucknall.
Derbs 4B 86
Aultibea. High 1H 165
Aultiphurst. High 2A 168
Aultivullin. High 2A 168
Aultmore. Mor 3B 160
Aultnamain Inn. High 5D 164
Aunby. Linc 4H 75
Aunsby. Linc 2H 75
Aust. S Glo 3A 34
Austerfield. S Yor 1D 86
Austin Fen. Linc 1C 88
Austrey. Warw 5G 73
Austwick. N Yor 3G 97
Authorpe. Linc 2D 88
Authorpe Row. Linc 3E 89
Avebury. Wilts 5G 35
Avebury Trusloe. Wilts 5F 35
Aveley. Thur 2G 39
Avening. Glos 2D 35
Averham. Notts 5E 87
Aveton Gifford. Devn 4C 8
Avielochan. High 2D 150
Aviemore. High 2C 150
Avington. Hants 3D 24
Avoch. High 3B 158
Avon. Hants 3G 15
Avonbridge. Falk 2C 128
Avon Dassett. Warw 5B 62
Avonmouth. Bris 4A 34
Avonwick. Devn 3D 8
Awbridge. Hants 4B 24
Awliscombe. Devn 2E 13
Awre. Glos 5C 48
Awsworth. Notts 1B 74
Axbridge. Som 1H 21
Axford. Hants 2E 24
Axford. Wilts 5H 35
Axminster. Devn 3F 13
Axmouth. Devn 3F 13
Aycliffe Village. Dur 2F 105
Aydon. Nmbd 3D 114
Aykley Heads. Dur 5F 115
Aylburton. Glos 5B 48
Aylburton Common.
Glos 5B 48
Ayle. Nmbd 5A 114
Aylesbeare. Devn 3D 12
Aylesbury. Buck 4G 51
Aylesby. NE Lin 4F 95
Aylescott. Devn 1G 11
Aylesford. Kent 5B 40
Aylesham. Kent 5G 41
Aylestone. Leic 5C 74
Aylmerton. Norf 2D 78
Aylsham. Norf 3D 78
Aylton. Here 2B 48
Aylworth. Glos 3G 49
Aymestrey. Here 4G 59
Aynho. Nptn 2D 50
Ayot Green. Herts 4C 52
Ayot St Lawrence.
Herts 4B 52
Ayot St Peter. Herts 4C 52
Ayr. S Ayr 2C 116
Ayres of Selivoe. Shet 7D 173
Ayreville. Torb 2E 9
Aysgarth. N Yor 1C 98
Ayshford. Devn 1D 12
Ayside. Cumb 1C 96
Ayston. Rut 5F 75
Ayton. Bord 3F 131
Aywick. Shet 3G 173
Azerley. N Yor 2E 99

B

Babbacombe. Torb 2F 9
Babbinswood. Shrp 2F 71
Babb's Green. Herts 4D 53
Babcary. Som 4A 22
Babel. Carm 2B 46
Babell. Flin 3D 82
Babingley. Norf 3F 77
Bablock Hythe. Oxon 5C 50
Babraham. Cambs 5E 65
Babworth. Notts 2D 86
Bac. W Isl 3G 171
Bachau. IOA 2D 80
Bacheldre. Powy 1E 59
Bachymbyd Fawr. Den 4C 82
Backaland. Orkn 4E 172
Backaskaill. Orkn 2D 172
Backbarrow. Cumb 1C 96
Backe. Carm 3G 43
Backfolds. Abers 3H 161
Backford. Ches W 3G 83
Backhill. Abers 5E 161
Backhill of Clackriach.
Abers 4G 161
Backies. High 3F 165
Backmuir of New Gilston.
Fife 3G 137
Back of Keppoch. High 5E 147
Back Street. Suff 5G 65
Backwell. N Som 5H 33
Backworth. Tyne 2G 115
Bacon End. Essx 4G 53
Baconsthorpe. Norf 2D 78
Bacton. Here 2G 47
Bacton. Norf 2F 79
Bacton. Suff 4C 66
Bacton Green. Norf 2F 79
Bacup. Lanc 2G 91
Badachonacher. High 1A 158
Badachro. High 1G 155
Badanloch Lodge. High 5H 167
Badavanich. High 3D 156
Badbury. Swin 3G 35
Badby. Nptn 5C 62
Badcall. High 3B 166
Badcaul. High 4E 163
Baddeley Green. Stoke 5D 84
Baddesley Clinton.
W Mid 3G 61
Baddesley Ensor. Warw 1G 61
Baddidarach. High 1E 163
Baddoch. Abers 5F 151
Badenscallie. High 3E 163
Badenscoth. Abers 5E 160
Badentarbat. High 2E 163
Badgall. Corn 4C 10
Badgers Mount. Kent 4F 39
Badgeworth. Glos 4E 49
Badgworth. Som 1G 21
Badicaul. High 1F 147
Badingham. Suff 4F 67
Badlesmere. Kent 5E 40
Badlipster. High 4E 169
Badluarach. High 4D 163
Badminton. S Glo 3D 34
Badnaban. High 1E 163
Badnabay. High 4C 166
Badnagie. High 5D 168
Badnellan. High 3F 165
Badninish. High 4E 165
Badrallach. High 4E 163
Badsey. Worc 1F 49
Badshot Lea. Surr 2G 25
Badsworth. W Yor 3E 93
Badwell Ash. Suff 4B 66
Bae Cinmel. Cnwy 2B 82
Bae Colwyn. Cnwy 3A 82
Bae Penrhyn. Cnwy 2H 81
Bagby. N Yor 1G 99
Bag Enderby. Linc 3C 88
Bagendon. Glos 5F 49
Bagginswood. Shrp 2A 60
Bagh a Chàise. W Isl 1E 170
Bagh a' Chaisteil. W Isl 9B 170
Bagham. Kent 5E 41
Baghasdal. W Isl 7C 170
Bagh Mor. W Isl 3D 170
Bagh Shiarabhagh.
W Isl 8C 170
Bagillt. Flin 3E 83
Baginton. Warw 3H 61
Baglan. Neat 2A 32
Bagley. Shrp 3G 71
Bagley. Som 2H 21
Bagnall. Staf 5D 84
Bagnor. W Ber 5C 36
Bagshot. Surr 4A 38
Bagshot. Wilts 5B 36
Bagstone. S Glo 3B 34
Bagthorpe. Norf 2G 77
Bagthorpe. Notts 5B 86
Bagworth. Leics 5B 74
Bagwy Llydiart. Here 3H 47
Baildon. W Yor 1B 92
Baildon Green. W Yor 1B 92
Baile. W Isl 1E 170
Baile Ailein. W Isl 5E 171
Baile an Truiseil. W Isl 2F 171
Baile Boidheach. Arg 2F 125
Baile Glas. W Isl 3D 170
Bailemeonach. Arg 4A 140
Baile Mhanaich. W Isl 3C 170
Baile Mhartainn. W Isl 1C 170
Baile MhicPhail. W Isl 1D 170
Baile Mòr. Arg 2A 132
Baile Mor. W Isl 2C 170
Baile nan Cailleach.
W Isl 3C 170
Baile Raghaill. W Isl 2C 170
Bailey Green. Hants 4E 25
Baileyhead. Cumb 1G 113
Baileysmill. Lis 4H 179
Bailiesward. Abers 5B 160
Bail' Iochdrach. W Isl 3D 170
Baillieston. Glas 3H 127
Bailrigg. Lanc 4D 97
Bail Uachdraich. W Isl 2D 170
Bail' Ur Tholastaidh.
W Isl 3H 171
Bainbridge. N Yor 5C 104
Bainsford. Falk 1B 128
Bainshole. Abers 5D 160
Bainton. E Yor 4D 100
Bainton. Oxon 3D 50
Bainton. Pet 5H 75
Baintown. Fife 3F 137
Baker Street. Thur 2H 39
Bakewell. Derbs 4G 85
Bala. Gwyn 2B 70
Balachuirn. High 4E 155
Balbeg. High 5G 157
(nr. Cannich)
Balbeg. High 1G 149
(nr. Loch Ness)
Balbeggie. Per 1D 136
Balblair. High 4C 164
(nr. Bonar Bridge)
Balblair. High 2B 158
(nr. Invergordon)
Balblair. High 4H 157
(nr. Inverness)
Balby. S Yor 4F 93
Balcathie. Ang 5F 145
Balchladich. High 1E 163
Balchraggan. High 4H 157
Balchrick. High 3B 166
Balcombe. W Sus 2E 27
Balcombe Lane. W Sus 2E 27
Balcurvie. Fife 3F 137
Baldersby. N Yor 2F 99
Baldersby St James.
N Yor 2F 99
Balderstone. Lanc 1E 91
Balderton. Ches W 4F 83
Balderton. Notts 5F 87
Baldinnie. Fife 2G 137
Baldock. Herts 2C 52
Baldrine. IOM 3D 108
Baldslow. E Sus 4C 28
Baldwin. IOM 3C 108
Baldwinholme. Cumb 4E 113
Baldwin's Gate. Staf 2B 72
Bale. Norf 2C 78
Balearn. Abers 3H 161
Balemartine. Arg 4A 138
Balephetrish. Arg 4B 138
Balephuil. Arg 4A 138
Balerno. Edin 3E 129
Balevullin. Arg 4A 138
Balfield. Ang 2E 145
Balfour. Orkn 6D 172
Balfron. Stir 1G 127
Balgaveny. Abers 4D 160
Balgonar. Fife 4C 136
Balgowan. High 4A 150
Balgown. High 2C 154
Balgrochan. E Dun 2H 127
Balgy. High 3H 155
Balhalgardy. Abers 1E 153
Baliasta. Shet 1H 173
Baligill. High 2A 168
Balintore. Ang 3B 144
Balintore. High 1C 158
Balintraid. High 1B 158
Balk. N Yor 1G 99
Balkeerie. Ang 4C 144
Balkholme. E Yor 2A 94
Ball. Shrp 3F 71
Ballabeg. IOM 4B 108
Ballacannell. IOM 3D 108
Ballacarnane Beg. IOM 3C 108
Ballachulish. High 3E 141
Ballagyr. IOM 3B 108
Ballajora. IOM 2D 108
Ballaleigh. IOM 3C 108
Ballamodha. IOM 4B 108
Ballantrae. S Ayr 1F 109
Ballards Gore. Essx 1D 40
Ballasalla. IOM 4B 108
(nr. Castletown)
Ballasalla. IOM 2C 108
(nr. Kirk Michael)
Ballater. Abers 4A 152
Ballaugh. IOM 2C 108
Ballencrieff. E Lot 2A 130
Ballencrieff Toll. W Lot 2C 128
Ballentoul. Per 2F 143
Ball Hill. Hants 5C 36
Ballidon. Derbs 5G 85
Balliemore. Arg 1B 126
(nr. Dunoon)
Balliemore. Arg 1F 133
(nr. Oban)
Ballieward. High 5E 159
Ballig. IOM 3B 108
Ballimore. Stir 2E 135
Ballinamallard. Ferm 7E 176
Ballindarragh. Ferm 6J 177
Ballingdon. Suff 1B 54
Ballinger Common. Buck 5H 51
Ballingham. Here 2A 48
Ballingry. Fife 4D 136
Ballinluig. Per 3G 143
Ballintoy. Moy 2G 175
Ballintuim. Per 3A 144
Balliveolan. Arg 4C 140
Balloan. High 3C 164
Balloch. High 4B 158
Balloch. N Lan 2A 128
Balloch. Per 2H 135
Balloch. W Dun 1E 127
Ballochan. Abers 4C 152
Ballochgoy. Arg 3B 126
Ballochmyle. E Ayr 2E 117
Ballochroy. Arg 4F 125
Balloo. Ards 3J 179
Balls Cross. W Sus 3A 26
Ball's Green. E Sus 2F 27
Ballsmill. New M 8D 178
Ballyalton. Down 5K 179
Ballybogy. Bmny 3F 174
Ballycarry. Lar 7L 175
Ballycassidy. Ferm 7E 176
Ballycastle. Moy 2H 175
Ballyclare. Newt 7J 175
Ballyeaston. Newt 7J 175
Ballygally. Lar 6K 175
Ballygawley. Dngn 4A 178
Ballygowan. Ards 3J 179
Ballygown. Arg 4F 139
Ballygrant. Arg 3B 124
Ballyhalbert. Ards 3L 179
Ballyholland. New M 7F 178
Ballyhornan. Down 5K 179
Ballykelly. Lim 4C 174
Ballykinler. Down 6J 179
Ballylesson. Lis 3H 179
Ballymagorry. Strab 2F 176
Ballymartin. New M 8H 179
Ballymena. Bmna 6H 175
Ballymichael. N Ayr 2D 122
Ballymoney. Bmny 4F 174
Ballymoney. Lim 6C 174
Ballynagard. Derr 4A 174
Ballynahinch. Down 4H 179
Ballynakilly. Dngn 3C 178
Ballynure. Newt 7K 175
Ballyrashane. Cole 3E 174
Ballyrobert. Newt 8J 175
Ballyronan. Cook 8F 174
Ballyroney. Ban 6G 179
Ballyscullion. Lim 3C 174
Ballystrudder. Lar 7L 175
Ballyvoy. Moy 2H 175
Ballyward. Ban 6G 179
Ballywater. Ards 3L 179
Ballywonard. Newt 1G 179
Balmacara. High 1G 147
Balmaclellan. Dum 2D 110
Balmacqueen. High 1D 154
Balmaha. Stir 4D 134
Balmalcolm. Fife 3F 137
Balmeanach. High 5E 155
Balmedie. Abers 2G 153
Balmerino. Fife 1F 137
Balmerlawn. Hants 2B 16
Balmore. E Dun 2H 127
Balmore. High 4B 154
Balmuir. Ang 5D 144
Balmullo. Fife 1G 137
Balmurrie. Dum 3H 109
Balnaboth. Ang 2C 144
Balnabruaich. High 1B 158
Balnabruich. High 5D 168
Balnacoil. High 2F 165
Balnacra. High 4B 156
Balnacroft. Abers 4G 151
Balnageith. Mor 3E 159
Balnaglaic. High 5G 157
Balnagrantach. High 5G 157
Balnaguard. Per 3G 143
Balnahard. Arg 4B 132
Balnain. High 5G 157
Balnakeil. High 2D 166
Balnaknock. High 2D 154
Balnamoon. Abers 3G 161
Balnamoon. Ang 2E 145
Balnamore. Bmny 4F 174
Balnapaling. High 2B 158
Balornock. Glas 3H 127
Balquhidder. Stir 1E 135
Balsall. W Mid 3G 61
Balsall Common. W Mid 3G 61
Balscote. Oxon 1B 50
Balsham. Cambs 5E 65
Balstonia. Thur 2A 40
Baltasound. Shet 1H 173
Balterley. Staf 5B 84
Baltersan. Dum 3B 110
Balthangie. Abers 3F 161
Baltonsborough. Som 3A 22
Balvaird. High 3H 157
Balvaird. Per 2D 136
Balvenie. Mor 4H 159
Balvicar. Arg 2E 133
Balvraid. High 2G 147
Balvraid Lodge. High 5C 158
Bamber Bridge. Lanc 2D 90
Bamber's Green. Essx 3F 53
Bamburgh. Nmbd 1F 121
Bamford. Derbs 2G 85
Bamfurlong. G Man 4D 90
Bampton. Cumb 3G 103
Bampton. Devn 4C 20
Bampton. Oxon 5B 50
Bampton Grange. Cumb 3G 103
Banavie. High 1F 141
Banbridge. Ban 5F 178
Banbury. Oxon 1C 50
Bancffosfelen. Carm 4E 45
Banchory. Abers 4D 152
Banchory-Devenick.
Abers 3G 153
Bancycapel. Carm 4E 45
Bancyfelin. Carm 3H 43
Banc-y-ffordd. Carm 2E 45
Banff. Abers 2D 160
Bangor. Gwyn 3E 81
Bangor. N Dwn 1K 179
Bangor-is-y-coed. Wrex 1F 71
Bangors. Corn 3C 10
Bangor's Green. Lanc 4B 90
Banham. Norf 2C 66
Bank. Hants 2A 16
Bankend. Dum 3B 112
Bankfoot. Per 5H 143
Bankglen. E Ayr 3E 117
Bankhead. Aber 2F 153
Bankhead. Abers 3D 152
Bankhead. S Lan 5B 128
Bankland. Som 4G 21
Bank Newton. N Yor 4B 98
Banknock. Falk 2A 128
Banks. Cumb 3G 113
Banks. Lanc 2B 90
Bankshill. Dum 1C 112
Bank Street. Worc 4A 60
Bank, The. Ches E 5C 84
Bank, The. Shrp 1A 60
Bank Top. Lanc 4D 90
Banners Gate. W Mid 1E 61
Banningham. Norf 3E 78
Banniskirk. High 3D 168
Bannister Green. Essx 3G 53
Bannockburn. Stir 4H 135
Banstead. Surr 5D 38
Bantham. Devn 4C 8
Banton. N Lan 2A 128
Banwell. N Som 1G 21
Banyard's Green. Suff 3F 67
Bapchild. Kent 4D 40
Bapton. Wilts 3E 23
Barabhas. W Isl 2F 171
Barabhas Iarach. W Isl 3F 171
Baramore. High 1A 140
Barassie. S Ayr 1C 116
Baravullin. Arg 4D 140
Barbaraville. High 1B 158
Barber Booth. Derbs 2F 85
Barber Green. Cumb 1C 96
Barbhas Uarach. W Isl 2F 171
Barbieston. S Ayr 3D 116
Barbon. Cumb 1F 97
Barbourne. Worc 5C 60
Barbridge. Ches E 5A 84
Barbrook. Devn 2H 19
Barby. Nptn 3C 62
Barby Nortoft. Nptn 3C 62
Barcaldine. Arg 4D 140
Barcheston. Warw 1A 50
Barclose. Cumb 3F 113
Barcombe. E Sus 4F 27
Barcombe Cross. E Sus 4F 27
Barden. N Yor 5E 105
Barden Scale. N Yor 4C 98
Bardfield End Green.
Essx 2G 53
Bardfield Saling. Essx 3G 53
Bardister. Shet 4E 173
Bardnabeinne. High 4E 164
Bardney. Linc 4A 88
Bardon. Leics 4B 74
Bardon Mill. Nmbd 3A 114
Bardowie. E Dun 2G 127
Bardrainney. Inv 2E 127
Bardsea. Cumb 2C 96
Bardsey. W Yor 5F 99
Bardsley. G Man 4H 91
Bardwell. Suff 3B 66
Bare. Lanc 3D 96
Barelees. Nmbd 1C 120
Barewood. Here 5F 59
Barford. Hants 3G 25
Barford. Norf 5D 78
Barford. Warw 4G 61
Barford St John. Oxon 2C 50
Barford St Martin. Wilts 3F 23
Barford St Michael. Oxon 2C 50
Barfrestone. Kent 5G 41
Bargeddie. N Lan 3A 128
Bargod. Cphy 2E 33
Bargoed. Cphy 2E 33
Bargrennan. Dum 2A 110
Barham. Cambs 3A 64
Barham. Kent 5G 41
Barham. Suff 5D 66
Barharrow. Dum 4D 110
Bar Hill. Cambs 4C 64
Barholm. Linc 4H 75
Barkby. Leics 5D 74
Barkestone-le-Vale. Leics 2E 75
Barkham. Wok 5F 37
Barking. G Lon 2F 39
Barking. Suff 5C 66
Barkingside. G Lon 2F 39
Barking Tye. Suff 5C 66
Barkisland. W Yor 3A 92
Barkston. Linc 1G 75
Barkston Ash. N Yor 1E 93
Barkway. Herts 2D 53
Barlanark. Glas 3H 127
Barlaston. Staf 2C 72
Barlavington. W Sus 4A 26
Barlborough. Derbs 3B 86
Barlby. N Yor 1G 93
Barlestone. Leics 5B 74
Barley. Herts 2D 53
Barley. Lanc 5H 97
Barley Mow. Tyne 4F 115
Barleythorpe. Rut 5F 75
Barling. Essx 2D 40
Barlings. Linc 3H 87
Barlow. Derbs 3H 85
Barlow. N Yor 2G 93
Barlow. Tyne 3E 115
Barmby Moor. E Yor 5B 100
Barmby on the Marsh.
E Yor 2G 93
Barmer. Norf 2H 77
Barming Heath. Kent 5B 40
Barmoor. Nmbd 1E 121
Barmouth. Gwyn 4F 69
Barmpton. Darl 3A 106
Barmston. E Yor 4F 101
Barmulloch. Glas 3H 127
Barnack. Pet 5H 75
Barnacle. Warw 2A 62
Barnard Castle. Dur 3D 104
Barnard Gate. Oxon 4C 50
Barnardiston. Suff 1H 53
Barnbarroch. Dum 4F 111
Barnburgh. S Yor 4E 93
Barnby. Suff 2G 67
Barnby Dun. S Yor 4G 93
Barnby in the Willows.
Notts 5F 87
Barnby Moor. Notts 2D 86
Barnes. G Lon 3D 38
Barnes Street. Kent 1H 27
Barnet. G Lon 1D 38
Barnetby le Wold.
N Lin 4D 94
Barney. Norf 2B 78
Barnham. Suff 3A 66
Barnham. W Sus 5A 26
Barnham Broom. Norf 5C 78
Barnhead. Ang 3F 145
Barnhill. D'dee 5D 145
Barnhill. Mor 3F 159
Barnhill. Per 1D 136
Barnhills. Dum 2E 109
Barningham. Dur 3D 105
Barningham. Suff 3B 66
Barnoldby le Beck. NE Lin 4F 95
Barnoldswick. Lanc 5A 98
Barns Green. W Sus 3C 26
Barnsley. Glos 5F 49
Barnsley. Shrp 1B 60
Barnsley. S Yor 4D 92
Barnstaple. Devn 3F 19
Barnston. Essx 4G 53
Barnston. Mers 2E 83
Barnstone. Notts 2E 75
Barnt Green. Worc 3E 61
Barnton. Ches W 3A 84
Barnwell. Cambs 5D 64
Barnwell. Nptn 2H 63
Barnwood. Glos 4D 48
Barons Cross. Here 5G 59
Barony, The. Orkn 5B 172
Barr. Dum 4G 117
Barr. S Ayr 5B 116
Barra Airport. W Isl 8C 170
Barrachan. Dum 5A 110
Barraglom. W Isl 4D 171
Barrahormid. Arg 1F 125
Barrapol. Arg 4A 138
Barrasford. Nmbd 2C 114
Barravullin. Arg 3F 133
Barregarrow. IOM 3C 108
Barrhead. E Ren 4G 127
Barrhill. S Ayr 1H 109
Barri. V Glam 5E 32
Barrington. Cambs 1D 53
Barrington. Som 1G 13
Barripper. Corn 3D 4
Barrmill. N Ayr 4E 127
Barrock. High 1E 169
Barrow. Lanc 1F 91
Barrow. Rut 4F 75
Barrow. Shrp 5A 72
Barrow. Som 3C 22
Barrow. Suff 4G 65
Barroway Drove. Norf 5E 77
Barrow Bridge. G Man 3E 91
Barrowburn. Nmbd 3C 120
Barrowby. Linc 2F 75
Barrowcliff. N Yor 1E 101
Barrow Common. N Som 5A 34
Barrowden. Rut 5G 75
Barrowford. Lanc 1G 91
Barrow Gurney. N Som 5A 34
Barrow Haven. N Lin 2D 94
Barrow Hill. Derbs 3B 86
Barrow-in-Furness.
Cumb 3B 96
Barrow Nook. Lanc 4C 90
Barrows Green. Cumb 1E 97
Barrow's Green. Hal 2H 83
Barrow Street. Wilts 3D 22
Barrow upon Humber.
N Lin 2D 94
Barrow upon Soar. Leics 4C 74
Barrow upon Trent.
Derbs 3A 74
Barry. Ang 5E 145
Barry. V Glam 5E 32
Barry Island. V Glam 5E 32
Barsby. Leics 4D 74
Barsham. Suff 2F 67
Barston. W Mid 3G 61
Bartestree. Here 1A 48
Barthol Chapel. Abers 5F 161
Bartholomew Green.
Essx 3H 53
Barthomley. Ches E 5B 84
Bartley. Hants 1B 16
Bartley Green. W Mid 2E 61
Bartlow. Cambs 1F 53
Barton. Cambs 5D 64
Barton. Ches W 5G 83
Barton. Cumb 2G 103
Barton. Glos 3G 49
Barton. IOW 4D 16
Barton. Lanc 4B 90
(nr. Ormskirk)
Barton. Lanc 1D 90
(nr. Preston)
Barton. N Som 1G 21
Barton. N Yor 4F 105
Barton. Oxon 5D 50
Barton. Torb 2F 9
Barton. Warw 5F 61
Barton Bendish. Norf 5G 77
Barton Gate. Staf 4F 73
Barton Green. Staf 4F 73
Barton Hartsthorn. Buck 2E 51
Barton Hill. N Yor 3B 100
Barton in Fabis. Notts 2C 74
Barton in the Beans.
Leics 5A 74
Barton-le-Clay. C Beds 2A 52
Barton-le-Street. N Yor 2B 100
Barton-le-Willows.
N Yor 3B 100
Barton Mills. Suff 3G 65
Barton on Sea. Hants 3H 15
Barton-on-the-Heath.
Warw 2A 50
Barton St David. Som 3A 22
Barton Seagrave. Nptn 3F 63
Barton Stacey. Hants 2C 24
Barton Town. Devn 2G 19
Barton Turf. Norf 3F 79
Barton-under-Needwood.
Staf 4F 73
Barton-upon-Humber.
N Lin 2D 94
Barton Waterside. N Lin 2D 94
Barugh Green. S Yor 4D 92
Barway. Cambs 3E 65
Barwell. Leics 1B 62
Barwick. Herts 4D 53
Barwick. Som 1A 14
Barwick in Elmet. W Yor 1D 93
Baschurch. Shrp 3G 71
Bascote. Warw 4B 62
Basford Green. Staf 5D 85
Bashall Eaves. Lanc 5F 97
Bashall Town. Lanc 5G 97
Bashley. Hants 3H 15
Basildon. Essx 2B 40
Basingstoke. Hants 1E 25
Baslow. Derbs 3G 85
Bason Bridge. Som 2G 21
Bassaleg. Newp 3F 33
Bassendean. Bord 5C 130
Bassenthwaite. Cumb 1D 102
Bassett. Sotn 1C 16
Bassingbourn. Cambs 1D 52
Bassingfield. Notts 2D 74
Bassingham. Linc 5G 87
Bassingthorpe. Linc 3G 75
Bassus Green. Herts 3D 52
Basta. Shet 2G 173
Baston. Linc 4A 76
Bastonford. Worc 5C 60
Bastwick. Norf 4G 79
Batchley. Worc 4E 61
Batchworth. Herts 1B 38
Batcombe. Dors 2B 14
Batcombe. Som 3B 22
Bate Heath. Ches E 3A 84
Bath. Bath 5C 34 & 192
Bathampton. Bath 5C 34
Bathealton. Som 4D 20
Batheaston. Bath 5C 34
Bathford. Bath 5C 34
Bathgate. W Lot 3C 128
Bathley. Notts 5E 87
Bathpool. Corn 5C 10
Bathpool. Som 4F 21
Bathville. W Lot 3C 128
Bathway. Som 1A 22
Batley. W Yor 2C 92
Batsford. Glos 2G 49
Batson. Devn 5D 8
Battersby. N Yor 4C 106
Battersea. G Lon 3D 39
Battisborough Cross. Devn 4C 8
Battisford. Suff 5C 66
Battisford Tye. Suff 5C 66
Battle. E Sus 4B 28
Battle. Powy 2D 46
Battleborough. Som 1G 21
Battledown. Glos 3E 49
Battlefield. Shrp 4H 71
Battlesbridge. Essx 1B 40
Battlesden. C Beds 3H 51
Battlesea Green. Suff 3E 66
Battleton. Som 4C 20
Battram. Leics 5B 74
Battramsley. Hants 3B 16
Batt's Corner. Surr 2G 25
Bauds of Cullen. Mor 2B 160
Baugh. Arg 4B 138
Baughton. Worc 1D 49
Baughurst. Hants 5D 36
Baulking. Oxon 2B 36
Baumber. Linc 3B 88
Baunton. Glos 5F 49
Baverstock. Wilts 3F 23
Bawburgh. Norf 5D 78
Bawdeswell. Norf 3C 78
Bawdrip. Som 3G 21
Bawdsey. Suff 1G 55
Bawdsey Manor. Suff 2G 55
Bawsey. Norf 4F 77
Bawtry. S Yor 1D 86
Baxenden. Lanc 2F 91
Baxterley. Warw 1G 61
Baxter's Green. Suff 5G 65
Bay. High 3B 154
Baybridge. Hants 4D 24
Baybridge. Nmbd 4C 114
Baycliff. Cumb 2B 96
Baydon. Wilts 4A 36
Bayford. Herts 5D 52
Bayford. Som 4C 22
Bayles. Cumb 5A 114
Baylham. Suff 5D 66
Baynard's Green. Oxon 3D 50
Bayston Hill. Shrp 5G 71
Baythorn End. Essx 1H 53
Baythorpe. Linc 1B 76
Bayton. Worc 3A 60
Bayton Common. Worc 3B 60
Bayworth. Oxon 5D 50
Beach. S Glo 4C 34
Beachampton. Buck 2F 51
Beachamwell. Norf 5G 77
Beachley. Glos 2A 34
Beacon. Devn 2E 13
Beacon End. Essx 3C 54
Beacon Hill. Surr 3G 25
Beacon's Bottom. Buck 2F 37
Beaconsfield. Buck 1A 38
Beacrabhaic. W Isl 8D 171
Beadlam. N Yor 1A 100
Beadnell. Nmbd 2G 121
Beaford. Devn 1F 11
Beal. Nmbd 5G 131
Beal. N Yor 2F 93
Bealsmill. Corn 5D 10
Beam Hill. Staf 3G 73
Beamhurst. Staf 2E 73
Beaminster. Dors 2H 13
Beamish. Dur 4F 115
Beamond End. Buck 1A 38
Beamsley. N Yor 4C 98
Bean. Kent 3G 39
Beanacre. Wilts 5E 35
Beanley. Nmbd 3E 121
Beaquoy. Orkn 5C 172
Beardwood. Bkbn 2E 91
Beare Green. Surr 1C 26
Bearley. Warw 4F 61
Bearpark. Dur 5F 115
Bearsbridge. Nmbd 4A 114
Bearsden. E Dun 2G 127
Bearsted. Kent 5B 40
Bearstone. Shrp 2B 72
Bearwood. Pool 3F 15
Bearwood. W Mid 2E 61
Beattock. Dum 4C 118
Beauchamp Roding. Essx 5F 53
Beauchief. S Yor 2H 85
Beaufort. Blae 4E 47
Beaulieu. Hants 2B 16
Beauly. High 4H 157

Beaumaris—Bournmoor

Beaumaris. *IOA* 3F **81**
Beaumont. *Cumb* 4E **113**
Beaumont. *Essx* 3E **55**
Beaumont Hill. *Darl* 3F **105**
Beaumont Leys. *Leic* 5C **74**
Beausale. *Warw* 3G **61**
Beauvale. *Notts* 1B **74**
Beauworth. *Hants* 4D **24**
Beaworthy. *Devn* 3E **11**
Beazley End. *Essx* 3H **53**
Bebington. *Mers* 2F **83**
Bebside. *Nmbd* 1F **115**
Beccles. *Suff* 2G **67**
Becconsall. *Lanc* 2C **90**
Beckbury. *Shrp* 5B **72**
Beckenham. *G Lon* 4E **39**
Beckermet. *Cumb* 4B **102**
Beckett End. *Norf* 1G **65**
Beckfoot. *Cumb* 1A **96**
(nr. Broughton in Furness)
Beck Foot. *Cumb* 5H **103**
(nr. Kendal)
Beckfoot. *Cumb* 4C **102**
(nr. Seascale)
Beckfoot. *Cumb* 5B **112**
(nr. Silloth)
Beckford. *Worc* 2E **49**
Beckhampton. *Wilts* 5F **35**
Beck Hole. *N Yor* 4F **107**
Beckingham. *Linc* 5F **87**
Beckingham. *Notts* 1E **87**
Beckington. *Som* 1D **22**
Beckley. *E Sus* 3C **28**
Beckley. *Hants* 3H **15**
Beckley. *Oxon* 4D **50**
Beck Row. *Suff* 3F **65**
Beck Side. *Cumb* 1C **96**
(nr. Cartmel)
Beckside. *Cumb* 1F **97**
(nr. Sedbergh)
Beck Side. *Cumb* 1B **96**
(nr. Ulverston)
Beckton. *G Lon* 2F **39**
Beckwithshaw. *N Yor* 4E **99**
Becontree. *G Lon* 2F **39**
Bedale. *N Yor* 1E **99**
Bedburn. *Dur* 1E **105**
Bedchester. *Dors* 1D **14**
Beddau. *Rhon* 3D **32**
Beddgelert. *Gwyn* 1E **69**
Beddingham. *E Sus* 5F **27**
Beddington. *G Lon* 4D **39**
Bedfield. *Suff* 4E **66**
Bedford. *Bed* 1A **52**
Bedford. *G Man* 4E **91**
Bedham. *W Sus* 3B **26**
Bedhampton. *Hants* 2F **17**
Bedingfield. *Suff* 4D **66**
Bedingham Green. *Norf* 1E **67**
Bedlam. *N Yor* 3E **99**
Bedlar's Green. *Essx* 4F **53**
Bedlington. *Nmbd* 1F **115**
Bedlinog. *Mer T* 5D **46**
Bedminster. *Bris* 4A **34**
Bedmond. *Herts* 5A **52**
Bednall. *Staf* 4D **72**
Bedrule. *Bord* 3A **120**
Bedstone. *Shrp* 3F **59**
Bedwas. *Cphy* 3E **33**
Bedwellty. *Cphy* 5E **47**
Bedworth. *Warw* 2A **62**
Beeby. *Leics* 5D **74**
Beech. *Hants* 3E **25**
Beech. *Staf* 2C **72**
Beechcliffe. *W Yor* 5C **98**
Beech Hill. *W Ber* 5E **37**
Beechingstoke. *Wilts* 1F **23**
Beedon. *W Ber* 4C **36**
Beeford. *E Yor* 4F **101**
Beeley. *Derbs* 4G **85**
Beelsby. *NE Lin* 4F **95**
Beenham. *W Ber* 5D **36**
Beeny. *Corn* 3B **10**
Beer. *Devn* 4F **13**
Beer. *Som* 3H **21**
Beercrocombe. *Som* 4G **21**
Beer Hackett. *Dors* 1B **14**
Beesands. *Devn* 4E **9**
Beesby. *Linc* 2D **88**
Beeson. *Devn* 4E **9**
Beeston. *C Beds* 1B **52**
Beeston. *Ches W* 5H **83**
Beeston. *Norf* 4B **78**
Beeston. *Notts* 2C **74**
Beeston. *W Yor* 1C **92**
Beeston Regis. *Norf* 1D **78**
Beeswing. *Dum* 3F **111**
Beetham. *Cumb* 2D **97**
Beetham. *Som* 1F **13**
Beetley. *Norf* 4B **78**
Beffcote. *Staf* 4C **72**
Began. *Card* 3F **33**
Begbroke. *Oxon* 4C **50**
Begdale. *Cambs* 5D **76**
Begelly. *Pemb* 4F **43**
Beggar Hill. *Essx* 5G **53**
Beggar's Bush. *Powy* 4E **59**
Beggearn Huish. *Som* 3D **20**
Beguildy. *Powy* 3D **58**
Beighton. *Norf* 5F **79**
Beighton. *S Yor* 2B **86**
Beighton Hill. *Derbs* 5G **85**
Beinn Casgro. *W Isl* 5G **171**
Beith. *N Ayr* 4E **127**
Bekesbourne. *Kent* 5F **41**
Belaugh. *Norf* 4E **79**
Belbroughton. *Worc* 3D **60**
Belchalwell. *Dors* 2C **14**
Belchalwell Street. *Dors* 2C **14**
Belchamp Otten. *Essx* 1B **54**
Belchamp St Paul. *Essx* 1A **54**
Belchamp Walter. *Essx* 1B **54**
Belchford. *Linc* 3B **88**
Belcoo. *Ferm* 6F **177**
Belfast. *Bel* 2H **179**
Belfast International Airport.
Ant 1F **179**
Belfatton. *Abers* 3H **161**
Belford. *Nmbd* 1F **121**
Belgrano. *Cnwy* 3B **82**
Belhaven. *E Lot* 2C **130**
Belhelvie. *Abers* 2G **153**
Belhinnie. *Abers* 1B **152**
Bellabeg. *Abers* 2A **152**
Belladrum. *High* 4H **157**
Bellaghy. *Mag* 7F **175**
Bellamore. *S Ayr* 1H **109**
Bellanaleck. *Ferm* 6H **177**
Bellanoch. *Arg* 4F **133**
Bell Busk. *N Yor* 4B **98**
Belleau. *Linc* 3D **88**
Belleek. *Ferm* 7B **176**
Belleek. *New M* 7D **178**
Belleheiglash. *Mor* 5F **159**
Bell End. *Worc* 3D **60**
Bellerby. *N Yor* 5E **105**
Bellerby Camp. *N Yor* 5D **105**
Bellever. *Devn* 5G **11**
Belle Vue. *Cumb* 1C **102**
Belle Vue. *Shrp* 4G **71**
Bellfield. *S Lan* 1H **117**
Belliehill. *Ang* 2E **145**
Bellingdon. *Buck* 5H **51**
Bellingham. *Nmbd* 1B **114**
Bellmount. *Norf* 3E **77**
Bellochantuy. *Arg* 2A **122**
Bellsbank. *E Ayr* 4D **117**
Bell's Cross. *Suff* 5D **66**
Bellshill. *N Lan* 4A **128**
Bellshill. *Nmbd* 1F **121**
Bellside. *N Lan* 4B **128**
Bellspool. *Bord* 1D **118**
Bellsquarry. *W Lot* 3D **128**
Bells Yew Green. *E Sus* 2H **27**
Belmaduthy. *High* 3A **158**
Belmesthorpe. *Rut* 4H **75**
Belmont. *Bkbn* 3E **91**
Belmont. *Shet* 1G **173**
Belmont. *S Ayr* 3C **116**
Belnacraig. *Abers* 2A **152**
Belnie. *Linc* 2B **76**
Belowda. *Corn* 2D **6**
Belper. *Derbs* 1A **74**
Belper Lane End. *Derbs* 1H **73**
Belph. *Derbs* 3C **86**
Belsay. *Nmbd* 2E **115**
Belsford. *Devn* 3D **8**
Belsize. *Herts* 5A **52**
Belstead. *Suff* 1E **55**
Belston. *S Ayr* 2C **116**
Belstone. *Devn* 3G **11**
Belstone Corner. *Devn* 3G **11**
Belthorn. *Lanc* 2F **91**
Beltinge. *Kent* 4F **41**
Beltoft. *N Lin* 4B **94**
Belton. *Leics* 3B **74**
Belton. *Linc* 2G **75**
Belton. *Norf* 5G **79**
Belton. *N Lin* 4A **94**
Belton-in-Rutland. *Rut* 5F **75**
Beltring. *Kent* 1A **28**
Belts of Collonach.
Abers 4D **152**
Belvedere. *G Lon* 3F **39**
Belvoir. *Leics* 2F **75**
Bembridge. *IOW* 4E **17**
Bemersyde. *Bord* 1H **119**
Bemerton. *Wilts* 3G **23**
Bempton. *E Yor* 2F **101**
Benacre. *Suff* 2H **67**
Ben Alder Lodge. *High* 1C **142**
Ben Armine Lodge. *High* 2E **164**
Benbecula Airport.
W Isl 3C **170**
Benbuie. *Dum* 5G **117**
Benburb. *Dngn* 4C **178**
Benchill. *G Man* 2C **84**
Benderloch. *Arg* 5D **140**
Bendish. *Herts* 3B **52**
Bendooragh. *Bmny* 4F **174**
Bendronaig Lodge. *High* 5C **156**
Benenden. *Kent* 2C **28**
Benfieldside. *Dur* 4D **115**
Bengate. *Norf* 3F **79**
Bengeworth. *Worc* 1F **49**
Bengrove. *Glos* 2E **49**
Benhall Green. *Suff* 4F **67**
Benholm. *Abers* 2H **145**
Beningbrough. *N Yor* 4H **99**
Benington. *Herts* 3C **52**
Benington. *Linc* 1C **76**
Benington Sea End. *Linc* 1D **76**
Benllech. *IOA* 2E **81**
Benmore Lodge. *High* 2H **163**
Bennacott. *Corn* 3D **10**
Bennah. *Devn* 4B **12**
Bennecarrigan. *N Ayr* 3D **122**
Bennethead. *Cumb* 2F **103**
Benniworth. *Linc* 2B **88**
Benover. *Kent* 1B **28**
Benson. *Oxon* 2E **36**
Benston. *Shet* 6F **173**
Benstonhall. *Orkn* 4E **172**
Bent. *Abers* 1F **145**
Benthall. *Shrp* 5A **72**
Bentham. *Glos* 4E **49**
Benthoul. *Aber* 3F **153**
Bentlawnt. *Shrp* 5F **71**
Bentley. *E Yor* 1D **94**
Bentley. *Hants* 2F **25**
Bentley. *S Yor* 4F **93**
Bentley. *Suff* 2E **54**
Bentley. *Warw* 1G **61**
Bentley. *W Mid* 1D **61**
Bentley Heath. *Herts* 1D **38**
Bentley Heath. *W Mid* 3F **61**
Bentpath. *Dum* 5F **119**
Bents. *W Lot* 3C **128**
Bentworth. *Hants* 2E **25**
Benvie. *D'dee* 5C **144**
Benville. *Dors* 2A **14**
Benwell. *Tyne* 3F **115**
Benwick. *Cambs* 1C **64**
Beoley. *Worc* 4E **61**
Beoraidbeg. *High* 4E **147**
Bepton. *W Sus* 1G **17**
Beragh. *Omag* 3L **177**
Berden. *Essx* 3E **53**
Bere Alston. *Devn* 2A **8**
Bere Ferrers. *Devn* 2A **8**
Berepper. *Corn* 4D **4**
Bere Regis. *Dors* 3D **14**
Bergh Apton. *Norf* 5F **79**
Berinsfield. *Oxon* 2D **36**
Berkeley. *Glos* 2B **34**
Berkhamsted. *Herts* 5H **51**
Berkley. *Som* 2D **22**
Berkswell. *W Mid* 3G **61**
Bermondsey. *G Lon* 3E **39**
Bernera. *High* 1G **147**
Bernice. *Arg* 4A **134**
Bernisdale. *High* 3D **154**
Berrick Salome. *Oxon* 2E **36**
Berriedale. *High* 1H **165**
Berrier. *Cumb* 2F **103**
Berriew. *Powy* 5D **70**
Berrington. *Nmbd* 5G **131**
Berrington. *Shrp* 5H **71**
Berrington. *Worc* 4H **59**
Berrington Green. *Worc* 4H **59**
Berrington Law. *Nmbd* 5F **131**
Berrow. *Som* 1G **21**
Berrow Green. *Worc* 5B **60**
Berry Cross. *Devn* 1E **11**
Berry Down Cross. *Devn* 2F **19**
Berry Hill. *Glos* 4A **48**
Berry Hill. *Pemb* 1A **44**
Berryhillock. *Mor* 2C **160**
Berrynarbor. *Devn* 2F **19**
Berry Pomeroy. *Devn* 2E **9**
Berryscaur. *Dum* 5D **118**
Berry's Green. *G Lon* 5F **39**
Bersham. *Wrex* 1F **71**
Berthengam. *Flin* 3D **82**
Berwick. *E Sus* 5G **27**
Berwick Bassett. *Wilts* 4G **35**
Berwick Hill. *Nmbd* 2E **115**
Berwick St James. *Wilts* 3F **23**
Berwick St John. *Wilts* 4E **23**
Berwick St Leonard. *Wilts* 3E **23**
Berwick-upon-Tweed.
Nmbd 4G **131**
Berwyn. *Den* 1D **70**
Bescaby. *Leics* 3F **75**
Bescar. *Lanc* 3B **90**
Besford. *Worc* 1E **49**
Bessacarr. *S Yor* 4G **93**
Bessbrook. *New M* 7E **178**
Bessels Leigh. *Oxon* 5C **50**
Bessingby. *E Yor* 3F **101**
Bessingham. *Norf* 2D **78**
Best Beech Hill. *E Sus* 2H **27**
Besthorpe. *Norf* 1C **66**
Besthorpe. *Notts* 4F **87**
Bestwood Village. *Notts* 1C **74**
Beswick. *E Yor* 5E **101**
Betchworth. *Surr* 5D **38**
Bethania. *Cdgn* 4E **57**
Bethania. *Gwyn* 1G **69**
(nr. Blaenau Ffestiniog)
Bethania. *Gwyn* 5F **81**
(nr. Caernarfon)
Bethel. *Gwyn* 2B **70**
(nr. Bala)
Bethel. *Gwyn* 4E **81**
(nr. Caernarfon)
Bethel. *IOA* 3C **80**
Bethersden. *Kent* 1D **28**
Bethesda. *Gwyn* 4F **81**
Bethesda. *Pemb* 3E **43**
Bethlehem. *Carm* 3G **45**
Bethnal Green. *G Lon* 2E **39**
Betley. *Staf* 1B **72**
Betsham. *Kent* 3H **39**
Betteshanger. *Kent* 5H **41**
Bettiscombe. *Dors* 3H **13**
Bettisfield. *Wrex* 2G **71**
Betton. *Shrp* 2A **72**
Betton Strange. *Shrp* 5H **71**
Bettws. *B'end* 3C **32**
Bettws. *Newp* 2F **33**
Bettws Bledrws. *Cdgn* 5E **57**
Bettws Cedewain. *Powy* 1D **58**
Bettws Gwerfil Goch. *Den* 1C **70**
Bettws Ifan. *Cdgn* 1D **44**
Bettws Newydd. *Mon* 5G **47**
Bettyhill. *High* 2H **167**
Betws. *Carm* 4G **45**
Betws Garmon. *Gwyn* 5E **81**
Betws-y-Coed. *Cnwy* 5G **81**
Betws-yn-Rhos. *Cnwy* 3B **82**
Beulah. *Cdgn* 1C **44**
Beulah. *Powy* 5B **58**
Beul an Atha. *Arg* 3B **124**
Bevendean. *Brig* 5E **27**
Bevercotes. *Notts* 3E **86**
Beverley. *E Yor* 1D **94**
Beverston. *Glos* 2D **34**
Bevington. *Glos* 2B **34**
Bewaldeth. *Cumb* 1D **102**
Bewcastle. *Cumb* 2G **113**
Bewdley. *Worc* 3B **60**
Bewerley. *N Yor* 3D **98**
Bewholme. *E Yor* 4F **101**
Bexfield. *Norf* 3C **78**
Bexhill. *E Sus* 5B **28**
Bexley. *G Lon* 3F **39**
Bexleyheath. *G Lon* 3F **39**
Bexleyhill. *W Sus* 3A **26**
Bexwell. *Norf* 5F **77**
Beyton. *Suff* 4B **66**
Bhalton. *W Isl* 4C **171**
Bhatarsaigh. *W Isl* 9B **170**
Bibbington. *Derbs* 3E **85**
Bibury. *Glos* 5G **49**
Bicester. *Oxon* 3D **50**
Bickenhall. *Som* 1F **13**
Bickenhill. *W Mid* 2F **61**
Bicker. *Linc* 2B **76**
Bicker Bar. *Linc* 2B **76**
Bicker Gauntlet. *Linc* 2B **76**
Bickershaw. *G Man* 4E **91**
Bickerstaffe. *Lanc* 4C **90**
Bickerton. *Ches E* 5H **83**
Bickerton. *Nmbd* 4D **121**
Bickerton. *N Yor* 4G **99**
Bickford. *Staf* 4C **72**
Bickington. *Devn* 3F **19**
(nr. Barnstaple)
Bickington. *Devn* 5B **12**
(nr. Newton Abbot)
Bickleigh. *Devn* 2B **8**
(nr. Plymouth)
Bickleigh. *Devn* 2C **12**
(nr. Tiverton)
Bickleton. *Devn* 3F **19**
Bickley. *N Yor* 5G **107**
Bickley Moss. *Ches W* 1H **71**
Bickmarsh. *Warw* 5F **61**
Bicknacre. *Essx* 5A **54**
Bicknoller. *Som* 3E **20**
Bicknor. *Kent* 5C **40**
Bickton. *Hants* 1G **15**
Bicton. *Here* 4G **59**
Bicton. *Shrp* 2E **59**
(nr. Bishop's Castle)
Bicton. *Shrp* 4G **71**
(nr. Shrewsbury)
Bicton Heath. *Shrp* 4G **71**
Bidborough. *Kent* 1G **27**
Biddenden. *Kent* 2C **28**
Biddenden Green. *Kent* 1C **28**
Biddenham. *Bed* 1A **52**
Biddestone. *Wilts* 4D **34**
Biddisham. *Som* 1G **21**
Biddlesden. *Buck* 1E **51**
Biddlestone. *Nmbd* 4D **120**
Biddulph. *Staf* 5C **84**
Biddulph Moor. *Staf* 5D **84**
Bideford. *Devn* 4E **19**
Bidford-on-Avon. *Warw* 5E **61**
Bidlake. *Devn* 4F **11**
Bidston. *Mers* 2E **83**
Bielby. *E Yor* 5B **100**
Bieldside. *Aber* 3F **153**
Bierley. *IOW* 5D **16**
Bierley. *W Yor* 1B **92**
Bierton. *Buck* 4G **51**
Bigbury. *Devn* 4C **8**
Bigbury-on-Sea. *Devn* 4C **8**
Bigby. *Linc* 4D **94**
Biggar. *Cumb* 3A **96**
Biggar. *S Lan* 1C **118**
Biggin. *Derbs* 5F **85**
(nr. Hartington)
Biggin. *Derbs* 1G **73**
(nr. Hulland)
Biggin. *N Yor* 1F **93**
Biggings. *Shet* 5C **173**
Biggin Hill. *G Lon* 5F **39**
Biggleswade. *C Beds* 1B **52**
Bighouse. *High* 2A **168**
Bighton. *Hants* 3E **24**
Biglands. *Cumb* 4D **112**
Bignall End. *Staf* 5C **84**
Bignor. *W Sus* 4A **26**
Bigrigg. *Cumb* 3B **102**
Big Sand. *High* 1G **155**
Bigton. *Shet* 9E **173**
Bilberry. *Corn* 2E **6**
Bilborough. *Nott* 1C **74**
Bilbrook. *Som* 2D **20**
Bilbrook. *Staf* 5C **72**
Bilbrough. *N Yor* 5H **99**
Bilbster. *High* 3E **169**
Bilby. *Notts* 2D **86**
Bildershaw. *Dur* 2F **105**
Bildeston. *Suff* 1C **54**
Billericay. *Essx* 1A **40**
Billesdon. *Leics* 5E **74**
Billesley. *Warw* 5F **61**
Billingborough. *Linc* 2A **76**
Billinge. *Mers* 4D **90**
Billingford. *Norf* 3C **78**
(nr. Dereham)
Billingford. *Norf* 3D **66**
(nr. Diss)
Billingham. *Stoc T* 2B **106**
Billinghay. *Linc* 5A **88**
Billingley. *S Yor* 4E **93**
Billingshurst. *W Sus* 3B **26**
Billingsley. *Shrp* 2B **60**
Billington. *C Beds* 3H **51**
Billington. *Lanc* 1F **91**
Billington. *Staf* 3C **72**
Billockby. *Norf* 4G **79**
Billy Row. *Dur* 1E **105**
Bilsborrow. *Lanc* 5E **97**
Bilsby. *Linc* 3D **88**
Bilsham. *W Sus* 5A **26**
Bilsington. *Kent* 2E **29**
Bilson Green. *Glos* 4B **48**
Bilsthorpe. *Notts* 4D **86**
Bilston. *Midl* 3F **129**
Bilston. *W Mid* 1D **60**
Bilstone. *Leics* 5A **74**
Bilting. *Kent* 1E **29**
Bilton. *E Yor* 1E **95**
Bilton. *Nmbd* 3G **121**
Bilton. *N Yor* 4E **99**
Bilton. *Warw* 3B **62**
Bilton in Ainsty. *N Yor* 5G **99**
Bimbister. *Orkn* 6C **172**
Binbrook. *Linc* 1B **88**
Binchester. *Dur* 1F **105**
Bincombe. *Dors* 4B **14**
Bindal. *High* 5G **165**
Binegar. *Som* 2B **22**
Bines Green. *W Sus* 4C **26**
Binfield. *Brac* 4G **37**
Binfield Heath. *Oxon* 4F **37**
Bingfield. *Nmbd* 2C **114**
Bingham. *Notts* 1E **74**
Bingham's Melcombe.
Dors 2C **14**
Bingley. *W Yor* 1B **92**
Bings Heath. *Shrp* 4H **71**
Binham. *Norf* 2B **78**
Binley. *Hants* 1C **24**
Binley. *W Mid* 3A **62**
Binnegar. *Dors* 4D **15**
Binniehill. *Falk* 2B **128**
Binsoe. *N Yor* 2E **99**
Binstead. *IOW* 3D **16**
Binstead. *W Sus* 5A **26**
Binsted. *Hants* 2F **25**
Binton. *Warw* 5F **61**
Bintree. *Norf* 3C **78**
Binweston. *Shrp* 5F **71**
Birch. *Essx* 4C **54**
Birchall. *Staf* 5D **85**
Bircham Newton. *Norf* 2G **77**
Bircham Tofts. *Norf* 2G **77**
Birchanger. *Essx* 3F **53**
Birchburn. *N Ayr* 3D **122**
Birch Cross. *Staf* 2F **73**
Bircher. *Here* 4G **59**
Birch Green. *Essx* 4C **54**
Birchgrove. *Card* 4E **33**
Birchgrove. *Swan* 3G **31**
Birch Heath. *Ches W* 4H **83**
Birch Hill. *Ches W* 3H **83**
Birchill. *Devn* 2G **13**
Birchington. *Kent* 4G **41**
Birch Langley. *G Man* 4G **91**
Birchley Heath. *Warw* 1G **61**
Birchmoor. *Warw* 5G **73**
Birchmoor Green. *C Beds* 2H **51**
Birchover. *Derbs* 4G **85**
Birch Vale. *Derbs* 2E **85**
Birchview. *Mor* 5F **159**
Birchwood. *Linc* 4G **87**
Birchwood. *Som* 1F **13**
Birchwood. *Warr* 1A **84**
Bircotes. *Notts* 1D **86**
Birdbrook. *Essx* 1H **53**
Birdham. *W Sus* 2G **17**
Birdholme. *Derbs* 4A **86**
Birdingbury. *Warw* 4B **62**
Birdlip. *Glos* 4E **49**
Birdsall. *N Yor* 3C **100**
Birds Edge. *W Yor* 4C **92**
Birds Green. *Essx* 5F **53**
Birdsgreen. *Shrp* 2B **60**
Birdsmoorgate. *Dors* 2G **13**
Birdston. *E Dun* 2H **127**
Birdwell. *S Yor* 4D **92**
Birdwood. *Glos* 4C **48**
Birgham. *Bord* 1B **120**
Birichen. *High* 4E **165**
Birkby. *Cumb* 1B **102**
Birkby. *N Yor* 4A **106**
Birkdale. *Mers* 3B **90**
Birkenhead. *Mers* 2F **83**
Birkenhills. *Abers* 4E **161**
Birkenshaw. *N Lan* 3H **127**
Birkenshaw. *W Yor* 2C **92**
Birkhall. *Abers* 4H **151**
Birkhill. *Ang* 5C **144**
Birkholme. *Linc* 3G **75**
Birkin. *N Yor* 2F **93**
Birley. *Here* 5G **59**
Birling. *Kent* 4A **40**
Birling. *Nmbd* 4G **121**
Birling Gap. *E Sus* 5G **27**
Birlingham. *Worc* 1E **49**
Birmingham.
W Mid 2E **61** & **192**
Birmingham Airport.
W Mid 2F **61** & **205**
Birnam. *Per* 4H **143**
Birse. *Abers* 4C **152**
Birsemore. *Abers* 4C **152**
Birstall. *Leics* 5C **74**
Birstall. *W Yor* 2C **92**
Birstall Smithies. *W Yor* 2C **92**
Birstwith. *N Yor* 4E **99**
Birthorpe. *Linc* 2A **76**
Birtle. *Lanc* 3G **91**
Birtley. *Here* 4F **59**
Birtley. *Nmbd* 2B **114**
Birtley. *Tyne* 4F **115**
Birtsmorton. *Worc* 2D **48**
Birts Street. *Worc* 2C **48**
Bisbrooke. *Rut* 1F **63**
Bisham. *Wind* 3G **37**
Bishampton. *Worc* 5D **61**
Bish Mill. *Devn* 4H **19**
Bishop Auckland. *Dur* 2F **105**
Bishopbridge. *Linc* 1H **87**
Bishopbriggs. *E Dun* 2H **127**
Bishop Burton. *E Yor* 1C **94**
Bishopdown. *Wilts* 3G **23**
Bishop Middleham. *Dur* 1A **106**
Bishopmill. *Mor* 2G **159**
Bishop Monkton. *N Yor* 3F **99**
Bishop Norton. *Linc* 1G **87**
Bishopsbourne. *Kent* 5F **41**
Bishops Cannings. *Wilts* 5F **35**
Bishop's Castle. *Shrp* 2F **59**
Bishop's Caundle. *Dors* 1B **14**
Bishop's Cleeve. *Glos* 3E **49**
Bishops Court. *Down* 5K **179**
Bishop's Down. *Dors* 1B **14**
Bishop's Frome. *Here* 1B **48**
Bishop's Green. *Essx* 4G **53**
Bishop's Green. *Hants* 5D **36**
Bishop's Hull. *Som* 4F **21**
Bishop's Itchington.
Warw 5A **62**
Bishops Lydeard. *Som* 4E **21**
Bishop's Norton. *Glos* 3D **48**
Bishop's Nympton. *Devn* 4A **20**
Bishop's Offley. *Staf* 3B **72**
Bishop's Stortford. *Herts* 3E **53**
Bishops Sutton. *Hants* 3E **24**
Bishop's Tachbrook.
Warw 4H **61**
Bishop's Tawton. *Devn* 3F **19**
Bishopsteignton. *Devn* 5C **12**
Bishopstoke. *Hants* 1C **16**
Bishopston. *Swan* 4E **31**
Bishopstone. *Buck* 4G **51**
Bishopstone. *E Sus* 5F **27**
Bishopstone. *Here* 1H **47**
Bishopstone. *Swin* 3H **35**
Bishopstone. *Wilts* 4F **23**
Bishopstrow. *Wilts* 2D **23**
Bishop Sutton. *Bath* 1A **22**
Bishop's Waltham. *Hants* 1D **16**
Bishopswood. *Som* 1F **13**
Bishops Wood. *Staf* 5C **72**
Bishopsworth. *Bris* 5A **34**
Bishop Thornton. *N Yor* 3E **99**
Bishopthorpe. *York* 5H **99**
Bishopton. *Darl* 2A **106**
Bishopton. *Dum* 5B **110**
Bishopton. *N Yor* 2F **99**
Bishopton. *Ren* 2F **127**
Bishopton. *Warw* 5F **61**
Bishop Wilton. *E Yor* 4B **100**
Bishton. *Newp* 3G **33**
Bishton. *Staf* 3E **73**
Bisley. *Glos* 5E **49**
Bisley. *Surr* 5A **38**
Bispham. *Bkpl* 5C **96**
Bispham Green. *Lanc* 3C **90**
Bissoe. *Corn* 4B **6**
Bisterne. *Hants* 2G **15**
Bisterne Close. *Hants* 2H **15**
Bitchfield. *Linc* 3G **75**
Bittadon. *Devn* 2F **19**
Bittaford. *Devn* 3C **8**
Bittering. *Norf* 4B **78**
Bitterley. *Shrp* 3H **59**
Bitterne. *Sotn* 1C **16**
Bitteswell. *Leics* 2C **62**
Bitton. *S Glo* 5B **34**
Bix. *Oxon* 3F **37**
Bixter. *Shet* 6E **173**
Blaby. *Leics* 1C **62**
Blackawton. *Devn* 3E **9**
Black Bank. *Cambs* 2E **65**
Black Barn. *Linc* 3D **76**
Blackborough. *Devn* 2D **12**
Blackborough. *Norf* 4F **77**
Blackborough End. *Norf* 4F **77**
Black Bourton. *Oxon* 5A **50**
Blackboys. *E Sus* 3G **27**
Blackbrook. *Derbs* 1H **73**
Blackbrook. *Mers* 1H **83**
Blackbrook. *Staf* 2B **72**
Blackbrook. *Surr* 1C **26**
Blackburn. *Abers* 2F **153**
Blackburn. *Bkbn* 2E **91**
Blackburn. *W Lot* 3C **128**
Black Callerton. *Tyne* 3E **115**
Black Carr. *Norf* 1C **66**
Black Clauchrie. *S Ayr* 1H **109**
Black Corries. *High* 3G **141**
Black Crofts. *Arg* 5D **140**
Black Cross. *Corn* 2D **6**
Blackden Heath. *Ches E* 3B **84**
Blackditch. *Oxon* 5C **50**
Blackdog. *Abers* 2G **153**
Black Dog. *Devn* 2B **12**
Blackdown. *Dors* 2G **13**
Blackdyke. *Cumb* 4C **112**
Blacker Hill. *S Yor* 4D **92**
Blackfen. *G Lon* 3F **39**
Blackfield. *Hants* 2C **16**
Blackford. *Cumb* 3E **113**
Blackford. *Per* 3A **136**
Blackford. *Shrp* 2H **59**
Blackford. *Som* 2H **21**
(nr. Burnham-on-Sea)
Blackford. *Som* 4B **22**
(nr. Wincanton)
Blackfordby. *Leics* 4H **73**
Blackgang. *IOW* 5C **16**
Blackhall. *Edin* 2F **129**
Blackhall. *Ren* 3F **127**
Blackhall Colliery. *Dur* 1B **106**
Blackhall Mill. *Tyne* 4E **115**
Blackhall Rocks. *Dur* 1B **106**
Blackham. *E Sus* 2F **27**
Blackheath. *Essx* 3D **54**
Blackheath. *G Lon* 3E **39**
Blackheath. *Suff* 3G **67**
Blackheath. *Surr* 1B **26**
Blackheath. *W Mid* 2D **61**
Black Heddon. *Nmbd* 2D **115**
Blackhill. *Abers* 4H **161**
Blackhill. *High* 3C **154**
Black Hill. *Warw* 5G **61**
Blackhills. *Abers* 2G **161**
Blackhills. *High* 3D **158**
Blackjack. *Linc* 2B **76**
Blackland. *Wilts* 5F **35**
Black Lane. *G Man* 4F **91**
Blackleach. *Lanc* 1C **90**
Blackley. *G Man* 4G **91**
Blackley. *W Yor* 3B **92**
Blacklunans. *Per* 2A **144**
Blackmill. *B'end* 3C **32**
Blackmoor. *G Man* 4E **91**
Blackmoor. *Hants* 3F **25**
Blackmoor Gate. *Devn* 2G **19**
Blackmore. *Essx* 5G **53**
Blackmore End. *Essx* 2H **53**
Blackmore End. *Herts* 4B **52**
Black Mount. *Arg* 4G **141**
Blackness. *Falk* 2D **128**
Blacknest. *Hants* 2F **25**
Blackney. *Dors* 3H **13**
Blacknoll. *Dors* 4D **14**
Black Notley. *Essx* 3A **54**
Blacko. *Lanc* 5A **98**
Black Pill. *Swan* 3F **31**
Blackpool. *Bkpl* 1B **90** & **192**
Blackpool. *Devn* 4E **9**
Blackpool Airport. *Lanc* 1B **90**
Blackpool Corner. *Devn* 3G **13**
Blackpool Gate. *Cumb* 2G **113**
Blackridge. *W Lot* 3C **128**
Blackrock. *Arg* 3B **124**
Blackrock. *Mon* 4F **47**
Blackrod. *G Man* 3E **90**
Blackshaw. *Dum* 3B **112**
Blackshaw Head. *W Yor* 2H **91**
Blackshaw Moor. *Staf* 5E **85**
Blackskull. *Cgvn* 4F **178**
Blacksmith's Green. *Suff* 4D **66**
Blacksnape. *Bkbn* 2F **91**
Blackstone. *W Sus* 4D **26**
Black Street. *Suff* 2H **67**
Black Tar. *Pemb* 4D **43**
Blackthorn. *Oxon* 4E **50**
Blackthorpe. *Suff* 4B **66**
Blacktoft. *E Yor* 2B **94**
Blacktop. *Aber* 3F **153**
Black Torrington. *Devn* 2E **11**
Blacktown. *Newp* 3F **33**
Blackwall Tunnel. *G Lon* 2E **39**
Blackwater. *Corn* 4B **6**
Blackwater. *Hants* 1G **25**
Blackwater. *IOW* 4D **16**
Blackwater. *Som* 1F **13**
Blackwaterfoot. *N Ayr* 3C **122**
Blackwatertown. *Arm* 4C **178**
Blackwell. *Darl* 3F **105**
Blackwell. *Derbs* 5B **86**
(nr. Alfreton)
Blackwell. *Derbs* 3F **85**
(nr. Buxton)
Blackwell. *Som* 4D **20**
Blackwell. *Warw* 1H **49**
Blackwell. *Worc* 3D **61**
Blackwood. *Cphy* 2E **33**
Blackwood. *Dum* 1G **111**
Blackwood. *S Lan* 5A **128**
Blackwood Hill. *Staf* 5D **84**
Blacon. *Ches W* 4F **83**
Bladnoch. *Dum* 4B **110**
Bladon. *Oxon* 4C **50**
Blaenannerch. *Cdgn* 1C **44**
Blaenau Dolwyddelan.
Cnwy 5F **81**
Blaenau Ffestiniog. *Gwyn* 1G **69**
Blaenavon. *Torf* 5F **47**
Blaenawey. *Mon* 4F **47**
Blaen Celyn. *Cdgn* 5C **56**
Blaen Clydach. *Rhon* 2C **32**
Blaencwm. *Rhon* 2C **32**
Blaendulais. *Neat* 5B **46**
Blaenffos. *Pemb* 1F **43**
Blaengarw. *B'end* 2C **32**
Blaen-geuffordd. *Cdgn* 2F **57**
Blaengwrach. *Neat* 5B **46**
Blaengwynfi. *Neat* 2B **32**
Blaenllechau. *Rhon* 2D **32**
Blaenpennal. *Cdgn* 4F **57**
Blaenplwyf. *Cdgn* 3E **57**
Blaenporth. *Cdgn* 1C **44**
Blaenrhondda. *Rhon* 2C **32**
Blaenwaun. *Carm* 2G **43**
Blaen-y-coed. *Carm* 2H **43**
Blagdon. *N Som* 1A **22**
Blagdon. *Torb* 2E **9**
Blagdon Hill. *Som* 1F **13**
Blagill. *Cumb* 5A **114**
Blaguegate. *Lanc* 4C **90**
Blaich. *High* 1E **141**
Blain. *High* 2A **140**
Blaina. *Blae* 5F **47**
Blair Atholl. *Per* 2F **143**
Blair Drummond. *Stir* 4G **135**
Blairgowrie. *Per* 4A **144**
Blairhall. *Fife* 1D **128**
Blairingone. *Per* 4B **136**
Blairlogie. *Stir* 4H **135**
Blairmore. *Abers* 5B **160**
Blairmore. *Arg* 1C **126**
Blairmore. *High* 3B **166**
Blairquhanan. *W Dun* 1F **127**
Blaisdon. *Glos* 4C **48**
Blakebrook. *Worc* 3C **60**
Blakedown. *Worc* 3C **60**
Blake End. *Essx* 3H **53**
Blakemere. *Here* 1G **47**
Blakeney. *Glos* 5B **48**
Blakeney. *Norf* 1C **78**
Blakenhall. *Ches E* 1B **72**
Blakenhall. *W Mid* 1C **60**
Blakeshall. *Worc* 2C **60**
Blakesley. *Nptn* 5D **62**
Blanchland. *Nmbd* 4C **114**
Blandford Camp. *Dors* 2E **15**
Blandford Forum. *Dors* 2D **15**
Blandford St Mary. *Dors* 2D **15**
Bland Hill. *N Yor* 4E **98**
Blandy. *High* 3G **167**
Blanefield. *Stir* 2G **127**
Blankney. *Linc* 4H **87**
Blantyre. *S Lan* 4H **127**
Blarmachfoldach. *High* 2E **141**
Blarnalearoch. *High* 4F **163**
Blashford. *Hants* 2G **15**
Blaston. *Leics* 1F **63**
Blatchbridge. *Som* 2C **22**
Blathaisbhal. *W Isl* 1D **170**
Blatherwycke. *Nptn* 1G **63**
Blawith. *Cumb* 1B **96**
Blaxhall. *Suff* 5F **67**
Blaxton. *S Yor* 4G **93**
Blaydon. *Tyne* 3E **115**
Bleadney. *Som* 2H **21**
Bleadon. *N Som* 1G **21**
Blean. *Kent* 4F **41**
Bleary. *Cgvn* 4E **178**
Bleasby. *Linc* 2A **88**
Bleasby. *Notts* 1E **74**
Bleasby Moor. *Linc* 2A **88**
Blebocraigs. *Fife* 2G **137**
Bleddfa. *Powy* 4E **58**
Bledington. *Glos* 3H **49**
Bledlow. *Buck* 5F **51**
Bledlow Ridge. *Buck* 2F **37**
Blencarn. *Cumb* 1H **103**
Blencogo. *Cumb* 5C **112**
Blendworth. *Hants* 1F **17**
Blenheim. *Oxon* 5D **50**
Blennerhasset. *Cumb* 5C **112**
Bletchingdon. *Oxon* 4D **50**
Bletchingley. *Surr* 5E **39**
Bletchley. *Mil* 2G **51**
Bletchley. *Shrp* 2A **72**
Bletherston. *Pemb* 2E **43**
Bletsoe. *Bed* 5H **63**
Blewbury. *Oxon* 3D **36**
Blickling. *Norf* 3D **78**
Blidworth. *Notts* 5C **86**
Blindburn. *Nmbd* 3C **120**
Blindcrake. *Cumb* 1C **102**
Blindley Heath. *Surr* 1E **27**
Blindmoor. *Som* 1F **13**
Blisland. *Corn* 5A **10**
Blissford. *Hants* 1G **15**
Bliss Gate. *Worc* 3B **60**
Blists Hill. *Telf* 5A **72**
Blisworth. *Nptn* 5E **63**
Blithbury. *Staf* 3E **73**
Blitterlees. *Cumb* 4C **112**
Blockley. *Glos* 2G **49**
Blofield. *Norf* 5F **79**
Blofield Heath. *Norf* 4F **79**
Blo' Norton. *Norf* 3C **66**
Bloomfield. *Bord* 2H **119**
Blore. *Staf* 1F **73**
Blount's Green. *Staf* 2E **73**
Bloxham. *Oxon* 2C **50**
Bloxholm. *Linc* 5H **87**
Bloxwich. *W Mid* 5E **73**
Bloxworth. *Dors* 3D **15**
Blubberhouses. *N Yor* 4D **98**
Blue Anchor. *Som* 2D **20**
Blue Anchor. *Swan* 3E **31**
Blue Bell Hill. *Kent* 4B **40**
Blue Row. *Essx* 4D **54**
Bluetown. *Kent* 5D **40**
Blundeston. *Suff* 1H **67**
Blunham. *C Beds* 5A **64**
Blunsdon St Andrew.
Swin 3G **35**
Bluntington. *Worc* 3C **60**
Bluntisham. *Cambs* 3C **64**
Blunts. *Corn* 2H **7**
Blurton. *Stoke* 1C **72**
Blyborough. *Linc* 1G **87**
Blyford. *Suff* 3G **67**
Blymhill. *Staf* 4C **72**
Blymhill Lawns. *Staf* 4C **72**
Blyth. *Nmbd* 1G **115**
Blyth. *Notts* 2D **86**
Blyth. *Bord* 5E **129**
Blyth Bank. *Bord* 5E **129**
Blyth Bridge. *Bord* 5E **129**
Blythburgh. *Suff* 3G **67**
Blythe Bridge. *Staf* 1D **72**
Blythe Marsh. *Staf* 1D **72**
Blythe, The. *Staf* 3E **73**
Blyton. *Linc* 1F **87**
Boardmills. *Lis* 4H **179**
Boarhills. *Fife* 2H **137**
Boarhunt. *Hants* 2E **16**
Boarshead. *E Sus* 2G **27**
Boar's Head. *G Man* 4D **90**
Boars Hill. *Oxon* 5C **50**
Boarstall. *Buck* 4E **51**
Boasley Cross. *Devn* 3E **11**
Boath. *High* 1H **157**
Boat of Garten. *High* 2D **150**
Bobbing. *Kent* 4C **40**
Bobbington. *Staf* 1C **60**
Bobbingworth. *Essx* 5F **53**
Bocaddon. *Corn* 3F **7**
Bocking. *Essx* 3A **54**
Bocking Churchstreet.
Essx 3A **54**
Boddam. *Abers* 4H **161**
Boddam. *Shet* 10E **173**
Boddington. *Glos* 3D **49**
Bodedern. *IOA* 2C **80**
Bodelwyddan. *Den* 3C **82**
Bodenham. *Here* 5H **59**
Bodenham. *Wilts* 4G **23**
Bodewryd. *IOA* 1C **80**
Bodfari. *Den* 3C **82**
Bodffordd. *IOA* 3D **80**
Bodham. *Norf* 1D **78**
Bodiam. *E Sus* 3B **28**
Bodicote. *Oxon* 2C **50**
Bodieve. *Corn* 1D **6**
Bodinnick. *Corn* 3F **7**
Bodle Street Green.
E Sus 4A **28**
Bodmin. *Corn* 2E **7**
Bodnant. *Cnwy* 3H **81**
Bodney. *Norf* 1H **65**
Bodorgan. *IOA* 4C **80**
Bodrane. *Corn* 2G **7**
Bodsham. *Kent* 1F **29**
Boduan. *Gwyn* 2C **68**
Bodymoor Heath. *Warw* 1F **61**
Bogallan. *High* 3A **158**
Bogbrae Croft. *Abers* 5H **161**
Bogend. *S Ayr* 1C **116**
Boghall. *Midl* 3F **129**
Boghall. *W Lot* 3C **128**
Boghead. *S Lan* 5A **128**
Bogindollo. *Ang* 3D **144**
Bogmoor. *Mor* 2A **160**
Bogniebrae. *Abers* 4C **160**
Bognor Regis. *W Sus* 3H **17**
Bograxie. *Abers* 2E **152**
Bogside. *N Lan* 4B **128**
Bog, The. *Shrp* 1F **59**
Bogton. *Abers* 3D **160**
Bogue. *Dum* 1D **110**
Bohenie. *High* 5E **149**
Bohortha. *Corn* 5C **6**
Boirseam. *W Isl* 9C **171**
Bokiddick. *Corn* 2E **7**
Bolam. *Dur* 2E **105**
Bolam. *Nmbd* 1D **115**
Bolberry. *Devn* 5C **8**
Bold Heath. *Mers* 2H **83**
Boldon. *Tyne* 3G **115**
Boldon Colliery. *Tyne* 3G **115**
Boldre. *Hants* 3B **16**
Boldron. *Dur* 3D **104**
Bole. *Notts* 2E **87**
Bolehill. *Staf* 5G **73**
Bolehill. *Derbs* 5G **85**
Bolenowe. *Corn* 5A **6**
Boleside. *Bord* 1G **119**
Bolham. *Devn* 1C **12**
Bolham Water. *Devn* 1E **13**
Bolingey. *Corn* 3B **6**
Bollington. *Ches E* 3D **84**
Bolney. *W Sus* 3D **26**
Bolnhurst. *Bed* 5H **63**
Bolshan. *Ang* 3F **145**
Bolsover. *Derbs* 3B **86**
Bolsterstone. *S Yor* 1G **85**
Bolstone. *Here* 2A **48**
Boltachan. *Per* 3F **143**
Boltby. *N Yor* 1G **99**
Bolton. *Cumb* 2H **103**
Bolton. *E Lot* 2B **130**
Bolton. *E Yor* 4B **100**
Bolton. *G Man* 4F **91**
Bolton. *Nmbd* 3F **121**
Bolton Abbey. *N Yor* 4C **98**
Bolton-by-Bowland. *Lanc* 5G **97**
Boltonfellend. *Cumb* 3F **113**
Boltongate. *Cumb* 5D **112**
Bolton Green. *Lanc* 3D **90**
Bolton-le-Sands. *Lanc* 3D **97**
Bolton Low Houses.
Cumb 5D **112**
Bolton New Houses.
Cumb 5D **112**
Bolton-on-Swale. *N Yor* 5F **105**
Bolton Percy. *N Yor* 5H **99**
Bolton Town End. *Lanc* 3D **97**
Bolton upon Dearne.
S Yor 4E **93**
Bolton Wood Lane.
Cumb 5D **112**
Bolventor. *Corn* 5B **10**
Bomarsund. *Nmbd* 1F **115**
Bomere Heath. *Shrp* 4G **71**
Bonar Bridge. *High* 4D **164**
Bonawe. *Arg* 5E **141**
Bonby. *N Lin* 3D **94**
Boncath. *Pemb* 1G **43**
Bonchester Bridge.
Bord 3H **119**
Bonchurch. *IOW* 5D **16**
Bond End. *Staf* 4F **73**
Bondleigh. *Devn* 2G **11**
Bonds. *Lanc* 5D **97**
Bonehill. *Devn* 5H **11**
Bonehill. *Staf* 5F **73**
Bo'ness. *Falk* 1C **128**
Boney Hay. *Staf* 4E **73**
Bonham. *Wilts* 3C **22**
Bonhill. *W Dun* 2E **127**
Boningale. *Shrp* 5C **72**
Bonjedward. *Bord* 2A **120**
Bonkle. *N Lan* 4B **128**
Bonnanaboigh. *Lim* 5C **174**
Bonnington. *Ang* 5E **145**
Bonnington. *Edin* 3E **129**
Bonnington. *Kent* 2E **29**
Bonnybank. *Fife* 3F **137**
Bonnybridge. *Falk* 1B **128**
Bonnykelly. *Abers* 3F **161**
Bonnyrigg. *Midl* 3G **129**
Bonnyton. *Ang* 5C **144**
Bonnytown. *Fife* 2H **137**
Bonsall. *Derbs* 5G **85**
Bont. *Mon* 4G **47**
Bontddu. *Gwyn* 4F **69**
Bont Dolgadfan. *Powy* 5A **70**
Bontgoch. *Cdgn* 2F **57**
Bonthorpe. *Linc* 3D **89**
Bontnewydd. *Cdgn* 4F **57**
Bont-newydd. *Cnwy* 3C **82**
Bontnewydd. *Gwyn* 4D **81**
(nr. Caernarfon)
Bont Newydd. *Gwyn* 1G **69**
(nr. Llan Ffestiniog)
Bontuchel. *Den* 5C **82**
Bonvilston. *V Glam* 4D **32**
Bon-y-maen. *Swan* 3F **31**
Booker. *Buck* 2G **37**
Booley. *Shrp* 3H **71**
Boorley Green. *Hants* 1D **16**
Boosbeck. *Red C* 3D **106**
Boot. *Cumb* 4C **102**
Booth. *W Yor* 2A **92**
Boothby Graffoe. *Linc* 5G **87**
Boothby Pagnell. *Linc* 2G **75**
Booth Green. *Ches E* 2D **84**
Booth of Toft. *Shet* 4F **173**
Boothstown. *G Man* 4F **91**
Boothville. *Nptn* 4E **63**
Booth Wood. *W Yor* 3A **92**
Bootle. *Cumb* 1A **96**
Bootle. *Mers* 1F **83**
Booton. *Norf* 3D **78**
Booze. *N Yor* 4D **104**
Boquhan. *Stir* 1G **127**
Boraston. *Shrp* 3A **60**
Borden. *Kent* 4C **40**
Borden. *W Sus* 4G **25**
Bordlands. *Bord* 5E **129**
Bordley. *N Yor* 3B **98**
Bordon. *Hants* 3G **25**
Boreham. *Essx* 5A **54**
Boreham. *Wilts* 2D **23**
Boreham Street.
E Sus 4A **28**
Borehamwood. *Herts* 1C **38**
Boreland. *Dum* 5D **118**
Boreston. *Devn* 3D **8**
Borestone Brae. *Stir* 4H **135**
Boreton. *Shrp* 5H **71**
Borgh. *W Isl* 8B **170**
(on Barra)
Borgh. *W Isl* 3C **170**
(on Benbecula)
Borgh. *W Isl* 1E **170**
(on Berneray)
Borgh. *W Isl* 2G **171**
(on Isle of Lewis)
Borghasdal. *W Isl* 9C **171**
Borghastan. *W Isl* 3D **171**
Borgh na Sgiotaig. *High* 1C **154**
Borgie. *High* 3G **167**
Borgue. *Dum* 5D **110**
Borgue. *High* 1H **165**
Borley. *Essx* 1B **54**
Borley Green. *Essx* 1B **54**
Borley Green. *Suff* 4B **66**
Borlum. *High* 1H **149**
Bornais. *W Isl* 6C **170**
Bornesketaig. *High* 1C **154**
Boroughbridge. *N Yor* 3F **99**
Borough Green. *Kent* 5H **39**
Borras Head. *Wrex* 5F **83**
Borreraig. *High* 3A **154**
Borrobol Lodge. *High* 1F **165**
Borrodale. *High* 4A **154**
Borrowash. *Derb* 2B **74**
Borrowby. *N Yor* 1G **99**
(nr. Northallerton)
Borrowby. *N Yor* 3E **107**
(nr. Whitby)
Borrowston. *High* 4F **169**
Borrowstonehill. *Orkn* 7D **172**
Borrowstoun. *Falk* 1C **128**
Borstal. *Medw* 4B **40**
Borth. *Cdgn* 2F **57**
Borthwick. *Midl* 4G **129**
Borth-y-Gest. *Gwyn* 2E **69**
Borve. *High* 4D **154**
Borwick. *Lanc* 2E **97**
Bosbury. *Here* 1B **48**
Boscastle. *Corn* 3A **10**
Boscombe. *Bour* 3G **15**
Boscombe. *Wilts* 3H **23**
Boscoppa. *Corn* 3E **7**
Bosham. *W Sus* 2G **17**
Bosherston. *Pemb* 5D **42**
Bosley. *Ches E* 4D **84**
Bossall. *N Yor* 3B **100**
Bossiney. *Corn* 4A **10**
Bossingham. *Kent* 1F **29**
Bossington. *Som* 2B **20**
Bostadh. *W Isl* 3D **171**
Bostock Green. *Ches W* 4A **84**
Boston. *Linc* 1C **76**
Boston Spa. *W Yor* 5G **99**
Boswarthen. *Corn* 3B **4**
Boswinger. *Corn* 4D **6**
Botallack. *Corn* 3A **4**
Botany Bay. *G Lon* 1D **39**
Botcheston. *Leics* 5B **74**
Botesdale. *Suff* 3C **66**
Bothal. *Nmbd* 1F **115**
Bothampstead. *W Ber* 4D **36**
Bothamsall. *Notts* 3D **86**
Bothel. *Cumb* 1C **102**
Bothenhampton. *Dors* 3H **13**
Bothwell. *S Lan* 4H **127**
Botley. *Buck* 5H **51**
Botley. *Hants* 1D **16**
Botley. *Oxon* 5C **50**
Botloe's Green. *Glos* 3C **48**
Botolph Claydon. *Buck* 3F **51**
Botolphs. *W Sus* 5C **26**
Bottacks. *High* 2G **157**
Bottesford. *Leics* 2F **75**
Bottesford. *N Lin* 4B **94**
Bottisham. *Cambs* 4E **65**
Bottlesford. *Wilts* 1G **23**
Bottomcraig. *Fife* 1F **137**
Bottom o' th' Moor.
G Man 3E **91**
Botton. *N Yor* 4D **107**
Botton Head. *Lanc* 3F **97**
Bottreaux Mill. *Devn* 4B **20**
Botus Fleming. *Corn* 2A **8**
Botwnnog. *Gwyn* 2B **68**
Bough Beech. *Kent* 1F **27**
Boughrood. *Powy* 2E **47**
Boughspring. *Glos* 2A **34**
Boughton. *Norf* 5F **77**
Boughton. *Nptn* 4E **63**
Boughton. *Notts* 4D **86**
Boughton Aluph. *Kent* 1E **29**
Boughton Green. *Kent* 5B **40**
Boughton Lees. *Kent* 1E **28**
Boughton Malherbe. *Kent* 1C **28**
Boughton Monchelsea.
Kent 5B **40**
Boughton under Blean.
Kent 5E **41**
Boulby. *Red C* 3E **107**
Bouldnor. *IOW* 4B **16**
Bouldon. *Shrp* 2H **59**
Boulmer. *Nmbd* 3G **121**
Boulston. *Pemb* 3D **42**
Boultham. *Linc* 4G **87**
Boulton. *Derb* 2A **74**
Boundary. *Staf* 1D **73**
Bounds. *Here* 2B **48**
Bourn. *Cambs* 5C **64**
Bournbrook. *W Mid* 2E **61**
Bourne. *Linc* 3H **75**
Bourne End. *Bed* 4H **63**
Bourne End. *Buck* 3G **37**
Bourne End. *C Beds* 1H **51**
Bourne End. *Herts* 5A **52**
Bournemouth.
Bour 3F **15** & **192**
Bournemouth Airport.
Dors 3G **15**
Bournes Green. *Glos* 5E **49**
Bournes Green. *S'end* 2D **40**
Bourne, The. *Surr* 2G **25**
Bournheath. *Worc* 3D **60**
Bournmoor. *Dur* 4G **115**

Bournville—Burley

Bournville. W Mid 2E 61
Bourton. Dors 3C 22
Bourton. N Som 5G 33
Bourton. Oxon 3H 35
Bourton. Shrp 1H 59
Bourton. Wilts 5F 35
Bourton on Dunsmore.
Warw 3B 62
Bourton-on-the-Hill. Glos 2G 49
Bourton-on-the-Water.
Glos 3G 49
Bousd. Arg 2D 138
Bousta. Shet 6D 173
Boustead Hill. Cumb 4D 112
Bouth. Cumb 1C 96
Bouthwaite. N Yor 2D 98
Boveney. Buck 3A 38
Boveridge. Dors 1F 15
Boverton. V Glam 5C 32
Bovey Tracey. Devn 5B 12
Bovingdon. Herts 5A 52
Bovingdon Green. Buck 3G 37
Bovinger. Essx 5F 53
Bovington Camp. Dors 4D 14
Bow. Devn 2H 11
Bowbank. Dur 2C 104
Bow Brickhill. Mil 2H 51
Bowbridge. Glos 5D 48
Bowburn. Dur 1A 106
Bowcombe. IOW 4C 16
Bowd. Devn 4E 12
Bowden. Devn 4E 9
Bowden. Bord 1H 119
Bowden Hill. Wilts 5E 35
Bowdens. Som 4H 21
Bowderdale. Cumb 4H 103
Bowdon. G Man 2B 84
Bower. Nmbd 1A 114
Bowerchalke. Wilts 4F 23
Bowerhill. Wilts 5E 35
Bower Hinton. Som 1H 13
Bowermadden. High 2E 169
Bowers. Staf 2C 72
Bowers Gifford. Essx 2B 40
Bowershall. Fife 4C 136
Bowertower. High 2E 169
Bowes. Dur 3C 104
Bowgreave. Lanc 5D 97
Bowhousebog. N Lan 4B 128
Bowithick. Corn 4B 10
Bowland Bridge. Cumb 1D 96
Bowlees. Dur 2C 104
Bowley. Here 5H 59
Bowlhead Green. Surr 2A 26
Bowling. W Dun 2F 127
Bowling. W Yor 1B 92
Bowling Bank. Wrex 1F 71
Bowling Green. Worc 5C 60
Bowlish. Som 2B 22
Bowmanstead. Cumb 5E 102
Bowmore. Arg 4B 124
Bowness-on-Solway.
Cumb 3D 112
Bowness-on-Windermere.
Cumb 5F 103
Bow of Fife. Fife 2F 137
Bowriefauld. Ang 4E 145
Bowscale. Cumb 1E 103
Bowsden. Nmbd 5F 131
Bowside Lodge. High 2A 168
Bowston. Cumb 5F 103
Bow Street. Cdgn 2F 57
Bowthorpe. Norf 5D 78
Box. Glos 5D 48
Box. Wilts 5D 34
Boxbush. Glos 3B 48
Box End. Bed 1A 52
Boxford. Suff 1C 54
Boxford. W Ber 4C 36
Boxgrove. W Sus 5A 26
Box Hill. Wilts 5D 34
Boxley. Kent 5B 40
Boxmoor. Herts 5A 52
Box's Shop. Corn 2C 10
Boxted. Essx 2C 54
Boxted. Suff 5H 65
Boxted Cross. Essx 2D 54
Boxworth. Cambs 4C 64
Boxworth End. Cambs 4C 64
Boyden End. Suff 5G 65
Boyden Gate. Kent 4G 41
Boylestone. Derbs 2F 73
Boylestonfield. Derbs 2F 73
Boyndie. Abers 2D 160
Boynton. E Yor 3F 101
Boys Hill. Dors 1B 14
Boythorpe. Derbs 4A 86
Boyton. Corn 3D 10
Boyton. Suff 1G 55
Boyton. Wilts 3E 23
Boyton Cross. Essx 5G 53
Boyton End. Essx 2G 53
Boyton End. Suff 1H 53
Bozeat. Nptn 5G 63
Braaid. IOM 4C 108
Braal Castle. High 2D 168
Brabling Green. Suff 4E 67
Brabourne. Kent 1F 29
Brabourne Lees. Kent 1E 29
Brabster. High 2F 169
Bracadale. High 5C 154
Bracara. High 4F 147
Braceborough. Linc 4H 75
Bracebridge. Linc 4G 87
Bracebridge Heath. Linc 4G 87
Braceby. Linc 2H 75
Bracewell. Lanc 5A 98
Brackenber. Cumb 3A 104
Brackenfield. Derbs 5A 86
Brackenlands. Cumb 5D 112
Brackenthwaite. Cumb 5D 112
Brackenthwaite. N Yor 4E 99
Brackla. B'end 4C 32
Brackla. High 3C 158
Bracklesham. W Sus 3G 17
Brackletter. High 5D 148
Brackley. Nptn 2D 50
Brackley Hatch. Nptn 1E 51
Brackloch. High 1F 163
Bracknell. Brac 5G 37
Braco. Per 3H 135
Bracobrae. Mor 3C 160
Bracon. N Lin 4A 94
Bracon Ash. Norf 1D 66
Bradbourne. Derbs 5G 85
Bradbury. Dur 2A 106
Bradda. IOM 4A 108
Bradden. Nptn 1E 51
Bradenham. Buck 2G 37
Bradenham. Norf 5B 78
Bradenstoke. Wilts 4F 35
Bradfield. Essx 2E 55
Bradfield. Norf 2E 79
Bradfield. W Ber 4E 36
Bradfield Combust. Suff 5A 66
Bradfield Green. Ches E 5A 84
Bradfield Heath. Essx 3E 55
Bradfield St Clare. Suff 5B 66
Bradfield St George. Suff 4B 66
Bradford. Derbs 4G 85
Bradford. Devn 2E 11
Bradford. Nmbd 1F 121
Bradford. W Yor 1B 92 & 192
Bradford Abbas. Dors 1A 14
Bradford Barton. Devn 1B 12
Bradford Leigh. Wilts 5D 34
Bradford-on-Avon. Wilts 5D 34
Bradford-on-Tone. Som 4E 21
Bradford Peverell. Dors 3B 14
Bradiford. Devn 3F 19
Brading. IOW 4E 16
Bradley. Ches W 3H 83
Bradley. Derbs 1G 73
Bradley. Glos 2C 34
Bradley. Hants 2E 25
Bradley. NE Lin 4F 95
Bradley. N Yor 1C 98
Bradley. Staf 4C 72
Bradley. W Mid 1D 60
Bradley. W Yor 2B 92
Bradley. Wrex 5F 83
Bradley Cross. Som 1H 21
Bradley Green. Ches W 1H 71
Bradley Green. Som 3F 21
Bradley Green. Warw 5G 73
Bradley Green. Worc 4D 61
Bradley in the Moors.
Staf 1E 73
Bradley Mount. Ches E 3D 84
Bradley Stoke. S Glo 3B 34
Bradlow. Here 2C 48
Bradmore. Notts 2C 74
Bradmore. W Mid 1C 60
Bradninch. Devn 2D 12
Bradnop. Staf 5E 85
Bradpole. Dors 3H 13
Bradshaw. G Man 3F 91
Bradstone. Devn 4D 11
Bradwall Green. Ches E 4B 84
Bradway. S Yor 2H 85
Bradwell. Derbs 2F 85
Bradwell. Essx 3B 54
Bradwell. Mil 2G 51
Bradwell. Norf 5H 79
Bradwell-on-Sea. Essx 5D 54
Bradwell Waterside. Essx 5C 54
Bradworthy. Devn 1D 10
Brae. High 5C 162
Brae. Shet 5E 173
Braeantra. High 1H 157
Braefield. High 5G 157
Braefindon. High 3A 158
Braegrum. Per 1C 136
Braehead. Ang 3F 145
Braehead. Dum 4B 110
Braehead. Mor 4G 159
Braehead. Orkn 3D 172
Braehead. S Lan 1H 117
(nr. Coalburn)
Braehead. S Lan 4C 128
(nr. Forth)
Braehoulland. Shet 4D 173
Braemar. Abers 4F 151
Braemore. High 5C 168
(nr. Dunbeath)
Braemore. High 1D 156
(nr. Ullapool)
Brae of Achnahaird.
High 2E 163
Brae Roy Lodge. High 4F 149
Braeside. Abers 5G 161
Braeside. Inv 2D 126
Braes of Coul. Ang 3B 144
Braeswick. Orkn 4F 172
Braetongue. High 3F 167
Braeval. Stir 3E 135
Braevallich. Arg 3G 133
Braewick. Shet 6E 173
Brafferton. Darl 2F 105
Brafferton. N Yor 2G 99
Brafield-on-the-Green.
Nptn 5F 63
Bragar. W Isl 3E 171
Bragbury End. Herts 3C 52
Bragleenbeg. Arg 1G 133
Braichmelyn. Gwyn 4F 81
Braides. Lanc 4D 96
Braidwood. S Lan 5B 128
Braigo. Arg 3A 124
Brailsford. Derbs 1G 73
Braintree. Essx 3A 54
Braiseworth. Suff 3D 66
Braishfield. Hants 4B 24
Braithwaite. Cumb 2D 102
Braithwaite. S Yor 3G 93
Braithwaite. W Yor 5C 98
Braithwell. S Yor 1C 86
Brakefield Green. Norf 5C 78
Bramber. W Sus 4C 26
Brambledown. Kent 3D 40
Brambridge. Hants 4C 24
Bramcote. Notts 2C 74
Bramcote. Warw 2B 62
Bramdean. Hants 4E 24
Bramerton. Norf 5E 79
Bramfield. Herts 4C 52
Bramfield. Suff 3F 67
Bramford. Suff 1E 54
Bramhall. G Man 2C 84
Bramham. W Yor 5G 99
Bramhope. W Yor 5E 99
Bramley. Hants 1E 25
Bramley. S Yor 1B 86
Bramley. Surr 1B 26
Bramley. W Yor 1C 92
Bramley Green. Hants 1E 25
Bramley Head. N Yor 4D 98
Bramley Vale. Derbs 4B 86
Bramling. Kent 5G 41
Brampford Speke. Devn 3C 12
Brampton. Cambs 3B 64
Brampton. Cumb 2H 103
(nr. Appleby-in-Westmorland)
Brampton. Cumb 3G 113
(nr. Carlisle)
Brampton. Linc 3F 87
Brampton. Norf 3E 78
Brampton. S Yor 4E 93
Brampton. Suff 2G 67
Brampton Abbotts. Here 3B 48
Brampton Ash. Nptn 2E 63
Brampton Bryan. Here 3F 59
Brampton en le Morthen.
S Yor 2B 86
Bramshall. Staf 2E 73
Bramshaw. Hants 1A 16
Bramshill. Hants 5F 37
Bramshott. Hants 3G 25
Branault. High 2G 139
Brancaster. Norf 1G 77
Brancaster Staithe. Norf 1G 77
Brancepeth. Dur 1F 105
Branch End. Nmbd 3D 114
Branchill. Mor 3E 159
Brand End. Linc 1C 76
Branderburgh. Mor 1G 159
Brandesburton. E Yor 5F 101
Brandeston. Suff 4E 67
Brand Green. Glos 3C 48
Brandhill. Shrp 3G 59
Brandis Corner. Devn 2E 11
Brandish Street. Som 2C 20
Brandiston. Norf 3D 78
Brandon. Dur 1F 105
Brandon. Linc 1G 75
Brandon. Nmbd 3E 121
Brandon. Suff 2G 65
Brandon. Warw 3B 62
Brandon Bank. Cambs 2F 65
Brandon Creek. Norf 1F 65
Brandon Parva. Norf 5C 78
Brandsby. N Yor 2H 99
Brandy Wharf. Linc 1H 87
Brane. Corn 4B 4
Bran End. Essx 3G 53
Branksome. Pool 3F 15
Bransbury. Hants 2C 24
Bransby. Linc 3G 87
Branscombe. Devn 4E 13
Bransford. Worc 5B 60
Bransgore. Hants 3G 15
Bransholme. Hull 1D 94
Bransley. Shrp 3A 60
Branston. Leics 3F 75
Branston. Linc 4H 87
Branston. Staf 3G 73
Branston Booths. Linc 4H 87
Branstone. IOW 4D 16
Bransty. Cumb 3A 102
Brant Broughton. Linc 5G 87
Brantham. Suff 2E 54
Branthwaite. Cumb 1D 102
(nr. Caldbeck)
Branthwaite. Cumb 2B 102
(nr. Workington)
Brantingham. E Yor 2C 94
Branton. Nmbd 3E 121
Branton. S Yor 4G 93
Branton Green. N Yor 3G 99
Branxholme. Bord 3G 119
Branxton. Nmbd 1C 120
Brassington. Derbs 5G 85
Brasted. Kent 5F 39
Brasted Chart. Kent 5F 39
Bratch, The. Staf 1C 60
Brathens. Abers 4D 152
Bratoft. Linc 4D 88
Brattleby. Linc 2G 87
Bratton. Som 2C 20
Bratton. Telf 4A 72
Bratton. Wilts 1E 23
Bratton Clovelly. Devn 3E 11
Bratton Fleming. Devn 3G 19
Bratton Seymour. Som 4B 22
Braughing. Herts 3D 53
Braulen Lodge. High 5E 157
Braunston. Nptn 4C 62
Braunstone Town. Leic 5C 74
Braunston-in-Rutland.
Rut 5F 75
Braunton. Devn 3E 19
Brawby. N Yor 2B 100
Brawl. High 2A 168
Brawlbin. High 3C 168
Bray. Wind 3A 38
Braybrooke. Nptn 2E 63
Brayford. Devn 3G 19
Bray Shop. Corn 5D 10
Braystones. Cumb 4B 102
Brayton. N Yor 1G 93
Bray Wick. Wind 4G 37
Brazacott. Corn 3C 10
Brea. Corn 4A 6
Breach. W Sus 2F 17
Breachwood Green. Herts 3B 52
Breacleit. W Isl 4D 171
Breaden Heath. Shrp 2G 71
Breadsall. Derbs 1A 74
Breadstone. Glos 5C 48
Breage. Corn 4D 4
Breakachy. High 4G 157
Breakish. High 1E 147
Bream. Glos 5B 48
Breamore. Hants 1G 15
Bream's Meend. Glos 5B 48
Brean. Som 1F 21
Breanais. W Isl 5B 171
Brearton. N Yor 3F 99
Breascleit. W Isl 4E 171
Breaston. Derbs 2B 74
Brecais Àrd. High 1E 147
Brecais Iosal. High 1E 147
Brechfa. Carm 2F 45
Brechin. Ang 3F 145
Breckles. Norf 1B 66
Brecon. Powy 3D 46
Brecon Beacons. Powy 3C 46
Bredbury. G Man 1D 84
Brede. E Sus 4C 28
Bredenbury. Here 5A 60
Bredfield. Suff 5E 67
Bredgar. Kent 4C 40
Bredhurst. Kent 4B 40
Bredicot. Worc 5D 60
Bredon. Worc 2E 49
Bredon's Norton. Worc 2E 49
Bredwardine. Here 1G 47
Breedon on the Hill. Leics 3B 74
Breibhig. W Isl 9B 170
(on Barra)
Breibhig. W Isl 4G 171
(on Isle of Lewis)
Breich. W Lot 3C 128
Breightmet. G Man 3F 91
Breighton. E Yor 1H 93
Breinton. Here 2H 47
Breinton Common. Here 2H 47
Breiwick. Shet 7F 173
Brelston Green. Here 3A 48
Bremhill. Wilts 4E 35
Brenachie. High 1B 158
Brenchley. Kent 1A 28
Brendon. Devn 2A 20
Brent Cross. G Lon 2D 38
Brent Eleigh. Suff 1C 54
Brentford. G Lon 3C 38
Brentingby. Leics 4E 75
Brent Knoll. Som 1G 21
Brent Pelham. Herts 2E 53
Brentwood. Essx 1H 39
Brenzett. Kent 3E 28
Brereton. Staf 4E 73
Brereton Cross. Staf 4E 73
Brereton Green. Ches E 4B 84
Brereton Heath. Ches E 4C 84
Bressingham. Norf 2C 66
Bretby. Derbs 3G 73
Bretford. Warw 3B 62
Bretforton. Worc 1F 49
Bretherdale Head. Cumb 4G 103
Bretherton. Lanc 2C 90
Brettabister. Shet 6F 173
Brettenham. Norf 2B 66
Brettenham. Suff 5B 66
Bretton. Flin 4F 83
Bretton. Pet 5A 76
Brewer Street. Surr 5E 39
Brewlands Bridge. Ang 2A 144
Brewood. Staf 5C 72
Briantspuddle. Dors 3D 14
Bricket Wood. Herts 5B 52
Bricklehampton. Worc 1E 49
Bride. IOM 1D 108
Bridekirk. Cumb 1C 102
Bridell. Pemb 1B 44
Bridestowe. Devn 4F 11
Brideswell. Abers 5C 160
Bridford. Devn 4B 12
Bridge. Corn 4A 6
Bridge. Kent 5F 41
Bridge. Som 2G 13
Bridge End. Bed 5H 63
Bridge End. Cumb 5D 102
(nr. Broughton in Furness)
Bridge End. Cumb 5E 113
(nr. Dalston)
Bridge End. Linc 2A 76
Bridge End. Shet 8E 173
Bridgefoot. Ang 5C 144
Bridgefoot. Cumb 2B 102
Bridge Green. Essx 2E 53
Bridgehampton. Som 4A 22
Bridge Hewick. N Yor 2F 99
Bridgehill. Dur 4D 115
Bridgemary. Hants 2D 16
Bridgemere. Ches E 1B 72
Bridgemont. Derbs 2E 85
Bridgend. Abers 5C 160
(nr. Huntly)
Bridgend. Abers 5H 161
(nr. Peterhead)
Bridgend. Ang 2E 145
(nr. Brechin)
Bridgend. Ang 4C 144
(nr. Kirriemuir)
Bridgend. Arg 4F 133
(nr. Lochgilphead)
Bridgend. Arg 3B 124
(on Islay)
Bridgend. B'end 3C 32
Bridgend. Cumb 3F 103
Bridgend. Devn 4B 8
Bridgend. Fife 2F 137
Bridgend. High 3F 157
Bridgend. Mor 5A 160
Bridgend. Per 1D 136
Bridgend. W Lot 2D 128
Bridgend of Lintrathen.
Ang 3B 144
Bridgeness. Falk 1D 128
Bridge of Alford. Abers 2C 152
Bridge of Allan. Stir 4G 135
Bridge of Avon. Mor 5F 159
Bridge of Awe. Arg 1H 133
Bridge of Balgie. Per 4C 142
Bridge of Brown. High 1F 151
Bridge of Cally. Per 3A 144
Bridge of Canny. Abers 4D 152
Bridge of Dee. Dum 3E 111
Bridge of Don. Aber 2G 153
Bridge of Dun. Ang 3F 145
Bridge of Dye. Abers 5D 152
Bridge of Earn. Per 2D 136
Bridge of Ericht. Per 3C 142
Bridge of Feugh. Abers 4E 152
Bridge of Gairn. Abers 4A 152
Bridge of Gaur. Per 3C 142
Bridge of Muchalls.
Abers 4F 153
Bridge of Oich. High 3F 149
Bridge of Orchy. Arg 5H 141
Bridge of Walls. Shet 6D 173
Bridge of Weir. Ren 3E 127
Bridge Reeve. Devn 1G 11
Bridgerule. Devn 2C 10
Bridge Sollers. Here 1H 47
Bridge Street. Suff 1B 54
Bridgetown. Devn 2E 9
Bridgetown. Som 3C 20
Bridge Town. Warw 5G 61
Bridge Trafford. Ches W 3G 83
Bridgeyate. S Glo 4B 34
Bridgham. Norf 2B 66
Bridgnorth. Shrp 1B 60
Bridgtown. Staf 5D 73
Bridgwater. Som 3G 21
Bridlington. E Yor 3F 101
Bridport. Dors 3H 13
Bridstow. Here 3A 48
Brierfield. Lanc 1G 91
Brierley. Glos 4B 48
Brierley. Here 5G 59
Brierley. S Yor 3E 93
Brierley Hill. W Mid 2D 60
Brierton. Hart 1B 106
Briestfield. W Yor 3C 92
Brigg. N Lin 4D 94
Briggate. Norf 3F 79
Briggswath. N Yor 4F 107
Brigham. Cumb 1B 102
Brigham. E Yor 4E 101
Brighouse. W Yor 2B 92
Brighstone. IOW 4C 16
Brightgate. Derbs 5G 85
Brighthampton. Oxon 5B 50
Brightholmlee. S Yor 1G 85
Brightley. Devn 3G 11
Brightling. E Sus 3A 28
Brightlingsea. Essx 4D 54
Brighton. Brig 5E 27 & 192
Brighton. Corn 3D 6
Brighton Hill. Hants 2E 24
Brightons. Falk 2C 128
Brightwalton. W Ber 4C 36
Brightwalton Green.
W Ber 4C 36
Brightwell. Suff 1F 55
Brightwell Baldwin. Oxon 2E 37
Brightwell-cum-Sotwell.
Oxon 2D 36
Brigmerston. Wilts 2G 23
Brignall. Dur 3D 104
Brig o' Turk. Stir 3E 135
Brigsley. NE Lin 4F 95
Brigsteer. Cumb 1D 97
Brigstock. Nptn 2G 63
Brill. Buck 4E 51
Brill. Corn 4E 5
Brilley. Here 1F 47
Brimaston. Pemb 2D 42
Brimfield. Here 4H 59
Brimington. Derbs 3B 86
Brimley. Devn 5B 12
Brimpsfield. Glos 4E 49
Brimpton. W Ber 5D 36
Brims. Orkn 9B 172
Brimscombe. Glos 5D 48
Brimstage. Mers 2F 83
Brincliffe. S Yor 2H 85
Brind. E Yor 1H 93
Brindister. Shet 6D 173
(nr. West Burrafirth)
Brindister. Shet 8F 173
(nr. West Lerwick)
Brindle. Lanc 2E 90
Brindley. Ches E 5H 83
Brindley Ford. Stoke 5C 84
Brineton. Staf 4C 72
Bringhurst. Leics 1F 63
Bringsty Common. Here 5A 60
Brington. Cambs 3H 63
Brinian. Orkn 5D 172
Briningham. Norf 2C 78
Brinkhill. Linc 3C 88
Brinkley. Cambs 5F 65
Brinklow. Warw 3B 62
Brinkworth. Wilts 3F 35
Brinscall. Lanc 2E 91
Brinscombe. Som 1H 21
Brinsley. Notts 1B 74
Brinsworth. S Yor 2B 86
Brinton. Norf 2C 78
Brisco. Cumb 4F 113
Brisley. Norf 3B 78
Brislington. Bris 4B 34
Brissenden Green. Kent 2D 28
Bristol. Bris 4A 34 & 193
Bristol International Airport.
N Som 5A 34
Briston. Norf 2C 78
Britannia. Lanc 2G 91
Britford. Wilts 4G 23
Brithdir. Cphy 5E 47
Brithdir. Cdgn 1D 44
Brithdir. Gwyn 4G 69
Briton Ferry. Neat 3G 31
Britwell Salome. Oxon 2E 37
Brixham. Torb 3F 9
Brixton. Devn 3B 8
Brixton. G Lon 3E 39
Brixton Deverill. Wilts 3D 22
Brixworth. Nptn 3E 63
Brize Norton. Oxon 5B 50
Broad Alley. Worc 4C 60
Broad Blunsdon. Swin 2G 35
Broadbottom. G Man 1D 85
Broadbridge. W Sus 2G 17
Broadbridge Heath.
W Sus 2C 26
Broad Campden. Glos 2G 49
Broad Chalke. Wilts 4F 23
Broadclyst. Devn 3C 12
Broadfield. Inv 2E 127
Broadfield. Pemb 4F 43
Broadfield. W Sus 2D 26
Broadford. High 1E 147
Broadford Bridge. W Sus 3B 26
Broadgate. Cumb 1A 96
Broad Green. Cambs 5F 65
Broad Green. C Beds 1H 51
Broad Green. Worc 3D 61
(nr. Bromsgrove)
Broad Green. Worc 5B 60
(nr. Worcester)
Broadhaven. High 3F 169
Broad Haven. Pemb 3C 42
Broadheath. G Man 2B 84
Broad Heath. Staf 3C 72
Broadheath. Worc 4A 60
Broadhembury. Devn 2E 12
Broadhempston. Devn 2E 9
Broad Hill. Cambs 3E 65
Broad Hinton. Wilts 4G 35
Broadholm. Derbs 1A 74
Broadholme. Linc 3F 87
Broadlay. Carm 5D 44
Broad Laying. Hants 5C 36
Broadley. Lanc 3G 91
Broadley. Mor 2A 160
Broadley Common. Essx 5E 53
Broad Marston. Worc 1G 49
Broadmayne. Dors 4C 14
Broadmere. Hants 2E 24
Broadmoor. Pemb 4E 43
Broad Oak. Carm 3F 45
Broad Oak. Cumb 5C 102
Broad Oak. Devn 3D 12
Broadoak. Dors 3H 13
(nr. Bridport)
Broad Oak. Dors 1C 14
(nr. Sturminster Newton)
Broad Oak. E Sus 4C 28
(nr. Hastings)
Broad Oak. E Sus 3H 27
(nr. Heathfield)
Broadoak. Glos 4B 48
Broadoak. Hants 1C 16
Broad Oak. Here 3H 47
Broad Oak. Kent 4F 41
Broadrashes. Mor 3B 160
Broads. Norf 5G 79
Broadsea. Abers 2G 161
Broad's Green. Essx 4G 53
Broadshard. Som 1H 13
Broadstairs. Kent 4H 41
Broadstone. Pool 3F 15
Broadstone. Shrp 2H 59
Broad Street. E Sus 4C 28
Broad Street. Kent 1F 29
(nr. Ashford)
Broad Street. Kent 5C 40
(nr. Maidstone)
Broad Street Green. Essx 5B 54
Broad, The. Here 4G 59
Broad Town. Wilts 4F 35
Broadwas. Worc 5B 60
Broadwath. Cumb 4F 113
Broadway. Carm 5D 45
(nr. Kidwelly)
Broadway. Carm 3G 43
(nr. Laugharne)
Broadway. Pemb 3C 42
Broadway. Som 1G 13
Broadway. Suff 3F 67
Broadway. Worc 2G 49
Broadwell. Glos 4A 48
(nr. Cinderford)
Broadwell. Glos 3H 49
(nr. Stow-on-the-Wold)
Broadwell. Oxon 5A 50
Broadwell. Warw 4B 62
Broadwell House. Nmbd 4C 114
Broadwey. Dors 4B 14
Broadwindsor. Dors 2H 13
Broadwoodkelly. Devn 2G 11
Broadwoodwidger. Devn 4E 11
Broallan. High 4G 157
Brobury. Here 1G 47
Brochel. High 4E 155
Brockaghboy. Cole 5E 174
Brockamin. Worc 5B 60
Brockbridge. Hants 1E 16
Brockdish. Norf 3E 66
Brockencote. Worc 3C 60
Brockenhurst. Hants 2A 16
Brocketsbrae. S Lan 1H 117
Brockford Street. Suff 4D 66
Brockhall. Nptn 4D 62
Brockham. Surr 1C 26
Brockhampton. Glos 3E 49
(nr. Bishop's Cleeve)
Brockhampton. Glos 3F 49
(nr. Sevenhampton)
Brockhampton. Here 2A 48
Brockhill. Bord 2F 119
Brockholes. W Yor 3B 92
Brockhurst. Hants 2D 16
Brocklesby. Linc 3E 95
Brockley. N Som 5H 33
Brockley Corner. Suff 3H 65
Brockley Green. Suff 1H 53
(nr. Bury St Edmunds)
Brockley Green. Suff 5H 65
(nr. Haverhill)
Brockleymoor. Cumb 1F 103
Brockmoor. W Mid 2C 60
Brockton. Shrp 2F 59
(nr. Bishop's Castle)
Brockton. Shrp 5B 72
(nr. Madeley)
Brockton. Shrp 1H 59
(nr. Much Wenlock)
Brockton. Shrp 5F 71
(nr. Pontesbury)
Brockton. Staf 2C 72
Brockton. Telf 4B 72
Brockweir. Glos 5A 48
Brockworth. Glos 4D 49
Brocton. Staf 4D 72
Brodick. N Ayr 2E 123
Brodie. Mor 3D 159
Brodiesord. Abers 3C 160
Brodsworth. S Yor 4F 93
Brogaig. High 2D 154
Brogborough. C Beds 2H 51
Brokenborough. Wilts 3E 35
Broken Cross. Ches E 3C 84
Bromborough. Mers 2F 83
Bromdon. Shrp 2A 60
Brome. Suff 3D 66
Brome Street. Suff 3D 66
Bromeswell. Suff 5F 67
Bromfield. Cumb 5C 112
Bromfield. Shrp 3G 59
Bromford. W Mid 1F 61
Bromham. Bed 5H 63
Bromham. Wilts 5E 35
Bromley. G Lon 4F 39
Bromley. Herts 3E 53
Bromley. Shrp 1B 60
Bromley Cross. G Man 3F 91
Bromley Green. Kent 2D 28
Bromley Wood. Staf 3F 73
Brompton. Medw 4B 40
Brompton. N Yor 5A 106
(nr. Northallerton)
Brompton. N Yor 1D 100
(nr. Scarborough)
Brompton. Shrp 5H 71
Brompton-on-Swale.
N Yor 5F 105
Brompton Ralph. Som 3D 20
Brompton Regis. Som 3C 20
Bromsash. Here 3B 48
Bromsberrow. Glos 2C 48
Bromsberrow Heath.
Glos 2C 48
Bromsgrove. Worc 3D 60
Bromstead Heath. Staf 4B 72
Bromyard. Here 5A 60
Bromyard Downs.
Here 5A 60
Bronaber. Gwyn 2G 69
Broncroft. Shrp 2H 59
Brongest. Cdgn 1D 44
Brongwyn. Cdgn 1C 44
Bronington. Wrex 2G 71
Bronllys. Powy 2E 47
Bronnant. Cdgn 4F 57
Bronwydd Arms. Carm 3E 45
Bronydd. Powy 1F 47
Bronygarth. Shrp 2E 71
Brook. Carm 4G 43
Brook. Hants 1A 16
(nr. Cadnam)
Brook. Hants 4B 24
(nr. Romsey)
Brook. IOW 4B 16
Brook. Kent 1E 29
Brook. Surr 1B 26
(nr. Guildford)
Brook. Surr 2A 26
(nr. Haslemere)
Brooke. Norf 1E 67
Brooke. Rut 5F 75
Brookeborough. Ferm 8F 176
Brookenby. Linc 1B 88
Brookend. Glos 5B 48
Brook End. Worc 1D 48
Brookfield. Lanc 1D 90
Brookfield. Ren 3F 127
Brookhouse. Lanc 3E 97
Brookhouse. S Yor 2C 86
Brookhouse Green.
Ches E 4C 84
Brookhouses. Staf 1D 73
Brookhurst. Mers 2F 83
Brookland. Kent 3D 28
Brooklands. G Man 1B 84
Brooklands. Shrp 1H 71
Brookmans Park. Herts 5C 52
Brooks. Powy 1D 58
Brooksby. Leics 4D 74
Brooks Green. W Sus 3C 26
Brook Street. Essx 1G 39
Brook Street. Kent 2D 28
Brook Street. W Sus 3E 27
Brookthorpe. Glos 4D 48
Brookville. Norf 1G 65
Brookwood. Surr 5A 38
Broom. C Beds 1B 52
Broom. Fife 3F 137
Broom. Warw 5E 61
Broome. Norf 1F 67
Broome. Shrp 1H 59
(nr. Cardington)
Broome. Shrp 2G 59
(nr. Craven Arms)
Broome. Worc 3D 60
Broomedge. Warr 2B 84
Broomend. Abers 2E 153
Broome Park. Nmbd 3F 121
Broomer's Corner. W Sus 3C 26
Broomfield. Abers 5G 161
Broomfield. Essx 4H 53
Broomfield. Kent 4F 41
(nr. Herne Bay)
Broomfield. Kent 5C 40
(nr. Maidstone)
Broomfield. Som 3F 21
Broomfleet. E Yor 2B 94
Broom Green. Norf 3B 78
Broomhall. Ches E 1A 72
Broomhall. Wind 4A 38
Broomhaugh. Nmbd 3D 114
Broom Hill. Dors 2F 15
Broomhill. High 1D 151
(nr. Grantown-on-Spey)
Broomhill. High 1B 158
(nr. Invergordon)
Broomhill. Norf 5F 77
Broomhill. S Yor 4E 93
Broom Hill. Worc 3D 60
Broomhillbank. Dum 5D 118
Broomholm. Norf 2F 79
Broomlands. Dum 4C 118
Broomley. Nmbd 3D 114
Broom of Moy. Mor 3E 159
Broompark. Dur 5F 115
Broom's Green. Glos 2C 48
Brora. High 3G 165
Broseley. Shrp 5A 72
Brotherhouse Bar. Linc 4B 76
Brotheridge Green. Worc 1D 48
Brotherlee. Dur 1C 104
Brothertoft. Linc 1B 76
Brotherton. N Yor 2E 93
Brotton. Red C 2D 107
Broubster. High 2C 168
Brough. Cumb 3A 104
Brough. Derbs 2F 85
Brough. E Yor 2C 94
Brough. High 1E 169
Brough. Notts 5F 87
Brough. Orkn 6C 172
(nr. Finstown)
Brough. Orkn 9D 172
(nr. St Margaret's Hope)
Brough. Shet 6F 173
(nr. Benston)
Brough. Shet 4F 173
(nr. Booth of Toft)
Brough. Shet 7G 173
(on Bressay)
Brough. Shet 5G 173
(on Whalsay)
Broughall. Shrp 1H 71
Brougham. Cumb 2G 103
Brough Lodge. Shet 2G 173
Broughshane. Bmna 6H 175
Brough Sowerby. Cumb 3A 104
Broughton. Cambs 3B 64
Broughton. Flin 4F 83
Broughton. Hants 3B 24
Broughton. Lanc 1D 90
Broughton. Mil 2G 51
Broughton. Nptn 3F 63
Broughton. N Lin 4C 94
Broughton. N Yor 2B 100
(nr. Malton)
Broughton. N Yor 4B 98
(nr. Skipton)
Broughton. Orkn 3D 172
Broughton. Oxon 2C 50
Broughton. Bord 1D 118
Broughton. Staf 2B 72
Broughton. V Glam 4C 32
Broughton Astley. Leics 1C 62
Broughton Beck. Cumb 1B 96
Broughton Cross. Cumb 1B 102
Broughton Gifford. Wilts 5D 35
Broughton Green. Worc 4D 60
Broughton Hackett. Worc 5D 60
Broughton in Furness.
Cumb 1B 96
Broughton Mills. Cumb 5D 102
Broughton Moor. Cumb 1B 102
Broughton Park. G Man 4G 91
Broughton Poggs. Oxon 5H 49
Broughtown. Orkn 3F 172
Broughty Ferry. D'dee 5D 144
Browland. Shet 6D 173
Brownbread Street. E Sus 4A 28
Brown Candover. Hants 3D 24
Brown Edge. Lanc 3B 90
Brown Edge. Staf 5D 84
Brownhill. Bkbn 1E 91
Brownhill. Shrp 3G 71
Brownhills. Shrp 2A 72
Brownhills. W Mid 5E 73
Brown Knowl. Ches W 5G 83
Brownlow. Ches E 4C 84
Brownlow Heath. Ches E 4C 84
Brown's Green. W Mid 1E 61
Brownshill. Glos 5D 49
Brownston. Devn 3C 8
Brownstone. Devn 2A 12
Browston Green. Norf 5G 79
Broxa. N Yor 5G 107
Broxbourne. Herts 5D 52
Broxburn. E Lot 2C 130
Broxburn. W Lot 2D 129
Broxholme. Linc 3G 87
Broxted. Essx 3F 53
Broxton. Ches W 5G 83
Broxwood. Here 5F 59
Broyle Side. E Sus 4F 27
Brù. W Isl 3F 171
Bruach Mairi. W Isl 4G 171
Bruairnis. W Isl 8C 170
Bruan. High 5F 169
Bruar Lodge. Per 1F 143
Brucehill. W Dun 2E 127
Brucklay. Abers 3G 161
Bruera. Ches W 4G 83
Bruern Abbey. Oxon 3A 50
Bruichladdich. Arg 3A 124
Bruisyard. Suff 4F 67
Bruisyard Street. Suff 4F 67
Brumby. N Lin 4B 94
Brund. Staf 4F 85
Brundall. Norf 5F 79
Brundish. Norf 1F 67
Brundish. Suff 4E 67
Brundish Street. Suff 3E 67
Brunery. High 1B 140
Brunswick Village. Tyne 2F 115
Brunthwaite. W Yor 5C 98
Bruntingthorpe. Leics 1D 62
Brunton. Fife 1F 137
Brunton. Nmbd 2G 121
Brunton. Wilts 1H 23
Brushford. Devn 2G 11
Brushford. Som 4C 20
Brusta. W Isl 1E 170
Bruton. Som 3B 22
Bryansford. Down 6H 179
Bryanston. Dors 2D 15
Bryant's Bottom. Buck 2G 37
Brydekirk. Dum 2C 112
Brymbo. Cnwy 3H 81
Brymbo. Wrex 5E 83
Brympton D'Evercy. Som 1A 14
Bryn. Carm 5F 45
Bryn. G Man 4D 90
Bryn. Neat 2B 32
Bryn. Shrp 2E 59
Brynamman. Carm 4H 45
Brynberian. Pemb 1F 43
Brynbryddan. Neat 2A 32
Bryncae. Rhon 3C 32
Bryncethin. B'end 3C 32
Bryncir. Gwyn 1D 69
Bryn-coch. Neat 3G 31
Bryncroes. Gwyn 2B 68
Bryncrug. Gwyn 5F 69
Bryn Du. IOA 3C 80
Bryn Eden. Gwyn 3G 69
Bryneglwys. Den 1D 70
Bryn Eglwys. Gwyn 4F 81
Brynford. Flin 3D 82
Bryn Gates. G Man 4D 90
Bryn Golau. Rhon 3D 32
Bryngwran. IOA 3C 80
Bryngwyn. Mon 5G 47
Bryngwyn. Powy 1E 47
Bryn-henllan. Pemb 1E 43
Brynhoffnant. Cdgn 5C 56
Bryn-llwyn. Flin 2C 82
Brynllywarch. Powy 2D 58
Brynmawr. Blae 4E 47
Bryn-mawr. Gwyn 2B 68
Brynmenyn. B'end 3C 32
Brynmill. Swan 3F 31
Brynna. Rhon 3C 32
Brynrefail. Gwyn 4E 81
Brynrefail. IOA 2D 81
Brynsadler. Rhon 3D 32
Bryn-Saith Marchog. Den 5C 82
Brynsiencyn. IOA 4D 81
Brynteg. IOA 2D 81
Brynteg. Wrex 5F 83
Brynygwenyn. Mon 4G 47
Bryn-y-maen. Cnwy 3H 81
Buaile nam Bodach.
W Isl 8C 170
Bualintur. High 1C 146
Bubbenhall. Warw 3A 62
Bubwith. E Yor 1H 93
Buccleuch. Bord 3F 119
Buchanan Smithy. Stir 1F 127
Buchanhaven. Abers 4H 161
Buchanty. Per 1B 136
Buchany. Stir 3G 135
Buchley. E Dun 2G 127
Buchlyvie. Stir 4E 135
Buckabank. Cumb 5E 113
Buckden. Cambs 4A 64
Buckden. N Yor 2B 98
Buckenham. Norf 5F 79
Buckerell. Devn 2E 13
Buckfast. Devn 2D 8
Buckfastleigh. Devn 2D 8
Buckhaven. Fife 4F 137
Buckholm. Bord 1G 119
Buckholt. Here 4A 48
Buckhorn Weston. Dors 4C 22
Buckhurst Hill. Essx 1F 39
Buckie. Mor 2B 160
Buckingham. Buck 2E 51
Buckland. Buck 4G 51
Buckland. Glos 2F 49
Buckland. Here 5H 59
Buckland. Herts 2D 52
Buckland. Kent 1H 29
Buckland. Oxon 2B 36
Buckland. Surr 5D 38
Buckland Brewer. Devn 4E 19
Buckland Common. Buck 5H 51
Buckland Dinham. Som 1C 22
Buckland Filleigh. Devn 2E 11
Buckland in the Moor.
Devn 5H 11
Buckland Monachorum.
Devn 2A 8
Buckland Newton. Dors 2B 14
Buckland Ripers. Dors 4B 14
Buckland St Mary. Som 1F 13
Buckland-tout-Saints.
Devn 4D 8
Bucklebury. W Ber 4D 36
Bucklegate. Linc 2C 76
Buckleigh. Devn 4E 19
Buckler's Hard. Hants 3C 16
Bucklesham. Suff 1F 55
Buckley. Flin 4E 83
Buckley Green. Warw 4F 61
Buckley Hill. Mers 1F 83
Bucklow Hill. Ches E 2B 84
Buckminster. Leics 3F 75
Bucknall. Linc 4A 88
Bucknall. Stoke 1D 72
Bucknell. Oxon 3D 50
Bucknell. Shrp 3F 59
Buckpool. Mor 2B 160
Bucksburn. Aber 3F 153
Buck's Cross. Devn 4D 18
Bucks Green. W Sus 2B 26
Buckshaw Village. Lanc 2D 90
Bucks Hill. Herts 5A 52
Bucks Horn Oak. Hants 2G 25
Buck's Mills. Devn 4D 18
Buckton. E Yor 2F 101
Buckton. Here 3F 59
Buckton. Nmbd 1E 121
Buckton Vale. G Man 4H 91
Buckworth. Cambs 3A 64
Budby. Notts 4D 86
Bude. Corn 2C 10
Budge's Shop. Corn 3H 7
Budlake. Devn 2C 12
Budle. Nmbd 1F 121
Budleigh Salterton. Devn 4D 12
Budock Water. Corn 5B 6
Buerton. Ches E 1A 72
Buffler's Holt. Buck 2E 51
Bugbrooke. Nptn 5D 62
Buglawton. Ches E 4C 84
Bugle. Corn 3E 6
Bugthorpe. E Yor 4B 100
Buildwas. Shrp 5A 72
Builth Road. Powy 5C 58
Builth Wells. Powy 5C 58
Bulbourne. Herts 4H 51
Bulby. Linc 3H 75
Bulcote. Notts 1D 74
Buldoo. High 2B 168
Bulford. Wilts 2G 23
Bulford Camp. Wilts 2G 23
Bulkeley. Ches E 5H 83
Bulkington. Warw 2A 62
Bulkington. Wilts 1E 23
Bulkworthy. Devn 1D 11
Bullamoor. N Yor 5A 106
Bull Bay. IOA 1D 80
Bullbridge. Derbs 5A 86
Bullgill. Cumb 1B 102
Bull Hill. Hants 3B 16
Bullinghope. Here 2A 48
Bull's Green. Herts 4C 52
Bullwood. Arg 2C 126
Bulmer. Essx 1B 54
Bulmer. N Yor 3A 100
Bulmer Tye. Essx 2B 54
Bulphan. Thur 2H 39
Bulverhythe. E Sus 5B 28
Bulwark. Abers 4G 161
Bulwell. Nott 1C 74
Bulwick. Nptn 1G 63
Bumble's Green. Essx 5E 53
Bun Abhainn Eadarra.
W Isl 7D 171
Bunacaimb. High 5E 147
Bun a' Mhuillinn. W Isl 7C 170
Bunarkaig. High 5D 148
Bunbury. Ches E 5H 83
Bunchrew. High 4A 158
Bundalloch. High 1A 148
Buness. Shet 1H 173
Bunessan. Arg 1A 132
Bungay. Suff 2F 67
Bunkegivie. High 2H 149
Bunker's Hill. Cambs 5D 76
Bunkers Hill. Linc 5B 88
Bunker's Hill. Norf 5H 79
Bunloit. High 1H 149
Bunnahabhain. Arg 2C 124
Bunny. Notts 3C 74
Bunoich. High 3F 149
Bunree. High 2E 141
Bunroy. High 5E 149
Buntait. High 5F 157
Buntingford. Herts 3D 52
Buntings Green. Essx 2B 54
Bunwell. Norf 1D 66
Burbage. Derbs 3E 85
Burbage. Leics 1B 62
Burbage. Wilts 5H 35
Burcher. Here 4F 59
Burchett's Green. Wind 3G 37
Burcombe. Wilts 3F 23
Burcot. Oxon 2D 36
Burcot. Worc 3D 61
Burcote. Shrp 1B 60
Burcott. Buck 3G 51
Burcott. Som 2A 22
Burdale. N Yor 3C 100
Burdrop. Oxon 2B 50
Bures. Suff 2C 54
Burford. Oxon 4A 50
Burford. Shrp 4H 59
Burf, The. Worc 4C 60
Burg. Arg 4E 139
Burgate Great Green. Suff 3C 66
Burgate Little Green. Suff 3C 66
Burgess Hill. W Sus 4E 27
Burgh. Suff 5E 67
Burgh by Sands. Cumb 4E 113
Burgh Castle. Norf 5G 79
Burghclere. Hants 5C 36
Burghead. Mor 2F 159
Burghfield. W Ber 5E 37
Burghfield Common.
W Ber 5E 37
Burghfield Hill. W Ber 5E 37
Burgh Heath. Surr 5D 38
Burghill. Here 1H 47
Burgh le Marsh. Linc 4E 89
Burgh Muir. Abers 2E 153
Burgh next Aylsham.
Norf 3E 78
Burgh on Bain. Linc 2B 88
Burgh St Margaret. Norf 4G 79
Burgh St Peter. Norf 1G 67
Burghwallis. S Yor 3F 93
Burham. Kent 4B 40
Buriton. Hants 4F 25
Burland. Ches E 5A 84
Burland. Shet 8E 173
Burlawn. Corn 2D 6
Burleigh. Brac 3A 38
Burleigh. Glos 5D 48
Burlescombe. Devn 1D 12
Burleston. Dors 3C 14
Burlestone. Devn 4E 9
Burley. Hants 2H 15

A-Z Great Britain Road Atlas 209

Charlton—Connor Downs

Charlton. *Nmbd* 1B **114**
Charlton. *Oxon* 3C **36**
Charlton. *Som* 1B **22**
(nr. Radstock)
Charlton. *Som* 2B **22**
(nr. Shepton Mallet)
Charlton. *Som* 4F **21**
(nr. Taunton)
Charlton. *Telf* 4H **71**
Charlton. *W Sus* 1G **17**
Charlton. *Wilts* 3E **35**
(nr. Malmesbury)
Charlton. *Wilts* 1G **23**
(nr. Pewsey)
Charlton. *Wilts* 4G **23**
(nr. Salisbury)
Charlton. *Wilts* 4E **23**
(nr. Shaftesbury)
Charlton. *Worc* 1F **49**
(nr. Evesham)
Charlton. *Worc* 3C **60**
(nr. Stourport-on-Severn)
Charlton Abbots. *Glos* 3F **49**
Charlton Adam. *Som* 4A **22**
Charlton Down. *Dors* 3B **14**
Charlton Horethorne. *Som* 4B **22**
Charlton Kings. *Glos* 3E **49**
Charlton Mackrell. *Som* 4A **22**
Charlton Marshall. *Dors* 2E **15**
Charlton Musgrove. *Som* 4C **22**
Charlton-on-Otmoor. *Oxon* 4D **50**
Charlton on the Hill. *Dors* 2D **15**
Charlwood. *Hants* 3E **25**
Charlwood. *Surr* 1D **26**
Charlynch. *Som* 3F **21**
Charminster. *Dors* 3B **14**
Charmouth. *Dors* 3G **13**
Charndon. *Buck* 3E **51**
Charney Bassett. *Oxon* 2B **36**
Charnock Green. *Lanc* 3D **90**
Charnock Richard. *Lanc* 3D **90**
Charsfield. *Suff* 5E **67**
Chart Corner. *Kent* 5B **40**
Charter Alley. *Hants* 1D **24**
Charterhouse. *Som* 1H **21**
Charterville Allotments. *Oxon* 4B **50**
Chartham. *Kent* 5F **41**
Chartham Hatch. *Kent* 5F **41**
Chartridge. *Buck* 5H **51**
Chart Sutton. *Kent* 5B **40**
Chart, The. *Kent* 5F **39**
Charvil. *Wok* 4F **37**
Charwelton. *Nptn* 5C **62**
Chase Terrace. *Staf* 5E **73**
Chasetown. *Staf* 5E **73**
Chastleton. *Oxon* 3H **49**
Chasty. *Devn* 2D **10**
Chatburn. *Lanc* 5G **97**
Chatcull. *Staf* 2B **72**
Chatham. *Medw* 4B **40** & **Medway 197**
Chatham Green. *Essx* 4H **53**
Chathill. *Nmbd* 2F **121**
Chatley. *Worc* 4C **60**
Chattenden. *Medw* 3B **40**
Chatteris. *Cambs* 2C **64**
Chattisham. *Suff* 1D **54**
Chatton. *Nmbd* 2E **121**
Chatwall. *Shrp* 1H **59**
Chaulden. *Herts* 5A **52**
Chaul End. *C Beds* 3A **52**
Chawleigh. *Devn* 1H **11**
Chawley. *Oxon* 5C **50**
Chawston. *Bed* 5A **64**
Chawton. *Hants* 3F **25**
Chaxhill. *Glos* 4C **48**
Cheadle. *G Man* 2C **84**
Cheadle. *Staf* 1E **73**
Cheadle Hulme. *G Man* 2C **84**
Cheam. *Surr* 4D **38**
Cheapside. *Wind* 4A **38**
Chearsley. *Buck* 4F **51**
Chebsey. *Staf* 3C **72**
Checkendon. *Oxon* 3E **37**
Checkley. *Ches E* 1B **72**
Checkley. *Here* 2A **48**
Checkley. *Staf* 2E **73**
Chedburgh. *Suff* 5G **65**
Cheddar. *Som* 1H **21**
Cheddington. *Buck* 4H **51**
Cheddleton. *Staf* 5D **84**
Cheddon Fitzpaine. *Som* 4F **21**
Chedglow. *Wilts* 2E **35**
Chedgrave. *Norf* 1F **67**
Chedington. *Dors* 2H **13**
Chediston. *Suff* 3F **67**
Chediston Green. *Suff* 3F **67**
Chedworth. *Glos* 4F **49**
Chedzoy. *Som* 3G **21**
Cheeseman's Green. *Kent* 2E **29**
Cheetham Hill. *G Man* 4G **91**
Cheglinch. *Devn* 2F **19**
Cheldon. *Devn* 1H **11**
Chelford. *Ches E* 3C **84**
Chellaston. *Derb* 2A **74**
Chellington. *Bed* 5G **63**
Chelmarsh. *Shrp* 2B **60**
Chelmick. *Shrp* 1G **59**
Chelmondiston. *Suff* 2F **55**
Chelmorton. *Derbs* 4F **85**
Chelmsford. *Essx* 5H **53**
Chelsea. *G Lon* 3D **39**
Chelsfield. *G Lon* 4F **39**
Chelsham. *Surr* 5E **39**
Chelston. *Som* 4E **21**
Chelsworth. *Suff* 1C **54**
Cheltenham. *Glos* 3E **49** & **193**
Chelveston. *Nptn* 4G **63**
Chelvey. *N Som* 5H **33**
Chelwood. *Bath* 5B **34**
Chelwood Common. *E Sus* 3F **27**
Chelwood Gate. *E Sus* 3F **27**
Chelworth. *Wilts* 2E **35**
Chelworth Lower Green. *Wilts* 2F **35**
Chelworth Upper Green. *Wilts* 2F **35**
Chelynch. *Som* 2B **22**
Cheney Longville. *Shrp* 2G **59**
Chenies. *Buck* 1B **38**
Chepstow. *Mon* 2A **34**
Chequerfield. *W Yor* 2E **93**
Chequers Corner. *Norf* 5D **77**
Cherhill. *Wilts* 4F **35**
Cherington. *Glos* 2E **35**
Cherington. *Warw* 2A **50**
Cheriton. *Devn* 2H **19**
Cheriton. *Hants* 4D **24**
Cheriton. *Kent* 2G **29**
Cheriton. *Pemb* 5D **43**
Cheriton. *Swan* 3D **30**
Cheriton Bishop. *Devn* 3A **12**
Cheriton Cross. *Devn* 3A **12**
Cheriton Fitzpaine. *Devn* 2B **12**
Cherrington. *Telf* 3A **72**
Cherrybank. *Per* 1D **136**
Cherry Burton. *E Yor* 5D **101**
Cherry Green. *Herts* 3D **52**
Cherry Hinton. *Cambs* 5D **65**
Cherry Willingham. *Linc* 3H **87**
Chertsey. *Surr* 4B **38**
Cheselbourne. *Dors* 3C **14**
Chesham. *Buck* 5H **51**
Chesham. *G Man* 3G **91**
Chesham Bois. *Buck* 1A **38**
Cheshunt. *Herts* 5D **52**
Cheslyn Hay. *Staf* 5D **73**
Chessetts Wood. *Warw* 3F **61**
Chessington. *G Lon* 4C **38**
Chester. *Ches W* 4G **83** & **194**
Chesterblade. *Som* 2B **22**
Chesterfield. *Derbs* 3A **86**
Chesterfield. *Staf* 5F **73**
Chesterhope. *Nmbd* 1C **114**
Chester-le-Street. *Dur* 4F **115**
Chester Moor. *Dur* 5F **115**
Chesters. *Bord* 3A **120**
Chesterton. *Cambs* 4D **64**
(nr. Cambridge)
Chesterton. *Cambs* 1A **64**
(nr. Peterborough)
Chesterton. *Glos* 5F **49**
Chesterton. *Oxon* 3D **50**
Chesterton. *Shrp* 1B **60**
Chesterton. *Staf* 1C **72**
Chesterton Green. *Warw* 5H **61**
Chesterwood. *Nmbd* 3B **114**
Chestfield. *Kent* 4F **41**
Cheston. *Devn* 3C **8**
Cheswardine. *Shrp* 2B **72**
Cheswell. *Telf* 4B **72**
Cheswick. *Nmbd* 5G **131**
Cheswick Green. *W Mid* 3F **61**
Chetnole. *Dors* 2B **14**
Chettiscombe. *Devn* 1C **12**
Chettisham. *Cambs* 2E **65**
Chettle. *Dors* 1E **15**
Chetton. *Shrp* 1A **60**
Chetwode. *Buck* 3E **51**
Chetwynd Aston. *Telf* 4B **72**
Cheveley. *Cambs* 4F **65**
Chevening. *Kent* 5F **39**
Chevington. *Suff* 5G **65**
Chevithorne. *Devn* 1C **12**
Chew Magna. *Bath* 5A **34**
Chew Moor. *G Man* 4E **91**
Chew Stoke. *Bath* 5A **34**
Chewton Keynsham. *Bath* 5B **34**
Chewton Mendip. *Som* 1A **22**
Chichacott. *Devn* 3G **11**
Chicheley. *Mil* 1H **51**
Chichester. *W Sus* 2G **17**
Chickerell. *Dors* 4B **14**
Chickering. *Suff* 3E **66**
Chicklade. *Wilts* 3E **23**
Chicksands. *C Beds* 2B **52**
Chickward. *Here* 5E **59**
Chidden. *Hants* 1E **17**
Chiddingfold. *Surr* 2A **26**
Chiddingly. *E Sus* 4G **27**
Chiddingstone. *Kent* 1G **27**
Chiddingstone Causeway. *Kent* 1G **27**
Chiddingstone Hoath. *Kent* 1F **27**
Chideock. *Dors* 3H **13**
Chidgley. *Som* 3D **20**
Chidham. *W Sus* 2F **17**
Chieveley. *W Ber* 4C **36**
Chignall St James. *Essx* 5G **53**
Chignall Smealy. *Essx* 4G **53**
Chigwell. *Essx* 1F **39**
Chigwell Row. *Essx* 1F **39**
Chilbolton. *Hants* 2B **24**
Chilcomb. *Hants* 4D **24**
Chilcombe. *Dors* 3A **14**
Chilcompton. *Som* 1B **22**
Chilcote. *Leics* 4G **73**
Childer Thornton. *Ches W* 3F **83**
Child Okeford. *Dors* 1D **14**
Childrey. *Oxon* 3B **36**
Child's Ercall. *Shrp* 3A **72**
Childswickham. *Worc* 2F **49**
Childwall. *Mers* 2G **83**
Childwick Green. *Herts* 4B **52**
Chilfrome. *Dors* 3A **14**
Chilgrove. *W Sus* 1G **17**
Chilham. *Kent* 5E **41**
Chilhampton. *Wilts* 3F **23**
Chilla. *Devn* 2E **11**
Chilland. *Hants* 3D **24**
Chillaton. *Devn* 4E **11**
Chillenden. *Kent* 5G **41**
Chillerton. *IOW* 4C **16**
Chillesford. *Suff* 5F **67**
Chillingham. *Nmbd* 2E **121**
Chillington. *Devn* 4D **9**
Chillington. *Som* 1G **13**
Chilmark. *Wilts* 3E **23**
Chilmington Green. *Kent* 1D **28**
Chilson. *Oxon* 4B **50**
Chilsworthy. *Corn* 5E **11**
Chilsworthy. *Devn* 2D **10**
Chiltern Green. *C Beds* 4B **52**
Chilthorne Domer. *Som* 1A **14**
Chilton. *Buck* 4E **51**
Chilton. *Devn* 2B **12**
Chilton. *Dur* 2F **105**
Chilton. *Oxon* 3C **36**
Chilton Candover. *Hants* 2D **24**
Chilton Cantelo. *Som* 4A **22**
Chilton Foliat. *Wilts* 4B **36**
Chilton Lane. *Dur* 1A **106**
Chilton Polden. *Som* 3G **21**
Chilton Street. *Suff* 1A **54**
Chilton Trinity. *Som* 3F **21**
Chilwell. *Notts* 2C **74**
Chilworth. *Hants* 1C **16**
Chilworth. *Surr* 1B **26**
Chimney. *Oxon* 5B **50**
Chimney Street. *Suff* 1H **53**
Chineham. *Hants* 1E **25**
Chingford. *G Lon* 1E **39**
Chinley. *Derbs* 2E **85**
Chinnor. *Oxon* 5F **51**
Chipley. *Som* 4E **20**
Chipnall. *Shrp* 2B **72**
Chippenham. *Cambs* 4F **65**
Chippenham. *Wilts* 4E **35**
Chipperfield. *Herts* 5A **52**
Chipping. *Herts* 2D **52**
Chipping. *Lanc* 5F **97**
Chipping Campden. *Glos* 2G **49**
Chipping Hill. *Essx* 4B **54**
Chipping Norton. *Oxon* 3B **50**
Chipping Ongar. *Essx* 5F **53**
Chipping Sodbury. *S Glo* 3C **34**
Chipping Warden. *Nptn* 1C **50**
Chipstable. *Som* 4D **20**
Chipstead. *Kent* 5G **39**
Chipstead. *Surr* 5D **38**
Chirbury. *Shrp* 1E **59**
Chirk. *Wrex* 2E **71**
Chirmorie. *S Ayr* 2H **109**
Chirnside. *Bord* 4E **131**
Chirnsidebridge. *Bord* 4E **131**
Chirton. *Wilts* 1F **23**
Chisbridge Cross. *Buck* 3G **37**
Chisbury. *Wilts* 5A **36**
Chiselborough. *Som* 1H **13**
Chiseldon. *Swin* 4G **35**
Chiselhampton. *Oxon* 2D **36**
Chiserley. *W Yor* 2A **92**
Chislehurst. *G Lon* 4F **39**
Chislet. *Kent* 4G **41**
Chiswell. *Dors* 5B **14**
Chiswell Green. *Herts* 5B **52**
Chiswick. *G Lon* 3D **38**
Chisworth. *Derbs* 1D **85**
Chitcombe. *E Sus* 3C **28**
Chithurst. *W Sus* 4G **25**
Chittering. *Cambs* 4D **65**
Chitterley. *Devn* 2C **12**
Chitterne. *Wilts* 2E **23**
Chittlehamholt. *Devn* 4G **19**
Chittlehampton. *Devn* 4G **19**
Chittoe. *Wilts* 5E **35**
Chivelstone. *Devn* 5D **9**
Chivenor. *Devn* 3F **19**
Chobham. *Surr* 4A **38**
Cholderton. *Wilts* 2H **23**
Cholesbury. *Buck* 5H **51**
Chollerford. *Nmbd* 2C **114**
Chollerton. *Nmbd* 2C **114**
Cholsey. *Oxon* 3D **36**
Cholstrey. *Here* 5G **59**
Chop Gate. *N Yor* 5C **106**
Choppington. *Nmbd* 1F **115**
Chopwell. *Tyne* 4E **115**
Chorley. *Ches E* 5H **83**
Chorley. *Lanc* 3D **90**
Chorley. *Shrp* 2A **60**
Chorley. *Staf* 4E **73**
Chorleywood. *Herts* 1B **38**
Chorlton. *Ches E* 5B **84**
Chorlton-cum-Hardy. *G Man* 1C **84**
Chorlton Lane. *Ches W* 1G **71**
Choulton. *Shrp* 2F **59**
Chrishall. *Essx* 2E **53**
Christchurch. *Cambs* 1D **65**
Christchurch. *Dors* 3G **15**
Christchurch. *Glos* 4A **48**
Christian Malford. *Wilts* 4E **35**
Christleton. *Ches W* 4G **83**
Christmas Common. *Oxon* 2F **37**
Christon. *N Som* 1G **21**
Christon Bank. *Nmbd* 2G **121**
Christow. *Devn* 4B **12**
Chryston. *N Lan* 2H **127**
Chuck Hatch. *E Sus* 2F **27**
Chudleigh. *Devn* 5B **12**
Chudleigh Knighton. *Devn* 5B **12**
Chulmleigh. *Devn* 1G **11**
Chunal. *Derbs* 1E **85**
Church. *Lanc* 2F **91**
Churcham. *Glos* 4C **48**
Church Aston. *Telf* 4B **72**
Church Brampton. *Nptn* 4E **62**
Church Brough. *Cumb* 3A **104**
Church Broughton. *Derbs* 2G **73**
Church Corner. *Suff* 2G **67**
Church Crookham. *Hants* 1G **25**
Churchdown. *Glos* 4D **48**
Church Eaton. *Staf* 4C **72**
Church End. *Cambs* 5D **65**
(nr. Cambridge)
Church End. *Cambs* 2B **64**
(nr. Sawtry)
Church End. *Cambs* 3C **64**
(nr. Willingham)
Church End. *Cambs* 5C **76**
(nr. Wisbech)
Church End. *C Beds* 3H **51**
(nr. Dunstable)
Church End. *C Beds* 2B **52**
(nr. Stotfold)
Church End. *E Yor* 4E **101**
Church End. *Essx* 3H **53**
(nr. Braintree)
Churchend. *Essx* 3G **53**
(nr. Great Dunmow)
Church End. *Essx* 1F **53**
(nr. Saffron Walden)
Churchend. *Essx* 1E **40**
(nr. Southend-on-Sea)
Church End. *Glos* 5C **48**
Church End. *Hants* 1E **25**
Church End. *Linc* 2B **76**
(nr. Donington)
Church End. *Linc* 1D **88**
(nr. North Somercotes)
Church End. *Norf* 4E **77**
Church End. *Warw* 1G **61**
(nr. Coleshill)
Church End. *Warw* 1G **61**
(nr. Nuneaton)
Church End. *Wilts* 4F **35**
Church Enstone. *Oxon* 3B **50**
Church Fenton. *N Yor* 1F **93**
Church Green. *Devn* 3E **13**
Church Gresley. *Derbs* 4G **73**
Church Hanborough. *Oxon* 4C **50**
Church Hill. *Ches W* 4A **84**
Church Hill. *Worc* 4E **61**
Church Hougham. *Kent* 1G **29**
Church Houses. *N Yor* 5D **106**
Churchill. *Devn* 2G **13**
(nr. Axminster)
Churchill. *Devn* 2F **19**
(nr. Barnstaple)
Churchill. *N Som* 1H **21**
Churchill. *Oxon* 3A **50**
Churchill. *Worc* 3C **60**
(nr. Kidderminster)
Churchill. *Worc* 5D **60**
(nr. Worcester)
Churchinford. *Som* 1F **13**
Church Knowle. *Dors* 4E **15**
Church Laneham. *Notts* 3F **87**
Church Langley. *Essx* 5E **53**
Church Langton. *Leics* 1E **62**
Church Lawford. *Warw* 3B **62**
Church Lawton. *Ches E* 5C **84**
Church Leigh. *Staf* 2E **73**
Church Lench. *Worc* 5E **61**
Church Mayfield. *Staf* 1F **73**
Church Minshull. *Ches E* 4A **84**
Church Norton. *W Sus* 3G **17**
Churchover. *Warw* 2C **62**
Church Preen. *Shrp* 1H **59**
Church Pulverbatch. *Shrp* 5G **71**
Churchstanton. *Som* 1E **13**
Church Stoke. *Powy* 1E **59**
Churchstow. *Devn* 4D **8**
Church Stowe. *Nptn* 5D **62**
Church Street. *Kent* 3B **40**
Church Stretton. *Shrp* 1G **59**
Churchthorpe. *Linc* 1C **88**
Churchtown. *Cumb* 5E **113**
Churchtown. *Derbs* 4G **85**
Churchtown. *Devn* 2G **19**
Churchtown. *Down* 5K **179**
Churchtown. *IOM* 2D **108**
Churchtown. *Lanc* 5D **97**
Church Town. *Leics* 4A **74**
Churchtown. *Mers* 3B **90**
Church Town. *N Lin* 4A **94**
Churchtown. *Shrp* 2E **59**
Church Village. *Rhon* 3D **32**
Church Warsop. *Notts* 4C **86**
Church Westcote. *Glos* 3H **49**
Church Wilne. *Derbs* 2B **74**
Churnsike Lodge. *Nmbd* 2H **113**
Churston Ferrers. *Torb* 3F **9**
Churt. *Surr* 3G **25**
Churton. *Ches W* 5G **83**
Churwell. *W Yor* 2C **92**
Chute Standen. *Wilts* 1B **24**
Chwilog. *Gwyn* 2D **68**
Chwitffordd. *Flin* 3D **82**
Chyandour. *Corn* 3B **4**
Cilan Uchaf. *Gwyn* 3B **68**
Cilcain. *Flin* 4D **82**
Cilcennin. *Cdgn* 4E **57**
Cilfrew. *Neat* 5A **46**
Cilfynydd. *Rhon* 2D **32**
Cilgerran. *Pemb* 1B **44**
Cilgeti. *Pemb* 4F **43**
Cilgwyn. *Carm* 3H **45**
Cilgwyn. *Pemb* 1E **43**
Ciliau Aeron. *Cdgn* 5D **57**
Cill Amhlaidh. *W Isl* 4C **170**
Cill Donnain. *W Isl* 6C **170**
Cille a' Bhacstair. *High* 2C **154**
Cille Bhrighde. *W Isl* 7C **170**
Cille Pheadair. *W Isl* 7C **170**
Cilmaengwyn. *Neat* 5H **45**
Cilmeri. *Powy* 5C **58**
Cilmery. *Powy* 5C **58**
Cilrhedyn. *Pemb* 1G **43**
Cilsan. *Carm* 3F **45**
Ciltalgarth. *Gwyn* 1A **70**
Ciltwrch. *Powy* 1E **47**
Cilybebyll. *Neat* 5H **45**
Cilycwm. *Carm* 2A **46**
Cimla. *Neat* 2A **32**
Cinderford. *Glos* 4B **48**
Cinderhill. *Derbs* 1A **74**
Cippenham. *Slo* 2A **38**
Cippyn. *Pemb* 1B **44**
Cirbhig. *W Isl* 3D **171**
Circebost. *W Isl* 4D **171**
Cirencester. *Glos* 5F **49**
City. *Powy* 1E **58**
City. *V Glam* 4C **32**
City Centre. *Stoke* 1C **72** & **Stoke 202**
City Dulas. *IOA* 2D **80**
City (London) Airport. *G Lon* 2F **39**
City of Derry Airport. *Derr* 4B **174**
City of London. *G Lon* 2E **39**
City, The. *Buck* 2F **37**
Civiltown. *Ban* 5F **178**
Clabby. *Ferm* 4K **177**
Clabhach. *Arg* 3C **138**
Clachaig. *Arg* 1C **126**
Clachaig. *High* 3F **141**
(nr. Kinlochleven)
Clachaig. *High* 2E **151**
(nr. Nethy Bridge)
Clachamish. *High* 3C **154**
Clachan. *Arg* 4F **125**
(on Kintyre)
Clachan. *Arg* 4C **140**
(on Lismore)
Clachan. *High* 2H **167**
(nr. Bettyhill)
Clachan. *High* 2D **155**
(nr. Staffin)
Clachan. *High* 1C **154**
(nr. Uig)
Clachan. *High* 5E **155**
(on Raasay)
Clachan Farm. *Arg* 2A **134**
Clachan na Luib. *W Isl* 2D **170**
Clachan of Campsie. *E Dun* 2H **127**
Clachan of Glendaruel. *Arg* 1A **126**
Clachan-Seil. *Arg* 2E **133**
Clachan Shannda. *W Isl* 1D **170**
Clachan Strachur. *Arg* 3H **133**
Clachbreck. *Arg* 2F **125**
Clachnaharry. *High* 4A **158**
Clachtoll. *High* 1E **163**
Clackmannan. *Clac* 4B **136**
Clackmannanshire Bridge. *Falk* 1C **128**
Clackmarras. *Mor* 3G **159**
Clacton-on-Sea. *Essx* 4E **55**
Cladach a Chaolais. *W Isl* 2C **170**
Cladach Chairinis. *W Isl* 3D **170**
Cladach Chirceboist. *W Isl* 2C **170**
Cladach Iolaraigh. *W Isl* 2C **170**
Cladich. *Arg* 1H **133**
Cladswell. *Worc* 5E **61**
Clady. *Mag* 6F **175**
Clady. *Strab* 3E **176**
Claggan. *High* 1F **141**
(nr. Fort William)
Claggan. *High* 4A **140**
(nr. Lochaline)
Claigan. *High* 3B **154**
Clandown. *Bath* 1B **22**
Clanfield. *Hants* 1E **17**
Clanfield. *Oxon* 5A **50**
Clanville. *Hants* 2B **24**
Clanville. *Som* 3B **22**
Claonaig. *Arg* 4G **125**
Clapgate. *Dors* 2F **15**
Clapgate. *Herts* 3E **53**
Clapham. *Bed* 5H **63**
Clapham. *Devn* 4B **12**
Clapham. *G Lon* 3D **39**
Clapham. *N Yor* 3G **97**
Clapham. *W Sus* 5B **26**
Clap Hill. *Kent* 2E **29**
Clappers. *Bord* 4F **131**
Clappersgate. *Cumb* 4E **103**
Clapphoull. *Shet* 9F **173**
Clapton. *Som* 2H **13**
(nr. Crewkerne)
Clapton. *Som* 1B **22**
(nr. Radstock)
Clapton-in-Gordano. *N Som* 4H **33**
Clapton-on-the-Hill. *Glos* 4G **49**
Clapworthy. *Devn* 4G **19**
Clara Vale. *Tyne* 3E **115**
Clarbeston. *Pemb* 2E **43**
Clarbeston Road. *Pemb* 2E **43**
Clarborough. *Notts* 2E **87**
Clare. *Arm* 5E **178**
Clare. *Suff* 1A **54**
Clarebrand. *Dum* 3E **111**
Clarencefield. *Dum* 3B **112**
Clarilaw. *Bord* 3H **119**
Clark's Green. *Surr* 2C **26**
Clark's Hill. *Linc* 3C **76**
Clarkston. *E Ren* 4G **127**
Clasheddy. *High* 2G **167**
Clashindarroch. *Abers* 5B **160**
Clashmore. *High* 5E **165**
(nr. Dornoch)
Clashmore. *High* 1E **163**
(nr. Stoer)
Clashnessie. *High* 5A **166**
Clashnoir. *Mor* 1G **151**
Clate. *Shet* 5G **173**
Clathick. *Per* 1H **135**
Clathy. *Per* 2B **136**
Clatt. *Abers* 1C **152**
Clatter. *Powy* 1B **58**
Clatterford. *IOW* 4C **16**
Clatworthy. *Som* 3D **20**
Claudy. *Derr* 6B **174**
Claughton. *Lanc* 3E **97**
(nr. Caton)
Claughton. *Lanc* 5E **97**
(nr. Garstang)
Claughton. *Mers* 2F **83**
Claverdon. *Warw* 4F **61**
Claverham. *N Som* 5H **33**
Clavering. *Essx* 2E **53**
Claverley. *Shrp* 1B **60**
Claverton. *Bath* 5C **34**
Clawdd-coch. *V Glam* 4D **32**
Clawdd-newydd. *Den* 5C **82**
Clawson Hill. *Leics* 3E **75**
Clawton. *Devn* 3D **10**
Claxby. *Linc* 3D **88**
(nr. Alford)
Claxby. *Linc* 1A **88**
(nr. Market Rasen)
Claxton. *Norf* 5F **79**
Claxton. *N Yor* 4A **100**
Claybrooke Magna. *Leics* 2B **62**
Claybrooke Parva. *Leics* 2B **62**
Clay Common. *Suff* 2G **67**
Clay Coton. *Nptn* 3C **62**
Clay Cross. *Derbs* 4A **86**
Claydon. *Oxon* 5B **62**
Claydon. *Suff* 5D **66**
Clay End. *Herts* 3D **52**
Claygate. *Dum* 2E **113**
Claygate. *Kent* 1B **28**
Claygate. *Surr* 4C **38**
Claygate Cross. *Kent* 5H **39**
Clayhall. *Hants* 3E **16**
Clayhanger. *Devn* 4D **20**
Clayhanger. *W Mid* 5E **73**
Clayhidon. *Devn* 1E **13**
Clay Hill. *Bris* 4B **34**
Clayhill. *E Sus* 3C **28**
Clayhill. *Hants* 2B **16**
Clayhithe. *Cambs* 4E **65**
Clayholes. *Ang* 5E **145**
Clay Lake. *Linc* 3B **76**
Clayock. *High* 3D **168**
Claypits. *Glos* 5C **48**
Claypole. *Linc* 1F **75**
Claythorpe. *Linc* 3D **88**
Clayton. *G Man* 1C **84**
Clayton. *S Yor* 4E **93**
Clayton. *Staf* 1C **72**
Clayton. *W Sus* 4E **27**
Clayton. *W Yor* 1B **92**
Clayton Green. *Lanc* 2D **90**
Clayton-le-Moors. *Lanc* 1F **91**
Clayton-le-Woods. *Lanc* 2D **90**
Clayton West. *W Yor* 3C **92**
Clayworth. *Notts* 2E **87**
Cleadale. *High* 5C **146**
Cleadon. *Tyne* 3G **115**
Clearbrook. *Devn* 2B **8**
Clearwell. *Glos* 5A **48**
Cleasby. *N Yor* 3F **105**
Cleat. *Orkn* 3D **172**
(nr. Braehead)
Cleat. *Orkn* 9D **172**
(nr. St Margaret's Hope)
Cleatlam. *Dur* 3E **105**
Cleator. *Cumb* 3B **102**
Cleator Moor. *Cumb* 3B **102**
Cleckheaton. *W Yor* 2B **92**
Cleedownton. *Shrp* 2H **59**
Cleehill. *Shrp* 3H **59**
Cleekhimin. *N Lan* 4A **128**
Clee St Margaret. *Shrp* 2H **59**
Cleestanton. *Shrp* 3H **59**
Cleethorpes. *NE Lin* 4G **95**
Cleeton St Mary. *Shrp* 3A **60**
Cleeve. *N Som* 5H **33**
Cleeve. *Oxon* 3E **36**
Cleeve Hill. *Glos* 3E **49**
Cleeve Prior. *Worc* 1F **49**
Clehonger. *Here* 2H **47**
Cleigh. *Arg* 1F **133**
Cleish. *Per* 4C **136**
Cleland. *N Lan* 4B **128**
Clench Common. *Wilts* 5G **35**
Clenchwarton. *Norf* 3E **77**
Clennell. *Nmbd* 4D **120**
Clent. *Worc* 3D **60**
Cleobury Mortimer. *Shrp* 3A **60**
Cleobury North. *Shrp* 2A **60**
Clephanton. *High* 3C **158**
Clerkhill. *High* 2H **167**
Clestrain. *Orkn* 7C **172**
Clevancy. *Wilts* 4F **35**
Clevedon. *N Som* 4H **33**
Cleveley. *Oxon* 3B **50**
Cleveleys. *Lanc* 5C **96**
Clevelode. *Worc* 1D **48**
Cleverton. *Wilts* 3E **35**
Clewer. *Som* 1H **21**
Cley next the Sea. *Norf* 1C **78**
Cliaid. *W Isl* 8B **170**
Cliasmol. *W Isl* 7C **171**
Clibberswick. *Shet* 1H **173**
Cliburn. *Cumb* 2G **103**
Cliddesden. *Hants* 2E **25**
Clieves Hills. *Lanc* 4B **90**
Cliff. *Warw* 1G **61**
Cliffburn. *Ang* 4F **145**
Cliffe. *Medw* 3B **40**
Cliffe. *N Yor* 3F **105**
(nr. Darlington)
Cliffe. *N Yor* 1G **93**
(nr. Selby)
Cliff End. *E Sus* 4C **28**
Cliffe Woods. *Medw* 3B **40**
Clifford. *Here* 1F **47**
Clifford. *W Yor* 5G **99**
Clifford Chambers. *Warw* 5F **61**
Clifford's Mesne. *Glos* 3B **48**
Cliffsend. *Kent* 4H **41**
Clifton. *Bris* 4A **34**
Clifton. *C Beds* 2B **52**
Clifton. *Cumb* 2G **103**
Clifton. *Derbs* 1F **73**
Clifton. *Devn* 2G **19**
Clifton. *G Man* 4F **91**
Clifton. *Lanc* 1C **90**
Clifton. *Nmbd* 1F **115**
Clifton. *N Yor* 5D **98**
Clifton. *Nott* 2C **74**
Clifton. *Oxon* 2C **50**
Clifton. *S Yor* 1C **86**
Clifton. *Stir* 5H **141**
Clifton. *W Yor* 2B **92**
Clifton. *Worc* 1D **48**
Clifton. *York* 4H **99**
Clifton Campville. *Staf* 4G **73**
Clifton Hampden. *Oxon* 2D **36**
Clifton Hill. *Worc* 4B **60**
Clifton Reynes. *Mil* 5G **63**
Clifton upon Dunsmore. *Warw* 3C **62**
Clifton upon Teme. *Worc* 4B **60**
Cliftonville. *Kent* 3H **41**
Cliftonville. *Norf* 2F **79**
Climping. *W Sus* 5A **26**
Climpy. *S Lan* 4C **128**
Clint. *N Yor* 4E **99**
Clint Green. *Norf* 4C **78**
Clintmains. *Bord* 1A **120**
Cliobh. *W Isl* 4C **171**
Clipiau. *Gwyn* 4H **69**
Clippesby. *Norf* 4G **79**
Clippings Green. *Norf* 4C **78**
Clipsham. *Rut* 4G **75**
Clipston. *Nptn* 2E **62**
Clipston. *Notts* 2D **74**
Clipstone. *Notts* 4C **86**
Clitheroe. *Lanc* 5G **97**
Cliuthar. *W Isl* 8D **171**
Clive. *Shrp* 3H **71**
Clivocast. *Shet* 1H **173**
Clixby. *Linc* 4D **94**
Clocaenog. *Den* 5C **82**
Clochan. *Mor* 2B **160**
Clochforbie. *Abers* 3F **161**
Clock Face. *Mers* 1H **83**
Cloddiau. *Powy* 5E **70**
Cloddymoss. *Mor* 2D **159**
Clodock. *Here* 3G **47**
Cloford. *Som* 2C **22**
Clogh. *Bmna* 5G **175**
Clogher. *Dngn* 4L **177**
Cloghmills. *Bmny* 5G **175**
Clola. *Abers* 4H **161**
Clonoe. *Dngn* 3C **178**
Clonvaraghan. *Down* 5H **179**
Clophill. *C Beds* 2A **52**
Clopton. *Nptn* 2H **63**
Clopton Corner. *Suff* 5E **66**
Clopton Green. *Suff* 5G **65**
Closeburn. *Dum* 5A **118**
Close Clark. *IOM* 4B **108**
Closworth. *Som* 1A **14**
Clothall. *Herts* 2C **52**
Clotton. *Ches W* 4H **83**
Clough. *Down* 5J **179**
Clough. *G Man* 3H **91**
Clough. *W Yor* 3A **92**
Cloughey. *Ards* 4L **179**
Clough Foot. *W Yor* 2H **91**
Cloughton. *N Yor* 5H **107**
Cloughton Newlands. *N Yor* 5H **107**
Clousta. *Shet* 6E **173**
Clouston. *Orkn* 6B **172**
Clova. *Abers* 1B **152**
Clova. *Ang* 1C **144**
Clovelly. *Devn* 4D **18**
Clovenfords. *Bord* 1G **119**
Clovenstone. *Abers* 2E **153**
Clovullin. *High* 2E **141**
Clowne. *Derbs* 3B **86**
Clows Top. *Worc* 3B **60**
Cloy. *Wrex* 1F **71**
Cloyfin. *Cole* 3E **174**
Cluanie Inn. *High* 2C **148**
Cluanie Lodge. *High* 2C **148**
Cluddley. *Telf* 5A **72**
Clun. *Shrp* 2F **59**
Clunas. *High* 4C **158**
Clunbury. *Shrp* 2F **59**
Clunderwen. *Pemb* 3F **43**
Clune. *High* 1B **150**
Clunes. *High* 5E **148**
Clungunford. *Shrp* 3F **59**
Clunie. *Per* 4A **144**
Clunton. *Shrp* 2F **59**
Cluny. *Fife* 4E **137**
Clutton. *Bath* 1B **22**
Clutton. *Ches W* 5G **83**
Clwt-y-bont. *Gwyn* 4E **81**
Clwydfagwyr. *Mer T* 5D **46**
Clydach. *Mon* 4F **47**
Clydach. *Swan* 5G **45**
Clydach Vale. *Rhon* 2C **32**
Clydebank. *W Dun* 2G **127**
Clydey. *Pemb* 1G **43**
Clyffe Pypard. *Wilts* 4F **35**
Clynder. *Arg* 1D **126**
Clyne. *Neat* 5B **46**
Clynelish. *High* 3F **165**
Clynnog-fawr. *Gwyn* 1D **68**
Clyro. *Powy* 1F **47**
Clyst Honiton. *Devn* 3C **12**
Clyst Hydon. *Devn* 2D **12**
Clyst St George. *Devn* 4C **12**
Clyst St Lawrence. *Devn* 2D **12**
Clyst St Mary. *Devn* 3C **12**
Clyth. *High* 5E **169**
Cnip. *W Isl* 4C **171**
Cnoc Amhlaigh. *W Isl* 4H **171**
Cnwcau. *Pemb* 1C **44**
Cnwch Coch. *Cdgn* 3F **57**
Coad's Green. *Corn* 5C **10**
Coagh. *Cook* 2C **178**
Coal Aston. *Derbs* 3A **86**
Coalbrookdale. *Telf* 5A **72**
Coalbrookvale. *Blae* 5F **47**
Coalburn. *S Lan* 1H **117**
Coalburns. *Tyne* 3E **115**
Coalcleugh. *Nmbd* 5B **114**
Coaley. *Glos* 5C **48**
Coalford. *Abers* 4F **153**
Coalhall. *E Ayr* 3D **116**
Coalhill. *Essx* 1B **40**
Coalisland. *Dngn* 3C **178**
Coalpit Heath. *S Glo* 3B **34**
Coal Pool. *W Mid* 5E **73**
Coalport. *Telf* 5B **72**
Coalsnaughton. *Clac* 4B **136**
Coaltown of Balgonie. *Fife* 4F **137**
Coaltown of Wemyss. *Fife* 4F **137**
Coalville. *Leics* 4B **74**
Coalway. *Glos* 4A **48**
Coanwood. *Nmbd* 4H **113**
Coat. *Som* 4H **21**
Coatbridge. *N Lan* 3A **128**
Coatdyke. *N Lan* 3A **128**
Coate. *Swin* 3G **35**
Coate. *Wilts* 5F **35**
Coates. *Cambs* 1C **64**
Coates. *Glos* 5E **49**
Coates. *Linc* 2G **87**
Coates. *W Sus* 4A **26**
Coatham. *Red C* 2C **106**
Coatham Mundeville. *Darl* 2F **105**
Cobbaton. *Devn* 4G **19**
Coberley. *Glos* 4E **49**
Cobhall Common. *Here* 2H **47**
Cobham. *Kent* 4A **40**
Cobham. *Surr* 4C **38**
Cobnash. *Here* 4G **59**
Coburg. *Devn* 5B **12**
Cockayne. *N Yor* 5D **106**
Cockayne Hatley. *C Beds* 1C **52**
Cock Bank. *Wrex* 1F **71**
Cock Bridge. *Abers* 3G **151**
Cockburnspath. *Bord* 2D **130**
Cock Clarks. *Essx* 5B **54**
Cockenzie and Port Seton. *E Lot* 2H **129**
Cockerham. *Lanc* 4D **96**
Cockermouth. *Cumb* 1C **102**
Cockernhoe. *Herts* 3B **52**
Cockfield. *Dur* 2E **105**
Cockfield. *Suff* 5B **66**
Cockfosters. *G Lon* 1D **39**
Cock Gate. *Here* 4G **59**
Cock Green. *Essx* 4G **53**
Cocking. *W Sus* 1G **17**
Cocking Causeway. *W Sus* 1G **17**
Cockington. *Torb* 2F **9**
Cocklake. *Som* 2H **21**
Cocklaw. *Abers* 4H **161**
Cocklaw. *Nmbd* 2C **114**
Cockley Beck. *Cumb* 4D **102**
Cockley Cley. *Norf* 5G **77**
Cockmuir. *Abers* 3G **161**
Cockpole Green. *Wind* 3G **37**
Cockshutford. *Shrp* 2H **59**
Cockshutt. *Shrp* 3G **71**
Cockthorpe. *Norf* 1B **78**
Cockwood. *Devn* 4C **12**
Cockyard. *Derbs* 3E **85**
Cockyard. *Here* 2H **47**
Codda. *Corn* 5B **10**
Coddenham. *Suff* 5D **66**
Coddenham Green. *Suff* 5D **66**
Coddington. *Ches W* 5G **83**
Coddington. *Here* 1C **48**
Coddington. *Notts* 5F **87**
Codford St Mary. *Wilts* 3E **23**
Codford St Peter. *Wilts* 3E **23**
Codicote. *Herts* 4C **52**
Codmore Hill. *W Sus* 3B **26**
Codnor. *Derbs* 1B **74**
Codrington. *S Glo* 4C **34**
Codsall. *Staf* 5C **72**
Codsall Wood. *Staf* 5C **72**
Coed Duon. *Cphy* 2E **33**
Coedely. *Rhon* 3D **32**
Coedglasson. *Powy* 4C **58**
Coedkernew. *Newp* 3F **33**
Coed Morgan. *Mon* 4G **47**
Coedpoeth. *Wrex* 5E **83**
Coedway. *Powy* 4F **71**
Coed-y-bryn. *Cdgn* 1D **44**
Coed-y-paen. *Mon* 2G **33**
Coed Ystumgwern. *Gwyn* 3E **69**
Coelbren. *Powy* 4B **46**
Coffinswell. *Devn* 2E **9**
Cofton Hackett. *Worc* 3E **61**
Cogan. *V Glam* 4E **33**
Cogenhoe. *Nptn* 4F **63**
Cogges. *Oxon* 5B **50**
Coggeshall. *Essx* 3B **54**
Coggeshall Hamlet. *Essx* 3B **54**
Coggins Mill. *E Sus* 3G **27**
Coignafearn Lodge. *High* 2A **150**
Coig Peighinnean. *W Isl* 1H **171**
Coig Peighinnean Bhuirgh. *W Isl* 2G **171**
Coilleag. *W Isl* 7C **170**
Coillemore. *High* 1A **158**
Coillore. *High* 5C **154**
Coire an Fhuarain. *W Isl* 4E **171**
Coity. *B'end* 3C **32**
Cokhay Green. *Derbs* 3G **73**
Col. *W Isl* 3G **171**
Colaboll. *High* 2C **164**
Colan. *Corn* 2C **6**
Colaton Raleigh. *Devn* 4D **12**
Colbost. *High* 4B **154**
Colburn. *N Yor* 5E **105**
Colby. *Cumb* 2H **103**
Colby. *IOM* 4B **108**
Colby. *Norf* 2E **78**
Colchester. *Essx* 3D **54**
Cold Ash. *W Ber* 5D **36**
Cold Ashby. *Nptn* 3D **62**
Cold Ashton. *S Glo* 4C **34**
Cold Aston. *Glos* 4G **49**
Coldbackie. *High* 3G **167**
Cold Blow. *Pemb* 3F **43**
Cold Brayfield. *Mil* 5G **63**
Cold Cotes. *N Yor* 2G **97**
Coldean. *Brig* 5E **27**
Coldeast. *Devn* 5B **12**
Colden. *W Yor* 2H **91**
Colden Common. *Hants* 4C **24**
Coldfair Green. *Suff* 4G **67**
Coldham. *Cambs* 5D **76**
Coldham. *Staf* 5C **72**
Cold Hanworth. *Linc* 2H **87**
Coldharbour. *Corn* 4B **6**
Cold Harbour. *Dors* 3E **15**
Coldharbour. *Glos* 5A **48**
Coldharbour. *Kent* 5G **39**
Coldharbour. *Surr* 1C **26**
Cold Hatton. *Telf* 3A **72**
Cold Hatton Heath. *Telf* 3A **72**
Cold Hesledon. *Dur* 5H **115**
Cold Hiendley. *W Yor* 3D **92**
Cold Higham. *Nptn* 5D **62**
Coldingham. *Bord* 3F **131**
Cold Kirby. *N Yor* 1H **99**
Coldmeece. *Staf* 2C **72**
Cold Northcott. *Corn* 4C **10**
Cold Norton. *Essx* 5B **54**
Cold Overton. *Leics* 4F **75**
Coldrain. *Per* 3C **136**
Coldred. *Kent* 1G **29**
Coldridge. *Devn* 2G **11**
Cold Row. *Lanc* 5C **96**
Coldstream. *Bord* 5E **131**
Coldwaltham. *W Sus* 4B **26**
Coldwell. *Here* 2H **47**
Coldwells. *Abers* 5H **161**
Coldwells Croft. *Abers* 1C **152**
Cole. *Shet* 5E **173**
Cole. *Som* 3B **22**
Colebatch. *Shrp* 2F **59**
Colebrook. *Devn* 2D **12**
Colebrooke. *Devn* 2A **12**
Coleburn. *Mor* 3G **159**
Coleby. *Linc* 4G **87**
Coleby. *N Lin* 3B **94**
Cole End. *Warw* 2G **61**
Coleford. *Devn* 2A **12**
Coleford. *Glos* 4A **48**
Coleford. *Som* 2B **22**
Colegate End. *Norf* 2D **66**
Cole Green. *Herts* 4C **52**
Cole Henley. *Hants* 1C **24**
Colehill. *Dors* 2F **15**
Coleman Green. *Herts* 4B **52**
Coleman's Hatch. *E Sus* 2F **27**
Colemere. *Shrp* 2G **71**
Colemore. *Hants* 3F **25**
Colemore Green. *Shrp* 1B **60**
Coleorton. *Leics* 4B **74**
Coleraine. *Cole* 3E **174**
Colerne. *Wilts* 4D **34**
Colesbourne. *Glos* 4E **49**
Colesden. *Bed* 5A **64**
Coles Green. *Worc* 5B **60**
Coleshill. *Buck* 1A **38**
Coleshill. *Oxon* 2H **35**
Coleshill. *Warw* 2G **61**
Colestocks. *Devn* 2D **12**
Colethrop. *Glos* 4D **48**
Coley. *Bath* 1A **22**
Colgate. *W Sus* 2D **26**
Colinsburgh. *Fife* 3G **137**
Colinton. *Edin* 3F **129**
Colintraive. *Arg* 2B **126**
Colkirk. *Norf* 3B **78**
Collace. *Per* 5B **144**
Collam. *W Isl* 8D **171**
Collaton. *Devn* 5D **8**
Collaton St Mary. *Torb* 2E **9**
College of Roseisle. *Mor* 2F **159**
Collessie. *Fife* 2E **137**
Collier Row. *G Lon* 1F **39**
Colliers End. *Herts* 3D **52**
Collier Street. *Kent* 1B **28**
Colliery Row. *Tyne* 5G **115**
Collieston. *Abers* 1H **153**
Collin. *Dum* 2B **112**
Collingbourne Ducis. *Wilts* 1H **23**
Collingbourne Kingston. *Wilts* 1H **23**
Collingham. *Notts* 4F **87**
Collingham. *W Yor* 5F **99**
Collingtree. *Nptn* 5E **63**
Collins Green. *Warr* 1H **83**
Collins Green. *Worc* 5B **60**
Colliston. *Ang* 4F **145**
Colliton. *Devn* 2D **12**
Collydean. *Fife* 3E **137**
Collyweston. *Nptn* 5G **75**
Colmonell. *S Ayr* 1G **109**
Colmworth. *Bed* 5A **64**
Colnbrook. *Slo* 3B **38**
Colne. *Cambs* 3C **64**
Colne. *Lanc* 5A **98**
Colne Engaine. *Essx* 2B **54**
Colney. *Norf* 5D **78**
Colney Heath. *Herts* 5C **52**
Colney Street. *Herts* 5B **52**
Coln Rogers. *Glos* 5F **49**
Coln St Aldwyns. *Glos* 5G **49**
Coln St Dennis. *Glos* 4F **49**
Colpitts Grange. *Nmbd* 4C **114**
Colpy. *Abers* 5D **160**
Colscott. *Devn* 1D **10**
Colsterdale. *N Yor* 1D **98**
Colsterworth. *Linc* 3G **75**
Colston Bassett. *Notts* 2D **74**
Colstoun House. *E Lot* 2B **130**
Coltfield. *Mor* 2F **159**
Colthouse. *Cumb* 5E **103**
Coltishall. *Norf* 4E **79**
Coltness. *N Lan* 4A **128**
Colton. *Cumb* 1C **96**
Colton. *Norf* 5D **78**
Colton. *N Yor* 5H **99**
Colton. *Staf* 3E **73**
Colton. *W Yor* 1D **92**
Colt's Hill. *Kent* 1H **27**
Col Uarach. *W Isl* 4G **171**
Colvend. *Dum* 4F **111**
Colvister. *Shet* 2G **173**
Colwall. *Here* 1C **48**
Colwall Green. *Here* 1C **48**
Colwell. *Nmbd* 2C **114**
Colwich. *Staf* 3E **73**
Colwick. *Notts* 1D **74**
Colwinston. *V Glam* 4C **32**
Colworth. *W Sus* 5A **26**
Colwyn Bay. *Cnwy* 3A **82**
Colyford. *Devn* 3F **13**
Colyton. *Devn* 3F **13**
Combe. *Devn* 2D **8**
Combe. *Here* 4F **59**
Combe. *Oxon* 4C **50**
Combe. *W Ber* 5B **36**
Combe Almer. *Dors* 3E **15**
Combebow. *Devn* 4E **11**
Combe Down. *Bath* 5C **34**
Combe Fishacre. *Devn* 2E **9**
Combe Florey. *Som* 3E **21**
Combe Hay. *Bath* 1C **22**
Combeinteignhead. *Devn* 5C **12**
Combe Martin. *Devn* 2F **19**
Combe Moor. *Here* 4F **59**
Comber. *Ards* 3J **179**
Combe Raleigh. *Devn* 2E **13**
Comberbach. *Ches W* 3A **84**
Comberford. *Staf* 5F **73**
Comberton. *Cambs* 5C **64**
Comberton. *Here* 4G **59**
Combe St Nicholas. *Som* 1G **13**
Combpyne. *Devn* 3F **13**
Combridge. *Staf* 2E **73**
Combrook. *Warw* 5H **61**
Combs. *Derbs* 3E **85**
Combs. *Suff* 5C **66**
Combs Ford. *Suff* 5C **66**
Combwich. *Som* 2F **21**
Comers. *Abers* 3D **152**
Comhampton. *Worc* 4C **60**
Comins Coch. *Cdgn* 2F **57**
Comley. *Shrp* 1G **59**
Commercial End. *Cambs* 4E **65**
Commins. *Powy* 3D **70**
Commins Coch. *Powy* 5H **69**
Commondale. *N Yor* 3D **106**
Common End. *Cumb* 2B **102**
Common Hill. *Here* 2A **48**
Common Moor. *Corn* 2G **7**
Commonside. *Ches W* 3H **83**
Common Side. *Derbs* 3H **85**
(nr. Chesterfield)
Commonside. *Derbs* 1G **73**
(nr. Derby)
Common, The. *Wilts* 3H **23**
(nr. Salisbury)
Common, The. *Wilts* 3F **35**
(nr. Swindon)
Compstall. *G Man* 1D **84**
Compton. *Devn* 2E **9**
Compton. *Hants* 4C **24**
Compton. *Staf* 2C **60**
Compton. *Surr* 1A **26**
Compton. *W Ber* 3D **36**
Compton. *W Sus* 1F **17**
Compton. *Wilts* 1G **23**
Compton Abbas. *Dors* 1D **14**
Compton Abdale. *Glos* 4F **49**
Compton Bassett. *Wilts* 4F **35**
Compton Beauchamp. *Oxon* 3A **36**
Compton Bishop. *Som* 1G **21**
Compton Chamberlayne. *Wilts* 4F **23**
Compton Dando. *Bath* 5B **34**
Compton Dundon. *Som* 3H **21**
Compton Greenfield. *S Glo* 3A **34**
Compton Martin. *Bath* 1A **22**
Compton Pauncefoot. *Som* 4B **22**
Compton Valence. *Dors* 3A **14**
Comrie. *Fife* 1D **128**
Comrie. *Per* 1G **135**
Conaglen. *High* 2E **141**
Conchra. *Arg* 1B **126**
Conchra. *High* 1A **148**
Conder Green. *Lanc* 4D **96**
Conderton. *Worc* 2E **49**
Condicote. *Glos* 3G **49**
Condorrat. *N Lan* 2A **128**
Condover. *Shrp* 5G **71**
Coneyhurst Common. *W Sus* 3C **26**
Coneyisland. *Down* 6K **179**
Coneysthorpe. *N Yor* 2B **100**
Coneythorpe. *N Yor* 4F **99**
Coney Weston. *Suff* 3B **66**
Conford. *Hants* 3G **25**
Congdon's Shop. *Corn* 5C **10**
Congerstone. *Leics* 5A **74**
Congham. *Norf* 3G **77**
Congleton. *Ches E* 4C **84**
Congl-y-wal. *Gwyn* 1G **69**
Congresbury. *N Som* 5H **33**
Congreve. *Staf* 4D **72**
Conham. *S Glo* 4B **34**
Conicaval. *Mor* 3D **159**
Coningsby. *Linc* 5B **88**
Conington. *Cambs* 4C **64**
(nr. Fenstanton)
Conington. *Cambs* 2A **64**
(nr. Sawtry)
Conisbrough. *S Yor* 1C **86**
Conisby. *Arg* 3A **124**
Conisholme. *Linc* 1D **88**
Coniston. *Cumb* 5E **102**
Coniston. *E Yor* 1E **95**
Coniston Cold. *N Yor* 4B **98**
Conistone. *N Yor* 3B **98**
Conlig. *N Dwn* 2K **179**
Connah's Quay. *Flin* 4E **83**
Connel. *Arg* 5D **140**
Connel Park. *E Ayr* 3F **117**
Connista. *High* 1D **154**
Connor. *Bmna* 7H **175**
Connor Downs. *Corn* 3C **4**

A-Z Great Britain Road Atlas 211

Conock—Dalton-on-Tees

Conock. Wilts 1F 23
Conon Bridge. High 3H 157
Cononley. N Yor 5B 98
Cononsyth. Ang 4E 145
Conordan. High 5E 155
Consall. Staf 1D 73
Consett. Dur 4E 115
Constable Burton. N Yor 5E 105
Constantine. Corn 4E 5
Constantine Bay. Corn 1C 6
Contin. High 3G 157
Contullich. High 1A 158
Conwy. Cnwy 3G 81
Conyer. Kent 4D 40
Conyer's Green. Suff 4A 66
Cooden. E Sus 5B 28
Cooil. IOM 4C 108
Cookbury. Devn 2E 11
Cookbury Wick. Devn 2D 11
Cookham. Wind 3G 37
Cookham Dean. Wind 3G 37
Cookham Rise. Wind 3G 37
Cookhill. Worc 5E 61
Cookley. Suff 3F 67
Cookley. Worc 2C 60
Cookley Green. Oxon 2E 37
Cookney. Abers 4F 153
Cooksbridge. E Sus 4F 27
Cooksey Green. Worc 4D 60
Cookshill. Staf 1D 72
Cooksmill Green. Essx 5G 53
Cookstown. Cook 2C 178
Coolham. W Sus 3C 26
Cooling. Medw 3B 40
Cooling Street. Medw 3B 40
Coombe. Corn 1C 10
(nr. Bude)
Coombe. Corn 3D 6
(nr. St Austell)
Coombe. Corn 4C 6
(nr. Truro)
Coombe. Devn 3E 12
(nr. Sidmouth)
Coombe. Devn 5C 12
(nr. Teignmouth)
Coombe. Glos 2C 34
Coombe. Hants 4E 25
Coombe. Wilts 1G 23
Coombe Bissett. Wilts 4G 23
Coombe Hill. Glos 3D 49
Coombe Keynes. Dors 4D 14
Coombes. W Sus 5C 26
Coopersale Common. Essx 5E 53
Coopersale Street. Essx 5E 53
Cooper's Corner. Kent 1F 27
Cooper Street. Kent 5H 41
Cootham. W Sus 4B 26
Copalder Corner. Cambs 1C 64
Copdock. Suff 1E 54
Copford. Essx 3C 54
Copford Green. Essx 3C 54
Copgrove. N Yor 3F 99
Copister. Shet 4F 173
Cople. Bed 1B 52
Copley. Dur 2D 105
Coplow Dale. Derbs 3F 85
Copmanthorpe. York 5H 99
Copp. Lanc 1C 90
Coppathorne. Corn 2C 10
Coppenhall. Ches E 5B 84
Coppenhall. Staf 4D 72
Coppenhall Moss. Ches E 5B 84
Copperhouse. Corn 3C 4
Coppicegate. Shrp 2B 60
Coppingford. Cambs 2A 64
Copplestone. Devn 2A 12
Coppull. Lanc 3D 90
Coppull Moor. Lanc 3D 90
Copsale. W Sus 3C 26
Copshaw Holm. Bord 1F 113
Copster Green. Lanc 1E 91
Copston Magna. Warw 2B 62
Copt Green. Warw 4F 61
Copthall Green. Essx 5E 53
Copt Heath. W Mid 3F 61
Copt Hewick. N Yor 2F 99
Copthill. Dur 5B 114
Copthorne. W Sus 2E 27
Coptiviney. Shrp 2G 71
Copy's Green. Norf 2B 78
Copythorne. Hants 1B 16
Corbridge. Nmbd 3C 114
Corby. Nptn 2F 63
Corby Glen. Linc 3H 75
Cordon. N Ayr 2E 123
Coreley. Shrp 3A 60
Corfe. Som 1F 13
Corfe Castle. Dors 4E 15
Corfe Mullen. Dors 3E 15
Corfton. Shrp 2G 59
Corgarff. Abers 3G 151
Corhampton. Hants 4E 24
Corkey. Bmny 4G 175
Corlae. Dum 5F 117
Corlannau. Neat 2A 32
Corley. Warw 2H 61
Corley Ash. Warw 2G 61
Corley Moor. Warw 2G 61
Cormiston. S Lan 1C 118
Cornaa. IOM 3D 108
Cornaigbeg. Arg 4A 138
Cornaigmore. Arg 2D 138
(on Coll)
Cornaigmore. Arg 4A 138
(on Tiree)
Corner Row. Lanc 1C 90
Corney. Cumb 5C 102
Cornforth. Dur 1A 106
Cornhill. Abers 3C 160
Cornhill. High 4C 164
Cornhill-on-Tweed. Nmbd 1C 120
Cornholme. W Yor 2H 91
Cornish Hall End. Essx 2G 53
Cornquoy. Orkn 7E 172
Cornriggs. Dur 5B 114
Cornsay. Dur 5E 115
Cornsay Colliery. Dur 5E 115
Corntown. High 3H 157
Corntown. V Glam 4C 32
Cornwell. Oxon 3A 50
Cornwood. Devn 3C 8
Cornworthy. Devn 3E 9
Corpach. High 1E 141
Corpusty. Norf 3D 78
Corra. Dum 3F 111
Corran. High 2E 141
(nr. Arnisdale)
Corran. High 3A 148
(nr. Fort William)
Corrany. IOM 3D 108
Corribeg. High 1D 141
Corrie. N Ayr 5B 126
Corrie Common. Dum 1D 112
Corriecravie. N Ayr 3D 122
Corriekinloch. High 1A 164
Corriemoillie. High 2F 157
Corrievarkie Lodge. Per 1C 142
Corrievorrie. High 1B 150
Corrigall. Orkn 6C 172
Corrimony. High 5F 157
Corringham. Linc 1F 87
Corringham. Thur 2B 40
Corris. Gwyn 5G 69
Corris Uchaf. Gwyn 5G 69
Corrour Shooting Lodge. High 2B 142
Corry. High 1E 147
Corrybrough. High 1C 150
Corrygills. N Ayr 2E 123
Corry of Ardnagrask. High 4H 157
Corsback. High 1E 169
(nr. Dunnet)
Corsback. High 3E 169
(nr. Halkirk)
Corscombe. Dors 2A 14
Corse. Abers 4D 160
Corse. Glos 3C 48
Corsehill. Abers 3G 161
Corse Lawn. Worc 2D 48
Corse of Kinnoir. Abers 4C 160
Corsham. Wilts 4D 34
Corsley. Wilts 2D 22
Corsley Heath. Wilts 2D 22
Corsock. Dum 2E 111
Corston. Bath 5B 34
Corston. Wilts 3E 35
Corstorphine. Edin 2F 129
Cortachy. Ang 3C 144
Corton. Suff 1H 67
Corton. Wilts 2E 23
Corton Denham. Som 4B 22
Corwar House. S Ayr 1H 109
Corwen. Den 1C 70
Coryates. Dors 4B 14
Coryton. Devn 4E 11
Coryton. Thur 2B 40
Cosby. Leics 1C 62
Coscote. Oxon 3D 36
Coseley. W Mid 1D 60
Cosgrove. Nptn 1F 51
Cosham. Port 2E 17
Cosheston. Pemb 4E 43
Coskills. N Lin 3D 94
Cosmeston. V Glam 5E 33
Cossall. Notts 1B 74
Cossington. Leics 4D 74
Cossington. Som 2G 21
Costa. Orkn 5C 172
Costessey. Norf 4D 78
Costock. Notts 2C 74
Coston. Leics 3F 75
Coston. Norf 5C 78
Cote. Oxon 5B 50
Cotebrook. Ches W 4H 83
Cotehill. Cumb 4F 113
Cotes. Cumb 1D 97
Cotes. Leics 3C 74
Cotes. Staf 2C 72
Cotesbach. Leics 2C 62
Cotes Heath. Staf 2C 72
Cotford St Luke. Som 4E 21
Cotgrave. Notts 2D 74
Cothall. Abers 2F 153
Cotham. Notts 1E 75
Cothelstone. Som 3E 21
Cotheridge. Worc 5B 60
Cotherstone. Dur 3D 104
Cothill. Oxon 2C 36
Cotland. Mon 5A 48
Cotleigh. Devn 2F 13
Cotmanhay. Derbs 1B 74
Coton. Cambs 5D 64
Coton. Nptn 3D 62
Coton. Staf 3C 72
(nr. Gnosall)
Coton. Staf 2D 73
(nr. Stone)
Coton. Staf 5F 73
(nr. Tamworth)
Coton Clanford. Staf 3C 72
Coton Hayes. Staf 2D 73
Coton Hill. Shrp 4G 71
Coton in the Clay. Staf 3F 73
Coton in the Elms. Derbs 4G 73
Cotonwood. Shrp 2H 71
Cotonwood. Staf 3C 72
Cott. Devn 2D 9
Cott. Orkn 5F 172
Cottam. E Yor 3D 101
Cottam. Lanc 1D 90
Cottam. Notts 3F 87
Cottartown. High 5E 159
Cottarville. Nptn 4E 63
Cottenham. Cambs 4D 64
Cotterdale. N Yor 5B 104
Cottered. Herts 3D 52
Cotterstock. Nptn 1H 63
Cottesbrooke. Nptn 3E 62
Cottesmore. Rut 4G 75
Cotteylands. Devn 1C 12
Cottingham. E Yor 1D 94
Cottingham. Nptn 1F 63
Cottingley. W Yor 1B 92
Cottisford. Oxon 2D 50
Cotton. Staf 1E 73
Cotton. Suff 4C 66
Cotton End. Bed 1A 52
Cottown. Abers 4F 161
Cotts. Devn 2A 8
Cotwalton. Staf 2D 72
Couch's Mill. Corn 3F 7
Coughton. Here 3A 48
Coughton. Warw 4E 61
Coulags. High 4B 156
Coulby Newham. Midd 3C 106
Coulderton. Cumb 4A 102
Coulin Lodge. High 3C 156
Coull. Abers 3C 152
Coulport. Arg 1D 126
Coulsdon. Surr 5D 39
Coulston. Wilts 1E 23
Coulter. S Lan 1C 118
Coultershaw Bridge. W Sus 4A 26
Coultings. Som 2F 21
Coulton. N Yor 2A 100
Cound. Shrp 5H 71
Coundon. Dur 2F 105
Coundon Grange. Dur 2F 105
Countersett. N Yor 1B 98
Countess. Wilts 2G 23
Countess Cross. Essx 2B 54
Countesthorpe. Leics 1C 62
Countisbury. Devn 2H 19
Coupar Angus. Per 4B 144
Coupe Green. Lanc 2D 90
Coupland. Cumb 3A 104
Coupland. Nmbd 1D 120
Cour. Arg 5G 125
Courance. Dum 5C 118
Court-at-Street. Kent 2E 29
Courteachan. High 4E 147
Courteenhall. Nptn 5E 63
Court Henry. Carm 3F 45
Courtsend. Essx 1E 41
Courtway. Som 3F 21
Cousland. Midl 3G 129
Cousley Wood. E Sus 2A 28
Coustonn. Arg 2B 126
Cove. Arg 1D 126
Cove. Devn 1C 12
Cove. Hants 1G 25
Cove. High 4C 162
Cove. Bord 2D 130
Cove Bay. Aber 3G 153
Covehithe. Suff 2H 67
Coven. Staf 5D 72
Coveney. Cambs 2D 65
Covenham St Bartholomew. Linc 1C 88
Covenham St Mary. Linc 1C 88
Coven Heath. Staf 5D 72
Coventry. W Mid 3H 61 & 194
Coverack. Corn 5E 5
Coverham. N Yor 1D 98
Covesea. Mor 1F 159
Covingham. Swin 3G 35
Covington. Cambs 3H 63
Covington. S Lan 1B 118
Cowan Bridge. Lanc 2F 97
Cowan Head. Cumb 5F 103
Cowbar. Red C 3E 107
Cowbeech. E Sus 4H 27
Cowbit. Linc 4B 76
Cowbridge. V Glam 4C 32
Cowden. Kent 1F 27
Cowdenbeath. Fife 4D 136
Cowdenburn. Bord 4F 129
Cowdenend. Fife 4D 136
Cowers Lane. Derbs 1H 73
Cowes. IOW 3C 16
Cowesby. N Yor 1G 99
Cowfold. W Sus 3D 26
Cowfords. Mor 3H 159
Cowgill. Cumb 1G 97
Cowie. Abers 5F 153
Cowie. Stir 1B 128
Cowlam. E Yor 3D 100
Cowley. Devn 3C 12
Cowley. Glos 4E 49
Cowley. G Lon 2B 38
Cowley. Oxon 5D 50
Cowley. Staf 4C 72
Cowleymoor. Devn 1C 12
Cowling. Lanc 3D 90
Cowling. N Yor 1E 99
(nr. Bedale)
Cowling. N Yor 5B 98
(nr. Glusburn)
Cowlinge. Suff 5G 65
Cowmes. W Yor 3B 92
Cowpe. Lanc 2G 91
Cowpen. Nmbd 1F 115
Cowpen Bewley. Stoc T 2B 106
Cowplain. Hants 1E 17
Cowshill. Dur 5B 114
Cowslip Green. N Som 5H 33
Cowstrandburn. Fife 4C 136
Cowthorpe. N Yor 4G 99
Coxall. Here 3F 59
Coxbank. Ches E 1A 72
Coxbench. Derbs 1A 74
Cox Common. Suff 2G 67
Coxford. Norf 3H 77
Coxgreen. Staf 2C 60
Cox Green. Surr 2B 26
Cox Green. Tyne 4G 115
Coxheath. Kent 5B 40
Coxhoe. Dur 1A 106
Coxley. Som 2A 22
Coxwold. N Yor 2H 99
Coychurch. V Glam 3C 32
Coylton. S Ayr 3D 116
Coylumbridge. High 2D 150
Coynach. Abers 3B 152
Coynachie. Abers 5B 160
Coytrahen. B'end 3B 32
Crabbs Cross. Worc 4E 61
Crabgate. Norf 3C 78
Crab Orchard. Dors 2F 15
Crabtree. W Sus 3D 26
Crabtree Green. Wrex 1F 71
Crackaig. High 2G 165
Crackenthorpe. Cumb 2H 103
Crackington Haven. Corn 3B 10
Crackley. Staf 5C 84
Crackley. Warw 3G 61
Crackleybank. Shrp 4B 72
Crackpot. N Yor 5C 104
Cracoe. N Yor 3B 98
Craddock. Devn 1D 12
Cradhlastadh. W Isl 4C 171
Cradley. Here 1C 48
Cradley. W Mid 2D 60
Cradoc. Powy 2D 46
Crafthole. Corn 3H 7
Crafton. Buck 4G 51
Cragabus. Arg 5B 124
Crag Foot. Lanc 2D 97
Craggan. High 1E 151
Cragganmore. Mor 5F 159
Cragganvallie. High 5H 157
Craggie. High 1F 165
Craggiemore. High 5B 158
Cragg Vale. W Yor 2A 92
Craghead. Dur 4F 115
Crai. Powy 3B 46
Craibstone. Aber 2F 153
Craichie. Ang 4E 145
Craig. Arg 5E 141
Craig. Dum 2D 111
Craig. High 4C 156
(nr. Achnashellach)
Craig. High 2G 155
(nr. Lower Diabaig)
Craig. High 5H 155
(nr. Stromeferry)
Craiganour Lodge. Per 3D 142
Craigavon. Cgvn 4E 178
Craigbrack. Arg 4A 134
Craig-cefn-parc. Swan 5G 45
Craigdallie. Per 1E 137
Craigdam. Abers 5F 161
Craigdarragh. Derr 6B 174
Craigdarroch. E Ayr 4F 117
Craigdarroch. High 3G 157
Craigdhu. High 4G 157
Craigearn. Abers 2E 152
Craigellachie. Mor 4G 159
Craigend. Per 1D 136
Craigendoran. Arg 1E 126
Craigends. Ren 3F 127
Craigenputtock. Dum 1E 111
Craigens. E Ayr 3E 117
Craighall. Edin 2E 129
Craighead. Fife 2H 137
Craighouse. Arg 3D 124
Craigie. Abers 2G 153
Craigie. D'dee 5D 144
Craigie. Per 4A 144
(nr. Blairgowrie)
Craigie. Per 1D 136
(nr. Perth)
Craigie. S Ayr 1D 116
Craigielaw. E Lot 2A 130
Craiglemine. Dum 5B 110
Craig-llwyn. Shrp 3E 71
Craiglockhart. Edin 2F 129
Craig Lodge. Arg 2B 126
Craigmalloch. E Ayr 5D 117
Craigmaud. Abers 3F 161
Craigmill. Stir 4H 135
Craigmillar. Edin 2F 129
Craigmore. Arg 3C 126
Craigmuie. Dum 1F 111
Craignair. Dum 3F 111
Craignant. Shrp 2E 71
Craigneuk. N Lan 3A 128
(nr. Airdrie)
Craigneuk. N Lan 4A 128
(nr. Motherwell)
Craignure. Arg 5B 140
Craigo. Abers 2F 145
Craigrory. High 4A 158
Craigrothie. Fife 2F 137
Craigs. Dum 2D 112
Craigshill. W Lot 3D 128
Craigs, The. High 4B 164
Craigton. Aber 3F 153
Craigton. Abers 3E 152
Craigton. Ang 5E 145
(nr. Carnoustie)
Craigton. Ang 3C 144
(nr. Kirriemuir)
Craigton. High 4A 158
Craigtown. High 3A 168
Craig-y-Duke. Neat 5H 45
Craig-y-nos. Powy 4B 46
Craik. Bord 4F 119
Crail. Fife 3H 137
Crailing. Bord 2A 120
Crailinghall. Bord 2A 120
Crakehill. N Yor 2G 99
Crakemarsh. Staf 2E 73
Crambe. N Yor 3B 100
Crambeck. N Yor 3B 100
Cramlington. Nmbd 2F 115
Cramond. Edin 2E 129
Cramond Bridge. Edin 2E 129
Cranage. Ches E 4B 84
Cranagh. Strab 7B 174
Cranberry. Staf 2C 72
Cranborne. Dors 1F 15
Cranbourne. Brac 3A 38
Cranbrook. Devn 3D 12
Cranbrook. Kent 2B 28
Cranbrook Common. Kent 2B 28
Crane Moor. S Yor 4D 92
Crane's Corner. Norf 4B 78
Cranfield. C Beds 1H 51
Cranford. G Lon 3B 38
Cranford St Andrew. Nptn 3G 63
Cranford St John. Nptn 3G 63
Cranham. Glos 4D 49
Cranham. G Lon 2G 39
Crank. Mers 1H 83
Cranleigh. Surr 2B 26
Cranley. Suff 3D 66
Cranloch. Mor 3G 159
Cranmer Green. Suff 3C 66
Cranmore. IOW 3B 16
Cranmore. Linc 5A 76
Crannich. Arg 4G 139
Crannoch. Mor 3B 160
Cranoe. Leics 1E 63
Cransford. Suff 4F 67
Cranshaws. Bord 3C 130
Cranstal. IOM 1D 108
Crantock. Corn 2B 6
Cranwell. Linc 1H 75
Cranwich. Norf 1G 65
Cranworth. Norf 5B 78
Craobh Haven. Arg 3E 133
Craobhnaclag. High 4G 157
Crapstone. Devn 2B 8
Crarae. Arg 4G 133
Crask. High 2H 167
Crask Inn. High 1C 164
Crask of Aigas. High 4G 157
Craster. Nmbd 3G 121
Cratfield. Suff 3F 67
Crathes. Abers 4E 153
Crathie. Abers 4G 151
Crathie. High 4H 149
Crathorne. N Yor 4B 106
Craven Arms. Shrp 2G 59
Crawcrook. Tyne 3E 115
Crawford. Lanc 4D 90
Crawford. S Lan 2B 118
Crawforddyke. S Lan 4B 128
Crawfordjohn. S Lan 2A 118
Crawfordsburn. N Dwn 1J 179
Crawick. Dum 3G 117
Crawley. Devn 2F 13
Crawley. Hants 3C 24
Crawley. Oxon 4B 50
Crawley. W Sus 2D 26
Crawley Down. W Sus 2E 27
Crawley End. Essx 1E 53
Crawley Side. Dur 5C 114
Crawshawbooth. Lanc 2G 91
Crawton. Abers 5F 153
Cray. N Yor 2B 98
Cray. Per 2A 144
Crayford. G Lon 3G 39
Crayke. N Yor 2H 99
Craymere Beck. Norf 2C 78
Crays Hill. Essx 1B 40
Cray's Pond. Oxon 3E 37
Crazies Hill. Wok 3F 37
Creacombe. Devn 1B 12
Creagan. Arg 4D 141
Creag Aoil. High 1F 141
Creag Ghoraidh. W Isl 4C 170
Creaguaineach Lodge. High 2H 141
Creamore Bank. Shrp 2H 71
Creaton. Nptn 3E 62
Creca. Dum 2D 112
Credenhill. Here 1H 47
Crediton. Devn 2B 12
Creebridge. Dum 3B 110
Creech. Dors 4E 15
Creech Heathfield. Som 4F 21
Creech St Michael. Som 4F 21
Creed. Corn 4D 6
Creekmoor. Pool 3E 15
Creekmouth. G Lon 2F 39
Creeting St Mary. Suff 5C 66
Creeting St Peter. Suff 5C 66
Creeton. Linc 3H 75
Creetown. Dum 4B 110
Creggan. New M 8D 178
Creggan. Omag 2A 178
Creggans. Arg 3H 133
Cregneash. IOM 5A 108
Cregrina. Powy 5D 58
Creich. Arg 2B 132
Creich. Fife 1F 137
Creighton. Staf 2E 73
Creigiau. Card 3D 32
Cremyll. Corn 3A 8
Crendell. Dors 1F 15
Crepkill. High 4D 154
Cressage. Shrp 5H 71
Cressbrook. Derbs 3F 85
Cresselly. Pemb 4E 43
Cressing. Essx 3A 54
Cresswell. Nmbd 5G 121
Cresswell. Staf 2D 73
Cresswell Quay. Pemb 4E 43
Creswell. Derbs 3C 86
Creswell Green. Staf 4E 73
Cretingham. Suff 4E 67
Crewe. Ches E 5B 84
Crewe-by-Farndon. Ches W 5G 83
Crewgreen. Powy 4F 71
Crewkerne. Som 2H 13
Crews Hill. G Lon 5D 52
Crewton. Derb 2A 74
Crianlarich. Stir 1C 134
Cribbs Causeway. S Glo 3A 34
Cribyn. Cdgn 5E 57
Criccieth. Gwyn 2D 69
Crich. Derbs 5A 86
Crichton. Midl 3G 129
Crick. Mon 2H 33
Crick. Nptn 3C 62
Crickadarn. Powy 1D 46
Cricket Hill. Hants 5G 37
Cricket Malherbie. Som 1G 13
Cricket St Thomas. Som 2G 13
Crickham. Som 2H 21
Crickheath. Shrp 3E 71
Crickhowell. Powy 4F 47
Cricklade. Wilts 2F 35
Cricklewood. G Lon 2D 38
Cridling Stubbs. N Yor 2F 93
Crieff. Per 1A 136
Criftins. Shrp 2F 71
Criggion. Powy 4E 71
Crigglestone. W Yor 3D 92
Crimchard. Som 2G 13
Crimdon Park. Dur 1B 106
Crimond. Abers 3H 161
Crimonmogate. Abers 3H 161
Crimplesham. Norf 5F 77
Crimscote. Warw 1H 49
Crinan. Arg 4E 133
Cringleford. Norf 5D 78
Crinow. Pemb 3F 43
Cripplesease. Corn 3C 4
Cripplestyle. Dors 1F 15
Cripp's Corner. E Sus 3B 28
Croanford. Corn 5A 10
Crockenhill. Kent 4G 39
Crocker End. Oxon 3F 37
Crockerhill. Hants 2D 16
Crockernwell. Devn 3A 12
Crocker's Ash. Here 4A 48
Crockerton. Wilts 2D 22
Crocketford. Dum 2F 111
Crockey Hill. York 5A 100
Crockham Hill. Kent 5F 39
Crockhurst Street. Kent 1H 27
Crockleford Heath. Essx 3D 54
Croeserw. Neat 2B 32
Croes-Goch. Pemb 1C 42
Croes Hywel. Mon 4G 47
Croes-lan. Cdgn 1D 45
Croesor. Gwyn 1F 69
Croesoswallt. Shrp 3E 71
Croesyceiliog. Carm 4E 45
Croesyceiliog. Torf 2G 33
Croes-y-mwyalch. Torf 2G 33
Croesywaun. Gwyn 5E 81
Croford. Som 4E 20
Croft. Leics 1C 62
Croft. Linc 4E 89
Croft. Warr 1A 84
Croftamie. Stir 1F 127
Croftfoot. Glas 3G 127
Croftmill. Per 5F 143
Crofton. Cumb 4E 112
Crofton. W Yor 3D 93
Crofton. Wilts 5A 36
Croft-on-Tees. N Yor 4F 105
Crofts. Dum 2E 111
Crofts of Benachielt. High 5D 169
Crofts of Dipple. Mor 3H 159
Crofty. Swan 3E 31
Croggan. Arg 1E 132
Croglin. Cumb 5G 113
Croich. High 4B 164
Croick. High 3A 168
Croig. Arg 3E 139
Cromarty. High 2B 158
Crombie. Fife 1D 128
Cromdale. High 1E 151
Cromer. Herts 3C 52
Cromer. Norf 1E 78
Cromford. Derbs 5G 85
Cromhall. S Glo 2B 34
Cromor. W Isl 5G 171
Cromra. High 5H 149
Cromwell. Notts 4E 87
Cronberry. E Ayr 2F 117
Crondall. Hants 2F 25
Cronk, The. IOM 2C 108
Cronk-y-Voddy. IOM 3C 108
Cronton. Mers 2G 83
Crook. Cumb 5F 103
Crook. Dur 1E 105
Crookdake. Cumb 5C 112
Crooke. G Man 4D 90
Crookedholm. E Ayr 1D 116
Crooked Soley. Wilts 4B 36
Crookes. S Yor 2H 85
Crookgate Bank. Dur 4E 115
Crookhall. Dur 4E 115
Crookham. Nmbd 1D 120
Crookham. W Ber 5D 36
Crookham Village. Hants 1F 25
Crooklands. Cumb 1E 97
Crook of Devon. Per 3C 136
Crookston. Ren 3G 127
Cropredy. Oxon 1C 50
Cropston. Leics 4C 74
Cropthorne. Worc 1E 49
Cropton. N Yor 1B 100
Cropwell Bishop. Notts 2D 74
Cropwell Butler. Notts 2D 74
Cros. W Isl 1H 171
Crosbie. N Ayr 5D 126
Crosbost. W Isl 5F 171
Crosby. Cumb 1B 102
Crosby. IOM 4C 108
Crosby. Mers 1F 83
Crosby. N Lin 3B 94
Crosby Court. N Yor 5A 106
Crosby Garrett. Cumb 4A 104
Crosby Ravensworth. Cumb 3H 103
Crosby Villa. Cumb 1B 102
Croscombe. Som 2A 22
Crosland Moor. W Yor 3B 92
Cross. Som 1H 21
Crossaig. Arg 4G 125
Crossapol. Arg 4A 138
Cross Ash. Mon 4H 47
Cross-at-Hand. Kent 1B 28
Crossbush. W Sus 5B 26
Crosscanonby. Cumb 1B 102
Crossdale Street. Norf 2E 79
Cross End. Essx 2B 54
Crossens. Mers 3B 90
Crossford. Fife 1D 129
Crossford. S Lan 5B 128
Cross Foxes. Gwyn 4G 69
Crossgar. Down 4J 179
Crossgate. Orkn 6D 172
Crossgate. Staf 2D 72
Crossgatehall. E Lot 3G 129
Crossgates. Fife 1E 129
Crossgates. N Yor 1E 101
Crossgates. Powy 4C 58
Cross Gates. W Yor 1D 93
Crossgill. Lanc 3E 97
Cross Green. Devn 4D 11
Cross Green. Staf 5D 72
Cross Green. Suff 5A 66
(nr. Cockfield)
Cross Green. Suff 5B 66
(nr. Hitcham)
Cross Hands. Carm 4F 45
(nr. Ammanford)
Crosshands. Carm 2F 43
(nr. Whitland)
Crosshands. E Ayr 1D 117
Cross Hill. Derbs 1B 74
Crosshill. E Ayr 2D 117
Crosshill. Fife 4D 136
Cross Hill. Glos 2A 34
Crosshill. S Ayr 4C 116
Crosshills. High 1A 158
Cross Hills. N Yor 5C 98
Cross Holme. N Yor 5C 106
Crosshouse. E Ayr 1C 116
Cross Houses. Shrp 5H 71
Crossings. Cumb 2G 113
Cross in Hand. E Sus 3G 27
Cross Inn. Cdgn 4E 57
(nr. Aberaeron)
Cross Inn. Cdgn 5C 56
(nr. New Quay)
Cross Inn. Rhon 3D 32
Crosskeys. Cphy 2F 33
Crosskirk. High 2C 168
Crosslands. Cumb 1C 96
Cross Lane Head. Shrp 1B 60
Cross Lanes. Corn 4D 5
Cross Lanes. Dur 3D 104
Cross Lanes. N Yor 3H 99
Crosslanes. Shrp 4F 71
Cross Lanes. Wrex 1F 71
Crosslee. Ren 3F 127
Crossmaglen. New M 8D 178
Crossmichael. Dum 3E 111
Crossmoor. Lanc 1C 90
Crossnacreevy. Cast 3H 179
Cross Oak. Powy 3E 46
Cross of Jackston. Abers 5E 161
Cross o' th' Hands. Derbs 1G 73
Crossroads. Abers 3G 153
(nr. Aberdeen)
Crossroads. Abers 4E 153
(nr. Banchory)
Crossroads. E Ayr 1D 116
Cross Side. Devn 4B 20
Cross Street. Suff 3D 66
Crosston. Ang 3E 145
Cross Town. Ches E 3B 84
Crossway. Mon 4H 47
Crossway. Powy 5C 58
Crossway Green. Mon 2A 34
Crossway Green. Worc 4C 60
Crossways. Dors 4C 14
Crosswell. Pemb 1F 43
Crosswood. Cdgn 3F 57
Crosthwaite. Cumb 5F 103
Croston. Lanc 3C 90
Crostwick. Norf 4E 79
Crostwight. Norf 3F 79
Crothair. W Isl 4D 171
Crouch. Kent 5H 39
Croucheston. Wilts 4F 23
Crouch Hill. Dors 1C 14
Croughton. Nptn 2D 50
Crovie. Abers 2F 161
Crow. Hants 2G 15
Crowan. Corn 3D 4
Crowborough. E Sus 2G 27
Crowcombe. Som 3E 21
Crowcroft. Worc 5B 60
Crowdecote. Derbs 4F 85
Crowden. Derbs 1E 85
Crowden. Devn 3E 11
Crowdhill. Hants 1C 16
Crowdon. N Yor 5G 107
Crow Edge. S Yor 4B 92
Crow End. Cambs 5C 64
Crowfield. Nptn 1E 50
Crowfield. Suff 5D 66
Crow Green. Essx 1G 39
Crow Hill. Here 3B 48
Crowhurst. E Sus 4B 28
Crowhurst. Surr 1E 27
Crowhurst Lane End. Surr 1E 27
Crowland. Linc 4B 76
Crowland. Suff 3C 66
Crowlas. Corn 3C 4
Crowle. N Lin 3A 94
Crowle. Worc 5D 60
Crowle Green. Worc 5D 60
Crowmarsh Gifford. Oxon 3E 36
Crown Corner. Suff 3E 67
Crownthorpe. Norf 5C 78
Crowntown. Corn 3D 4
Crows-an-wra. Corn 4A 4
Crowshill. Norf 5B 78
Crowthorne. Brac 5G 37
Crowton. Ches W 3H 83
Croxall. Staf 4F 73
Croxby. Linc 1A 88
Croxdale. Dur 1F 105
Croxden. Staf 2E 73
Croxley Green. Herts 1B 38
Croxton. Cambs 4B 64
Croxton. Norf 2B 78
(nr. Fakenham)
Croxton. Norf 2A 66
(nr. Thetford)
Croxton. N Lin 3D 94
Croxton. Staf 2B 72
Croxtonbank. Staf 2B 72
Croxton Green. Ches E 5H 83
Croxton Kerrial. Leics 3F 75
Croy. High 4B 158
Croy. N Lan 2A 128
Croyde. Devn 3E 19
Croydon. Cambs 1D 52
Croydon. G Lon 4E 39
Crubenbeg. High 4A 150
Crubenmore Lodge. High 4A 150
Cruckmeole. Shrp 5G 71
Cruckton. Shrp 4G 71
Cruden Bay. Abers 5H 161
Crudgington. Telf 4A 72
Crudie. Abers 3E 161
Crudwell. Wilts 2E 35
Cruft. Devn 3F 11
Crug. Powy 3D 58
Crughywel. Powy 4F 47
Crugmeer. Corn 1D 6
Crugybar. Carm 2G 45
Crug-y-byddar. Powy 2D 58
Crulabhig. W Isl 4D 171
Crumlin. Ant 2F 179
Crumlin. Cphy 2F 33
Crumpsall. G Man 4G 91
Crumpsbrook. Shrp 3A 60
Crundale. Kent 1E 29
Crundale. Pemb 3D 42
Cruwys Morchard. Devn 1B 12
Crux Easton. Hants 1C 24
Cruxton. Dors 3B 14
Crwbin. Carm 4E 45
Cryers Hill. Buck 2G 37
Crymych. Pemb 1F 43
Crynant. Neat 5A 46
Crystal Palace. G Lon 3E 39
Cuaich. High 5A 150
Cuaig. High 3G 155
Cuan. Arg 2E 133
Cubbington. Warw 4H 61
Cubert. Corn 3B 6
Cubley. S Yor 4C 92
Cubley Common. Derbs 2F 73
Cublington. Buck 3G 51
Cublington. Here 2H 47
Cuckfield. W Sus 3E 27
Cucklington. Som 4C 22
Cuckney. Notts 3C 86
Cuckron. Shet 6F 173
Cuddesdon. Oxon 5E 50
Cuddington. Buck 4F 51
Cuddington. Ches W 3A 84
Cuddington Heath. Ches W 1G 71
Cuddy Hill. Lanc 1C 90
Cudham. G Lon 5F 39
Cudlipptown. Devn 5F 11
Cudworth. Som 1G 13
Cudworth. S Yor 4D 93
Cudworth. Surr 1D 26
Cuerdley Cross. Warr 2H 83
Cuffley. Herts 5D 52
Cuidhir. W Isl 8B 170
Cuidhsiadar. W Isl 2H 171
Cuidhtinis. W Isl 9C 171
Culbo. High 2A 158
Culbokie. High 3A 158
Culburnie. High 4G 157
Culcabock. High 4A 158
Culcavy. Lis 3G 179
Culcharry. High 3C 158
Culcheth. Warr 1A 84
Culduie. High 4G 155
Culeave. High 4C 164
Culford. Suff 4H 65
Culgaith. Cumb 2H 103
Culham. Oxon 2D 36
Culkein. High 1E 163
Culkein Drumbeg. High 5B 166
Culkerton. Glos 2E 35
Cullaville. New M 8C 178
Cullen. Mor 2C 160
Cullercoats. Tyne 2G 115
Cullicudden. High 2A 158
Cullingworth. W Yor 1A 92
Cullipool. Arg 2E 133
Cullivoe. Shet 1G 173
Culloch. Per 2G 135
Culloden. High 4B 158
Cullompton. Devn 2D 12
Cullybackey. Bmna 6G 175
Cullycapple. Cole 4E 174
Cullyhanna. New M 7D 178
Culm Davy. Devn 1E 13
Culmington. Shrp 2G 59
Culmore. Derr 4A 174
Culmstock. Devn 1E 12
Cul na Caepaich. High 5E 147
Culnacnoc. High 2E 155
Culnacraig. High 3E 163
Culnady. Mag 6E 174
Culrain. High 4C 164
Culross. Fife 1C 128
Culroy. S Ayr 3C 116
Culswick. Shet 7D 173
Cults. Aber 3F 153
Cults. Abers 5C 160
Cults. Fife 2F 137
Cultybraggan Camp. Per 1G 135
Culver. Devn 3B 12
Culverlane. Devn 2D 8
Culverstone Green. Kent 4H 39
Culverthorpe. Linc 1H 75
Culworth. Nptn 1D 50
Culzie Lodge. High 1H 157
Cumberlow Green. Herts 2D 52
Cumbernauld. N Lan 2A 128
Cumbernauld Village. N Lan 2A 128
Cumberworth. Linc 3E 89
Cumdivock. Cumb 5E 113
Cuminestown. Abers 3F 161
Cumledge Mill. Bord 4D 130
Cumlewick. Shet 9F 173
Cummersdale. Cumb 4E 113
Cummertrees. Dum 3C 112
Cummingstown. Mor 2F 159
Cumnock. E Ayr 3E 117
Cumnor. Oxon 5C 50
Cumrew. Cumb 4G 113
Cumwhinton. Cumb 4F 113
Cumwhitton. Cumb 4G 113
Cundall. N Yor 2G 99
Cunninghamhead. N Ayr 5E 127
Cunning Park. S Ayr 3C 116
Cunningsburgh. Shet 9F 173
Cunnister. Shet 2G 173
Cupar. Fife 2F 137
Cupar Muir. Fife 2F 137
Cupernham. Hants 4B 24
Curbar. Derbs 3G 85
Curborough. Staf 4F 73
Curbridge. Hants 1D 16
Curbridge. Oxon 5B 50
Curdridge. Hants 1D 16
Curdworth. Warw 1F 61
Curland. Som 1F 13
Curland Common. Som 1F 13
Curran. Mag 7E 174
Curridge. W Ber 4C 36
Currie. Edin 3E 129
Curry Mallet. Som 4G 21
Curry Rivel. Som 4G 21
Curtisden Green. Kent 1B 28
Curtisknowle. Devn 3D 8
Cury. Corn 4D 5
Cusgarne. Corn 4B 6
Cushendall. Moy 4J 175
Cushendun. Moy 3J 175
Cusop. Here 1F 47
Cusworth. S Yor 4F 93
Cutcombe. Som 3C 20
Cuthill. E Lot 2G 129
Cutiau. Gwyn 4F 69
Cutlers Green. Essx 2F 53
Cutmadoc. Corn 2E 7
Cutnall Green. Worc 4C 60
Cutsdean. Glos 2F 49
Cutthorpe. Derbs 3H 85
Cuttiford's Door. Som 1G 13
Cuttivett. Corn 2H 7
Cutts. Shet 8F 173
Cuttybridge. Pemb 3D 42
Cuttyhill. Abers 3H 161
Cuxham. Oxon 2E 37
Cuxton. Medw 4B 40
Cuxwold. Linc 4E 95
Cwm. Blae 5E 47
Cwm. Den 3C 82
Cwm. Powy 1E 59
Cwmafan. Neat 2A 32
Cwmaman. Rhon 2C 32
Cwmann. Carm 1F 45
Cwmbach. Carm 2G 43
Cwmbach. Powy 2E 47
Cwmbach. Rhon 5D 46
Cwmbach Llechrhyd. Powy 5C 58
Cwmbelan. Powy 2B 58
Cwmbran. Torf 2F 33
Cwmbrwyno. Cdgn 2G 57
Cwm Capel. Carm 5E 45
Cwmcarn. Cphy 2F 33
Cwmcarvan. Mon 5H 47
Cwm-celyn. Blae 5F 47
Cwmcerdinen. Swan 5G 45
Cwm-Cewydd. Gwyn 4A 70
Cwm-cou. Cdgn 1C 44
Cwmcych. Pemb 1G 43
Cwmdare. Rhon 5C 46
Cwmdu. Carm 2G 45
Cwmdu. Powy 3E 47
Cwmduad. Carm 2D 45
Cwm Dulais. Swan 5G 45
Cwmerfyn. Cdgn 2F 57
Cwmfelin. B'end 3B 32
Cwmfelin Boeth. Carm 3F 43
Cwmfelinfach. Cphy 2E 33
Cwmfelin Mynach. Carm 2G 43
Cwmffrwd. Carm 4E 45
Cwmgiedd. Powy 4A 46
Cwmgors. Neat 4H 45
Cwmgwili. Carm 4F 45
Cwmgwrach. Neat 5B 46
Cwmhiraeth. Carm 1H 43
Cwmifor. Carm 3G 45
Cwmisfael. Carm 4E 45
Cwm-Llinau. Powy 5H 69
Cwmllynfell. Neat 4H 45
Cwm-mawr. Carm 4F 45
Cwm-miles. Carm 2F 43
Cwmorgan. Carm 1G 43
Cwmparc. Rhon 2C 32
Cwm Penmachno. Cnwy 1G 69
Cwmpennar. Rhon 5D 46
Cwm Plysgog. Pemb 1B 44
Cwmrhos. Powy 3E 47
Cwmsychpant. Cdgn 1E 45
Cwmsyfiog. Cphy 5E 47
Cwmsymlog. Cdgn 2F 57
Cwmtillery. Blae 5F 47
Cwm-twrch Isaf. Powy 5A 46
Cwm-twrch Uchaf. Powy 4A 46
Cwm-y-glo. Gwyn 4E 81
Cwmyoy. Mon 3G 47
Cwmystwyth. Cdgn 3G 57
Cwrt. Gwyn 5F 69
Cwrtnewydd. Cdgn 1E 45
Cwrt-y-Cadno. Carm 1G 45
Cydweli. Carm 5E 45
Cyffylliog. Den 5C 82
Cymau. Flin 5E 83
Cymer. Neat 2B 32
Cymmer. Neat 2B 32
Cymmer. Rhon 2D 32
Cyncoed. Card 3E 33
Cynghordy. Carm 2B 46
Cynghordy. Swan 5G 45
Cynheidre. Carm 5E 45
Cynonville. Neat 2B 32
Cynwyd. Den 1C 70
Cynwyl Elfed. Carm 3D 44
Cywarch. Gwyn 4A 70

D

Dacre. Cumb 2F 103
Dacre. N Yor 3D 98
Dacre Banks. N Yor 3D 98
Daddry Shield. Dur 1B 104
Dadford. Buck 2E 51
Dadlington. Leics 1B 62
Dafen. Carm 5F 45
Daffy Green. Norf 5B 78
Dagdale. Staf 2E 73
Dagenham. G Lon 2F 39
Daggons. Dors 1G 15
Daglingworth. Glos 5E 49
Dagnall. Buck 4H 51
Dagtail End. Worc 4E 61
Dail. Arg 5E 141
Dail Beag. W Isl 3E 171
Dail bho Dheas. W Isl 1G 171
Dailly. S Ayr 4B 116
Dail Mor. W Isl 3E 171
Dairsie. Fife 2G 137
Daisy Bank. W Mid 1E 61
Daisy Hill. G Man 4E 91
Daisy Hill. W Yor 1B 92
Dalabrog. W Isl 6C 170
Dalavich. Arg 2G 133
Dalbeattie. Dum 3F 111
Dalblair. E Ayr 3F 117
Dalbury. Derbs 2G 73
Dalby. IOM 4B 108
Dalby Wolds. Leics 3D 74
Dalchalm. High 3G 165
Dalcharn. High 3G 167
Dalchork. High 2C 164
Dalchreichart. High 2E 149
Dalchruin. Per 2G 135
Dalcross. High 4B 158
Dalderby. Linc 4B 88
Dale. Cumb 5G 113
Dale. Pemb 4C 42
Dale Abbey. Derbs 2B 74
Dalebank. Derbs 4A 86
Dale Bottom. Cumb 2D 102
Dale Head. Cumb 3F 103
Dalehouse. N Yor 3E 107
Dalelia. High 2B 140
Dale of Walls. Shet 6C 173
Dalgarven. N Ayr 5D 126
Dalgety Bay. Fife 1E 129
Dalginross. Per 1G 135
Dalguise. Per 4G 143
Dalhalvaig. High 3A 168
Dalham. Suff 4G 65
Dalintart. Arg 1F 133
Dalkeith. Midl 3G 129
Dallas. Mor 3F 159
Dalleagles. E Ayr 3E 117
Dall House. Per 3C 142
Dallinghoo. Suff 5E 67
Dallington. E Sus 4A 28
Dallow. N Yor 2D 98
Dalmally. Arg 1A 134
Dalmarnock. Glas 3H 127
Dalmellington. E Ayr 4D 117
Dalmeny. Edin 2E 129
Dalmigavie. High 2B 150
Dalmilling. S Ayr 2C 116
Dalmore. High 2A 158
(nr. Alness)
Dalmore. High 3E 164
(nr. Rogart)
Dalmuir. W Dun 2F 127
Dalmunach. Mor 4G 159
Dalnabreck. High 2B 140
Dalnacardoch Lodge. Per 1E 142
Dalnamein Lodge. Per 2E 143
Dalnaspidal Lodge. Per 1D 142
Dalnatrat. High 3D 140
Dalnavie. High 1A 158
Dalnawillan Lodge. High 4C 168
Dalness. High 3F 141
Dalnessie. High 2D 164
Dalqueich. Per 3C 136
Dalquhairn. S Ayr 5C 116
Dalreavoch. High 3E 165
Dalreoch. Per 2C 136
Dalry. Edin 2F 129
Dalry. N Ayr 5D 126
Dalrymple. E Ayr 3C 116
Dalscote. Nptn 5D 62
Dalserf. S Lan 4A 128
Dalsmirren. Arg 4A 122
Dalston. Cumb 4E 113
Dalswinton. Dum 1G 111
Dalton. Dum 2C 112
Dalton. Lanc 4C 90
Dalton. Nmbd 4C 114
(nr. Hexham)
Dalton. Nmbd 2E 115
(nr. Ponteland)
Dalton. N Yor 4E 105
(nr. Richmond)
Dalton. N Yor 2G 99
(nr. Thirsk)
Dalton. S Lan 4H 127
Dalton. S Yor 1B 86
Dalton-in-Furness. Cumb 2B 96
Dalton-le-Dale. Dur 5H 115
Dalton Magna. S Yor 1B 86
Dalton-on-Tees. N Yor 4F 105

Dalton Piercy—Easter Ord

Dalton Piercy. Hart 1B 106
Daltot. Arg 1F 125
Dalvey. High 5F 159
Dalwhinnie. High 5A 150
Dalwood. Devn 2F 13
Damerham. Hants 1G 15
Damgate. Norf 5G 79 (nr. Acle)
Damgate. Norf 4G 79 (nr. Martham)
Dam Green. Norf 2C 66
Damhead. Mor 3E 159
Danaway. Kent 4C 40
Danbury. Essx 5A 54
Danby. N Yor 4E 107
Danby Botton. N Yor 4D 107
Danby Wiske. N Yor 5A 106
Danderhall. Midl 3G 129
Danebank. Ches E 2D 85
Danebridge. Ches E 4D 84
Dane End. Herts 3D 52
Danehill. E Sus 3F 27
Danesford. Shrp 1B 60
Daneshill. Hants 1E 25
Danesmoor. Derbs 4A 86
Danestone. Aber 2G 153
Dangerous Corner. Lanc 3D 90
Daniel's Water. Kent 1D 28
Dan's Castle. Dur 1E 105
Danzey Green. Warw 4F 61
Dapple Heath. Staf 3E 73
Daren. Powy 4F 47
Darenth. Kent 3G 39
Daresbury. Hal 2H 83
Darfield. S Yor 4E 93
Dargate. Kent 4E 41
Dargill. Per 2A 136
Darite. Corn 2G 7
Darkley. Arm 6C 178
Darlaston. W Mid 1D 60
Darley. N Yor 4E 98
Darley Abbey. Derb 2A 74
Darley Bridge. Derbs 4G 85
Darley Dale. Derbs 4G 85
Darley Head. N Yor 4D 98
Darlingscott. Warw 1H 49
Darlington. Darl 3F 105
Darliston. Shrp 2H 71
Darlton. Notts 3E 87
Darmsden. Suff 5C 66
Darnall. S Yor 2A 86
Darnford. Abers 4E 153
Darnford. Staf 5F 73
Darnhall. Ches W 4A 84
Darnick. Bord 1H 119
Darowen. Powy 5H 69
Darra. Abers 4E 161
Darracott. Devn 3E 19
Darragh Cross. Down 4J 179
Darras Hall. Nmbd 2E 115
Darrington. W Yor 3E 93
Darrow Green. Norf 2E 67
Darsham. Suff 4G 67
Dartfield. Abers 3H 161
Dartford. Kent 3G 39
Dartford-Thurrock River Crossing. Kent 3G 39
Dartington. Devn 2D 9
Dartmeet. Devn 5G 11
Dartmoor. Devn 4F 11
Dartmouth. Devn 3E 9
Darton. S Yor 3D 92
Darvel. E Ayr 1E 117
Darwen. Bkbn 2E 91
Dassels. Herts 3D 53
Datchet. Wind 3A 38
Datchworth. Herts 4C 52
Datchworth Green. Herts 4C 52
Daubhill. G Man 4F 91
Dauntsey. Wilts 3E 35
Dauntsey Green. Wilts 3E 35
Dauntsey Lock. Wilts 3E 35
Dava. Mor 5E 159
Davenham. Ches W 3A 84
Daventry. Nptn 4C 62
Davidson's Mains. Edin 2F 129
Davidston. High 2B 158
Davidstow. Corn 4B 10
David's Well. Powy 3C 58
Davington. Dum 4E 119
Daviot. Abers 1E 153
Daviot. High 5B 158
Davyhulme. G Man 1B 84
Daw Cross. N Yor 4E 99
Dawdon. Dur 5H 115
Dawesgreen. Surr 1D 26
Dawley. Telf 5A 72
Dawlish. Devn 5C 12
Dawlish Warren. Devn 5C 12
Dawn. Cnwy 3A 82
Daws Heath. Essx 2C 40
Dawshill. Worc 5C 60
Daw's House. Corn 4D 10
Dawsmere. Linc 2D 76
Dayhills. Staf 2D 72
Dayhouse Bank. Worc 3D 60
Daylesford. Glos 3H 49
Daywall. Shrp 2E 71
Ddol. Flin 3D 82
Ddol Cownwy. Powy 4C 70
Deadman's Cross. C Beds 1B 52
Deadwater. Nmbd 5A 120
Deaf Hill. Dur 1A 106
Deal. Kent 5H 41
Dean. Cumb 2B 102
Dean. Devn 2G 19 (nr. Combe Martin)
Dean. Devn 2H 19 (nr. Lynton)
Dean. Dors 1E 15
Dean. Hants 1D 16 (nr. Bishop's Waltham)
Dean. Hants 3C 24 (nr. Winchester)
Dean. Oxon 3B 50
Dean. Som 2B 22
Dean Bank. Dur 1F 105
Deanburnhaugh. Bord 3F 119
Dean Cross. Devn 2F 19
Deane. Hants 1D 24
Deanich Lodge. High 5A 164
Deanland. Dors 1E 15
Deanlane End. W Sus 1F 17
Dean Park. Shrp 4H 59
Dean Prior. Devn 2D 8
Dean Row. Ches E 2C 84
Deans. W Lot 3D 128
Deanscales. Cumb 2B 102
Deanshanger. Nptn 2F 51
Deanston. Stir 3G 135
Dearham. Cumb 1B 102
Dearne. S Yor 4E 93
Dearne Valley. S Yor 4D 93
Debach. Suff 5E 67
Debden. Essx 2F 53
Debden Green. Essx 1F 39 (nr. Loughton)
Debden Green. Essx 2F 53 (nr. Saffron Walden)
Debenham. Suff 4D 66
Dechmont. W Lot 2D 128
Deddington. Oxon 2C 50
Dedham. Essx 2D 54
Dedham Heath. Essx 2D 54
Deebank. Abers 4D 152
Deene. Nptn 1G 63
Deenethorpe. Nptn 1G 63
Deepcar. S Yor 1G 85
Deepcut. Surr 5A 38
Deepdale. Cumb 1G 97
Deepdale. N Lin 3D 94
Deepdale. N Yor 2A 98
Deeping Gate. Pet 5A 76
Deeping St James. Linc 5A 76
Deeping St Nicholas. Linc 4B 76
Deerhill. Mor 3B 160
Deerhurst. Glos 3D 48
Deerhurst Walton. Glos 3D 49
Deerness. Orkn 7E 172
Defford. Worc 1E 49
Defynnog. Powy 3C 46
Deganwy. Cnwy 3G 81
Deighton. N Yor 4A 106
Deighton. W Yor 3B 92
Deighton. York 5A 100
Deiniolen. Gwyn 4E 81
Delabole. Corn 4A 10
Delamere. Ches W 4H 83
Delfour. High 3C 150
Delliefure. High 5E 159
Dell, The. Suff 1G 67
Delly End. Oxon 4B 50
Delny. High 1B 158
Delph. G Man 4H 91
Delves. Dur 5E 115
Delves, The. W Mid 1E 61
Delvin End. Essx 2A 54
Dembleby. Linc 2H 75
Demelza. Corn 2D 6
Denaby Main. S Yor 1B 86
Denbeath. Fife 4F 137
Denbigh. Den 4C 82
Denbury. Devn 2E 9
Denby. Derbs 1A 74
Denby Common. Derbs 1B 74
Denby Dale. W Yor 4C 92
Denchworth. Oxon 2B 36
Dendron. Cumb 2B 96
Deneside. Dur 5H 115
Denford. Nptn 3G 63
Dengie. Essx 5C 54
Denham. Buck 2B 38
Denham. Suff 4G 65 (nr. Bury St Edmunds)
Denham. Suff 3D 66 (nr. Eye)
Denham Green. Buck 2B 38
Denham Street. Suff 3D 66
Denhead. Abers 5G 161 (nr. Ellon)
Denhead. Abers 3G 161 (nr. Strichen)
Denhead. Fife 2G 137
Denholm. Bord 3H 119
Denholme. W Yor 1A 92
Denholme Clough. W Yor 1A 92
Denholme Gate. W Yor 1A 92
Denio. Gwyn 2C 68
Denmead. Hants 1E 17
Dennington. Suff 4E 67
Denny. Falk 1B 128
Denny End. Cambs 4D 65
Dennyloanhead. Falk 1B 128
Den of Lindores. Fife 2E 137
Denshaw. G Man 3H 91
Denside. Abers 4F 153
Densole. Kent 1G 29
Denston. Suff 5G 65
Denstone. Staf 1F 73
Denstroude. Kent 4F 41
Dent. Cumb 1G 97
Den, The. N Ayr 4E 127
Denton. Cambs 2A 64
Denton. Darl 3F 105
Denton. E Sus 5F 27
Denton. G Man 1D 84
Denton. Kent 1G 29
Denton. Linc 2F 75
Denton. Norf 2E 67
Denton. Nptn 5F 63
Denton. N Yor 5D 98
Denton. Oxon 5D 50
Denver. Norf 5F 77
Denwick. Nmbd 3G 121
Deopham. Norf 5C 78
Deopham Green. Norf 1C 66
Depden. Suff 5G 65
Depden Green. Suff 5G 65
Deptford. G Lon 3E 39
Deptford. Wilts 3F 23
Derby. Derb 2A 74 & 194
Derbyhaven. IOM 5B 108
Derculich. Per 3F 143
Dereham. Norf 4B 78
Deri. Cphy 5E 47
Derril. Devn 2D 10
Derringstone. Kent 1G 29
Derrington. Shrp 1A 60
Derrington. Staf 3C 72
Derriton. Devn 2D 10
Derry. Derr 5A 174
Derryboye. Down 4J 179
Derrycrin. Cook 2D 178
Derrygonnelly. Ferm 7D 176
Derryguaig. Arg 5F 139
Derry Hill. Wilts 4E 35
Derrykeighan. Bmny 3F 175
Derrylin. Ferm 7H 177
Derrymacash. Cgvn 3E 178
Derrythorpe. N Lin 4B 94
Derrytrasna. Cgvn 3D 178
Dersingham. Norf 2F 77
Dervaig. Arg 3F 139
Dervock. Bmny 3F 175
Derwen. Den 5C 82
Derwen Gam. Cdgn 5D 56
Derwenlas. Powy 1G 57
Desborough. Nptn 2F 63
Desertmartin. Mag 7E 174
Desford. Leics 5B 74
Detchant. Nmbd 1E 121
Dethick. Derbs 5H 85
Detling. Kent 5B 40
Deuchar. Ang 2D 144
Deuddwr. Powy 4E 71
Devauden. Mon 2H 33
Devil's Bridge. Cdgn 3G 57
Devitts Green. Warw 1G 61
Devizes. Wilts 5F 35
Devonport. Plym 3A 8
Devonside. Clac 4B 136
Devoran. Corn 5B 6
Dewartown. Midl 3G 129
Dewlish. Dors 3C 14
Dewsall Court. Here 2H 47
Dewsbury. W Yor 2C 92
Dexbeer. Devn 2C 10
Dhoon. IOM 3D 108
Dhoor. IOM 2D 108
Dhowin. IOM 1D 108
Dial Green. W Sus 3A 26
Dial Post. W Sus 4C 26
Diamond, The. Cook 2D 178
Dibberford. Dors 2H 13
Dibden. Hants 2C 16
Dibden Purlieu. Hants 2C 16
Dickleburgh. Norf 2D 66
Didbrook. Glos 2F 49
Didcot. Oxon 2D 36
Diddington. Cambs 4A 64
Diddlebury. Shrp 2H 59
Didley. Here 2H 47
Didling. W Sus 1G 17
Didmarton. Glos 3D 34
Didsbury. G Man 1C 84
Didworthy. Devn 2C 8
Digby. Linc 5H 87
Digg. High 2D 154
Diggle. G Man 4A 92
Digmoor. Lanc 4C 90
Digswell. Herts 4C 52
Dihewyd. Cdgn 5D 57
Dilham. Norf 3F 79
Dilhorne. Staf 1D 72
Dillarburn. S Lan 5B 128
Dillington. Cambs 4A 64
Dilston. Nmbd 3C 114
Dilton Marsh. Wilts 2D 22
Dilwyn. Here 5G 59
Dimmer. Som 3B 22
Dimple. G Man 3F 91
Dinas. Carm 1G 43
Dinas. Gwyn 5D 81 (nr. Caernarfon)
Dinas. Gwyn 2B 68 (nr. Tudweiliog)
Dinas Cross. Pemb 1E 43
Dinas Dinlle. Gwyn 5D 80
Dinas Mawddwy. Gwyn 4A 70
Dinas Powys. V Glam 4E 33
Dinbych. Den 4C 82
Dinbych-y-Pysgod. Pemb 4F 43
Dinckley. Lanc 1E 91
Dinder. Som 2A 22
Dinedor. Here 2A 48
Dinedor Cross. Here 2A 48
Dingestow. Mon 4H 47
Dingle. Mers 2F 83
Dingleden. Kent 2C 28
Dingleton. Bord 1H 119
Dingley. Nptn 2E 63
Dingwall. High 3H 157
Dinmael. Cnwy 1C 70
Dinnet. Abers 4B 152
Dinnington. Som 1H 13
Dinnington. S Yor 2C 86
Dinnington. Tyne 2F 115
Dinorwig. Gwyn 4E 81
Dinton. Buck 4F 51
Dinton. Wilts 3F 23
Dinworthy. Devn 1D 10
Dipley. Hants 1F 25
Dippen. Arg 2B 122
Dippenhall. Surr 2G 25
Dippertown. Devn 4E 11
Dippin. N Ayr 3E 123
Dipple. S Ayr 4B 116
Diptford. Devn 3D 8
Dipton. Dur 4E 115
Dirleton. E Lot 1B 130
Dirt Pot. Nmbd 5B 114
Discoed. Powy 4E 59
Diseworth. Leics 3B 74
Dishes. Orkn 5F 172
Dishforth. N Yor 2F 99
Disley. Ches E 2D 85
Diss. Norf 3D 66
Disserth. Powy 5C 58
Distington. Cumb 2B 102
Ditchampton. Wilts 3F 23
Ditcheat. Som 3B 22
Ditchingham. Norf 1F 67
Ditchling. E Sus 4E 27
Ditteridge. Wilts 5D 34
Dittisham. Devn 3E 9
Ditton. Hal 2G 83
Ditton. Kent 5B 40
Ditton Green. Cambs 5F 65
Ditton Priors. Shrp 2A 60
Divach. High 1G 149
Dixonfield. High 2D 168
Dixton. Glos 2E 49
Dixton. Mon 4A 48
Dizzard. Corn 3B 10
Doagh. Newt 8J 175
Dobcross. G Man 4H 91
Dobs Hill. Flin 4F 83
Dobson's Bridge. Shrp 2G 71
Dobwalls. Corn 2G 7
Doccombe. Devn 4A 12
Dochgarroch. High 4A 158
Docking. Norf 2G 77
Docklow. Here 5H 59
Dockray. Cumb 2E 103
Doc Penfro. Pemb 4D 42 & 204
Dodbrooke. Devn 4D 8
Doddenham. Worc 5B 60
Doddinghurst. Essx 1G 39
Doddington. Cambs 1C 64
Doddington. Kent 5D 40
Doddington. Linc 4G 87
Doddington. Nmbd 1D 121
Doddington. Shrp 3A 60
Doddiscombsleigh. Devn 4B 12
Doddshill. Norf 2G 77
Dodford. Nptn 4D 62
Dodford. Worc 3D 60
Dodington. Som 2E 21
Dodington. S Glo 4C 34
Dodleston. Ches W 4F 83
Dods Leigh. Staf 2E 73
Dodworth. S Yor 4D 92
Doe Lea. Derbs 4B 86
Dogdyke. Linc 5B 88
Dogmersfield. Hants 1F 25
Dogsthorpe. Pet 5B 76
Dog Village. Devn 3C 12
Dolanog. Powy 4C 70
Dolau. Powy 4D 58
Dolau. Rhon 3D 32
Dolbenmaen. Gwyn 1E 69
Doley. Staf 3B 72
Dol-fâch. Powy 5B 70 (nr. Llanbrynmair)
Dolfach. Powy 3B 58 (nr. Llanidloes)
Dolfor. Powy 2D 58
Dolgarrog. Cnwy 4G 81
Dolgellau. Gwyn 4G 69
Dolgoch. Gwyn 5F 69
Dol-gran. Carm 2E 45
Dolhelfa. Powy 3B 58
Doll. High 3F 165
Dollar. Clac 4B 136
Dolley Green. Powy 4E 59
Dollingstown. Cgvn 4F 178
Dollwen. Cdgn 2F 57
Dolphin. Flin 3D 82
Dolphingstone. E Lot 2G 129
Dolphinholme. Lanc 4E 97
Dolphinton. S Lan 5E 129
Dolton. Devn 1F 11
Dolwen. Cnwy 3A 82
Dolwyddelan. Cnwy 5G 81
Dol-y-Bont. Cdgn 2F 57
Dolyhir. Powy 5E 59
Domgay. Powy 4E 71
Donagh. Ferm 7J 177
Donaghadee. Ards 2K 179
Donaghcloney. Cgvn 4F 178
Donaghmore. Dngn 3B 178
Doncaster. S Yor 4F 93
Donhead St Andrew. Wilts 4E 23
Donhead St Mary. Wilts 4E 23
Doniford. Som 2D 20
Donington. Linc 2B 76
Donington. Shrp 5C 72
Donington Eaudike. Linc 2B 76
Donington le Heath. Leics 4B 74
Donington on Bain. Linc 2B 88
Donington South Ing. Linc 2B 76
Donisthorpe. Leics 4H 73
Donkey Street. Kent 2F 29
Donkey Town. Surr 4A 38
Donna Nook. Linc 1D 88
Donnington. Glos 3G 49
Donnington. Here 2C 48
Donnington. Shrp 5H 71
Donnington. Telf 4B 72
Donnington. W Ber 5C 36
Donnington. W Sus 2G 17
Donyatt. Som 1G 13
Doomsday Green. W Sus 2C 26
Doonfoot. S Ayr 3C 116
Doonholm. S Ayr 3C 116
Dorback Lodge. High 2E 151
Dorchester. Dors 3B 14
Dorchester on Thames. Oxon 2D 36
Dordon. Warw 5G 73
Dore. S Yor 2H 85
Dores. High 5H 157
Dorking. Surr 1C 26
Dorking Tye. Suff 2C 54
Dormansland. Surr 1F 27
Dormans Park. Surr 1E 27
Dormanstown. Red C 2C 106
Dormington. Here 1A 48
Dormston. Worc 5D 61
Dorn. Glos 2H 49
Dorney. Buck 3A 38
Dornie. High 1A 148
Dornoch. High 5E 165
Dornock. Dum 3D 112
Dorrery. High 3C 168
Dorridge. W Mid 3F 61
Dorrington. Linc 5H 87
Dorrington. Shrp 5G 71
Dorsington. Warw 1G 49
Dorstone. Here 1G 47
Dorton. Buck 4E 51
Dosthill. Staf 5G 73
Dotham. IOA 3C 80
Dottery. Dors 3H 13
Doublebois. Corn 2F 7
Dougarie. N Ayr 2C 122
Doughton. Glos 2D 35
Douglas. IOM 4C 108
Douglas. S Lan 1H 117
Douglas Bridge. Strab 3F 176
Douglastown. Ang 4D 144
Douglas Water. S Lan 1A 118
Doulting. Som 2B 22
Dounby. Orkn 5B 172
Doune. High 3C 150 (nr. Kingussie)
Doune. High 3B 164 (nr. Lairg)
Doune. Stir 3G 135
Dounie. High 4C 164 (nr. Bonar Bridge)
Dounie. High 5D 164 (nr. Tain)
Dounreay. High 2B 168
Doura. N Ayr 5E 127
Dousland. Devn 2B 8
Dovaston. Shrp 3F 71
Dove Holes. Derbs 3E 85
Dovenby. Cumb 1B 102
Dover. Kent 1H 29 & 194
Dovercourt. Essx 2F 55
Doverdale. Worc 4C 60
Doveridge. Derbs 2F 73
Doversgreen. Surr 1D 26
Dowally. Per 4H 143
Dowbridge. Lanc 1C 90
Dowdeswell. Glos 4F 49
Dowlais. Mer T 5D 46
Dowland. Devn 1F 11
Dowlands. Devn 3F 13
Dowles. Worc 3B 60
Dowlesgreen. Wok 5G 37
Dowlish Wake. Som 1G 13
Downall Green. Mers 4D 90
Down Ampney. Glos 2F 35
Downderry. Corn 3H 7 (nr. Looe)
Downderry. Corn 3D 6 (nr. St Austell)
Downe. G Lon 4F 39
Downend. IOW 4D 16
Downend. S Glo 4B 34
Downend. W Ber 4C 36
Down Field. Cambs 3F 65
Downfield. D'dee 5C 144
Downgate. Corn 5D 10 (nr. Kelly Bray)
Downgate. Corn 5C 10 (nr. Upton Cross)
Downham. Essx 1B 40
Downham. Lanc 5G 97
Downham. Nmbd 1C 120
Downham Market. Norf 5F 77
Down Hatherley. Glos 3D 48
Downhead. Som 2B 22 (nr. Frome)
Downhead. Som 4A 22 (nr. Yeovil)
Downhill. Cole 3D 174
Downholland Cross. Lanc 4B 90
Downholme. N Yor 5E 105
Downies. Abers 4G 153
Downley. Buck 2G 37
Downpatrick. Down 5J 179
Down St Mary. Devn 2H 11
Downside. Som 1B 22 (nr. Chilcompton)
Downside. Som 2B 22 (nr. Shepton Mallet)
Downside. Surr 5C 38
Down, The. Shrp 1A 60
Down Thomas. Devn 3B 8
Downton. Hants 3A 16
Downton. Wilts 4G 23
Downton on the Rock. Here 3G 59
Dowsby. Linc 3A 76
Dowsdale. Linc 4B 76
Dowthwaitehead. Cumb 2E 103
Doxey. Staf 3D 72
Doxford. Nmbd 2F 121
Doynton. S Glo 4C 34
Drabblegate. Norf 3E 78
Draethen. Cphy 3F 33
Draffan. S Lan 5A 128
Dragonby. N Lin 3C 94
Dragons Green. W Sus 3C 26
Drakelow. Worc 2C 60
Drakemyre. N Ayr 4D 126
Drakes Broughton. Worc 1E 49
Drakes Cross. Worc 3E 61
Drakewalls. Corn 5E 11
Draperstown. Mag 7D 174
Draughton. Nptn 3E 63
Draughton. N Yor 4C 98
Drax. N Yor 2G 93
Draycot. Oxon 5E 51
Draycote. Warw 4B 62
Draycot Foliat. Swin 4G 35
Draycott. Derbs 2B 74
Draycott. Glos 2G 49
Draycott. Shrp 1C 60
Draycott. Som 1H 21 (nr. Cheddar)
Draycott. Som 4A 22 (nr. Yeovil)
Draycott. Worc 1D 48
Draycott in the Clay. Staf 3F 73
Draycott in the Moors. Staf 1D 73
Drayford. Devn 1A 12
Drayton. Leics 1F 63
Drayton. Linc 2B 76
Drayton. Norf 4D 78
Drayton. Nptn 4C 62
Drayton. Oxon 2C 36 (nr. Abingdon)
Drayton. Oxon 1C 50 (nr. Banbury)
Drayton. Port 2E 17
Drayton. Som 4H 21
Drayton. Warw 5F 61
Drayton. Worc 3D 60
Drayton Bassett. Staf 5F 73
Drayton Beauchamp. Buck 4H 51
Drayton Parslow. Buck 3G 51
Drayton St Leonard. Oxon 2D 36
Drebley. N Yor 4C 98
Dreenhill. Pemb 3D 42
Drefach. Carm 4F 45 (nr. Meidrim)
Drefach. Carm 2D 44 (nr. Newcastle Emlyn)
Drefach. Carm 2G 43 (nr. Tumble)
Drefach. Cdgn 1E 45
Dreghorn. N Ayr 1C 116
Drellingore. Kent 1G 29
Drem. E Lot 2B 130
Dreumasdal. W Isl 5C 170
Drewsteignton. Devn 3H 11
Driby. Linc 3C 88
Driffield. E Yor 4E 101
Driffield. Glos 2F 35
Drift. Corn 4B 4
Drigg. Cumb 5B 102
Drighlington. W Yor 2C 92
Drimnin. High 3G 139
Drimpton. Dors 2H 13
Dringhoe. E Yor 4F 101
Drinisiadar. W Isl 8D 171
Drinkstone. Suff 4B 66
Drinkstone Green. Suff 4B 66
Drointon. Staf 3E 73
Droitwich Spa. Worc 4C 60
Droman. High 3B 166
Dromara. Lis 5G 179
Dromore. Ban 4G 179
Dromore. Omag 6F 176
Dron. Per 2D 136
Dronfield. Derbs 3A 86
Dronfield Woodhouse. Derbs 3H 85
Drongan. E Ayr 3D 116
Dronley. Ang 5C 144
Droop. Dors 2C 14
Drope. V Glam 4E 32
Droxford. Hants 1E 16
Droylsden. G Man 1C 84
Druggers End. Worc 2C 48
Druid. Den 1C 70
Druid's Heath. W Mid 5E 73
Druidston. Pemb 3C 42
Druim. High 3D 158
Druimarbin. High 1E 141
Druim Fhearna. High 2E 147
Druimindarroch. High 5E 147
Druim Saighdinis. W Isl 2D 170
Drum. Per 3C 136
Drumaness. Down 5H 179
Drumaroad. Down 5H 179
Drumbeg. High 5B 166
Drumblade. Abers 4C 160
Drumbo. Lis 3H 179
Drumbuie. Dum 1C 110
Drumbuie. High 5G 155
Drumburgh. Cumb 4D 112
Drumburn. Dum 3A 112
Drumchapel. Glas 2G 127
Drumchardine. High 4H 157
Drumchork. High 5C 162
Drumclog. S Lan 1F 117
Drumeldrie. Fife 3G 137
Drumelzier. Bord 1D 118
Drumfearn. High 2E 147
Drumgask. High 4A 150
Drumgelloch. N Lan 3A 128
Drumgley. Ang 3D 144
Drumguish. High 4B 150
Drumin. Mor 5F 159
Drumindorsair. High 4G 157
Drumintee. New M 8E 178
Drumlamford House. S Ayr 2H 109
Drumlasie. Abers 3D 152
Drumlemble. Arg 4A 122
Drumlithie. Abers 5E 153
Drummoddie. Dum 5A 110
Drummond. High 2A 158
Drummore. Dum 5E 109
Drummuir. Mor 4A 160
Drumnacanvy. Cgvn 4E 178
Drumnadrochit. High 5H 157
Drumnagorrach. Mor 3C 160
Drumnakilly. Omag 2L 177
Drumoak. Abers 4E 153
Drumquin. Omag 5F 176
Drumraighland. Lim 4C 174
Drumrunie. High 3F 163
Drumry. W Dun 2G 127
Drums. Abers 1G 153
Drumsleet. Dum 2G 111
Drumsmittal. High 4A 158
Drums of Park. Abers 3C 160
Drumsturdy. Ang 5D 145
Drumsurn. Lim 5D 174
Drumtochty Castle. Abers 5D 152
Drumuie. High 4D 154
Drumuillie. High 1D 150
Drumvaich. Stir 3F 135
Drumwhindle. Abers 5G 161
Drunkendub. Ang 4F 145
Drury. Flin 4E 83
Drury Square. Norf 4B 78
Drybeck. Cumb 3H 103
Drybridge. Mor 2B 160
Drybridge. N Ayr 1C 116
Drybrook. Glos 4B 48
Drybrook. Here 4A 48
Dryburgh. Bord 1H 119
Dry Doddington. Linc 1F 75
Dry Drayton. Cambs 4C 64
Drym. Corn 3D 4
Drymen. Stir 1F 127
Drymuir. Abers 4G 161
Drynachan Lodge. High 5C 158
Drynie Park. High 3H 157
Drynoch. High 5D 154
Dry Sandford. Oxon 5C 50
Dryslwyn. Carm 3F 45
Dry Street. Essx 2A 40
Dryton. Shrp 5H 71
Dubford. Abers 2E 161
Dubiton. Abers 3D 160
Dubton. Ang 3E 145
Duchally. High 2A 164
Duck End. Essx 3G 53
Duckington. Ches W 5G 83
Ducklington. Oxon 5B 50
Duckmanton. Derbs 3B 86
Duck Street. Hants 2B 24
Dudbridge. Glos 5D 48
Duddenhoe End. Essx 2E 53
Duddingston. Edin 2F 129
Duddington. Nptn 5G 75
Duddleswell. E Sus 3F 27
Duddo. Nmbd 5F 131
Duddon. Ches W 4H 83
Duddon Bridge. Cumb 1A 96
Dudleston. Shrp 2F 71
Dudleston Heath. Shrp 2F 71
Dudley. Tyne 2F 115
Dudley. W Mid 2D 60
Dudston. Shrp 1E 59
Dudwells. Pemb 2D 42
Duffield. Derbs 1H 73
Duffryn. Neat 2B 32
Dufftown. Mor 4H 159
Duffus. Mor 2F 159
Dufton. Cumb 2H 103
Duggleby. N Yor 3C 100
Duirinish. High 5G 155
Duisdalemore. High 2E 147
Duisdeil Mòr. High 2E 147
Duisky. High 1E 141
Dukesfield. Nmbd 4C 114
Dukestown. Blae 5E 47
Dukinfield. G Man 1D 84
Dulas. IOA 2D 81
Dulcote. Som 2A 22
Dulford. Devn 2D 12
Dull. Per 4F 143
Dullatur. N Lan 2A 128
Dullingham. Cambs 5F 65
Dullingham Ley. Cambs 5F 65
Dulnain Bridge. High 1D 151
Duloe. Bed 4A 64
Duloe. Corn 3G 7
Dulverton. Som 4C 20
Dulwich. G Lon 3E 39
Dumbarton. W Dun 2F 127
Dumbleton. Glos 2F 49
Dumfin. Arg 1E 127
Dumfries. Dum 2A 112 & 194
Dumgoyne. Stir 1G 127
Dummer. Hants 2D 24
Dumpford. W Sus 4G 25
Dun. Ang 2F 145
Dunadry. Ant 1F 179
Dunaghy. Bmny 4F 175
Dunagoil. Arg 4B 126
Dunalastair. Per 3E 142
Dunan. High 1D 147
Dunball. Som 2G 21
Dunbar. E Lot 2C 130
Dunbeath. High 5D 168
Dunbeg. Arg 5C 140
Dunblane. Stir 3G 135
Dunbog. Fife 2E 137
Dunbridge. Hants 4B 24
Duncanston. Abers 1C 152
Duncanston. High 3H 157
Dun Charlabhaigh. W Isl 3D 171
Dunchideock. Devn 4B 12
Dunchurch. Warw 3B 62
Duncote. Nptn 5D 62
Duncow. Dum 1A 112
Duncrievie. Per 3D 136
Duncton. W Sus 4A 26
Dundee. D'dee 5D 144 & 194
Dundee Airport. D'dee 1F 137
Dundon. Som 3H 21
Dundonald. Cast 2J 179
Dundonald. S Ayr 1C 116
Dundonnell. High 5E 163
Dundraw. Cumb 5D 112
Dundreggan. High 2F 149
Dundrennan. Dum 5E 111
Dundridge. Hants 1D 16
Dundrod. Lis 2G 179
Dundrum. Down 6J 179
Dundry. N Som 5A 34
Dunecht. Abers 3E 153
Dunfermline. Fife 1D 129
Dunford Bridge. S Yor 4B 92
Dungannon. Dngn 3B 178
Dungate. Kent 5D 40
Dunge. Wilts 1D 23
Dungeness. Kent 4E 29
Dungiven. Lim 6C 174
Dungworth. S Yor 2G 85
Dunham-on-the-Hill. Ches W 3G 83
Dunham-on-Trent. Notts 3F 87
Dunhampton. Worc 4C 60
Dunham Town. G Man 2B 84
Dunham Woodhouses. G Man 2B 84
Dunholme. Linc 3H 87
Dunino. Fife 2H 137
Dunipace. Falk 1B 128
Dunira. Per 1G 135
Dunkeld. Per 4H 143
Dunkerton. Bath 1C 22
Dunkeswell. Devn 2E 13
Dunkeswick. N Yor 5F 99
Dunkirk. Kent 5E 41
Dunkirk. S Glo 3C 34
Dunkirk. Staf 5C 84
Dunkirk. Wilts 5E 35
Dunk's Green. Kent 5H 39
Dunlappie. Ang 2E 145
Dunley. Hants 1C 24
Dunley. Worc 4B 60
Dunlichity Lodge. High 5A 158
Dunlop. E Ayr 5F 127
Dunloy. Bmny 5G 175
Dunmaglass Lodge. High 1H 149
Dunmore. Arg 3F 125
Dunmore. Falk 1B 128
Dunmore. High 4H 157
Dunmurry. Lis 3G 179
Dunnamanagh. Strab 6A 174
Dunnaval. New M 8G 179
Dunnet. High 1E 169
Dunnichen. Ang 4E 145
Dunning. Per 2C 136
Dunnington. E Yor 4F 101
Dunnington. Warw 5E 61
Dunnington. York 4A 100
Dunningwell. Cumb 1A 96
Dunnockshaw. Lanc 2G 91
Dunoon. Arg 2C 126
Dunphail. Mor 4E 159
Dunragit. Dum 4G 109
Dunrostan. Arg 1F 125
Duns. Bord 4D 130
Dunsby. Linc 3A 76
Dunscar. G Man 3F 91
Dunscore. Dum 1F 111
Dunscroft. S Yor 4G 93
Dunsdale. Red C 3D 106
Dunsden Green. Oxon 4F 37
Dunsfold. Surr 2B 26
Dunsford. Devn 4B 12
Dunshalt. Fife 2E 137
Dunshillock. Abers 4G 161
Dunsley. N Yor 3F 107
Dunsley. Staf 2C 60
Dunsmore. Buck 5G 51
Dunsop Bridge. Lanc 4F 97
Dunstable. C Beds 3A 52
Dunstal. Staf 3E 73
Dunstall. Staf 3F 73
Dunstall Green. Suff 4G 65
Dunstall Hill. W Mid 1D 60
Dunstan. Nmbd 3G 121
Dunster. Som 2C 20
Duns Tew. Oxon 3C 50
Dunston. Linc 4H 87
Dunston. Norf 5E 79
Dunston. Staf 4D 72
Dunston. Tyne 3F 115
Dunstone. Devn 3B 8
Dunston Heath. Staf 4D 72
Dunsville. S Yor 4G 93
Dunswell. E Yor 1D 94
Dunsyre. S Lan 5D 128
Dunterton. Devn 5D 11
Duntisbourne Abbots. Glos 5E 49
Duntisbourne Leer. Glos 5E 49
Duntisbourne Rouse. Glos 5E 49
Duntish. Dors 2B 14
Duntocher. W Dun 2F 127
Dunton. Buck 3G 51
Dunton. C Beds 1C 52
Dunton. Norf 2A 78
Dunton Bassett. Leics 1C 62
Dunton Green. Kent 5G 39
Dunton Patch. Norf 2A 78
Duntulm. High 1D 154
Dunure. S Ayr 3B 116
Dunvant. Swan 3E 31
Dunvegan. High 4B 154
Dunwich. Suff 3G 67
Dunwood. Staf 5D 84
Durdar. Cumb 4F 113
Durgates. E Sus 2H 27
Durham. Dur 5F 115 & 194
Durham Tees Valley Airport. Darl 3A 106
Durisdeer. Dum 4A 118
Durisdeermill. Dum 4A 118
Durkar. W Yor 3D 92
Durleigh. Som 3F 21
Durley. Hants 1D 16
Durley. Wilts 5H 35
Durley Street. Hants 1D 16
Durlow Common. Here 2B 48
Durnamuck. High 4E 163
Durness. High 2E 166
Durno. Abers 1E 152
Durns Town. Hants 3A 16
Duror. High 3D 141
Durran. Arg 3G 133
Durran. High 2D 169
Durrant Green. Kent 2C 28
Durrants. Hants 1F 17
Durrington. W Sus 5C 26
Durrington. Wilts 2G 23
Dursley. Glos 2C 34
Dursley Cross. Glos 4B 48
Durston. Som 4F 21
Durweston. Dors 2D 14
Dury. Shet 6F 173
Duston. Nptn 4E 62
Duthil. High 1D 150
Dutlas. Powy 3E 58
Duton Hill. Essx 3G 53
Dutson. Corn 4D 10
Dutton. Ches W 3H 83
Duxford. Cambs 1E 53
Duxford. Oxon 2B 36
Dwygyfylchi. Cnwy 3G 81
Dwyran. IOA 4D 80
Dyce. Aber 2F 153
Dyffryn. B'end 2B 32
Dyffryn. Carm 2H 43
Dyffryn. Pemb 1D 42
Dyffryn. V Glam 4D 32
Dyffryn Ardudwy. Gwyn 3E 69
Dyffryn Castell. Cdgn 2G 57
Dyffryn Ceidrych. Carm 3H 45
Dyffryn Cellwen. Neat 5B 46
Dyke. Linc 3A 76
Dyke. Mor 3D 159
Dykehead. Ang 2C 144
Dykehead. N Lan 3B 128
Dykehead. Stir 4E 135
Dykend. Ang 3B 144
Dykesfield. Cumb 4E 112
Dylife. Powy 1A 58
Dymchurch. Kent 3F 29
Dymock. Glos 2C 48
Dyrham. S Glo 4C 34
Dysart. Fife 4F 137
Dyserth. Den 3C 82

E

Eachwick. Nmbd 2E 115
Eadar Dha Fhadhail. W Isl 4C 171
Eagland Hill. Lanc 5D 96
Eagle. Linc 4F 87
Eagle Barnsdale. Linc 4F 87
Eagle Moor. Linc 4F 87
Eaglescliffe. Stoc T 3B 106
Eaglesfield. Cumb 2B 102
Eaglesfield. Dum 2D 112
Eaglesham. E Ren 4G 127
Eaglethorpe. Nptn 1H 63
Eagley. G Man 3F 91
Eairy. IOM 4B 108
Eakley Lanes. Mil 5F 63
Eakring. Notts 4D 86
Ealand. N Lin 3A 94
Ealing. G Lon 2C 38
Eallabus. Arg 3B 124
Eals. Nmbd 4H 113
Eamont Bridge. Cumb 2G 103
Earby. Lanc 5B 98
Earcroft. Bkbn 2E 91
Eardington. Shrp 1B 60
Eardisland. Here 5G 59
Eardisley. Here 1G 47
Eardiston. Shrp 3F 71
Eardiston. Worc 4A 60
Earith. Cambs 3C 64
Earlais. High 2C 154
Earle. Nmbd 2D 121
Earlesfield. Linc 2G 75
Earlestown. Mers 1H 83
Earley. Wok 4F 37
Earlham. Norf 5D 78
Earlish. High 2C 154
Earls Barton. Nptn 4F 63
Earls Colne. Essx 3B 54
Earls Common. Worc 5D 60
Earl's Croome. Worc 1D 48
Earlsdon. W Mid 3H 61
Earlsferry. Fife 3G 137
Earlsford. Abers 5F 161
Earl's Green. Suff 4C 66
Earlsheaton. W Yor 2C 92
Earl Shilton. Leics 1B 62
Earl Soham. Suff 4E 67
Earl Sterndale. Derbs 4E 85
Earlston. E Ayr 1D 116
Earlston. Bord 1H 119
Earl Stonham. Suff 5D 66
Earlstoun. Dum 1D 110
Earlswood. Mon 2H 33
Earlswood. Warw 3F 61
Earlyvale. Bord 4F 129
Earnley. W Sus 3G 17
Earsairidh. W Isl 9C 170
Earsdon. Tyne 2G 115
Earsham. Norf 2F 67
Earsham Street. Suff 3E 67
Earswick. York 4A 100
Eartham. W Sus 5A 26
Earthcott Green. S Glo 3B 34
Easby. N Yor 4C 106 (nr. Great Ayton)
Easby. N Yor 4E 105 (nr. Richmond)
Easdale. Arg 2E 133
Easebourne. W Sus 4G 25
Easenhall. Warw 3B 62
Eashing. Surr 1A 26
Easington. Buck 4E 51
Easington. Dur 5H 115
Easington. E Yor 3G 95
Easington. Nmbd 1F 121
Easington. Oxon 2C 50 (nr. Banbury)
Easington. Oxon 2E 37 (nr. Watlington)
Easington. Red C 3E 107
Easington Colliery. Dur 5H 115
Easington Lane. Tyne 5G 115
Easingwold. N Yor 3H 99
Eassie. Ang 4C 144
Eassie and Nevay. Ang 4C 144
East Aberthaw. V Glam 5D 32
Eastacombe. Devn 4F 19
Eastacott. Devn 4G 19
East Allington. Devn 4D 8
East Anstey. Devn 4B 20
East Anton. Hants 2B 24
East Appleton. N Yor 5F 105
East Ardsley. W Yor 2D 92
East Ashley. Devn 1G 11
East Ashling. W Sus 2G 17
East Aston. Hants 2C 24
East Ayton. N Yor 1D 101
East Barkwith. Linc 2A 88
East Barnby. N Yor 3F 107
East Barnet. G Lon 1D 39
East Barns. E Lot 2D 130
East Barsham. Norf 2B 78
East Beach. W Sus 3G 17
East Beckham. Norf 1D 78
East Bedfont. G Lon 3B 38
East Bennan. N Ayr 3D 123
East Bergholt. Suff 2D 54
East Bierley. W Yor 2B 92
East Bilney. Norf 4B 78
East Blatchington. E Sus 5F 27
East Bloxworth. Dors 3D 15
East Boldre. Hants 2B 16
East Bolton. Nmbd 3F 121
Eastbourne. Darl 3F 105
Eastbourne. E Sus 5H 27 & 194
East Brent. Som 1G 21
East Bridge. Suff 4G 67
East Bridgford. Notts 1D 74
East Briscoe. Dur 3C 104
East Buckland. Devn 3G 19 (nr. Barnstaple)
East Buckland. Devn 4C 8 (nr. Thurlestone)
East Budleigh. Devn 4D 12
Eastburn. W Yor 5C 98
East Burnham. Buck 2A 38
East Burrafirth. Shet 6E 173
East Burton. Dors 4D 14
Eastbury. Herts 1B 38
Eastbury. W Ber 4B 36
East Butsfield. Dur 5E 115
East Butterleigh. Devn 2C 12
East Butterwick. N Lin 4B 94
Eastby. N Yor 4C 98
East Calder. W Lot 3D 129
East Carleton. Norf 5D 78
East Carlton. Nptn 2F 63
East Carlton. W Yor 5E 98
East Chaldon. Dors 4C 14
East Challow. Oxon 3B 36
East Charleton. Devn 4D 8
East Chelborough. Dors 2A 14
East Chiltington. E Sus 4E 27
East Chinnock. Som 1H 13
East Chisenbury. Wilts 1G 23
Eastchurch. Kent 3D 40
East Clandon. Surr 5B 38
East Claydon. Buck 3F 51
East Clevedon. N Som 4H 33
East Clyne. High 3F 165
East Clyth. High 5E 169
East Coker. Som 1A 14
Eastcombe. Glos 5D 49
East Combe. Som 3E 21
East Common. N Yor 1G 93
East Compton. Som 2B 22
East Cornworthy. Devn 3E 9
Eastcote. G Lon 2C 38
Eastcote. Nptn 5D 62
Eastcote. W Mid 3F 61
Eastcott. Corn 1C 10
Eastcott. Wilts 1F 23
East Cottingwith. E Yor 5B 100
Eastcourt. Wilts 5H 35 (nr. Pewsey)
Eastcourt. Wilts 2E 35 (nr. Tetbury)
East Cowes. IOW 3D 16
East Cowick. E Yor 2G 93
East Cowton. N Yor 4A 106
East Cramlington. Nmbd 2F 115
East Cranmore. Som 2B 22
East Creech. Dors 4E 15
East Croachy. High 1A 150
East Dean. E Sus 5G 27
East Dean. Glos 3B 48
East Dean. Hants 4A 24
East Dean. W Sus 4A 26
East Down. Devn 2G 19
East Drayton. Notts 3E 87
East Dundry. N Som 5A 34
East Ella. Hull 2D 94
East End. Cambs 3C 64
East End. Dors 3E 15
East End. E Yor 4F 101 (nr. Ulrome)
East End. E Yor 2F 95 (nr. Withernsea)
East End. Hants 3B 16 (nr. Lymington)
East End. Hants 5C 36 (nr. Newbury)
East End. Herts 3E 53
East End. Kent 3D 40 (nr. Minster)
East End. Kent 2C 28 (nr. Tenterden)
East End. N Som 4H 33
East End. Oxon 4B 50
East End. Som 1A 22
East End. Suff 2E 54
Easter Ardross. High 1A 158
Easter Balgedie. Per 3D 136
Easter Balmoral. Abers 4G 151
Easter Brae. High 2A 158
Easter Buckieburn. Stir 1A 128
Easter Bush. Midl 3F 129
Easter Compton. S Glo 3A 34
Easter Fearn. High 5D 164
Easter Galcantray. High 4C 158
Eastergate. W Sus 5A 26
Easterhouse. Glas 3H 127
Easter Howgate. Midl 3F 129
Easter Kinkell. High 3H 157
Easter Lednathie. Ang 2C 144
Easter Ogil. Ang 2D 144
Easter Ord. Abers 3F 153

F

Firby—Golant

Firby. N Yor 1E 99
(nr. Bedale)
Firby. N Yor 3B 100
(nr. Malton)
Firgrove. G Man 3H 91
Firle. E Sus 5F 27
Firsby. Linc 4D 88
Firsdown. Wilts 3H 23
First Coast. High 4D 162
Firth. Shet 4F 173
Fir Tree. Dur 1E 105
Fishbourne. IOW 3D 16
Fishbourne. W Sus 2G 17
Fishburn. Dur 1A 106
Fishcross. Clac 4B 136
Fisherford. Abers 5D 160
Fisherrow. E Lot 2G 129
Fisher's Pond. Hants 4C 24
Fisher's Row. Lanc 5D 96
Fisherstreet. W Sus 2A 26
Fisherton. High 3B 158
Fisherton. S Ayr 3B 116
Fisherton de la Mere. Wilts 3E 23
Fishguard. Pemb 1D 42
Fishlake. S Yor 3G 93
Fishley. Norf 4G 79
Fishnish. Arg 4A 140
Fishpond Bottom. Dors 3G 13
Fishponds. Bris 4B 34
Fishpool. Glos 3B 48
Fishpool. G Man 4G 91
Fishpools. Powy 4D 58
Fishtoft. Linc 1C 76
Fishtoft Drove. Linc 1C 76
Fishwick. Bord 4F 131
Fiskavaig. High 5C 154
Fiskerton. Linc 3H 87
Fiskerton. Notts 5E 87
Fitch. Shet 7E 173
Fitling. E Yor 1F 95
Fittleton. Wilts 2G 23
Fittleworth. W Sus 4B 26
Fitton End. Cambs 4D 76
Fitz. Shrp 4G 71
Fitzhead. Som 4E 20
Fitzwilliam. W Yor 3E 93
Fiunary. High 4A 140
Five Ash Down. E Sus 3F 27
Five Ashes. E Sus 3G 27
Five Bells. Som 2D 20
Five Bridges. Here 1B 48
Fivehead. Som 4G 21
Five Lane Ends. Lanc 4E 97
Fivelanes. Corn 4C 10
Fivemiletown. Dngn 5K 177
Five Oak Green. Kent 1H 27
Five Oaks. W Sus 3B 26
Five Roads. Carm 5E 45
Five Ways. Warw 3G 61
Flack's Green. Essx 4A 54
Flackwell Heath. Buck 3G 37
Fladbury. Worc 1E 49
Fladda. Shet 3E 173
Fladdabister. Shet 8F 173
Flagg. Derbs 4F 85
Flamborough. E Yor 2G 101
Flamstead. Herts 4A 52
Flansham. W Sus 5A 26
Flasby. N Yor 4B 98
Flash. Staf 4E 85
Flashader. High 3C 154
Flatt, The. Cumb 2G 113
Flaunden. Herts 5A 52
Flawborough. Notts 1E 75
Flawith. N Yor 3G 99
Flax Bourton. N Som 5A 34
Flaxby. N Yor 4F 99
Flaxholme. Derbs 1H 73
Flaxley. Glos 4B 48
Flaxley Green. Staf 4E 73
Flaxpool. Som 3E 21
Flaxton. N Yor 3A 100
Fleck. Shet 10E 173
Fleckney. Leics 1D 62
Flecknoe. Warw 4C 62
Fledborough. Notts 3F 87
Fleet. Dors 4B 14
Fleet. Hants 1G 25
(nr. Farnborough)
Fleet. Hants 2F 17
(nr. South Hayling)
Fleet. Linc 3C 76
Fleet Hargate. Linc 3C 76
Fleetville. Herts 5B 52
Fleetwood. Lanc 5C 96
Fleggburgh. Norf 4G 79
Fleisirin. W Isl 4H 171
Flemingston. V Glam 4D 32
Flemington. S Lan 3H 127
(nr. Glasgow)
Flemington. S Lan 5A 128
(nr. Strathaven)
Flempton. Suff 4H 65
Fleoideabhagh. W Isl 9C 171
Fletcher's Green. Kent 1G 27
Fletchertown. Cumb 5D 112
Fletching. E Sus 3F 27
Fleuchary. High 4E 165
Flexbury. Corn 2C 10
Flexford. Surr 5A 38
Flimby. Cumb 1B 102
Flimwell. E Sus 2B 28
Flint. Flin 3E 83
Flintham. Notts 1E 75
Flint Mountain. Flin 3E 83
Flinton. E Yor 1F 95
Flintsham. Here 5F 59
Flishinghurst. Kent 2B 28
Flitcham. Norf 3G 77
Flitton. C Beds 2A 52
Flitwick. C Beds 2A 52
Flixborough. N Lin 3B 94
Flixton. G Man 1B 84
Flixton. N Yor 2E 101
Flixton. Suff 2F 67
Flockton. W Yor 3C 92
Flodden. Nmbd 1D 120
Flodigarry. High 1D 154
Flood's Ferry. Cambs 1C 64
Flookburgh. Cumb 2C 96
Flordon. Norf 1D 66
Flore. Nptn 4D 62
Flotterton. Nmbd 4E 121
Flowton. Suff 1D 54
Flushing. Abers 4H 161
Flushing. Corn 5C 6
Fluxton. Devn 3D 12
Flyford Flavell. Worc 5D 61
Fobbing. Thur 2B 40
Fochabers. Mor 3H 159
Fochriw. Cphy 5E 46
Fockerby. N Lin 3B 94
Fodderty. High 3H 157
Foddington. Som 4A 22
Foel. Powy 4B 70
Foffarty. Ang 4D 144
Foggathorpe. E Yor 1A 94
Fogo. Bord 5D 130
Fogorig. Bord 5D 130
Foindle. High 4B 166
Folda. Ang 2A 144
Fole. Staf 2E 73
Foleshill. W Mid 2A 62
Foley Park. Worc 3C 60
Folke. Dors 1B 14
Folkestone. Kent 2G 29 & 195
Folkingham. Linc 2H 75
Folkington. E Sus 5G 27
Folksworth. Cambs 1A 64
Folkton. N Yor 2E 101
Folla Rule. Abers 5E 161
Follifoot. N Yor 4F 99
Folly Gate. Devn 3F 11
Folly, The. Herts 4B 52
Folly, The. W Ber 5C 36
Fonmon. V Glam 5D 32
Fonthill Bishop. Wilts 3E 23
Fonthill Gifford. Wilts 3E 23
Fontmell Magna. Dors 1D 14
Fontwell. W Sus 5A 26
Font-y-gary. V Glam 5D 32
Foodieash. Fife 2F 137
Foolow. Derbs 3F 85
Footdee. Aber 3G 153
Footherley. Staf 5F 73
Foots Cray. G Lon 3F 39
Forbestown. Abers 2A 152
Force Forge. Cumb 5E 103
Force Mills. Cumb 5E 103
Forcett. N Yor 3E 105
Ford. Arg 3F 133
Ford. Buck 5F 51
Ford. Derbs 2B 86
Ford. Devn 4E 19
(nr. Bideford)
Ford. Devn 3C 8
(nr. Holbeton)
Ford. Devn 4D 9
(nr. Salcombe)
Ford. Glos 3F 49
Ford. Nmbd 1D 120
Ford. Plym 3A 8
Ford. Shrp 4G 71
Ford. Som 1A 22
(nr. Wells)
Ford. Som 4D 20
(nr. Wiveliscombe)
Ford. Staf 5E 85
Ford. W Sus 5B 26
Ford. Wilts 4D 34
(nr. Chippenham)
Ford. Wilts 3G 23
(nr. Salisbury)
Forda. Devn 3E 19
Ford Barton. Devn 1C 12
Fordcombe. Kent 1G 27
Fordell. Fife 1E 129
Forden. Powy 5E 71
Ford End. Essx 4G 53
Forder Green. Devn 2D 9
Ford Green. Lanc 5D 97
Fordham. Cambs 3F 65
Fordham. Essx 3C 54
Fordham. Norf 1F 65
Fordham Heath. Essx 3C 54
Ford Heath. Shrp 4G 71
Fordhouses. W Mid 5D 72
Fordie. Per 1G 135
Fordingbridge. Hants 1G 15
Fordington. Linc 3D 88
Fordon. E Yor 2E 101
Fordoun. Abers 1G 145
Ford Street. Essx 3C 54
Ford Street. Som 1E 13
Fordton. Devn 3B 12
Fordwells. Oxon 4B 50
Fordwich. Kent 5F 41
Fordyce. Abers 2C 160
Forebridge. Staf 3D 72
Foremark. Derbs 3H 73
Forest. N Yor 4F 105
Forestburn Gate. Nmbd 5E 121
Foresterseat. Mor 3F 159
Forest Green. Glos 2D 34
Forest Green. Surr 1C 26
Forest Hall. Cumb 4G 103
Forest Head. Cumb 4G 113
Forest Hill. Oxon 5D 50
Forest-in-Teesdale. Dur 2B 104
Forest Lodge. Per 1G 143
Forest Mill. Clac 4B 136
Forest Row. E Sus 2F 27
Forestside. W Sus 1F 17
Forest Town. Notts 4C 86
Forfar. Ang 3D 144
Forgandenny. Per 2C 136
Forge. Powy 1G 57
Forge Side. Torf 5F 47
Forge, The. Here 5F 59
Forgewood. N Lan 4A 128
Forgie. Mor 3A 160
Forgue. Abers 4D 160
Forkill. New M 8E 178
Formby. Mers 4A 90
Forncett End. Norf 1D 66
Forncett St Mary. Norf 1D 66
Forncett St Peter. Norf 1D 66
Forneth. Per 4H 143
Fornham All Saints. Suff 4H 65
Fornham St Martin. Suff 4A 66
Forres. Mor 3E 159
Forrestfield. N Lan 3B 128
Forrest Lodge. Dum 1C 110
Forsbrook. Staf 1D 72
Forse. High 5E 169
Forsinard. High 4A 168
Forss. High 2C 168
Forstal, The. Kent 2E 29
Forston. Dors 3B 14
Fort Augustus. High 3F 149
Forteviot. Per 2C 136
Fort George. High 3B 158
Forth. S Lan 4C 128
Forthampton. Glos 2D 48
Forthay. Glos 2C 34
Forth Road Bridge. Fife 2E 129
Fortingall. Per 4E 143
Fort Matilda. Inv 2D 126
Forton. Hants 2C 24
Forton. Lanc 4D 97
Forton. Shrp 4G 71
Forton. Som 2G 13
Forton. Staf 3B 72
Forton Heath. Shrp 4G 71
Fortrie. Abers 4D 160
Fortrose. High 3B 158
Fortuneswell. Dors 5B 14
Fort William. High 1F 141
Forty Green. Buck 1A 38
Forty Hill. G Lon 1E 39
Forward Green. Suff 5C 66
Fosbury. Wilts 1B 24
Foscot. Oxon 3H 49
Fosdyke. Linc 2C 76
Foss. Per 3E 143
Fossebridge. Glos 4F 49
Foster Street. Essx 5E 53
Foston. Derbs 2F 73
Foston. Leics 1D 62
Foston. Linc 1F 75
Foston. N Yor 3A 100
Foston on the Wolds. E Yor 4F 101
Fotherby. Linc 1C 88
Fothergill. Cumb 1B 102
Fotheringhay. Nptn 1H 63
Foubister. Orkn 7E 172
Foula Airport. Shet 8A 173
Foul Anchor. Cambs 4D 76
Foulbridge. Cumb 5F 113
Foulden. Norf 1G 65
Foulden. Bord 4F 131
Foul Mile. E Sus 4H 27
Foulridge. Lanc 5A 98
Foulsham. Norf 3C 78
Fountainhall. Bord 5H 129
Four Alls, The. Shrp 2A 72
Four Ashes. Staf 5D 72
(nr. Cannock)
Four Ashes. Staf 2C 60
(nr. Kinver)
Four Ashes. Suff 3C 66
Four Crosses. Powy 5C 70
(nr. Llanerfyl)
Four Crosses. Powy 4E 71
(nr. Llanymynech)
Four Crosses. Staf 5D 72
Four Elms. Kent 1F 27
Four Forks. Som 3F 21
Four Gotes. Cambs 4D 76
Four Lane End. S Yor 4C 92
Four Lane Ends. Lanc 4E 97
Four Lanes. Corn 5A 6
Fourlanes End. Ches E 5B 84
Four Marks. Hants 3E 25
Four Mile Bridge. IOA 3B 80
Four Oaks. E Sus 3C 28
Four Oaks. Glos 3B 48
Four Oaks. W Mid 2G 61
Four Roads. Carm 5E 45
Four Roads. IOM 5B 108
Fourstones. Nmbd 3B 114
Four Throws. Kent 3B 28
Fovant. Wilts 4F 23
Foveran. Abers 1G 153
Fowey. Corn 3F 7
Fowlershill. Abers 2G 153
Fowley Common. Warr 1A 84
Fowlis. Ang 5C 144
Fowlis Wester. Per 1B 136
Fowlmere. Cambs 1E 53
Fownhope. Here 2A 48
Foxcombe Hill. Oxon 5C 50
Fox Corner. Surr 5A 38
Foxcote. Glos 4F 49
Foxcote. Som 1C 22
Foxdale. IOM 4B 108
Foxearth. Essx 1B 54
Foxfield. Cumb 1B 96
Foxham. Wilts 4E 35
Fox Hatch. Essx 1G 39
Foxhole. Corn 3D 6
Foxholes. N Yor 2E 101
Foxhunt Green. E Sus 4G 27
Fox Lane. Hants 1G 25
Foxley. Norf 3C 78
Foxley. Nptn 5D 62
Foxley. Wilts 3D 35
Foxlydiate. Worc 4E 61
Fox Street. Essx 3D 54
Foxt. Staf 1E 73
Foxton. Cambs 1E 53
Foxton. Dur 2A 106
Foxton. Leics 2D 62
Foxton. N Yor 5B 106
Foxup. N Yor 2A 98
Foxwist Green. Ches W 4A 84
Foxwood. Shrp 3A 60
Foy. Here 3A 48
Foyers. High 1G 149
Foynesfield. High 3C 158
Fraddam. Corn 3C 4
Fraddon. Corn 3D 6
Fradley. Staf 4F 73
Fradley South. Staf 4F 73
Fradswell. Staf 2D 73
Fraisthorpe. E Yor 3F 101
Framfield. E Sus 3F 27
Framingham Earl. Norf 5E 79
Framingham Pigot. Norf 5E 79
Framlingham. Suff 4E 67
Frampton. Dors 3B 14
Frampton. Linc 2C 76
Frampton Cotterell. S Glo 3B 34
Frampton Mansell. Glos 5E 49
Frampton on Severn. Glos 5C 48
Frampton West End. Linc 1B 76
Framsden. Suff 5D 66
Framwellgate Moor. Dur 5F 115
Franche. Worc 3C 60
Frandley. Ches W 3A 84
Frankby. Mers 2E 83
Frankfort. Norf 3F 79
Frankley. Worc 2D 61
Frank's Bridge. Powy 5D 58
Frankton. Warw 3B 62
Frankwell. Shrp 4G 71
Frant. E Sus 2G 27
Fraserburgh. Abers 2G 161
Frating Green. Essx 3D 54
Fratton. Port 2E 17
Freathy. Corn 3A 8
Freckenham. Suff 3F 65
Freckleton. Lanc 2C 90
Freeby. Leics 3F 75
Freefolk Priors. Hants 2C 24
Freehay. Staf 1E 73
Freeland. Oxon 4C 50
Freester. Shet 6F 173
Freethorpe. Norf 5G 79
Freiston. Linc 1C 76
Freiston Shore. Linc 1C 76
Fremington. Devn 3F 19
Fremington. N Yor 5D 104
Frenchay. S Glo 4B 34
Frenchbeer. Devn 4G 11
French Street. Kent 5F 39
Frenich. Stir 3D 134
Frensham. Surr 2G 25
Frenze. Norf 2D 66
Fresgoe. High 2B 168
Freshfield. Mers 4A 90
Freshford. Bath 5C 34
Freshwater. IOW 4B 16
Freshwater Bay. IOW 4B 16
Freshwater East. Pemb 5E 43
Fressingfield. Suff 3E 67
Freston. Suff 2E 55
Freswick. High 2F 169
Fretherne. Glos 5C 48
Frettenham. Norf 4E 79
Freuchie. Fife 3E 137
Freystrop. Pemb 3D 42
Friar's Gate. E Sus 2F 27
Friar Waddon. Dors 4B 14
Friday Bridge. Cambs 5D 76
Friday Street. E Sus 5H 27
Friday Street. Surr 1C 26
Fridaythorpe. E Yor 4C 100
Friden. Derbs 4F 85
Friern Barnet. G Lon 1D 39
Friesthorpe. Linc 2H 87
Frieston. Linc 1G 75
Frieth. Buck 2F 37
Friezeland. Notts 5B 86
Frilford. Oxon 2C 36
Frilsham. W Ber 4D 36
Frimley. Surr 1G 25
Frimley Green. Surr 1G 25
Frindsbury. Medw 4B 40
Fring. Norf 2G 77
Fringford. Oxon 3E 50
Frinsted. Kent 5C 40
Frinton-on-Sea. Essx 4F 55
Friockheim. Ang 4E 145
Friog. Gwyn 4F 69
Frisby. Leics 5E 74
Frisby on the Wreake. Leics 4D 74
Friskney. Linc 5D 88
Friskney Eaudyke. Linc 5D 88
Friston. E Sus 5G 27
Friston. Suff 4G 67
Fritchley. Derbs 5A 86
Fritham. Hants 1H 15
Frith Bank. Linc 1C 76
Frith Common. Worc 4A 60
Frithelstock. Devn 1E 11
Frithelstock Stone. Devn 1E 11
Frithsden. Herts 5A 52
Frithville. Linc 5C 88
Frittenden. Kent 1C 28
Frittiscombe. Devn 4E 9
Fritton. Norf 5G 79
(nr. Great Yarmouth)
Fritton. Norf 1E 67
(nr. Long Stratton)
Fritwell. Oxon 3D 50
Frizinghall. W Yor 1B 92
Frizington. Cumb 3B 102
Frobost. W Isl 6C 170
Frocester. Glos 5C 48
Frochas. Powy 5D 70
Frodesley. Shrp 5H 71
Frodingham. N Lin 3C 94
Frodsham. Ches W 3H 83
Froggatt. Derbs 3G 85
Froghall. Staf 1E 73
Frogham. Hants 1G 15
Frogham. Kent 5G 41
Frogmore. Devn 4D 8
Frogmore. Hants 5G 37
Frogmore. Herts 5B 52
Frognall. Linc 4A 76
Frogshall. Norf 2E 79
Frogwell. Corn 2H 7
Frolesworth. Leics 1C 62
Frome. Som 2C 22
Fromefield. Som 2C 22
Frome St Quintin. Dors 2A 14
Fromes Hill. Here 1B 48
Fron. Gwyn 2C 68
Fron. Powy 1C 58
(nr. Llandrindod Wells)
Fron. Powy 1D 58
(nr. Newtown)
Fron. Powy 5E 71
(nr. Welshpool)
Froncysyllte. Wrex 1E 71
Frongoch. Gwyn 2B 70
Fron Isaf. Wrex 1E 71
Fronoleu. Gwyn 2G 69
Frosterley. Dur 1D 104
Frotoft. Orkn 5D 172
Froxfield. C Beds 2H 51
Froxfield. Wilts 5A 36
Froxfield Green. Hants 4F 25
Fryern Hill. Hants 4C 24
Fryerning. Essx 5G 53
Fryton. N Yor 2A 100
Fugglestone St Peter. Wilts 3G 23
Fulbeck. Linc 5G 87
Fulbourn. Cambs 5D 65
Fulbrook. Oxon 4A 50
Fulflood. Hants 3C 24
Fulford. Som 4F 21
Fulford. Staf 2D 72
Fulford. York 5A 100
Fulham. G Lon 3D 38
Fulking. W Sus 4D 26
Fuller's Moor. Ches W 5G 83
Fuller Street. Essx 4H 53
Fullerton. Hants 3B 24
Fulletby. Linc 3B 88
Full Sutton. E Yor 4B 100
Fullwood. E Ayr 4F 127
Fulmer. Buck 2A 38
Fulmodestone. Norf 2B 78
Fulnetby. Linc 3H 87
Fulney. Linc 3B 76
Fulstow. Linc 1C 88
Fulthorpe. Stoc T 2B 106
Fulwell. Tyne 4G 115
Fulwood. Lanc 1D 90
Fulwood. Notts 5B 86
Fulwood. Som 1F 13
Fulwood. S Yor 2G 85
Fundenhall. Norf 1D 66
Funtington. W Sus 2G 17
Funtley. Hants 2D 16
Funzie. Shet 2H 173
Furley. Devn 2F 13
Furnace. Arg 3H 133
Furnace. Carm 5F 45
Furnace. Cdgn 1F 57
Furner's Green. E Sus 3F 27
Furness Vale. Derbs 2E 85
Furneux Pelham. Herts 3E 53
Furzebrook. Dors 4E 15
Furzehill. Devn 2H 19
Furzehill. Dors 2F 15
Furzeley Corner. Hants 1E 17
Furzey Lodge. Hants 2B 16
Furzley. Hants 1A 16
Fyfield. Essx 5F 53
Fyfield. Glos 5H 49
Fyfield. Hants 2A 24
Fyfield. Oxon 2C 36
Fyfield. Wilts 5G 35
Fylde, The. Lanc 1B 90
Fylingthorpe. N Yor 4G 107
Fyning. W Sus 4G 25
Fyvie. Abers 5E 161

G

Gabhsann bho Dheas. W Isl 2G 171
Gabhsann bho Thuath. W Isl 2G 171
Gabroc Hill. E Ayr 4F 127
Gadbrook. Surr 1D 26
Gaddesby. Leics 4D 74
Gadfa. IOA 2D 80
Gadgirth. S Ayr 2D 116
Gaer. Powy 3E 47
Gaerwen. IOA 3D 81
Gagingwell. Oxon 3C 50
Gaick Lodge. High 5B 150
Gailey. Staf 4D 72
Gainford. Dur 3E 105
Gainsborough. Linc 1F 87
Gainsborough. Suff 1E 55
Gainsford End. Essx 2H 53
Gairletter. Arg 1C 126
Gairloch. Abers 3E 153
Gairloch. High 1H 155
Gairlochy. High 5D 148
Gairney Bank. Per 4D 136
Gairnshiel Lodge. Abers 3G 151
Gaisgill. Cumb 4H 103
Gaitsgill. Cumb 5E 113
Galashiels. Bord 1G 119
Galgate. Lanc 4D 97
Galgorm. Bmna 6G 175
Galhampton. Som 4B 22
Gallatown. Fife 4E 137
Galley Common. Warw 1H 61
Galleyend. Essx 5H 53
Galleywood. Essx 5H 53
Gallin. Per 4C 142
Gallowfauld. Ang 4D 144
Gallowhill. E Dun 2H 127
Gallowhill. Per 5A 144
Gallowhill. Ren 3F 127
Gallowhills. Abers 3H 161
Gallows Green. Staf 1E 73
Gallows Green. Worc 4D 60
Gallowstree Common. Oxon 3E 37
Galltair. High 1G 147
Gallt Melyd. Den 2C 82
Galmington. Som 4F 21
Galmisdale. High 5C 146
Galmpton. Devn 4C 8
Galmpton. Torb 3E 9
Galmpton Warborough. Torb 3E 9
Galphay. N Yor 2E 99
Galston. E Ayr 1D 117
Galton. Dors 4C 14
Galtrigill. High 3A 154
Gamblesby. Cumb 1H 103
Gamblestown. Cgvn 4F 178
Gamelsby. Cumb 4D 112
Gamesley. Derbs 1E 85
Gamlingay. Cambs 5B 64
Gamlingay Cinques. Cambs 5B 64
Gamlingay Great Heath. C Beds 5B 64
Gammaton. Devn 4E 19
Gammersgill. N Yor 1C 98
Gamston. Notts 2D 74
(nr. Nottingham)
Gamston. Notts 3E 86
(nr. Retford)
Ganarew. Here 4A 48
Ganavan. Arg 5C 140
Ganborough. Glos 3G 49
Gang. Corn 2H 7
Ganllwyd. Gwyn 3G 69
Gannochy. Ang 1E 145
Gannochy. Per 1D 136
Gansclet. High 4F 169
Ganstead. E Yor 1E 95
Ganthorpe. N Yor 2A 100
Ganton. N Yor 2D 101
Gants Hill. G Lon 2F 39
Gappah. Devn 5B 12
Garafad. High 2D 155
Garboldisham. Norf 2C 66
Garden City. Flin 4F 83
Gardeners Green. Wok 5G 37
Gardenstown. Abers 2F 161
Garden Village. S Yor 1G 85
Garden Village. Swan 3E 31
Garderhouse. Shet 7E 173
Gardham. E Yor 5D 100
Gardie. Shet 5D 173
(on Papa Stour)
Gardie. Shet 1H 173
(on Unst)
Gardie Ho. Shet 7F 173
Gare Hill. Som 2C 22
Garelochhead. Arg 4B 134
Garford. Oxon 2C 36
Garforth. W Yor 1E 93
Gargrave. N Yor 4B 98
Gargunnock. Stir 4G 135
Garleffin. S Ayr 1F 109
Garlieston. Dum 5B 110
Garlinge Green. Kent 5F 41
Garlogie. Abers 3E 153
Garmelow. Staf 3B 72
Garmond. Abers 3F 161
Garmondsway. Dur 1A 106
Garmony. Arg 4A 140
Garmouth. Mor 2H 159
Garmston. Shrp 5A 72
Garnant. Carm 4G 45
Garndiffaith. Torf 5F 47
Garndolbenmaen. Gwyn 1D 69
Garnett Bridge. Cumb 5G 103
Garnfadryn. Gwyn 2B 68
Garnkirk. N Lan 3H 127
Garnlydan. Blae 4E 47
Garnsgate. Linc 3D 76
Garnswllt. Swan 5G 45
Garn-yr-erw. Torf 4F 47
Garrabost. W Isl 4H 171
Garrallan. E Ayr 3E 117
Garras. Corn 4E 5
Garreg. Gwyn 1F 69
Garrigill. Cumb 5A 114
Garriston. Ferm 7B 176
Garriston. N Yor 5E 105
Garrogie Lodge. High 2H 149
Garros. High 2D 155
Garrow. Per 4F 143
Garsdale. Cumb 1G 97
Garsdale Head. Cumb 5A 104
Garsdon. Wilts 3E 35
Garshall Green. Staf 2D 72
Garsington. Oxon 5D 50
Garstang. Lanc 5D 97
Garston. Mers 2G 83
Garswood. Mers 1H 83
Gartcosh. N Lan 3H 127
Garth. B'end 2B 32
Garth. Cdgn 2F 57
Garth. Gwyn 2E 69
Garth. IOM 4C 108
Garth. Powy 1C 46
(nr. Builth Wells)
Garth. Powy 3E 59
(nr. Knighton)
Garth. Shet 6D 173
(nr. Sandness)
Garth. Shet 5F 173
(nr. Skellister)
Garth. Wrex 1E 71
Garthamlock. Glas 3H 127
Garthbrengy. Powy 2D 46
Garthdee. Aber 3G 153
Gartheli. Cdgn 5E 57
Garthmyl. Powy 1D 58
Garthorpe. Leics 3F 75
Garthorpe. N Lin 3B 94
Garth Owen. Powy 1D 58
Garth Row. Cumb 5G 103
Gartly. Abers 5C 160
Gartmore. Stir 4E 135
Gartness. N Lan 3A 128
Gartness. Stir 1G 127
Gartocharn. W Dun 1F 127
Garton. E Yor 1F 95
Garton-on-the-Wolds. E Yor 4D 101
Gartsherrie. N Lan 3A 128
Gartymore. High 2H 165
Garvagh. Cole 5E 174
Garvaghy. Omag 3L 177
Garvald. E Lot 2B 130
Garvamore. High 4H 149
Garvard. Arg 4A 132
Garvault. High 5H 167
Garve. High 2F 157
Garvestone. Norf 5C 78
Garvetagh. Strab 4E 176
Garvie. Arg 4H 133
Garvock. Abers 1G 145
Garvock. Inv 2D 126
Garway. Here 3H 47
Garway Common. Here 3H 47
Garway Hill. Here 3H 47
Garwick. Linc 1A 76
Gaskan. High 1B 140
Gasper. Wilts 3C 22
Gastard. Wilts 5D 35
Gasthorpe. Norf 2B 66
Gatcombe. IOW 4C 16
Gateacre. Mers 2G 83
Gatebeck. Cumb 1E 97
Gate Burton. Linc 2F 87
Gateforth. N Yor 2F 93
Gatehead. E Ayr 1C 116
Gate Helmsley. N Yor 4A 100
Gatehouse. Nmbd 1A 114
Gatehouse of Fleet. Dum 4D 110
Gatelawbridge. Dum 5B 118
Gateley. Norf 3B 78
Gatenby. N Yor 1F 99
Gatesgarth. Cumb 3C 102
Gateshead. Tyne 3F 115
Gatesheath. Ches W 4G 83
Gateside. Ang 4D 144
(nr. Forfar)
Gateside. Ang 4C 144
(nr. Kirriemuir)
Gateside. Fife 3D 136
Gateside. N Ayr 4E 127
Gathurst. G Man 4D 90
Gatley. G Man 2C 84
Gatton. Surr 5D 39
Gattonside. Bord 1H 119
Gatwick (London) Airport. W Sus 1D 27 & 205
Gaufron. Powy 4B 58
Gaulby. Leics 5D 74
Gauldry. Fife 1F 137
Gaultree. Norf 5D 77
Gaunt's Common. Dors 2F 15
Gaunt's Earthcott. S Glo 3B 34
Gautby. Linc 3A 88
Gavinton. Bord 4D 130
Gawber. S Yor 4D 92
Gawcott. Buck 2E 51
Gawsworth. Ches E 4C 84
Gawthorpe. W Yor 2C 92
Gawthrop. Cumb 1F 97
Gawthwaite. Cumb 1B 96
Gay Bowers. Essx 5A 54
Gaydon. Warw 5A 62
Gayfield. Orkn 2D 172
Gayhurst. Mil 1G 51
Gayle. N Yor 1A 98
Gayles. N Yor 4E 105
Gay Street. W Sus 3B 26
Gayton. Mers 2E 83
Gayton. Norf 4G 77
Gayton. Nptn 5E 62
Gayton. Staf 3D 73
Gayton le Marsh. Linc 2D 88
Gayton le Wold. Linc 2B 88
Gayton Thorpe. Norf 4G 77
Gaywood. Norf 3F 77
Gazeley. Suff 4G 65
Geanies. High 1C 158
Gearraidh Bhailteas. W Isl 6C 170
Gearraidh Bhaird. W Isl 6F 171
Gearraidh ma Monadh. W Isl 7C 170
Gearraidh na h-Aibhne. W Isl 4E 171
Geary. High 2B 154
Geddes. High 3C 158
Gedding. Suff 5B 66
Geddington. Nptn 2F 63
Gedintailor. High 5E 155
Gedling. Notts 1D 74
Gedney. Linc 3D 76
Gedney Broadgate. Linc 3D 76
Gedney Drove End. Linc 3D 76
Gedney Dyke. Linc 3D 76
Gedney Hill. Linc 4C 76
Gee Cross. G Man 1D 84
Geeston. Rut 5G 75
Geilston. Arg 2E 127
Geirinis. W Isl 4C 170
Geise. High 2D 168
Geisiadar. W Isl 4D 171
Gelder Shiel. Abers 5G 151
Geldeston. Norf 1F 67
Gell. Cnwy 4A 82
Gelli. Pemb 3E 43
Gelli. Rhon 2C 32
Gellifor. Den 4D 82
Gelligaer. Cphy 2E 33
Gellilydan. Gwyn 2F 69
Gellinudd. Neat 5H 45
Gellyburn. Per 5H 143
Gellywen. Carm 2G 43
Gelston. Dum 4E 111
Gelston. Linc 1G 75
Gembling. E Yor 4F 101
Geneva. Cdgn 5D 56
Gentleshaw. Staf 4E 73
Geocrab. W Isl 8D 171
George Best Belfast City Airport. Bel 2H 179
George Green. Buck 2A 38
Georgeham. Devn 3E 19
George Nympton. Devn 4H 19
Georgetown. Blae 5E 47
Georgetown. Ren 3F 127
Georth. Orkn 5C 172
Gerlan. Gwyn 4F 81
Germansweek. Devn 3E 11
Germoe. Corn 4C 4
Gerrans. Corn 5C 6
Gerrard's Bromley. Staf 2B 72
Gerrards Cross. Buck 2A 38
Gerston. High 3D 168
Gestingthorpe. Essx 2B 54
Gethsemane. Pemb 1A 44
Geuffordd. Powy 4E 70
Gibraltar. Buck 4F 51
Gibraltar. Linc 5E 89
Gibraltar. Suff 5D 66
Gibsmere. Notts 1E 74
Giddeahall. Wilts 4D 34
Gidea Park. G Lon 2G 39
Gidleigh. Devn 4G 11
Giffnock. E Ren 4G 127
Gifford. E Lot 3B 130
Giffordtown. Fife 2E 137
Giggetty. Staf 1C 60
Giggleswick. N Yor 3H 97
Gignog. Pemb 2C 42
Gilberdyke. E Yor 2B 94
Gilbert's End. Worc 1D 48
Gilbert's Green. Warw 3F 61
Gilchriston. E Lot 3A 130
Gilcrux. Cumb 1C 102
Gildersome. W Yor 2C 92
Gildingwells. S Yor 2C 86
Gilesgate Moor. Dur 5F 115
Gileston. V Glam 5D 32
Gilfach. Cphy 2E 33
Gilfach Goch. Rhon 2C 32
Gilfachreda. Cdgn 5D 56
Gilford. Ban 5E 178
Gilgarran. Cumb 2B 102
Gillamoor. N Yor 5D 107
Gillan. Corn 4E 5
Gillar's Green. Mers 1G 83
Gillen. High 3B 154
Gilling East. N Yor 2A 100
Gillingham. Dors 4D 22
Gillingham. Medw 4B 40 & **Medway** 197
Gillingham. Norf 1G 67
Gilling West. N Yor 4E 105
Gillock. High 3E 169
Gillow Heath. Staf 5C 84
Gills. High 1F 169
Gill's Green. Kent 2B 28
Gilmanscleuch. Bord 2F 119
Gilmerton. Edin 3F 129
Gilmerton. Per 1A 136
Gilmonby. Dur 3C 104
Gilmorton. Leics 2C 62
Gilsland. Nmbd 3H 113
Gilsland Spa. Cumb 3H 113
Gilston. Midl 4H 129
Giltbrook. Notts 1B 74
Gilwern. Mon 4F 47
Gimingham. Norf 2E 79
Giosla. W Isl 5D 171
Gipping. Suff 4C 66
Gipsey Bridge. Linc 1B 76
Gipton. W Yor 1D 92
Girdle Toll. N Ayr 5E 127
Girlsta. Shet 6F 173
Girsby. N Yor 4A 106
Girthon. Dum 4D 110
Girton. Cambs 4D 64
Girton. Notts 4F 87
Girvan. S Ayr 5A 116
Gisburn. Lanc 5H 97
Gisleham. Suff 2H 67
Gislingham. Suff 3C 66
Gissing. Norf 2D 66
Gittisham. Devn 3E 13
Gladestry. Powy 5E 59
Gladsmuir. E Lot 2A 130
Glaichbea. High 5H 157
Glais. Swan 5H 45
Glaisdale. N Yor 4E 107
Glame. High 4E 155
Glamis. Ang 4C 144
Glanaman. Carm 4G 45
Glan-Conwy. Cnwy 5H 81
Glandford. Norf 1C 78
Glan Duar. Carm 1F 45
Glandwr. Blae 5F 47
Glandwr. Pemb 2F 43
Glan-Dwyfach. Gwyn 1D 69
Glandy Cross. Carm 2F 43
Glandyfi. Cdgn 1F 57
Glangrwyney. Powy 4F 47
Glanmule. Powy 1D 58
Glanrhyd. Gwyn 2B 68
Glanrhyd. Pemb 1B 44
(nr. Cardigan)
Glan-rhyd. Pemb 1F 43
(nr. Crymych)
Glan-rhyd. Powy 5A 46
Glanton. Nmbd 3E 121
Glanton Pyke. Nmbd 3E 121
Glanvilles Wootton. Dors 2B 14
Glan-y-don. Flin 3D 82
Glan-y-nant. Powy 2B 58
Glan-yr-afon. Gwyn 1C 70
Glan-yr-afon. IOA 2F 81
Glan-yr-afon. Powy 5C 70
Glan-y-wern. Gwyn 2F 69
Glapthorn. Nptn 1H 63
Glapwell. Derbs 4B 86
Glarryford. Bmna 5G 175
Glas Aird. Arg 4A 132
Glas-allt Shiel. Abers 5G 151
Glasbury. Powy 2E 47
Glaschoil. High 5E 159
Glascoed. Den 3B 82
Glascoed. Mon 5G 47
Glascote. Staf 5G 73
Glascwm. Powy 5D 58
Glasfryn. Cnwy 5B 82
Glasgow. Glas 3G 127 & 195
Glasgow Airport. Ren 3F 127 & 205
Glasgow Prestwick Airport. S Ayr 2C 116
Glashvin. High 2D 154
Glasinfryn. Gwyn 4E 81
Glas na Cardaich. High 4E 147
Glasnacardoch. High 4E 147
Glasnakille. High 2D 146
Glaspwll. Cdgn 1G 57
Glassburn. High 5F 157
Glassenbury. Kent 2B 28
Glasserton. Dum 5B 110
Glassford. S Lan 5A 128
Glassgreen. Mor 2G 159
Glasshouse. Glos 3C 48
Glasshouses. N Yor 3D 98
Glasson. Cumb 3D 112
Glasson. Lanc 4D 96
Glassonby. Cumb 1G 103
Glasswater. Down 4J 179
Glasterlaw. Ang 3E 145
Glaston. Rut 5F 75
Glastonbury. Som 3H 21
Glatton. Cambs 2A 64
Glazebrook. Warr 1A 84
Glazebury. Warr 1A 84
Glazeley. Shrp 2B 60
Gleadless. S Yor 2A 86
Gleadsmoss. Ches E 4C 84
Gleann Dail bho Dheas. W Isl 7C 170
Gleann Tholastaidh. W Isl 3H 171
Gleann Uige. High 1A 140
Gleaston. Cumb 2B 96
Glebe. Strab 3F 176
Glecknabae. Arg 3B 126
Gledrid. Shrp 2E 71
Gleiniant. Powy 1B 58
Glemsford. Suff 1B 54
Glen. Dum 4C 110
Glenancross. High 4E 147
Glenanne. Arm 6D 178
Glenariff. Moy 4J 175
Glenarm. Lar 5K 175
Glen Auldyn. IOM 2D 108
Glenavy. Lis 2F 179
Glenbarr. Arg 2A 122
Glenbeg. High 2G 139
Glen Bernisdale. High 4D 154
Glenbervie. Abers 5E 153
Glenboig. N Lan 3A 128
Glenborrodale. High 2A 140
Glenbranter. Arg 4A 134
Glenbreck. Bord 2C 118
Glenbrein Lodge. High 2G 149
Glenbrittle. High 1C 146
Glenbuchat Lodge. Abers 2H 151
Glenbuck. E Ayr 2G 117
Glenburn. Ren 3F 127
Glencalvie Lodge. High 5B 164
Glencaple. Dum 3A 112
Glencarron Lodge. High 3C 156
Glencarse. Per 1D 136
Glencassley Castle. High 3B 164
Glencat. Abers 4C 152
Glencoe. High 3F 141
Glen Cottage. High 5E 147
Glencraig. Fife 4D 136
Glendale. High 4A 154
Glendevon. Per 3B 136
Glendoebeg. High 3G 149
Glendoick. Per 1E 136
Glendoune. S Ayr 5A 116
Glenduckie. Fife 2E 137
Gleneagles. Per 3B 136
Glenegedale. Arg 4B 124
Glenegedale Lots. Arg 4B 124
Glenelg. High 2G 147
Glenernie. Mor 4E 159
Glenesslin. Dum 1F 111
Glenfarg. Per 2D 136
Glenfarquhar Lodge. Abers 5E 152
Glenferness Mains. High 4D 158
Glenfeshie Lodge. High 4C 150
Glenfiddich Lodge. Mor 5H 159
Glenfield. Leics 5C 74
Glenfinnan. High 5B 148
Glenfintaig Lodge. High 5E 149
Glenfoot. Per 2D 136
Glenfyne Lodge. Arg 2B 134
Glengap. Dum 4D 110
Glengarnock. N Ayr 4E 126
Glengolly. High 2D 168
Glengorm Castle. Arg 3F 139
Glengormley. Newt 1H 179
Glengrasco. High 4D 154
Glenhead Farm. Ang 2B 144
Glenholm. Bord 1D 118
Glen House. Bord 1E 119
Glenhurich. High 2C 140
Glenkerry. Bord 3E 119
Glenkiln. Dum 2F 111
Glenkindie. Abers 2B 152
Glenkinglass Lodge. Arg 5F 141
Glenkirk. Bord 2C 118
Glenlean. Arg 1B 126
Glenlee. Dum 1D 110
Glenleraig. High 5B 166
Glenlichorn. Per 2G 135
Glenlivet. Mor 1F 151
Glenlochar. Dum 3E 111
Glenlochsie Lodge. Per 1H 143
Glenluce. Dum 4G 109
Glenmassan. Arg 1C 126
Glenmavis. N Lan 3A 128
Glen Maye. IOM 4B 108
Glenmazeran Lodge. High 1B 150
Glenmidge. Dum 1F 111
Glen Mona. IOM 3D 108
Glenmore. High 2G 139
(nr. Glenborrodale)
Glenmore. High 3D 151
(nr. Kingussie)
Glenmore. High 4D 154
(on Isle of Skye)
Glenmoy. Ang 2D 144
Glennoe. Arg 5E 141
Glen of Coachford. Abers 4B 160
Glenogil. Ang 2D 144
Glen Parva. Leics 1C 62
Glenprosen Village. Ang 2C 144
Glenree. N Ayr 3D 122
Glenridding. Cumb 3E 103
Glenrosa. N Ayr 2E 123
Glenrothes. Fife 3E 137
Glensanda. High 4C 140
Glensaugh. Abers 1F 145
Glenshero Lodge. High 4H 149
Glensluain. Arg 4H 133
Glenstockadale. Dum 3F 109
Glenstriven. Arg 2B 126
Glen Tanar House. Abers 4B 152
Glentham. Linc 1H 87
Glenton. Abers 1D 152
Glentress. Bord 1E 119
Glentromie Lodge. High 4B 150
Glentrool Lodge. Dum 1B 110
Glentrool Village. Dum 2A 110
Glentruim House. High 4A 150
Glentworth. Linc 2G 87
Glenuig. High 1A 140
Glen View. New M 6E 178
Glen Village. Falk 2B 128
Glen Vine. IOM 4C 108
Glenwhilly. Dum 2G 109
Glenzierfoot. Dum 2E 113
Glespin. S Lan 2H 117
Gletness. Shet 6F 173
Glewstone. Here 3A 48
Glib Cheois. W Isl 5F 171
Glinton. Pet 5A 76
Glooston. Leics 1E 63
Glossop. Derbs 1E 85
Gloster Hill. Nmbd 4G 121
Gloucester. Glos 4D 48 & 195
Gloucestershire Airport. Glos 3D 49
Gloup. Shet 1G 173
Glusburn. N Yor 5C 98
Glutt Lodge. High 5B 168
Glutton Bridge. Staf 4E 85
Gluvian. Corn 2D 6
Glympton. Oxon 3C 50
Glyn. Cnwy 3A 82
Glynarthen. Cdgn 1D 44
Glynbrochan. Powy 2B 58
Glyn Ceiriog. Wrex 2E 70
Glyncoch. Rhon 2D 32
Glyncorrwg. Neat 2B 32
Glynde. E Sus 5F 27
Glyndebourne. E Sus 4F 27
Glyndyfrdwy. Den 1D 70
Glyn Ebwy. Blae 5E 47
Glynn. Lar 7L 175
Glyn-neath. Neat 5B 46
Glynogwr. B'end 3C 32
Glyntaff. Rhon 3D 32
Glyntawe. Powy 4B 46
Glynteg. Carm 2D 44
Gnosall. Staf 3C 72
Gnosall Heath. Staf 3C 72
Goadby. Leics 1E 63
Goadby Marwood. Leics 3E 75
Goatacre. Wilts 4F 35
Goathill. Dors 1B 14
Goathland. N Yor 4F 107
Goathurst. Som 3F 21
Goathurst Common. Kent 5F 39
Goat Lees. Kent 1E 28
Gobernuisgach Lodge. High 4E 167
Gobernuisgeach. High 5B 168
Gobhaig. W Isl 7C 171
Gobowen. Shrp 2F 71
Godalming. Surr 1A 26
Goddard's Corner. Suff 4E 67
Goddard's Green. Kent 2C 28
(nr. Benenden)
Goddard's Green. Kent 2B 28
(nr. Cranbrook)
Goddards Green. W Sus 3D 27
Godford Cross. Devn 2E 13
Godleybrook. Staf 1D 73
Godmanchester. Cambs 3B 64
Godmanstone. Dors 3B 14
Godmersham. Kent 5E 41
Godolphin Cross. Corn 3D 4
Godre'r-graig. Neat 5A 46
Godshill. Hants 1G 15
Godshill. IOW 4D 16
Godstone. Staf 2E 73
Godstone. Surr 5E 39
Goetre. Mon 5G 47
Goff's Oak. Herts 5D 52
Gogar. Edin 2E 129
Goginan. Cdgn 2F 57
Golan. Gwyn 1E 69
Golant. Corn 3F 7

Golberdon—Harlyn Bay

Golberdon. Corn 5D 10
Golborne. G Man 1A 84
Golcar. W Yor 3A 92
Goldcliff. Newp 3G 33
Golden Cross. E Sus 4G 27
Golden Green. Kent 1H 27
Golden Grove. Carm 4F 45
Golden Grove. N Yor 4F 107
Golden Hill. Pemb 2D 43
Goldenhill. Stoke 5C 84
Golden Pot. Hants 2F 25
Golden Valley. Glos 3E 49
Golders Green. G Lon 2D 38
Goldhanger. Essx 5C 54
Gold Hill. Norf 1E 65
Golding. Shrp 5H 71
Goldington. Bed 5H 63
Goldsborough. N Yor 4F 99 (nr. Harrogate)
Goldsborough. N Yor 3F 107 (nr. Whitby)
Goldsithney. Corn 3C 4
Goldstone. Kent 4G 41
Goldstone. Shrp 3B 72
Goldthorpe. S Yor 4E 93
Goldworthy. Devn 4D 19
Golfa. Powy 3D 70
Gollanfield. High 3C 158
Gollinglith Foot. N Yor 1D 98
Golsoncott. Som 3D 20
Golspie. High 4F 165
Gomeldon. Wilts 3G 23
Gomersal. W Yor 2C 92
Gometra House. Arg 4E 139
Gomshall. Surr 1B 26
Gonalston. Notts 1D 74
Gonerby Hill Foot. Linc 2G 75
Gonfirth. Shet 5E 173
Good Easter. Essx 4G 53
Gooderstone. Norf 5G 77
Goodleigh. Devn 3G 19
Goodmanham. E Yor 5C 100
Goodmayes. G Lon 2F 39
Goodnestone. Kent 5G 41 (nr. Aylesham)
Goodnestone. Kent 4E 41 (nr. Faversham)
Goodrich. Here 4A 48
Goodrington. Torb 3E 9
Goodshaw. Lanc 2G 91
Goodshaw Fold. Lanc 2G 91
Goodstone. Devn 5A 12
Goodwick. Pemb 1D 42
Goodworth Clatford. Hants 2B 24
Goole. E Yor 2H 93
Goom's Hill. Worc 5E 61
Goonabarn. Corn 3D 6
Goonbell. Corn 4B 6
Goonhavern. Corn 3B 6
Goonvrea. Corn 4B 6
Goose Green. Cumb 1E 97
Goose Green. S Glo 3C 34
Gooseham. Corn 1C 10
Goosewell. Plym 3B 8
Goosey. Oxon 2B 36
Goosnargh. Lanc 1D 90
Goostrey. Ches E 3B 84
Gorcott Hill. Warw 4E 61
Gord. Shet 9F 173
Gordon. Bord 5C 130
Gordonbush. High 3F 165
Gordonstown. Abers 3C 160 (nr. Cornhill)
Gordonstown. Abers 5E 160 (nr. Fyvie)
Gorebridge. Midl 3G 129
Gorefield. Cambs 4D 76
Gores. Wilts 1G 23
Gorgie. Edin 2F 129
Goring. Oxon 3E 36
Goring-by-Sea. W Sus 5C 26
Goring Heath. Oxon 4E 37
Gorleston-on-Sea. Norf 5H 79
Gornalwood. W Mid 1D 60
Gorran Churchtown. Corn 4D 6
Gorran Haven. Corn 4E 6
Gorran High Lanes. Corn 4D 6
Gors. Cdgn 3F 57
Gorsedd. Flin 3D 82
Gorseinon. Swan 3E 31
Gorseness. Orkn 6D 172
Gorseybank. Derbs 5G 85
Gorsgoch. Cdgn 5D 57
Gorslas. Carm 4F 45
Gorsley. Glos 3B 48
Gorsley Common. Here 3B 48
Gorstan. High 2F 157
Gorstella. Ches W 4F 83
Gorsty Common. Here 2H 47
Gorsty Hill. Staf 3E 73
Gortantaoid. Arg 2B 124
Gorteneorn. High 2A 140
Gortenfern. High 2A 140
Gortin. Omag 8A 174
Gortnahey. Lim 5C 174
Gorton. G Man 1C 84
Gosbeck. Suff 5D 66
Gosberton. Linc 2B 76
Gosberton Cheal. Linc 3B 76
Gosberton Clough. Linc 3A 76
Goseley Dale. Derbs 3H 73
Gosfield. Essx 3A 54
Gosford. Oxon 4D 50
Gosforth. Cumb 4B 102
Gosforth. Tyne 3F 115
Gosmore. Herts 3B 52
Gospel End Village. Staf 1C 60
Gosport. Hants 2E 16
Gossabrough. Shet 3G 173
Gossington. Glos 5C 48
Gossops Green. W Sus 2D 26
Goswick. Nmbd 5G 131
Gotham. Notts 2C 74
Gotherington. Glos 3E 49
Gott. Arg 4B 138
Gott. Shet 7F 173
Goudhurst. Kent 2B 28
Goulceby. Linc 3B 88
Gourdon. Abers 1H 145
Gourock. Inv 2D 126
Govan. Glas 3G 127
Govanhill. Glas 3G 127
Goverton. Notts 1E 74
Goveton. Devn 4D 8
Govilon. Mon 4F 47
Gowanhill. Abers 2H 161
Gowdall. E Yor 2G 93
Gowdystown. Ban 4F 179
Gowerton. Swan 3E 31
Gowkhall. Fife 1D 128
Gowthorpe. E Yor 4B 100
Goxhill. E Yor 5F 101
Goxhill. N Lin 2E 94
Goxhill Haven. N Lin 2E 94
Goytre. Neat 3A 32
Grabhair. W Isl 6F 171
Graby. Linc 3H 75
Gracehill. Bmna 6G 175
Graffham. W Sus 4A 26
Grafham. Cambs 4A 64
Grafham. Surr 1B 26
Grafton. Here 2H 47
Grafton. N Yor 3G 99
Grafton. Oxon 5A 50
Grafton. Shrp 4G 71
Grafton. Worc 2E 49 (nr. Evesham)
Grafton. Worc 4H 59 (nr. Leominster)
Grafton Flyford. Worc 5D 60
Grafton Regis. Nptn 1F 51
Grafton Underwood. Nptn 2G 63
Grafty Green. Kent 1C 28
Graianrhyd. Den 5E 82
Graig. Carm 5E 45
Graig. Cnwy 3H 81
Graig. Den 3C 82
Graig-fechan. Den 5D 82
Graig Penllyn. V Glam 4C 32
Grain. Medw 3C 40
Grainsby. Linc 1B 88
Grainthorpe. Linc 1C 88
Grainthorpe Fen. Linc 1C 88
Graiselound. N Lin 1E 87
Gramasdail. W Isl 3D 170
Grampound. Corn 4D 6
Grampound Road. Corn 3D 6
Granborough. Buck 3F 51
Granby. Notts 2E 75
Grandborough. Warw 4B 62
Grandpont. Oxon 5D 50
Grandtully. Per 3G 143
Grange. Cumb 3D 102
Grange. E Ayr 1D 116
Grange. Here 3G 59
Grange. Mers 2E 83
Grange. Per 1E 137
Grange Corner. Bmna 7G 175
Grange Crossroads. Mor 3B 160
Grange Hill. G Lon 1F 39
Grangemill. Derbs 5G 85
Grange Moor. W Yor 3C 92
Grangemouth. Falk 1C 128
Grange of Lindores. Fife 2E 137
Grange-over-Sands. Cumb 2D 96
Grangepans. Falk 1D 128
Grange Park. Down 5J 179
Grange, The. N Yor 5C 106
Grangetown. Card 4E 33
Grangetown. Red C 2C 106
Grange Villa. Dur 4F 115
Granish. High 2C 150
Granston. Pemb 1C 42
Grantchester. Cambs 5D 64
Grantham. Linc 2G 75
Grantley. N Yor 3E 99
Grantlodge. Abers 2E 152
Granton. Edin 2F 129
Grantown-on-Spey. High 1E 151
Grantshouse. Bord 3E 130
Grappenhall. Warr 2A 84
Grasby. Linc 4D 94
Grasmere. Cumb 4E 103
Grasscroft. G Man 4H 91
Grassendale. Mers 2F 83
Grassgarth. Cumb 5E 113
Grassholme. Dur 2C 104
Grassington. N Yor 3C 98
Grassmoor. Derbs 4B 86
Grassthorpe. Notts 4E 87
Grateley. Hants 2A 24
Gratton. Devn 1D 11
Gratton. Staf 5D 84
Gratwich. Staf 2E 73
Graveley. Cambs 4B 64
Graveley. Herts 3C 52
Gravelhill. Shrp 4G 71
Gravel Hole. G Man 4H 91
Gravelly Hill. W Mid 1F 61
Graven. Shet 4F 173
Graveney. Kent 4E 41
Gravesend. Kent 3H 39
Grayingham. Linc 1G 87
Grayrigg. Cumb 5G 103
Grays. Thur 3H 39
Grayshott. Hants 3G 25
Grayson Green. Cumb 2A 102
Grayswood. Surr 2A 26
Graythorp. Hart 2C 106
Grazeley. Wok 5E 37
Grealin. High 2E 155
Greasbrough. S Yor 1B 86
Greasby. Mers 2E 83
Great Abington. Cambs 1F 53
Great Addington. Nptn 3G 63
Great Alne. Warw 5F 61
Great Altcar. Lanc 4B 90
Great Amwell. Herts 4D 52
Great Asby. Cumb 3H 103
Great Ashfield. Suff 4B 66
Great Ayton. N Yor 3C 106
Great Baddow. Essx 5H 53
Great Bardfield. Essx 2G 53
Great Barford. Bed 5A 64
Great Barr. W Mid 1E 61
Great Barrington. Glos 4H 49
Great Barrow. Ches W 4G 83
Great Barton. Suff 4A 66
Great Barugh. N Yor 2B 100
Great Bavington. Nmbd 1C 114
Great Bealings. Suff 1F 55
Great Bedwyn. Wilts 5A 36
Great Bentley. Essx 3E 54
Great Billing. Nptn 4F 63
Great Bircham. Norf 2G 77
Great Blakenham. Suff 5D 66
Great Blencow. Cumb 1F 103
Great Bolas. Telf 3A 72
Great Bookham. Surr 5C 38
Great Bosullow. Corn 3B 4
Great Bourton. Oxon 1C 50
Great Bowden. Leics 2E 63
Great Bradley. Suff 5F 65
Great Braxted. Essx 4B 54
Great Bricett. Suff 5C 66
Great Brickhill. Buck 2H 51
Great Bridgeford. Staf 3C 72
Great Brington. Nptn 4D 62
Great Bromley. Essx 3D 54
Great Broughton. Cumb 1B 102
Great Broughton. N Yor 4C 106
Great Budworth. Ches W 3A 84
Great Burdon. Darl 3A 106
Great Burstead. Essx 1A 40
Great Busby. N Yor 4C 106
Great Canfield. Essx 4F 53
Great Carlton. Linc 2D 88
Great Casterton. Rut 5H 75
Great Chalfield. Wilts 5D 34
Great Chart. Kent 1D 28
Great Chatwell. Staf 4B 72
Great Chesterford. Essx 1F 53
Great Cheverell. Wilts 1E 23
Great Chilton. Dur 1F 105
Great Chishill. Cambs 2E 53
Great Clacton. Essx 4E 55
Great Cliff. W Yor 3D 92
Great Clifton. Cumb 2B 102
Great Coates. NE Lin 3F 95
Great Comberton. Worc 1E 49
Great Corby. Cumb 4F 113
Great Cornard. Suff 1B 54
Great Cowden. E Yor 5G 101
Great Coxwell. Oxon 2A 36
Great Crakehall. N Yor 1E 99
Great Cransley. Nptn 3F 63
Great Cressingham. Norf 5H 77
Great Crosby. Mers 1F 83
Great Cubley. Derbs 2F 73
Great Dalby. Leics 4E 75
Great Doddington. Nptn 4F 63
Great Doward. Here 4A 48
Great Dunham. Norf 4A 78
Great Dunmow. Essx 3G 53
Great Durnford. Wilts 3G 23
Great Easton. Essx 3G 53
Great Easton. Leics 1F 63
Great Eccleston. Lanc 5D 96
Great Edstone. N Yor 1B 100
Great Ellingham. Norf 1C 66
Great Elm. Som 2C 22
Great Eppleton. Tyne 5G 115
Great Eversden. Cambs 5C 64
Great Fencote. N Yor 5F 105
Great Finborough. Suff 5C 66
Greatford. Linc 4H 75
Great Fransham. Norf 4A 78
Great Gaddesden. Herts 4A 52
Great Gate. Staf 1E 73
Great Gidding. Cambs 2A 64
Great Givendale. E Yor 4C 100
Great Glemham. Suff 4F 67
Great Glen. Leics 1D 62
Great Gonerby. Linc 2G 75
Great Gransden. Cambs 5B 64
Great Green. Norf 2E 67
Great Green. Suff 5B 66 (nr. Lavenham)
Great Green. Suff 3D 66 (nr. Palgrave)
Great Habton. N Yor 2B 100
Great Hale. Linc 1A 76
Great Hallingbury. Essx 4F 53
Greatham. Hants 3F 25
Greatham. Hart 2B 106
Greatham. W Sus 4B 26
Great Hampden. Buck 5G 51
Great Harrowden. Nptn 3F 63
Great Harwood. Lanc 1F 91
Great Haseley. Oxon 5E 51
Great Hatfield. E Yor 5F 101
Great Haywood. Staf 3D 73
Great Heath. W Mid 2H 61
Great Heck. N Yor 2F 93
Great Henny. Essx 2B 54
Great Hinton. Wilts 1E 23
Great Hockham. Norf 1B 66
Great Holland. Essx 4F 55
Great Horkesley. Essx 2C 54
Great Hormead. Herts 2E 53
Great Horton. W Yor 1B 92
Great Horwood. Buck 2F 51
Great Houghton. Nptn 5E 63
Great Houghton. S Yor 4E 93
Great Hucklow. Derbs 3F 85
Great Kelk. E Yor 4F 101
Great Kendale. E Yor 3E 101
Great Kimble. Buck 5G 51
Great Kingshill. Buck 2G 37
Great Langdale. Cumb 4D 102
Great Langton. N Yor 5F 105
Great Leighs. Essx 4H 53
Great Limber. Linc 4E 95
Great Linford. Mil 1G 51
Great Livermere. Suff 3A 66
Great Longstone. Derbs 3G 85
Great Lumley. Dur 5F 115
Great Lyth. Shrp 5G 71
Great Malvern. Worc 1C 48
Great Maplestead. Essx 2B 54
Great Marton. Bkpl 1B 90
Great Massingham. Norf 3G 77
Great Melton. Norf 5D 78
Great Milton. Oxon 5E 51
Great Missenden. Buck 5G 51
Great Mitton. Lanc 1F 91
Great Mongeham. Kent 5H 41
Great Moulton. Norf 1D 66
Great Munden. Herts 3D 52
Great Musgrave. Cumb 3A 104
Great Ness. Shrp 4F 71
Great Notley. Essx 3H 53
Great Oak. Mon 5G 47
Great Oakley. Essx 3E 55
Great Oakley. Nptn 2F 63
Great Offley. Herts 3B 52
Great Ormside. Cumb 3A 104
Great Orton. Cumb 4E 113
Great Ouseburn. N Yor 3G 99
Great Oxendon. Nptn 2E 63
Great Oxney Green. Essx 5G 53
Great Parndon. Essx 5E 53
Great Paxton. Cambs 4B 64
Great Plumpton. Lanc 1B 90
Great Plumstead. Norf 4F 79
Great Ponton. Linc 2G 75
Great Potheridge. Devn 1F 11
Great Preston. W Yor 2E 93
Great Raveley. Cambs 2B 64
Great Rissington. Glos 4G 49
Great Rollright. Oxon 2B 50
Great Ryburgh. Norf 3B 78
Great Ryle. Nmbd 3E 121
Great Ryton. Shrp 5G 71
Great Saling. Essx 3G 53
Great Salkeld. Cumb 1G 103
Great Sampford. Essx 2G 53
Great Sankey. Warr 2H 83
Great Saredon. Staf 5D 72
Great Saxham. Suff 4G 65
Great Shefford. W Ber 4B 36
Great Shelford. Cambs 5D 64
Great Shoddesden. Hants 2A 24
Great Smeaton. N Yor 4A 106
Great Snoring. Norf 2B 78
Great Somerford. Wilts 3E 35
Great Stainton. Darl 2A 106
Great Stambridge. Essx 1C 40
Great Staughton. Cambs 4A 64
Great Steeping. Linc 4D 88
Great Stonar. Kent 5H 41
Greatstone-on-Sea. Kent 3E 29
Great Strickland. Cumb 2G 103
Great Stukeley. Cambs 3B 64
Great Sturton. Linc 3B 88
Great Sutton. Ches W 3F 83
Great Sutton. Shrp 2H 59
Great Swinburne. Nmbd 2C 114
Great Tew. Oxon 3B 50
Great Tey. Essx 3B 54
Great Thirkleby. N Yor 2G 99
Great Thorness. IOW 3C 16
Great Thurlow. Suff 5F 65
Great Torr. Devn 4C 8
Great Torrington. Devn 1E 11
Great Tosson. Nmbd 4E 121
Great Totham North. Essx 4B 54
Great Totham South. Essx 4B 54
Great Tows. Linc 1B 88
Great Urswick. Cumb 2B 96
Great Wakering. Essx 2D 40
Great Waldingfield. Suff 1C 54
Great Walsingham. Norf 2B 78
Great Waltham. Essx 4G 53
Great Warley. Essx 1G 39
Great Washbourne. Glos 2E 49
Great Wenham. Suff 2D 54
Great Whelnetham. Suff 5A 66
Great Whittington. Nmbd 2D 114
Great Wigborough. Essx 4C 54
Great Wilbraham. Cambs 5E 65
Great Wilne. Derbs 2B 74
Great Wishford. Wilts 3F 23
Great Witchingham. Norf 3D 78
Great Witcombe. Glos 4E 49
Great Witley. Worc 4B 60
Great Wolford. Warw 2H 49
Greatworth. Nptn 1D 50
Great Wratting. Suff 1G 53
Great Wymondley. Herts 3C 52
Great Wyrley. Staf 5D 73
Great Wytheford. Shrp 4H 71
Great Yarmouth. Norf 5H 79
Great Yeldham. Essx 2A 54
Grebby. Linc 4D 88
Greeba Castle. IOM 3C 108
Greenbank. Shet 1G 173
Greenbottom. Corn 4B 6
Greenburn. W Lot 3C 128
Greencastle. Omag 1L 177
Greencroft. Dur 4E 115
Greencroft Park. Dur 5E 115
Greendown. Som 1A 22
Greendykes. Nmbd 2E 121
Green End. Bed 1A 52 (nr. Bedford)
Green End. Bed 4A 64 (nr. St Neots)
Green End. Herts 2D 52 (nr. Buntingford)
Green End. Herts 3D 52 (nr. Stevenage)
Green End. N Yor 4F 107
Green End. Warw 2G 61
Greenfield. Arg 4B 134
Greenfield. C Beds 2A 52
Greenfield. Flin 3D 82
Greenfield. G Man 4H 91
Greenfield. Oxon 2F 37
Greenfoot. N Lan 3A 128
Greenford. G Lon 2C 38
Greengairs. N Lan 2A 128
Greengate. Norf 4C 78
Greengill. Cumb 1C 102
Greenhalgh. Lanc 1C 90
Greenham. Dors 2H 13
Greenham. Som 4D 20
Greenham. W Ber 5C 36
Green Hammerton. N Yor 4G 99
Greenhaugh. Nmbd 1A 114
Greenhead. Nmbd 3H 113
Green Heath. Staf 4D 73
Greenhill. Dum 2C 112
Greenhill. Falk 2B 128
Greenhill. Kent 4F 41
Greenhill. S Yor 2H 85
Greenhill. Worc 3C 60
Greenhills. N Ayr 4E 127
Greenhithe. Kent 3G 39
Greenholm. E Ayr 1E 117
Greenhow Hill. N Yor 3D 98
Greenigoe. Orkn 7D 172
Greenisland. Carr 8K 175
Greenland. High 2E 169
Greenland Mains. High 2E 169
Greenlands. Worc 4E 61
Green Lane. Shrp 3A 72
Green Lane. Warw 4E 61
Greenlaw. Bord 5D 130
Greenlea. Dum 2B 112
Greenloaning. Per 3H 135
Greenmount. G Man 3F 91
Greenmow. Shet 9F 173
Greenock. Inv 2D 126
Greenock Mains. E Ayr 2F 117
Greenodd. Cumb 1C 96
Green Ore. Som 1A 22
Greenrow. Cumb 4C 112
Greens. Abers 4F 161
Greensgate. Norf 4D 78
Greenside. Tyne 3E 115
Greensidehill. Nmbd 3D 121
Greens Norton. Nptn 1E 51
Greenstead Green. Essx 3B 54
Greensted Green. Essx 5F 53
Green Street. Herts 1C 38
Green Street. Suff 3D 66
Green Street Green. G Lon 4F 39
Green Street Green. Kent 3G 39
Greenstreet Green. Suff 1D 54
Green, The. Cumb 1A 96
Green, The. Wilts 3D 22
Green Tye. Herts 4E 53
Greenwall. Orkn 7E 172
Greenway. Pemb 2E 43
Greenway. V Glam 4D 32
Greenwell. Cumb 4G 113
Greenwich. G Lon 3E 39
Greet. Glos 2F 49
Greete. Shrp 3H 59
Greetham. Linc 3C 88
Greetham. Rut 4G 75
Greetland. W Yor 2A 92
Gregson Lane. Lanc 2D 90
Grein. W Isl 8B 170
Greinetobht. W Isl 1D 170
Greinton. Som 3H 21
Gremista. Shet 7F 173
Grenaby. IOM 4B 108
Grendon. Nptn 4F 63
Grendon. Warw 1G 61
Grendon Common. Warw 1G 61
Grendon Green. Here 5H 59
Grendon Underwood. Buck 3E 51
Grenofen. Devn 5E 11
Grenoside. S Yor 1H 85
Greosabhagh. W Isl 8D 171
Gresford. Wrex 5F 83
Gresham. Norf 2D 78
Greshornish. High 3C 154
Gressenhall. Norf 4B 78
Gressingham. Lanc 3E 97
Greta Bridge. Dur 3D 105
Gretna. Dum 3E 112
Gretna Green. Dum 3E 112
Gretton. Glos 2F 49
Gretton. Nptn 1G 63
Gretton. Shrp 1H 59
Grewelthorpe. N Yor 2E 99
Greyabbey. Ards 3K 179
Greygarth. N Yor 2D 98
Grey Green. N Lin 4A 94
Greylake. Som 3G 21
Greysouthen. Cumb 2B 102
Greysteel. Lim 4B 174
Greystoke. Cumb 1F 103
Greystoke Gill. Cumb 2F 103
Greystone. Ang 4E 145
Greystones. S Yor 2H 85
Greywell. Hants 1F 25
Griais. W Isl 3G 171
Grianan. W Isl 4G 171
Gribthorpe. E Yor 1A 94
Gribun. Arg 5F 139
Griff. Warw 2A 62
Griffithstown. Torf 2F 33
Griffydam. Leics 4B 74
Griggs Green. Hants 3G 25
Grimbister. Orkn 6C 172
Grimeford Village. Lanc 3E 90
Grimeston. Orkn 6C 172
Grimethorpe. S Yor 4E 93
Griminis. W Isl 3C 170 (on Benbecula)
Griminis. W Isl 1C 170 (on North Uist)
Grimister. Shet 2F 173
Grimley. Worc 4C 60
Grimness. Orkn 8D 172
Grimoldby. Linc 2C 88
Grimpo. Shrp 3F 71
Grimsargh. Lanc 1D 90
Grimsby. NE Lin 3F 95
Grimscote. Nptn 5D 62
Grimscott. Corn 2C 10
Grimshaw. Bkbn 2F 91
Grimshaw Green. Lanc 3C 90
Grimsthorpe. Linc 3H 75
Grimston. E Yor 1F 95
Grimston. Leics 3D 74
Grimston. Norf 3G 77
Grimston. York 4A 100
Grimstone. Dors 3B 14
Grimstone End. Suff 4B 66
Grinacombe Moor. Devn 3E 11
Grindale. E Yor 2F 101
Grindhill. Devn 3E 11
Grindiscol. Shet 8F 173
Grindle. Shrp 5B 72
Grindleford. Derbs 3G 85
Grindleton. Lanc 5G 97
Grindley. Staf 3E 73
Grindley Brook. Shrp 1H 71
Grindlow. Derbs 3F 85
Grindon. Nmbd 5F 131
Grindon. Staf 5E 85
Gringley on the Hill. Notts 1E 87
Grinsdale. Cumb 4E 113
Grinshill. Shrp 3H 71
Grinton. N Yor 5D 104
Griomsidar. W Isl 5G 171
Grishipoll. Arg 3C 138
Grisling Common. E Sus 3F 27
Gristhorpe. N Yor 1E 101
Griston. Norf 1B 66
Gritley. Orkn 7E 172
Grittenham. Wilts 3F 35
Grittleton. Wilts 4D 34
Grizebeck. Cumb 1B 96
Grizedale. Cumb 5E 103
Grobister. Orkn 5F 172
Grobsness. Shet 5E 173
Groby. Leics 5C 74
Groes. Cnwy 4C 82
Groes. Neat 3A 32
Groes-faen. Rhon 3D 32
Groesffordd. Gwyn 2B 68
Groesffordd. Powy 3D 46
Groeslon. Gwyn 5D 81
Groes-lwyd. Powy 4E 70
Groes-wen. Cphy 3E 33
Grogport. Arg 5G 125
Groigearraidh. W Isl 4C 170
Gromford. Suff 5F 67
Gronant. Flin 2C 82
Groombridge. E Sus 2G 27
Groomsport. N Dwn 1K 179
Grosmont. Mon 3H 47
Grosmont. N Yor 4F 107
Groton. Suff 1C 54
Grove. Dors 5C 14
Grove. Kent 4G 41
Grove. Notts 3E 87
Grove. Oxon 2B 36
Grovehill. E Yor 1D 94
Grove Park. G Lon 3F 39
Grovesend. Swan 5F 45
Grove, The. Dum 2A 112
Grove, The. Worc 1D 48
Grub Street. Staf 3B 72
Grudie. High 2F 157
Gruids. High 3C 164
Gruinard House. High 4D 162
Gruinart. Arg 3A 124
Grulinbeg. Arg 3A 124
Gruline. Arg 4G 139
Grummore. High 5G 167
Grundisburgh. Suff 5E 66
Gruting. Shet 7D 173
Grutness. Shet 10F 173
Gualachulain. High 4F 141
Gualin House. High 3D 166
Guardbridge. Fife 2G 137
Guarlford. Worc 1D 48
Guay. Per 4H 143
Gubblecote. Herts 4H 51
Guestling Green. E Sus 4C 28
Guestling Thorn. E Sus 4C 28
Guestwick. Norf 3C 78
Guestwick Green. Norf 3C 78
Guide. Bkbn 2F 91
Guide Post. Nmbd 1F 115
Guilden Down. Shrp 2F 59
Guilden Morden. Cambs 1C 52
Guilden Sutton. Ches W 4G 83
Guildford. Surr 1A 26 & 195
Guildtown. Per 5A 144
Guilsborough. Nptn 3D 62
Guilsfield. Powy 4E 70
Guineaford. Devn 3F 19
Guisborough. Red C 3D 106
Guiseley. W Yor 5D 98
Guist. Norf 3B 78
Guiting Power. Glos 3F 49
Gulberwick. Shet 8F 173
Gulladuff. Mag 7F 174
Gullane. E Lot 1A 130
Gulling Green. Suff 5H 65
Gulval. Corn 3B 4
Gumfreston. Pemb 4F 43
Gumley. Leics 1D 62
Gunby. E Yor 1H 93
Gunby. Linc 3G 75
Gundleton. Hants 3E 24
Gun Green. Kent 2B 28
Gun Hill. E Sus 4G 27
Gunn. Devn 3G 19
Gunnerside. N Yor 5C 104
Gunnerton. Nmbd 2C 114
Gunness. N Lin 3B 94
Gunnislake. Corn 5E 11
Gunnista. Shet 7F 173
Gunsgreenhill. Bord 3F 131
Gunstone. Staf 5C 72
Gunthorpe. Norf 2C 78
Gunthorpe. N Lin 1F 87
Gunthorpe. Notts 1D 74
Gunthorpe. Pet 5A 76
Gunville. IOW 4C 16
Gupworthy. Som 3C 20
Gurnard. IOW 3C 16
Gurney Slade. Som 2B 22
Gurnos. Powy 5A 46
Gussage All Saints. Dors 1F 15
Gussage St Andrew. Dors 1E 15
Gussage St Michael. Dors 1E 15
Guston. Kent 1H 29
Gutcher. Shet 2G 173
Guthram Gowt. Linc 3A 76
Guthrie. Ang 3E 145
Guyhirn. Cambs 5D 76
Guyhirn Gull. Cambs 5C 76
Guy's Head. Linc 3D 77
Guy's Marsh. Dors 4D 22
Guyzance. Nmbd 4G 121
Gwaelod-y-garth. Card 3E 32
Gwaenynog Bach. Den 4C 82
Gwaenysgor. Flin 2C 82
Gwalchmai. IOA 3C 80
Gwastad. Pemb 2E 43
Gwaun-Cae-Gurwen. Neat 4H 45
Gwaun-y-bara. Cphy 3E 33
Gwbert. Cdgn 1B 44
Gweek. Corn 4E 5
Gwehelog. Mon 5G 47
Gwenddwr. Powy 1D 46
Gwennap. Corn 4B 6
Gwenter. Corn 5E 5
Gwernaffield. Flin 4E 82
Gwernesney. Mon 5H 47
Gwernogle. Carm 2F 45
Gwern-y-go. Powy 1E 58
Gwernymynydd. Flin 4E 82
Gwersyllt. Wrex 5F 83
Gwespyr. Flin 2D 82
Gwinear. Corn 3C 4
Gwithian. Corn 2C 4
Gwredog. IOA 2D 80
Gwyddelwern. Den 1C 70
Gwyddgrug. Carm 2E 45
Gwynfryn. Wrex 5E 83
Gwystre. Powy 4C 58
Gwytherin. Cnwy 4A 82
Gyfelia. Wrex 1F 71
Gyffin. Cnwy 3G 81

H

Haa of Houlland. Shet 1G 173
Habberley. Shrp 5F 71
Habblesthorpe. Notts 2E 87
Habergham. Lanc 1G 91
Habin. W Sus 4G 25
Habrough. NE Lin 3E 95
Haceby. Linc 2H 75
Hacheston. Suff 5F 67
Hackenthorpe. S Yor 2B 86
Hackford. Norf 5C 78
Hackforth. N Yor 5F 105
Hackland. Orkn 5C 172
Hackleton. Nptn 5F 63
Hackman's Gate. Worc 3C 60
Hackness. N Yor 5G 107
Hackness. Orkn 8C 172
Hackney. G Lon 2E 39
Hackthorn. Linc 2G 87
Hackthorpe. Cumb 2G 103
Haclait. W Isl 4D 170
Haconby. Linc 3A 76
Hadden. Bord 1B 120
Haddenham. Buck 5F 51
Haddenham. Cambs 3D 64
Haddenham End. Cambs 3D 64
Haddington. E Lot 2B 130
Haddington. Linc 4G 87
Haddiscoe. Norf 1G 67
Haddo. Abers 5F 161
Haddon. Cambs 1A 64
Hademore. Staf 5F 73
Hadfield. Derbs 1E 85
Hadham Cross. Herts 4E 53
Hadham Ford. Herts 3E 53
Hadleigh. Essx 2C 40
Hadleigh. Suff 1D 54
Hadleigh Heath. Suff 1C 54
Hadley. Telf 4A 72
Hadley. Worc 4C 60
Hadley End. Staf 3F 73
Hadley Wood. G Lon 1D 38
Hadlow. Kent 1H 27
Hadlow Down. E Sus 3G 27
Hadnall. Shrp 3H 71
Hadstock. Essx 1F 53
Hadston. Nmbd 5G 121
Hady. Derbs 3A 86
Hadzor. Worc 4D 60
Haffenden Quarter. Kent 1C 28
Haggate. Lanc 1G 91
Haggbeck. Cumb 2F 113
Haggersta. Shet 7E 173
Haggerston. Nmbd 5G 131
Haggrister. Shet 4E 173
Hagley. Here 1A 48
Hagley. Worc 2D 60
Hagnaby. Linc 4C 88
Hagworthingham. Linc 4C 88
Haigh. G Man 4E 90
Haigh Moor. W Yor 2C 92
Haighton Green. Lanc 1D 90
Haile. Cumb 4B 102
Hailes. Glos 2F 49
Hailey. Herts 4D 52
Hailey. Oxon 4B 50
Hailsham. E Sus 5G 27
Hail Weston. Cambs 4A 64
Hainault. G Lon 1F 39
Hainford. Norf 4E 78
Hainton. Linc 2A 88
Hainworth. W Yor 1A 92
Haisthorpe. E Yor 3F 101
Hakin. Pemb 4C 42
Halam. Notts 5D 86
Halbeath. Fife 1E 129
Halberton. Devn 1D 12
Halcro. High 2E 169
Hale. Cumb 2E 97
Hale. G Man 2B 84
Hale. Hal 2G 83
Hale. Hants 1G 15
Hale. Surr 2G 25
Hale Bank. Hal 2G 83
Halebarns. G Man 2B 84
Hales. Norf 1F 67
Hales. Staf 2B 72
Halesgate. Linc 3C 76
Hales Green. Derbs 1F 73
Halesowen. W Mid 2D 60
Hale Street. Kent 1A 28
Halesworth. Suff 3F 67
Halewood. Mers 2G 83
Halford. Shrp 2G 59
Halford. Warw 1A 50
Halfpenny. Cumb 1E 97
Halfpenny Furze. Carm 3G 43
Halfpenny Green. Shrp 1C 60
Halfway. Carm 2G 45
Halfway. Powy 2B 46
Halfway. S Yor 2B 86
Halfway. W Ber 5C 36
Halfway House. Shrp 4F 71
Halfway Houses. Kent 3D 40
Halgabron. Corn 4A 10
Halifax. W Yor 2A 92
Halistra. High 3B 154
Halket. E Ayr 4F 127
Halkirk. High 3D 168
Halkyn. Flin 3E 82
Hall. E Ren 4F 127
Hallam Fields. Derbs 1B 74
Halland. E Sus 4G 27
Hallands, The. N Lin 2D 94
Hallaton. Leics 1E 63
Hallatrow. Bath 1B 22
Hallbank. Cumb 5H 103
Hallbankgate. Cumb 4G 113
Hall Dunnerdale. Cumb 5D 102
Hallen. S Glo 3A 34
Hall End. Bed 1A 52
Hallgarth. Dur 5G 115
Hall Green. Ches E 5C 84
Hall Green. Norf 2D 66
Hall Green. W Mid 2F 61
Hall Green. W Yor 3D 92
Hall Green. Wrex 1G 71
Halliburton. Bord 5C 130
Hallin. High 3B 154
Halling. Medw 4B 40
Hallington. Linc 2C 88
Hallington. Nmbd 2C 114
Halloughton. Notts 5D 86
Hallow. Worc 5C 60
Hallow Heath. Worc 5C 60
Hallowsgate. Ches W 4H 83
Hallsands. Devn 5E 9
Hall's Green. Herts 3C 52
Hallspill. Devn 4E 19
Hallthwaites. Cumb 1A 96
Hall Waberthwaite. Cumb 5C 102
Hallwood Green. Glos 2B 48
Hallworthy. Corn 4B 10
Hallyne. Bord 5E 129
Halmer End. Staf 1C 72
Halmond's Frome. Here 1B 48
Halmore. Glos 5B 48
Halnaker. W Sus 5A 26
Halsall. Lanc 3B 90
Halse. Nptn 1D 50
Halse. Som 4E 21
Halsetown. Corn 3C 4
Halsham. E Yor 2F 95
Halsinger. Devn 3F 19
Halstead. Essx 2B 54
Halstead. Kent 4F 39
Halstead. Leics 5E 75
Halstock. Dors 2A 14
Halsway. Som 3E 21
Haltcliff Bridge. Cumb 1E 103
Haltham. Linc 4B 88
Haltoft End. Linc 1C 76
Halton. Buck 5G 51
Halton. Hal 2H 83
Halton. Lanc 3E 97
Halton. Nmbd 3C 114
Halton. W Yor 1D 92
Halton. Wrex 2F 71
Halton East. N Yor 4C 98
Halton Fenside. Linc 4D 88
Halton Gill. N Yor 2A 98
Halton Holegate. Linc 4D 88
Halton Lea Gate. Nmbd 4H 113
Halton Moor. W Yor 1D 92
Halton Shields. Nmbd 3D 114
Halton West. N Yor 4H 97
Haltwhistle. Nmbd 3A 114
Halvergate. Norf 5G 79
Halwell. Devn 3D 9
Halwill. Devn 3E 11
Halwill Junction. Devn 3E 11
Ham. Devn 2F 13
Ham. Glos 2B 34
Ham. G Lon 3C 38
Ham. High 1E 169
Ham. Kent 5H 41
Ham. Plym 3A 8
Ham. Shet 8A 173
Ham. Som 1F 13 (nr. Ilminster)
Ham. Som 4F 21 (nr. Taunton)
Ham. Som 4E 21 (nr. Wellington)
Ham. Wilts 5B 36
Hambleden. Buck 3F 37
Hambledon. Hants 1E 17
Hambledon. Surr 2A 26
Hamble-le-Rice. Hants 2C 16
Hambleton. Lanc 5C 96
Hambleton. N Yor 1F 93
Hambridge. Som 4G 21
Hambrook. S Glo 4B 34
Hambrook. W Sus 2F 17
Ham Common. Dors 4D 22
Hameringham. Linc 4C 88
Hamerton. Cambs 3A 64
Ham Green. Here 1C 48
Ham Green. Kent 4C 40
Ham Green. N Som 4A 34
Ham Green. Worc 4E 61
Ham Hill. Kent 4A 40
Hamilton. Leics 5D 74
Hamilton. S Lan 4A 128
Hamiltonsbawn. Arm 5D 178
Hamister. Shet 5G 173
Hammer. W Sus 3G 25
Hammersmith. G Lon 3D 38
Hammerwich. Staf 5E 73
Hammerwood. E Sus 2F 27
Hammill. Kent 5G 41
Hammond Street. Herts 5D 52
Hammoon. Dors 1D 14
Hamnavoe. Shet 3D 173 (nr. Braehoulland)
Hamnavoe. Shet 8E 173 (nr. Burland)
Hamnavoe. Shet 4F 173 (nr. Lunna)
Hamnavoe. Shet 3F 173 (on Yell)
Hamp. Som 3G 21
Hampden Park. E Sus 5H 27
Hampen. Glos 4F 49
Hamperden End. Essx 2F 53
Hamperley. Shrp 2G 59
Hampnett. Glos 4F 49
Hampole. S Yor 3F 93
Hampreston. Dors 3F 15
Hampstead. G Lon 2D 38
Hampstead Norreys. W Ber 4D 36
Hampsthwaite. N Yor 4E 99
Hampton. Devn 3F 13
Hampton. G Lon 3C 38
Hampton. Kent 4F 41
Hampton. Shrp 2B 60
Hampton. Swin 2G 35
Hampton. Worc 1F 49
Hampton Bishop. Here 2A 48
Hampton Fields. Glos 2D 35
Hampton Hargate. Pet 1A 64
Hampton Heath. Ches W 1H 71
Hampton in Arden. W Mid 2G 61
Hampton Loade. Shrp 2B 60
Hampton Lovett. Worc 4C 60
Hampton Lucy. Warw 5G 61
Hampton Magna. Warw 4G 61
Hampton on the Hill. Warw 4G 61
Hampton Poyle. Oxon 4D 50
Hampton Wick. G Lon 4C 38
Hamptworth. Wilts 1H 15
Hamrow. Norf 3B 78
Hamsey. E Sus 4F 27
Hamsey Green. Surr 5E 39
Hamstall Ridware. Staf 4F 73
Hamstead. IOW 3C 16
Hamstead. W Mid 1E 61
Hamstead Marshall. W Ber 5C 36
Hamsterley. Dur 4E 115 (nr. Consett)
Hamsterley. Dur 1E 105 (nr. Wolsingham)
Hamsterley Mill. Dur 4E 115
Hamstreet. Kent 2E 28
Ham Street. Som 3A 22
Hamworthy. Pool 3E 15
Hanbury. Staf 3F 73
Hanbury. Worc 4D 60
Hanbury Woodend. Staf 3F 73
Hanby. Linc 2H 75
Hanchurch. Staf 1C 72
Hand and Pen. Devn 3D 12
Handbridge. Ches W 4G 83
Handcross. W Sus 3D 26
Handforth. Ches E 2C 84
Handley. Ches W 5G 83
Handley. Derbs 4A 86
Handsacre. Staf 4E 73
Handsworth. S Yor 2B 86
Handsworth. W Mid 1E 61
Handy Cross. Buck 2G 37
Hanford. Dors 1D 14
Hanford. Stoke 1C 72
Hangersley. Hants 2G 15
Hanging Houghton. Nptn 3E 63
Hanging Langford. Wilts 3F 23
Hangleton. Brig 5D 26
Hangleton. W Sus 5B 26
Hanham. S Glo 4B 34
Hanham Green. S Glo 4B 34
Hankelow. Ches E 1A 72
Hankerton. Wilts 2E 35
Hankham. E Sus 5H 27
Hanley. Stoke 1C 72 & **Stoke 202**
Hanley Castle. Worc 1D 48
Hanley Childe. Worc 4A 60
Hanley Swan. Worc 1D 48
Hanley William. Worc 4A 60
Hanlith. N Yor 3B 98
Hanmer. Wrex 2G 71
Hannaborough. Devn 2F 11
Hannaford. Devn 4G 19
Hannah. Linc 3E 89
Hannington. Hants 1D 24
Hannington. Nptn 3F 63
Hannington. Swin 2G 35
Hannington Wick. Swin 2G 35
Hanscombe End. C Beds 2B 52
Hanslope. Mil 1G 51
Hanthorpe. Linc 3H 75
Hanwell. G Lon 2C 38
Hanwell. Oxon 1C 50
Hanwood. Shrp 5G 71
Hanworth. G Lon 3C 38
Hanworth. Norf 2D 78
Happas. Ang 4D 144
Happendon. S Lan 1A 118
Happisburgh. Norf 2F 79
Happisburgh Common. Norf 3F 79
Hapsford. Ches W 3G 83
Hapton. Lanc 1F 91
Hapton. Norf 1D 66
Harberton. Devn 3D 9
Harbertonford. Devn 3D 9
Harbledown. Kent 5F 41
Harborne. W Mid 2E 61
Harborough Magna. Warw 3B 62
Harbottle. Nmbd 4D 120
Harbourneford. Devn 2D 8
Harbours Hill. Worc 4D 60
Harbridge. Hants 1G 15
Harbury. Warw 4A 62
Harby. Leics 2E 75
Harby. Notts 3F 87
Harcombe. Devn 3E 13
Harcombe Bottom. Devn 3G 13
Harcourt. Corn 5C 6
Harden. W Yor 1A 92
Hardenhuish. Wilts 4E 35
Hardgate. Abers 3E 153
Hardgate. Dum 3F 111
Hardham. W Sus 4B 26
Hardingham. Norf 5C 78
Hardingstone. Nptn 5E 63
Hardings Wood. Ches E 5C 84
Hardington. Som 1C 22
Hardington Mandeville. Som 1A 14
Hardington Marsh. Som 2A 14
Hardington Moor. Som 1A 14
Hardley. Hants 2C 16
Hardley Street. Norf 5F 79
Hardmead. Mil 1H 51
Hardraw. N Yor 5B 104
Hardstoft. Derbs 4B 86
Hardway. Hants 2E 16
Hardway. Som 3C 22
Hardwick. Buck 4G 51
Hardwick. Cambs 5C 64
Hardwick. Norf 2E 66
Hardwick. Nptn 4F 63
Hardwick. Oxon 3D 50 (nr. Bicester)
Hardwick. Oxon 5B 50 (nr. Witney)
Hardwick. Shrp 1F 59
Hardwick. S Yor 2B 86
Hardwick. Stoc T 2B 106
Hardwick. W Mid 1E 61
Hardwicke. Glos 3E 49 (nr. Cheltenham)
Hardwicke. Glos 4C 48 (nr. Gloucester)
Hardwicke. Here 1F 47
Hardwick Village. Notts 3D 86
Hardy's Green. Essx 3C 54
Hare. Som 1F 13
Hareby. Linc 4C 88
Hareden. Lanc 4F 97
Harefield. G Lon 1B 38
Hare Green. Essx 3D 54
Hare Hatch. Wok 4G 37
Harehill. Derbs 2F 73
Harehills. W Yor 1D 92
Harehope. Nmbd 2E 121
Harelaw. Dum 2F 113
Harelaw. Dur 4E 115
Hareplain. Kent 2C 28
Harescough. Cumb 5H 113
Harescombe. Glos 4D 48
Haresfield. Glos 4D 48
Haresfinch. Mers 1H 83
Hareshaw. N Lan 3B 128
Hare Street. Essx 5E 53
Hare Street. Herts 3D 53
Harewood. W Yor 5F 99
Harewood End. Here 3A 48
Harford. Devn 3C 8
Hargate. Norf 1D 66
Hargatewall. Derbs 3F 85
Hargrave. Ches W 4G 83
Hargrave. Nptn 3H 63
Hargrave. Suff 5G 65
Harker. Cumb 3E 113
Harkland. Shet 3F 173
Harkstead. Suff 2E 55
Harlaston. Staf 4G 73
Harlaxton. Linc 2F 75
Harlech. Gwyn 2E 69
Harlequin. Notts 2D 74
Harlescott. Shrp 4H 71
Harleston. Devn 4D 9
Harleston. Norf 2E 67
Harleston. Suff 4C 66
Harlestone. Nptn 4E 62
Harley. Shrp 5H 71
Harley. S Yor 1A 86
Harling Road. Norf 2B 66
Harlington. C Beds 2A 52
Harlington. G Lon 3B 38
Harlington. S Yor 4E 93
Harlosh. High 4B 154
Harlow. Essx 4E 53
Harlow Hill. Nmbd 3D 115
Harlsey Castle. N Yor 5B 106
Harlthorpe. E Yor 1H 93
Harlton. Cambs 5C 64
Harlyn Bay. Corn 1C 6

Harman's Cross—Holme next the Sea

Harman's Cross. *Dors* 4E **15**
Harmby. *N Yor* 1D **98**
Harmer Green. *Herts* 4C **52**
Harmer Hill. *Shrp* 3G **71**
Harmondsworth. *G Lon* 3B **38**
Harmston. *Linc* 4G **87**
Harnage. *Shrp* 5H **71**
Harnham. *Nmbd* 1D **115**
Harnhill. *Glos* 5F **49**
Harold Hill. *G Lon* 1G **39**
Haroldston West. *Pemb* 3C **42**
Haroldswick. *Shet* 1H **173**
Harold Wood. *G Lon* 1G **39**
Harome. *N Yor* 1A **100**
Harpenden. *Herts* 4B **52**
Harpford. *Devn* 3D **12**
Harpham. *E Yor* 3E **101**
Harpley. *Norf* 3G **77**
Harpley. *Worc* 4A **60**
Harpole. *Nptn* 4D **62**
Harpsdale. *High* 3D **168**
Harpsden. *Oxon* 3F **37**
Harpswell. *Linc* 2G **87**
Harpurhey. *G Man* 4G **91**
Harpur Hill. *Derbs* 3E **85**
Harraby. *Cumb* 4F **113**
Harracott. *Devn* 4F **19**
Harrapool. *High* 1E **147**
Harrapul. *High* 1E **147**
Harrietfield. *Per* 1B **136**
Harrietsham. *Kent* 5C **40**
Harrington. *Cumb* 2A **102**
Harrington. *Linc* 3C **88**
Harrington. *Nptn* 2E **63**
Harringworth. *Nptn* 1G **63**
Harriseahead. *Staf* 5C **84**
Harriston. *Cumb* 5C **112**
Harrogate. *N Yor* 4F **99** & **196**
Harrold. *Bed* 5G **63**
Harrop Dale. *G Man* 4A **92**
Harrow. *G Lon* 2C **38**
Harrowbarrow. *Corn* 2H **7**
Harrowden. *Bed* 1A **52**
Harrowgate Hill. *Darl* 3F **105**
Harrow on the Hill. *G Lon* 2C **38**
Harrow Weald. *G Lon* 1C **38**
Harry Stoke. *S Glo* 4B **34**
Harston. *Cambs* 5D **64**
Harston. *Leics* 2F **75**
Harswell. *E Yor* 5C **100**
Hart. *Hart* 1B **106**
Hartburn. *Nmbd* 1D **115**
Hartburn. *Stoc T* 3B **106**
Hartest. *Suff* 5H **65**
Hartfield. *E Sus* 2F **27**
Hartford. *Cambs* 3B **64**
Hartford. *Ches W* 3A **84**
Hartford. *Som* 4C **20**
Hartfordbridge. *Hants* 1F **25**
Hartford End. *Essx* 4G **53**
Harthill. *Ches W* 5H **83**
Harthill. *N Lan* 3C **128**
Harthill. *S Yor* 2B **86**
Hartington. *Derbs* 4F **85**
Hartland. *Devn* 4C **18**
Hartland Quay. *Devn* 4C **18**
Hartle. *Worc* 3D **60**
Hartlebury. *Worc* 3C **60**
Hartlepool. *Hart* 1C **106**
Hartley. *Cumb* 4A **104**
Hartley. *Kent* 2B **28**
(nr. Cranbrook)
Hartley. *Kent* 4H **39**
(nr. Dartford)
Hartley. *Nmbd* 2G **115**
Hartley Green. *Staf* 2D **73**
Hartley Mauditt. *Hants* 3F **25**
Hartley Wespall. *Hants* 1E **25**
Hartley Wintney. *Hants* 1F **25**
Hartlip. *Kent* 4C **40**
Hartmount. *High* 1B **158**
Hartoft End. *N Yor* 5E **107**
Harton. *N Yor* 3B **100**
Harton. *Shrp* 2G **59**
Harton. *Tyne* 3G **115**
Hartpury. *Glos* 3C **48**
Hartshead. *W Yor* 2B **92**
Hartshill. *Warw* 1H **61**
Hartshorne. *Derbs* 3H **73**
Hartsop. *Cumb* 3F **103**
Hart Station. *Hart* 1B **106**
Hartswell. *Som* 4D **20**
Hartwell. *Nptn* 5E **63**
Hartwood. *Lanc* 3D **90**
Hartwood. *N Lan* 4B **128**
Harvel. *Kent* 4A **40**
Harvington. *Worc* 1F **49**
(nr. Evesham)
Harvington. *Worc* 3C **60**
(nr. Kidderminster)
Harwell. *Oxon* 3C **36**
Harwich. *Essx* 2F **55** & **204**
Harwood. *Dur* 1B **104**
Harwood. *G Man* 3F **91**
Harwood Dale. *N Yor* 5G **107**
Harworth. *Notts* 1D **86**
Hascombe. *Surr* 2A **26**
Haselbech. *Nptn* 3E **62**
Haselbury Plucknett.
Som 1H **13**
Haseley. *Warw* 4G **61**
Haselor. *Warw* 5F **61**
Hasfield. *Glos* 3D **48**
Hasguard. *Pemb* 4C **42**
Haskayne. *Lanc* 4B **90**
Hasketon. *Suff* 5E **67**
Hasland. *Derbs* 4A **86**
Haslemere. *Surr* 2A **26**
Haslingden. *Lanc* 2F **91**
Haslingden Grane. *Lanc* 2F **91**
Haslingfield. *Cambs* 5D **64**
Haslington. *Ches E* 5B **84**
Hassall. *Ches E* 5B **84**
Hassall Green. *Ches E* 5B **84**
Hassell Street. *Kent* 1E **29**
Hassendean. *Bord* 2H **119**
Hassingham. *Norf* 5F **79**
Hassocks. *W Sus* 4E **27**
Hassop. *Derbs* 3G **85**
Haster. *High* 3F **169**
Hasthorpe. *Linc* 4D **89**
Hastigrow. *High* 2E **169**
Hastingleigh. *Kent* 1E **29**
Hastings. *E Sus* 5C **28**
Hastingwood. *Essx* 5E **53**
Hastoe. *Herts* 5H **51**
Haston. *Shrp* 3H **71**
Haswell. *Dur* 5G **115**
Haswell Plough. *Dur* 5G **115**
Hatch. *C Beds* 1B **52**
Hatch Beauchamp. *Som* 4G **21**
Hatch End. *G Lon* 1C **38**
Hatch Green. *Som* 1G **13**
Hatching Green. *Herts* 4B **52**
Hatchmere. *Ches W* 3H **83**
Hatch Warren. *Hants* 2E **24**
Hatcliffe. *NE Lin* 4F **95**
Hatfield. *Here* 5H **59**
Hatfield. *Herts* 5C **52**
Hatfield. *S Yor* 4G **93**
Hatfield. *Worc* 5C **60**
Hatfield Broad Oak. *Essx* 4F **53**
Hatfield Garden Village.
Herts 5C **52**
Hatfield Heath. *Essx* 4F **53**
Hatfield Hyde. *Herts* 4C **52**
Hatfield Peverel. *Essx* 4A **54**
Hatfield Woodhouse.
S Yor 4G **93**
Hatford. *Oxon* 2B **36**
Hatherden. *Hants* 1B **24**
Hatherleigh. *Devn* 2F **11**
Hathern. *Leics* 3C **74**
Hatherop. *Glos* 5G **49**
Hathersage. *Derbs* 2G **85**
Hathersage Booths.
Derbs 2G **85**
Hatherton. *Ches E* 1A **72**
Hatherton. *Staf* 4D **72**
Hatley St George. *Cambs* 5B **64**
Hatt. *Corn* 2H **7**
Hattersley. *G Man* 1D **85**
Hattingley. *Hants* 3E **25**
Hatton. *Abers* 5H **161**
Hatton. *Derbs* 2G **73**
Hatton. *G Lon* 3B **38**
Hatton. *Linc* 3A **88**
Hatton. *Shrp* 1G **59**
Hatton. *Warr* 2H **83**
Hatton. *Warw* 4G **61**
Hattoncrook. *Abers* 1F **153**
Hatton Heath. *Ches W* 4G **83**
Hatton of Fintray. *Abers* 2F **153**
Haugh. *E Ayr* 2D **117**
Haugh. *Linc* 3D **88**
Haugham. *Linc* 2C **88**
Haugh Head. *Nmbd* 2E **121**
Haughley. *Suff* 4C **66**
Haughley Green. *Suff* 4C **66**
Haugh of Ballechin. *Per* 3G **143**
Haugh of Glass. *Mor* 5B **160**
Haugh of Urr. *Dum* 3F **111**
Haughton. *Ches E* 5H **83**
Haughton. *Notts* 3D **86**
Haughton. *Shrp* 1A **60**
(nr. Bridgnorth)
Haughton. *Shrp* 3F **71**
(nr. Oswestry)
Haughton. *Shrp* 5B **72**
(nr. Shifnal)
Haughton. *Shrp* 4H **71**
(nr. Shrewsbury)
Haughton. *Staf* 3C **72**
Haughton Green. *G Man* 1D **84**
Haughton le Skerne.
Darl 3A **106**
Haultwick. *Herts* 3D **52**
Haunn. *Arg* 4E **139**
Haunn. *W Isl* 7C **170**
Haunton. *Staf* 4G **73**
Hauxton. *Cambs* 5D **64**
Havannah. *Ches E* 4C **84**
Havant. *Hants* 2F **17**
Haven. *Here* 5G **59**
Haven Bank. *Linc* 5B **88**
Havenside. *E Yor* 2E **95**
Havenstreet. *IOW* 3D **16**
Haven, The. *W Sus* 2B **26**
Havercroft. *W Yor* 3D **93**
Haverfordwest. *Pemb* 3D **42**
Haverhill. *Suff* 1G **53**
Haverigg. *Cumb* 2A **96**
Havering-atte-Bower.
G Lon 1G **39**
Havering's Grove. *Essx* 1A **40**
Haversham. *Mil* 1G **51**
Haverthwaite. *Cumb* 1C **96**
Haverton Hill. *Stoc T* 2B **106**
Havyatt. *Som* 3A **22**
Hawarden. *Flin* 4F **83**
Hawbridge. *Worc* 1E **49**
Hawcoat. *Cumb* 2B **96**
Hawcross. *Glos* 2C **48**
Hawen. *Cdgn* 1D **44**
Hawes. *N Yor* 1A **98**
Hawes Green. *Norf* 1E **67**
Hawick. *Bord* 3H **119**
Hawkchurch. *Devn* 2G **13**
Hawkedon. *Suff* 5G **65**
Hawkenbury. *Kent* 1C **28**
Hawkeridge. *Wilts* 1D **22**
Hawkerland. *Devn* 4D **12**
Hawkesbury. *S Glo* 3C **34**
Hawkesbury. *W Mid* 2A **62**
Hawkesbury Upton. *S Glo* 3C **34**
Hawkes End. *W Mid* 2G **61**
Hawk Green. *G Man* 2D **84**
Hawkhurst. *Kent* 2B **28**
Hawkhurst Common.
E Sus 4G **27**
Hawkinge. *Kent* 1G **29**
Hawkley. *Hants* 4F **25**
Hawkridge. *Som* 3B **20**
Hawksdale. *Cumb* 5E **113**
Hawkshaw. *G Man* 3F **91**
Hawkshead. *Cumb* 5E **103**
Hawkshead Hill. *Cumb* 5E **103**
Hawkswick. *N Yor* 2B **98**
Hawksworth. *Notts* 1E **75**
Hawksworth. *W Yor* 5D **98**
Hawkwell. *Essx* 1C **40**
Hawley. *Hants* 1G **25**
Hawley. *Kent* 3G **39**
Hawling. *Glos* 3F **49**
Hawnby. *N Yor* 1H **99**
Haworth. *W Yor* 1A **92**
Hawstead. *Suff* 5A **66**
Hawthorn. *Dur* 5H **115**
Hawthorn Hill. *Brac* 4G **37**
Hawthorn Hill. *Linc* 5B **88**
Hawthorpe. *Linc* 3H **75**
Hawton. *Notts* 5E **87**
Haxby. *York* 4A **100**
Haxey. *N Lin* 1E **87**
Haybridge. *Shrp* 3A **60**
Haybridge. *Som* 2A **22**
Haydock. *Mers* 1H **83**
Haydon. *Bath* 1B **22**
Haydon. *Dors* 1B **14**
Haydon. *Som* 4F **21**
Haydon Bridge. *Nmbd* 3B **114**
Haydon Wick. *Swin* 3G **35**
Haye. *Corn* 2H **7**
Hayes. *G Lon* 4F **39**
(nr. Bromley)
Hayes. *G Lon* 2B **38**
(nr. Uxbridge)
Hayfield. *Derbs* 2E **85**
Hay Green. *Norf* 4E **77**
Hayhill. *E Ayr* 3D **116**
Haylands. *IOW* 3D **16**
Hayle. *Corn* 3C **4**
Hayley Green. *W Mid* 2D **60**
Hayling Island. *Hants* 3F **17**
Hayne. *Devn* 2B **12**
Haynes. *C Beds* 1A **52**
Haynes West End.
C Beds 1A **52**
Hay-on-Wye. *Powy* 1F **47**
Hayscastle. *Pemb* 2C **42**
Hayscastle Cross. *Pemb* 2D **42**
Haysden. *Kent* 1G **27**
Hayshead. *Ang* 4F **145**
Hay Street. *Herts* 3D **53**
Hayton. *Aber* 3G **153**
Hayton. *Cumb* 5C **112**
(nr. Aspatria)
Hayton. *Cumb* 4G **113**
(nr. Brampton)
Hayton. *E Yor* 5C **100**
Hayton. *Notts* 2E **87**
Hayton's Bent. *Shrp* 2H **59**
Haytor Vale. *Devn* 5A **12**
Haytown. *Devn* 1D **11**
Haywards Heath. *W Sus* 3E **27**
Haywood. *S Lan* 4C **128**
Hazelbank. *S Lan* 5B **128**
Hazelbury Bryan. *Dors* 2C **14**
Hazeleigh. *Essx* 5B **54**
Hazeley. *Hants* 1F **25**
Hazel Grove. *G Man* 2D **84**
Hazelhead. *S Yor* 4B **92**
Hazelslade. *Staf* 4E **73**
Hazel Street. *Kent* 2A **28**
Hazelton Walls. *Fife* 1F **137**
Hazelwood. *Derbs* 1H **73**
Hazlemere. *Buck* 2G **37**
Hazler. *Shrp* 1G **59**
Hazlerigg. *Tyne* 2F **115**
Hazles. *Staf* 1E **73**
Hazleton. *Glos* 4F **49**
Hazon. *Nmbd* 4F **121**
Heacham. *Norf* 2F **77**
Headbourne Worthy.
Hants 3C **24**
Headcorn. *Kent* 1C **28**
Headingley. *W Yor* 1C **92**
Headington. *Oxon* 5D **50**
Headlam. *Dur* 3E **105**
Headless Cross. *Worc* 4E **61**
Headley. *Hants* 3G **25**
(nr. Haslemere)
Headley. *Hants* 5D **36**
(nr. Kingsclere)
Headley. *Surr* 5D **38**
Headley Down. *Hants* 3G **25**
Headley Heath. *Worc* 3E **61**
Headley Park. *Bris* 5A **34**
Head of Muir. *Falk* 1B **128**
Headon. *Notts* 3E **87**
Heads Nook. *Cumb* 4F **113**
Heage. *Derbs* 5A **86**
Healaugh. *N Yor* 5D **104**
(nr. Grinton)
Healaugh. *N Yor* 5H **99**
(nr. York)
Heald Green. *G Man* 2C **84**
Heale. *Devn* 2G **19**
Healey. *G Man* 3G **91**
Healey. *Nmbd* 4D **114**
Healey. *N Yor* 1D **98**
Healeyfield. *Dur* 5D **114**
Healey Hall. *Nmbd* 4D **114**
Healing. *NE Lin* 3F **95**
Heamoor. *Corn* 3B **4**
Heanish. *Arg* 4B **138**
Heanor. *Derbs* 1B **74**
Heanton Punchardon.
Devn 3F **19**
Heapham. *Linc* 2F **87**
Heartsease. *Powy* 4D **58**
Heasley Mill. *Devn* 3H **19**
Heaste. *High* 2E **147**
Heath. *Derbs* 4B **86**
Heath and Reach. *C Beds* 3H **51**
Heath Common. *W Sus* 4C **26**
Heathcote. *Derbs* 4F **85**
Heath Cross. *Devn* 3H **11**
Heathencote. *Nptn* 1F **51**
Heath End. *Derbs* 3A **74**
Heath End. *Hants* 5D **36**
Heath End. *W Mid* 5E **73**
Heather. *Leics* 4A **74**
Heatherfield. *High* 4D **155**
Heatherton. *Derb* 2H **73**
Heathfield. *Cambs* 1E **53**
Heathfield. *Cumb* 5C **112**
Heathfield. *Devn* 5B **12**
Heathfield. *E Sus* 3G **27**
Heathfield. *Ren* 3E **126**
Heathfield. *Som* 3E **21**
(nr. Lydeard St Lawrence)
Heathfield. *Som* 4E **21**
(nr. Norton Fitzwarren)
Heath Green. *Worc* 3E **61**
Heathhall. *Dum* 2A **112**
Heath Hayes. *Staf* 4E **73**
Heath Hill. *Shrp* 4B **72**
Heath House. *Som* 2H **21**
Heathrow (London) Airport.
G Lon 3B **38** & **205**
Heathstock. *Devn* 2F **13**
Heath, The. *Norf* 3E **79**
(nr. Buxton)
Heath, The. *Norf* 3B **78**
(nr. Fakenham)
Heath, The. *Norf* 3D **78**
(nr. Hevingham)
Heath, The. *Staf* 2E **73**
Heath, The. *Suff* 2E **55**
Heathton. *Shrp* 1C **60**
Heathtop. *Derbs* 2F **73**
Heath Town. *W Mid* 1D **60**
Heatley. *G Man* 2B **84**
Heatley. *Staf* 3E **73**
Heaton. *Lanc* 3D **96**
Heaton. *Staf* 4D **84**
Heaton. *Tyne* 3F **115**
Heaton. *W Yor* 1B **92**
Heaton Moor. *G Man* 1C **84**
Heaton's Bridge. *Lanc* 3C **90**
Heaverham. *Kent* 5G **39**
Heavitree. *Devn* 3C **12**
Hebburn. *Tyne* 3G **115**
Hebden. *N Yor* 3C **98**
Hebden Bridge. *W Yor* 2H **91**
Hebden Green. *Ches W* 4A **84**
Hebing End. *Herts* 3D **52**
Hebron. *Carm* 2F **43**
Hebron. *Nmbd* 1E **115**
Heck. *Dum* 1B **112**
Heckdyke. *Notts* 1E **87**
Heckfield. *Hants* 5F **37**
Heckfield Green. *Suff* 3D **66**
Heckfordbridge. *Essx* 3C **54**
Heckington. *Linc* 1A **76**
Heckmondwike. *W Yor* 2C **92**
Heddington. *Wilts* 5E **35**
Heddle. *Orkn* 6C **172**
Heddon. *Devn* 4G **19**
Heddon-on-the-Wall.
Nmbd 3E **115**
Hedenham. *Norf* 1F **67**
Hedge End. *Hants* 1C **16**
Hedgerley. *Buck* 2A **38**
Hedging. *Som* 4G **21**
Hedley on the Hill.
Nmbd 4D **115**
Hednesford. *Staf* 4E **73**
Hedon. *E Yor* 2E **95**
Hegdon Hill. *Here* 5H **59**
Heglibister. *Shet* 6E **173**
Heighington. *Darl* 2F **105**
Heighington. *Linc* 4H **87**
Heightington. *Worc* 3B **60**
Heights of Brae. *High* 2H **157**
Heights of Fodderty.
High 2H **157**
Heights of Kinlochewe.
High 2C **156**
Heiton. *Bord* 1B **120**
Hele. *Devn* 2C **12**
(nr. Exeter)
Hele. *Devn* 3D **10**
(nr. Holsworthy)
Hele. *Devn* 2F **19**
(nr. Ilfracombe)
Hele. *Torb* 2F **9**
Helen's Bay. *N Dwn* 1J **179**
Helensburgh. *Arg* 1D **126**
Helford. *Corn* 4E **5**
Helhoughton. *Norf* 3A **78**
Helions Bumpstead. *Essx* 1G **53**
Helland. *Corn* 5A **10**
Helland. *Som* 4G **21**
Hellandbridge. *Corn* 5A **10**
Hellesdon. *Norf* 4E **78**
Hellesveor. *Corn* 2C **4**
Hellidon. *Nptn* 5C **62**
Hellifield. *N Yor* 4A **98**
Hellingly. *E Sus* 4G **27**
Hellington. *Norf* 5F **79**
Hellister. *Shet* 7E **173**
Helmdon. *Nptn* 1D **50**
Helmingham. *Suff* 5D **66**
Helmington Row. *Dur* 1E **105**
Helmsdale. *High* 2H **165**
Helmshore. *Lanc* 2F **91**
Helmsley. *N Yor* 1A **100**
Helperby. *N Yor* 3G **99**
Helperthorpe. *N Yor* 2D **100**
Helpringham. *Linc* 1A **76**
Helpston. *Pet* 5A **76**
Helsby. *Ches W* 3G **83**
Helsey. *Linc* 3E **89**
Helston. *Corn* 4D **4**
Helstone. *Corn* 4A **10**
Helton. *Cumb* 2G **103**
Helwith. *N Yor* 4D **105**
Helwith Bridge. *N Yor* 3H **97**
Helygain. *Flin* 3E **82**
Hemblington. *Norf* 4F **79**
Hemel Hempstead. *Herts* 5A **52**
Hemerdon. *Devn* 3B **8**
Hemingbrough. *N Yor* 1G **93**
Hemingby. *Linc* 3B **88**
Hemingfield. *S Yor* 4D **93**
Hemingford Abbots.
Cambs 3B **64**
Hemingford Grey. *Cambs* 3B **64**
Hemingstone. *Suff* 5D **66**
Hemington. *Leics* 3B **74**
Hemington. *Nptn* 2H **63**
Hemington. *Som* 1C **22**
Hemley. *Suff* 1F **55**
Hemlington. *Midd* 3B **106**
Hempholme. *E Yor* 4E **101**
Hempnall. *Norf* 1E **67**
Hempnall Green. *Norf* 1E **67**
Hempriggs. *High* 4F **169**
Hemp's Green. *Essx* 3C **54**
Hempstead. *Essx* 2G **53**
Hempstead. *Medw* 4B **40**
Hempstead. *Norf* 2D **78**
(nr. Holt)
Hempstead. *Norf* 3G **79**
(nr. Stalham)
Hempsted. *Glos* 4D **48**
Hempton. *Norf* 3B **78**
Hempton. *Oxon* 2C **50**
Hemsby. *Norf* 4G **79**
Hemswell. *Linc* 1G **87**
Hemswell Cliff. *Linc* 2G **87**
Hemsworth. *Dors* 2E **15**
Hemsworth. *W Yor* 3E **93**
Hem, The. *Shrp* 5B **72**
Hemyock. *Devn* 1E **13**
Henallt. *Carm* 3E **45**
Henbury. *Bris* 4A **34**
Henbury. *Ches E* 3C **84**
Hendomen. *Powy* 1E **58**
Hendon. *G Lon* 2D **38**
Hendon. *Tyne* 4H **115**
Hendra. *Corn* 3D **6**
Hendre. *B'end* 3C **32**
Hendreforgan. *Rhon* 3C **32**
Hendy. *Carm* 5F **45**
Heneglwys. *IOA* 3D **80**
Henfeddau Fawr. *Pemb* 1G **43**
Henfield. *S Glo* 4B **34**
Henfield. *W Sus* 4D **26**
Henford. *Devn* 3D **10**
Hengoed. *Cphy* 2E **33**
Hengoed. *Shrp* 2E **71**
Hengrave. *Suff* 4H **65**
Henham. *Essx* 3F **53**
Heniarth. *Powy* 5D **70**
Henlade. *Som* 4F **21**
Henley. *Dors* 2B **14**
Henley. *Shrp* 2G **59**
(nr. Church Stretton)
Henley. *Shrp* 3H **59**
(nr. Ludlow)
Henley. *Som* 3H **21**
Henley. *Suff* 5D **66**
Henley. *W Sus* 4G **25**
Henley-in-Arden. *Warw* 4F **61**
Henley-on-Thames. *Oxon* 3F **37**
Henley's Down. *E Sus* 4B **28**
Henley Street. *Kent* 4A **40**
Henllan. *Cdgn* 1D **44**
Henllan. *Den* 4C **82**
Henllan. *Mon* 3F **47**
Henllan Amgoed. *Carm* 3F **43**
Henllys. *Torf* 2F **33**
Henlow. *C Beds* 2B **52**
Hennock. *Devn* 4B **12**
Henny Street. *Essx* 2B **54**
Henryd. *Cnwy* 3G **81**
Henry's Moat. *Pemb* 2E **43**
Hensall. *N Yor* 2F **93**
Henshaw. *Nmbd* 3A **114**
Hensingham. *Cumb* 3A **102**
Henstead. *Suff* 2G **67**
Hensting. *Hants* 4C **24**
Henstridge. *Som* 1C **14**
Henstridge Ash. *Som* 4C **22**
Henstridge Bowden. *Som* 4B **22**
Henstridge Marsh. *Som* 4C **22**
Henton. *Oxon* 5F **51**
Henton. *Som* 2H **21**
Henwood. *Corn* 5C **10**
Heogan. *Shet* 7F **173**
Heol Senni. *Powy* 3C **46**
Heol-y-Cyw. *B'end* 3C **32**
Hepburn. *Nmbd* 2E **121**
Hepple. *Nmbd* 4D **121**
Hepscott. *Nmbd* 1F **115**
Heptonstall. *W Yor* 2H **91**
Hepworth. *Suff* 3B **66**
Hepworth. *W Yor* 4B **92**
Herbrandston. *Pemb* 4C **42**
Hereford. *Here* 2A **48**
Heribusta. *High* 1D **154**
Heriot. *Bord* 4H **129**
Hermiston. *Edin* 2E **129**
Hermitage. *Dors* 2B **14**
Hermitage. *Bord* 5H **119**
Hermitage. *W Ber* 4D **36**
Hermitage. *W Sus* 2F **17**
Hermon. *Carm* 3G **45**
(nr. Llandeilo)
Hermon. *Carm* 2D **44**
(nr. Newcastle Emlyn)
Hermon. *IOA* 4C **80**
Hermon. *Pemb* 1G **43**
Herne. *Kent* 4F **41**
Herne Bay. *Kent* 4F **41**
Herne Common. *Kent* 4F **41**
Herne Pound. *Kent* 5A **40**
Herner. *Devn* 4F **19**
Hernhill. *Kent* 4E **41**
Herodsfoot. *Corn* 2G **7**
Heronden. *Kent* 5G **41**
Herongate. *Essx* 1H **39**
Heronsford. *S Ayr* 1G **109**
Heronsgate. *Herts* 1B **38**
Heron's Ghyll. *E Sus* 3F **27**
Herra. *Shet* 2H **173**
Herriard. *Hants* 2E **25**
Herringfleet. *Suff* 1G **67**
Herringswell. *Suff* 4G **65**
Herrington. *Tyne* 4G **115**
Hersden. *Kent* 4G **41**
Hersham. *Corn* 2C **10**
Hersham. *Surr* 4C **38**
Herstmonceux. *E Sus* 4H **27**
Herston. *Dors* 5F **15**
Herston. *Orkn* 8D **172**
Hertford. *Herts* 4D **52**
Hertford Heath. *Herts* 4D **52**
Hertingfordbury. *Herts* 4D **52**
Hesketh. *Lanc* 2C **90**
Hesketh Bank. *Lanc* 2C **90**
Hesketh Lane. *Lanc* 5F **97**
Hesket Newmarket.
Cumb 1E **103**
Heskin Green. *Lanc* 3D **90**
Hesleden. *Dur* 1B **106**
Hesleyside. *Nmbd* 1B **114**
Heslington. *York* 4A **100**
Hessay. *York* 4H **99**
Hessenford. *Corn* 3H **7**
Hessett. *Suff* 4B **66**
Hessilhead. *N Ayr* 4E **127**
Hessle. *Hull* 2D **94**
Hestaford. *Shet* 6D **173**
Hest Bank. *Lanc* 3D **96**
Hester's Way. *Glos* 3E **49**
Hestinsetter. *Shet* 7D **173**
Heston. *G Lon* 3C **38**
Hestwall. *Orkn* 6B **172**
Heswall. *Mers* 2E **83**
Hethe. *Oxon* 3D **50**
Hethelpit Cross. *Glos* 3C **48**
Hethersett. *Norf* 5D **78**
Hethersgill. *Cumb* 3F **113**
Hetherside. *Cumb* 3F **113**
Hethpool. *Nmbd* 2C **120**
Hett. *Dur* 1F **105**
Hetton. *N Yor* 4B **98**
Hetton-le-Hole. *Tyne* 5G **115**
Hetton Steads. *Nmbd* 1E **121**
Heugh. *Nmbd* 2D **115**
Heugh-head. *Abers* 2A **152**
Heveningham. *Suff* 3F **67**
Hever. *Kent* 1F **27**
Heversham. *Cumb* 1D **97**
Hevingham. *Norf* 3D **78**
Hewas Water. *Corn* 4D **6**
Hewelsfield. *Glos* 5A **48**
Hewish. *N Som* 5G **33**
Hewish. *Som* 2H **13**
Hewood. *Dors* 2G **13**
Heworth. *York* 4A **100**
Hexham. *Nmbd* 3C **114**
Hextable. *Kent* 3G **39**
Hexton. *Herts* 2B **52**
Hexworthy. *Devn* 5G **11**
Heybridge. *Essx* 1H **39**
(nr. Brentwood)
Heybridge. *Essx* 5B **54**
(nr. Maldon)
Heybridge Basin. *Essx* 5B **54**
Heybrook Bay. *Devn* 4A **8**
Heydon. *Cambs* 1E **53**
Heydon. *Norf* 3D **78**
Heydour. *Linc* 2H **75**
Heylipol. *Arg* 4A **138**
Heyop. *Powy* 3E **59**
Heysham. *Lanc* 3D **96**
Heyshott. *W Sus* 1G **17**
Heytesbury. *Wilts* 2E **23**
Heythrop. *Oxon* 3B **50**
Heywood. *G Man* 3G **91**
Heywood. *Wilts* 1D **22**
Hibaldstow. *N Lin* 4C **94**
Hickleton. *S Yor* 4E **93**
Hickling. *Norf* 3G **79**
Hickling. *Notts* 3D **74**
Hickling Green. *Norf* 3G **79**
Hickling Heath. *Norf* 3G **79**
Hickstead. *W Sus* 3D **26**
Hidcote Bartrim. *Glos* 1G **49**
Hidcote Boyce. *Glos* 1G **49**
Higford. *Shrp* 5B **72**
High Ackworth. *W Yor* 3E **93**
Higham. *Derbs* 5A **86**
Higham. *Kent* 3B **40**
Higham. *Lanc* 1G **91**
Higham. *S Yor* 4D **92**
Higham. *Suff* 2D **54**
(nr. Ipswich)
Higham. *Suff* 4G **65**
(nr. Newmarket)
Higham Dykes. *Nmbd* 2E **115**
Higham Ferrers. *Nptn* 4G **63**
Higham Gobion. *C Beds* 2B **52**
Higham on the Hill. *Leics* 1A **62**
Highampton. *Devn* 2E **11**
Higham Wood. *Kent* 1G **27**
High Angerton. *Nmbd* 1D **115**
High Auldgirth. *Dum* 1G **111**
High Bankhill. *Cumb* 5G **113**
High Banton. *N Lan* 1A **128**
High Barnet. *G Lon* 1D **38**
High Beech. *Essx* 1F **39**
High Bentham. *N Yor* 3F **97**
High Bickington. *Devn* 4G **19**
High Biggins. *Cumb* 2F **97**
High Birkwith. *N Yor* 2H **97**
High Blantyre. *S Lan* 4H **127**
High Bonnybridge. *Falk* 2B **128**
High Borrans. *Cumb* 4F **103**
High Bradfield. *S Yor* 1G **85**
High Bray. *Devn* 3G **19**
Highbridge. *Cumb* 5E **113**
Highbridge. *High* 5D **148**
Highbridge. *Som* 2G **21**
Highbrook. *W Sus* 2E **27**
High Brooms. *Kent* 1G **27**
High Bullen. *Devn* 4F **19**
Highburton. *W Yor* 3B **92**
Highbury. *Som* 2B **22**
High Buston. *Nmbd* 4G **121**
High Callerton. *Nmbd* 2E **115**
High Carlingill. *Cumb* 4H **103**
High Catton. *E Yor* 4B **100**
High Church. *Nmbd* 1E **115**
Highclere. *Hants* 5C **36**
Highcliffe. *Dors* 3H **15**
High Cogges. *Oxon* 5B **50**
High Common. *Norf* 5B **78**
High Coniscliffe. *Darl* 3F **105**
High Crosby. *Cumb* 4F **113**
High Cross. *Hants* 4F **25**
High Cross. *Herts* 4D **52**
High Easter. *Essx* 4G **53**
High Eggborough. *N Yor* 2F **93**
High Ellington. *N Yor* 1D **98**
Higher Alham. *Som* 2B **22**
Higher Ansty. *Dors* 2C **14**
Higher Ashton. *Devn* 4B **12**
Higher Ballam. *Lanc* 1B **90**
Higher Bartle. *Lanc* 1D **90**
Higher Bockhampton.
Dors 3C **14**
Higher Bojewyan. *Corn* 3A **4**
High Ercall. *Telf* 4H **71**
Higher Cheriton. *Devn* 2E **12**
Higher Clovelly. *Devn* 4D **18**
Higher Compton. *Plym* 3A **8**
Higher Dean. *Devn* 2D **8**
Higher Dinting. *Derbs* 1E **85**
Higher Dunstone. *Devn* 5H **11**
Higher End. *G Man* 4D **90**
Higherford. *Lanc* 5A **98**
Higher Gabwell. *Devn* 2F **9**
Higher Halstock Leigh.
Dors 2A **14**
Higher Heysham. *Lanc* 3D **96**
Higher Hurdsfield.
Ches E 3D **84**
Higher Kingcombe. *Dors* 3A **14**
Higher Kinnerton. *Flin* 4F **83**
Higher Melcombe. *Dors* 2C **14**
Higher Penwortham.
Lanc 2D **90**
Higher Porthpean. *Corn* 3E **7**
Higher Poynton. *Ches E* 2D **84**
Higher Shotton. *Flin* 4F **83**
Higher Shurlach. *Ches W* 3A **84**
Higher Slade. *Devn* 2F **19**
Higher Tale. *Devn* 2D **12**
Highertown. *Corn* 4C **6**
Higher Town. *IOS* 1B **4**
Higher Town. *Som* 2C **20**
Higher Vexford. *Som* 3E **20**
Higher Walton. *Lanc* 2D **90**
Higher Walton. *Warr* 2H **83**
Higher Whatcombe. *Dors* 2D **14**
Higher Wheelton. *Lanc* 2E **90**
Higher Whiteleigh. *Corn* 3C **10**
Higher Whitley. *Ches W* 3A **84**
Higher Wincham. *Ches W* 3A **84**
Higher Wraxall. *Dors* 2A **14**
Higher Wych. *Wrex* 1G **71**
Higher Yalberton. *Torb* 3E **9**
High Etherley. *Dur* 2E **105**
High Ferry. *Linc* 1C **76**
Highfield. *E Yor* 1H **93**
Highfield. *N Ayr* 4E **126**
Highfield. *Tyne* 4E **115**
Highfields Caldecote.
Cambs 5C **64**
High Garrett. *Essx* 3A **54**
Highgate. *G Lon* 2D **39**
Highgate. *N Ayr* 4E **127**
Highgate. *Powy* 1D **58**
High Grange. *Dur* 1E **105**
High Green. *Cumb* 4F **103**
High Green. *Norf* 5D **78**
High Green. *Shrp* 2B **60**
High Green. *S Yor* 1H **85**
High Green. *W Yor* 3B **92**
High Green. *Worc* 1D **49**
Highgreen Manor.
Nmbd 5C **120**
High Halden. *Kent* 2C **28**
High Halstow. *Medw* 3B **40**
High Ham. *Som* 3H **21**
High Harrington. *Cumb* 2B **102**
High Haswell. *Dur* 5G **115**
High Hatton. *Shrp* 3A **72**
High Hawsker. *N Yor* 4G **107**
High Hesket. *Cumb* 5F **113**
High Hesleden. *Dur* 1B **106**
High Hoyland. *S Yor* 3C **92**
High Hunsley. *E Yor* 1C **94**
High Hurstwood. *E Sus* 3F **27**
High Hutton. *N Yor* 3B **100**
High Ireby. *Cumb* 1D **102**
High Keil. *Arg* 5A **122**
High Kelling. *Norf* 1D **78**
High Kilburn. *N Yor* 2H **99**
High Knipe. *Cumb* 3G **103**
High Lands. *Dur* 2E **105**
Highlands, The. *Shrp* 2A **60**
Highlane. *Ches E* 4C **84**
Highlane. *Derbs* 2B **86**
High Lane. *G Man* 2D **84**
High Lane. *Here* 4A **60**
High Laver. *Essx* 5F **53**
Highlaws. *Cumb* 5C **112**
Highleadon. *Glos* 3C **48**
High Legh. *Ches E* 2A **84**
Highleigh. *W Sus* 3G **17**
High Leven. *Stoc T* 3B **106**
Highley. *Shrp* 2B **60**
High Littleton. *Bath* 1B **22**
High Longthwaite.
Cumb 5D **112**
High Lorton. *Cumb* 2C **102**
High Marishes. *N Yor* 2C **100**
High Marnham. *Notts* 3F **87**
High Melton. *S Yor* 4F **93**
High Mickley. *Nmbd* 3D **115**
Highmoor. *Cumb* 5D **112**
High Moor. *Lanc* 3D **90**
Highmoor. *Oxon* 3F **37**
Highmoor Cross. *Oxon* 3F **37**
Highmoor Hill. *Mon* 3H **33**
High Mowthorpe. *N Yor* 3C **100**
Highnam. *Glos* 4C **48**
High Newport. *Tyne* 4G **115**
High Newton. *Cumb* 1D **96**
High Newton-by-the-Sea.
Nmbd 2G **121**
High Nibthwaite. *Cumb* 1B **96**
High Offley. *Staf* 3B **72**
High Ongar. *Essx* 5F **53**
High Onn. *Staf* 4C **72**
High Orchard. *Glos* 4D **48**
High Park. *Mers* 3B **90**
High Roding. *Essx* 4G **53**
High Row. *Cumb* 1E **103**
High Salvington. *W Sus* 5C **26**
High Scales. *Cumb* 5C **112**
High Shaw. *N Yor* 5B **104**
High Shincliffe. *Dur* 5F **115**
High Side. *Cumb* 1D **102**
High Spen. *Tyne* 3E **115**
Highsted. *Kent* 4D **40**
High Stoop. *Dur* 5E **115**
High Street. *Corn* 3D **6**
High Street. *Suff* 5G **67**
(nr. Aldeburgh)
High Street. *Suff* 2F **67**
(nr. Bungay)
High Street. *Suff* 3G **67**
(nr. Yoxford)
Highstreet Green. *Essx* 2A **54**
High Street Green. *Suff* 5C **66**
Highstreet Green. *Surr* 2A **26**
Hightae. *Dum* 2B **112**
High Throston. *Hart* 1B **106**
Hightown. *Ches E* 4C **84**
Hightown. *Mers* 4A **90**
High Town. *Staf* 4D **73**
Hightown Green. *Suff* 5B **66**
High Toynton. *Linc* 4B **88**
High Trewhitt. *Nmbd* 4E **121**
High Valleyfield. *Fife* 1D **128**
Highway. *Here* 1H **47**
Highweek. *Devn* 5B **12**
High Westwood. *Dur* 4E **115**
Highwood. *Staf* 2E **73**
Highwood. *Worc* 4A **60**
High Worsall. *N Yor* 4A **106**
Highworth. *Swin* 2H **35**
High Wray. *Cumb* 5E **103**
High Wych. *Herts* 4E **53**
High Wycombe. *Buck* 2G **37**
Hilborough. *Norf* 5H **77**
Hilcott. *Wilts* 1G **23**
Hildenborough. *Kent* 1G **27**
Hildersham. *Cambs* 1F **53**
Hilderstone. *Staf* 2D **72**
Hilderthorpe. *E Yor* 3F **101**
Hilfield. *Dors* 2B **14**
Hilgay. *Norf* 1F **65**
Hill. *S Glo* 2B **34**
Hill. *Warw* 4B **62**
Hill. *Worc* 1E **49**
Hillam. *N Yor* 2F **93**
Hillbeck. *Cumb* 3A **104**
Hillberry. *IOM* 4C **108**
Hillborough. *Kent* 4G **41**
Hillbourne. *Pool* 3F **15**
Hillbrae. *Abers* 4D **160**
(nr. Aberchirder)
Hillbrae. *Abers* 1E **153**
(nr. Inverurie)
Hillbrae. *Abers* 5F **161**
(nr. Methlick)
Hill Brow. *Hants* 4F **25**
Hillbutts. *Dors* 2E **15**
Hillclifflane. *Derbs* 1G **73**
Hillcommon. *Som* 4E **21**
Hill Deverill. *Wilts* 2D **22**
Hilldyke. *Linc* 1C **76**
Hill End. *Dur* 1D **104**
Hillend. *Fife* 1E **129**
(nr. Inverkeithing)
Hill End. *Fife* 4C **136**
(nr. Saline)
Hillend. *N Lan* 3B **128**
Hill End. *N Yor* 4C **98**
Hillend. *Shrp* 1C **60**
Hillend. *Swan* 3D **30**
Hillersland. *Glos* 4A **48**
Hillerton. *Devn* 3H **11**
Hillesden. *Buck* 3E **51**
Hillesley. *Glos* 3C **34**
Hillfarrance. *Som* 4E **21**
Hill Furze. *Worc* 1E **49**
Hill Gate. *Here* 3H **47**
Hill Green. *Essx* 2E **53**
Hillgreen. *W Ber* 4C **36**
Hillhall. *Lis* 3G **179**
Hillhead. *Abers* 5C **160**
Hill Head. *Hants* 2D **16**
Hillhead. *S Ayr* 3D **116**
Hillhead. *Torb* 3F **9**
Hillhead of Auchentumb.
Abers 3G **161**
Hilliard's Cross. *Staf* 4F **73**
Hilliclay. *High* 2D **168**
Hillingdon. *G Lon* 2B **38**
Hillington. *Norf* 3G **77**
Hillington. *Ren* 3G **127**
Hillmorton. *Warw* 3C **62**
Hill of Beath. *Fife* 4D **136**
Hill of Fearn. *High* 1C **158**
Hill of Fiddes. *Abers* 1G **153**
Hill of Keillor. *Ang* 4B **144**
Hill of Overbrae. *Abers* 2F **161**
Hill Ridware. *Staf* 4E **73**
Hillsborough. *Lis* 4G **179**
Hillsborough. *S Yor* 1H **85**
Hillside. *Abers* 4G **153**
Hillside. *Ang* 2G **145**
Hillside. *Devn* 2D **8**
Hillside. *Mers* 3B **90**
Hillside. *Orkn* 5C **172**
Hillside. *Shet* 5F **173**
Hillside. *Shrp* 2A **60**
Hill Side. *W Yor* 3B **92**
Hillside. *Worc* 4B **60**
Hillside of Prieston. *Ang* 5C **144**
Hill Somersal. *Derbs* 2F **73**
Hillstown. *Derbs* 4B **86**
Hillstreet. *Hants* 1B **16**
Hillswick. *Shet* 4D **173**
Hill, The. *Cumb* 1A **96**
Hill Top. *Dur* 2C **104**
(nr. Barnard Castle)
Hill Top. *Dur* 5F **115**
(nr. Durham)
Hill Top. *Dur* 4E **115**
(nr. Stanley)
Hilltown. *New M* 7G **179**
Hill View. *Dors* 3E **15**
Hillwell. *Shet* 10E **173**
Hill Wootton. *Warw* 4H **61**
Hillyland. *Per* 1C **136**
Hilmarton. *Wilts* 4F **35**
Hilperton. *Wilts* 1D **22**
Hilperton Marsh. *Wilts* 1D **22**
Hilsea. *Port* 2E **17**
Hilston. *E Yor* 1F **95**
Hiltingbury. *Hants* 4C **24**
Hilton. *Cambs* 4B **64**
Hilton. *Cumb* 2A **104**
Hilton. *Derbs* 2G **73**
Hilton. *Dors* 2C **14**
Hilton. *Dur* 2E **105**
Hilton. *High* 5E **165**
Hilton. *Shrp* 1B **60**
Hilton. *Staf* 5E **73**
Hilton. *Stoc T* 3B **106**
Hilton of Cadboll. *High* 1C **158**
Himbleton. *Worc* 5D **60**
Himley. *Staf* 1C **60**
Hincaster. *Cumb* 1E **97**
Hinchcliffe Mill. *W Yor* 4B **92**
Hinchwick. *Glos* 2G **49**
Hinckley. *Leics* 1B **62**
Hinderclay. *Suff* 3C **66**
Hinderwell. *N Yor* 3E **107**
Hindford. *Shrp* 2F **71**
Hindhead. *Surr* 3G **25**
Hindley. *G Man* 4E **90**
Hindley. *Nmbd* 4D **114**
Hindley Green. *G Man* 4E **91**
Hindlip. *Worc* 5C **60**
Hindolveston. *Norf* 3C **78**
Hindon. *Wilts* 3E **23**
Hindringham. *Norf* 2B **78**
Hingham. *Norf* 5C **78**
Hinksford. *Staf* 2C **60**
Hinstock. *Shrp* 3A **72**
Hintlesham. *Suff* 1D **54**
Hinton. *Hants* 3H **15**
Hinton. *Here* 2G **47**
Hinton. *Nptn* 5C **62**
Hinton. *Shrp* 5G **71**
Hinton. *S Glo* 4C **34**
Hinton Ampner. *Hants* 4D **24**
Hinton Blewett. *Bath* 1A **22**
Hinton Charterhouse.
Bath 1C **22**
Hinton-in-the-Hedges.
Nptn 2D **50**
Hinton Martell. *Dors* 2F **15**
Hinton on the Green.
Worc 1F **49**
Hinton Parva. *Swin* 3H **35**
Hinton St George. *Som* 1H **13**
Hinton St Mary. *Dors* 1C **14**
Hinton Waldrist. *Oxon* 2B **36**
Hints. *Shrp* 3A **60**
Hints. *Staf* 5F **73**
Hinwick. *Bed* 4G **63**
Hinxhill. *Kent* 1E **29**
Hinxton. *Cambs* 1E **53**
Hinxworth. *Herts* 1C **52**
Hipley. *Hants* 1E **16**
Hipperholme. *W Yor* 2B **92**
Hipsburn. *Nmbd* 3G **121**
Hipswell. *N Yor* 5E **105**
Hiraeth. *Carm* 2F **43**
Hirn. *Abers* 3E **153**
Hirnant. *Powy* 3C **70**
Hirst. *N Lan* 3B **128**
Hirst. *Nmbd* 1F **115**
Hirst Courtney. *N Yor* 2G **93**
Hirwaen. *Den* 4D **82**
Hirwaun. *Rhon* 5C **46**
Hiscott. *Devn* 4F **19**
Histon. *Cambs* 4D **64**
Hitcham. *Suff* 5B **66**
Hitchin. *Herts* 3B **52**
Hittisleigh. *Devn* 3H **11**
Hittisleigh Barton. *Devn* 3H **11**
Hive. *E Yor* 1B **94**
Hixon. *Staf* 3E **73**
Hoaden. *Kent* 5G **41**
Hoar Cross. *Staf* 3F **73**
Hoarwithy. *Here* 3A **48**
Hoath. *Kent* 4G **41**
Hobarris. *Shrp* 3F **59**
Hobbister. *Orkn* 7C **172**
Hobbles Green. *Suff* 5G **65**
Hobbs Cross. *Essx* 1F **39**
Hobkirk. *Bord* 3H **119**
Hobson. *Dur* 4E **115**
Hoby. *Leics* 4D **74**
Hockering. *Norf* 4C **78**
Hockering Heath. *Norf* 4C **78**
Hockerton. *Notts* 5E **86**
Hockley. *Essx* 1C **40**
Hockley. *Staf* 5G **73**
Hockley. *W Mid* 3G **61**
Hockley Heath. *W Mid* 3F **61**
Hockliffe. *C Beds* 3H **51**
Hockwold cum Wilton.
Norf 2G **65**
Hockworthy. *Devn* 1D **12**
Hoddesdon. *Herts* 5D **52**
Hoddlesden. *Bkbn* 2F **91**
Hoddomcross. *Dum* 2C **112**
Hodgeston. *Pemb* 5E **43**
Hodley. *Powy* 1D **58**
Hodnet. *Shrp* 3A **72**
Hodsoll Street. *Kent* 4H **39**
Hodson. *Swin* 3G **35**
Hodthorpe. *Derbs* 3C **86**
Hoe. *Norf* 4B **78**
Hoe Gate. *Hants* 1E **17**
Hoe, The. *Plym* 3A **8**
Hoff. *Cumb* 3H **103**
Hoffleet Stow. *Linc* 2B **76**
Hogaland. *Shet* 4E **173**
Hogben's Hill. *Kent* 5E **41**
Hoggard's Green. *Suff* 5A **66**
Hoggeston. *Buck* 3G **51**
Hoggrill's End. *Warw* 1G **61**
Hogha Gearraidh. *W Isl* 1C **170**
Hoghton. *Lanc* 2E **90**
Hoghton Bottoms. *Lanc* 2E **91**
Hognaston. *Derbs* 5G **85**
Hogsthorpe. *Linc* 3E **89**
Hogstock. *Dors* 2E **15**
Holbeach. *Linc* 3C **76**
Holbeach Bank. *Linc* 3C **76**
Holbeach Clough. *Linc* 3C **76**
Holbeach Drove. *Linc* 4C **76**
Holbeach Hurn. *Linc* 3C **76**
Holbeach St Johns. *Linc* 4C **76**
Holbeach St Marks. *Linc* 2C **76**
Holbeach St Matthew.
Linc 2D **76**
Holbeck. *Notts* 3C **86**
Holbeck. *W Yor* 1C **92**
Holbeck Woodhouse.
Notts 3C **86**
Holberrow Green. *Worc* 5E **61**
Holbeton. *Devn* 3C **8**
Holborn. *G Lon* 2E **39**
Holbrook. *Derbs* 1A **74**
Holbrook. *S Yor* 2B **86**
Holbrook. *Suff* 2E **55**
Holburn. *Nmbd* 1E **121**
Holbury. *Hants* 2C **16**
Holcombe. *Devn* 5C **12**
Holcombe. *G Man* 3F **91**
Holcombe. *Som* 2B **22**
Holcombe Brook. *G Man* 3F **91**
Holcombe Rogus. *Devn* 1D **12**
Holcot. *Nptn* 4E **63**
Holden. *Lanc* 5G **97**
Holdenby. *Nptn* 4D **62**
Holder's Green. *Essx* 3G **53**
Holdgate. *Shrp* 2H **59**
Holdingham. *Linc* 1H **75**
Holditch. *Dors* 2G **13**
Holemoor. *Devn* 2E **11**
Hole Street. *W Sus* 4C **26**
Holford. *Som* 2E **21**
Holker. *Cumb* 2C **96**
Holkham. *Norf* 1A **78**
Hollacombe. *Devn* 2D **11**
Holland. *Orkn* 2D **172**
(on Papa Westray)
Holland. *Orkn* 5F **172**
(on Stronsay)
Holland Fen. *Linc* 1B **76**
Holland Lees. *Lanc* 4D **90**
Holland-on-Sea. *Essx* 4F **55**
Holland Park. *W Mid* 5E **73**
Hollandstoun. *Orkn* 2G **172**
Hollesley. *Suff* 1G **55**
Hollinfare. *Warr* 1A **84**
Hollingbourne. *Kent* 5C **40**
Hollingbury. *Brig* 5E **27**
Hollingdon. *Buck* 3G **51**
Hollingrove. *E Sus* 3A **28**
Hollington. *Derbs* 1G **73**
Hollington. *E Sus* 4B **28**
Hollington. *Staf* 2E **73**
Hollington Grove. *Derbs* 2G **73**
Hollingworth. *G Man* 1E **85**
Hollins. *Derbs* 3H **85**
Hollins. *G Man* 4G **91**
(nr. Bury)
Hollins. *G Man* 4G **91**
(nr. Middleton)
Hollinsclough. *Staf* 4E **85**
Hollinswood. *Telf* 5A **72**
Hollinthorpe. *W Yor* 1D **93**
Hollinwood. *G Man* 4H **91**
Hollinwood. *Shrp* 2H **71**
Hollocombe. *Devn* 1G **11**
Holloway. *Derbs* 5H **85**
Hollow Court. *Worc* 5D **61**
Hollowell. *Nptn* 3D **62**
Hollow Meadows. *S Yor* 2G **85**
Hollows. *Dum* 2E **113**
Hollybush. *Cphy* 5E **47**
Hollybush. *E Ayr* 3C **116**
Hollybush. *Worc* 2C **48**
Holly End. *Norf* 5D **77**
Holly Hill. *N Yor* 4E **105**
Hollyhurst. *Ches E* 1H **71**
Hollym. *E Yor* 2G **95**
Hollywood. *Worc* 3E **61**
Holmacott. *Devn* 4F **19**
Holmbridge. *W Yor* 4B **92**
Holmbury St Mary. *Surr* 1C **26**
Holmbush. *Corn* 3E **7**
Holmcroft. *Staf* 3D **72**
Holme. *Cambs* 2A **64**
Holme. *Cumb* 2E **97**
Holme. *N Lin* 4C **94**
Holme. *N Yor* 1F **99**
Holme. *Notts* 5F **87**
Holme. *W Yor* 4B **92**
Holmebridge. *Dors* 4D **15**
Holme Chapel. *Lanc* 2G **91**
Holme Hale. *Norf* 5A **78**
Holme Lacy. *Here* 2A **48**
Holme Marsh. *Here* 5F **59**
Holmend. *Dum* 4C **118**
Holme next the Sea.
Norf 1G **77**

Holme-on-Spalding-Moor—Keyham

Holme-on-Spalding-Moor. E Yor 1B 94
Holme on the Wolds. E Yor 5D 100
Holme Pierrepont. Notts 2D 74
Holmer. Here 1A 48
Holmer Green. Buck 1A 38
Holmes. Lanc 3C 90
Holme St Cuthbert. Cumb 5C 112
Holmes Chapel. Ches E 4B 84
Holmesfield. Derbs 3H 85
Holmeswood. Lanc 3C 90
Holmewood. Derbs 4B 86
Holmfirth. W Yor 4B 92
Holmhead. E Ayr 2E 117
Holmisdale. High 4A 154
Holm of Drumlanrig. Dum 5H 117
Holmpton. E Yor 2G 95
Holmrook. Cumb 5B 102
Holmsgarth. Shet 7F 173
Holmside. Dur 5F 115
Holmwrangle. Cumb 5G 113
Holne. Devn 2D 8
Holsworthy. Devn 2D 10
Holsworthy Beacon. Devn 2D 10
Holt. Dors 2F 15
Holt. Norf 2C 78
Holt. Wilts 5D 34
Holt. Worc 4C 60
Holt. Wrex 5G 83
Holtby. York 4A 100
Holt End. Hants 3E 25
Holt End. Worc 4E 61
Holt Fleet. Worc 4C 60
Holt Green. Lanc 4B 90
Holt Heath. Dors 2F 15
Holt Heath. Worc 4C 60
Holton. Oxon 5E 50
Holton. Som 4B 22
Holton. Suff 3F 67
Holton cum Beckering. Linc 2A 88
Holton Heath. Dors 3E 15
Holton le Clay. Linc 4F 95
Holton le Moor. Linc 1H 87
Holton St Mary. Suff 2D 54
Holt Pound. Hants 2G 25
Holtsmere End. Herts 4A 52
Holtye. E Sus 2F 27
Holwell. Dors 1C 14
Holwell. Herts 2B 52
Holwell. Leics 3E 75
Holwell. Oxon 5H 49
Holwell. Som 2C 22
Holwick. Dur 2C 104
Holworth. Dors 4C 14
Holybourne. Hants 2F 25
Holy City. Devn 2G 13
Holy Cross. Worc 3D 60
Holyfield. Essx 5D 53
Holyhead. IOA 2B 80
Holy Island. Nmbd 5H 131
Holymoorside. Derbs 4H 85
Holyport. Wind 4G 37
Holystone. Nmbd 4D 120
Holytown. N Lan 3A 128
Holywell. Cambs 3C 64
Holywell. Corn 3B 6
Holywell. Dors 2A 14
Holywell. Flin 3D 82
Holywell. Glos 2C 34
Holywell. Nmbd 2G 115
Holywell. Warw 4F 61
Holywell Bay. Corn 3B 6
Holywell Green. W Yor 3A 92
Holywell Lake. Som 4E 20
Holywell Row. Suff 3G 65
Holywood. Dum 1G 111
Holywood. N Dwn 2J 179
Homer. Shrp 5A 72
Homer Green. Mers 4B 90
Homersfield. Suff 2E 67
Hom Green. Here 3A 48
Homington. Wilts 4G 23
Honeyborough. Pemb 4D 42
Honeybourne. Worc 1G 49
Honeychurch. Devn 2G 11
Honeydon. Bed 5A 64
Honey Hill. Kent 4F 41
Honey Street. Wilts 5G 35
Honey Tye. Suff 2C 54
Honeywick. C Beds 3H 51
Honiley. Warw 3G 61
Honing. Norf 3F 79
Honingham. Norf 4D 78
Honington. Linc 1G 75
Honington. Suff 3B 66
Honington. Warw 1A 50
Honiton. Devn 2E 13
Honley. W Yor 3B 92
Honnington. Telf 4B 72
Hoo. Suff 5E 67
Hoobrook. Worc 3C 60
Hood Green. S Yor 4D 92
Hooe. E Sus 5A 28
Hooe. Plym 3B 8
Hooe Common. E Sus 4A 28
Hoo Green. Ches E 2B 84
Hoohill. Bkpl 1B 90
Hook. Cambs 1D 64
Hook. E Yor 2A 94
Hook. G Lon 4C 38
Hook. Hants 1F 25 (nr. Basingstoke)
Hook. Hants 2D 16 (nr. Fareham)
Hook. Pemb 3D 43
Hook. Wilts 3F 35
Hook-a-Gate. Shrp 5G 71
Hook Bank. Worc 1D 48
Hooke. Dors 2A 14
Hooker Gate. Tyne 4E 115
Hookgate. Staf 2B 72
Hook Green. Kent 2A 28 (nr. Lamberhurst)
Hook Green. Kent 3H 39 (nr. Longfield)
Hook Green. Kent 4H 39 (nr. Meopham)
Hook Norton. Oxon 2B 50
Hook's Cross. Herts 3C 52
Hook Street. Glos 2B 34
Hookway. Devn 3B 12
Hookwood. Surr 1D 26
Hoole. Ches W 4G 83
Hooley. Surr 5D 39
Hooley Bridge. G Man 3G 91
Hooley Brow. G Man 3G 91
Hoo St Werburgh. Medw 3B 40
Hooton. Ches W 3F 83
Hooton Levitt. S Yor 1C 86
Hooton Pagnell. S Yor 4E 93
Hooton Roberts. S Yor 1B 86
Hoove. Shet 7E 173
Hope. Derbs 2F 85
Hope. Flin 5F 83
Hope. High 2E 167
Hope. Powy 5E 71
Hope. Shrp 5F 71
Hope. Staf 5F 85
Hope Bagot. Shrp 3H 59
Hope Bowdler. Shrp 1G 59
Hopedale. Staf 5F 85
Hope Green. Ches E 2D 84
Hopeman. Mor 2F 159
Hope Mansell. Here 4B 48
Hopesay. Shrp 2F 59
Hope's Green. Essx 2B 40
Hopetown. W Yor 2D 93
Hope under Dinmore. Here 5H 59
Hopley's Green. Here 5F 59
Hopperton. N Yor 4G 99
Hop Pole. Linc 4A 76
Hopstone. Shrp 1B 60
Hopton. Derbs 5G 85
Hopton. Powy 1E 59
Hopton. Shrp 3F 71 (nr. Oswestry)
Hopton. Shrp 3H 71 (nr. Wem)
Hopton. Staf 3D 72
Hopton. Suff 3B 66
Hopton Cangeford. Shrp 2H 59
Hopton Castle. Shrp 3F 59
Hoptonheath. Shrp 3F 59
Hopton Heath. Staf 3D 72
Hopton on Sea. Norf 5H 79
Hopton Wafers. Shrp 3A 60
Hopwas. Staf 5F 73
Hopwood. Worc 3E 61
Horam. E Sus 4G 27
Horbling. Linc 2A 76
Horbury. W Yor 3C 92
Horcott. Glos 5G 49
Horden. Dur 5H 115
Horderley. Shrp 2G 59
Hordle. Hants 3A 16
Hordley. Shrp 2F 71
Horeb. Carm 3F 45 (nr. Brechfa)
Horeb. Carm 5E 45 (nr. Llanelli)
Horeb. Cdgn 1D 45
Horfield. Bris 4B 34
Horgabost. W Isl 8C 171
Horham. Suff 3E 66
Horkesley Heath. Essx 3C 54
Horkstow. N Lin 3C 94
Horley. Oxon 1C 50
Horley. Surr 1D 27
Horn Ash. Dors 2G 13
Hornblotton Green. Som 3A 22
Hornby. Lanc 3E 97
Hornby. N Yor 4A 106 (nr. Appleton Wiske)
Hornby. N Yor 5F 105 (nr. Catterick Garrison)
Horncastle. Linc 4B 88
Hornchurch. G Lon 2G 39
Horncliffe. Nmbd 5F 131
Horndean. Hants 1E 17
Horndean. Bord 5E 131
Horndon. Devn 4F 11
Horndon on the Hill. Thur 2A 40
Horne. Surr 1E 27
Horner. Som 2C 20
Horning. Norf 4F 79
Horninghold. Leics 1F 63
Horninglow. Staf 3G 73
Horningsea. Cambs 4D 65
Horningsham. Wilts 2D 22
Horningtoft. Norf 3B 78
Hornsbury. Som 1G 13
Hornsby. Cumb 4G 113
Hornsbygate. Cumb 4G 113
Horns Corner. Kent 3B 28
Horns Cross. Devn 4D 19
Hornsea. E Yor 5G 101
Hornsea Burton. E Yor 5G 101
Hornsey. G Lon 2E 39
Hornton. Oxon 1B 50
Horpit. Swin 3H 35
Horrabridge. Devn 2B 8
Horringer. Suff 4H 65
Horringford. IOW 4D 16
Horrocks Fold. G Man 3F 91
Horrocksford. Lanc 5G 97
Horsbrugh Ford. Bord 1E 119
Horsebridge. Devn 5E 11
Horsebridge. E Sus 4G 27
Horsebridge. Hants 3B 24
Horse Bridge. Staf 5D 84
Horsebrook. Staf 4C 72
Horsecastle. N Som 5H 33
Horsehay. Telf 5A 72
Horseheath. Cambs 1G 53
Horsehouse. N Yor 1C 98
Horsell. Surr 5A 38
Horseman's Green. Wrex 1G 71
Horsenden. Buck 5F 51
Horseway. Cambs 2D 64
Horsey. Norf 3G 79
Horsey. Som 3G 21
Horsford. Norf 4D 78
Horsforth. W Yor 1C 92
Horsham. W Sus 2C 26
Horsham St Faith. Norf 4E 78
Horsington. Linc 4A 88
Horsington. Som 4C 22
Horsley. Derbs 1A 74
Horsley. Glos 2D 34
Horsley. Nmbd 3D 115 (nr. Prudhoe)
Horsley. Nmbd 5C 120 (nr. Rochester)
Horsley Cross. Essx 3E 54
Horsleycross Street. Essx 3E 54
Horsleyhill. Bord 3H 119
Horsleyhope. Dur 5D 114
Horsley Woodhouse. Derbs 1A 74
Horsmonden. Kent 1A 28
Horspath. Oxon 5D 50
Horstead. Norf 4E 79
Horsted Keynes. W Sus 3E 27
Horton. Buck 4H 51
Horton. Dors 2F 15
Horton. Lanc 4A 98
Horton. Nptn 5F 63
Horton. Shrp 2G 71
Horton. Som 1G 13
Horton. S Glo 3C 34
Horton. Staf 5D 84
Horton. Swan 4D 30
Horton. Wind 3B 38
Horton Cross. Som 1G 13
Horton-cum-Studley. Oxon 4D 50
Horton Grange. Nmbd 2F 115
Horton Green. Ches W 1G 71
Horton Heath. Hants 1C 16
Horton in Ribblesdale. N Yor 2H 97
Horton Kirby. Kent 4G 39
Hortonwood. Telf 4A 72
Horwich. G Man 3E 91
Horwich End. Derbs 2E 85
Horwood. Devn 4F 19
Hoscar. Lanc 3C 90
Hose. Leics 3E 75
Hosh. Per 1A 136
Hosta. W Isl 1C 170
Hoswick. Shet 9F 173
Hotham. E Yor 1B 94
Hothfield. Kent 1D 28
Hoton. Leics 3C 74
Houbie. Shet 2H 173
Hough. Arg 4A 138
Hough. Ches E 5B 84 (nr. Crewe)
Hough. Ches E 3C 84 (nr. Wilmslow)
Hougham. Linc 1F 75
Hough Green. Hal 2G 83
Hough-on-the-Hill. Linc 1G 75
Houghton. Cambs 3B 64
Houghton. Cumb 4F 113
Houghton. Hants 3B 24
Houghton. Nmbd 3E 115
Houghton. Pemb 4D 43
Houghton. W Sus 4B 26
Houghton Bank. Darl 2F 105
Houghton Conquest. C Beds 1A 52
Houghton Green. E Sus 3D 28
Houghton-le-Side. Darl 2F 105
Houghton-le-Spring. Tyne 5G 115
Houghton on the Hill. Leics 5D 74
Houghton Regis. C Beds 3A 52
Houghton St Giles. Norf 2B 78
Houlland. Shet 6E 173 (on Mainland)
Houlland. Shet 4G 173 (on Yell)
Houlsyke. N Yor 4E 107
Hound. Hants 2C 16
Hound Green. Hants 1F 25
Houndslow. Bord 5C 130
Houndsmoor. Som 4E 21
Houndwood. Bord 3E 131
Hounsdown. Hants 1B 16
Hounslow. G Lon 3C 38
Housabister. Shet 6F 173
Housay. Shet 4H 173
Househill. High 3C 158
Housetter. Shet 3E 173
Houss. Shet 8E 173
Houston. Ren 3F 127
Housty. High 5D 168
Houton. Orkn 7C 172
Hove. Brig 5D 27 & 192
Hoveringham. Notts 1E 74
Hoveton. Norf 4F 79
Hovingham. N Yor 2A 100
How. Cumb 4G 113
How Caple. Here 2B 48
Howden. E Yor 2H 93
Howden-le-Wear. Dur 1E 105
Howe. High 2F 169
Howe. Norf 5E 79
Howe. N Yor 1F 99
Howe Green. Essx 5H 53 (nr. Chelmsford)
Howegreen. Essx 5B 54 (nr. Maldon)
Howe Green. Warw 2H 61
Howell. Linc 1A 76
How End. C Beds 1A 52
Howe of Teuchar. Abers 4E 161
Howes. Dum 3C 112
Howe Street. Essx 4G 53 (nr. Chelmsford)
Howe Street. Essx 2G 53 (nr. Finchingfield)
Howe, The. Cumb 1D 96
Howe, The. IOM 5A 108
Howey. Powy 5C 58
Howgate. Midl 4F 129
Howgill. Lanc 5H 97
Howgill. N Yor 4C 98
How Green. Kent 1F 27
How Hill. Norf 4F 79
Howick. Nmbd 3G 121
Howle. Telf 3A 72
Howle Hill. Here 3B 48
Howleigh. Som 1F 13
Howlett End. Essx 2F 53
Howley. Som 2F 13
Howley. Warr 2A 84
Hownam. Bord 3B 120
Howsham. N Lin 4D 94
Howsham. N Yor 3B 100
Howtel. Nmbd 1C 120
Howt Green. Kent 4C 40
Howton. Here 3H 47
Howwood. Ren 3E 127
Hoxne. Suff 3D 66
Hoylake. Mers 2E 82
Hoyland. S Yor 4D 92
Hoylandswaine. S Yor 4C 92
Hoyle. W Sus 4A 26
Hubberholme. N Yor 2B 98
Hubberston. Pemb 4C 42
Hubbert's Bridge. Linc 1B 76
Huby. N Yor 5E 99 (nr. Harrogate)
Huby. N Yor 3H 99 (nr. York)
Hucclecote. Glos 4D 48
Hucking. Kent 5C 40
Hucknall. Notts 1C 74
Huddersfield. W Yor 3B 92
Huddington. Worc 5D 60
Huddlesford. Staf 5F 73
Hudswell. N Yor 4E 105
Huggate. E Yor 4C 100
Hugglescote. Leics 4B 74
Hughenden Valley. Buck 2G 37
Hughley. Shrp 1H 59
Hughton. High 4G 157
Hugh Town. IOS 1B 4
Hugus. Corn 4B 6
Huish. Devn 1F 11
Huish. Wilts 5G 35
Huish Champflower. Som 4D 20
Huish Episcopi. Som 4H 21
Huisinis. W Isl 6B 171
Hulcote. Nptn 5E 62
Hulcott. Buck 4G 51
Hulham. Devn 4D 12
Hull. Hull 2D 94 & 196
Hulland. Derbs 1G 73
Hulland Moss. Derbs 1G 73
Hulland Ward. Derbs 1G 73
Hullavington. Wilts 3D 35
Hullbridge. Essx 1C 40
Hulme. G Man 1C 84
Hulme. Staf 1D 72
Hulme End. Staf 5F 85
Hulme Walfield. Ches E 4C 84
Hulverstone. IOW 4B 16
Hulver Street. Suff 2G 67
Humber. Devn 5C 12
Humber. Here 5H 59
Humber Bridge. N Lin 2D 94
Humberside International Airport. N Lin 3D 94
Humberston. NE Lin 4G 95
Humberstone. Leic 5D 74
Humbie. E Lot 3A 130
Humbleton. E Yor 1F 95
Humbleton. Nmbd 2D 121
Humby. Linc 2H 75
Hume. Bord 5D 130
Humshaugh. Nmbd 2C 114
Huna. High 1F 169
Huncoat. Lanc 1F 91
Huncote. Leics 1C 62
Hundall. Derbs 3A 86
Hunderthwaite. Dur 2C 104
Hundleby. Linc 4C 88
Hundle Houses. Linc 5B 88
Hundleton. Pemb 4D 42
Hundon. Suff 1H 53
Hundred Acres. Hants 1D 16
Hundred House. Powy 5D 58
Hundred, The. Here 4H 59
Hungarton. Leics 5D 74
Hungerford. Hants 1G 15
Hungerford. Shrp 2H 59
Hungerford. Som 2D 20
Hungerford. W Ber 5B 36
Hungerford Newtown. W Ber 4B 36
Hunger Hill. G Man 4E 91
Hungerton. Linc 2F 75
Hungladder. High 1C 154
Hungryhatton. Shrp 3A 72
Hunmanby. N Yor 2E 101
Hunmanby Sands. N Yor 2F 101
Hunningham. Warw 4A 62
Hunnington. Worc 2D 60
Hunny Hill. IOW 4C 16
Hunsdon. Herts 4E 53
Hunsdonbury. Herts 4E 53
Hunsingore. N Yor 4G 99
Hunslet. W Yor 1D 92
Hunslet Carr. W Yor 2D 92
Hunsonby. Cumb 1G 103
Hunspow. High 1E 169
Hunstanton. Norf 1F 77
Hunstanworth. Dur 5C 114
Hunston. Suff 4B 66
Hunston. W Sus 2G 17
Hunstrete. Bath 5B 34
Hunt End. Worc 4E 61
Hunterfield. Midl 3G 129
Hunters Forstal. Kent 4F 41
Hunter's Quay. Arg 2C 126
Huntham. Som 4G 21
Hunthill Lodge. Ang 1D 144
Huntingdon. Cambs 3B 64
Huntingfield. Suff 3F 67
Huntingford. Wilts 3D 22
Huntington. Ches W 4G 83
Huntington. E Lot 2A 130
Huntington. Here 5E 59
Huntington. Staf 4D 72
Huntington. Telf 5A 72
Huntington. York 4A 100
Huntingtower. Per 1C 136
Huntley. Glos 4C 48
Huntley. Staf 1E 73
Huntly. Abers 4C 160
Huntlywood. Bord 5C 130
Hunton. Hants 3C 24
Hunton. Kent 1B 28
Hunton. N Yor 5E 105
Hunton Bridge. Herts 5A 52
Hunt's Corner. Norf 2C 66
Huntscott. Som 2C 20
Hunt's Cross. Mers 2G 83
Hunts Green. Warw 1F 61
Huntsham. Devn 4D 20
Huntshaw. Devn 4F 19
Huntspill. Som 2G 21
Huntstile. Som 3F 21
Huntworth. Som 3G 21
Hunwick. Dur 1E 105
Hunworth. Norf 2C 78
Hurcott. Som 1G 13 (nr. Ilminster)
Hurcott. Som 4A 22 (nr. Somerton)
Hurdcott. Wilts 3G 23
Hurdley. Powy 1E 59
Hurdsfield. Ches E 3D 84
Hurlet. Glas 3G 127
Hurley. Warw 1G 61
Hurley. Wind 3G 37
Hurlford. E Ayr 1D 116
Hurliness. Orkn 9B 172
Hurlston Green. Lanc 3B 90
Hurn. Dors 3G 15
Hursey. Dors 2H 13
Hursley. Hants 4C 24
Hurst. G Man 4H 91
Hurst. N Yor 4D 104
Hurst. Som 1H 13
Hurst. Wok 4F 37
Hurstbourne Priors. Hants 2C 24
Hurstbourne Tarrant. Hants 1B 24
Hurst Green. Ches E 1H 71
Hurst Green. E Sus 3B 28
Hurst Green. Essx 4D 54
Hurst Green. Lanc 1E 91
Hurst Green. Surr 5E 39
Hurstley. Here 1G 47
Hurstpierpoint. W Sus 4D 27
Hurstway Common. Here 1F 47
Hurst Wickham. W Sus 4D 27
Hurstwood. Lanc 1G 91
Hurtmore. Surr 1A 26
Hurworth-on-Tees. Darl 3A 106
Hurworth Place. Darl 3F 105
Hury. Dur 3C 104
Husbands Bosworth. Leics 2D 62
Husborne Crawley. C Beds 2H 51
Husthwaite. N Yor 2H 99
Hutcherleigh. Devn 3D 9
Hut Green. N Yor 2F 93
Huthwaite. Notts 5B 86
Huttoft. Linc 3E 89
Hutton. Cumb 2F 103
Hutton. E Yor 4E 101
Hutton. Essx 1H 39
Hutton. Lanc 2C 90
Hutton. N Som 1G 21
Hutton. Bord 4F 131
Hutton Bonville. N Yor 4A 106
Hutton Buscel. N Yor 1D 100
Hutton Conyers. N Yor 2F 99
Hutton Cranswick. E Yor 4E 101
Hutton End. Cumb 1F 103
Hutton Gate. Red C 3C 106
Hutton Henry. Dur 1B 106
Hutton-le-Hole. N Yor 1B 100
Hutton Magna. Dur 3E 105
Hutton Mulgrave. N Yor 4F 107
Hutton Roof. Cumb 2E 97 (nr. Kirkby Lonsdale)
Hutton Roof. Cumb 1E 103 (nr. Penrith)
Hutton Rudby. N Yor 4B 106
Huttons Ambo. N Yor 3B 100
Hutton Sessay. N Yor 2G 99
Hutton Village. Red C 3D 106
Hutton Wandesley. N Yor 4H 99
Huxham. Devn 3C 12
Huxham Green. Som 3A 22
Huxley. Ches W 4H 83
Huxter. Shet 6C 173 (on Mainland)
Huxter. Shet 5G 173 (on Whalsay)
Huyton. Mers 1G 83
Hwlffordd. Pemb 3D 42
Hycemoor. Cumb 1A 96
Hyde. Glos 5D 49 (nr. Stroud)
Hyde. Glos 3F 49 (nr. Winchcombe)
Hyde. G Man 1D 84
Hyde Heath. Buck 5H 51
Hyde Lea. Staf 3D 72
Hyde Park. S Yor 4F 93
Hydestile. Surr 1A 26
Hyndford Bridge. S Lan 5C 128
Hynish. Arg 5A 138
Hyssington. Powy 1F 59
Hythe. Hants 2C 16
Hythe. Kent 2F 29
Hythe End. Wind 3B 38
Hythie. Abers 3H 161
Hyton. Cumb 1A 96

I

Ianstown. Mor 2B 160
Iarsiadar. W Isl 4D 171
Ibberton. Dors 2C 14
Ible. Derbs 5G 85
Ibrox. Glas 3G 127
Ibsley. Hants 2G 15
Ibstock. Leics 4B 74
Ibstone. Buck 2F 37
Ibthorpe. Hants 1B 24
Iburndale. N Yor 4F 107
Ibworth. Hants 1D 24
Icelton. N Som 5G 33
Ichrachan. Arg 5E 141
Ickburgh. Norf 1H 65
Ickenham. G Lon 2B 38
Ickenthwaite. Cumb 1C 96
Ickford. Buck 5E 51
Ickham. Kent 5G 41
Ickleford. Herts 2B 52
Icklesham. E Sus 4C 28
Ickleton. Cambs 1E 53
Icklingham. Suff 3G 65
Ickwell. C Beds 1B 52
Icomb. Glos 3H 49
Idbury. Oxon 3H 49
Iddesleigh. Devn 2F 11
Ide. Devn 3B 12
Ideford. Devn 5B 12
Ide Hill. Kent 5F 39
Iden. E Sus 3D 28
Iden Green. Kent 2B 28 (nr. Benenden)
Iden Green. Kent 2C 28 (nr. Goudhurst)
Idle. W Yor 1B 92
Idless. Corn 4C 6
Idlicote. Warw 1A 50
Idmiston. Wilts 3G 23
Idole. Carm 4E 45
Idridgehay. Derbs 1G 73
Idrigill. High 2C 154
Idstone. Oxon 3A 36
Iffley. Oxon 5D 50
Ifield. W Sus 2D 26
Ifieldwood. W Sus 2D 26
Ifold. W Sus 2B 26
Iford. E Sus 5F 27
Ifton Heath. Shrp 2F 71
Ightfield. Shrp 2H 71
Ightham. Kent 5G 39
Iken. Suff 5G 67
Ilam. Staf 5F 85
Ilchester. Som 4A 22
Ilderton. Nmbd 2E 121
Ilford. G Lon 2F 39
Ilford. Som 1G 13
Ilfracombe. Devn 2F 19
Ilkeston. Derbs 1B 74
Ilketshall St Andrew. Suff 2F 67
Ilketshall St Lawrence. Suff 2F 67
Ilketshall St Margaret. Suff 2F 67
Ilkley. W Yor 5D 98
Illand. Corn 5C 10
Illey. W Mid 2D 61
Illidge Green. Ches E 4B 84
Illington. Norf 2B 66
Illingworth. W Yor 2A 92
Illogan. Corn 4A 6
Illogan Highway. Corn 4A 6
Illston on the Hill. Leics 1E 62
Ilmer. Buck 5F 51
Ilmington. Warw 1H 49
Ilminster. Som 1G 13
Ilsington. Devn 5A 12
Ilsington. Dors 3C 14
Ilston. Swan 3E 31
Ilton. N Yor 2D 98
Ilton. Som 1G 13
Imachar. N Ayr 5G 125
Imber. Wilts 2E 23
Immingham. NE Lin 3E 95
Immingham Dock. NE Lin 3E 95
Impington. Cambs 4D 64
Ince. Ches W 3G 83
Ince Blundell. Mers 4B 90
Ince-in-Makerfield. G Man 4D 90
Inchbae Lodge. High 2G 157
Inchbare. Ang 2F 145
Inchberry. Mor 3H 159
Inchbraoch. Ang 3G 145
Inchbrook. Glos 5D 48
Incheril. High 2C 156
Inchinnan. Ren 3F 127
Inchlaggan. High 3D 148
Inchmichael. Per 1E 137
Inchnadamph. High 1G 163
Inchree. High 2E 141
Inchture. Per 1E 137
Inchyra. Per 1D 136
Indian Queens. Corn 3D 6
Ingatestone. Essx 1H 39
Ingbirchworth. S Yor 4C 92
Ingestre. Staf 3D 73
Ingham. Linc 2G 87
Ingham. Norf 3F 79
Ingham. Suff 3A 66
Ingham Corner. Norf 3F 79
Ingleborough. Norf 4D 76
Ingleby. Derbs 3H 73
Ingleby Arncliffe. N Yor 4B 106
Ingleby Barwick. Stoc T 3B 106
Ingleby Greenhow. N Yor 4C 106
Ingleigh Green. Devn 2G 11
Inglemire. Hull 1D 94
Inglesbatch. Bath 5C 34
Ingleton. Dur 2E 105
Ingleton. N Yor 2F 97
Inglewhite. Lanc 5E 97
Ingoe. Nmbd 2D 114
Ingol. Lanc 1D 90
Ingoldisthorpe. Norf 2F 77
Ingoldmells. Linc 4E 89
Ingoldsby. Linc 2H 75
Ingon. Warw 5G 61
Ingram. Nmbd 3E 121
Ingrave. Essx 1H 39
Ingrow. W Yor 1A 92
Ings. Cumb 5F 103
Ingst. S Glo 3A 34
Ingthorpe. Rut 5G 75
Ingworth. Norf 3D 78
Inishrush. Mag 6F 174
Inkberrow. Worc 5E 61
Inkford. Worc 3E 61
Inkpen. W Ber 5B 36
Inkstack. High 1E 169
Innellan. Arg 3C 126
Inner Hope. Devn 5C 8
Innerleith. Fife 2E 137
Innerleithen. Bord 1F 119
Innerleven. Fife 3F 137
Innermessan. Dum 3F 109
Innerwick. E Lot 2D 130
Innerwick. Per 4C 142
Innsworth. Glos 3D 48
Insch. Abers 1D 152
Insh. High 3C 150
Inshegra. High 3C 166
Inshore. High 1D 166
Inskip. Lanc 1C 90
Instow. Devn 3E 19
Intwood. Norf 5D 78
Inver. Abers 4G 151
Inver. High 5F 165
Inver. Per 4H 143
Inverailort. High 5F 147
Inveralligin. High 3H 155
Inverallochy. Abers 2H 161
Inveramsay. Abers 1E 153
Inveran. High 4C 164
Inveraray. Arg 3H 133
Inverarish. High 5E 155
Inverarity. Ang 4D 144
Inverarnan. Arg 2C 134
Inverarnie. High 5A 158
Inverbeg. Arg 4C 134
Inverbervie. Abers 1H 145
Inverboyndie. Abers 2D 160
Invercassley. High 3B 164
Invercharnan. High 4F 141
Inverchoran. High 3E 157
Invercreran. Arg 4E 141
Inverdruie. High 2D 150
Inverebrie. Abers 5G 161
Invereck. Arg 1C 126
Inveresk. E Lot 2G 129
Inveresragan. Arg 5D 141
Inverey. Abers 5E 151
Inverfarigaig. High 1H 149
Invergarry. High 3F 149
Invergeldie. Per 1G 135
Invergordon. High 2B 158
Invergowrie. Per 5C 144
Inverguseran. High 3F 147
Inverharroch. Mor 5A 160
Inverie. High 3F 147
Inverinan. Arg 2G 133
Inverinate. High 1B 148
Inverkeilor. Ang 4F 145
Inverkeithing. Fife 1E 129
Inverkeithny. Abers 4D 160
Inverkip. Inv 2D 126
Inverkirkaig. High 2E 163
Inverlael. High 5F 163
Inverliever Lodge. Arg 3F 133
Inverliver. Arg 5E 141
Inverlochlarig. Stir 2D 134
Inverlochy. High 1F 141
Inverlussa. Arg 1E 125
Inver Mallie. High 5D 148
Invermarkie. Abers 5B 160
Invermoriston. High 2G 149
Invernaver. High 2H 167
Inverneil House. Arg 1G 125
Inverness. High 4A 158 & 196
Inverness Airport. High 3B 158
Invernettie. Abers 4H 161
Inverpolly Lodge. High 2E 163
Inverquhomery. Abers 4H 161
Inverroy. High 5E 149
Inversanda. High 3D 140
Invershiel. High 2B 148
Invershin. High 4C 164
Invershore. High 5E 169
Inversnaid. Stir 3C 134
Inverugie. Abers 4H 161
Inveruglas. Arg 3C 134
Inverurie. Abers 1E 153
Invervar. Per 4D 142
Inverythan. Abers 4E 161
Inwardleigh. Devn 3F 11
Inworth. Essx 4B 54
Iochdar. W Isl 4C 170
Iping. W Sus 4G 25
Ipplepen. Devn 2E 9
Ipsden. Oxon 3E 37
Ipstones. Staf 1E 73
Ipswich. Suff 1E 55 & 196
Irby. Mers 2E 83
Irby in the Marsh. Linc 4D 88
Irby upon Humber. NE Lin 4E 95
Irchester. Nptn 4G 63
Ireby. Cumb 1D 102
Ireby. Lanc 2F 97
Ireland. Shet 9E 173
Ireleth. Cumb 2B 96
Ireshopeburn. Dur 1B 104
Ireton Wood. Derbs 1G 73
Irlam. G Man 1B 84
Irnham. Linc 3H 75
Iron Acton. S Glo 3B 34
Iron Bridge. Cambs 1D 65
Ironbridge. Telf 5A 72
Iron Cross. Warw 5E 61
Ironville. Derbs 5B 86
Irstead. Norf 3F 79
Irthington. Cumb 3F 113
Irthlingborough. Nptn 3G 63
Irton. N Yor 1E 101
Irvine. N Ayr 1C 116
Irvine Mains. N Ayr 1C 116
Irvinestown. Ferm 7E 176
Isabella Pit. Nmbd 1G 115
Isauld. High 2B 168
Isbister. Orkn 6C 172
Isbister. Shet 2E 173 (on Mainland)
Isbister. Shet 5G 173 (on Whalsay)
Isfield. E Sus 4F 27
Isham. Nptn 3F 63
Island Carr. N Lin 4C 94
Islay Airport. Arg 4B 124
Isle Abbotts. Som 4G 21
Isle Brewers. Som 4G 21
Isleham. Cambs 3F 65
Isle of Man Airport. IOM 5B 108
Isle of Thanet. Kent 4H 41
Isle of Whithorn. Dum 5B 110
Isleornsay. High 2F 147
Islesburgh. Shet 5E 173
Isles of Scilly (St Mary's) Airport. IOS 1B 4
Islesteps. Dum 2A 112
Isleworth. G Lon 3C 38
Isley Walton. Leics 3B 74
Islibhig. W Isl 5B 171
Islington. G Lon 2E 39
Islington. Telf 3B 72
Islip. Nptn 3G 63
Islip. Oxon 4D 50
Islwyn. Cphy 2F 33
Isombridge. Telf 4A 72
Istead Rise. Kent 4H 39
Itchen. Sotn 1C 16
Itchen Abbas. Hants 3D 24
Itchen Stoke. Hants 3D 24
Itchingfield. W Sus 3C 26
Itchington. S Glo 3B 34
Itlaw. Abers 3D 160
Itteringham. Norf 2D 78
Itteringham Common. Norf 3D 78
Itton. Devn 3G 11
Itton Common. Mon 2H 33
Ivegill. Cumb 5F 113
Ivelet. N Yor 5C 104
Iverchaolain. Arg 2B 126
Iver Heath. Buck 2B 38
Iveston. Dur 4E 115
Ivetsey Bank. Staf 4C 72
Ivinghoe. Buck 4H 51
Ivinghoe Aston. Buck 4H 51
Ivington. Here 5G 59
Ivington Green. Here 5G 59
Ivybridge. Devn 3C 8
Ivychurch. Kent 3E 29
Ivy Hatch. Kent 5G 39
Ivy Todd. Norf 5A 78
Iwade. Kent 4D 40
Iwerne Courtney. Dors 1D 14
Iwerne Minster. Dors 1D 14
Ixworth. Suff 3B 66
Ixworth Thorpe. Suff 3B 66

J

Jackfield. Shrp 5A 72
Jack Hill. N Yor 4E 98
Jacksdale. Notts 5B 86
Jackton. S Lan 4G 127
Jacobstow. Corn 3B 10
Jacobstowe. Devn 2F 11
Jacobswell. Surr 5A 38
Jameston. Pemb 5E 43
Jamestown. Dum 5F 119
Jamestown. Fife 1E 129
Jamestown. High 3G 157
Jamestown. W Dun 1E 127
Janetstown. High 3C 168 (nr. Thurso)
Janetstown. High 3F 169 (nr. Wick)
Jarrow. Tyne 3G 115
Jarvis Brook. E Sus 3G 27
Jasper's Green. Essx 3H 53
Jaywick. Essx 4E 55
Jedburgh. Bord 2A 120
Jeffreyston. Pemb 4E 43
Jemimaville. High 2B 158
Jenkins Park. High 3F 149
Jersey Marine. Neat 3G 31
Jesmond. Tyne 3F 115
Jevington. E Sus 5G 27
Jingle Street. Mon 4H 47
Jockey End. Herts 4A 52
Jodrell Bank. Ches E 3B 84
Johnby. Cumb 1F 103
John o' Gaunts. W Yor 2D 92
John o' Groats. High 1F 169
John's Cross. E Sus 3B 28
Johnshaven. Abers 2G 145
Johnson Street. Norf 4F 79
Johnston. Pemb 3D 42
Johnstone. Ren 3F 127
Johnstonebridge. Dum 5C 118
Johnstown. Carm 4D 45
Johnstown. Wrex 1F 71
Jonesborough. New M 8E 178
Joppa. Edin 2G 129
Joppa. S Ayr 3D 116
Jordan Green. Norf 3C 78
Jordans. Buck 1A 38
Jordanston. Pemb 1D 42
Jump. S Yor 4D 93
Jumpers Common. Dors 3G 15
Juniper. Nmbd 4C 114
Juniper Green. Edin 3E 129
Jurby East. IOM 2C 108
Jurby West. IOM 2C 108
Jury's Gap. E Sus 4D 28

K

Kaber. Cumb 3A 104
Kaimend. S Lan 5C 128
Kaimes. Edin 3F 129
Kaimrig End. Bord 5D 129
Kames. Arg 2A 126
Kames. E Ayr 2F 117
Katesbridge. Ban 5G 179
Kea. Corn 4C 6
Keadby. N Lin 3B 94
Keady. Arm 6C 178
Keal Cotes. Linc 4C 88
Kearsley. G Man 4F 91
Kearsney. Kent 1G 29
Kearstwick. Cumb 1F 97
Kearton. N Yor 5C 104
Kearvaig. High 1C 166
Keasden. N Yor 3G 97
Keason. Corn 2H 7
Keckwick. Hal 2H 83
Keddington. Linc 2C 88
Keddington Corner. Linc 2C 88
Kedington. Suff 1H 53
Kedleston. Derbs 1H 73
Kedlock Feus. Fife 2F 137
Keekle. Cumb 3B 102
Keelby. Linc 3E 95
Keele. Staf 1C 72
Keeley Green. Bed 1A 52
Keeston. Pemb 3D 42
Keevil. Wilts 1E 23
Kegworth. Leics 3B 74
Kehelland. Corn 2D 4
Keig. Abers 2D 152
Keighley. W Yor 5C 98
Keilarsbrae. Clac 4A 136
Keillmore. Arg 1E 125
Keillor. Per 4B 144
Keillour. Per 1B 136
Keills. Arg 3C 124
Keiloch. Abers 4F 151
Keils. Arg 3D 124
Keinton Mandeville. Som 3A 22
Keir Mill. Dum 5A 118
Keirsleywell Row. Nmbd 4A 114
Keisby. Linc 3H 75
Keisley. Cumb 2A 104
Keiss. High 2F 169
Keith. Mor 3B 160
Keith Inch. Abers 4H 161
Kelbrook. Lanc 5B 98
Kelby. Linc 1H 75
Keld. Cumb 3G 103
Keld. N Yor 4B 104
Keldholme. N Yor 1B 100
Kelfield. N Lin 4B 94
Kelfield. N Yor 1F 93
Kelham. Notts 5E 87
Kellacott. Devn 4E 11
Kellan. Arg 4G 139
Kellas. Ang 5D 144
Kellas. Mor 3F 159
Kellaton. Devn 5E 9
Kelleth. Cumb 4H 103
Kelling. Norf 1C 78
Kellingley. N Yor 2F 93
Kellington. N Yor 2F 93
Kelloe. Dur 1A 106
Kelloholm. Dum 3G 117
Kells. Bmna 7H 175
Kells. Cumb 3A 102
Kelly. Devn 4D 11
Kelly Bray. Corn 5D 10
Kelmarsh. Nptn 3E 63
Kelmscott. Oxon 2A 36
Kelsale. Suff 4F 67
Kelsall. Ches W 4H 83
Kelshall. Herts 2D 52
Kelsick. Cumb 4C 112
Kelso. Bord 1B 120
Kelstedge. Derbs 4H 85
Kelstern. Linc 1B 88
Kelsterton. Flin 3E 83
Kelston. Bath 5C 34
Keltneyburn. Per 4E 143
Kelton. Dum 2A 112
Kelton Hill. Dum 4E 111
Kelty. Fife 4D 136
Kelvedon. Essx 4B 54
Kelvedon Hatch. Essx 1G 39
Kelvinside. Glas 3G 127
Kelynack. Corn 3A 4
Kemback. Fife 2G 137
Kemberton. Shrp 5B 72
Kemble. Glos 2E 35
Kemerton. Worc 2E 49
Kemeys Commander. Mon 5G 47
Kemnay. Abers 2E 153
Kempe's Corner. Kent 1E 29
Kempley. Glos 3B 48
Kempley Green. Glos 3B 48
Kempsey. Worc 1D 48
Kempsford. Glos 2G 35
Kemps Green. Warw 3F 61
Kempshott. Hants 1E 24
Kempston. Bed 1A 52
Kempston Hardwick. Bed 1A 52
Kempton. Shrp 2F 59
Kemp Town. Brig 5E 27
Kemsing. Kent 5G 39
Kemsley. Kent 4D 40
Kenardington. Kent 2D 28
Kenchester. Here 1H 47
Kencot. Oxon 5A 50
Kendal. Cumb 5G 103
Kendleshire. S Glo 4B 34
Kendray. S Yor 4D 92
Kenfig. B'end 3B 32
Kenfig Hill. B'end 3B 32
Kengharair. Arg 4F 139
Kenilworth. Warw 3G 61
Kenknock. Stir 5B 142
Kenley. G Lon 5E 39
Kenley. Shrp 5H 71
Kenmore. High 3G 155
Kenmore. Per 4E 143
Kenn. Devn 4C 12
Kenn. N Som 5H 33
Kennacraig. Arg 3G 125
Kenneggy Downs. Corn 4C 4
Kennerleigh. Devn 2B 12
Kennet. Clac 4B 136
Kennethmont. Abers 1C 152
Kennett. Cambs 4G 65
Kennford. Devn 4C 12
Kenninghall. Norf 2C 66
Kennington. Kent 1E 29
Kennington. Oxon 5D 50
Kennoway. Fife 3F 137
Kennyhill. Suff 3F 65
Kennythorpe. N Yor 3B 100
Kenovay. Arg 4A 138
Kensaleyre. High 3D 154
Kensington. G Lon 3D 38
Kenstone. Shrp 3H 71
Kensworth. C Beds 4A 52
Kensworth Common. C Beds 4A 52
Kentallen. High 3E 141
Kentchurch. Here 3H 47
Kentford. Suff 4G 65
Kent International Airport. Kent 4H 41
Kentisbeare. Devn 2D 12
Kentisbury. Devn 2G 19
Kentisbury Ford. Devn 2G 19
Kentmere. Cumb 4F 103
Kenton. Devn 4C 12
Kenton. G Lon 2C 38
Kenton. Suff 4D 66
Kenton Bankfoot. Tyne 3F 115
Kentra. High 2A 140
Kentrigg. Cumb 5G 103
Kents Bank. Cumb 2C 96
Kent's Green. Glos 3C 48
Kent's Oak. Hants 4B 24
Kent Street. E Sus 4B 28
Kent Street. Kent 5A 40
Kent Street. W Sus 3D 26
Kenwick. Shrp 2G 71
Kenwyn. Corn 4C 6
Kenyon. Warr 1A 84
Keoldale. High 2D 166
Keppoch. High 1B 148
Kepwick. N Yor 5B 106
Keresley. W Mid 2H 61
Keresley Newland. Warw 2H 61
Keristal. IOM 4C 108
Kerne Bridge. Here 4A 48
Kerridge. Ches E 3D 84
Kerris. Corn 4B 4
Kerrow. High 5F 157
Kerry. Powy 2D 58
Kerrycroy. Arg 3C 126
Kerry's Gate. Here 2G 47
Kersall. Notts 4E 86
Kersbrook. Devn 4D 12
Kerse. Ren 4E 127
Kersey. Suff 1D 54
Kershopefoot. Cumb 1F 113
Kersoe. Worc 1E 49
Kerswell. Devn 2D 12
Kerswell Green. Worc 1D 48
Kesgrave. Suff 1F 55
Kesh. Ferm 6D 176
Kessingland. Suff 2H 67
Kessingland Beach. Suff 2H 67
Kestle. Corn 4D 6
Kestle Mill. Corn 3C 6
Keston. G Lon 4F 39
Keswick. Cumb 2D 102
Keswick. Norf 2F 79 (nr. North Walsham)
Keswick. Norf 5E 78 (nr. Norwich)
Ketsby. Linc 3C 88
Kettering. Nptn 3F 63
Ketteringham. Norf 5D 78
Kettins. Per 5B 144
Kettlebaston. Suff 5B 66
Kettlebridge. Fife 3F 137
Kettlebrook. Staf 5G 73
Kettleburgh. Suff 4E 67
Kettleholm. Dum 2C 112
Kettleness. N Yor 3F 107
Kettleshulme. Ches E 3D 85
Kettlesing. N Yor 4E 99
Kettlesing Bottom. N Yor 4E 99
Kettlestone. Norf 2B 78
Kettlethorpe. Linc 3F 87
Kettletoft. Orkn 4F 172
Kettlewell. N Yor 2B 98
Ketton. Rut 5G 75
Kew. G Lon 3C 38
Kewaigue. IOM 4C 108
Kewstoke. N Som 5G 33
Kexbrough. S Yor 4D 92
Kexby. Linc 2F 87
Kexby. York 4B 100
Keyford. Som 2C 22
Key Green. Ches E 4C 84
Key Green. N Yor 4F 107
Keyham. Leics 5D 74

Keyhaven—Leckwith

Keyhaven. Hants 3B 16
Keyhead. Abers 3H 161
Keyingham. E Yor 2F 95
Keymer. W Sus 4E 27
Keynsham. Bath 5B 34
Keysoe. Bed 4H 63
Keysoe Row. Bed 4H 63
Key's Toft. Linc 5D 89
Keyston. Cambs 3H 63
Key Street. Kent 4C 40
Keyworth. Notts 2D 74
Kibblesworth. Tyne 4F 115
Kibworth Beauchamp. Leics 1D 62
Kibworth Harcourt. Leics 1D 62
Kidbrooke. G Lon 3F 39
Kidburngill. Cumb 2B 102
Kiddemore Green. Staf 5C 72
Kidderminster. Worc 3C 60
Kiddington. Oxon 3C 50
Kidd's Moor. Norf 5D 78
Kidlington. Oxon 4C 50
Kidmore End. Oxon 4E 37
Kidnal. Ches W 1G 71
Kidsgrove. Staf 5C 84
Kidstones. N Yor 1B 98
Kidwelly. Carm 5E 45
Kiel Crofts. Arg 5D 140
Kielder. Nmbd 5A 120
Kilbagie. Fife 4B 136
Kilbarchan. Ren 3F 127
Kilbeg. High 3E 147
Kilberry. Arg 3F 125
Kilbirnie. N Ayr 4E 126
Kilbride. Arg 1F 133
Kilbride. High 1D 147
Kilbucho Place. Bord 1C 118
Kilburn. Derbs 1A 74
Kilburn. G Lon 2D 38
Kilburn. N Yor 2H 99
Kilby. Leics 1D 62
Kilchattan. Arg 4A 132
Kilchattan Bay. Arg 4C 126
Kilchenzie. Arg 3A 122
Kilcheran. Arg 5C 140
Kilchiaran. Arg 3A 124
Kilchoan. High 4F 147 (nr. Inverie)
Kilchoan. High 2F 139 (nr. Tobermory)
Kilchoman. Arg 3A 124
Kilchrenan. Arg 1H 133
Kilclief. Down 5K 179
Kilconquhar. Fife 3G 137
Kilcoo. Down 6G 179
Kilcot. Glos 3B 48
Kilcoy. High 3H 157
Kilcreggan. Arg 1D 126
Kildale. N Yor 4D 106
Kildary. High 1B 158
Kildermorie Lodge. High 1H 157
Kildonan. Dum 4F 109
Kildonan. High 1G 165 (nr. Helmsdale)
Kildonan. High 3C 154 (on Isle of Skye)
Kildonan. N Ayr 3E 123
Kildonnan. High 5C 146
Kildrummy. Abers 2B 152
Kildwick. N Yor 5C 98
Kilfillan. Dum 4H 109
Kilfinan. Arg 2H 125
Kilfinnan. High 4E 149
Kilgetty. Pemb 4F 43
Kilgour. Fife 3E 136
Kilgrammie. S Ayr 4B 116
Kilham. E Yor 3E 101
Kilham. Nmbd 1C 120
Kilkeel. New M 8H 179
Kilkenneth. Arg 4A 138
Kilkhampton. Corn 1C 10
Killadeas. Ferm 7E 176
Killamarsh. Derbs 2B 86
Killandrist. Arg 4C 140
Killay. Swan 3F 31
Killean. Arg 5E 125
Killearn. Stir 1G 127
Killeen. Dngn 3C 178
Killellan. Arg 4A 122
Killen. High 3A 158
Killen. Strab 4E 176
Killerby. Darl 3E 105
Killeter. Strab 4E 176
Killichonan. Per 3C 142
Killiechronan. Arg 4G 139
Killiecrankie. Per 2G 143
Killilan. High 5B 156
Killimster. High 3F 169
Killin. Stir 5C 142
Killinchy. Ards 3K 179
Killinghall. N Yor 4E 99
Killington. Cumb 1F 97
Killingworth. Tyne 2F 115
Killin Lodge. High 3H 149
Killinochonoch. Arg 4F 133
Killochyett. Bord 5A 130
Killough. Down 6K 179
Killowen. New M 8F 179
Killundine. High 4G 139
Killylea. Arm 5B 178
Killyleagh. Down 4K 179
Killyrammer. Bmny 4F 175
Kilmacolm. Inv 3E 127
Kilmahog. Stir 3F 135
Kilmahumaig. Arg 4E 133
Kilmalieu. High 3C 140
Kilmaluag. High 1D 154
Kilmany. Fife 1F 137
Kilmarie. High 2D 146
Kilmarnock. E Ayr 1D 116 & 196
Kilmaron. Fife 2F 137
Kilmartin. Arg 4F 133
Kilmaurs. E Ayr 5F 127
Kilmelford. Arg 2F 133
Kilmeny. Arg 3B 124
Kilmersdon. Som 1B 22
Kilmeston. Hants 4D 24
Kilmichael Glassary. Arg 4F 133
Kilmichael of Inverlussa. Arg 1F 125
Kilmington. Devn 3F 13
Kilmington. Wilts 3C 22
Kilmoluaig. Arg 4A 138
Kilmorack. High 4G 157
Kilmore. Arg 1F 133
Kilmore. Arm 4D 178
Kilmore. Down 4J 179
Kilmore. High 3E 147
Kilmory. Arg 2F 125
Kilmory. High 1G 139 (nr. Kilchoan)
Kilmory. High 3B 146 (on Rùm)
Kilmory. N Ayr 3D 122
Kilmory Lodge. Arg 3E 132
Kilmote. High 2G 165
Kilmuir. High 4B 154 (nr. Dunvegan)
Kilmuir. High 1B 158 (nr. Invergordon)
Kilmuir. High 4A 158 (nr. Inverness)
Kilmuir. High 1C 154 (nr. Uig)

Kilnun. Arg 1C 126
Kilnave. Arg 2A 124
Kilncadzow. S Lan 5B 128
Kilndown. Kent 2B 28
Kiln Green. Here 4B 48
Kiln Green. Wind 4G 37
Kilnhill. Cumb 1D 102
Kilnhurst. S Yor 1B 86
Kilninian. Arg 4E 139
Kilninver. Arg 1F 133
Kiln Pit Hill. Nmbd 4D 114
Kilnsea. E Yor 3H 95
Kilnsey. N Yor 3B 98
Kilnwick. E Yor 5D 101
Kiloran. Arg 4A 132
Kilpatrick. N Ayr 3D 122
Kilpeck. Here 2H 47
Kilpin. E Yor 2A 94
Kilpin Pike. E Yor 2A 94
Kilrea. Cole 5F 174
Kilrenny. Fife 3H 137
Kilsby. Nptn 3C 62
Kilspindie. Per 1E 136
Kilsyth. N Lan 2A 128
Kiltarlity. High 4H 157
Kilton. Som 2E 21
Kilton Thorpe. Red C 3D 107
Kilvaxter. High 2C 154
Kilve. Som 2E 21
Kilvington. Notts 1F 75
Kilwinning. N Ayr 5D 126
Kimberley. Norf 5C 78
Kimberley. Notts 1B 74
Kimblesworth. Dur 5F 115
Kimble Wick. Buck 5G 51
Kimbolton. Cambs 4H 63
Kimbolton. Here 4H 59
Kimcote. Leics 2C 62
Kimmeridge. Dors 5E 15
Kimmerston. Nmbd 1D 120
Kimpton. Hants 2A 24
Kimpton. Herts 4B 52
Kinallen. Ban 5G 179
Kinawley. Ferm 6H 177
Kinbeachie. High 2A 158
Kinbrace. High 5A 168
Kinbuck. Stir 3G 135
Kincaple. Fife 2G 137
Kincardine. Fife 1C 128
Kincardine. High 5D 164
Kincardine Bridge. Fife 1C 128
Kincardine O'Neil. Abers 4C 152
Kinchrackine. Arg 1A 134
Kincorth. Aber 3G 153
Kincraig. High 3C 150
Kincraigie. Per 4G 143
Kindallachan. Per 3G 143
Kineton. Glos 3F 49
Kineton. Warw 5H 61
Kinfauns. Per 1D 136
Kingairloch. High 3C 140
Kingarth. Arg 4B 126
Kingcoed. Mon 5H 47
King Edward. Abers 3E 160
Kingerby. Linc 1H 87
Kingham. Oxon 3A 50
Kingholm Quay. Dum 2A 112
Kinghorn. Fife 1F 129
Kingie. High 3D 148
Kinglassie. Fife 4E 137
Kingledores. Bord 2D 118
Kingodie. Per 1F 137
King o' Muirs. Clac 4A 136
King's Acre. Here 1H 47
Kingsand. Corn 3A 8
Kingsash. Buck 5G 51
Kingsbarns. Fife 2H 137
Kingsbridge. Devn 4D 8
Kingsbridge. Som 3C 20
King's Bromley. Staf 4F 73
Kingsburgh. High 3C 154
Kingsbury. G Lon 2C 38
Kingsbury. Warw 1G 61
Kingsbury Episcopi. Som 4H 21
Kings Caple. Here 3A 48
Kingscavil. W Lot 2D 128
Kingsclere. Hants 1D 24
King's Cliffe. Nptn 1H 63
Kings Clipstone. Notts 4D 86
Kingscote. Glos 2D 34
Kingscott. Devn 1F 11
Kings Coughton. Warw 5E 61
Kingscross. N Ayr 3E 123
Kingsdon. Som 4A 22
Kingsdown. Kent 1H 29
Kingsdown. Swin 3G 35
Kingsdown. Wilts 5D 34
Kingseat. Fife 4D 136
Kingsey. Buck 5F 51
Kingsfold. Lanc 2D 90
Kingsfold. W Sus 2C 26
Kingsford. E Ayr 5F 127
Kingsford. Worc 2C 60
Kingsforth. N Lin 3D 94
Kingsgate. Kent 3H 41
King's Green. Glos 2C 48
Kingshall Street. Suff 4B 66
Kingsheanton. Devn 3F 19
King's Heath. W Mid 2E 61
Kings Hill. Kent 5A 40
Kingsholm. Glos 4D 48
Kingshouse. High 3G 141
Kingshouse. Stir 1E 135
Kingshurst. W Mid 2F 61
Kingskerswell. Devn 2E 9
Kingskettle. Fife 3F 137
Kingsland. Here 4G 59
Kingsland. IOA 2B 80
Kings Langley. Herts 5A 52
Kingsley. Ches W 3H 83
Kingsley. Hants 3F 25
Kingsley. Staf 1E 73
Kingsley Green. W Sus 3G 25
Kingsley Holt. Staf 1E 73
King's Lynn. Norf 3F 77
King's Meaburn. Cumb 2H 103
Kings Moss. Mers 4D 90
Kingsmuir. Ang 4D 145
Kingsmuir. Fife 3H 137
Kings Muir. Bord 1E 119
King's Newnham. Warw 3B 62
King's Newton. Derbs 3A 74
Kingsnorth. Kent 2E 28
Kingsnorth. Medw 3C 40
King's Norton. Leics 5D 74
King's Norton. W Mid 3E 61
King's Nympton. Devn 1G 11
King's Pyon. Here 5G 59
Kings Ripton. Cambs 3B 64
King's Somborne. Hants 3B 24
King's Stag. Dors 1C 14
King's Stanley. Glos 5D 48
King's Sutton. Nptn 2C 50
Kingstanding. W Mid 1E 61
Kingsteignton. Devn 5B 12
Kingsteps. High 3D 158
King's Thorn. Here 2A 48
Kingsthorpe. Nptn 4E 63
Kingston. Cambs 5C 64
Kingston. Devn 4C 8
Kingston. Dors 2C 14 (nr. Sturminster Newton)
Kingston. Dors 5E 15 (nr. Swanage)
Kingston. E Lot 1B 130
Kingston. Hants 2G 15

Kingston. IOW 4C 16
Kingston. Kent 5F 41
Kingston. Mor 2H 159
Kingston. W Sus 5B 26
Kingston Bagpuize. Oxon 2C 36
Kingston Blount. Oxon 2F 37
Kingston by Sea. W Sus 5D 26
Kingston Deverill. Wilts 3D 22
Kingstone. Here 2H 47
Kingstone. Som 1G 13
Kingstone. Staf 3E 73
Kingston Lisle. Oxon 3B 36
Kingston Maurward. Dors 3C 14
Kingston near Lewes. E Sus 5E 27
Kingston on Soar. Notts 3C 74
Kingston Russell. Dors 3A 14
Kingston St Mary. Som 4F 21
Kingston Seymour. N Som 5H 33
Kingston Stert. Oxon 5F 51
Kingston upon Hull. Hull 2D 94 & 196
Kingston upon Thames. G Lon 4C 38
King's Walden. Herts 3B 52
Kingswear. Devn 3E 9
Kingswells. Aber 3F 153
Kingswinford. W Mid 2C 60
Kingswood. Buck 4E 51
Kingswood. Glos 2C 34
Kingswood. Here 5E 59
Kingswood. Kent 5C 40
Kingswood. Per 5H 143
Kingswood. Powy 5E 71
Kingswood. Som 3E 20
Kingswood. S Glo 4B 34
Kingswood. Surr 5D 38
Kingswood. Warw 3F 61
Kingswood Common. Staf 5C 72
Kings Worthy. Hants 3C 24
Kingthorpe. Linc 3A 88
Kington. Here 5E 59
Kington. S Glo 2B 34
Kington. Worc 5D 61
Kington Langley. Wilts 4E 35
Kington Magna. Dors 4C 22
Kington St Michael. Wilts 4E 35
Kingussie. High 3B 150
Kingweston. Som 3A 22
Kinharrachie. Abers 5G 161
Kinhrive. High 1B 158
Kinkell Bridge. Per 2B 136
Kinknockie. Abers 4H 161
Kinkry Hill. Cumb 2G 113
Kinlet. Shrp 2B 60
Kinloch. High 5D 166 (nr. Loch More)
Kinloch. High 3A 140 (nr. Lochaline)
Kinloch. High 4C 146 (on Rùm)
Kinloch. Per 4A 144
Kinlochard. Stir 3D 134
Kinlochbervie. High 3C 166
Kinlocheil. High 1D 141
Kinlochewe. High 2C 156
Kinloch Hourn. High 3B 148
Kinloch Laggan. High 5H 149
Kinlochleven. High 2F 141
Kinloch Lodge. High 3F 167
Kinlochmoidart. High 1B 140
Kinlochmore. High 2F 141
Kinloch Rannoch. Per 3D 142
Kinlochspelve. Arg 1D 132
Kinloid. High 5E 147
Kinloss. Mor 2E 159
Kinmel Bay. Cnwy 2B 82
Kinmuck. Abers 2F 153
Kinnadie. Abers 4G 161
Kinnaird. Per 1E 137
Kinneff. Abers 1H 145
Kinnelhead. Dum 4C 118
Kinnell. Ang 3F 145
Kinnerley. Shrp 3F 71
Kinnernie. Abers 2E 152
Kinnersley. Here 1G 47
Kinnersley. Worc 1D 48
Kinnerton. Powy 4E 59
Kinnerton. Shrp 1F 59
Kinnesswood. Per 3D 136
Kinninvie. Dur 2D 104
Kinnordy. Ang 3C 144
Kinoulton. Notts 2D 74
Kinross. Per 3D 136
Kinrossie. Per 5A 144
Kinsbourne Green. Herts 4B 52
Kinsey Heath. Ches E 1A 72
Kinsham. Here 4F 59
Kinsham. Worc 2E 49
Kinsley. W Yor 3E 93
Kinson. Bour 3F 15
Kintbury. W Ber 5B 36
Kintessack. Mor 2E 159
Kintillo. Per 2D 136
Kinton. Here 3G 59
Kinton. Shrp 4F 71
Kintore. Abers 2E 153
Kintour. Arg 4C 124
Kintra. Arg 2B 132
Kintraw. Arg 3F 133
Kinveachy. High 2D 150
Kinver. Staf 2C 60
Kinwarton. Warw 5F 61
Kiplingcotes. E Yor 5D 100
Kippax. W Yor 1E 93
Kippen. Stir 4F 135
Kippford. Dum 4F 111
Kipping's Cross. Kent 1H 27
Kirbister. Orkn 7C 172 (nr. Hobbister)
Kirbister. Orkn 6B 172 (nr. Quholm)
Kirbuster. Orkn 5F 172
Kirby Bedon. Norf 5E 79
Kirby Bellars. Leics 4E 74
Kirby Cane. Norf 1F 67
Kirby Cross. Essx 3F 55
Kirby Fields. Leics 5C 74
Kirby Green. Norf 1F 67
Kirby Grindalythe. N Yor 3D 100
Kirby Hill. N Yor 4E 105 (nr. Richmond)
Kirby Hill. N Yor 3F 99 (nr. Ripon)
Kirby Knowle. N Yor 1G 99
Kirby-le-Soken. Essx 3F 55
Kirby Misperton. N Yor 2B 100
Kirby Muxloe. Leics 5C 74
Kirby Sigston. N Yor 5B 106
Kirby Underdale. E Yor 4C 100
Kirby Wiske. N Yor 1F 99
Kircubbin. Ards 3L 179
Kirdford. W Sus 3B 26
Kirk. High 3E 169
Kirkabister. Shet 8F 173 (on Bressay)
Kirkabister. Shet 6F 173 (on Mainland)
Kirkandrews. Dum 5D 110
Kirkandrews-on-Eden. Cumb 4E 113

Kirkapol. Arg 4B 138
Kirkbampton. Cumb 4E 112
Kirkbean. Dum 4A 112
Kirk Bramwith. S Yor 3G 93
Kirkbride. Cumb 4D 112
Kirkbridge. N Yor 5F 105
Kirkbuddo. Ang 4E 145
Kirkburn. E Yor 4D 101
Kirkburton. W Yor 3B 92
Kirkby. Linc 1H 87
Kirkby. Mers 1G 83
Kirkby. N Yor 4C 106
Kirkby Fenside. Linc 4C 88
Kirkby Fleetham. N Yor 5F 105
Kirkby Green. Linc 5H 87
Kirkby-in-Ashfield. Notts 5C 86
Kirkby-in-Furness. Cumb 1B 96
Kirkby la Thorpe. Linc 1A 76
Kirkby Lonsdale. Cumb 2F 97
Kirkby Malham. N Yor 3A 98
Kirkby Mallory. Leics 5B 74
Kirkby Malzeard. N Yor 2E 99
Kirkby Mills. N Yor 1B 100
Kirkbymoorside. N Yor 1A 100
Kirkby on Bain. Linc 4B 88
Kirkby Overblow. N Yor 5F 99
Kirkby Stephen. Cumb 4A 104
Kirkby Thore. Cumb 2H 103
Kirkby Underwood. Linc 3H 75
Kirkby Wharfe. N Yor 5H 99
Kirkcaldy. Fife 4E 137
Kirkcambeck. Cumb 3G 113
Kirkcolm. Dum 3F 109
Kirkconnel. Dum 3G 117
Kirkconnell. Dum 3A 112
Kirkcowan. Dum 3A 110
Kirkcudbright. Dum 4D 111
Kirkdale. Mers 1F 83
Kirk Deighton. N Yor 4F 99
Kirk Ella. E Yor 2D 94
Kirkfieldbank. S Lan 5B 128
Kirkforthar Feus. Fife 3E 137
Kirkgunzeon. Dum 3F 111
Kirk Hallam. Derbs 1B 74
Kirkham. Lanc 1C 90
Kirkham. N Yor 3B 100
Kirkhamgate. W Yor 2C 92
Kirk Hammerton. N Yor 4G 99
Kirkharle. Nmbd 1D 114
Kirkheaton. Nmbd 2D 114
Kirkheaton. W Yor 3B 92
Kirkhill. Ang 2F 145
Kirkhill. High 4H 157
Kirkhope. S Lan 4B 118
Kirkhouse. Bord 1F 119
Kirkibost. High 2D 146
Kirkinch. Ang 4C 144
Kirkinner. Dum 4B 110
Kirkintilloch. E Dun 2H 127
Kirk Ireton. Derbs 5G 85
Kirkland. Cumb 3B 102 (nr. Cleator Moor)
Kirkland. Cumb 1H 103 (nr. Penrith)
Kirkland. Cumb 5D 112 (nr. Wigton)
Kirkland. Dum 3G 117 (nr. Kirkconnel)
Kirkland. Dum 5H 117 (nr. Moniaive)
Kirkland Guards. Cumb 5C 112
Kirk Langley. Derbs 2G 73
Kirklauchline. Dum 4F 109
Kirkleatham. Red C 2C 106
Kirklevington. Stoc T 4B 106
Kirkley. Suff 1H 67
Kirklington. N Yor 1F 99
Kirklington. Notts 5D 86
Kirklinton. Cumb 3F 113
Kirkliston. Edin 2E 129
Kirkmabreck. Dum 4B 110
Kirkmaiden. Dum 5E 109
Kirk Merrington. Dur 1F 105
Kirk Michael. IOM 2C 108
Kirkmichael. Per 3H 143
Kirkmichael. S Ayr 4C 116
Kirkmuirhill. S Lan 5A 128
Kirknewton. Nmbd 1D 120
Kirknewton. W Lot 3E 129
Kirkney. Abers 5C 160
Kirk of Shotts. N Lan 3B 128
Kirkoswald. Cumb 5G 113
Kirkoswald. S Ayr 4B 116
Kirkpatrick. Dum 5B 118
Kirkpatrick Durham. Dum 2E 111
Kirkpatrick-Fleming. Dum 2D 112
Kirk Sandall. S Yor 4G 93
Kirksanton. Cumb 1A 96
Kirk Smeaton. N Yor 3F 93
Kirkstall. W Yor 1C 92
Kirkstile. Dum 5F 119
Kirkstyle. High 1F 169
Kirkthorpe. W Yor 2D 92
Kirkton. Abers 2D 152 (nr. Alford)
Kirkton. Abers 1D 152 (nr. Insch)
Kirkton. Abers 4F 161 (nr. Turriff)
Kirkton. Ang 5D 144 (nr. Dundee)
Kirkton. Ang 4D 144 (nr. Forfar)
Kirkton. Ang 5B 152 (nr. Tarfside)
Kirkton. Dum 1A 112
Kirkton. Fife 1F 137
Kirkton. High 4E 165 (nr. Golspie)
Kirkton. High 1G 147 (nr. Kyle of Lochalsh)
Kirkton. High 4B 156 (nr. Lochcarron)
Kirkton. Bord 3H 119
Kirkton. S Lan 2B 118
Kirktonhill. W Dun 2E 127
Kirkton Manor. Bord 1E 118
Kirkton of Airlie. Ang 3C 144
Kirkton of Auchterhouse. Ang 5C 144
Kirkton of Bourtie. Abers 1F 153
Kirkton of Collace. Per 5A 144
Kirkton of Craig. Ang 3G 145
Kirkton of Culsalmond. Abers 5D 160
Kirkton of Durris. Abers 4E 153
Kirkton of Glenbuchat. Abers 2A 152
Kirkton of Glenisla. Ang 2B 144
Kirkton of Kingoldrum. Ang 3C 144
Kirkton of Largo. Fife 3G 137
Kirkton of Lethendy. Per 4A 144
Kirkton of Logie Buchan. Abers 1G 153
Kirkton of Maryculter. Abers 4F 153
Kirkton of Menmuir. Ang 2E 145
Kirkton of Monikie. Ang 5E 145
Kirkton of Oyne. Abers 1D 152
Kirkton of Rayne. Abers 5D 160
Kirkton of Skene. Abers 3F 153

Kirktown. Abers 2G 161 (nr. Fraserburgh)
Kirktown. Abers 3H 161 (nr. Peterhead)
Kirktown of Alvah. Abers 2D 160
Kirktown of Auchterless. Abers 4E 160
Kirktown of Deskford. Mor 2C 160
Kirktown of Fetteresso. Abers 5F 153
Kirktown of Mortlach. Mor 5H 159
Kirktown of Slains. Abers 1H 153
Kirkurd. Bord 5E 129
Kirkwall. Orkn 6D 172
Kirkwall Airport. Orkn 7D 172
Kirkwhelpington. Nmbd 1C 114
Kirk Yetholm. Bord 2C 120
Kirmington. N Lin 3E 94
Kirmond le Mire. Linc 1A 88
Kirn. Arg 2C 126
Kirriemuir. Ang 3C 144
Kirstead Green. Norf 1E 67
Kirtlebridge. Dum 2D 112
Kirtleton. Dum 2D 112
Kirtling. Cambs 5F 65
Kirtling Green. Cambs 5F 65
Kirtlington. Oxon 4D 50
Kirtomy. High 2H 167
Kirton. Linc 2C 76
Kirton. Notts 4D 86
Kirton. Suff 2F 55
Kirton End. Linc 1B 76
Kirton Holme. Linc 1B 76
Kirton in Lindsey. N Lin 1G 87
Kishorn. High 4H 155
Kislingbury. Nptn 5D 62
Kite Hill. IOW 3D 16
Kites Hardwick. Warw 4B 62
Kittisford. Som 4D 20
Kittle. Swan 4E 31
Kittybrewster. Aber 3G 153
Kitwood. Hants 3E 25
Kivernoll. Here 2H 47
Kiveton Park. S Yor 2B 86
Knaith. Linc 2F 87
Knaith Park. Linc 2F 87
Knaphill. Surr 5A 38
Knapp. Hants 4C 24
Knapp. Per 5B 144
Knapp. Som 4G 21
Knapperfield. High 3E 169
Knapton. Norf 2F 79
Knapton. York 4H 99
Knapton Green. Here 5G 59
Knapwell. Cambs 4C 64
Knaresborough. N Yor 4F 99
Knarsdale. Nmbd 4H 113
Knatts Valley. Kent 4G 39
Knaven. Abers 4F 161
Knayton. N Yor 1G 99
Knebworth. Herts 3C 52
Knedlington. E Yor 2H 93
Kneesall. Notts 4E 86
Kneesworth. Cambs 1D 52
Kneeton. Notts 1E 74
Knelston. Swan 4D 30
Knenhall. Staf 2D 72
Knightacott. Devn 3G 19
Knightcote. Warw 5B 62
Knightcott. N Som 1G 21
Knightley. Staf 3C 72
Knightley Dale. Staf 3C 72
Knightlow Hill. Warw 3B 62
Knighton. Devn 4B 8
Knighton. Dors 1B 14
Knighton. Leic 5D 74
Knighton. Powy 3E 59
Knighton. Som 2E 21
Knighton. Staf 3B 72 (nr. Eccleshall)
Knighton. Staf 1B 72 (nr. Woore)
Knighton. Wilts 4A 36
Knighton. Worc 5E 61
Knighton Common. Worc 3A 60
Knight's End. Cambs 1D 64
Knightswood. Glas 3G 127
Knightwick. Worc 5B 60
Knill. Here 4E 59
Knipton. Leics 2F 75
Knitsley. Dur 5E 115
Kniveton. Derbs 5G 85
Knock. Arg 5G 139
Knock. Cumb 2H 103
Knock. Mor 3C 160
Knockally. High 5D 168
Knockan. Arg 1B 132
Knockan. High 2G 163
Knockandhu. Mor 1G 151
Knockando. Mor 4F 159
Knockarthur. High 3E 165
Knockbain. High 3A 158
Knockbreck. High 2B 154
Knockcloghrim. Mag 7E 174
Knockdee. High 2D 168
Knockdolian. S Ayr 1G 109
Knockdon. S Ayr 3C 116
Knockdown. Glos 3D 34
Knockenbaird. Abers 1D 152
Knockenkelly. N Ayr 3E 123
Knockentiber. E Ayr 1C 116
Knockfarrel. High 3H 157
Knockglass. High 2C 168
Knockholt. Kent 5F 39
Knockholt Pound. Kent 5F 39
Knockie Lodge. High 2G 149
Knockin. Shrp 3F 71
Knockinlaw. E Ayr 1D 116
Knockinnon. High 5D 169
Knocknacarry. Moy 3J 175
Knockrome. Arg 2D 124
Knocksharry. IOM 3B 108
Knockshinnoch. E Ayr 3D 116
Knockvennie. Dum 2E 111
Knockvologan. Arg 3B 132
Knodishall. Suff 4G 67
Knole. Som 4H 21
Knollbury. Mon 3H 33
Knolls Green. Ches E 3C 84
Knolton. Wrex 2F 71
Knook. Wilts 2E 23
Knossington. Leics 5F 75
Knott. High 3C 154
Knott End-on-Sea. Lanc 5C 96
Knotting. Bed 4H 63
Knotting Green. Bed 4H 63
Knottingley. W Yor 2E 93
Knotts. Cumb 2F 103
Knotty Ash. Mers 1G 83
Knotty Green. Buck 1A 38
Knowbury. Shrp 3H 59
Knowe. Dum 2A 110
Knowefield. Cumb 4F 113
Knowehead. Dum 5F 117
Knowes. E Lot 2C 130
Knowesgate. Nmbd 1C 114
Knoweside. S Ayr 3B 116
Knowes of Elrick. Abers 3D 160
Knowle. Bris 4A 34

Knowle. Devn 3E 19 (nr. Braunton)
Knowle. Devn 4D 12 (nr. Budleigh Salterton)
Knowle. Devn 2A 12 (nr. Crediton)
Knowle. Shrp 3H 59
Knowle. W Mid 3F 61
Knowle Green. Lanc 1E 91
Knowle St Giles. Som 1G 13
Knowlesands. Shrp 1B 60
Knowle Village. Hants 2D 16
Knowl Hill. Wind 4G 37
Knowlton. Kent 5G 41
Knowsley. Mers 1G 83
Knowstone. Devn 4B 20
Knucklas. Powy 3E 59
Knuston. Nptn 4G 63
Knutsford. Ches E 3B 84
Knypersley. Staf 5C 84
Krumlin. W Yor 3A 92
Kuggar. Corn 5E 5
Kyleakin. High 1F 147
Kyle of Lochalsh. High 1F 147
Kylerhea. High 1F 147
Kylesku. High 5C 166
Kyles Lodge. W Isl 9B 171
Kylesmorar. High 4G 147
Kylestrome. High 5C 166
Kymin. Mon 4A 48
Kynaston. Here 2B 48
Kynaston. Shrp 3F 71
Kynnersley. Telf 4A 72
Kyre Green. Worc 4A 60
Kyre Park. Worc 4A 60
Kyrewood. Worc 4A 60

L

Labost. W Isl 3E 171
Lacasaidh. W Isl 5F 171
Lacasdail. W Isl 4G 171
Laceby. NE Lin 4F 95
Lacey Green. Buck 5G 51
Lach Dennis. Ches W 3B 84
Lache. Ches W 4F 83
Lack. Ferm 6E 176
Lackagh. Lim 5C 174
Lackford. Suff 3G 65
Lacock. Wilts 5E 35
Ladbroke. Warw 5B 62
Laddingford. Kent 1A 28
Lade Bank. Linc 5C 88
Ladock. Corn 3C 6
Lady. Orkn 3F 172
Ladybank. Fife 2F 137
Ladycross. Corn 4D 10
Lady Green. Mers 4B 90
Lady Hall. Cumb 1A 96
Ladykirk. Bord 5E 131
Ladysford. Abers 2G 161
Ladywood. W Mid 2E 61
Ladywood. Worc 4C 60
Laga. High 2A 140
Lagavulin. Arg 5C 124
Lagg. Arg 2D 125
Lagg. N Ayr 3D 122
Laggan. Arg 4A 124
Laggan. High 4E 149 (nr. Fort Augustus)
Laggan. High 4A 150 (nr. Newtonmore)
Laggan. Mor 5H 159
Lagganlia. High 3C 150
Lagganulva. Arg 4F 139
Laghey Corner. Dngn 3C 178
Laglingarten. Arg 3A 134
Lagness. W Sus 2G 17
Laid. High 3E 166
Laide. High 4D 162
Laigh Fenwick. E Ayr 5F 127
Laindon. Essx 2A 40
Lairg. High 3C 164
Lairg Muir. High 3C 164
Laithes. Cumb 1F 103
Laithkirk. Dur 2C 104
Lake. Devn 3F 19
Lake. IOW 4D 16
Lake. Wilts 3G 23
Lake District. Cumb 3E 103
Lakenham. Norf 5E 79
Lakenheath. Suff 2G 65
Lakesend. Norf 1E 65
Lakeside. Cumb 1C 96
Laleham. Surr 4B 38
Laleston. B'end 3B 32
Lamancha. Bord 4F 129
Lamarsh. Essx 2B 54
Lamas. Norf 3E 79
Lamb Corner. Essx 2D 54
Lambden. Bord 5D 130
Lamberhead Green. G Man 4D 90
Lamberhurst. Kent 2A 28
Lamberhurst Quarter. Kent 2A 28
Lamberton. Bord 4F 131
Lambeth. G Lon 3E 39
Lambfell Moar. IOM 3B 108
Lambhill. Glas 3G 127
Lambley. Nmbd 4H 113
Lambley. Notts 1D 74
Lambourn. W Ber 4B 36
Lambourne End. Essx 1F 39
Lambourn Woodlands. W Ber 4B 36
Lambrook. Som 4F 21
Lambs Green. Dors 3E 15
Lambs Green. W Sus 2D 26
Lambston. Pemb 3D 42
Lamellion. Corn 2G 7
Lamerton. Devn 5E 11
Lamesley. Tyne 4F 115
Laminess. Orkn 4F 172
Lamington. High 1B 158
Lamington. S Lan 1B 118
Lamlash. N Ayr 2E 123
Lamonby. Cumb 1F 103
Lamorick. Corn 2E 7
Lamorna. Corn 4B 4
Lamorran. Corn 4C 6
Lampeter. Cdgn 1F 45
Lampeter Velfrey. Pemb 3F 43
Lamphey. Pemb 4E 43
Lamplugh. Cumb 2B 102
Lamport. Nptn 3E 63
Lamyatt. Som 3B 22
Lana. Devn 3D 10 (nr. Ashwater)
Lana. Devn 2D 10 (nr. Holsworthy)
Lanark. S Lan 5B 128
Lanarth. Corn 4E 5
Lancaster. Lanc 3D 97
Lanchester. Dur 5E 115
Lancing. W Sus 5C 26
Landbeach. Cambs 4D 64
Landcross. Devn 4E 19
Landerberry. Abers 3E 153
Landford. Wilts 1A 16
Land Gate. G Man 4D 90
Landhallow. High 5D 169
Landimore. Swan 3D 30
Landkey. Devn 3F 19
Landkey Newland. Devn 3F 19
Landore. Swan 3F 31

Landport. Port 2E 17
Landrake. Corn 2H 7
Landscove. Devn 2D 9
Land's End (St Just) Airport. Corn 4A 4
Landshipping. Pemb 3E 43
Landulph. Corn 2A 8
Landywood. Staf 5D 73
Lane. Corn 2C 6
Laneast. Corn 4C 10
Lane Bottom. Lanc 1G 91
Lane End. Buck 2G 37
Lane End. Hants 4D 24
Lane End. IOW 4E 17
Lane End. Wilts 2D 22
Lane Ends. Derbs 2G 73
Lane Ends. Dur 1E 105
Lane Ends. Lanc 4G 97
Laneham. Notts 3F 87
Lanehead. Dur 5B 114 (nr. Cowshill)
Lane Head. Dur 3E 105 (nr. Hutton Magna)
Lane Head. Dur 2D 105 (nr. Woodland)
Lane Head. G Man 1A 84
Lanehead. Nmbd 1A 114
Lane Head. W Yor 4B 92
Lane Heads. Lanc 1C 90
Lanercost. Cumb 3G 113
Laneshaw Bridge. Lanc 5B 98
Laney Green. Staf 5D 72
Langais. W Isl 2D 170
Langal. High 2B 140
Langar. Notts 2E 74
Langbank. Ren 2E 127
Langbar. N Yor 4C 98
Langburnshiels. Bord 4H 119
Langcliffe. N Yor 3H 97
Langdale End. N Yor 5G 107
Langdon. Corn 3C 10
Langdon Beck. Dur 1B 104
Langdon Cross. Corn 4D 10
Langdon Hills. Essx 2A 40
Langdown. Hants 2C 16
Langdyke. Fife 3F 137
Langenhoe. Essx 4D 54
Langford. C Beds 1B 52
Langford. Devn 2D 12
Langford. Essx 5B 54
Langford. Notts 5F 87
Langford. Oxon 5H 49
Langford. Som 4F 21
Langford Budville. Som 4E 20
Langham. Dors 4C 22
Langham. Essx 2D 54
Langham. Norf 1C 78
Langham. Rut 4F 75
Langham. Suff 4B 66
Langho. Lanc 1F 91
Langholm. Dum 1E 113
Langland. Swan 4F 31
Langleeford. Nmbd 2D 120
Langley. Ches E 3D 84
Langley. Derbs 1B 74
Langley. Essx 2E 53
Langley. Glos 3F 49
Langley. Hants 2C 16
Langley. Herts 3C 52
Langley. Kent 5C 40
Langley. Nmbd 3B 114
Langley. Slo 3B 38
Langley. Som 4D 20
Langley. Warw 4F 61
Langley. W Sus 4G 25
Langley Burrell. Wilts 4E 35
Langleybury. Herts 5A 52
Langley Common. Derbs 2G 73
Langley Green. Derbs 2G 73
Langley Green. Norf 5F 79
Langley Green. Warw 4F 61
Langley Green. W Sus 2D 26
Langley Heath. Kent 5C 40
Langley Marsh. Som 4D 20
Langley Moor. Dur 5F 115
Langley Park. Dur 5F 115
Langley Street. Norf 5F 79
Langney. E Sus 5H 27
Langold. Notts 2C 86
Langore. Corn 4D 10
Langport. Som 4H 21
Langrick. Linc 1B 76
Langridge. Bath 5C 34
Langridgeford. Devn 4F 19
Langrigg. Cumb 5C 112
Langrish. Hants 4F 25
Langsett. S Yor 4C 92
Langshaw. Bord 1H 119
Langstone. Hants 2F 17
Langthorne. N Yor 5F 105
Langthorpe. N Yor 3F 99
Langthwaite. N Yor 4D 104
Langtoft. E Yor 3E 101
Langtoft. Linc 4A 76
Langton. Dur 3E 105
Langton. Linc 4B 88 (nr. Horncastle)
Langton. Linc 3C 88 (nr. Spilsby)
Langton. N Yor 3B 100
Langton by Wragby. Linc 3A 88
Langton Green. Kent 2G 27
Langton Herring. Dors 4B 14
Langton Long Blandford. Dors 2E 15
Langton Matravers. Dors 5F 15
Langtree. Devn 1E 11
Langwathby. Cumb 1G 103
Langwith. Derbs 4C 86
Langworth. Linc 3H 87
Lanivet. Corn 2E 7
Lanjeth. Corn 3D 6
Lank. Corn 5A 10
Lanlivery. Corn 3E 7
Lanner. Corn 5B 6
Lanreath. Corn 3F 7
Lansallos. Corn 3F 7
Lansdown. Bath 5C 34
Lansdown. Glos 3E 49
Lanteglos Highway. Corn 3F 7
Lanton. Nmbd 1D 120
Lanton. Bord 2A 120
Lapford. Devn 2H 11
Lapford Cross. Devn 2H 11
Laphroaig. Arg 5B 124
Lapley. Staf 4C 72
Lapworth. Warw 3F 61
Larachbeg. High 4A 140
Larbert. Falk 1B 128
Larden Green. Ches E 5H 83
Larel. High 3D 169
Largie. Abers 5D 160
Largiemore. Arg 1H 125
Largoward. Fife 3G 137
Largs. N Ayr 4D 126
Largue. Abers 4D 160
Largybeg. N Ayr 3E 123
Largymeanoch. N Ayr 3E 123
Largymore. N Ayr 3E 123
Larkfield. Inv 2D 126
Larkfield. Kent 5A 40
Larkhall. Bath 5C 34
Larkhall. S Lan 4A 128
Larkhill. Wilts 2G 23
Larling. Norf 2B 66
Larne. Lar 6L 175
Larport. Here 2A 48

Lartington. Dur 3D 104
Lary. Abers 3H 151
Lasham. Hants 2E 25
Lashenden. Kent 1C 28
Lassodie. Fife 4D 136
Lasswade. Midl 3G 129
Lastingham. N Yor 5E 107
Latchford. Herts 3D 53
Latchford. Oxon 5E 51
Latchingdon. Essx 5B 54
Latchley. Corn 5E 11
Latchmere Green. Hants 5E 37
Lathbury. Mil 1G 51
Latheron. High 5D 169
Latheronwheel. High 5D 169
Lathom. Lanc 4C 90
Lathones. Fife 3G 137
Latimer. Buck 1B 38
Latteridge. S Glo 3B 34
Lattiford. Som 4B 22
Latton. Wilts 2F 35
Laudale House. High 3B 140
Lauder. Bord 5B 130
Laugharne. Carm 3H 43
Laughterton. Linc 3F 87
Laughton. E Sus 4G 27
Laughton. Leics 2D 62
Laughton. Linc 1F 87 (nr. Gainsborough)
Laughton. Linc 2H 75 (nr. Grantham)
Laughton Common. S Yor 2C 86
Laughton en le Morthen. S Yor 2C 86
Launcells. Corn 2C 10
Launceston. Corn 4D 10
Launcherley. Som 2A 22
Launton. Oxon 3E 50
Laurencekirk. Abers 1G 145
Laurieston. Dum 3D 111
Laurieston. Falk 2C 128
Lavendon. Mil 5G 63
Lavenham. Suff 1C 54
Laverhay. Dum 5D 118
Laversdale. Cumb 3F 113
Laverstock. Wilts 3G 23
Laverstoke. Hants 2C 24
Laverton. Glos 2F 49
Laverton. N Yor 2E 99
Laverton. Som 1C 22
Lavister. Wrex 5F 83
Law. S Lan 4B 128
Lawers. Per 5D 142
Lawford. Essx 2D 54
Lawhitton. Corn 4D 10
Lawkland. N Yor 3G 97
Lawley. Telf 5A 72
Lawnhead. Staf 3C 72
Lawrencetown. Ban 5E 178
Lawrenny. Pemb 4E 43
Lawshall. Suff 5A 66
Lawton. Here 5F 59
Laxey. IOM 3D 108
Laxfield. Suff 3E 67
Laxfirth. Shet 6F 173
Laxo. Shet 5F 173
Laxton. E Yor 2A 94
Laxton. Nptn 1G 63
Laxton. Notts 4E 86
Laycock. W Yor 5C 98
Layer Breton. Essx 4C 54
Layer-de-la-Haye. Essx 3C 54
Layer Marney. Essx 4C 54
Layland's Green. W Ber 5B 36
Laymore. Dors 2G 13
Laysters Pole. Here 4H 59
Layter's Green. Buck 1A 38
Laytham. E Yor 1H 93
Lazenby. Red C 3C 106
Lazonby. Cumb 1G 103
Lea. Derbs 5H 85
Lea. Here 3B 48
Lea. Linc 2F 87
Lea. Shrp 2F 59 (nr. Bishop's Castle)
Lea. Shrp 5G 71 (nr. Shrewsbury)
Lea. Wilts 3E 35
Leabrooks. Derbs 5B 86
Leac a Li. W Isl 8D 171
Leachd. Arg 4H 133
Leachkin. High 4A 158
Leachpool. Pemb 3D 42
Leadburn. Midl 4F 129
Leadenham. Linc 5G 87
Leaden Roding. Essx 4F 53
Leaderfoot. Bord 1H 119
Leadgate. Cumb 5A 114
Leadgate. Dur 4E 115
Leadgate. Nmbd 4E 115
Leadhills. S Lan 3A 118
Leadingcross Green. Kent 5C 40
Lea End. Worc 3E 61
Leafield. Oxon 4B 50
Leagrave. Lutn 3A 52
Lea Hall. W Mid 2F 61
Lea Heath. Staf 3E 73
Leake. N Yor 5B 106
Leake Common Side. Linc 5C 88
Leake Fold Hill. Linc 5D 88
Leake Hurn's End. Linc 1D 76
Lealholm. N Yor 4E 107
Lealt. Arg 4D 132
Lealt. High 2E 155
Leam. Derbs 3G 85
Lea Marston. Warw 1G 61
Leamington Hastings. Warw 4B 62
Leamington Spa, Royal. Warw 4H 61
Leamonsley. Staf 5F 73
Leamside. Dur 5G 115
Leargybreck. Arg 2D 124
Lease Rigg. N Yor 4F 107
Leasgill. Cumb 1D 97
Leasingham. Linc 1H 75
Leasingthorne. Dur 1F 105
Leasowe. Mers 1E 83
Leatherhead. Surr 5C 38
Leathley. N Yor 5E 99
Leaths. Dum 3E 111
Leaton. Shrp 4G 71
Leaton. Telf 4A 72
Lea Town. Lanc 1C 90
Leaveland. Kent 5E 40
Leavenheath. Suff 2C 54
Leavening. N Yor 3B 100
Leaves Green. G Lon 4F 39
Lea Yeat. Cumb 1G 97
Leazes. Dur 4E 115
Lebberston. N Yor 1E 101
Lechlade on Thames. Glos 2H 35
Leck. Lanc 2F 97
Leckford. Hants 3B 24
Leckfurin. High 3H 167
Leckgruinart. Arg 3A 124
Leckhampstead. Buck 2F 51
Leckhampstead. W Ber 4C 36
Leckhampstead Street. W Ber 4C 36
Leckhampton. Glos 4E 49
Leckmelm. High 4F 163
Leckwith. V Glam 4E 33

Maxted Street—Mynydd Isa

Maxted Street. *Kent* 1F **29**
Maxton. *Kent* 1G **29**
Maxton. *Bord* 1A **120**
Maxwellheugh. *Bord* 1B **120**
Maxwelltown. *Dum* 2A **112**
Maxworthy. *Corn* 3C **10**
Mayals. *Swan* 4F **31**
Maybole. *S Ayr* 4C **116**
Maybush. *Sotn* 1B **16**
Maydown. *Derr* 5A **174**
Mayes Green. *Surr* 2C **26**
Mayfield. *E Sus* 3G **27**
Mayfield. *Midl* 3G **129**
Mayfield. *Per* 1C **136**
Mayfield. *Staf* 1F **73**
Mayford. *Surr* 5A **38**
Mayhill. *Swan* 3F **31**
Mayland. *Essx* 5C **54**
Maylandsea. *Essx* 5C **54**
Maynard's Green. *E Sus* 4G **27**
Mayobridge. *New M* 7F **179**
Maypole. *IOS* 1B **4**
Maypole. *Kent* 4G **41**
Maypole. *Mon* 4H **47**
Maypole Green. *Norf* 1G **67**
Maypole Green. *Suff* 5B **66**
Maywick. *Shet* 9E **173**
Mazetown. *Lis* 3G **179**
Mead. *Devn* 1C **10**
Meadgate. *Bath* 1B **22**
Meadle. *Buck* 5G **51**
Meadowbank. *Ches W* 4A **84**
Meadowfield. *Dur* 1F **105**
Meadow Green. *Here* 5B **60**
Meadowmill. *E Lot* 2H **129**
Meadows. *Nott* 2C **74**
Meadowtown. *Shrp* 5F **71**
Meadwell. *Devn* 4E **11**
Meaford. *Staf* 2C **72**
Mealabost. *W Isl* 2G **171** (nr. Borgh)
Mealabost. *W Isl* 4G **171** (nr. Stornoway)
Mealasta. *W Isl* 5B **171**
Meal Bank. *Cumb* 5G **103**
Mealrigg. *Cumb* 5C **112**
Mealsgate. *Cumb* 5D **112**
Meanwood. *W Yor* 1C **92**
Mearbeck. *N Yor* 3H **97**
Meare. *Som* 2H **21**
Meare Green. *Som* 4F **21** (nr. Curry Mallet)
Meare Green. *Som* 4G **21** (nr. Stoke St Gregory)
Mears Ashby. *Nptn* 4F **63**
Measham. *Leics* 4H **73**
Meath Green. *Surr* 1D **27**
Meathop. *Cumb* 1D **96**
Meaux. *E Yor* 1D **94**
Meavy. *Devn* 2B **8**
Medbourne. *Leics* 1E **63**
Medburn. *Nmbd* 2E **115**
Meddon. *Devn* 1C **10**
Meden Vale. *Notts* 4C **86**
Medlam. *Linc* 5C **88**
Medlicott. *Shrp* 1G **59**
Medmenham. *Buck* 3G **37**
Medomsley. *Dur* 4E **115**
Medstead. *Hants* 3E **25**
Medway Towns. *Medw* 4B **40** & **197**
Meerbrook. *Staf* 4D **85**
Meer End. *W Mid* 3G **61**
Meers Bridge. *Linc* 2D **89**
Meesden. *Herts* 2E **53**
Meeson. *Telf* 3A **72**
Meeth. *Devn* 2F **11**
Meeting Green. *Suff* 5G **65**
Meeting House Hill. *Norf* 3F **79**
Meidrim. *Carm* 2G **43**
Meifod. *Powy* 4D **70**
Meigh. *New M* 7E **178**
Meigle. *Per* 4B **144**
Meikle Earnock. *S Lan* 4A **128**
Meikle Kilchattan Butts. *Arg* 4B **126**
Meikleour. *Per* 5A **144**
Meikle Tarty. *Abers* 1G **153**
Meikle Wartle. *Abers* 5E **160**
Meinciau. *Carm* 4E **45**
Meir. *Stoke* 1D **72**
Meir Heath. *Staf* 1D **72**
Melbourn. *Cambs* 1D **53**
Melbourne. *Derbs* 3A **74**
Melbourne. *E Yor* 5B **100**
Melbury Abbas. *Dors* 4D **23**
Melbury Bubb. *Dors* 2A **14**
Melbury Osmond. *Dors* 2A **14**
Melbury Sampford. *Dors* 2A **14**
Melby. *Shet* 6C **173**
Melchbourne. *Bed* 4H **63**
Melcombe Bingham. *Dors* 2C **14**
Melcombe Regis. *Dors* 4B **14**
Meldon. *Devn* 3F **11**
Meldon. *Nmbd* 1E **115**
Meldreth. *Cambs* 1D **53**
Melfort. *Arg* 2F **133**
Melgarve. *High* 4G **149**
Meliden. *Den* 2C **82**
Melinbyrhedyn. *Powy* 1H **57**
Melincourt. *Neat* 5B **46**
Melin-y-coed. *Cnwy* 4H **81**
Melin-y-ddol. *Powy* 5C **70**
Melin-y-wig. *Den* 1C **70**
Melkington. *Nmbd* 5E **131**
Melkinthorpe. *Cumb* 2G **103**
Melkridge. *Nmbd* 3A **114**
Melksham. *Wilts* 5E **35**
Mellangaun. *High* 5C **162**
Melldalloch. *Arg* 2H **125**
Mellguards. *Cumb* 5F **113**
Melling. *Lanc* 2E **97**
Melling. *Mers* 4B **90**
Melling Mount. *Mers* 4C **90**
Mellis. *Suff* 3C **66**
Mellon Charles. *High* 4C **162**
Mellon Udrigle. *High* 4C **162**
Mellor. *G Man* 2D **85**
Mellor. *Lanc* 1E **91**
Mellor Brook. *Lanc* 1E **91**
Mells. *Som* 2C **22**
Melmerby. *Cumb* 1H **103**
Melmerby. *N Yor* 1C **98** (nr. Middleham)
Melmerby. *N Yor* 2F **99** (nr. Ripon)
Melplash. *Dors* 3H **13**
Melrose. *Bord* 1H **119**
Melsetter. *Orkn* 9B **172**
Melsonby. *N Yor* 4E **105**
Meltham. *W Yor* 3A **92**
Meltham Mills. *W Yor* 3B **92**
Melton. *E Yor* 2C **94**
Melton. *Suff* 5E **67**
Meltonby. *E Yor* 4B **100**
Melton Constable. *Norf* 2C **78**
Melton Mowbray. *Leics* 4E **75**
Melton Ross. *N Lin* 3D **94**
Melvaig. *High* 5B **162**
Melverley. *Shrp* 4F **71**
Melverley Green. *Shrp* 4F **71**
Melvich. *High* 2A **168**
Membury. *Devn* 2F **13**
Memsie. *Abers* 2G **161**
Memus. *Ang* 3D **144**
Menabilly. *Corn* 3E **7**
Menai Bridge. *IOA* 3E **81**
Mendham. *Suff* 2E **67**
Mendlesham. *Suff* 4D **66**
Mendlesham Green. *Suff* 4C **66**
Menethorpe. *N Yor* 3B **100**
Menheniot. *Corn* 2G **7**
Menithwood. *Worc* 4B **60**
Menna. *Corn* 3D **6**
Mennock. *Dum* 4H **117**
Menston. *W Yor* 5D **98**
Menstrie. *Clac* 4H **135**
Menthorpe. *N Yor* 1H **93**
Mentmore. *Buck* 4H **51**
Meole Brace. *Shrp* 4G **71**
Meols. *Mers* 2E **83**
Meon. *Hants* 2D **16**
Meonstoke. *Hants* 4E **24**
Meopham. *Kent* 4H **39**
Meopham Green. *Kent* 4H **39**
Meopham Station. *Kent* 4H **39**
Mepal. *Cambs* 2D **64**
Meppershall. *C Beds* 2B **52**
Merbach. *Here* 1G **47**
Mercaston. *Derbs* 1G **73**
Merchiston. *Edin* 2F **129**
Mere. *Ches E* 2B **84**
Mere. *Wilts* 3D **22**
Mere Brow. *Lanc* 3C **90**
Mereclough. *Lanc* 1G **91**
Mere Green. *W Mid* 1F **61**
Mere Green. *Worc* 4D **60**
Mere Heath. *Ches W* 3A **84**
Mereside. *Bkpl* 1B **90**
Meretown. *Staf* 3B **72**
Mereworth. *Kent* 5A **40**
Meriden. *W Mid* 2G **61**
Merkadale. *High* 5C **154**
Merkland. *S Ayr* 5B **116**
Merkland Lodge. *High* 1A **164**
Merley. *Pool* 3F **15**
Merlin's Bridge. *Pemb* 3D **42**
Merridge. *Som* 3F **21**
Merrington. *Shrp* 3G **71**
Merrion. *Pemb* 5D **42**
Merriott. *Som* 1H **13**
Merrivale. *Devn* 5F **11**
Merrow. *Surr* 5B **38**
Merrybent. *Darl* 3F **105**
Merry Lees. *Leics* 5B **74**
Merrymeet. *Corn* 2G **7**
Mersham. *Kent* 2E **29**
Merstham. *Surr* 5D **39**
Merston. *W Sus* 2G **17**
Merstone. *IOW* 4D **16**
Merther. *Corn* 4C **6**
Merthyr. *Carm* 3D **44**
Merthyr Cynog. *Powy* 2C **46**
Merthyr Dyfan. *V Glam* 4E **32**
Merthyr Mawr. *B'end* 4B **32**
Merthyr Tudful. *Mer T* 5D **46**
Merthyr Tydfil. *Mer T* 5D **46**
Merthyr Vale. *Mer T* 5D **46**
Merton. *Devn* 1F **11**
Merton. *G Lon* 4D **38**
Merton. *Norf* 1B **66**
Merton. *Oxon* 4D **50**
Meshaw. *Devn* 1A **12**
Messing. *Essx* 4B **54**
Messingham. *N Lin* 4B **94**
Metcombe. *Devn* 3D **12**
Metfield. *Suff* 2E **67**
Metherell. *Corn* 2A **8**
Metheringham. *Linc* 4H **87**
Methil. *Fife* 4F **137**
Methilhill. *Fife* 4F **137**
Methley. *W Yor* 2D **93**
Methley Junction. *W Yor* 2D **93**
Methlick. *Abers* 5F **161**
Methven. *Per* 1C **136**
Methwold. *Norf* 1G **65**
Methwold Hythe. *Norf* 1G **65**
Mettingham. *Suff* 1F **67**
Metton. *Norf* 2D **78**
Mevagissey. *Corn* 4E **6**
Mexborough. *S Yor* 4E **93**
Mey. *High* 1E **169**
Meysey Hampton. *Glos* 2G **35**
Miabhag. *W Isl* 8D **171**
Miabhag. *W Isl* 7C **171** (nr. Cliasmol)
Miabhaig. *W Isl* 4C **171** (nr. Timsgearraidh)
Mial. *High* 1G **155**
Michaelchurch. *Here* 3A **48**
Michaelchurch Escley. *Here* 2G **47**
Michaelchurch-on-Arrow. *Powy* 5E **59**
Michaelston-le-Pit. *V Glam* 4E **33**
Michaelston-y-Fedw. *Newp* 3F **33**
Michaelstow. *Corn* 5A **10**
Michelcombe. *Devn* 2C **8**
Micheldever. *Hants* 3D **24**
Micheldever Station. *Hants* 2D **24**
Michelmersh. *Hants* 4B **24**
Mickfield. *Suff* 4D **66**
Micklebring. *S Yor* 1C **86**
Mickleby. *N Yor* 3F **107**
Micklefield. *W Yor* 1E **93**
Micklefield Green. *Herts* 1B **38**
Mickleham. *Surr* 5C **38**
Mickleover. *Derb* 2H **73**
Micklethwaite. *Cumb* 4D **112**
Micklethwaite. *W Yor* 5D **98**
Mickleton. *Dur* 2C **104**
Mickleton. *Glos* 1G **49**
Mickletown. *W Yor* 2D **93**
Mickle Trafford. *Ches W* 4G **83**
Mickley. *N Yor* 2E **99**
Mickley Green. *Suff* 5H **65**
Mickley Square. *Nmbd* 3D **115**
Mid Ardlaw. *Abers* 2G **161**
Midbea. *Orkn* 3D **172**
Mid Beltie. *Abers* 3D **152**
Mid Calder. *W Lot* 3D **129**
Mid Clyth. *High* 5E **169**
Middle Assendon. *Oxon* 3F **37**
Middle Aston. *Oxon* 3C **50**
Middle Barton. *Oxon* 3C **50**
Middlebie. *Dum* 2D **112**
Middle Chinnock. *Som* 1H **13**
Middle Claydon. *Buck* 3F **51**
Middlecliffe. *S Yor* 4E **93**
Middlecott. *Devn* 4H **11**
Middle Drums. *Ang* 3E **145**
Middle Duntisbourne. *Glos* 5E **49**
Middle Essie. *Abers* 3H **161**
Middleforth Green. *Lanc* 2D **90**
Middleham. *N Yor* 1D **98**
Middle Handley. *Derbs* 3B **86**
Middle Harling. *Norf* 2B **66**
Middlehope. *Shrp* 2G **59**
Middle Littleton. *Worc* 1F **49**
Middle Maes-coed. *Here* 2G **47**
Middlemarsh. *Dors* 2B **14**
Middle Marwood. *Devn* 3F **19**
Middle Mayfield. *Staf* 1F **73**
Middlemoor. *Devn* 5E **11**
Middlemuir. *Abers* 4F **161** (nr. New Deer)
Middlemuir. *Abers* 3G **161** (nr. Strichen)
Middle Rainton. *Tyne* 5G **115**
Middle Rasen. *Linc* 2H **87**
Middlesbrough. *Midd* 3B **106** & **197**
Middlesceugh. *Cumb* 5E **113**
Middleshaw. *Cumb* 1E **97**
Middlesmoor. *N Yor* 2C **98**
Middles, The. *Dur* 4F **115**
Middlestone. *Dur* 1F **105**
Middlestone Moor. *Dur* 1F **105**
Middle Stoughton. *Som* 2H **21**
Middlestown. *W Yor* 3C **92**
Middle Street. *Glos* 5C **48**
Middle Taphouse. *Corn* 2F **7**
Middleton. *Ang* 4E **145**
Middleton. *Arg* 4A **138**
Middleton. *Cumb* 1F **97**
Middleton. *Derbs* 4F **85** (nr. Bakewell)
Middleton. *Derbs* 5G **85** (nr. Wirksworth)
Middleton. *Essx* 2B **54**
Middleton. *G Man* 4G **91**
Middleton. *Hants* 2C **24**
Middleton. *Hart* 1C **106**
Middleton. *Here* 4H **59**
Middleton. *IOW* 4B **16**
Middleton. *Lanc* 4D **96**
Middleton. *Midl* 4G **129**
Middleton. *Norf* 4F **77**
Middleton. *Nptn* 1F **63**
Middleton. *Nmbd* 1F **121** (nr. Belford)
Middleton. *Nmbd* 1D **114** (nr. Morpeth)
Middleton. *N Yor* 5D **98** (nr. Ilkley)
Middleton. *N Yor* 1B **100** (nr. Pickering)
Middleton. *Per* 3D **136**
Middleton. *Shrp* 3H **59** (nr. Ludlow)
Middleton. *Shrp* 3F **71** (nr. Oswestry)
Middleton. *Suff* 4G **67**
Middleton. *Swan* 4D **30**
Middleton. *Warw* 1F **61**
Middleton. *W Yor* 2D **92**
Middleton Cheney. *Nptn* 1D **50**
Middleton Green. *Staf* 2D **73**
Middleton Hall. *Nmbd* 2D **121**
Middleton-in-Teesdale. *Dur* 2C **104**
Middleton One Row. *Darl* 3A **106**
Middleton-on-Leven. *N Yor* 4B **106**
Middleton-on-Sea. *W Sus* 5A **26**
Middleton on the Hill. *Here* 4H **59**
Middleton-on-the-Wolds. *E Yor* 5D **100**
Middleton Priors. *Shrp* 1A **60**
Middleton Quernhow. *N Yor* 2F **99**
Middleton St George. *Darl* 3A **106**
Middleton Scriven. *Shrp* 2A **60**
Middleton Stoney. *Oxon* 3D **50**
Middleton Tyas. *N Yor* 4F **105**
Middletown. *Arm* 6B **178**
Middletown. *Cumb* 4A **102**
Middle Town. *IOS* 1B **4**
Middletown. *Powy* 4F **71**
Middle Tysoe. *Warw* 1B **50**
Middle Wallop. *Hants* 3A **24**
Middlewich. *Ches E* 4B **84**
Middle Winterslow. *Wilts* 3H **23**
Middlewood. *Corn* 5C **10**
Middlewood. *S Yor* 1H **85**
Middle Woodford. *Wilts* 3G **23**
Middlewood Green. *Suff* 4C **66**
Middleyard. *Glos* 5D **48**
Middlezoy. *Som* 3G **21**
Middridge. *Dur* 2F **105**
Midelney. *Som* 4H **21**
Midfield. *High* 2F **167**
Midford. *Bath* 5C **34**
Mid Garrary. *Dum* 2C **110**
Midge Hall. *Lanc* 2D **90**
Midgeholme. *Cumb* 4H **113**
Midgham. *W Ber* 5D **36**
Midgley. *W Yor* 2A **92** (nr. Halifax)
Midgley. *W Yor* 3C **92** (nr. Horbury)
Mid Ho. *Shet* 2G **173**
Midhopestones. *S Yor* 1G **85**
Midhurst. *W Sus* 4G **25**
Mid Kirkton. *N Ayr* 4C **126**
Mid Lambrook. *Som* 1H **13**
Midland. *Orkn* 7C **172**
Mid Lavant. *W Sus* 2G **17**
Midlem. *Bord* 2H **119**
Midney. *Som* 4A **22**
Midsomer Norton. *Bath* 1B **22**
Midton. *Inv* 2D **126**
Midtown. *High* 5C **162** (nr. Poolewe)
Midtown. *High* 2F **167** (nr. Tongue)
Midville. *Linc* 5C **88**
Mid Walls. *Shet* 7C **173**
Mid Yell. *Shet* 2G **173**
Migdale. *High* 4D **164**
Migvie. *Abers* 3B **152**
Milborne Port. *Som* 1B **14**
Milborne St Andrew. *Dors* 3D **14**
Milborne Wick. *Som* 4B **22**
Milbourne. *Nmbd* 2E **115**
Milbourne. *Wilts* 3E **35**
Milburn. *Cumb* 2H **103**
Milbury Heath. *S Glo* 2B **34**
Milby. *N Yor* 3G **99**
Milcombe. *Oxon* 2C **50**
Milden. *Suff* 1C **54**
Mildenhall. *Suff* 3G **65**
Mildenhall. *Wilts* 5H **35**
Milebrook. *Powy* 3F **59**
Milebush. *Kent* 1B **28**
Mile End. *Cambs* 2F **65**
Mile End. *Essx* 3C **54**
Mileham. *Norf* 4B **78**
Mile Oak. *Brig* 5D **26**
Miles Green. *Staf* 5C **84**
Miles Hope. *Here* 4H **59**
Milesmark. *Fife* 1D **128**
Mile Town. *Kent* 3D **40**
Milfield. *Nmbd* 1D **120**
Milford. *Arm* 5C **178**
Milford. *Derbs* 1A **74**
Milford. *Devn* 4C **18**
Milford. *Powy* 1C **58**
Milford. *Staf* 3D **72**
Milford. *Surr* 1A **26**
Milford Haven. *Pemb* 4D **42**
Milford on Sea. *Hants* 3A **16**
Milkwall. *Glos* 5A **48**
Milkwell. *Wilts* 4E **23**
Milland. *W Sus* 4G **25**
Millbank. *High* 2D **168**
Millbank. *Newt* 1G **179**
Mill Bank. *W Yor* 2A **92**
Millbay. *Lar* 7L **175**
Millbeck. *Cumb* 2D **102**
Millbounds. *Orkn* 4E **172**
Millbreck. *Abers* 4H **161**
Millbridge. *Surr* 2G **25**
Millbrook. *C Beds* 2A **52**
Millbrook. *Corn* 3A **8**
Millbrook. *G Man* 1D **85**
Millbrook. *Lar* 6K **175**
Millbrook. *Sotn* 1B **16**
Mill Common. *Suff* 2G **67**
Mill Corner. *E Sus* 3C **28**
Milldale. *Staf* 5F **85**
Millden Lodge. *Ang* 1E **145**
Milldens. *Ang* 3E **145**
Millearn. *Per* 2B **136**
Mill End. *Buck* 3F **37**
Mill End. *Cambs* 5F **65**
Millend. *Glos* 2C **34** (nr. Dursley)
Mill End. *Glos* 4G **49** (nr. Northleach)
Mill End. *Herts* 2D **52**
Millerhill. *Midl* 3G **129**
Miller's Dale. *Derbs* 3F **85**
Millers Green. *Derbs* 5G **85**
Millerston. *N Lan* 3H **127**
Millfield. *Abers* 4B **152**
Millfield. *Pet* 1A **64**
Millgate. *Lanc* 3G **91**
Mill Green. *Essx* 5G **53**
Mill Green. *Norf* 2D **66**
Mill Green. *Shrp* 3A **72**
Mill Green. *Staf* 3E **73**
Mill Green. *Suff* 1C **54**
Millhalf. *Here* 1F **47**
Millhall. *E Ren* 4G **127**
Millhayes. *Devn* 2F **13** (nr. Honiton)
Millhayes. *Devn* 1E **13** (nr. Wellington)
Millhead. *Lanc* 2D **97**
Millheugh. *S Lan* 4A **128**
Mill Hill. *Bkbn* 2E **91**
Mill Hill. *G Lon* 1D **38**
Millholme. *Cumb* 5G **103**
Millhouse. *Arg* 2A **126**
Millhouse. *Cumb* 1E **103**
Millhousebridge. *Dum* 1C **112**
Millhouses. *S Yor* 2H **85**
Millikenpark. *Ren* 3F **127**
Millington. *E Yor* 4C **100**
Millington Green. *Derbs* 1G **73**
Millisle. *Ards* 2K **179**
Mill Knowe. *Arg* 3B **122**
Mill Lane. *Hants* 1F **25**
Millmeece. *Staf* 2C **72**
Mill of Craigievar. *Abers* 2C **152**
Mill of Fintray. *Abers* 2F **153**
Mill of Haldane. *W Dun* 1F **127**
Millom. *Cumb* 1A **96**
Millow. *C Beds* 1C **52**
Millpool. *Corn* 5B **10**
Millport. *N Ayr* 4C **126**
Mill Side. *Cumb* 1D **96**
Mill Street. *Norf* 4C **78** (nr. Lyng)
Mill Street. *Norf* 4C **78** (nr. Swanton Morley)
Millthorpe. *Derbs* 3H **85**
Millthorpe. *Linc* 2A **76**
Millthrop. *Cumb* 5H **103**
Milltimber. *Aber* 3F **153**
Milltown. *Abers* 3G **151** (nr. Corgarff)
Milltown. *Abers* 2B **152** (nr. Lumsden)
Mill Town. *Ant* 8H **175** (nr. Antrim)
Milltown. *Ant* 7G **175** (nr. Toome)
Milltown. *Arm* 5D **178**
Milltown. *Ban* 5F **178**
Milltown. *Corn* 3F **7**
Milltown. *Cgvn* 3D **178**
Milltown. *Derbs* 4A **86**
Milltown. *Devn* 3F **19**
Milltown. *Dum* 2E **113**
Milltown of Aberdalgie. *Per* 1C **136**
Milltown of Auchindoun. *Mor* 4A **160**
Milltown of Campfield. *Abers* 3D **152**
Milltown of Edinvillie. *Mor* 4G **159**
Milltown of Rothiemay. *Mor* 4C **160**
Milltown of Towie. *Abers* 2B **152**
Milnacraig. *Ang* 3B **144**
Milnathort. *Per* 3D **136**
Milngavie. *E Dun* 2G **127**
Milnholm. *Stir* 1A **128**
Milnrow. *G Man* 3H **91**
Milnthorpe. *Cumb* 1D **97**
Milnthorpe. *W Yor* 3D **92**
Milson. *Shrp* 3A **60**
Milstead. *Kent* 5D **40**
Milston. *Wilts* 2G **23**
Milthorpe. *Nptn* 1D **50**
Milton. *Ang* 4C **144**
Milton. *Cambs* 4D **65**
Milton. *Cumb* 3G **113** (nr. Brampton)
Milton. *Cumb* 1E **97** (nr. Crooklands)
Milton. *Derbs* 3H **73**
Milton. *Dum* 2F **111** (nr. Crocketford)
Milton. *Dum* 4H **109** (nr. Glenluce)
Milton. *E Ayr* 2D **116**
Milton. *Glas* 2G **127**
Milton. *High* 3F **157** (nr. Achnasheen)
Milton. *High* 4G **155** (nr. Applecross)
Milton. *High* 5G **157** (nr. Drumnadrochit)
Milton. *High* 1B **158** (nr. Invergordon)
Milton. *High* 4H **157** (nr. Inverness)
Milton. *High* 3F **169** (nr. Wick)
Milton. *Mor* 2C **160** (nr. Cullen)
Milton. *Mor* 2F **151** (nr. Tomintoul)
Milton. *N Som* 5G **33**
Milton. *Notts* 3E **86**
Milton. *Oxon* 2C **50** (nr. Bloxham)
Milton. *Oxon* 2C **36** (nr. Didcot)
Milton. *Pemb* 4E **43**
Milton. *Port* 3E **17**
Milton. *Som* 4H **21**
Milton. *Stir* 3E **135** (nr. Aberfoyle)
Milton. *Stir* 4D **134** (nr. Drymen)
Milton. *Stoke* 5D **84**
Milton. *W Dun* 2F **127**
Milton Abbas. *Dors* 2D **14**
Milton Abbot. *Devn* 5E **11**
Milton Auchlossan. *Abers* 3C **152**
Milton Bridge. *Midl* 3F **129**
Milton Bryan. *C Beds* 2H **51**
Milton Clevedon. *Som* 3B **22**
Milton Coldwells. *Abers* 5G **161**
Milton Combe. *Devn* 2A **8**
Milton Common. *Oxon* 5E **51**
Milton Damerel. *Devn* 1D **11**
Miltonduff. *Mor* 2F **159**
Milton End. *Glos* 5G **49**
Milton Ernest. *Bed* 5H **63**
Milton Green. *Ches W* 5G **83**
Milton Hill. *Devn* 5C **12**
Milton Hill. *Oxon* 2C **36**
Milton Keynes. *Mil* 2G **51** & **200**
Milton Keynes Village. *Mil* 2G **51**
Milton Lilbourne. *Wilts* 5G **35**
Milton Malsor. *Nptn* 5E **63**
Milton Morenish. *Per* 5D **142**
Milton of Auchinhove. *Abers* 3C **152**
Milton of Balgonie. *Fife* 3F **137**
Milton of Barras. *Abers* 1H **145**
Milton of Campsie. *E Dun* 2H **127**
Milton of Cultoquhey. *Per* 1A **136**
Milton of Cushnie. *Abers* 2C **152**
Milton of Finavon. *Ang* 3D **145**
Milton of Gollanfield. *High* 3B **158**
Milton of Lesmore. *Abers* 1B **152**
Milton of Leys. *High* 4A **158**
Milton of Tullich. *Abers* 4A **152**
Milton on Stour. *Dors* 4C **22**
Milton Regis. *Kent* 4C **40**
Milton Street. *E Sus* 5G **27**
Milton-under-Wychwood. *Oxon* 4A **50**
Milverton. *Som* 4E **20**
Milverton. *Warw* 4H **61**
Milwich. *Staf* 2D **72**
Mimbridge. *Surr* 4A **38**
Minard. *Arg* 4G **133**
Minchington. *Dors* 1E **15**
Minchinhampton. *Glos* 5D **49**
Mindrum. *Nmbd* 1C **120**
Minehead. *Som* 2C **20**
Minera. *Wrex* 5E **83**
Minerstown. *Down* 6J **179**
Minety. *Wilts* 2F **35**
Minffordd. *Gwyn* 2E **69**
Mingarrypark. *High* 2A **140**
Mingary. *High* 2G **139**
Mingearraidh. *W Isl* 6C **170**
Miningsby. *Linc* 4C **88**
Minions. *Corn* 5C **10**
Minishant. *S Ayr* 3C **116**
Minllyn. *Gwyn* 4A **70**
Minnigaff. *Dum* 3B **110**
Minorca. *IOM* 3D **108**
Minskip. *N Yor* 3F **99**
Minstead. *Hants* 1A **16**
Minsted. *W Sus* 4G **25**
Minster. *Kent* 4H **41** (nr. Ramsgate)
Minster. *Kent* 3D **40** (nr. Sheerness)
Minsteracres. *Nmbd* 4D **114**
Minsterley. *Shrp* 5F **71**
Minster Lovell. *Oxon* 4B **50**
Minsterworth. *Glos* 4C **48**
Minterne Magna. *Dors* 2B **14**
Minterne Parva. *Dors* 2B **14**
Minting. *Linc* 3A **88**
Mintlaw. *Abers* 4H **161**
Minto. *Bord* 2H **119**
Minton. *Shrp* 1G **59**
Minwear. *Pemb* 3E **43**
Minworth. *W Mid* 1F **61**
Miodar. *Arg* 4B **138**
Mirbister. *Orkn* 5C **172**
Mirehouse. *Cumb* 3A **102**
Mireland. *High* 2F **169**
Mirfield. *W Yor* 3C **92**
Miserden. *Glos* 5E **49**
Miskin. *Rhon* 3D **32**
Misson. *Notts* 1D **86**
Misterton. *Leics* 2C **62**
Misterton. *Notts* 1E **87**
Misterton. *Som* 2H **13**
Mistley. *Essx* 2E **54**
Mistley Heath. *Essx* 2E **55**
Mitcham. *G Lon* 4D **39**
Mitcheldean. *Glos* 4B **48**
Mitchell. *Corn* 3C **6**
Mitchel Troy. *Mon* 4H **47**
Mitcheltroy Common. *Mon* 5H **47**
Mitford. *Nmbd* 1E **115**
Mithian. *Corn* 3B **6**
Mitton. *Staf* 4C **72**
Mixbury. *Oxon* 2E **50**
Mixenden. *W Yor* 2A **92**
Mixon. *Staf* 5E **85**
Moaness. *Orkn* 7B **172**
Moarfield. *Shet* 1G **173**
Moat. *Cumb* 2F **113**
Moats Tye. *Suff* 5C **66**
Mobberley. *Ches E* 3B **84**
Mobberley. *Staf* 1E **73**
Moccas. *Here* 1G **47**
Mochdre. *Cnwy* 3H **81**
Mochdre. *Powy* 2C **58**
Mochrum. *Dum* 5A **110**
Mockbeggar. *Hants* 2G **15**
Mockerkin. *Cumb* 2B **102**
Modbury. *Devn* 3C **8**
Moddershall. *Staf* 2D **72**
Modsarie. *High* 2G **167**
Moelfre. *Cnwy* 3B **82**
Moelfre. *IOA* 2E **81**
Moelfre. *Powy* 3D **70**
Moffat. *Dum* 4C **118**
Moggerhanger. *C Beds* 1B **52**
Mogworthy. *Devn* 1B **12**
Moira. *Leics* 4H **73**
Moira. *Lis* 3F **178**
Molash. *Kent* 5E **41**
Mol-chlach. *High* 2C **146**
Mold. *Flin* 4E **83**
Molehill Green. *Essx* 3F **53**
Molescroft. *E Yor* 5E **101**
Molesden. *Nmbd* 1E **115**
Molesworth. *Cambs* 3H **63**
Moll. *High* 5E **155**
Molland. *Devn* 4B **20**
Mollington. *Ches W* 3F **83**
Mollington. *Oxon* 1C **50**
Mollinsburn. *N Lan* 2A **128**
Monachty. *Cdgn* 4E **57**
Monachyle. *Stir* 2D **134**
Monar Lodge. *High* 4E **156**
Monaughty. *Powy* 4E **59**
Monea. *Ferm* 7D **176**
Monewden. *Suff* 5E **67**
Moneydie. *Per* 1C **136**
Moneyglass. *Ant* 7G **175**
Moneymore. *Cook* 1C **178**
Moneyneany. *Mag* 7D **174**
Moneyreagh. *Cast* 3J **179**
Moneyrow Green. *Wind* 4G **37**
Moneyslane. *Ban* 6G **179**
Moniaive. *Dum* 5G **117**
Monifieth. *Ang* 5E **145**
Monikie. *Ang* 5E **145**
Monimail. *Fife* 2E **137**
Monington. *Pemb* 1B **44**
Monk Bretton. *S Yor* 4D **92**
Monken Hadley. *G Lon* 1D **38**
Monk Fryston. *N Yor* 2F **93**
Monk Hesleden. *Dur* 1B **106**
Monkhide. *Here* 1B **48**
Monkhill. *Cumb* 4E **113**
Monkhopton. *Shrp* 1A **60**
Monkland. *Here* 5G **59**
Monkleigh. *Devn* 4E **19**
Monknash. *V Glam* 4C **32**
Monkokehampton. *Devn* 2F **11**
Monkseaton. *Tyne* 2G **115**
Monks Eleigh. *Suff* 1C **54**
Monk's Gate. *W Sus* 3D **26**
Monk's Heath. *Ches E* 3C **84**
Monk Sherborne. *Hants* 1E **24**
Monkshill. *Abers* 4E **161**
Monksilver. *Som* 3D **20**
Monks Kirby. *Warw* 2B **62**
Monk Soham. *Suff* 4E **66**
Monk Soham Green. *Suff* 4E **66**
Monkspath. *W Mid* 3F **61**
Monks Risborough. *Buck* 5G **51**
Monksthorpe. *Linc* 4D **88**
Monkstown. *Newt* 1H **179**
Monk Street. *Essx* 3G **53**
Monkswood. *Mon* 5G **47**
Monkton. *Devn* 2E **13**
Monkton. *Kent* 4G **41**
Monkton. *Pemb* 4D **42**
Monkton. *S Ayr* 2C **116**
Monkton Combe. *Bath* 5C **34**
Monkton Deverill. *Wilts* 3D **22**
Monkton Farleigh. *Wilts* 5D **34**
Monkton Heathfield. *Som* 4F **21**
Monktonhill. *S Ayr* 2C **116**
Monkton Up Wimborne. *Dors* 1F **15**
Monkton Wyld. *Dors* 3G **13**
Monkwearmouth. *Tyne* 4H **115**
Monkwood. *Dors* 3H **13**
Monkwood. *Hants* 3E **25**
Monmarsh. *Here* 1A **48**
Monmouth. *Mon* 4A **48**
Monnington on Wye. *Here* 1G **47**
Monreith. *Dum* 5A **110**
Montacute. *Som* 1H **13**
Monteith. *Ban* 5F **179**
Montford. *Arg* 3C **126**
Montford. *Shrp* 4G **71**
Montford Bridge. *Shrp* 4G **71**
Montgarrie. *Abers* 2C **152**
Montgarswood. *E Ayr* 2E **117**
Montgomery. *Powy* 1E **58**
Montgreenan. *N Ayr* 5E **127**
Montrave. *Fife* 3F **137**
Montrose. *Ang* 3G **145**
Monxton. *Hants* 2B **24**
Monyash. *Derbs* 4F **85**
Monymusk. *Abers* 2D **152**
Monzie. *Per* 1A **136**
Moodiesburn. *N Lan* 2H **127**
Moon's Green. *Kent* 3C **28**
Moonzie. *Fife* 2F **137**
Moor. *Som* 1H **13**
Moor Allerton. *W Yor* 1C **92**
Moorbath. *Dors* 3H **13**
Moorbrae. *Shet* 3F **173**
Moorby. *Linc* 4B **88**
Moorcot. *Here* 5F **59**
Moor Crichel. *Dors* 2E **15**
Moor Cross. *Devn* 3C **8**
Moordown. *Bour* 3F **15**
Moore. *Hal* 2H **83**
Moorend. *Dum* 2D **112**
Moor End. *E Yor* 1B **94**
Moorend. *Glos* 5C **48** (nr. Dursley)
Moorend. *Glos* 4D **48** (nr. Gloucester)
Moorends. *S Yor* 3G **93**
Moorfields. *Bmna* 7H **175**
Moorgate. *S Yor* 1B **86**
Moorgreen. *Hants* 1C **16**
Moorgreen. *Notts* 1B **74**
Moor Green. *Wilts* 5D **34**
Moorhaigh. *Notts* 4C **86**
Moorhall. *Derbs* 3H **85**
Moorhampton. *Here* 1G **47**
Moorhouse. *Cumb* 4E **113** (nr. Carlisle)
Moorhouse. *Cumb* 4D **112** (nr. Wigton)
Moorhouse. *Notts* 4E **87**
Moorhouse. *Surr* 5F **39**
Moorhouses. *Linc* 5B **88**
Moorland. *Som* 3G **21**
Moorlinch. *Som* 3H **21**
Moor Monkton. *N Yor* 4H **99**
Moor of Granary. *Mor* 3E **159**
Moor Row. *Cumb* 3B **102** (nr. Whitehaven)
Moor Row. *Cumb* 5D **112** (nr. Wigton)
Moorsholm. *Red C* 3D **107**
Moorside. *Dors* 1C **14**
Moorside. *G Man* 4H **91**
Moor, The. *Kent* 3B **28**
Moortown. *Cook* 2D **178**
Moortown. *Devn* 3D **10**
Moortown. *Hants* 2G **15**
Moortown. *IOW* 4C **16**
Moortown. *Linc* 1H **87**
Moortown. *Telf* 4A **72**
Moortown. *W Yor* 1D **92**
Morangie. *High* 5E **165**
Morar. *High* 4E **147**
Morborne. *Cambs* 1A **64**
Morchard Bishop. *Devn* 2A **12**
Morcombelake. *Dors* 3H **13**
Morcott. *Rut* 5G **75**
Morda. *Shrp* 3E **71**
Morden. *G Lon* 4D **38**
Mordiford. *Here* 2A **48**
Mordon. *Dur* 2A **106**
More. *Shrp* 1F **59**
Morebath. *Devn* 4C **20**
Morebattle. *Bord* 2B **120**
Morecambe. *Lanc* 3D **96**
Morefield. *High* 4F **163**
Moreleigh. *Devn* 3D **8**
Morenish. *Per* 5C **142**
Moresby Parks. *Cumb* 3A **102**
Morestead. *Hants* 4D **24**
Moreton. *Dors* 4D **14**
Moreton. *Essx* 5F **53**
Moreton. *Here* 4H **59**
Moreton. *Mers* 1E **83**
Moreton. *Oxon* 5E **51**
Moreton. *Staf* 4B **72**
Moreton Corbet. *Shrp* 3H **71**
Moretonhampstead. *Devn* 4A **12**
Moreton-in-Marsh. *Glos* 2H **49**
Moreton Jeffries. *Here* 1B **48**
Moreton Morrell. *Warw* 5H **61**
Moreton on Lugg. *Here* 1A **48**
Moreton Pinkney. *Nptn* 1D **50**
Moreton Say. *Shrp* 2A **72**
Moreton Valence. *Glos* 5C **48**
Morfa. *Cdgn* 5C **56**
Morfa Bach. *Carm* 4D **44**
Morfa Bychan. *Gwyn* 2E **69**
Morfa Glas. *Neat* 5B **46**
Morfa Nefyn. *Gwyn* 1B **68**
Morganstown. *Card* 3E **33**
Morgan's Vale. *Wilts* 4G **23**
Morham. *E Lot* 2B **130**
Moriah. *Cdgn* 3F **57**
Morland. *Cumb* 2G **103**
Morley. *Ches E* 2C **84**
Morley. *Derbs* 1A **74**
Morley. *Dur* 2E **105**
Morley. *W Yor* 2C **92**
Morley St Botolph. *Norf* 1C **66**
Morningside. *Edin* 2F **129**
Morningside. *N Lan* 4B **128**
Morningthorpe. *Norf* 1E **66**
Morpeth. *Nmbd* 1F **115**
Morrey. *Staf* 4F **73**
Morridge Side. *Staf* 5E **85**
Morridge Top. *Staf* 4E **85**
Morrington. *Dum* 1F **111**
Morris Green. *Essx* 2H **53**
Morriston. *Swan* 3F **31**
Morston. *Norf* 1C **78**
Mortehoe. *Devn* 2E **19**
Morthen. *S Yor* 2B **86**
Mortimer. *W Ber* 5E **37**
Mortimer's Cross. *Here* 4G **59**
Mortimer West End. *Hants* 5E **37**
Mortomley. *S Yor* 1H **85**
Morton. *Cumb* 1F **103** (nr. Calthwaite)
Morton. *Cumb* 4E **113** (nr. Carlisle)
Morton. *Derbs* 4B **86**
Morton. *Linc* 3H **75** (nr. Bourne)
Morton. *Linc* 1F **87** (nr. Gainsborough)
Morton. *Linc* 4F **87** (nr. Lincoln)
Morton. *Norf* 4D **78**
Morton. *Notts* 5E **87**
Morton. *Shrp* 3E **71**
Morton. *S Glo* 2B **34**
Morton Bagot. *Warw* 4F **61**
Morton Mill. *Shrp* 3H **71**
Morton-on-Swale. *N Yor* 5A **106**
Morton Tinmouth. *Dur* 2E **105**
Morvah. *Corn* 3B **4**
Morval. *Corn* 3G **7**
Morvich. *High* 3E **165** (nr. Golspie)
Morvich. *High* 1B **148** (nr. Shiel Bridge)
Morvil. *Pemb* 1E **43**
Morville. *Shrp* 1A **60**
Morwenstow. *Corn* 1C **10**
Morwick Hall. *Nmbd* 4G **121**
Mosborough. *S Yor* 2B **86**
Moscow. *E Ayr* 5F **127**
Mose. *Shrp* 1B **60**
Mosedale. *Cumb* 1E **103**
Moseley. *W Mid* 2E **61** (nr. Birmingham)
Moseley. *W Mid* 5D **72** (nr. Wolverhampton)
Moseley. *Worc* 5C **60**
Moss. *Arg* 4A **138**
Moss. *High* 2A **140**
Moss. *S Yor* 3F **93**
Moss. *Wrex* 5F **83**
Mossatt. *Abers* 2B **152**
Moss Bank. *Mers* 1H **83**
Mossbank. *Shet* 4F **173**
Mossblown. *S Ayr* 2D **116**
Mossbrow. *G Man* 2B **84**
Mossburnford. *Bord* 3A **120**
Mossdale. *Dum* 2D **110**
Mossedge. *Cumb* 3F **113**
Mossend. *N Lan* 3A **128**
Mossgate. *Staf* 2D **72**
Moss Lane. *Ches E* 3D **84**
Mossley. *Ches E* 4C **84**
Mossley. *G Man* 4H **91**
Mossley. *Newt* 1H **179**
Mossley Hill. *Mers* 2F **83**
Moss of Barmuckity. *Mor* 2G **159**
Mosspark. *Glas* 3G **127**
Mosspaul. *Bord* 5G **119**
Moss Side. *Cumb* 4C **112**
Moss Side. *G Man* 1C **84**
Moss-side. *High* 3C **158**
Moss Side. *Lanc* 1B **90** (nr. Blackpool)
Moss Side. *Lanc* 2D **90** (nr. Preston)
Moss Side. *Mers* 4B **90**
Moss-Side. *Moy* 3G **175**
Moss-side of Cairness. *Abers* 2H **161**
Mosstodloch. *Mor* 2H **159**
Mosswood. *Nmbd* 4D **114**
Mossy Lea. *Lanc* 3D **90**
Mosterton. *Dors* 2H **13**
Moston. *Shrp* 3H **71**
Moston Green. *Ches E* 4B **84**
Mostyn. *Flin* 2D **82**
Mostyn Quay. *Flin* 2D **82**
Motcombe. *Dors* 4D **22**
Mothecombe. *Devn* 4C **8**
Motherby. *Cumb* 2F **103**
Motherwell. *N Lan* 4A **128**
Mottingham. *G Lon* 3F **39**
Mottisfont. *Hants* 4B **24**
Mottistone. *IOW* 4C **16**
Mottram in Longdendale. *G Man* 1D **85**
Mottram St Andrew. *Ches E* 3C **84**
Mott's Mill. *E Sus* 2G **27**
Mouldsworth. *Ches W* 3H **83**
Moulin. *Per* 3G **143**
Moulsecoomb. *Brig* 5E **27**
Moulsford. *Oxon* 3D **36**
Moulsoe. *Mil* 1H **51**
Moulton. *Ches W* 4A **84**
Moulton. *Linc* 3C **76**
Moulton. *Nptn* 4E **63**
Moulton. *N Yor* 4F **105**
Moulton. *Suff* 4F **65**
Moulton. *V Glam* 4D **32**
Moulton Chapel. *Linc* 4B **76**
Moulton Eaugate. *Linc* 4B **76**
Moulton St Mary. *Norf* 5F **79**
Moulton Seas End. *Linc* 3C **76**
Mount. *Corn* 2F **7** (nr. Bodmin)
Mount. *Corn* 3B **6** (nr. Newquay)
Mountain Ash. *Rhon* 2D **32**
Mountain Cross. *Bord* 5E **129**
Mountain Street. *Kent* 5E **41**
Mountain Water. *Pemb* 2D **42**
Mount Ambrose. *Corn* 4B **6**
Mountbenger. *Bord* 2F **119**
Mountblow. *W Dun* 2F **127**
Mount Bures. *Essx* 2C **54**
Mountfield. *E Sus* 3B **28**
Mountfield. *Omag* 2L **177**
Mountgerald. *High* 2H **157**
Mount Hawke. *Corn* 4B **6**
Mount High. *High* 2A **158**
Mountjoy. *Corn* 2C **6**
Mountjoy. *Omag* 2K **177**
Mount Lothian. *Midl* 4F **129**
Mountnessing. *Essx* 1H **39**
Mountnorris. *Arm* 6D **178**
Mounton. *Mon* 2A **34**
Mount Pleasant. *Buck* 2E **51**
Mount Pleasant. *Ches E* 5C **84**
Mount Pleasant. *Derbs* 1H **73** (nr. Derby)
Mount Pleasant. *Derbs* 4G **73** (nr. Swadlincote)
Mount Pleasant. *E Sus* 4F **27**
Mount Pleasant. *Fife* 2E **137**
Mount Pleasant. *Hants* 3A **16**
Mount Pleasant. *Norf* 1B **66**
Mount Skippett. *Oxon* 4B **50**
Mountsorrel. *Leics* 4C **74**
Mount Stuart. *Arg* 4C **126**
Mousehole. *Corn* 4B **4**
Mouswald. *Dum* 2B **112**
Mow Cop. *Ches E* 5C **84**
Mowden. *Darl* 3F **105**
Mowhaugh. *Bord* 2C **120**
Mowmacre Hill. *Leic* 5C **74**
Mowsley. *Leics* 2D **62**
Moy. *Dngn* 4C **178**
Moy. *High* 5B **158**
Moygashel. *Dngn* 3C **178**
Moylgrove. *Pemb* 1B **44**
Moy Lodge. *High* 5G **149**
Muasdale. *Arg* 5E **125**
Muchalls. *Abers* 4G **153**
Much Birch. *Here* 2A **48**
Much Cowarne. *Here* 1B **48**
Much Dewchurch. *Here* 2H **47**
Muchelney. *Som* 4H **21**
Muchelney Ham. *Som* 4H **21**
Much Hadham. *Herts* 4E **53**
Much Hoole. *Lanc* 2C **90**
Muchlarnick. *Corn* 3G **7**
Much Marcle. *Here* 2B **48**
Muchrachd. *High* 5E **157**
Much Wenlock. *Shrp* 1A **60**
Mucking. *Thur* 2A **40**
Muckle Breck. *Shet* 5G **173**
Muckleford. *Dors* 3B **14**
Mucklestone. *Staf* 2B **72**
Muckleton. *Norf* 2H **77**
Muckleton. *Shrp* 3H **71**
Muckley. *Shrp* 1A **60**
Muckley Corner. *Staf* 5E **73**
Muckton. *Linc* 2C **88**
Mudale. *High* 5F **167**
Muddiford. *Devn* 3F **19**
Mudeford. *Dors* 3G **15**
Mudford. *Som* 1A **14**
Mudgley. *Som* 2H **21**
Mugdock. *Stir* 2G **127**
Mugeary. *High* 5D **154**
Muggington. *Derbs* 1G **73**
Muggintonlane End. *Derbs* 1G **73**
Muggleswick. *Dur* 4D **114**
Mugswell. *Surr* 5D **38**
Muie. *High* 3D **164**
Muirden. *Abers* 3E **160**
Muirdrum. *Ang* 5E **145**
Muiredge. *Per* 1E **137**
Muirend. *Glas* 3G **127**
Muirhead. *Ang* 5C **144**
Muirhead. *Fife* 3E **137**
Muirhead. *N Lan* 3H **127**
Muirhouses. *Falk* 1D **128**
Muirkirk. *E Ayr* 2F **117**
Muir of Alford. *Abers* 2C **152**
Muir of Fairburn. *High* 3G **157**
Muir of Fowlis. *Abers* 2C **152**
Muir of Miltonduff. *Mor* 3F **159**
Muir of Ord. *High* 3H **157**
Muir of Tarradale. *High* 3H **157**
Muirshearlich. *High* 5D **148**
Muirtack. *Abers* 5G **161**
Muirton. *High* 2B **158**
Muirton. *Per* 1D **136**
Muirton of Ardblair. *Per* 4A **144**
Muirtown. *Per* 2B **136**
Muiryfold. *Abers* 3E **161**
Muker. *N Yor* 5C **104**
Mulbarton. *Norf* 5D **78**
Mulben. *Mor* 3A **160**
Mulindry. *Arg* 4B **124**
Mulla. *Shet* 5F **173**
Mullach Charlabhaigh. *W Isl* 3E **171**
Mullacott. *Devn* 2F **19**
Mullaghbane. *New M* 8D **178**
Mullaghboy. *Lar* 6L **175**
Mullaghglass. *New M* 7E **178**
Mullion. *Corn* 5D **5**
Mullion Cove. *Corn* 5D **4**
Mumbles. *Swan* 4F **31**
Mumby. *Linc* 3E **89**
Munderfield Row. *Here* 5A **60**
Munderfield Stocks. *Here* 5A **60**
Mundesley. *Norf* 2F **79**
Mundford. *Norf* 1H **65**
Mundham. *Norf* 1F **67**
Mundon. *Essx* 5B **54**
Munerigie. *High* 3E **149**
Muness. *Shet* 1H **173**
Mungasdale. *High* 4D **162**
Mungrisdale. *Cumb* 1E **103**
Munlochy. *High* 3A **158**
Munsley. *Here* 1B **48**
Munslow. *Shrp* 2H **59**
Murchington. *Devn* 4G **11**
Murcot. *Worc* 1F **49**
Murcott. *Oxon* 4D **50**
Murdishaw. *Hal* 2H **83**
Murieston. *W Lot* 3D **128**
Murkle. *High* 2D **168**
Murlaggan. *High* 4C **148**
Murra. *Orkn* 7B **172**
Murrayfield. *Edin* 2F **129**
Murray, The. *S Lan* 4H **127**
Murrell Green. *Hants* 1F **25**
Murroes. *Ang* 5D **144**
Murrow. *Cambs* 5C **76**
Mursley. *Buck* 3G **51**
Murthly. *Per* 5H **143**
Murton. *Cumb* 2A **104**
Murton. *Dur* 5G **115**
Murton. *Nmbd* 5F **131**
Murton. *Swan* 4E **31**
Murton. *York* 4A **100**
Musbury. *Devn* 3F **13**
Muscoates. *N Yor* 1A **100**
Muscott. *Nptn* 4D **62**
Musselburgh. *E Lot* 2G **129**
Muston. *Leics* 2F **75**
Muston. *N Yor* 2E **101**
Mustow Green. *Worc* 3C **60**
Muswell Hill. *G Lon* 2D **39**
Mutehill. *Dum* 5D **111**
Mutford. *Suff* 2G **67**
Muthill. *Per* 2A **136**
Mutterton. *Devn* 2D **12**
Muxton. *Telf* 4B **72**
Mwmbwls. *Swan* 4F **31**
Mybster. *High* 3D **168**
Myddfai. *Carm* 2A **46**
Myddle. *Shrp* 3G **71**
Mydroilyn. *Cdgn* 5D **56**
Myerscough. *Lanc* 1C **90**
Mylor Bridge. *Corn* 5C **6**
Mylor Churchtown. *Corn* 5C **6**
Mynachlog-ddu. *Pemb* 1F **43**
Mynydd-bach. *Mon* 2H **33**
Mynydd Isa. *Flin* 4E **83**

Mynyddislwyn—Norton-Juxta-Twycross

Mynyddislwyn. *Cphy* 2E **33**
Mynydd Llandegai. *Gwyn* 4F **81**
Mynydd Mechell. *IOA* 1C **80**
Mynydd-y-briw. *Powy* 3D **70**
Mynyddygarreg. *Carm* 5E **45**
Mynytho. *Gwyn* 2C **68**
Myrebird. *Abers* 4E **153**
Myrelandhorn. *High* 3E **169**
Mytchett. *Surr* 1G **25**
Mythe, The. *Glos* 2D **49**
Mytholmroyd. *W Yor* 2A **92**
Myton-on-Swale. *N Yor* 3G **99**
Mytton. *Shrp* 4G **71**

N

Naast. *High* 5C **162**
Na Buirgh. *W Isl* 8C **171**
Naburn. *York* 5H **99**
Nab Wood. *W Yor* 1B **92**
Nackington. *Kent* 5F **41**
Nacton. *Suff* 1F **55**
Nafferton. *E Yor* 4E **101**
Na Gearrannan. *W Isl* 3D **171**
Nailbridge. *Glos* 4B **48**
Nailsbourne. *Som* 4F **21**
Nailsea. *N Som* 4H **33**
Nailstone. *Leics* 5B **74**
Nailsworth. *Glos* 2D **34**
Nairn. *High* 3C **158**
Nalderswood. *Surr* 1D **26**
Nancegollan. *Corn* 3D **4**
Nancledra. *Corn* 3B **4**
Nangreaves. *G Man* 3G **91**
Nanhyfer. *Pemb* 1A **44**
Nannerch. *Flin* 4D **82**
Nanpantan. *Leics* 4C **74**
Nanpean. *Corn* 3D **6**
Nanstallon. *Corn* 2E **7**
Nant-ddu. *Powy* 4D **46**
Nanternis. *Cdgn* 5C **56**
Nantgaredig. *Carm* 3E **45**
Nantgarw. *Rhon* 3E **33**
Nant Glas. *Powy* 4B **58**
Nantglyn. *Den* 4C **82**
Nantgwyn. *Powy* 3B **58**
Nantlle. *Gwyn* 5E **81**
Nantmawr. *Shrp* 3E **71**
Nantmel. *Powy* 4C **58**
Nantmor. *Gwyn* 1F **69**
Nant Peris. *Gwyn* 5F **81**
Nantwich. *Ches E* 5A **84**
Nant-y-bai. *Carm* 1A **46**
Nant-y-bwch. *Blae* 4E **47**
Nant-y-Derry. *Mon* 5G **47**
Nant-y-dugoed. *Powy* 4B **70**
Nant-y-felin. *Cnwy* 3F **81**
Nantyffyllon. *B'end* 2B **32**
Nantyglo. *Blae* 4E **47**
Nant-y-meichiaid. *Powy* 4D **70**
Nant-y-moel. *B'end* 2C **32**
Nant-y-Pandy. *Cnwy* 3F **81**
Naphill. *Buck* 2G **37**
Nappa. *Lanc* 4A **98**
Napton on the Hill. *Warw* 4B **62**
Narberth. *Pemb* 3F **43**
Narberth Bridge. *Pemb* 3F **43**
Narborough. *Leics* 1C **62**
Narborough. *Norf* 4G **77**
Narkurs. *Corn* 3H **7**
Narth, The. *Mon* 5A **48**
Narthwaite. *Cumb* 5A **104**
Nasareth. *Gwyn* 1D **68**
Naseby. *Nptn* 3D **62**
Nash. *Buck* 2F **51**
Nash. *Here* 4F **59**
Nash. *Kent* 5G **41**
Nash. *Newp* 3G **33**
Nash. *Shrp* 3A **60**
Nash Lee. *Buck* 5G **51**
Nassington. *Nptn* 1H **63**
Nasty. *Herts* 3D **52**
Natcott. *Devn* 4C **18**
Nateby. *Cumb* 4A **104**
Nateby. *Lanc* 5D **96**
Nately Scures. *Hants* 1F **25**
Natland. *Cumb* 1E **97**
Naughton. *Suff* 1D **54**
Naunton. *Glos* 3G **49**
Naunton. *Worc* 2D **49**
Naunton Beauchamp. *Worc* 5D **60**
Navenby. *Linc* 5G **87**
Navestock. *Essx* 1G **39**
Navestock Side. *Essx* 1G **39**
Navidale. *High* 2H **165**
Nawton. *N Yor* 1A **100**
Nayland. *Suff* 2C **54**
Nazeing. *Essx* 5E **53**
Neacroft. *Hants* 3G **15**
Nealhouse. *Cumb* 4E **113**
Neal's Green. *W Mid* 2H **61**
Neap House. *N Lin* 3B **94**
Near Sawrey. *Cumb* 5E **103**
Neasden. *G Lon* 2D **38**
Neasham. *Darl* 3A **106**
Neath. *Neat* 2A **32**
Neath Abbey. *Neat* 3G **31**
Neatishead. *Norf* 3F **79**
Neaton. *Norf* 5B **78**
Nebo. *Cdgn* 4E **57**
Nebo. *Cnwy* 5H **81**
Nebo. *Gwyn* 5D **81**
Nebo. *IOA* 1D **80**
Necton. *Norf* 5A **78**
Nedd. *High* 5B **166**
Nedderton. *Nmbd* 1F **115**
Nedging. *Suff* 1D **54**
Nedging Tye. *Suff* 1D **54**
Needham. *Norf* 2E **67**
Needham Market. *Suff* 5C **66**
Needham Street. *Suff* 4G **65**
Needingworth. *Cambs* 3C **64**
Needwood. *Staf* 3F **73**
Neen Savage. *Shrp* 3A **60**
Neen Sollars. *Shrp* 3A **60**
Neenton. *Shrp* 2A **60**
Nefyn. *Gwyn* 1C **68**
Neilston. *E Ren* 4F **127**
Neithrop. *Oxon* 1C **50**
Nelly Andrews Green. *Powy* 5E **71**
Nelson. *Cphy* 2E **32**
Nelson. *Lanc* 1G **91**
Nelson Village. *Nmbd* 2F **115**
Nemphlar. *S Lan* 5B **128**
Nempnett Thrubwell. *Bath* 5A **34**
Nene Terrace. *Linc* 5B **76**
Nenthall. *Cumb* 5A **114**
Nenthead. *Cumb* 5A **114**
Nenthorn. *Bord* 1A **120**
Nercwys. *Flin* 4E **83**
Neribus. *Arg* 4A **124**
Nerston. *S Lan* 4H **127**
Nesbit. *Nmbd* 1D **121**
Nesfield. *N Yor* 5C **98**
Ness. *Ches W* 3F **83**
Nesscliffe. *Shrp* 4F **71**
Ness of Tenston. *Orkn* 6B **172**
Neston. *Ches W* 3E **83**
Neston. *Wilts* 5D **34**
Nethanfoot. *S Lan* 5B **128**
Nether Alderley. *Ches E* 3C **84**
Netheravon. *Wilts* 2G **23**
Nether Blainslie. *Bord* 5B **130**
Netherbrae. *Abers* 3E **161**
Netherbrough. *Orkn* 6C **172**
Nether Broughton. *Leics* 3D **74**
Netherburn. *S Lan* 5B **128**
Nether Burrow. *Lanc* 2F **97**
Netherbury. *Dors* 3H **13**
Netherby. *Cumb* 2E **113**
Nether Careston. *Ang* 3E **145**
Nether Cerne. *Dors* 3B **14**
Nether Compton. *Dors* 1A **14**
Nethercote. *Glos* 3G **49**
Nethercote. *Warw* 4C **62**
Nethercott. *Devn* 3E **19**
Nethercott. *Oxon* 3C **50**
Nether Dallachy. *Mor* 2A **160**
Nether Durdie. *Per* 1E **136**
Nether End. *Derbs* 3G **85**
Netherend. *Glos* 5A **48**
Nether Exe. *Devn* 2C **12**
Netherfield. *E Sus* 4B **28**
Netherfield. *Notts* 1D **74**
Nethergate. *Norf* 3C **78**
Netherhampton. *Wilts* 4G **23**
Nether Handley. *Derbs* 3B **86**
Nether Haugh. *S Yor* 1B **86**
Nether Heage. *Derbs* 5A **86**
Nether Heyford. *Nptn* 5D **62**
Netherhouses. *Cumb* 1B **96**
Nether Howcleugh. *Dum* 3C **118**
Nether Kellet. *Lanc* 3E **97**
Nether Kinmundy. *Abers* 4H **161**
Netherland Green. *Staf* 2F **73**
Nether Langwith. *Notts* 3C **86**
Netherlaw. *Dum* 5E **111**
Netherley. *Abers* 4F **153**
Nethermill. *Dum* 1B **112**
Nethermills. *Mor* 3C **160**
Nether Moor. *Derbs* 4A **86**
Nether Padley. *Derbs* 3G **85**
Netherplace. *E Ren* 4G **127**
Nether Poppleton. *York* 4H **99**
Netherseal. *Derbs* 4G **73**
Nether Silton. *N Yor* 5B **106**
Nether Stowey. *Som* 3E **21**
Nether Street. *Essx* 4F **53**
Netherstreet. *Wilts* 5E **35**
Netherthird. *E Ayr* 3E **117**
Netherthong. *W Yor* 4B **92**
Netherton. *Ang* 3E **145**
Netherton. *Cumb* 1B **102**
Netherton. *Devn* 5B **12**
Netherton. *Hants* 1B **24**
Netherton. *Here* 3A **48**
Netherton. *Mers* 1F **83**
Netherton. *N Lan* 4A **128**
Netherton. *Nmbd* 4D **121**
Netherton. *Per* 3A **144**
Netherton. *Shrp* 2B **60**
Netherton. *Stir* 2G **127**
Netherton. *W Mid* 2D **60**
Netherton. *W Yor* 3C **92** (nr. Horbury)
Netherton. *W Yor* 3B **92** (nr. Huddersfield)
Netherton. *Worc* 1E **49**
Nethertown. *Cumb* 4A **102**
Nethertown. *High* 1F **169**
Nethertown. *Staf* 4F **73**
Nether Urquhart. *Fife* 3D **136**
Nether Wallop. *Hants* 3B **24**
Nether Wasdale. *Cumb* 4C **102**
Nether Welton. *Cumb* 5E **113**
Nether Westcote. *Glos* 3H **49**
Nether Whitacre. *Warw* 1G **61**
Nether Winchendon. *Buck* 4F **51**
Netherwitton. *Nmbd* 5F **121**
Nether Worton. *Oxon* 2C **50**
Nethy Bridge. *High* 1E **151**
Netley. *Hants* 2C **16**
Netley. *Shrp* 5G **71**
Netley Marsh. *Hants* 1B **16**
Nettlebed. *Oxon* 3F **37**
Nettlebridge. *Som* 2B **22**
Nettlecombe. *Dors* 3A **14**
Nettlecombe. *IOW* 5D **16**
Nettleden. *Herts* 4A **52**
Nettleham. *Linc* 3H **87**
Nettlestead. *Kent* 5A **40**
Nettlestead Green. *Kent* 5A **40**
Nettlestone. *IOW* 3E **16**
Nettlesworth. *Dur* 5F **115**
Nettleton. *Linc* 4E **94**
Nettleton. *Wilts* 4D **34**
Netton. *Devn* 4B **8**
Netton. *Wilts* 3G **23**
Neuadd. *Powy* 5C **70**
Neuk, The. *Abers* 4E **153**
Nevendon. *Essx* 1B **40**
Nevern. *Pemb* 1A **44**
New Abbey. *Dum* 3A **112**
New Aberdour. *Abers* 2F **161**
New Addington. *G Lon* 4E **39**
Newall. *W Yor* 5D **98**
New Alresford. *Hants* 3D **24**
New Alyth. *Per* 4B **144**
Newark. *Orkn* 3G **172**
Newark. *Pet* 5B **76**
Newark-on-Trent. *Notts* 5E **87**
New Arley. *Warw* 2G **61**
Newarthill. *N Lan* 4A **128**
New Ash Green. *Kent* 4H **39**
New Balderton. *Notts* 5F **87**
New Barn. *Kent* 4H **39**
New Barnetby. *N Lin* 3D **94**
Newbattle. *Midl* 3G **129**
New Bewick. *Nmbd* 2E **121**
Newbie. *Dum* 3C **112**
Newbiggin. *Cumb* 2H **103** (nr. Appleby)
Newbiggin. *Cumb* 3B **96** (nr. Barrow-in-Furness)
Newbiggin. *Cumb* 5G **113** (nr. Cumrew)
Newbiggin. *Cumb* 2F **103** (nr. Penrith)
Newbiggin. *Cumb* 5B **102** (nr. Seascale)
Newbiggin. *Dur* 5E **115** (nr. Consett)
Newbiggin. *Dur* 2C **104** (nr. Holwick)
Newbiggin. *Nmbd* 5C **114**
Newbiggin. *N Yor* 5C **104** (nr. Askrigg)
Newbiggin. *N Yor* 1F **101** (nr. Filey)
Newbiggin. *N Yor* 1B **98** (nr. Thoralby)
Newbiggin-by-the-Sea. *Nmbd* 1G **115**
Newbigging. *Ang* 5D **145** (nr. Monikie)
Newbigging. *Ang* 4B **144** (nr. Newtyle)
Newbigging. *Ang* 5D **144** (nr. Tealing)
Newbigging. *Edin* 2E **129**
Newbigging. *S Lan* 5D **128**
Newbiggin-on-Lune. *Cumb* 4A **104**
Newbold. *Derbs* 3A **86**
Newbold. *Leics* 4B **74**
Newbold on Avon. *Warw* 3B **62**
Newbold on Stour. *Warw* 1H **49**
Newbold Pacey. *Warw* 5G **61**
Newbold Verdon. *Leics* 5B **74**
New Bolingbroke. *Linc* 5C **88**
Newborough. *IOA* 4D **80**
Newborough. *Pet* 5B **76**
Newborough. *Staf* 3F **73**
Newbottle. *Nptn* 2D **50**
Newbottle. *Tyne* 4G **115**
New Boultham. *Linc* 3G **87**
Newbourne. *Suff* 1F **55**
New Brancepeth. *Dur* 5F **115**
Newbridge. *Cphy* 2F **33**
Newbridge. *Cdgn* 5E **57**
Newbridge. *Corn* 3B **4**
New Bridge. *Dum* 2G **111**
Newbridge. *Edin* 2E **129**
Newbridge. *Hants* 1A **16**
Newbridge. *IOW* 4C **16**
Newbridge. *N Yor* 1C **100**
Newbridge. *Pemb* 1D **42**
Newbridge. *Wrex* 1E **71**
Newbridge Green. *Worc* 2D **48**
Newbridge-on-Usk. *Mon* 2G **33**
Newbridge on Wye. *Powy* 5C **58**
New Brighton. *Flin* 4E **83**
New Brighton. *Hants* 2F **17**
New Brighton. *Mers* 1F **83**
New Brinsley. *Notts* 5B **86**
Newbrough. *Nmbd* 3B **114**
New Broughton. *Wrex* 5F **83**
New Buckenham. *Norf* 1C **66**
New Buildings. *Derr* 5A **174**
Newbuildings. *Devn* 2A **12**
Newburgh. *Abers* 1G **153**
Newburgh. *Fife* 2E **137**
Newburgh. *Lanc* 3C **90**
Newburn. *Tyne* 3E **115**
Newbury. *W Ber* 5C **36**
Newbury. *Wilts* 2D **22**
Newby. *Cumb* 2G **103**
Newby. *N Yor* 2G **97** (nr. Ingleton)
Newby. *N Yor* 1E **101** (nr. Scarborough)
Newby. *N Yor* 3C **106** (nr. Stokesley)
Newby Bridge. *Cumb* 1C **96**
Newby Cote. *N Yor* 2G **97**
Newby East. *Cumb* 4F **113**
Newby Head. *Cumb* 2G **103**
New Byth. *Abers* 3F **161**
Newby West. *Cumb* 4E **113**
Newby Wiske. *N Yor* 1F **99**
Newcastle. *Ards* 4L **179**
Newcastle. *B'end* 3B **32**
Newcastle. *Down* 6H **179**
Newcastle. *Mon* 4H **47**
Newcastle. *Shrp* 2E **59**
Newcastle Emlyn. *Carm* 1D **44**
Newcastle International Airport. *Tyne* 2E **115**
Newcastleton. *Bord* 1F **113**
Newcastle-under-Lyme. *Staf* 1C **72**
Newcastle Upon Tyne. *Tyne* 3F **115** & **197**
Newchapel. *Pemb* 1G **43**
Newchapel. *Powy* 2B **58**
Newchapel. *Staf* 5C **84**
Newchapel. *Surr* 1E **27**
New Cheriton. *Hants* 4D **24**
Newchurch. *Carm* 3D **45**
Newchurch. *Here* 5F **59**
Newchurch. *IOW* 4D **16**
Newchurch. *Kent* 2E **29**
Newchurch. *Lanc* 1G **91** (nr. Nelson)
Newchurch. *Lanc* 2G **91** (nr. Rawtenstall)
Newchurch. *Mon* 2H **33**
Newchurch. *Powy* 5E **58**
Newchurch. *Staf* 3F **73**
New Costessey. *Norf* 4D **78**
Newcott. *Devn* 2F **13**
New Cowper. *Cumb* 5C **112**
Newcraighall. *Edin* 2G **129**
New Crofton. *W Yor* 3D **93**
New Cross. *Cdgn* 3F **57**
New Cross. *Som* 1H **13**
New Cumnock. *E Ayr* 3F **117**
New Deer. *Abers* 4F **161**
New Denham. *Buck* 2B **38**
Newdigate. *Surr* 1C **26**
New Duston. *Nptn* 4E **62**
New Earswick. *York* 4A **100**
New Edlington. *S Yor* 1C **86**
New Elgin. *Mor* 2G **159**
New Ellerby. *E Yor* 1E **95**
Newell Green. *Brac* 4G **37**
New Eltham. *G Lon* 3F **39**
New End. *Warw* 4F **61**
New End. *Worc* 5E **61**
Newenden. *Kent* 3C **28**
New England. *Essx* 1H **53**
New England. *Pet* 5A **76**
Newent. *Glos* 3C **48**
New Ferry. *Mers* 2F **83**
Newfield. *Dur* 4F **115** (nr. Chester-le-Street)
Newfield. *Dur* 1F **105** (nr. Willington)
New Forest. *Hants* 1H **15**
Newfound. *Hants* 1D **24**
New Fryston. *W Yor* 2E **93**
Newgale. *Pemb* 2C **42**
New Galloway. *Dum* 2D **110**
Newgate. *Norf* 1C **78**
Newgate Street. *Herts* 5D **52**
New Greens. *Herts* 5B **52**
New Grimsby. *IOS* 1A **4**
New Hainford. *Norf* 4E **78**
Newhall. *Ches E* 1A **72**
Newhall. *Staf* 3G **73**
Newham. *Nmbd* 2F **121**
New Hartley. *Nmbd* 2G **115**
Newhaven. *Derbs* 4F **85**
Newhaven. *E Sus* 5F **27** & **204**
Newhaven. *Edin* 2F **129**
New Haw. *Surr* 4B **38**
New Hedges. *Pemb* 4F **43**
New Herrington. *Tyne* 4G **115**
Newhey. *G Man* 3H **91**
New Holkham. *Norf* 2A **78**
New Holland. *N Lin* 2D **94**
Newholm. *N Yor* 3F **107**
New Houghton. *Derbs* 4C **86**
New Houghton. *Norf* 3G **77**
Newhouse. *N Lan* 3A **128**
New Houses. *N Yor* 2H **97**
New Hutton. *Cumb* 5G **103**
New Hythe. *Kent* 5B **40**
Newick. *E Sus* 3F **27**
Newingreen. *Kent* 2F **29**
Newington. *Edin* 2F **129**
Newington. *Kent* 2F **29** (nr. Folkestone)
Newington. *Kent* 4C **40** (nr. Sittingbourne)
Newington. *Notts* 1D **86**
Newington. *Oxon* 2E **36**
Newington Bagpath. *Glos* 2D **34**
New Inn. *Carm* 2E **45**
New Inn. *Mon* 5H **47**
New Inn. *N Yor* 2H **97**
New Inn. *Torf* 5G **47**
New Invention. *Shrp* 3E **59**
New Kelso. *High* 4B **156**
New Lanark. *S Lan* 5B **128**
Newland. *Glos* 5A **48**
Newland. *Hull* 1D **94**
Newland. *N Yor* 2G **93**
Newland. *Som* 3B **20**
Newland. *Worc* 1C **48**
Newlandrig. *Midl* 3G **129**
Newlands. *Cumb* 1E **103**
Newlands. *Essx* 2C **40**
Newlands. *High* 4B **158**
Newlands. *Nmbd* 4D **115**
Newlands. *Staf* 3E **73**
Newlands of Geise. *High* 2C **168**
Newlands of Tynet. *Mor* 2A **160**
Newlands Park. *IOA* 2B **80**
New Lane. *Lanc* 3C **90**
New Lane End. *Warr* 1A **84**
New Langholm. *Dum* 1E **113**
New Leake. *Linc* 5D **88**
New Leeds. *Abers* 3G **161**
New Lenton. *Nott* 2C **74**
New Longton. *Lanc* 2D **90**
Newlot. *Orkn* 6E **172**
New Luce. *Dum* 3G **109**
Newlyn. *Corn* 4B **4**
Newmachar. *Abers* 2F **153**
Newmains. *N Lan* 4B **128**
New Mains of Ury. *Abers* 5F **153**
New Malden. *G Lon* 4D **38**
Newman's Green. *Suff* 1B **54**
Newmarket. *Suff* 4F **65**
Newmarket. *W Isl* 4G **171**
New Marske. *Red C* 2D **106**
New Marton. *Shrp* 2F **71**
New Micklefield. *W Yor* 1E **93**
New Mill. *Abers* 4E **160**
Newmill. *Ant* 8J **175**
New Mill. *Corn* 3B **4**
New Mill. *Herts* 4H **51**
Newmill. *Mor* 3B **160**
Newmill. *Bord* 3G **119**
New Mill. *W Yor* 4B **92**
New Mill. *Wilts* 5G **35**
Newmillerdam. *W Yor* 3D **92**
New Mills. *Corn* 3C **6**
Newmills. *Cgvn* 4E **178**
New Mills. *Derbs* 2E **85**
Newmills. *Dngn* 3C **178**
Newmills. *Fife* 1D **128**
Newmills. *High* 2A **158**
New Mills. *Mon* 5A **48**
New Mills. *Powy* 5C **70**
Newmiln. *Per* 5A **144**
Newmilns. *E Ayr* 1E **117**
New Milton. *Hants* 3H **15**
New Mistley. *Essx* 2E **54**
New Moat. *Pemb* 2E **43**
Newmore. *High* 3H **157** (nr. Dingwall)
Newmore. *High* 1A **158** (nr. Invergordon)
Newnham. *Cambs* 5D **64**
Newnham. *Glos* 4B **48**
Newnham. *Hants* 1F **25**
Newnham. *Herts* 2C **52**
Newnham. *Kent* 5D **40**
Newnham. *Nptn* 5C **62**
Newnham. *Warw* 4F **61**
Newnham Bridge. *Worc* 4A **60**
New Ollerton. *Notts* 4D **86**
New Oscott. *W Mid* 1F **61**
Newpark. *Fife* 2G **137**
New Park. *N Yor* 4E **99**
New Pitsligo. *Abers* 3F **161**
New Polzeath. *Corn* 1D **6**
Newport. *Corn* 4D **10**
Newport. *Devn* 3F **19**
Newport. *E Yor* 1B **94**
Newport. *Essx* 2F **53**
Newport. *Glos* 2B **34**
Newport. *High* 1H **165**
Newport. *IOW* 4D **16**
Newport. *Newp* 3G **33** & **200**
Newport. *Norf* 4H **79**
Newport. *Pemb* 1E **43**
Newport. *Som* 4G **21**
Newport. *Telf* 4B **72**
Newport-on-Tay. *Fife* 1G **137**
Newport Pagnell. *Mil* 1G **51**
Newpound Common. *W Sus* 3B **26**
New Prestwick. *S Ayr* 2C **116**
New Quay. *Cdgn* 5C **56**
Newquay. *Corn* 2C **6**
Newquay Cornwall Airport. *Corn* 2C **6**
New Rackheath. *Norf* 4E **79**
New Radnor. *Powy* 4E **58**
New Rent. *Cumb* 1F **103**
New Ridley. *Nmbd* 4D **114**
New Romney. *Kent* 3E **29**
New Rossington. *S Yor* 1D **86**
New Row. *Cdgn* 3G **57**
New Row. *Lanc* 1E **91**
Newry. *New M* 7E **178**
New Sauchie. *Clac* 4A **136**
Newsbank. *Ches E* 4C **84**
Newseat. *Abers* 5E **160**
Newsham. *Lanc* 1D **90**
Newsham. *Nmbd* 2G **115**
Newsham. *N Yor* 3E **105** (nr. Richmond)
Newsham. *N Yor* 1F **99** (nr. Thirsk)
New Sharlston. *W Yor* 3D **93**
Newsholme. *E Yor* 2H **93**
Newsholme. *Lanc* 4H **97**
New Shoreston. *Nmbd* 1F **121**
New Springs. *G Man* 4D **90**
Newstead. *Notts* 5C **86**
Newstead. *Bord* 1H **119**
New Stevenston. *N Lan* 4A **128**
New Street. *Here* 5F **59**
Newstreet Lane. *Shrp* 2A **72**
New Swanage. *Dors* 4F **15**
New Swannington. *Leics* 4B **74**
Newthorpe. *N Yor* 1E **93**
Newthorpe. *Notts* 1B **74**
Newton. *Arg* 4H **133**
Newton. *B'end* 4B **32**
Newton. *Cambs* 1E **53** (nr. Cambridge)
Newton. *Cambs* 4D **76** (nr. Wisbech)
Newton. *Ches W* 4G **83** (nr. Chester)
Newton. *Ches W* 5H **83** (nr. Tattenhall)
Newton. *Cumb* 2B **96**
Newton. *Derbs* 5B **86**
Newton. *Dors* 1C **14**
Newton. *Dum* 2D **112** (nr. Annan)
Newton. *Dum* 5D **118** (nr. Moffat)
Newton. *G Man* 1D **84**
Newton. *Here* 2G **47** (nr. Ewyas Harold)
Newton. *Here* 5H **59** (nr. Leominster)
Newton. *High* 2B **158** (nr. Cromarty)
Newton. *High* 4B **158** (nr. Inverness)
Newton. *High* 5C **166** (nr. Kylestrome)
Newton. *High* 4F **169** (nr. Wick)
Newton. *Lanc* 1B **90** (nr. Blackpool)
Newton. *Lanc* 2E **97** (nr. Carnforth)
Newton. *Lanc* 4F **97** (nr. Clitheroe)
Newton. *Linc* 2H **75**
Newton. *Mers* 2E **83**
Newton. *Mor* 2F **159**
Newton. *Norf* 4H **77**
Newton. *Nptn* 2F **63**
Newton. *Nmbd* 3D **114**
Newton. *Notts* 1D **74**
Newton. *Bord* 2A **120**
Newton. *Shet* 8E **173**
Newton. *Shrp* 1B **60** (nr. Bridgnorth)
Newton. *Shrp* 2G **71** (nr. Wem)
Newton. *Som* 3E **20**
Newton. *S Lan* 3H **127** (nr. Glasgow)
Newton. *S Lan* 1B **118** (nr. Lanark)
Newton. *Staf* 3E **73**
Newton. *Suff* 1C **54**
Newton. *Swan* 4F **31**
Newton. *Warw* 3C **62**
Newton. *W Lot* 2D **129**
Newton. *Wilts* 4H **23**
Newton Abbot. *Devn* 5B **12**
Newtonairds. *Dum* 1F **111**
Newton Arlosh. *Cumb* 4D **112**
Newton Aycliffe. *Dur* 2F **105**
Newton Bewley. *Hart* 2B **106**
Newton Blossomville. *Mil* 5G **63**
Newton Bromswold. *Bed* 4G **63**
Newton Burgoland. *Leics* 5A **74**
Newton by Toft. *Linc* 2H **87**
Newton Ferrers. *Devn* 4B **8**
Newton Flotman. *Norf* 1E **66**
Newtongrange. *Midl* 3G **129**
Newton Green. *Mon* 2A **34**
Newton Hall. *Dur* 5F **115**
Newton Hall. *Nmbd* 3D **114**
Newton Harcourt. *Leics* 1D **62**
Newton Heath. *G Man* 4G **91**
Newtonhill. *Abers* 4G **153**
Newtonhill. *High* 4H **157**
Newton Hill. *W Yor* 2D **92**
Newton Ketton. *Darl* 2A **106**
Newton Kyme. *N Yor* 5G **99**
Newton-le-Willows. *Mers* 1H **83**
Newton-le-Willows. *N Yor* 1E **98**
Newton Longville. *Buck* 2G **51**
Newton Mearns. *E Ren* 4G **127**
Newtonmore. *High* 4B **150**
Newton Morrell. *N Yor* 4F **105**
Newton Mulgrave. *N Yor* 3E **107**
Newton of Ardtoe. *High* 1A **140**
Newton of Balcanquhal. *Per* 2D **136**
Newton of Beltrees. *Ren* 4E **127**
Newton of Falkland. *Fife* 3E **137**
Newton of Mountblairy. *Abers* 3E **160**
Newton of Pitcairns. *Per* 2C **136**
Newton-on-Ouse. *N Yor* 4H **99**
Newton-on-Rawcliffe. *N Yor* 5F **107**
Newton on the Hill. *Shrp* 3G **71**
Newton-on-the-Moor. *Nmbd* 4F **121**
Newton on Trent. *Linc* 3F **87**
Newton Poppleford. *Devn* 4D **12**
Newton Purcell. *Oxon* 2E **51**
Newton Regis. *Warw* 5G **73**
Newton Reigny. *Cumb* 1F **103**
Newton Rigg. *Cumb* 1F **103**
Newton St Cyres. *Devn* 3B **12**
Newton St Faith. *Norf* 4E **78**
Newton St Loe. *Bath* 5C **34**
Newton St Petrock. *Devn* 1E **11**
Newton Solney. *Derbs* 3G **73**
Newton Stacey. *Hants* 2C **24**
Newton Stewart. *Dum* 3B **110**
Newton Toney. *Wilts* 2H **23**
Newton Tony. *Wilts* 2H **23**
Newton Tracey. *Devn* 4F **19**
Newton under Roseberry. *Red C* 3C **106**
Newton Unthank. *Leics* 5B **74**
Newton upon Ayr. *S Ayr* 2C **116**
Newton upon Derwent. *E Yor* 5B **100**
Newton Valence. *Hants* 3F **25**
Newton-with-Scales. *Lanc* 1C **90**
Newtown. *Abers* 2E **160**
Newtown. *Cambs* 4H **63**
Newtown. *Corn* 5C **10**
Newtown. *Cumb* 5B **112** (nr. Aspatria)
Newtown. *Cumb* 3G **113** (nr. Brampton)
Newtown. *Cumb* 2G **103** (nr. Penrith)
Newtown. *Derbs* 2D **85**
Newtown. *Devn* 4A **20**
Newtown. *Dors* 2H **13** (nr. Beaminster)
New Town. *Dors* 1E **15** (nr. Sixpenny Handley)
New Town. *E Lot* 2H **129**
Newtown. *Falk* 1C **128**
Newtown. *Glos* 5B **48** (nr. Lydney)
Newtown. *Glos* 2E **49** (nr. Tewkesbury)
Newtown. *Hants* 1D **16** (nr. Bishop's Waltham)
Newtown. *Hants* 3G **25** (nr. Liphook)
Newtown. *Hants* 1A **16** (nr. Lyndhurst)
Newtown. *Hants* 5C **36** (nr. Newbury)
Newtown. *Hants* 4B **24** (nr. Romsey)
Newtown. *Hants* 2C **16** (nr. Warsash)
Newtown. *Hants* 1E **16** (nr. Wickham)
Newtown. *Here* 2A **48** (nr. Little Dewchurch)
Newtown. *Here* 1B **48** (nr. Stretton Grandison)
Newtown. *High* 3F **149**
Newtown. *IOM* 4C **108**
Newtown. *IOW* 3C **16**
Newtown. *Lanc* 3D **90**
New Town. *Lutn* 3A **52**
Newtown. *Nmbd* 4E **121** (nr. Rothbury)
Newtown. *Nmbd* 2E **121** (nr. Wooler)
Newtown. *Pool* 3F **15**
Newtown. *Powy* 1D **58**
Newtown. *Rhon* 2D **32**
Newtown. *Shet* 3F **173**
Newtown. *Shrp* 2G **71**
Newtown. *Som* 1F **13**
Newtown. *Staf* 4D **84** (nr. Biddulph)
Newtown. *Staf* 5D **73** (nr. Cannock)
Newtown. *Staf* 4E **85** (nr. Longnor)
New Town. *W Yor* 2E **93**
Newtown. *Wilts* 4E **23**
Newtownabbey. *Newt* 1H **179**
Newtownards. *Ards* 2J **179**
Newtownbutler. *Ferm* 7K **177**
Newtown-Crommelin. *Bmna* 5H **175**
Newtownhamilton. *New M* 7D **178**
Newtown-in-St Martin. *Corn* 4E **5**
Newtown Linford. *Leics* 4C **74**
Newtown St Boswells. *Bord* 1H **119**
Newtownstewart. *Strab* 8A **174**
New Tredegar. *Cphy* 5E **47**
Newtyle. *Ang* 4B **144**
New Village. *E Yor* 1D **94**
New Village. *S Yor* 4F **93**
New Walsoken. *Cambs* 5D **76**
New Waltham. *NE Lin* 4F **95**
New Winton. *E Lot* 2H **129**
New World. *Cambs* 1C **64**
New Yatt. *Oxon* 4B **50**
Newyears Green. *G Lon* 2B **38**
New York. *Linc* 5B **88**
New York. *Tyne* 2G **115**
Nextend. *Here* 5F **59**
Neyland. *Pemb* 4D **42**
Nib Heath. *Shrp* 4G **71**
Nicholashayne. *Devn* 1E **12**
Nicholaston. *Swan* 4E **31**
Nidd. *N Yor* 3F **99**
Niddrie. *Edin* 2F **129**
Niddry. *Edin* 2D **129**
Nigg. *Aber* 3G **153**
Nigg. *High* 1C **158**
Nigg Ferry. *High* 2B **158**
Nightcott. *Som* 4B **20**
Nimmer. *Som* 1G **13**
Nine Ashes. *Essx* 5F **53**
Ninebanks. *Nmbd* 4A **114**
Nine Elms. *Swin* 3G **35**
Ninemile Bar. *Dum* 2F **111**
Nine Mile Burn. *Midl* 4E **129**
Ninfield. *E Sus* 4B **28**
Ningwood. *IOW* 4C **16**
Nisbet. *Bord* 2A **120**
Nisbet Hill. *Bord* 4D **130**
Niton. *IOW* 5D **16**
Nitshill. *E Ren* 4G **127**
Niwbwrch. *IOA* 4D **80**
Nixon's Corner. *Derr* 5A **174**
Noak Hill. *G Lon* 1G **39**
Nobold. *Shrp* 4G **71**
Nobottle. *Nptn* 4D **62**
Nocton. *Linc* 4H **87**
Nogdam End. *Norf* 5F **79**
Noke. *Oxon* 4D **50**
Nolton. *Pemb* 3C **42**
Nolton Haven. *Pemb* 3C **42**
No Man's Heath. *Ches W* 1H **71**
No Man's Heath. *Warw* 5G **73**
Nomansland. *Devn* 1B **12**
Nomansland. *Wilts* 1A **16**
Noneley. *Shrp* 3G **71**
Noness. *Shet* 9F **173**
Nonikiln. *High* 1A **158**
Nonington. *Kent* 5G **41**
Nook. *Cumb* 2F **113** (nr. Longtown)
Nook. *Cumb* 1E **97** (nr. Milnthorpe)
Noranside. *Ang* 2D **144**
Norbreck. *Bkpl* 5C **96**
Norbridge. *Here* 1C **48**
Norbury. *Ches E* 1H **71**
Norbury. *Derbs* 1F **73**
Norbury. *Shrp* 1F **59**
Norbury. *Staf* 3B **72**
Norby. *N Yor* 1G **99**
Norby. *Shet* 6C **173**
Norcross. *Lanc* 5C **96**
Nordelph. *Norf* 5E **77**
Norden. *G Man* 3G **91**
Nordley. *Shrp* 1A **60**
Norfolk Broads. *Norf* 5G **79**
Norham. *Nmbd* 5F **131**
Norland Town. *W Yor* 2A **92**
Norley. *Ches W* 3H **83**
Norleywood. *Hants* 3B **16**
Normanby. *N Lin* 3B **94**
Normanby. *N Yor* 1B **100**
Normanby. *Red C* 3C **106**
Normanby-by-Spital. *Linc* 2H **87**
Normanby le Wold. *Linc* 1A **88**
Norman Cross. *Cambs* 1A **64**
Normandy. *Surr* 5A **38**
Norman's Bay. *E Sus* 5A **28**
Norman's Green. *Devn* 2D **12**
Normanton. *Derb* 2H **73**
Normanton. *Leics* 1F **75**
Normanton. *Linc* 1G **75**
Normanton. *Notts* 5E **86**
Normanton. *W Yor* 2D **93**
Normanton le Heath. *Leics* 4A **74**
Normanton on Soar. *Notts* 3C **74**
Normanton-on-the-Wolds. *Notts* 2D **74**
Normanton on Trent. *Notts* 4E **87**
Normoss. *Lanc* 1B **90**
Norrington Common. *Wilts* 5D **35**
Norris Green. *Mers* 1F **83**
Norris Hill. *Leics* 4H **73**
Norristhorpe. *W Yor* 2C **92**
Northacre. *Norf* 1B **66**
Northall. *Buck* 3H **51**
Northallerton. *N Yor* 5A **106**
Northam. *Devn* 4E **19**
Northam. *Sotn* 1C **16**
Northampton. *Nptn* 4E **63** & **200**
North Anston. *S Yor* 2C **86**
North Ascot. *Brac* 4A **38**
North Aston. *Oxon* 3C **50**
Northaw. *Herts* 5C **52**
Northay. *Som* 1F **13**
North Baddesley. *Hants* 4B **24**
North Balfern. *Dum* 4B **110**
North Ballachulish. *High* 2E **141**
North Barrow. *Som* 4B **22**
North Barsham. *Norf* 2B **78**
Northbeck. *Linc* 1H **75**
North Benfleet. *Essx* 2B **40**
North Bersted. *W Sus* 5A **26**
North Berwick. *E Lot* 1B **130**
North Bitchburn. *Dur* 1E **105**
North Blyth. *Nmbd* 1G **115**
North Boarhunt. *Hants* 1E **16**
North Bockhampton. *Dors* 3G **15**
Northborough. *Pet* 5A **76**
Northbourne. *Kent* 5H **41**
Northbourne. *Oxon* 3D **36**
North Bovey. *Devn* 4H **11**
North Bowood. *Dors* 3H **13**
North Bradley. *Wilts* 1D **22**
North Brentor. *Devn* 4E **11**
North Brewham. *Som* 3C **22**
Northbrook. *Oxon* 3C **50**
North Brook End. *Cambs* 1C **52**
North Broomhill. *Nmbd* 4G **121**
North Buckland. *Devn* 2E **19**
North Burlingham. *Norf* 4F **79**
North Cadbury. *Som* 4B **22**
North Carlton. *Linc* 3G **87**
North Cave. *E Yor* 1B **94**
North Cerney. *Glos* 5F **49**
North Chailey. *E Sus* 3E **27**
Northchapel. *W Sus* 3A **26**
North Charford. *Hants* 1G **15**
North Charlton. *Nmbd* 2F **121**
North Cheriton. *Som* 4B **22**
North Chideock. *Dors* 3H **13**
Northchurch. *Herts* 5H **51**
North Cliffe. *E Yor* 1B **94**
North Clifton. *Notts* 3F **87**
North Close. *Dur* 1F **105**
North Cockerington. *Linc* 1C **88**
North Coker. *Som* 1A **14**
North Collafirth. *Shet* 3E **173**
North Common. *E Sus* 3E **27**
North Commonty. *Abers* 4F **161**
North Coombe. *Devn* 1B **12**
North Cornelly. *B'end* 3B **32**
North Cotes. *Linc* 4G **95**
Northcott. *Devn* 3D **10** (nr. Boyton)
Northcott. *Devn* 1D **12** (nr. Culmstock)
Northcourt. *Oxon* 2D **36**
North Cove. *Suff* 2G **67**
North Cowton. *N Yor* 4F **105**
North Craigo. *Ang* 2F **145**
North Crawley. *Mil* 1H **51**
North Cray. *G Lon* 3F **39**
North Creake. *Norf* 2A **78**
North Curry. *Som* 4G **21**
North Dalton. *E Yor* 4D **100**
North Deighton. *N Yor* 4F **99**
North Dronley. *Ang* 5C **144**
North Duffield. *N Yor* 1G **93**
Northdyke. *Orkn* 5B **172**
Northedge. *Derbs* 4A **86**
North Elkington. *Linc* 1B **88**
North Elmham. *Norf* 3B **78**
North Elmsall. *W Yor* 3E **93**
Northend. *Buck* 2F **37**
North End. *E Yor* 1F **95**
North End. *Essx* 4G **53** (nr. Great Dunmow)
North End. *Essx* 2A **54** (nr. Great Yeldham)
North End. *Hants* 5C **36**
North End. *Leics* 4C **74**
North End. *Linc* 1B **76**
North End. *Norf* 1B **66**
North End. *N Som* 5H **33**
North End. *Port* 2E **17**
Northend. *Warw* 5A **62**
North End. *W Sus* 5C **26**
North End. *Wilts* 2F **35**
North Erradale. *High* 5B **162**
North Evington. *Leic* 5D **74**
North Fambridge. *Essx* 1C **40**
North Fearns. *High* 5E **155**
North Featherstone. *W Yor* 2E **93**
North Feorline. *N Ayr* 3D **122**
North Ferriby. *E Yor* 2C **94**
Northfield. *Aber* 3F **153**
Northfield. *Hull* 2D **94**
Northfield. *Som* 3F **21**
Northfield. *W Mid* 3E **61**
Northfleet. *Kent* 3H **39**
North Frodingham. *E Yor* 4F **101**
Northgate. *Linc* 3A **76**
North Gluss. *Shet* 4E **173**
North Gorley. *Hants* 1G **15**
North Green. *Norf* 2E **66**
North Green. *Suff* 4F **67** (nr. Framlingham)
North Green. *Suff* 3F **67** (nr. Halesworth)
North Green. *Suff* 4F **67** (nr. Saxmundham)
North Greetwell. *Linc* 3H **87**
North Grimston. *N Yor* 3C **100**
North Halling. *Medw* 4B **40**
North Hayling. *Hants* 2F **17**
North Hazelrigg. *Nmbd* 1E **121**
North Heasley. *Devn* 3H **19**
North Heath. *W Sus* 3B **26**
North Hill. *Corn* 5C **10**
North Hinksey Village. *Oxon* 5C **50**
North Holmwood. *Surr* 1C **26**
North Huish. *Devn* 3D **8**
North Hykeham. *Linc* 4G **87**
Northiam. *E Sus* 3C **28**
Northill. *C Beds* 1B **52**
Northington. *Hants* 3D **24**
North Kelsey. *Linc* 4D **94**
North Kelsey Moor. *Linc* 4D **94**
North Kessock. *High* 4A **158**
North Killingholme. *N Lin* 3E **95**
North Kilvington. *N Yor* 1G **99**
North Kilworth. *Leics* 2D **62**
North Kyme. *Linc* 5A **88**
North Lancing. *W Sus* 5C **26**
Northlands. *Linc* 5C **88**
Northleach. *Glos* 4G **49**
North Lee. *Buck* 5G **51**
North Lees. *N Yor* 2E **99**
Northleigh. *Devn* 3G **19** (nr. Barnstaple)
Northleigh. *Devn* 3E **13** (nr. Honiton)
North Leigh. *Kent* 1F **29**
North Leigh. *Oxon* 4B **50**
North Leverton. *Notts* 2E **87**
Northlew. *Devn* 3F **11**
North Littleton. *Worc* 1F **49**
North Lopham. *Norf* 2C **66**
North Luffenham. *Rut* 5G **75**
North Marden. *W Sus* 1G **17**
North Marston. *Buck* 3F **51**
North Middleton. *Midl* 4G **129**
North Middleton. *Nmbd* 2E **121**
North Molton. *Devn* 4H **19**
North Moor. *N Yor* 1D **100**
Northmoor. *Oxon* 5C **50**
Northmoor Green. *Som* 3G **21**
North Moreton. *Oxon* 3D **36**
Northmuir. *Ang* 3C **144**
North Mundham. *W Sus* 2G **17**
North Murie. *Per* 1E **137**
North Muskham. *Notts* 5E **87**
North Ness. *Orkn* 8C **172**
North Newbald. *E Yor* 1C **94**
North Newington. *Oxon* 2C **50**
North Newnton. *Wilts* 1G **23**
North Newton. *Som* 3F **21**
Northney. *Hants* 2F **17**
North Nibley. *Glos* 2C **34**
North Oakley. *Hants* 1D **24**
North Ockendon. *G Lon* 2G **39**
Northolt. *G Lon* 2C **38**
Northop. *Flin* 4E **83**
Northop Hall. *Flin* 4E **83**
North Ormesby. *Midd* 3C **106**
North Ormsby. *Linc* 1B **88**
Northorpe. *Linc* 4H **75** (nr. Bourne)
Northorpe. *Linc* 2B **76** (nr. Donington)
Northorpe. *Linc* 1F **87** (nr. Gainsborough)
North Otterington. *N Yor* 1F **99**
Northover. *Som* 3H **21** (nr. Glastonbury)
Northover. *Som* 4A **22** (nr. Yeovil)
North Owersby. *Linc* 1H **87**
Northowram. *W Yor* 2B **92**
North Perrott. *Som* 2H **13**
North Petherton. *Som* 3F **21**
North Petherwin. *Corn* 4C **10**
North Pickenham. *Norf* 5A **78**
North Piddle. *Worc* 5D **60**
North Poorton. *Dors* 3A **14**
North Port. *Arg* 1H **133**
Northport. *Dors* 4E **15**
North Queensferry. *Fife* 1E **129**
North Radworthy. *Devn* 3A **20**
North Rauceby. *Linc* 1H **75**
Northrepps. *Norf* 2E **79**
North Rigton. *N Yor* 5E **99**
North Rode. *Ches E* 4C **84**
North Roe. *Shet* 3E **173**
North Ronaldsay Airport. *Orkn* 2G **172**
North Row. *Cumb* 1D **102**
North Runcton. *Norf* 4F **77**
North Sannox. *N Ayr* 5B **126**
North Scale. *Cumb* 2A **96**
North Scarle. *Linc* 4F **87**
North Seaton. *Nmbd* 1F **115**
North Seaton Colliery. *Nmbd* 1F **115**
North Sheen. *G Lon* 3C **38**
North Shian. *Arg* 4D **140**
North Shields. *Tyne* 3G **115**
North Shoebury. *S'end* 2D **40**
North Shore. *Bkpl* 1B **90**
North Side. *Cumb* 2B **102**
North Skelton. *Red C* 3D **106**
North Somercotes. *Linc* 1D **88**
North Stainley. *N Yor* 2E **99**
North Stainmore. *Cumb* 3B **104**
North Stifford. *Thur* 2H **39**
North Stoke. *Bath* 5C **34**
North Stoke. *Oxon* 3E **36**
North Stoke. *W Sus* 4B **26**
Northstowe. *Cambs* 4D **64**
North Street. *Hants* 3E **25**
North Street. *Kent* 5E **40**
North Street. *Medw* 3C **40**
North Street. *W Ber* 4E **37**
North Sunderland. *Nmbd* 1G **121**
North Tamerton. *Corn* 3D **10**
North Tawton. *Devn* 2G **11**
North Thoresby. *Linc* 1B **88**
North Tidworth. *Wilts* 2H **23**
North Town. *Devn* 2F **11**
Northtown. *Orkn* 8D **172**
North Town. *Shet* 10E **173**
North Tuddenham. *Norf* 4C **78**
North Walbottle. *Tyne* 3E **115**
Northwall. *Orkn* 3G **172**
North Walney. *Cumb* 3A **96**
North Walsham. *Norf* 2E **79**
North Waltham. *Hants* 2D **24**
North Warnborough. *Hants* 1F **25**
North Water Bridge. *Ang* 2F **145**
North Watten. *High* 3E **169**
Northway. *Glos* 2E **49**
Northway. *Swan* 4E **31**
North Weald Bassett. *Essx* 5F **53**
North Weston. *N Som* 4H **33**
North Weston. *Oxon* 5E **51**
North Wheatley. *Notts* 2E **87**
North Whilborough. *Devn* 2E **9**
Northwich. *Ches W* 3A **84**
North Wick. *Bath* 5A **34**
Northwick. *Som* 2G **21**
Northwick. *S Glo* 3A **34**
North Widcombe. *Bath* 1A **22**
North Willingham. *Linc* 2A **88**
North Wingfield. *Derbs* 4B **86**
North Witham. *Linc* 3G **75**
Northwold. *Norf* 1G **65**
Northwood. *Derbs* 4G **85**
Northwood. *G Lon* 1B **38**
Northwood. *IOW* 3C **16**
Northwood. *Kent* 4H **41**
Northwood. *Shrp* 2G **71**
Northwood. *Stoke* 1C **72**
Northwood Green. *Glos* 4C **48**
North Wootton. *Dors* 1B **14**
North Wootton. *Norf* 3F **77**
North Wootton. *Som* 2A **22**
North Wraxall. *Wilts* 4D **34**
North Wroughton. *Swin* 3G **35**
North Yardhope. *Nmbd* 4D **120**
North York Moors. *N Yor* 5D **107**
Norton. *Devn* 3E **9**
Norton. *Glos* 3D **48**
Norton. *Hal* 2H **83**
Norton. *Herts* 2C **52**
Norton. *IOW* 4B **16**
Norton. *Mon* 3H **47**
Norton. *Nptn* 4D **62**
Norton. *Notts* 3C **86**
Norton. *Powy* 4F **59**
Norton. *Shrp* 2G **59** (nr. Ludlow)
Norton. *Shrp* 5B **72** (nr. Madeley)
Norton. *Shrp* 5H **71** (nr. Shrewsbury)
Norton. *S Yor* 3F **93** (nr. Askern)
Norton. *S Yor* 2A **86** (nr. Sheffield)
Norton. *Stoc T* 2B **106**
Norton. *Suff* 4B **66**
Norton. *Swan* 4F **31**
Norton. *W Sus* 5A **26** (nr. Arundel)
Norton. *W Sus* 3G **17** (nr. Selsey)
Norton. *Wilts* 3D **35**
Norton. *Worc* 1F **49** (nr. Evesham)
Norton. *Worc* 5C **60** (nr. Worcester)
Norton Bavant. *Wilts* 2E **23**
Norton Bridge. *Staf* 2C **72**
Norton Canes. *Staf* 5E **73**
Norton Canon. *Here* 1G **47**
Norton Corner. *Norf* 3C **78**
Norton Disney. *Linc* 5F **87**
Norton East. *Staf* 5E **73**
Norton Ferris. *Wilts* 3C **22**
Norton Fitzwarren. *Som* 4F **21**
Norton Green. *IOW* 4B **16**
Norton Green. *Stoke* 5D **84**
Norton Hawkfield. *Bath* 5A **34**
Norton Heath. *Essx* 5G **53**
Norton in Hales. *Shrp* 2B **72**
Norton in the Moors. *Stoke* 5C **84**
Norton-Juxta-Twycross. *Leics* 5H **73**

Norton-le-Clay. N Yor 2G 99
Norton Lindsey. Warw 4G 61
Norton Little Green. Suff 4B 66
Norton Malreward. Bath 5B 34
Norton Mandeville. Essx 5F 53
Norton-on-Derwent.
  N Yor 2B 100
Norton St Philip. Som 1C 22
Norton Subcourse. Norf 1G 67
Norton sub Hamdon.
  Som 1H 13
Norton Woodseats. S Yor 2A 86
Norwell. Notts 4E 87
Norwell Woodhouse.
  Notts 4E 87
Norwich. Norf ....5E 79 & 200
Norwich International Airport.
  Norf 4E 79
Norwood. Derbs 2B 86
Norwood Green. W Yor 2B 92
Norwood Hill. Surr 1D 26
Norwood Park. Som 3A 22
Norwoodside. Cambs 1D 64
Noseley. Leics 1E 63
Noss. Shet 10E 173
Noss Mayo. Devn 4B 8
Nosterfield. N Yor 1E 99
Nostie. High 1A 148
Notgrove. Glos 3G 49
Nottage. B'end 4B 32
Nottingham. Nott ....1C 74 & 200
Nottington. Dors 4B 14
Notton. Dors 3B 14
Notton. W Yor 3D 92
Notton. Wilts 5E 35
Nounsley. Essx 4A 54
Noutard's Green. Worc 4B 60
Nox. Shrp 4G 71
Noyadd Trefawr. Cdgn 1C 44
Nuffield. Oxon 3E 37
Nunburnholme. E Yor 5C 100
Nuncargate. Notts 5B 86
Nunclose. Cumb 5F 113
Nuneaton. Warw 1A 62
Nuneham Courtenay.
  Oxon 2D 36
Nun Monkton. N Yor 4H 99
Nunnerie. S Lan 3B 118
Nunney. Som 2C 22
Nunnington. N Yor 2A 100
Nunnykirk. Nmbd 5E 121
Nunsthorpe. NE Lin 4F 95
Nunthorpe. Red C 3C 106
Nunthorpe. York 5H 99
Nunton. Wilts 4G 23
Nunwick. Nmbd 2B 114
Nunwick. N Yor 2F 99
Nupend. Glos 5C 48
Nursling. Hants 1B 16
Nursted. W Sus 4F 25
Nursteed. Wilts 5F 35
Nurston. V Glam 5D 32
Nutbourne. W Sus 2F 17
  (nr. Chichester)
Nutbourne. W Sus 4B 26
  (nr. Pulborough)
Nutfield. Surr 5E 39
Nuthall. Notts 1C 74
Nuthampstead. Herts 2E 53
Nuthurst. Warw 3F 61
Nuthurst. W Sus 3C 26
Nutley. E Sus 3F 27
Nuttall. G Man 3F 91
Nutwell. S Yor 4G 93
Nybster. High 2F 169
Nyetimber. W Sus 3G 17
Nyewood. W Sus 4G 25
Nymet Rowland. Devn 2H 11
Nymet Tracey. Devn 2H 11
Nympsfield. Glos 5D 48
Nynehead. Som 4E 21
Nyton. W Sus 5A 26

O

Oadby. Leics 5D 74
Oad Street. Kent 4C 40
Oakamoor. Staf 1E 73
Oakbank. Arg 5B 140
Oakbank. W Lot 3D 129
Oakdale. Cphy 2E 33
Oakdale. Pool 3F 15
Oake. Som 4E 21
Oaken. Staf 5C 72
Oakenclough. Lanc 5E 97
Oakengates. Telf 4B 72
Oakenholt. Flin 3E 83
Oakenshaw. Dur 1F 105
Oakenshaw. W Yor 2B 92
Oakerthorpe. Derbs 5A 86
Oakford. Cdgn 5D 56
Oakford. Devn 4C 20
Oakfordbridge. Devn 4C 20
Oakgrove. Ches E 4D 84
Oakham. Rut 5F 75
Oakhanger. Ches E 5B 84
Oakhanger. Hants 3F 25
Oakhill. Som 2B 22
Oakington. Cambs 4D 64
Oaklands. Powy 5C 58
Oakle Street. Glos 4C 48
Oakley. Bed 5H 63
Oakley. Buck 4E 51
Oakley. Fife 1D 128
Oakley. Hants 1D 24
Oakley. Suff 3D 66
Oakley Green. Wind 3A 38
Oakley Park. Powy 2B 58
Oakmere. Ches W 4H 83
Oakridge. Glos 5E 49
Oaks. Shrp 5G 71
Oaksey. Wilts 2E 35
Oaks Green. Derbs 2F 73
Oakshaw Ford. Cumb 2G 113
Oakshott. Hants 4F 25
Oakthorpe. Leics 4H 73
Oak Tree. Darl 3A 106
Oakwood. Derb 2A 74
Oakwood. W Yor 1D 92
Oakwoodhill. Surr 2C 26
Oakworth. W Yor 1A 92
Oape. High 3B 164
Oare. Kent 4E 40
Oare. Som 2B 20
Oare. W Ber 4D 36
Oare. Wilts 5G 35
Oareford. Som 2B 20
Oasby. Linc 2H 75
Oath. Som 4G 21
Oathlaw. Ang 3D 145
Oatlands. N Yor 4F 99
Oban. Arg ....1F 133 & 201
Oban. W Isl 7D 171
Oborne. Dors 1B 14
Obsdale. High 2A 158
Obthorpe. Linc 4H 75
Occlestone Green.
  Ches W 4A 84
Occold. Suff 3D 66
Ochiltree. E Ayr 2E 117
Ochtermuthill. Per 2H 135
Ochtertyre. Per 1H 135
Ockbrook. Derbs 2B 74
Ockeridge. Worc 4B 60
Ockham. Surr 5B 38

Ockle. High 1G 139
Ockley. Surr 1C 26
Ocle Pychard. Here 1A 48
Octofad. Arg 4A 124
Octomore. Arg 4A 124
Octon. E Yor 3E 101
Odcombe. Som 1A 14
Odd Down. Bath 5C 34
Oddingley. Worc 5D 60
Oddington. Oxon 4D 50
Oddsta. Shet 2G 173
Odell. Bed 5G 63
Odie. Orkn 5F 172
Odiham. Hants 1F 25
Odsey. Cambs 2C 52
Odstock. Wilts 4G 23
Odstone. Leics 5A 74
Offchurch. Warw 4A 62
Offenham. Worc 1F 49
Offenham Cross. Worc 1F 49
Offerton. G Man 2D 84
Offerton. Tyne 4G 115
Offham. E Sus 4F 27
Offham. Kent 5A 40
Offham. W Sus 5B 26
Offleyhay. Staf 3C 72
Offley Hoo. Herts 3B 52
Offleymarsh. Staf 3B 72
Offord Cluny. Cambs 4B 64
Offord D'Arcy. Cambs 4B 64
Offton. Suff 1D 54
Offwell. Devn 3E 13
Ogbourne Maizey. Wilts 4G 35
Ogbourne St Andrew.
Ogbourne St George.
  Wilts 4H 35
Ogden. G Man 3H 91
Ogle. Nmbd 2E 115
Ogmore. V Glam 4B 32
Ogmore-by-Sea. V Glam 4B 32
Ogmore Vale. B'end 2C 32
Okeford Fitzpaine. Dors 1D 14
Okehampton. Devn 3F 11
Okehampton Camp. Devn 3F 11
Okraquoy. Shet 8F 173
Okus. Swin 3G 35
Olchard. Devn 5B 12
Old. Nptn 3E 63
Old Aberdeen. Aber 3G 153
Old Alresford. Hants 3D 24
Oldany. High 5B 166
Old Arley. Warw 1G 61
Old Basford. Nott 1C 74
Old Basing. Hants 1E 25
Oldberrow. Warw 4F 61
Old Bewick. Nmbd 2E 121
Old Bexley. G Lon 3F 39
Old Blair. Per 2F 143
Old Bolingbroke. Linc 4C 88
Oldborough. Devn 2A 12
Old Brampton. Derbs 3H 85
Old Bridge of Tilt. Per 2F 143
Old Bridge of Urr. Dum 3E 111
Old Buckenham. Norf 1C 66
Old Burghclere. Hants 1C 24
Oldbury. Shrp 1B 60
Oldbury. Warw 1H 61
Oldbury. W Mid 2D 61
Oldbury-on-Severn.
  S Glo 2B 34
Oldbury on the Hill. Glos 3D 34
Old Byland. N Yor 1H 99
Old Cassop. Dur 1A 106
Old Catton. Norf 4E 79
Old Clee. NE Lin 4F 95
Old Cleeve. Som 2D 20
Old Colwyn. Cnwy 3A 82
Oldcotes. Notts 2C 86
Old Coulsdon. G Lon 5E 39
Old Dailly. S Ayr 5B 116
Old Dalby. Leics 3D 74
Old Dam. Derbs 3F 85
Old Deer. Abers 4G 161
Old Dilton. Wilts 2D 22
Old Down. S Glo 3B 34
Oldeamere. Cambs 1C 64
Old Edlington. S Yor 1C 86
Old Eldon. Dur 2F 105
Old Ellerby. E Yor 1E 95
Old Fallings. W Mid 5D 72
Oldfallow. Staf 4D 72
Old Felixstowe. Suff 2G 55
Oldfield. Shrp 2A 60
Oldfield. Worc 4C 60
Old Fletton. Pet 1A 64
Oldford. Som 1C 22
Old Forge. Here 4A 48
Old Glossop. Derbs 1E 85
Old Goole. E Yor 2H 93
Old Gore. Here 3B 48
Old Graitney. Dum 3E 112
Old Grimsby. IOS 1A 4
Old Hall Street. Norf 2F 79
Oldham. G Man 4H 91
Oldhamstocks. E Lot 2D 130
Old Heathfield. E Sus 3G 27
Old Hill. W Mid 2D 60
Old Hunstanton. Norf 1F 77
Oldhurst. Cambs 3B 64
Old Hutton. Cumb 1E 97
Old Kea. Corn 4C 6
Old Kilpatrick. W Dun 2F 127
Old Kinnernie. Abers 3E 152
Old Knebworth. Herts 3C 52
Oldland. S Glo 4B 34
Old Laxey. IOM 3D 108
Old Leake. Linc 5D 88
Old Lenton. Nott 2C 74
Old Llanberis. Gwyn 5F 81
Old Malton. N Yor 2B 100
Oldmeldrum. Abers 1F 153
Old Micklefield. W Yor 1E 93
Old Mill. Corn 5D 10
Old Milton. Hants 3H 15
Old Milverton. Warw 4G 61
Oldmixon. N Som 1G 21
Old Monkland. N Lan 3A 128
Old Newton. Suff 4C 66
Old Park. Telf 5A 72
Old Pentland. Midl 3F 129
Old Philpstoun. W Lot 2D 128
Old Quarrington. Dur 1A 106
Old Rayne. Abers 1D 152
Old Romney. Kent 3E 29
Old Scone. Per 1D 136
Oldshore Beg. High 3B 166
Oldshoremore. High 3C 166
Old Snydale. W Yor 2E 93
Old Sodbury. S Glo 3C 34
Old Somerby. Linc 2G 75
Old Spital. Dur 3C 104
Oldstead. N Yor 1H 99
Old Stratford. Nptn 1F 51
Old Swan. Mers 1F 83
Old Swarland. Nmbd 4F 121
Old Tebay. Cumb 4H 103
Old Town. Cumb 5F 113
Old Town. E Sus 5G 27
Old Town. High 2C 164
Old Town. IOS 1B 4
Old Town. Nmbd 5C 120
Old Trafford. G Man 1C 84
Old Tupton. Derbs 4A 86
Oldwall. Cumb 3F 113

Oldwalls. Swan 3D 31
Old Warden. C Beds 1B 52
Oldways End. Som 4B 20
Old Westhall. Abers 1D 152
Old Weston. Cambs 3H 63
Oldwhat. Abers 3F 161
Old Windsor. Wind 3A 38
Old Wives Lees. Kent 5E 41
Old Woking. Surr 5B 38
Old Woodstock. Oxon 4C 50
Olgrinmore. High 3C 168
Oliver's Battery. Hants 4C 24
Ollaberry. Shet 3E 173
Ollerton. Ches E 3B 84
Ollerton. Notts 4D 86
Ollerton. Shrp 3A 72
Olmarch. Cdgn 5F 57
Olmstead Green. Cambs 1G 53
Olney. Mil 5F 63
Olrig. High 2D 169
Olton. W Mid 2F 61
Olveston. S Glo 3B 34
Ombersley. Worc 4C 60
Ompton. Notts 4D 86
Omunsgarth. Shet 7E 173
Onchan. IOM 4D 108
Onecote. Staf 5E 85
Onehouse. Suff 5C 66
Onen. Mon 4H 47
Ongar Hill. Norf 3E 77
Ongar Street. Here 4F 59
Onibury. Shrp 3G 59
Onich. High 2E 141
Onllwyn. Neat 4B 46
Onneley. Shrp 1B 72
Onslow Green. Essx 4G 53
Onslow Village. Surr 1A 26
Onthank. E Ayr 1D 116
Openwoodgate. Derbs 1A 74
Opinan. High 1G 155
  (nr. Gairloch)
Opinan. High 4C 162
  (nr. Laide)
Orasaigh. W Isl 6F 171
Orbost. High 4B 154
Orby. Linc 4D 89
Orchard Hill. Devn 4E 19
Orchard Portman. Som 4F 21
Orcheston. Wilts 2F 23
Orcop. Here 3H 47
Orcop Hill. Here 3H 47
Ord. High 2E 147
Ordale. Shet 1H 173
Ordhead. Abers 2D 152
Ordie. Abers 3B 152
Ordiquish. Mor 3H 159
Ordley. Nmbd 4C 114
Ordsall. Notts 3E 86
Ore. E Sus 4C 28
Oreham Common. W Sus 4D 26
Oreton. Shrp 2A 60
Orford. Suff 1H 55
Orford. Warr 1A 84
Organford. Dors 3E 15
Orgil. Orkn 7B 172
Orgreave. Staf 4F 73
Oridge Street. Glos 3C 48
Orlestone. Kent 2D 28
Orleton. Here 4G 59
Orleton. Worc 4A 60
Orleton Common. Here 4G 59
Ormacleit. W Isl 5C 170
Ormathwaite. Cumb 2D 102
Ormesby. Midd 3C 106
Ormesby St Margaret.
  Norf 4G 79
Ormesby St Michael.
  Norf 4G 79
Ormiscaig. High 4C 162
Ormiston. E Lot 3H 129
Ormsaigbeg. High 2F 139
Ormsaigmore. High 2F 139
Ormsary. Arg 2F 125
Ormsgill. Cumb 2A 96
Ormskirk. Lanc 4C 90
Orphir. Orkn 7C 172
Orpington. G Lon 4F 39
Orrell. Lanc 4D 90
Orrell. Mers 1F 83
Orrisdale. IOM 2C 108
Orsett. Thur 2H 39
Orslow. Staf 4C 72
Orston. Notts 1E 75
Orthwaite. Cumb 1D 102
Orton. Cumb 4H 103
Orton. Mor 3H 159
Orton. Nptn 3F 63
Orton. Staf 1C 60
Orton Longueville. Pet 1A 64
Orton-on-the-Hill. Leics 5H 73
Orton Waterville. Pet 1A 64
Orton Wistow. Pet 1A 64
Orwell. Cambs 5C 64
Osbaldeston. Lanc 1E 91
Osbaldwick. York 4A 100
Osbaston. Leics 5B 74
Osbaston. Shrp 3F 71
Osbournby. Linc 2H 75
Osclay. High 5E 169
Oscroft. Ches W 4H 83
Ose. High 4C 154
Osgathorpe. Leics 4B 74
Osgodby. Linc 1H 87
Osgodby. N Yor 1E 101
  (nr. Scarborough)
Osgodby. N Yor 1G 93
  (nr. Selby)
Oskaig. High 5E 155
Oskamull. Arg 4F 139
Osleston. Derbs 2G 73
Osmaston. Derb 2A 74
Osmaston. Derbs 1G 73
Osmington. Dors 4C 14
Osmington Mills. Dors 4C 14
Osmondthorpe. W Yor 1D 92
Osmondwall. Orkn 9C 172
Osmotherley. N Yor 5B 106
Osnaburgh. Fife 2G 137
Ospisdale. High 5E 164
Ospringe. Kent 4E 40
Ossett. W Yor 2C 92
Ossington. Notts 4E 87
Ostend. Essx 1D 40
Ostend. Norf 2F 79
Osterley. G Lon 3C 38
Oswaldkirk. N Yor 2A 100
Oswaldtwistle. Lanc 2F 91
Oswestry. Shrp 3E 71
Otby. Linc 1A 88
Otford. Kent 5G 39
Otham. Kent 5B 40
Otherton. Staf 4D 72
Othery. Som 3G 21
Otley. Suff 5E 66
Otley. W Yor 5E 99
Otterburn. Nmbd 5C 120
Otterburn. N Yor 4A 98
Otterburn Camp. Nmbd 5C 120
Otterburn Hall. Nmbd 5C 120
Otterden Place. Kent 5D 40
Otterford. Som 1F 13
Otterham. Corn 3B 10
Otterhampton. Som 2F 21
Otterspool. Mers 2F 83

Otterham Quay. Kent 4C 40
Ottershaw. Surr 4B 38
Otterswick. Shet 3G 173
Otterton. Devn 4D 12
Ottery St Mary. Devn 3E 12
Ottinge. Kent 1F 29
Ottringham. E Yor 2F 95
Oughterby. Cumb 4D 112
Oughtershaw. N Yor 1A 98
Oughterside. Cumb 5C 112
Oughtibridge. S Yor 1H 85
Oulston. N Yor 2H 99
Oulton. Cumb 4D 112
Oulton. Norf 3D 78
Oulton. Staf 2D 72
  (nr. Gnosall Heath)
Oulton. Staf 2B 72
  (nr. Stone)
Oulton. Suff 1H 67
Oulton. W Yor 2D 92
Oulton Broad. Suff 1H 67
Oulton Street. Norf 3D 78
Oundle. Nptn 2H 63
Ousby. Cumb 1H 103
Ousdale. High 1H 165
Ousefleet. E Yor 2B 94
Ouston. Dur 4F 115
Ouston. Nmbd 4A 114
  (nr. Bearsbridge)
Ouston. Nmbd 2D 114
  (nr. Stamfordham)
Outer Hope. Devn 4C 8
Outertown. Orkn 6B 172
Outgate. Cumb 5E 103
Outhgill. Cumb 4A 104
Outlands. Staf 2B 72
Outlane. W Yor 3A 92
Out Newton. E Yor 2G 95
Out Rawcliffe. Lanc 5D 96
Outwell. Norf 5E 77
Outwick. Hants 1G 15
Outwood. Surr 1E 27
Outwood. W Yor 2D 92
Outwood. Worc 3D 60
Outwoods. Leics 4B 74
Outwoods. Staf 4B 72
Ouzlewell Green. W Yor 2D 92
Ovenden. W Yor 2A 92
Over. Cambs 3C 64
Over. Ches W 4A 84
Over. Glos 4D 48
Over. S Glo 3A 34
Overbister. Orkn 3F 172
Over Burrows. Derbs 2G 73
Overbury. Worc 2E 49
Overcombe. Dors 4B 14
Over Compton. Dors 1A 14
Over End. Cambs 1H 63
Over Finlarg. Ang 4D 144
Overgreen. Derbs 3H 85
Over Green. W Mid 1F 61
Over Haddon. Derbs 4G 85
Over Hulton. G Man 4E 91
Over Kellet. Lanc 2E 97
Over Kiddington. Oxon 3C 50
Overleigh. Som 3H 21
Overley. Staf 4F 73
Over Monnow. Mon 4A 48
Over Norton. Oxon 3B 50
Over Peover. Ches E 3B 84
Overpool. Ches W 3F 83
Overscaig. High 1B 164
Overseal. Derbs 4G 73
Over Silton. N Yor 5B 106
Oversland. Kent 5E 41
Overstone. Nptn 4F 63
Over Stowey. Som 3E 21
Overstrand. Norf 1E 79
Over Stratton. Som 1H 13
Over Street. Wilts 3F 23
Overthorpe. Nptn 1C 50
Overton. Aber 2F 153
Overton. Ches W 3H 83
Overton. Hants 2D 24
Overton. High 4G 96
Overton. Lanc 4D 96
Overton. N Yor 4H 99
Overton. Shrp 3H 59
  (nr. Bridgnorth)
Overton. Shrp 3H 59
  (nr. Ludlow)
Overton. Swan 4D 30
Overton. W Yor 3C 92
Overton. Wrex 1F 71
Overtown. Lanc 2F 97
Overtown. N Lan 4B 128
Overtown. Swin 4G 35
Over Wallop. Hants 3A 24
Over Whitacre. Warw 1G 61
Over Worton. Oxon 3C 50
Oving. Buck 3F 51
Oving. W Sus 5A 26
Ovingdean. Brig 5E 27
Ovingham. Nmbd 3D 115
Ovington. Dur 3E 105
Ovington. Essx 1A 54
Ovington. Hants 3D 24
Ovington. Norf 5B 78
Ovington. Nmbd 3D 114
Ower. Hants 1B 16
  (nr. Holbury)
Ower. Hants 1B 16
  (nr. Totton)
Owermoigne. Dors 4C 14
Owlbury. Shrp 1F 59
Owler Bar. Derbs 3G 85
Owlerton. S Yor 2H 85
Owlsmoor. Brac 5G 37
Owlswick. Buck 5F 51
Owmby. Linc 4D 94
Owmby-by-Spital. Linc 2H 87
Ownham. W Ber 4C 36
Owrtyn. Wrex 1F 71
Owslebury. Hants 4D 24
Owston. Leics 5E 75
Owston. S Yor 3F 93
Owston Ferry. N Lin 4B 94
Owstwick. E Yor 1F 95
Owthorne. E Yor 2G 95
Owthorpe. Notts 2D 74
Oxborough. Norf 5G 77
Oxbridge. Dors 3H 13
Oxcombe. Linc 3C 88
Oxen End. Essx 3G 53
Oxenhall. Glos 3C 48
Oxenholme. Cumb 5G 103
Oxen Park. Cumb 1C 96
Oxenpill. Som 2H 21
Oxenton. Glos 2E 49
Oxenwood. Wilts 1B 24
Oxford. Oxon ....5D 50 & 200
Oxgangs. Edin 3F 129
Oxhey. Herts 1C 38
Oxhill. Warw 1B 50
Oxley. W Mid 5D 72
Oxley Green. Essx 4C 54
Oxley's Green. E Sus 3A 28
Oxlode. Cambs 2D 65
Oxnam. Bord 3B 120
Oxshott. Surr 4C 38

Oxspring. S Yor 4C 92
Oxted. Surr 5E 39
Oxton. Mers 2E 83
Oxton. N Yor 5H 99
Oxton. Notts 5D 86
Oxton. Bord 4A 130
Oxwich. Swan 4D 31
Oxwich Green. Swan 4D 31
Oxwick. Norf 3B 78
Oykel Bridge. High 3A 164
Oyne. Abers 1D 152
Oystermouth. Swan 4F 31
Ozleworth. Glos 2C 34

P

Pabail Iarach. W Isl 4H 171
Pabail Uarach. W Isl 4H 171
Pachesham. Surr 5C 38
Packers Hill. Dors 1C 14
Packington. Leics 4A 74
Packmoor. Stoke 5C 84
Packmores. Warw 4G 61
Packwood. W Mid 3F 61
Packwood Gullet. W Mid 3F 61
Padanaram. Ang 3D 144
Padbury. Buck 2F 51
Paddington. G Lon 2D 38
Paddington. Warr 2A 84
Paddlesworth. Kent 2F 29
Paddock. Kent 5D 40
Paddockhole. Dum 1D 112
Paddock Wood. Kent 1A 28
Paddolgreen. Shrp 2H 71
Padeswood. Flin 4E 83
Padiham. Lanc 1F 91
Padside. N Yor 4D 98
Padson. Devn 3F 11
Padstow. Corn 1D 6
Padworth. W Ber 5E 36
Page Bank. Dur 1F 105
Pagham. W Sus 3G 17
Paglesham Churchend.
  Essx 1D 40
Paglesham Eastend. Essx 1D 40
Paibeil. W Isl 2C 170
  (on North Uist)
Paibeil. W Isl 8C 171
  (on Taransay)
Paiblesgearraidh. W Isl 2C 170
Paignton. Torb 2E 9
Pailton. Warw 2B 62
Paine's Corner. E Sus 3H 27
Painleyhill. Staf 2E 73
Painscastle. Powy 1E 47
Painshawfield. Nmbd 3D 114
Painsthorpe. E Yor 4C 100
Painswick. Glos 5D 48
Painter's Forstal. Kent 5D 40
Painthorpe. W Yor 3D 92
Pairc Shiabost. W Isl 3E 171
Paisley. Ren 3F 127
Pakefield. Suff 1H 67
Pakenham. Suff 4B 66
Pale. Gwyn 2B 70
Palehouse Common.
  E Sus 4F 27
Palestine. Hants 2A 24
Paley Street. Wind 4G 37
Palgowan. Dum 1A 110
Palgrave. Suff 3D 66
Pallington. Dors 3C 14
Palmarsh. Kent 2F 29
Palmer Moor. Derbs 2F 73
Palmers Cross. W Mid 5C 72
Palmerstown. V Glam 5E 33
Palnackie. Dum 4F 111
Palnure. Dum 3B 110
Palterton. Derbs 4B 86
Pamber End. Hants 1E 24
Pamber Green. Hants 1E 24
Pamber Heath. Hants 5E 36
Pamington. Glos 2E 49
Pamphill. Dors 2E 15
Pampisford. Cambs 1E 53
Panborough. Som 2H 21
Panbride. Ang 5E 145
Pancakehill. Glos 4F 49
Pancrasweek. Devn 2C 10
Pandy. Gwyn 3C 69
  (nr. Bala)
Pandy. Gwyn 5F 69
  (nr. Tywyn)
Pandy. Mon 3G 47
Pandy. Powy 5B 70
Pandy. Wrex 2D 70
Pandy Tudur. Cnwy 4A 82
Panfield. Essx 3H 53
Pangbourne. W Ber 4E 37
Pannal. N Yor 4F 99
Pannal Ash. N Yor 4E 99
Pannanich. Abers 4A 152
Pant. Shrp 3E 71
Pant. Wrex 1F 71
Pantasaph. Flin 3D 82
Pantersbridge. Corn 2F 7
Pant-glas. Shrp 2E 71
Pantglas. Shrp 1F 59
Pantgwyn. Carm 1C 44
Pantgwyn. Cdgn 1C 44
Pant-lasau. Swan 3F 31
Panton. Linc 3A 88
Pant-pastynog. Den 4C 82
Pantperthog. Gwyn 5G 69
Pant-teg. Carm 3E 45
Pant-y-Caws. Carm 2F 43
Pant-y-dwr. Powy 3B 58
Pant-y-ffridd. Powy 5D 70
Pantyffynnon. Carm 4G 45
Pantygasseg. Torf 5F 47
Pant-y-llyn. Carm 4G 45
Pant-yr-awel. B'end 3C 32
Panxworth. Norf 4F 79
Papa Stour Airport. Shet 6C 173
Papa Westray Airport.
  Orkn 2D 172
Papcastle. Cumb 1C 102
Papigoe. High 3F 169
Papil. Shet 8E 173
Papple. E Lot 2B 130
Papplewick. Notts 5C 86
Papworth Everard.
  Cambs 4B 64
Papworth St Agnes.

Par. Corn 3E 7
Paramour Street. Kent 4G 41
Parbold. Lanc 3C 90
Parbrook. Som 3A 22
Parbrook. W Sus 3B 26
Parc. Gwyn 2B 70
Parcllyn. Cdgn 5B 56
Parc-Seymour. Newp 2H 33
Pardown. Hants 2D 24
Pardshaw. Cumb 2B 102
Parham. Suff 4F 67
Park. Abers 4E 153
Park. Arg 4D 140
Park. Derr 6B 174
Park Bottom. Corn 4A 6
Parkburn. Abers 5E 161
Parkend. Glos 5B 48
Park End. Nmbd 2B 114
Parkeston. Essx 2F 55
Parkfield. Corn 2H 7
Parkgate. Ant 8J 175
Parkgate. Ches W 3E 83
Parkgate. Cumb 5D 112
Parkgate. Dum 1B 112
Parkgate. Surr 1D 26
Park Gate. Hants 2D 16
Park Gate. Worc 3D 60
Parkhall. W Dun 2F 127
Parkham. Devn 4E 19
Parkham Ash. Devn 4E 19
Parkhead. Cumb 5E 113
Parkhead. Glas 3H 127
Park Hill. Mers 4C 90
Parkhouse. Mon 5A 48
Parkhurst. IOW 3C 16
Park Lane. G Man 4F 91
Park Lane. Staf 5C 72
Parkmill. Swan 4E 31
Park Mill. W Yor 3C 92
Parkneuk. Abers 1G 145
Parkside. N Lan 4B 128
Parkstone. Pool 3F 15
Park Street. Herts 5B 52
Park Street. W Sus 2C 26
Park Town. Oxon 5D 50
Park Village. Nmbd 3H 113
Parkway. Here 2C 48
Parley Cross. Dors 3F 15
Parmoor. Buck 3F 37
Parr. Mers 1H 83
Parracombe. Devn 2G 19
Parrog. Pemb 1E 43
Parsonage Green.
  Essx 4H 53
Parsonby. Cumb 1C 102
Parson Cross. S Yor 1A 86
Parson Drove. Cambs 5C 76
Partick. Glas 3G 127
Partington. G Man 1B 84
Partney. Linc 4D 88
Parton. Cumb 2A 102
  (nr. Whitehaven)
Parton. Cumb 4D 112
  (nr. Wigton)
Parton. Dum 2D 111
Partridge Green. W Sus 4C 26
Parwich. Derbs 5F 85
Passenham. Nptn 2F 51
Passfield. Hants 3G 25
Passingford Bridge. Essx 1F 39
Paston. Norf 2F 79
Pasturefields. Staf 3D 73
Patchacott. Devn 3E 11
Patcham. Brig 5E 27
Patchetts Green. Herts 1C 38
Patching. W Sus 5B 26
Patchole. Devn 2G 19
Patchway. S Glo 3B 34
Pateley Bridge. N Yor 3D 98
Pathe. Som 3G 21
Pathfinder Village. Devn 3B 12
Pathhead. Abers 2G 145
Pathhead. E Ayr 3F 117
Pathhead. Fife 4E 137
Pathhead. Midl 3G 129
Pathlow. Warw 5F 61
Path of Condie. Per 2C 136
Pathstruie. Per 2C 136
Patmore Heath. Herts 3E 53
Patna. E Ayr 3D 116
Patney. Wilts 1F 23
Patrick. IOM 3B 108
Patrick Brompton. N Yor 5F 105
Patrington. E Yor 2G 95
Patrington Haven. E Yor 2G 95
Patrixbourne. Kent 5F 41
Patterdale. Cumb 3E 103
Pattiesmuir. Fife 1D 129
Pattingham. Staf 1C 60
Pattishall. Nptn 5D 62
Pattiswick. Essx 3B 54
Patton Bridge. Cumb 5G 103
Paul. Corn 4B 4
Paulerspury. Nptn 1F 51
Paull. E Yor 2E 95
Paulton. Bath 1B 22
Pauperhaugh. Nmbd 5F 121
Pave Lane. Telf 4B 72
Pavenham. Bed 5G 63
Pawlett. Som 2G 21
Pawston. Nmbd 1C 120
Paxford. Glos 2G 49
Paxton. Bord 4F 131
Payhembury. Devn 2D 12
Paythorne. Lanc 4H 97
Payton. Som 4E 20
Peacehaven. E Sus 5F 27
Peak Dale. Derbs 3E 85
Peak Forest. Derbs 3F 85
Peak Hill. Linc 4B 76
Peakirk. Pet 5A 76
Pearsie. Ang 3C 144
Peasedown St John. Bath 1C 22
Peaseland Green. Norf 4C 78
Peasemore. W Ber 4C 36
Peasenhall. Suff 4F 67
Pease Pottage. W Sus 2D 26
Peaslake. Surr 1B 26
Peasley Cross. Mers 1H 83
Peasmarsh. E Sus 3C 28
Peasmarsh. Som 1G 13
Peasmarsh. Surr 1A 26
Peaston. E Lot 3H 129
Peastonbank. E Lot 3H 129
Peathill. Abers 2G 161
Peat Inn. Fife 3G 137
Peatling Magna. Leics 1C 62
Peatling Parva. Leics 2C 62
Peaton. Arg 1D 126
Peaton. Shrp 2H 59
Peats Corner. Suff 4D 66
Pebmarsh. Essx 2B 54
Pebworth. Worc 1G 49
Pecket Well. W Yor 2H 91
Peckforton. Ches E 5H 83
Peckham Bush. Kent 5A 40
Peckleton. Leics 5B 74
Pedair-ffordd. Powy 3D 70
Pedham. Norf 4F 79
Pedlinge. Kent 2F 29
Pedmore. W Mid 2D 60
Pedwell. Som 3H 21
Peebles. Bord 5F 129
Peel. IOM 3B 108
Peel. Bord 1G 119
Peel Common. Hants 2D 16
Peening Quarter. Kent 3C 28
Peggs Green. Leics 4B 74
Pegsdon. C Beds 2B 52
Pegswood. Nmbd 1F 115
Peinchorran. High 5E 155
Peinlich. High 3D 154
Pelaw. Tyne 3F 115
Pelcomb Bridge. Pemb 3D 42
Pelcomb Cross. Pemb 3D 42
Peldon. Essx 4C 54
Pelsall. W Mid 5E 73
Pelton. Dur 4F 115
Pelutho. Cumb 5C 112
Pelynt. Corn 3G 7
Pemberton. Carm 5F 45
Pembrey. Carm 5E 45
Pembridge. Here 5F 59
Pembroke. Pemb 4D 43

Pembroke Dock.
  Pemb ....4D 42 & 204
Pembroke Ferry. Pemb 4D 43
Pembury. Kent 1H 27
Penallt. Mon 4A 48
Penally. Pemb 5F 43
Penalt. Here 3A 48
Penare. Corn 4D 6
Penarth. V Glam 4E 33
Penbeagle. Corn 3C 4
Penberth. Corn 4B 4
Pen-bont Rhydybeddau.
  Cdgn 2F 57
Penbryn. Cdgn 5B 56
Pencader. Carm 2E 45
Pen-cae. Cdgn 5D 56
Pencaenewydd. Gwyn 1D 68
Pencaerau. Neat 3G 31
Pencaitland. E Lot 3H 129
Pencarnisiog. IOA 3C 80
Pencarreg. Carm 1F 45
Pencarrow. Corn 5A 10
Pencelli. Powy 3D 46
Pen-clawdd. Swan 3E 31
Pencoed. B'end 3C 32
Pencombe. Here 5H 59
Pencraig. Here 3A 48
Pencraig. Powy 3C 70
Pendeen. Corn 3A 4
Penderyn. Rhon 5C 46
Pendine. Carm 4G 43
Pendlebury. G Man 4F 91
Pendleton. Lanc 1F 91
Pendock. Worc 2C 48
Pendoggett. Corn 5A 10
Pendomer. Som 1A 14
Pendoylan. V Glam 4D 32
Pendre. B'end 3C 32
Penegoes. Powy 5G 69
Penffordd. Pemb 2E 43
Penffordd-Lâs. Powy 1A 58
Penfro. Pemb 4D 43
Pengam. Cphy 2E 33
Pengam. Card 4F 33
Penge. G Lon 3E 39
Pengelly. Corn 4A 10
Pengenffordd. Powy 2E 47
Pengorffwysfa. IOA 1D 80
Pengover Green. Corn 2G 7
Pengwern. Den 3C 82
Penhale. Corn 5D 5
  (nr. Mullion)
Penhale. Corn 3D 6
  (nr. St Austell)
Penhale Camp. Corn 3B 6
Penhallow. Corn 3B 6
Penhalvean. Corn 5B 6
Penhelig. Gwyn 1F 57
Penhill. Swin 3G 35
Penhow. Newp 2H 33
Penhurst. E Sus 4A 28
Peniarth. Gwyn 5F 69
Penicuik. Midl 3F 129
Peniel. Carm 3E 45
Penifiler. High 4D 155
Peninver. Arg 3B 122
Penisa'r Waun. Gwyn 4E 81
Penistone. S Yor 4C 92
Penketh. Warr 2H 83
Penkill. S Ayr 5B 116
Penkridge. Staf 4D 72
Penley. Wrex 2G 71
Penllech. Gwyn 2B 68
Penllergaer. Swan 3F 31
Pen-llyn. IOA 2C 80
Penmachno. Cnwy 5G 81
Penmaen. Swan 4E 31
Penmaenmawr. Cnwy 3G 81
Penmaenpool. Gwyn 4F 69
Penmaen Rhos. Cnwy 3A 82
Penmark. V Glam 5D 32
Penmon. IOA 2F 81
Penmorfa. Gwyn 1E 69
Penmynydd. IOA 3E 81
Penn. Buck 1A 38
Penn. Dors 3G 13
Penn. W Mid 1C 60
Pennal. Gwyn 5G 69
Pennan. Abers 2F 161
Pennant. Cdgn 4E 57
Pennant. Den 2C 70
Pennant. Powy 1A 58
Pennant Melangell. Powy 3C 70
Pennar. Pemb 4D 42
Pennard. Swan 4E 31
Pennerley. Shrp 1F 59
Pennington. Cumb 2B 96
Pennington. G Man 1A 84
Pennington. Hants 3B 16
Pennorth. Powy 3E 47
Penn Street. Buck 1A 38
Pennsylvania. Devn 3C 12
Pennsylvania. S Glo 4C 34
Penny Bridge. Cumb 1C 96
Pennycross. Plym 3A 8
Pennygate. Norf 3F 79
Pennyghael. Arg 1C 132
Penny Hill. Linc 3C 76
Pennylands. Lanc 4C 90
Pennymoor. Devn 1B 12
Pennyvenie. E Ayr 4D 116
Pennywell. Tyne 4G 115
Penparc. Cdgn 1C 44
Penparcau. Cdgn 2E 57
Penpedairheol. Cphy 2E 33
Penperlleni. Mon 5G 47
Penpillick. Corn 3E 7
Penpol. Corn 5C 6
Penpoll. Corn 3F 7
Penpont. Corn 5A 10
Penpont. Dum 5H 117
Penprysg. B'end 3C 32
Penquit. Devn 3C 8
Penrherber. Carm 1G 43
Penrhiw. Pemb 1C 44
Penrhiwceiber. Rhon 2D 32
Pen-Rhiw-fawr. Neat 4H 45
Penrhiw-llan. Cdgn 1D 44
Penrhiw-pal. Cdgn 1D 44
Penrhos. Gwyn 2C 68
Penrhos. Here 5F 59
Penrhos. IOA 2B 80
Penrhos. Mon 4H 47
Penrhos. Powy 4B 46
Penrhos Garnedd. Gwyn 3E 81
Penrhyn. IOA 1C 80
Penrhyn Bay. Cnwy 2H 81
Penrhyn-coch. Cdgn 2F 57
Penrhyndeudraeth. Gwyn 2F 69
Penrhyn Side. Cnwy 2H 81
Penrice. Swan 4D 30
Penrith. Cumb 2G 103
Penrose. Corn 1C 6
Penruddock. Cumb 2F 103
Penryn. Corn 5B 6
Pensarn. Carm 4E 45
Pen-sarn. Gwyn 3E 69
Pensax. Worc 4B 60
Pensby. Mers 2E 83
Penselwood. Som 3C 22
Pensford. Bath 5B 34
Pensham. Worc 1E 49
Penshaw. Tyne 4G 115
Penshurst. Kent 1G 27
Pensilva. Corn 2G 7
Pensnett. W Mid 2D 60
Penston. E Lot 2H 129
Pentewan. Corn 4E 7
Pentir. Gwyn 4E 81
Pentire. Corn 2B 6
Pentlepoir. Pemb 4F 43
Pentlow. Essx 1B 54
Pentney. Norf 4G 77
Penton Mewsey. Hants 2B 24
Pentraeth. IOA 3E 81
Pentre. Powy 1D 58
  (nr. Church Stoke)
Pentre. Powy 2E 59
  (nr. Kerry)
Pentre. Powy 2D 58
  (nr. Mochdre)
Pentre. Rhon 2C 32
Pentre. Shrp 4F 71
Pentre. Wrex 2F 71
  (nr. Llanfyllin)
Pentre. Wrex 1E 71
  (nr. Rhosllanerchrugog)
Pentrebach. Carm 2B 46
Pentre-bach. Cdgn 1F 45
Pentrebach. Mer T 5D 46
Pentre-bach. Powy 2C 46
Pentrebeirdd. Powy 4D 70
Pentre Berw. IOA 3D 80
Pentre-bont. Cnwy 5G 81
Pentrecagal. Carm 1D 44
Pentre-celyn. Den 5D 82
Pentre-clawdd. Shrp 2E 71
Pentreclwydau. Neat 5B 46
Pentre-cwrt. Carm 2D 45
Pentre Dolau Honddu.
  Powy 1C 46
Pentre-dwr. Swan 3F 31
Pentrefelin. Carm 3G 45
Pentrefelin. Cdgn 1G 45
Pentrefelin. Cnwy 3H 81
Pentrefelin. Gwyn 2E 69
Pentrefoelas. Cnwy 5A 82
Pentre Galar. Pemb 1F 43
Pentregat. Cdgn 5C 56
Pentre Gwenlais. Carm 4G 45
Pentre Gwynfryn. Gwyn 3E 69
Pentre Halkyn. Flin 3E 83
Pentre Hodre. Shrp 3F 59
Pentre-Llanrhaeadr. Den 4C 82
Pentrellwyn. IOA 2E 81
Pentre-llwyn-llwyd. Powy 5B 58
Pentre-llyn-cymmer.
  Cnwy 5B 82
Pentre Meyrick. V Glam 4C 32
Pentre-piod. Gwyn 2A 70
Pentre-poeth. Newp 3F 33
Pentre'r beirdd. Powy 4D 70
Pentre'r-felin. Powy 2C 46
Pentre-uchaf. Gwyn 2C 68
Pentrich. Derbs 5A 86
Pentridge. Dors 1F 15
Pen-twyn. Cphy 5E 47
  (nr. Oakdale)
Pentwyn. Cphy 5F 47
  (nr. Rhymney)
Pentwyn. Card 3F 33
Pentyrch. Card 3E 32
Pentywyn. Carm 4G 43
Penuwch. Cdgn 4E 57
Penwithick. Corn 3E 7
Penwyllt. Powy 4B 46
  (nr. Ammanford)
Pen-y-banc. Carm 3G 45
  (nr. Llandeilo)
Penybont. Powy 4D 58
  (nr. Llandrindod Wells)
Pen-y-bont. Powy 1E 58
  (nr. Llanfyllin)
Pen-y-Bont Ar Ogwr.
  B'end 3C 32
Penybontfawr. Powy 3C 70
Penybryn. Cphy 2E 33
Pen-y-bryn. Pemb 1B 44
Pen-y-bryn. Wrex 1E 71
Pen-y-cae. Powy 4B 46
Penycae. Wrex 1E 71
Pen-y-cae mawr. Mon 2H 33
Penycaerau. Gwyn 3A 68
Pen-y-cefn. Flin 3D 82
Pen-y-clawdd. Mon 5H 47
Pen-y-coedcae. Rhon 3D 32
Penycwm. Pemb 2C 42
Pen-y-fai. B'end 3B 32
Penyffordd. Flin 4F 83
  (nr. Mold)
Pen-y-ffordd. Flin 2D 82
  (nr. Prestatyn)
Penyffridd. Gwyn 5E 81
Pen-y-garn. Cdgn 2F 57
Pen-y-garnedd. IOA 3E 81
Pen-y-garnedd. Powy 3D 70
Pen-y-graig. Gwyn 2B 68
Penygraig. Rhon 2D 32
Penygraigwen. IOA 2D 80
Pen-y-groes. Carm 4F 45
Penygroes. Gwyn 5D 80
Penygroes. Pemb 1F 43
Pen-y-Mynydd. Carm 5E 45
Penymynydd. Flin 4F 83
Penyrheol. Cphy 3E 33
Pen-yr-heol. Mon 4H 47
Penyrheol. Swan 3E 31
Pen-yr-Heolgerrig. Mer T 5D 46
Penysarn. IOA 1D 80
Pen-y-stryt. Den 5D 82
Penywaun. Rhon 5C 46
Penzance. Corn 3B 4
Peopleton. Worc 5D 60
Peover Heath. Ches E 3B 84
Peper Harow. Surr 1A 26
Peplow. Shrp 3A 72
Pepper Arden. N Yor 4F 105
Perceton. N Ayr 5E 127
Percyhorner. Abers 2G 161
Perham Down. Wilts 2A 24
Periton. Som 2C 20
Perkinsville. Dur 4F 115
Perlethorpe. Notts 3D 86
Perranarworthal. Corn 5B 6
Perranporth. Corn 3B 6
Perranuthnoe. Corn 4C 4
Perranwell. Corn 5B 6
Perranzabuloe. Corn 3B 6
Perrott's Brook. Glos 5F 49
Perry. W Mid 1E 61
Perry Barr. W Mid 1E 61
Perry Crofts. Staf 5G 73
Perry Green. Essx 3B 54
Perry Green. Herts 4E 53
Perry Green. Wilts 3E 35
Perry Street. Kent 3H 39
Perry Street. Som 2G 13

Perrywood—Rew

Perrywood. Kent 5E 41
Pershall. Staf 3C 72
Pershore. Worc 1E 49
Pertenhall. Bed 4H 63
Perth. Per 1D 136 & 201
Perthy. Shrp 2F 71
Perton. Staf 1C 60
Pertwood. Wilts 3D 23
Peterborough. Pet 1A 64 & 201
Peterburn. High 5B 162
Peterchurch. Here 2G 47
Peterculter. Aber 3F 153
Peterhead. Abers 4H 161
Peterlee. Dur 5H 115
Petersfield. Hants 4F 25
Petersfinger. Wilts 4G 23
Peter's Green. Herts 4B 52
Peters Marland. Devn 1E 11
Peterstone Wentlooge. Newp 3F 33
Peterston-super-Ely. V Glam 4D 32
Peterstow. Here 3A 48
Peter Tavy. Devn 5F 11
Petertown. Orkn 7C 172
Petham. Kent 5F 41
Petherwin Gate. Corn 4C 10
Petrockstowe. Devn 2F 11
Petsoe End. Mil 1G 51
Pett. E Sus 4C 28
Pettaugh. Suff 5D 66
Pett Bottom. Kent 5F 41
Petteridge. Kent 1A 28
Pettinain. S Lan 5C 128
Pettistree. Suff 5E 67
Petton. Devn 4D 20
Petton. Shrp 3G 71
Petts Wood. G Lon 4F 39
Pettycur. Fife 1F 129
Pettywell. Norf 3C 78
Petworth. W Sus 3A 26
Pevensey. E Sus 5A 28
Pevensey Bay. E Sus 5A 28
Pewsey. Wilts 5G 35
Pheasants Hill. Buck 3F 37
Philadelphia. Tyne 4G 115
Philham. Devn 4C 18
Philiphaugh. Bord 2G 119
Phillack. Corn 3C 4
Philleigh. Corn 5C 6
Philpstoun. W Lot 2D 128
Phocle Green. Here 3B 48
Phoenix Green. Hants 1F 25
Pibsbury. Som 4H 21
Pibwrlwyd. Carm 4E 45
Pica. Cumb 2B 102
Piccadilly. Warw 1G 61
Piccadilly Corner. Norf 2E 67
Piccotts End. Herts 5A 52
Pickering. N Yor 1B 100
Picket Piece. Hants 2B 24
Picket Post. Hants 2G 15
Pickford. W Mid 2G 61
Pickhill. N Yor 1F 99
Picklenash. Glos 3C 48
Picklescott. Shrp 1G 59
Pickletillem. Fife 1G 137
Pickmere. Ches E 3A 84
Pickstock. Telf 3B 72
Pickwell. Devn 2E 19
Pickwell. Leics 4E 75
Pickworth. Linc 2H 75
Pickworth. Rut 4G 75
Picton. Ches W 3G 83
Picton. Flin 2D 82
Picton. N Yor 4B 106
Pict's Hill. Som 4H 21
Piddinghoe. E Sus 5F 27
Piddington. Buck 2G 37
Piddington. Nptn 5F 63
Piddington. Oxon 4E 51
Piddlehinton. Dors 3C 14
Piddletrenthide. Dors 2C 14
Pidley. Cambs 3C 64
Pidney. Dors 2C 14
Pie Corner. Here 4A 60
Piercebridge. Darl 3F 105
Pierowall. Orkn 3D 172
Pigdon. Nmbd 1E 115
Pightley. Som 3F 21
Pikehall. Derbs 5F 85
Pikeshill. Hants 2A 16
Pilford. Dors 2F 15
Pilgrims Hatch. Essx 1G 39
Pilham. Linc 1F 87
Pill. N Som 4A 34
Pillaton. Corn 2H 7
Pillaton. Staf 4D 72
Pillerton Hersey. Warw 1A 50
Pillerton Priors. Warw 1A 50
Pilleth. Powy 4E 59
Pilley. Hants 3B 16
Pilley. S Yor 4D 92
Pillgwenlly. Newp 3G 33
Pilling. Lanc 5D 96
Pilling Lane. Lanc 5C 96
Pillowell. Glos 5B 48
Pill, The. Mon 3H 33
Pillwell. Dors 1C 14
Pilning. S Glo 3A 34
Pilsbury. Derbs 4F 85
Pilsdon. Dors 3H 13
Pilsgate. Pet 5H 75
Pilsley. Derbs 3G 85 (nr. Bakewell)
Pilsley. Derbs 4B 86 (nr. Clay Cross)
Pilson Green. Norf 4F 79
Piltdown. E Sus 3F 27
Pilton. Edin 2F 129
Pilton. Nptn 2H 63
Pilton. Rut 5G 75
Pilton. Som 2A 22
Pilton Green. Swan 4D 30
Pimperne. Dors 2E 15
Pinchbeck. Linc 3B 76
Pinchbeck Bars. Linc 3A 76
Pinchbeck West. Linc 3B 76
Pinfold. Lanc 3B 90
Pinford End. Suff 5H 65
Pinged. Carm 5E 45
Pinhoe. Devn 3C 12
Pinkerton. E Lot 2D 130
Pinkneys Green. Wind 3G 37
Pinley. W Mid 3A 62
Pinley Green. Warw 4G 61
Pinmill. Suff 2F 55
Pinmore. S Ayr 5B 116
Pinner. G Lon 2C 38
Pins Green. Worc 1C 48
Pinsley Green. Ches E 1H 71
Pinvin. Worc 1E 49
Pinwherry. S Ayr 1G 109
Pinxton. Derbs 5B 86
Pipe and Lyde. Here 1A 48
Pipe Aston. Here 3G 59
Pipe Gate. Shrp 1B 72
Pipehill. Staf 5E 73
Piperhill. High 3C 158
Pipe Ridware. Staf 4E 73
Pipers Pool. Corn 4C 10
Pipewell. Nptn 2F 63
Pippacott. Devn 3F 19
Pipton. Powy 2E 47
Pirbright. Surr 5A 38
Pirnmill. N Ayr 5G 125
Pirton. Herts 2B 52
Pirton. Worc 1D 49
Pisgah. Stir 3G 135
Pishill. Oxon 3F 37
Pistyll. Gwyn 1C 68
Pitagowan. Per 2F 143
Pitcairn. Per 3F 143
Pitcairngreen. Per 1C 136
Pitcalnie. High 1C 158
Pitcaple. Abers 1E 152
Pitchcombe. Glos 5D 48
Pitchcott. Buck 3F 51
Pitchford. Shrp 5H 71
Pitch Green. Buck 5F 51
Pitch Place. Surr 5A 38
Pitcombe. Som 3B 22
Pitcox. E Lot 2C 130
Pitcur. Per 5B 144
Pitfichie. Abers 2D 152
Pitgrudy. High 4E 165
Pitkennedy. Ang 3E 145
Pitlessie. Fife 3F 137
Pitlochry. Per 3G 143
Pitmachie. Abers 1D 152
Pitmaduthy. High 1B 158
Pitmedden. Abers 1F 153
Pitminster. Som 1F 13
Pitnacree. Per 3G 143
Pitney. Som 4H 21
Pitroddie. Per 1E 136
Pitscottie. Fife 2G 137
Pitsea. Essx 2B 40
Pitsford. Nptn 4E 63
Pitsford Hill. Som 3E 20
Pitsmoor. S Yor 2A 86
Pitstone. Buck 4H 51
Pitt. Hants 4C 24
Pitt Court. Glos 2C 34
Pittentrail. High 3E 164
Pittenweem. Fife 3H 137
Pittington. Dur 5G 115
Pitton. Swan 4D 30
Pitton. Wilts 3H 23
Pittswood. Kent 1H 27
Pittulie. Abers 2G 161
Pittville. Glos 3E 49
Pitversie. Per 2D 136
Pityme. Corn 1D 6
Pity Me. Dur 5F 115
Pixey Green. Suff 3E 67
Pixley. Here 2B 48
Place Newton. N Yor 2C 100
Plaidy. Abers 3E 161
Plaidy. Corn 3G 7
Plain Dealings. Pemb 3E 43
Plains. N Lan 3A 128
Plainsfield. Som 3E 21
Plaish. Shrp 1H 59
Plaistow. Here 2B 48
Plaistow. W Sus 2B 26
Plaitford. Wilts 1A 16
Plas Llwyd. Cnwy 3B 82
Plastow Green. Hants 5D 36
Plas yn Cefn. Den 3C 82
Platt. Kent 5H 39
Platt Bridge. G Man 4E 90
Platt Lane. Shrp 2H 71
Platts Common. S Yor 4D 92
Platt's Heath. Kent 5C 40
Platt, The. E Sus 2G 27
Plawsworth. Dur 5F 115
Plaxtol. Kent 5H 39
Playden. E Sus 3D 28
Playford. Suff 1F 55
Play Hatch. Oxon 4F 37
Playing Place. Corn 4C 6
Playley Green. Glos 2C 48
Plealey. Shrp 5G 71
Plean. Stir 1B 128
Pleasington. Bkbn 2E 91
Pleasley. Derbs 4C 86
Pledgdon Green. Essx 3F 53
Plenmeller. Nmbd 3A 114
Pleshey. Essx 4G 53
Plockton. High 5H 155
Plocrapol. W Isl 8D 171
Ploughfield. Here 1G 47
Plowden. Shrp 2F 59
Ploxgreen. Shrp 5F 71
Pluckley. Kent 1D 28
Plucks Gutter. Kent 4G 41
Plumbland. Cumb 1C 102
Plumbridge. Strab 7A 174
Plumgarths. Cumb 5F 103
Plumley. Ches E 3B 84
Plummers Plain. W Sus 3D 26
Plumpton. Cumb 1F 103
Plumpton. E Sus 4E 27
Plumpton. Nptn 1D 50
Plumpton Foot. Cumb 1F 103
Plumpton Green. E Sus 4E 27
Plumpton Head. Cumb 1G 103
Plumstead. G Lon 3F 39
Plumstead. Norf 2D 78
Plumtree. Notts 2D 74
Plumtree Park. Notts 2D 74
Plungar. Leics 2E 75
Plush. Dors 2C 14
Plushabridge. Corn 5D 10
Plwmp. Cdgn 5C 56
Plymouth. Plym 3A 8 & 201
Plympton. Plym 3B 8
Plymstock. Plym 3B 8
Plymtree. Devn 2D 12
Pockley. N Yor 1A 100
Pocklington. E Yor 5C 100
Pode Hole. Linc 3B 76
Podimore. Som 4A 22
Podington. Bed 4G 63
Podmore. Staf 2B 72
Poffley End. Oxon 4B 50
Point Clear. Essx 4D 54
Pointon. Linc 2A 76
Pokesdown. Bour 3G 15
Polbae. Dum 2H 109
Polbain. High 3E 163
Polbathic. Corn 3H 7
Polbeth. W Lot 3D 128
Polbrock. Corn 2E 6
Polchar. High 3C 150
Polebrook. Nptn 2H 63
Pole Elm. Worc 1D 48
Polegate. E Sus 5G 27
Pole Moor. W Yor 3A 92
Poles. High 4E 165
Polesworth. Warw 5G 73
Polglass. High 3E 163
Polgooth. Corn 3D 6
Poling. W Sus 5B 26
Poling Corner. W Sus 5B 26
Polio. High 1B 158
Polkerris. Corn 3E 7
Polla. High 3D 166
Pollard Street. Norf 2F 79
Pollicott. Buck 4F 51
Pollington. E Yor 3G 93
Polloch. High 2B 140
Pollok. Glas 3G 127
Pollokshaws. Glas 3G 127
Pollokshields. Glas 3G 127
Polmaily. High 5G 157
Polmassick. Corn 4D 6
Polmont. Falk 2C 128
Polnessan. E Ayr 3D 116
Polnish. High 5F 147
Polperro. Corn 3G 7
Polruan. Corn 3F 7
Polscoe. Corn 2F 7
Polsham. Som 2A 22
Polskeoch. Dum 4F 117
Polstead. Suff 2C 54
Polstead Heath. Suff 1C 54
Poltesco. Corn 5E 5
Poltimore. Devn 3C 12
Polton. Midl 3G 129
Polwarth. Bord 4D 130
Polyphant. Corn 4C 10
Polzeath. Corn 1D 6
Pomeroy. Cook 2A 178
Ponde. Powy 2E 46
Pondersbridge. Cambs 1B 64
Ponders End. G Lon 1E 39
Pond Street. Essx 2E 53
Pondtail. Hants 1G 25
Ponsanooth. Corn 5B 6
Ponsongath. Corn 5E 5
Ponsworthy. Devn 5H 11
Pontamman. Carm 4G 45
Pontantwn. Carm 4E 45
Pontardawe. Neat 5H 45
Pontarddulais. Swan 5F 45
Pontarfynach. Cdgn 3G 57
Pont-ar-gothi. Carm 3F 45
Pont ar Hydfer. Powy 3B 46
Pontarllechau. Carm 3H 45
Pontarsais. Carm 3E 45
Pontblyddyn. Flin 4E 83
Pontbren Llwyd. Rhon 5C 46
Pont Cyfyng. Cnwy 5G 81
Pontdolgoch. Powy 1C 58
Pontefract. W Yor 2E 93
Ponteland. Nmbd 2E 115
Ponterwyd. Cdgn 2G 57
Pontesbury. Shrp 5G 71
Pontesford. Shrp 5G 71
Pontfadog. Wrex 2E 71
Pontfaen. Pemb 1E 43
Pont-faen. Powy 2C 46
Pont-Faen. Shrp 2E 71
Pontgarreg. Cdgn 5C 56
Pont-Henri. Carm 5E 45
Ponthir. Torf 2G 33
Ponthirwaun. Cdgn 1C 44
Pont-iets. Carm 5E 45
Pontllanfraith. Cphy 2E 33
Pontlliw. Swan 5G 45
Pont Llogel. Powy 4C 70
Pontllyfni. Gwyn 5D 80
Pontlottyn. Cphy 5E 46
Pontneddfechan. Neat 5C 46
Pont-newydd. Carm 5E 45
Pont-newydd. Flin 4D 82
Pontnewydd. Torf 2F 33
Ponton. Shet 6E 173
Pont Pen-y-benglog. Gwyn 4F 81
Pontrhydfendigaid. Cdgn 4G 57
Pont Rhyd-y-cyff. B'end 3B 32
Pontrhydyfen. Neat 2A 32
Pont-rhyd-y-groes. Cdgn 3G 57
Pontrhydyrun. Torf 2F 33
Pont-Rhythallt. Gwyn 4E 81
Pontrilas. Here 3G 47
Pontrilas Road. Here 3G 47
Pontrobert. Powy 4D 70
Pont-rug. Gwyn 4E 81
Ponts Green. E Sus 4A 28
Pontshill. Here 3B 48
Pont-Sian. Cdgn 1E 45
Pontsticill. Mer T 4D 46
Pont-Walby. Neat 5B 46
Pontwelly. Carm 2E 45
Pontwgan. Cnwy 3G 81
Pontyates. Carm 5E 45
Pontyberem. Carm 4F 45
Pontybodkin. Flin 5E 83
Pontyclun. Rhon 3D 32
Pontycymer. B'end 2C 32
Pontyglazier. Pemb 1F 43
Pontygwaith. Rhon 2D 32
Pont-y-pant. Cnwy 5G 81
Pontypool. Torf 2G 33
Pontypridd. Rhon 2D 32
Pontypwl. Torf 2G 33
Pontywaun. Cphy 2F 33
Pooksgreen. Hants 1B 16
Pool. Corn 4A 6
Pool. W Yor 5E 99
Poole. N Yor 2E 93
Poole. Pool 3F 15 & 204
Poole. Som 4E 21
Poole Keynes. Glos 2E 35
Poolend. Staf 5D 84
Poolewe. High 5C 162
Pooley Bridge. Cumb 2F 103
Poolfold. Staf 5C 84
Pool Head. Here 5H 59
Pool Hey. Lanc 3B 90
Poolhill. Glos 3C 48
Poolmill. Here 3A 48
Pool o' Muckhart. Clac 3C 136
Pool Quay. Powy 4E 71
Poolsbrook. Derbs 3B 86
Pool Street. Essx 2A 54
Pootings. Kent 1F 27
Pope Hill. Pemb 3D 42
Pope's Hill. Glos 4B 48
Popeswood. Brac 5G 37
Popham. Hants 2D 24
Poplar. G Lon 2E 39
Popley. Hants 1E 25
Porchfield. IOW 3C 16
Porin. High 3F 157
Poringland. Norf 5E 79
Porkellis. Corn 5A 6
Porlock. Som 2B 20
Porlock Weir. Som 2B 20
Portachoillan. Arg 4F 125
Port Adhair Bheinn na Faoghla. W Isl 3C 170
Port Adhair Thirlodh. Arg 4B 138
Portadown. Cgvn 4E 178
Portaferry. Ards 4K 179
Port Ann. Arg 1H 125
Port Appin. Arg 4D 140
Port Asgaig. Arg 3C 124
Port Askaig. Arg 3C 124
Portavadie. Arg 3H 125
Portavogie. Ards 3L 179
Portballintrae. Cole 2F 174
Port Bannatyne. Arg 3B 126
Portbury. N Som 4A 34
Port Carlisle. Cumb 3D 112
Port Charlotte. Arg 4A 124
Portchester. Hants 2E 16
Port Clarence. Stoc T 2B 106
Port Dinorwig. Gwyn 4E 81
Port Driseach. Arg 2A 126
Port Dundas. Glas 3H 127
Port Ellen. Arg 5B 124
Port Elphinstone. Abers 1E 153
Portencalzie. Dum 2F 109
Portencross. N Ayr 5C 126
Port Erin. IOM 5A 108
Port Erroll. Abers 5H 161
Porter's Fen Corner. Norf 5E 77
Portesham. Dors 4B 14
Portessie. Mor 2B 160
Port e Vullen. IOM 2D 108
Port-Eynon. Swan 4D 30
Portfield. Som 4H 21
Portfield Gate. Pemb 3D 42
Portgate. Devn 4E 11
Port Gaverne. Corn 4A 10
Port Glasgow. Inv 2E 127
Portglenone. Bmna 6F 175
Portgordon. Mor 2A 160
Portgower. High 2H 165
Porth. Corn 2C 6
Porth. Rhon 2D 32
Porthaethwy. IOA 3E 81
Porthallow. Corn 3G 7 (nr. Looe)
Porthallow. Corn 4E 5 (nr. St Keverne)
Porthcawl. B'end 4B 32
Porthceri. V Glam 5D 32
Porthcothan. Corn 1C 6
Porthcurno. Corn 4A 4
Port Henderson. High 1G 155
Porthgain. Pemb 1C 42
Porthgwarra. Corn 4A 4
Porthill. Shrp 4G 71
Porthkerry. V Glam 5D 32
Porthleven. Corn 4D 4
Porthllechog. IOA 1D 80
Porthmadog. Gwyn 2E 69
Porthmeor. Corn 3B 4
Porth Navas. Corn 4E 5
Portholland. Corn 4D 6
Porthoustock. Corn 4F 5
Porthtowan. Corn 4A 6
Porth Tywyn. Carm 5E 45
Porth-y-felin. IOA 2B 80
Porthyrhyd. Carm 4F 45 (nr. Carmarthen)
Porthyrhyd. Carm 2H 45 (nr. Llandovery)
Porth-y-waen. Shrp 3E 71
Portincaple. Arg 4B 134
Portington. E Yor 1A 94
Portinnisherrich. Arg 2G 133
Portinscale. Cumb 2D 102
Port Isaac. Corn 1D 6
Portishead. N Som 4H 33
Portknockie. Mor 2B 160
Port Lamont. Arg 2B 126
Portlethen. Abers 4G 153
Portlethen Village. Abers 4G 153
Portling. Dum 4F 111
Port Lion. Pemb 4D 43
Portloe. Corn 5D 6
Port Logan. Dum 5F 109
Portmahomack. High 5G 165
Port Mead. Swan 3F 31
Portmeirion. Gwyn 2E 69
Portmellon. Corn 4E 6
Port Mholair. W Isl 4H 171
Port Mor. High 1F 139
Portmore. Hants 3B 16
Port Mulgrave. N Yor 3E 107
Portnacroish. Arg 4D 140
Portnahaven. Arg 4A 124
Portnalong. High 5C 154
Portnaluchaig. High 5E 147
Portnancon. High 2E 167
Port Nan Giuran. W Isl 4H 171
Port nan Long. W Isl 1D 170
Port Nis. W Isl 1H 171
Portobello. Edin 2G 129
Portobello. W Yor 3D 92
Port of Menteith. Stir 3E 135
Porton. Wilts 3G 23
Portormin. High 5D 168
Portpatrick. Dum 4F 109
Port Quin. Corn 1D 6
Port Ramsay. Arg 4C 140
Portreath. Corn 4A 6
Portree. High 4D 155
Port Righ. High 4D 155
Portrush. Cole 3E 174
Port St Mary. IOM 5B 108
Portscatho. Corn 5C 6
Portsea. Port 2E 17
Portskerra. High 2A 168
Portskewett. Mon 3A 34
Portslade-by-Sea. Brig 5D 26
Portsmouth. Port 3E 17 & 201
Portsmouth. W Yor 2H 91
Port Soderick. IOM 4C 108
Port Solent. Port 2E 17
Portsonachan. Arg 1H 133
Portsoy. Abers 2C 160
Portstewart. Cole 3E 174
Port Sunlight. Mers 2F 83
Portswood. Sotn 1C 16
Port Talbot. Neat 4G 31
Porttannachy. Mor 2A 160
Port Tennant. Swan 3F 31
Portuairk. High 2F 139
Portway. Here 1H 47
Portway. Worc 3E 61
Port Wemyss. Arg 4A 124
Port William. Dum 5A 110
Portwrinkle. Corn 3H 7
Poslingford. Suff 1A 54
Postbridge. Devn 5G 11
Postcombe. Oxon 2F 37
Post Green. Dors 3E 15
Postling. Kent 2F 29
Postlip. Glos 3F 49
Post-Mawr. Cdgn 5D 56
Postwick. Norf 5E 79
Potarch. Abers 4D 152
Potsgrove. C Beds 3H 51
Potten End. Herts 5A 52
Potter Brompton. N Yor 2D 101
Pottergate Street. Norf 1D 66
Potterhanworth. Linc 4H 87
Potterhanworth Booths. Linc 4H 87
Potter Heigham. Norf 4G 79
Potter Hill. Leics 3E 75
Potteries, The. Stoke 1C 72
Potterne. Wilts 1E 23
Potterne Wick. Wilts 1E 23
Potternewton. W Yor 1D 92
Potters Bar. Herts 5C 52
Potters Brook. Lanc 4D 97
Potter's Cross. Staf 2C 60
Potters Crouch. Herts 5B 52
Potter Somersal. Derbs 2F 73
Potterspury. Nptn 1F 51
Potter Street. Essx 5E 53
Potterton. Abers 2G 153
Potthorpe. Norf 3B 78
Pottle Street. Wilts 2D 22
Potto. N Yor 4B 106
Potton. C Beds 1C 52
Pott Row. Norf 3G 77
Pott Shrigley. Ches E 3D 84
Poughill. Corn 2C 10
Poughill. Devn 2B 12
Poulner. Hants 2G 15
Poulshot. Wilts 1E 23
Poulton. Glos 5G 49
Poulton-le-Fylde. Lanc 1B 90
Pound Bank. Worc 3B 60
Poundbury. Dors 3B 14
Poundfield. E Sus 2G 27
Poundgate. E Sus 3F 27
Pound Green. E Sus 3G 27
Pound Green. Suff 5G 65
Pound Hill. W Sus 2D 27
Poundland. S Ayr 1G 109
Poundon. Buck 3E 51
Poundsgate. Devn 5H 11
Poundstock. Corn 3C 10
Pound Street. Hants 5C 36
Pounsley. E Sus 3G 27
Powburn. Nmbd 3E 121
Powderham. Devn 4C 12
Powerstock. Dors 3A 14
Powfoot. Dum 3C 112
Powick. Worc 5C 60
Powmill. Per 4C 136
Poxwell. Dors 4C 14
Poyle. Slo 3B 38
Poynings. W Sus 4D 26
Poyntington. Dors 4B 22
Poynton. Ches E 2D 84
Poynton. Telf 4H 71
Poynton Green. Telf 4H 71
Poyntz Pass. Arm 6E 178
Poystreet Green. Suff 5B 66
Praa Sands. Corn 4C 4
Pratt's Bottom. G Lon 4F 39
Praze-an-Beeble. Corn 3D 4
Prees. Shrp 2H 71
Preesall. Lanc 5C 96
Preesall Park. Lanc 5C 96
Prees Green. Shrp 2H 71
Prees Higher Heath. Shrp 2H 71
Prendergast. Pemb 3D 42
Prendwick. Nmbd 3E 121
Pren-gwyn. Cdgn 1E 45
Prenteg. Gwyn 1E 69
Prenton. Mers 2F 83
Prescot. Mers 1G 83
Prescott. Devn 1D 12
Prescott. Shrp 3G 71
Preshute. Wilts 5G 35
Pressen. Nmbd 1C 120
Prestatyn. Den 2C 82
Prestbury. Ches E 3D 84
Prestbury. Glos 3E 49
Presteigne. Powy 4F 59
Presthope. Shrp 1H 59
Prestleigh. Som 2B 22
Preston. Brig 5E 27
Preston. Devn 5B 12
Preston. Dors 4C 14
Preston. E Lot 2B 130 (nr. East Linton)
Preston. E Lot 2G 129 (nr. Prestonpans)
Preston. E Yor 1E 95
Preston. Glos 5F 49
Preston. Herts 3B 52
Preston. Kent 4G 41 (nr. Canterbury)
Preston. Kent 4E 40 (nr. Faversham)
Preston. Lanc 2D 90 & 201
Preston. Nmbd 2F 121
Preston. Rut 5F 75
Preston. Bord 4D 130
Preston. Shrp 4H 71
Preston. Suff 5B 66
Preston. Wilts 4A 36 (nr. Aldbourne)
Preston. Wilts 4F 35 (nr. Lyneham)
Preston Bagot. Warw 4F 61
Preston Bissett. Buck 3E 51
Preston Bowyer. Som 4E 21
Preston Brockhurst. Shrp 3H 71
Preston Brook. Hal 3H 83
Preston Candover. Hants 2E 24
Preston Capes. Nptn 5C 62
Preston Cross. Glos 2B 48
Preston Gubbals. Shrp 4G 71
Preston-le-Skerne. Dur 2A 106
Preston Marsh. Here 1A 48
Prestonmill. Dum 4A 112
Preston on Stour. Warw 5G 61
Preston on the Hill. Hal 2H 83
Preston on Wye. Here 1G 47
Prestonpans. E Lot 2G 129
Preston Plucknett. Som 1A 14
Preston-under-Scar. N Yor 5D 104
Preston upon the Weald Moors. Telf 4A 72
Preston Wynne. Here 1A 48
Prestwich. G Man 4G 91
Prestwick. Nmbd 2E 115
Prestwick. S Ayr 2C 116
Prestwold. Leics 3C 74
Prestwood. Buck 5G 51
Prestwood. Staf 1E 73
Price Town. B'end 2C 32
Prickwillow. Cambs 2E 65
Priddy. Som 1A 22
Priestcliffe. Derbs 3F 85
Priesthill. Glas 3G 127
Priest Hutton. Lanc 2E 97
Priestland. E Ayr 1E 117
Priest Weston. Shrp 1E 59
Priestwood. Brac 4G 37
Priestwood. Kent 4A 40
Primethorpe. Leics 1C 62
Primrose Green. Norf 4C 78
Primrose Hill. Derbs 5B 86
Primrose Hill. Glos 5B 48
Primrose Hill. Lanc 4B 90
Primrose Valley. N Yor 2F 101
Primsidemill. Bord 2C 120
Princes Gate. Pemb 3F 43
Princes Risborough. Buck 5G 51
Princethorpe. Warw 3B 62
Princetown. Devn 5F 11
Prinsted. W Sus 2F 17
Prion. Den 4C 82
Prior Muir. Fife 2H 137
Prior's Frome. Here 2A 48
Priors Halton. Shrp 3G 59
Priors Hardwick. Warw 5B 62
Priorslee. Telf 4B 72
Priors Marston. Warw 5B 62
Prior's Norton. Glos 3D 48
Priory, The. W Ber 5B 36
Priory Wood. Here 1F 47
Priston. Bath 5B 34
Pristow Green. Norf 2D 66
Prittlewell. S'end 2C 40
Privett. Hants 4E 25
Prixford. Devn 3F 19
Probus. Corn 4D 6
Prospect. Cumb 5C 112
Prospect Village. Staf 4E 73
Provanmill. Glas 3H 127
Prudhoe. Nmbd 3D 115
Publow. Bath 5B 34
Puckeridge. Herts 3D 53
Puckington. Som 1G 13
Pucklechurch. S Glo 4B 34
Puckrup. Glos 2D 49
Puddinglake. Ches W 4B 84
Puddington. Ches W 3F 83
Puddington. Devn 1B 12
Puddlebrook. Glos 4B 48
Puddledock. Norf 1C 66
Puddletown. Dors 3C 14
Pudleston. Here 5H 59
Pudsey. W Yor 1C 92
Pulborough. W Sus 4B 26
Puleston. Telf 3B 72
Pulford. Ches W 5F 83
Pulham. Dors 2C 14
Pulham Market. Norf 2D 66
Pulham St Mary. Norf 2E 66
Pulley. Shrp 5G 71
Pulloxhill. C Beds 2A 52
Pulpit Hill. Arg 1F 133
Pulverbatch. Shrp 5G 71
Pumpherston. W Lot 3D 128
Pumsaint. Carm 1G 45
Puncheston. Pemb 2E 43
Puncknowle. Dors 4A 14
Punnett's Town. E Sus 3H 27
Purbrook. Hants 2E 17
Purfleet. Thur 3G 39
Puriton. Som 2G 21
Purleigh. Essx 5B 54
Purley. G Lon 4E 39
Purley on Thames. W Ber 4E 37
Purlogue. Shrp 3E 59
Purl's Bridge. Cambs 2D 65
Purse Caundle. Dors 1B 14
Purslow. Shrp 2F 59
Purston Jaglin. W Yor 3E 93
Purtington. Som 2G 13
Purton. Glos 5B 48 (nr. Lydney)
Purton. Glos 5B 48 (nr. Sharpness)
Purton. Wilts 3F 35
Purton Stoke. Wilts 2F 35
Pury End. Nptn 1F 51
Pusey. Oxon 2B 36
Putley. Here 2B 48
Putney. G Lon 3D 38
Putsborough. Devn 2E 19
Puttenham. Herts 4G 51
Puttenham. Surr 1A 26
Puttock End. Essx 1B 54
Puttock's End. Essx 4F 53
Puxey. Dors 1C 14
Puxton. N Som 5H 33
Pwll. Carm 5E 45
Pwll. Powy 5D 70
Pwllcrochan. Pemb 4D 42
Pwll-glas. Den 5D 82
Pwllgloyw. Powy 2D 46
Pwllheli. Gwyn 2C 68
Pwllmeyric. Mon 2A 34
Pwlltrap. Carm 3G 43
Pwll-y-glaw. Neat 2A 32
Pyecombe. W Sus 4D 27
Pye Corner. Herts 4E 53
Pye Corner. Newp 3G 33
Pye Green. Staf 4D 73
Pyewipe. NE Lin 3F 95
Pyle. B'end 3B 32
Pyle. IOW 5C 16
Pyle Hill. Surr 5A 38
Pylle. Som 3B 22
Pymoor. Cambs 2D 65
Pymoor. Dors 3H 13
Pyrford. Surr 5B 38
Pyrford Village. Surr 5B 38
Pyrton. Oxon 2E 37
Pytchley. Nptn 3F 63
Pyworthy. Devn 2D 10

Q

Quabbs. Shrp 2E 58
Quadring. Linc 2B 76
Quadring Eaudike. Linc 2B 76
Quainton. Buck 3F 51
Quaking Houses. Dur 4E 115
Quarley. Hants 2A 24
Quarndon. Derbs 1H 73
Quarrendon. Buck 4G 51
Quarrier's Village. Inv 3E 127
Quarrington. Linc 1H 75
Quarrington Hill. Dur 1A 106
Quarry Bank. W Mid 2D 60
Quarry, The. Glos 2C 34
Quarrywood. Mor 2F 159
Quartalehouse. Abers 4G 161
Quarter. N Ayr 3C 126
Quarter. S Lan 4A 128
Quatford. Shrp 1B 60
Quatt. Shrp 2B 60
Quebec. Dur 5E 115
Quedgeley. Glos 4D 48
Queen Adelaide. Cambs 2E 65
Queenborough. Kent 3D 40
Queen Camel. Som 4A 22
Queen Charlton. Bath 5B 34
Queen Dart. Devn 1B 12
Queenhill. Worc 2D 48
Queen Oak. Dors 3C 22
Queensbury. W Yor 2B 92
Queensferry. Flin 4F 83
Queenstown. Bkpl 1B 90
Queen Street. Kent 1A 28
Queenzieburn. N Lan 2H 127
Quemerford. Wilts 5F 35
Quendale. Shet 10E 173
Quendon. Essx 2F 53
Queniborough. Leics 4D 74
Quenington. Glos 5G 49
Quernmore. Lanc 3E 97
Quethiock. Corn 2H 7
Quholm. Orkn 6B 172
Quick's Green. W Ber 4D 36
Quidenham. Norf 2C 66
Quidhampton. Hants 1D 24
Quidhampton. Wilts 3G 23
Quilquox. Abers 5G 161
Quina Brook. Shrp 2H 71
Quindry. Orkn 8D 172
Quine's Hill. IOM 4C 108
Quinton. Nptn 5E 63
Quinton. W Mid 2D 61
Quintrell Downs. Corn 2C 6
Quixhill. Staf 1F 73
Quoditch. Devn 3E 11
Quorn. Leics 4C 74
Quorndon. Leics 4C 74
Quothquan. S Lan 1B 118
Quoyloo. Orkn 5B 172
Quoyness. Orkn 7B 172
Quoys. Shet 5F 173 (on Mainland)
Quoys. Shet 1H 173 (on Unst)

R

Rableyheath. Herts 4C 52
Raby. Cumb 4C 112
Raby. Mers 3F 83
Rachan Mill. Bord 1D 118
Rachub. Gwyn 4F 81
Rack End. Oxon 5C 50
Rackenford. Devn 1B 12
Rackham. W Sus 4B 26
Rackheath. Norf 4E 79
Racks. Dum 2B 112
Rackwick. Orkn 8A 172 (on Hoy)
Rackwick. Orkn 3D 172 (on Westray)
Radbourne. Derbs 2G 73
Radcliffe. G Man 4F 91
Radcliffe. Nmbd 4G 121
Radcliffe on Trent. Notts 2D 74
Radclive. Buck 2E 51
Radernie. Fife 2G 137
Radfall. Kent 4F 41
Radford. Bath 1B 22
Radford. Nott 1C 74
Radford. Oxon 3C 50
Radford. W Mid 2H 61
Radford. Worc 5E 61
Radford Semele. Warw 4H 61
Radipole. Dors 4B 14
Radlett. Herts 1C 38
Radley. Oxon 2D 36
Radnage. Buck 2F 37
Radstock. Bath 1B 22
Radstone. Nptn 1D 50
Radway. Warw 1B 50
Radway Green. Ches E 5B 84
Radwell. Bed 5H 63
Radwell. Herts 2C 52
Radwinter. Essx 2G 53
Radyr. Card 3E 33
RAF Coltishall. Norf 3E 79
Rafford. Mor 3E 159
Raffrey. Down 4J 179
Ragdale. Leics 4D 74
Ragdon. Shrp 1G 59
Ragged Appleshaw. Hants 2B 24
Raggra. High 4F 169
Raglan. Mon 5H 47
Ragnall. Notts 3F 87
Raholp. Down 5K 179
Raigbeg. High 1C 150
Rainford. Mers 4C 90
Rainford Junction. Mers 4C 90
Rainham. G Lon 2G 39
Rainham. Medw 4C 40
Rainhill. Mers 1G 83
Rainow. Ches E 3D 84
Rainton. N Yor 2F 99
Rainworth. Notts 5C 86
Raisbeck. Cumb 4H 103
Raise. Cumb 5A 114
Rait. Per 1E 137
Raithby. Linc 2C 88
Raithby by Spilsby. Linc 4C 88
Raithwaite. N Yor 3F 107
Rake. W Sus 4G 25
Rake End. Staf 4E 73
Rakeway. Staf 1E 73
Rakewood. G Man 3H 91
Ralia. High 4B 150
Ram Alley. Wilts 5H 35
Ramasaig. High 4A 154
Rame. Corn 4A 8 (nr. Millbrook)
Rame. Corn 5B 6 (nr. Penryn)
Ram Lane. Kent 1D 28
Ramnageo. Shet 1H 173
Rampisham. Dors 2A 14
Rampside. Cumb 3B 96
Rampton. Cambs 4D 64
Rampton. Notts 3E 87
Ramsbottom. G Man 3F 91
Ramsburn. Mor 3C 160
Ramsbury. Wilts 4A 36
Ramscraigs. High 1H 165
Ramsdean. Hants 4F 25
Ramsdell. Hants 1D 24
Ramsden. Oxon 4B 50
Ramsden. Worc 1E 49
Ramsden Bellhouse. Essx 1B 40
Ramsden Heath. Essx 1B 40
Ramsey. Cambs 2B 64
Ramsey. Essx 2F 55
Ramsey. IOM 2D 108
Ramsey Forty Foot. Cambs 2C 64
Ramsey Heights. Cambs 2B 64
Ramsey Island. Essx 5C 54
Ramsey Mereside. Cambs 2B 64
Ramsey St Mary's. Cambs 2B 64
Ramsgate. Kent 4H 41
Ramsgill. N Yor 2D 98
Ramshaw. Dur 5C 114
Ramshorn. Staf 1E 73
Ramsley. Devn 3G 11
Ramsnest Common. Surr 2A 26
Ramstone. Abers 2D 152
Ranais. W Isl 5G 171
Ranby. Linc 3B 88
Ranby. Notts 2D 86
Rand. Linc 3A 88
Randalstown. Ant 7G 175
Randwick. Glos 5D 48
Ranfurly. Ren 3E 127
Rangag. High 4D 168
Rangemore. Staf 3F 73
Rangeworthy. S Glo 3B 34
Rankinston. E Ayr 3D 116
Rank's Green. Essx 4H 53
Ranmore Common. Surr 5C 38
Rannoch Station. Per 3B 142
Ranochan. High 5G 147
Ranskill. Notts 2D 86
Ranton. Staf 3C 72
Ranton Green. Staf 3C 72
Ranworth. Norf 4F 79
Raploch. Stir 4G 135
Rapness. Orkn 3E 172
Rapps. Som 1G 13
Rascal Moor. E Yor 1B 94
Rascarrel. Dum 5E 111
Rasharkin. Bmny 5F 175
Rashfield. Arg 1C 126
Rashwood. Worc 4D 60
Raskelf. N Yor 2G 99
Rassau. Blae 4E 47
Rastrick. W Yor 2B 92
Ratagan. High 2B 148
Ratby. Leics 5C 74
Ratcliffe Culey. Leics 1H 61
Ratcliffe on Soar. Notts 3B 74
Ratcliffe on the Wreake. Leics 4D 74
Rathen. Abers 2H 161
Rathfriland. Ban 6F 179
Rathillet. Fife 1F 137
Rathmell. N Yor 4H 97
Ratho. Edin 2E 129
Ratho Station. Edin 2E 129
Rathven. Mor 2B 160
Ratley. Hants 4B 24
Ratley. Warw 1B 50
Ratlinghope. Shrp 1G 59
Rattar. High 1E 169
Ratten Row. Cumb 5E 113
Ratten Row. Lanc 5D 96
Rattery. Devn 2D 8
Rattlesden. Suff 5B 66
Ratton Village. E Sus 5G 27
Rattray. Abers 3H 161
Rattray. Per 4A 144
Raughton. Cumb 5E 113
Raughton Head. Cumb 5E 113
Raunds. Nptn 3G 63
Ravenfield. S Yor 1B 86
Ravenfield Common. S Yor 1B 86
Ravenglass. Cumb 5B 102
Ravenhills Green. Worc 5B 60
Raveningham. Norf 1F 67
Ravenscar. N Yor 4G 107
Ravensdale. IOM 2C 108
Ravensden. Bed 5H 63
Ravenseat. N Yor 4B 104
Ravenshead. Notts 5C 86
Ravensmoor. Ches E 5A 84
Ravensthorpe. Nptn 3D 62
Ravensthorpe. W Yor 2C 92
Ravenstone. Leics 4B 74
Ravenstone. Mil 5F 63
Ravenstonedale. Cumb 4A 104
Ravenstown. Cumb 2C 96
Ravenstruther. S Lan 5C 128
Ravensworth. N Yor 4E 105
Ravernet. Lis 3G 179
Raw. N Yor 4G 107
Rawcliffe. E Yor 2G 93
Rawcliffe. York 4H 99
Rawcliffe Bridge. E Yor 2G 93
Rawdon. W Yor 1C 92
Rawgreen. Nmbd 4C 114
Rawmarsh. S Yor 1B 86
Rawnsley. Staf 4E 73
Rawreth. Essx 1B 40
Rawridge. Devn 2F 13
Rawson Green. Derbs 1A 74
Rawtenstall. Lanc 2F 91
Raydon. Suff 2D 54
Raylees. Nmbd 5D 120
Rayleigh. Essx 1C 40
Raymond's Hill. Devn 3G 13
Rayne. Essx 3H 53
Rayners Lane. G Lon 2C 38
Reach. Cambs 4E 65
Read. Lanc 1F 91
Reading. Read 4F 37 & 201
Reading Green. Suff 3D 66
Reading Street. Kent 2D 28
Readymoney. Corn 3F 7
Reagill. Cumb 3H 103
Rearquhar. High 4E 165
Rearsby. Leics 4D 74
Reasby. Linc 3H 87
Reaseheath. Ches E 5A 84
Reaster. High 2E 169
Reawick. Shet 7E 173
Reay. High 2B 168
Rechullin. High 3A 156
Reculver. Kent 4G 41
Redberth. Pemb 4E 43
Redbourn. Herts 4B 52
Redbourne. N Lin 4C 94
Redbrook. Glos 4A 48
Redbrook. Wrex 1H 71
Redburn. High 4D 158
Redburn. Nmbd 3A 114
Redcar. Red C 2D 106
Redcastle. High 4H 157
Redcliff Bay. N Som 4H 33
Red Dial. Cumb 5D 112
Redding. Falk 2C 128
Reddingmuirhead. Falk 2C 128
Reddings, The. Glos 3E 49
Reddish. G Man 1C 84
Redditch. Worc 4E 61
Rede. Suff 5H 65
Redenhall. Norf 2E 67
Redesdale Camp. Nmbd 5C 120
Redesmouth. Nmbd 1B 114
Redford. Ang 4E 145
Redford. Dur 1D 105
Redford. W Sus 4G 25
Redfordgreen. Bord 3F 119
Redgate. Corn 2G 7
Redgrave. Suff 3C 66
Redhill. Abers 3E 153
Redhill. Herts 2C 52
Redhill. N Som 5H 33
Redhill. Shrp 4B 72
Redhill. Surr 5D 39
Red Hill. Warw 5F 61
Red Hill. W Yor 2E 93
Redhouses. Arg 3B 124
Redisham. Suff 2G 67
Redland. Bris 4A 34
Redland. Orkn 5C 172
Redlingfield. Suff 3D 66
Red Lodge. Suff 3F 65
Redlynch. Som 3C 22
Redlynch. Wilts 4H 23
Redmain. Cumb 1C 102
Redmarley. Worc 4B 60
Redmarley D'Abitot. Glos 2C 48
Redmarshall. Stoc T 2A 106
Redmile. Leics 2E 75
Redmire. N Yor 5D 104
Rednal. Shrp 3F 71
Redpath. Bord 1H 119
Redpoint. High 2G 155
Red Post. Corn 2C 10
Red Rock. G Man 4D 90
Red Roses. Carm 3G 43
Red Row. Nmbd 5G 121
Redruth. Corn 4B 6
Red Street. Staf 5C 84
Redvales. G Man 4F 91
Red Wharf Bay. IOA 2E 81
Redwick. Newp 3H 33
Redwick. S Glo 3A 34
Redworth. Darl 2F 105
Reed. Herts 2D 52
Reed End. Herts 2D 52
Reedham. Linc 5B 88
Reedham. Norf 5G 79
Reedness. E Yor 2B 94
Reeds Beck. Linc 4B 88
Reemshill. Abers 4E 161
Reepham. Linc 3H 87
Reepham. Norf 3C 78
Reeth. N Yor 5D 104
Regaby. IOM 2D 108
Regil. N Som 5A 34
Regoul. High 3C 158
Reiff. High 2D 162
Reigate. Surr 5D 38
Reighton. N Yor 2F 101
Reilth. Shrp 2E 59
Reinigeadal. W Isl 7E 171
Reisque. Abers 1F 153
Reiss. High 3F 169
Rejerrah. Corn 3B 6
Releath. Corn 5A 6
Relubbus. Corn 3C 4
Relugas. Mor 4D 159
Remenham. Wok 3F 37
Remenham Hill. Wok 3F 37
Rempstone. Notts 3C 74
Rendcomb. Glos 5F 49
Rendham. Suff 4F 67
Rendlesham. Suff 5F 67
Renfrew. Ren 3G 127
Renhold. Bed 5H 63
Renishaw. Derbs 3B 86
Rennington. Nmbd 3G 121
Renton. W Dun 2E 127
Renwick. Cumb 5G 113
Repps. Norf 4G 79
Repton. Derbs 3H 73
Rescassa. Corn 4D 6
Rescobie. Ang 3E 145
Rescorla. Corn 3E 7 (nr. Rosevean)
Rescorla. Corn 4D 6 (nr. St Ewe)
Resipole. High 2B 140
Resolfen. Neat 5B 46
Resolis. High 2A 158
Resolven. Neat 5B 46
Rest and be thankful. Arg 3B 134
Reston. Bord 3E 131
Restrop. Wilts 3F 35
Retford. Notts 2E 86
Retire. Corn 2E 6
Rettendon. Essx 1B 40
Revesby. Linc 4C 88
Rew. Devn 5D 8

Rewe—Sarsden

Rewe. *Devn* 3C **12**
Rew Street. *IOW* 3C **16**
Rexon. *Devn* 4E **11**
Reybridge. *Wilts* 5E **35**
Reydon. *Suff* 3H **67**
Reymerston. *Norf* 5C **78**
Reynalton. *Pemb* 4E **43**
Reynoldston. *Swan* 4D **31**
Rezare. *Corn* 5D **10**
Rhadyr. *Mon* 5G **47**
Rhaeadr Gwy. *Powy* 4B **58**
Rhandirmwyn. *Carm* 1A **46**
Rhayader. *Powy* 4B **58**
Rheindown. *High* 4H **157**
Rhemore. *High* 3G **139**
Rhenetra. *High* 3D **154**
Rhewl. *Den* 1D **70**
(nr. Llangollen)
Rhewl. *Den* 4D **82**
(nr. Ruthin)
Rhewl. *Shrp* 2F **71**
Rhewl-Mostyn. *Flin* 3D **82**
Rhian. *High* 2C **164**
Rhian Breck. *High* 3C **164**
Rhicarn. *High* 1E **163**
Rhiconich. *High* 3C **166**
Rhicullen. *High* 1A **158**
Rhidorroch. *High* 4F **163**
Rhifail. *High* 4H **167**
Rhigos. *Rhon* 5C **46**
Rhilochan. *High* 3E **165**
Rhiroy. *High* 5F **163**
Rhitongue. *High* 3G **167**
Rhiw. *Gwyn* 3B **68**
Rhiwabon. *Wrex* 1F **71**
Rhiwbina. *Card* 3E **33**
Rhiwbryfdir. *Gwyn* 1F **69**
Rhiwderin. *Newp* 3F **33**
Rhiwlas. *Gwyn* 2B **70**
(nr. Bala)
Rhiwlas. *Gwyn* 4E **81**
(nr. Bangor)
Rhiwlas. *Powy* 2D **70**
Rhodes. *G Man* 4G **91**
Rhodesia. *Notts* 2C **86**
Rhodes Minnis. *Kent* 1F **29**
Rhodiad-y-Brenin. *Pemb* 2B **42**
Rhondda. *Rhon* 2C **32**
Rhonehouse. *Dum* 4E **111**
Rhoose. *V Glam* 5D **32**
Rhos. *Carm* 2D **45**
Rhos. *Neat* 5H **45**
Rhosaman. *Carm* 4H **45**
Rhoscefnhir. *IOA* 3E **81**
Rhoscolyn. *IOA* 3B **80**
Rhos Common. *Powy* 4E **71**
Rhoscrowther. *Pemb* 4D **42**
Rhos-ddu. *Gwyn* 2B **68**
Rhosdylluan. *Gwyn* 3A **70**
Rhosesmor. *Flin* 4E **82**
Rhos-fawr. *Gwyn* 2C **68**
Rhosgadfan. *Gwyn* 5E **81**
Rhosgoch. *IOA* 2D **80**
Rhosgoch. *Powy* 1E **47**
Rhos Haminiog. *Cdgn* 4E **57**
Rhos-hill. *Pemb* 1B **44**
Rhoshirwaun. *Gwyn* 3A **68**
Rhoslan. *Gwyn* 1D **69**
Rhoslefain. *Gwyn* 5E **69**
Rhosllanerchrugog.
Wrex 1E **71**
Rhôs Lligwy. *IOA* 2D **81**
Rhosmaen. *Carm* 3G **45**
Rhosmeirch. *IOA* 3D **80**
Rhosneigr. *IOA* 3C **80**
Rhos-on-Sea. *Cnwy* 2H **81**
Rhossili. *Swan* 4D **30**
Rhosson. *Pemb* 2B **42**
Rhos, The. *Pemb* 3E **43**
Rhostrenwfa. *IOA* 3D **80**
Rhostryfan. *Gwyn* 5D **81**
Rhostyllen. *Wrex* 1F **71**
Rhoswiel. *Shrp* 2E **71**
Rhosybol. *IOA* 2D **80**
Rhos-y-brithdir. *Powy* 3D **70**
Rhos-y-garth. *Cdgn* 3F **57**
Rhos-y-gwaliau. *Gwyn* 2B **70**
Rhos-y-llan. *Gwyn* 2B **68**
Rhos-y-meirch. *Powy* 4E **59**
Rhu. *Arg* 1D **126**
Rhuallt. *Den* 3C **82**
Rhubha Stoer. *High* 1E **163**
Rhubodach. *Arg* 2B **126**
Rhuddall Heath. *Ches W* 4H **83**
Rhuddlan. *Cdgn* 1E **45**
Rhuddlan. *Den* 3C **82**
Rhue. *High* 4E **163**
Rhulen. *Powy* 1E **47**
Rhunahaorine. *Arg* 5F **125**
Rhuthun. *Den* 5D **82**
Rhuvoult. *High* 3C **166**
Rhyd. *Gwyn* 1F **69**
Rhydaman. *Carm* 4G **45**
Rhydargaeau. *Carm* 3E **45**
Rhydcymerau. *Carm* 2F **45**
Rhydd. *Worc* 1D **48**
Rhyd-Ddu. *Gwyn* 5E **81**
Rhydding. *Neat* 3G **31**
Rhydfudr. *Cdgn* 4E **57**
Rhydlanfair. *Cnwy* 5H **81**
Rhydlewis. *Cdgn* 1D **44**
Rhydlios. *Gwyn* 2A **68**
Rhydlydan. *Cnwy* 5A **82**
Rhyd-meirionydd. *Cdgn* 2F **57**
Rhydowen. *Cdgn* 1E **45**
Rhyd-Rosser. *Cdgn* 4E **57**
Rhydspence. *Powy* 1F **47**
Rhydtalog. *Flin* 5E **83**
Rhyd-uchaf. *Gwyn* 2B **70**
Rhydwyn. *IOA* 2C **80**
Rhyd-y-clafdy. *Gwyn* 2C **68**
Rhydycroesau. *Shrp* 2E **71**
Rhydyfelin. *Cdgn* 3E **57**
Rhydyfelin. *Rhon* 3E **32**
Rhyd-y-foel. *Cnwy* 3B **82**
Rhyd-y-fro. *Neat* 5H **45**
Rhydymain. *Gwyn* 3H **69**
Rhyd-y-meudwy. *Den* 5D **82**
Rhydymwyn. *Flin* 4E **82**
Rhyd-yr-onen. *Gwyn* 5F **69**
Rhyd-y-sarn. *Gwyn* 1F **69**
Rhyl. *Den* 2C **82**
Rhymney. *Cphy* 5E **46**
Rhymni. *Cphy* 5E **46**
Rhynd. *Per* 1D **136**
Rhynie. *Abers* 1B **152**
Ribbesford. *Worc* 3B **60**
Ribbleton. *Lanc* 1D **90**
Ribby. *Lanc* 1C **90**
Ribchester. *Lanc* 1E **91**
Riber. *Derbs* 5H **85**
Ribigill. *High* 3F **167**
Riby. *Linc* 4E **95**
Riccall. *N Yor* 1G **93**
Riccarton. *E Ayr* 1D **116**
Richards Castle. *Here* 4G **59**
Richborough Port. *Kent* 4H **41**
Richhill. *Arm* 5D **178**
Richings Park. *Buck* 3B **38**
Richmond. *G Lon* 3C **38**
Richmond. *N Yor* 4E **105**
Rickarton. *Abers* 5F **153**
Rickerby. *Cumb* 4F **113**
Rickerscote. *Staf* 3D **72**
Rickford. *N Som* 1H **21**
Rickham. *Devn* 5D **8**
Rickinghall. *Suff* 3C **66**
Rickleton. *Tyne* 4F **115**
Rickling. *Essx* 2E **53**
Rickling Green. *Essx* 3F **53**
Rickmansworth. *Herts* 1B **38**
Riddings. *Derbs* 5B **86**
Riddlecombe. *Devn* 1G **11**
Riddlesden. *W Yor* 5C **98**
Ridge. *Dors* 4E **15**
Ridge. *Herts* 5C **52**
Ridge. *Wilts* 3E **23**
Ridgebourne. *Powy* 4C **58**
Ridge Lane. *Warw* 1G **61**
Ridgeway. *Derbs* 5A **86**
(nr. Alfreton)
Ridgeway. *Derbs* 2B **86**
(nr. Sheffield)
Ridgeway. *Staf* 5C **84**
Ridgeway Cross. *Here* 1C **48**
Ridgeway Moor. *Derbs* 2B **86**
Ridgewell. *Essx* 1H **53**
Ridgewood. *E Sus* 3F **27**
Ridgmont. *C Beds* 2H **51**
Ridgwardine. *Shrp* 2A **72**
Riding Mill. *Nmbd* 3D **114**
Ridley. *Kent* 4H **39**
Ridley. *Nmbd* 3A **114**
Ridlington. *Norf* 2F **79**
Ridlington. *Rut* 5F **75**
Ridsdale. *Nmbd* 1C **114**
Riemore Lodge. *Per* 4H **143**
Rievaulx. *N Yor* 1H **99**
Rift House. *Hart* 1B **106**
Rigg. *Dum* 3D **112**
Riggend. *N Lan* 2A **128**
Rigsby. *Linc* 3D **88**
Rigside. *S Lan* 1A **118**
Riley Green. *Lanc* 2E **90**
Rileyhill. *Staf* 4F **73**
Rilla Mill. *Corn* 5C **10**
Rillington. *N Yor* 2C **100**
Rimington. *Lanc* 5H **97**
Rimpton. *Som* 4B **22**
Rimsdale. *High* 4H **167**
Rimswell. *E Yor* 2G **95**
Ringasta. *Shet* 10E **173**
Ringford. *Dum* 4D **111**
Ringing Hill. *Leics* 4B **74**
Ringinglow. *S Yor* 2G **85**
Ringland. *Norf* 4D **78**
Ringlestone. *Kent* 5C **40**
Ringmer. *E Sus* 4F **27**
Ringmore. *Devn* 4C **8**
(nr. Kingsbridge)
Ringmore. *Devn* 5C **12**
(nr. Teignmouth)
Ring o' Bells. *Lanc* 3C **90**
Ring's End. *Cambs* 5C **76**
Ringsfield. *Suff* 2G **67**
Ringsfield Corner. *Suff* 2G **67**
Ringshall. *Buck* 4H **51**
Ringshall. *Suff* 5C **66**
Ringshall Stocks. *Suff* 5C **66**
Ringstead. *Norf* 1G **77**
Ringstead. *Nptn* 3G **63**
Ringwood. *Hants* 2G **15**
Ringwould. *Kent* 1H **29**
Rinmore. *Abers* 2B **152**
Rinnigill. *Orkn* 8C **172**
Rinsey. *Corn* 4C **4**
Riof. *W Isl* 4D **171**
Ripe. *E Sus* 4G **27**
Ripley. *Derbs* 1B **74**
Ripley. *Hants* 3G **15**
Ripley. *N Yor* 3E **99**
Ripley. *Surr* 5B **38**
Riplingham. *E Yor* 1C **94**
Riplington. *Hants* 4E **25**
Ripon. *N Yor* 2F **99**
Rippingale. *Linc* 3H **75**
Ripple. *Kent* 1H **29**
Ripple. *Worc* 2D **48**
Ripponden. *W Yor* 3A **92**
Rireavach. *High* 4E **163**
Risabus. *Arg* 5B **124**
Risbury. *Here* 5H **59**
Risby. *E Yor* 1D **94**
Risby. *N Lin* 3C **94**
Risby. *Suff* 4G **65**
Risca. *Cphy* 2F **33**
Rise. *E Yor* 5F **101**
Riseden. *E Sus* 2H **27**
Riseden. *Kent* 2B **28**
Rise End. *Derbs* 5G **85**
Risegate. *Linc* 2B **76**
Riseholme. *Linc* 3G **87**
Riseley. *Bed* 4H **63**
Riseley. *Wok* 5F **37**
Rishangles. *Suff* 4D **66**
Rishton. *Lanc* 1F **91**
Rishworth. *W Yor* 3A **92**
Risley. *Derbs* 2B **74**
Risley. *Warr* 1A **84**
Risplith. *N Yor* 3E **99**
Rispond. *High* 2E **167**
Rivar. *Wilts* 5B **36**
Rivenhall. *Essx* 4B **54**
Rivenhall End. *Essx* 4B **54**
River. *Kent* 1G **29**
River. *W Sus* 3A **26**
River Bank. *Cambs* 4E **65**
Riverhead. *Kent* 5G **39**
Rivington. *Lanc* 3E **91**
Roach Bridge. *Lanc* 2D **90**
Roachill. *Devn* 4B **20**
Roade. *Nptn* 5E **63**
Road Green. *Norf* 1E **67**
Roadhead. *Cumb* 2G **113**
Roadmeetings. *S Lan* 5B **128**
Roadside. *High* 2D **168**
Roadside of Catterline.
Abers 1H **145**
Roadside of Kinneff.
Abers 1H **145**
Roadwater. *Som* 3D **20**
Road Weedon. *Nptn* 5D **62**
Roag. *High* 4B **154**
Roa Island. *Cumb* 3B **96**
Roath. *Card* 4E **33**
Roberton. *Bord* 3G **119**
Roberton. *S Lan* 2B **118**
Robertsbridge. *E Sus* 3B **28**
Robertstown. *Mor* 4G **159**
Robertstown. *Rhon* 5C **46**
Roberttown. *W Yor* 2B **92**
Robeston Back. *Pemb* 3E **43**
Robeston Wathen. *Pemb* 3E **43**
Robeston West. *Pemb* 4C **42**
Robin Hood. *Lanc* 3D **90**
Robin Hood. *W Yor* 2D **92**
Robin Hood Airport
Doncaster Sheffield.
S Yor 1D **86**
Robinhood End. *Essx* 2H **53**
Robin Hood's Bay.
N Yor 4G **107**
Roborough. *Devn* 1F **11**
(nr. Great Torrington)
Roborough. *Devn* 2B **8**
(nr. Plymouth)
Rob Roy's House. *Arg* 2A **134**
Roby Mill. *Lanc* 4D **90**
Rocester. *Staf* 2F **73**
Roch. *Pemb* 2C **42**
Rochdale. *G Man* 3G **91**
Roche. *Corn* 2D **6**
Rochester. *Medw*
4B **40** & **Medway 197**
Rochester. *Nmbd* 5C **120**
Rochford. *Essx* 1C **40**
Rock. *Corn* 1D **6**
Rock. *Nmbd* 2G **121**
Rock. *W Sus* 4C **26**
Rock. *Worc* 3B **60**
Rockbeare. *Devn* 3D **12**
Rockbourne. *Hants* 1G **15**
Rockcliffe. *Cumb* 3E **113**
Rockcliffe. *Dum* 4F **111**
Rockcliffe Cross. *Cumb* 3E **113**
Rock Ferry. *Mers* 2F **83**
Rockfield. *High* 5G **165**
Rockfield. *Mon* 4H **47**
Rockford. *Hants* 2G **15**
Rockgreen. *Shrp* 3H **59**
Rockhampton. *S Glo* 2B **34**
Rockhead. *Corn* 4A **10**
Rockingham. *Nptn* 1F **63**
Rockland All Saints. *Norf* 1B **66**
Rockland St Mary. *Norf* 5F **79**
Rockland St Peter. *Norf* 1B **66**
Rockley. *Wilts* 4G **35**
Rock, The. *Cook* 2B **178**
Rockwell End. *Buck* 3F **37**
Rockwell Green. *Som* 1E **13**
Rodborough. *Glos* 5D **48**
Rodbourne. *Wilts* 3E **35**
Rodd. *Here* 4F **59**
Roddam. *Nmbd* 2E **121**
Rodden. *Dors* 4B **14**
Roddenloft. *E Ayr* 2D **117**
Roddymoor. *Dur* 1E **105**
Rode. *Som* 1D **22**
Rodeheath. *Ches E* 4C **84**
(nr. Congleton)
Rode Heath. *Ches E* 5C **84**
(nr. Kidsgrove)
Rodel. *W Isl* 9C **171**
Roden. *Telf* 4H **71**
Rodhuish. *Som* 3D **20**
Rodington. *Telf* 4H **71**
Rodington Heath. *Telf* 4H **71**
Rodley. *Glos* 4C **48**
Rodmarton. *Glos* 2E **35**
Rodmell. *E Sus* 5F **27**
Rodmersham. *Kent* 4D **40**
Rodmersham Green.
Kent 4D **40**
Rodney Stoke. *Som* 2H **21**
Rodsley. *Derbs* 1G **73**
Rodway. *Som* 2F **21**
Rodway. *Telf* 4A **72**
Rodwell. *Dors* 5B **14**
Roecliffe. *N Yor* 3F **99**
Roe Green. *Herts* 2D **52**
Roehampton. *G Lon* 3D **38**
Roesound. *Shet* 5E **173**
Roffey. *W Sus* 2C **26**
Rogart. *High* 3E **165**
Rogate. *W Sus* 4G **25**
Roger Ground. *Cumb* 5E **103**
Rogerstone. *Newp* 3F **33**
Rogiet. *Mon* 3H **33**
Rogue's Alley. *Cambs* 5C **76**
Roke. *Oxon* 2E **37**
Rokemarsh. *Oxon* 2E **36**
Roker. *Tyne* 4H **115**
Rollesby. *Norf* 4G **79**
Rolleston. *Leics* 5E **75**
Rolleston. *Notts* 5E **87**
Rolleston on Dove. *Staf* 3G **73**
Rolston. *E Yor* 5G **101**
Rolvenden. *Kent* 2C **28**
Rolvenden Layne. *Kent* 2C **28**
Romaldkirk. *Dur* 2C **104**
Roman Bank. *Shrp* 1H **59**
Romanby. *N Yor* 5A **106**
Roman Camp. *W Lot* 2D **129**
Romannobridge. *Bord* 5E **129**
Romansleigh. *Devn* 4H **19**
Romers Common. *Worc* 4H **59**
Romesdal. *High* 3D **154**
Romford. *Dors* 2F **15**
Romford. *G Lon* 2G **39**
Romiley. *G Man* 1D **84**
Romsey. *Hants* 4B **24**
Romsley. *Shrp* 2B **60**
Romsley. *Worc* 3D **60**
Ronague. *IOM* 4B **108**
Ronaldsvoe. *Orkn* 8D **172**
Rookby. *Cumb* 3B **104**
Rookhope. *Dur* 5C **114**
Rooking. *Cumb* 3F **103**
Rookley. *IOW* 4D **16**
Rooks Bridge. *Som* 1G **21**
Rooksey Green. *Suff* 5B **66**
Rook's Nest. *Som* 3D **20**
Rookwood. *W Sus* 3F **17**
Roos. *E Yor* 1F **95**
Roosebeck. *Cumb* 3B **96**
Roosecote. *Cumb* 3B **96**
Rootfield. *High* 3H **157**
Rootham's Green. *Bed* 5A **64**
Rootpark. *S Lan* 4C **128**
Ropley. *Hants* 3E **25**
Ropley Dean. *Hants* 3E **25**
Ropsley. *Linc* 2G **75**
Rora. *Abers* 3H **161**
Rorandle. *Abers* 2D **152**
Rorrington. *Shrp* 5F **71**
Rose. *Corn* 3B **6**
Roseacre. *Lanc* 1C **90**
Rose Ash. *Devn* 4A **20**
Rosebank. *S Lan* 5B **128**
Rosebush. *Pemb* 2E **43**
Rosedale Abbey. *N Yor* 5E **107**
Roseden. *Nmbd* 2E **121**
Rose Green. *Essx* 3C **54**
Rose Green. *Suff* 1C **54**
Rosehall. *High* 3B **164**
Rosehearty. *Abers* 2G **161**
Rose Hill. *E Sus* 4F **27**
Rose Hill. *Lanc* 1G **91**
Rosehill. *Shrp* 2A **72**
(nr. Market Drayton)
Rosehill. *Shrp* 4G **71**
(nr. Shrewsbury)
Roseisle. *Mor* 2F **159**
Rosemarket. *Pemb* 4D **42**
Rosemarkie. *High* 3B **158**
Rosemary Lane. *Devn* 1E **13**
Rosemount. *Per* 4A **144**
Rosenannon. *Corn* 2D **6**
Roser's Cross. *E Sus* 3G **27**
Rosevean. *Corn* 3E **6**
Rosewell. *Midl* 3F **129**
Roseworth. *Stoc T* 2B **106**
Roseworthy. *Corn* 3D **4**
Rosgill. *Cumb* 3G **103**
Roshven. *High* 1B **140**
Roskhill. *High* 4B **154**
Roskorwell. *Corn* 4E **5**
Rosley. *Cumb* 5E **112**
Roslin. *Midl* 3F **129**
Rosliston. *Derbs* 4G **73**
Rosneath. *Arg* 1D **126**
Ross. *Dum* 5D **110**
Ross. *Nmbd* 1F **121**
Ross. *Per* 1G **135**
Ross. *Bord* 3F **131**
Rossendale. *Lanc* 2F **91**
Rossett. *Wrex* 5F **83**
Rossington. *S Yor* 1D **86**
Rosskeen. *High* 2A **158**
Rossland. *Ren* 2F **127**
Rosslea. *Ferm* 6L **177**
Ross-on-Wye. *Here* 3B **48**
Roster. *High* 4E **169**
Rostherne. *Ches E* 2B **84**
Rostholme. *S Yor* 4F **93**
Rosthwaite. *Cumb* 3D **102**
Roston. *Derbs* 1F **73**
Rostrevor. *New M* 8F **179**
Rosudgeon. *Corn* 4C **4**
Rosyth. *Fife* 1E **129**
Rothbury. *Nmbd* 4E **121**
Rotherby. *Leics* 4D **74**
Rotherfield. *E Sus* 3G **27**
Rotherfield Greys. *Oxon* 3F **37**
Rotherfield Peppard.
Oxon 3F **37**
Rotherham. *S Yor* 1B **86**
Rothersthorpe. *Nptn* 5E **62**
Rotherwick. *Hants* 1F **25**
Rothes. *Mor* 4G **159**
Rothesay. *Arg* 3B **126**
Rothienorman. *Abers* 5E **160**
Rothiesholm. *Orkn* 5F **172**
Rothley. *Leics* 4C **74**
Rothley. *Nmbd* 1D **114**
Rothwell. *Linc* 1A **88**
Rothwell. *Nptn* 2F **63**
Rothwell. *W Yor* 2D **92**
Rotsea. *E Yor* 4E **101**
Rottal. *Ang* 2C **144**
Rotten End. *Suff* 4F **67**
Rotten Row. *Norf* 4C **78**
Rotten Row. *W Ber* 4D **36**
Rotten Row. *W Mid* 3F **61**
Rottingdean. *Brig* 5E **27**
Rottington. *Cumb* 3A **102**
Roud. *IOW* 4D **16**
Rougham. *Norf* 3H **77**
Rougham. *Suff* 4B **66**
Rough Close. *Staf* 2D **72**
Rough Common. *Kent* 5F **41**
Roughcote. *Staf* 1D **72**
Roughfort. *Newt* 1G **179**
Rough Haugh. *High* 4H **167**
Rough Hay. *Staf* 3G **73**
Roughlee. *Lanc* 5H **97**
Roughley. *W Mid* 1F **61**
Roughsike. *Cumb* 2G **113**
Roughton. *Linc* 4B **88**
Roughton. *Norf* 2E **78**
Roughton. *Shrp* 1B **60**
Roundbush Green. *Essx* 4F **53**
Roundham. *Som* 2H **13**
Roundhay. *W Yor* 1D **92**
Round Hill. *Torb* 2F **9**
Roundhurst. *W Sus* 2A **26**
Round Maple. *Suff* 1C **54**
Round Oak. *Shrp* 2F **59**
Roundstreet Common.
W Sus 3B **26**
Roundthwaite. *Cumb* 4H **103**
Roundway. *Wilts* 5F **35**
Roundyhill. *Ang* 3C **144**
Rousdon. *Devn* 3F **13**
Rousham. *Oxon* 3C **50**
Rousky. *Omag* 8B **174**
Rous Lench. *Worc* 5E **61**
Routh. *E Yor* 5E **101**
Rout's Green. *Buck* 2F **37**
Row. *Corn* 5A **10**
Row. *Cumb* 1D **96**
(nr. Kendal)
Row. *Cumb* 1H **103**
(nr. Penrith)
Rowanburn. *Dum* 2F **113**
Rowanhill. *Abers* 3H **161**
Rowardennan. *Stir* 4C **134**
Rowarth. *Derbs* 2E **85**
Row Ash. *Hants* 1D **16**
Rowberrow. *Som* 1H **21**
Rowde. *Wilts* 5E **35**
Rowden. *Devn* 3G **11**
Rowen. *Cnwy* 3G **81**
Rowfoot. *Nmbd* 3H **113**
Row Green. *Essx* 3H **53**
Row Heath. *Essx* 4E **55**
Rowhedge. *Essx* 3D **54**
Rowhook. *W Sus* 2C **26**
Rowington. *Warw* 4G **61**
Rowland. *Derbs* 3G **85**
Rowland's Castle. *Hants* 1F **17**
Rowlands Gill. *Tyne* 4E **115**
Rowledge. *Surr* 2G **25**
Rowley. *Dur* 5D **115**
Rowley. *E Yor* 1C **94**
Rowley. *Shrp* 5F **71**
Rowley Hill. *W Yor* 3B **92**
Rowley Regis. *W Mid* 2D **60**
Rowlstone. *Here* 3G **47**
Rowly. *Surr* 1B **26**
Rowner. *Hants* 2D **16**
Rowney Green. *Worc* 3E **61**
Rownhams. *Hants* 1B **16**
Rowrah. *Cumb* 3B **102**
Rowsham. *Buck* 4G **51**
Rowsley. *Derbs* 4G **85**
Rowstock. *Oxon* 3C **36**
Rowston. *Linc* 5H **87**
Row, The. *Lanc* 2D **96**
Rowthorne. *Derbs* 4B **86**
Rowton. *Ches W* 4G **83**
Rowton. *Shrp* 2G **59**
(nr. Ludlow)
Rowton. *Shrp* 4F **71**
(nr. Shrewsbury)
Rowton. *Telf* 4A **72**
Row Town. *Surr* 4B **38**
Roxburgh. *Bord* 1B **120**
Roxby. *N Lin* 3C **94**
Roxby. *N Yor* 3E **107**
Roxhill. *Ant* 7G **175**
Roxton. *Bed* 5A **64**
Roxwell. *Essx* 5G **53**
Royal Leamington Spa.
Warw 4H **61**
Royal Oak. *Darl* 2F **105**
Royal Oak. *Lanc* 4C **90**
Royal Oak. *N Yor* 2F **101**
Royal's Green. *Ches E* 1A **72**
Royal Tunbridge Wells.
Kent 2G **27**
Royal Wootton Bassett.
Wilts 3F **35**
Roybridge. *High* 5E **149**
Roydon. *Essx* 4E **53**
Roydon. *Norf* 2C **66**
(nr. Diss)
Roydon. *Norf* 3G **77**
(nr. King's Lynn)
Roydon Hamlet. *Essx* 5E **53**
Royston. *Herts* 1D **52**
Royston. *S Yor* 3D **92**
Royston Water. *Som* 1F **13**
Royton. *G Man* 4H **91**
Ruabon. *Wrex* 1F **71**
Ruaig. *Arg* 4B **138**
Ruan High Lanes. *Corn* 5D **6**
Ruan Lanihorne. *Corn* 4C **6**
Ruan Major. *Corn* 5E **5**
Ruan Minor. *Corn* 5E **5**
Ruarach. *High* 1B **148**
Ruardean. *Glos* 4B **48**
Ruardean Hill. *Glos* 4B **48**
Ruardean Woodside.
Glos 4B **48**
Rubane. *Ards* 3L **179**
Rubery. *W Mid* 3D **61**
Ruchazie. *Glas* 3H **127**
Ruckcroft. *Cumb* 5G **113**
Ruckinge. *Kent* 2E **29**
Ruckland. *Linc* 3C **88**
Rucklers Lane. *Herts* 5A **52**
Ruckley. *Shrp* 5H **71**
Rudbaxton. *Pemb* 2D **42**
Rudby. *N Yor* 4B **106**
Ruddington. *Notts* 2C **74**
Rudford. *Glos* 3C **48**
Rudge. *Shrp* 1C **60**
Rudge. *Wilts* 1D **22**
Rudge Heath. *Shrp* 1B **60**
Rudgeway. *S Glo* 3B **34**
Rudgwick. *W Sus* 2B **26**
Rudhall. *Here* 3B **48**
Rudheath. *Ches W* 3A **84**
Rudley Green. *Essx* 5B **54**
Rudloe. *Wilts* 4D **34**
Rudry. *Cphy* 3E **33**
Rudston. *E Yor* 3E **101**
Rudyard. *Staf* 5D **84**
Rufford. *Lanc* 3C **90**
Rufforth. *York* 4H **99**
Rugby. *Warw* 3C **62**
Rugeley. *Staf* 4E **73**
Ruglen. *S Ayr* 4B **116**
Ruilick. *High* 4H **157**
Ruisaurie. *High* 4G **157**
Ruishton. *Som* 4F **21**
Ruisigearraidh. *W Isl* 1E **170**
Ruislip. *G Lon* 2B **38**
Ruislip Common. *G Lon* 2B **38**
Rumbling Bridge. *Per* 4C **136**
Rumburgh. *Suff* 2F **67**
Rumford. *Corn* 1C **6**
Rumford. *Falk* 2C **128**
Rumney. *Card* 4F **33**
Rumwell. *Som* 4E **21**
Runcorn. *Hal* 2H **83**
Runcton. *W Sus* 2G **17**
Runcton Holme. *Norf* 5F **77**
Rundlestone. *Devn* 5F **11**
Runfold. *Surr* 2G **25**
Runhall. *Norf* 5C **78**
Runham. *Norf* 4G **79**
Runnington. *Som* 4E **20**
Runshaw Moor. *Lanc* 3D **90**
Runswick. *N Yor* 3F **107**
Runtaleave. *Ang* 2B **144**
Runwell. *Essx* 1B **40**
Ruscombe. *Wok* 4F **37**
Rushall. *Here* 2B **48**
Rushall. *Norf* 2D **66**
Rushall. *W Mid* 5E **73**
Rushall. *Wilts* 1G **23**
Rushbrooke. *Suff* 4A **66**
Rushbury. *Shrp* 1H **59**
Rushden. *Herts* 2D **52**
Rushden. *Nptn* 4G **63**
Rushenden. *Kent* 3D **40**
Rushford. *Devn* 5E **11**
Rushford. *Suff* 2B **66**
Rush Green. *Herts* 3C **52**
Rushlake Green. *E Sus* 4H **27**
Rushmere. *Suff* 2G **67**
Rushmere St Andrew.
Suff 1E **55**
Rushmoor. *Surr* 2G **25**
Rushock. *Worc* 3C **60**
Rusholme. *G Man* 1C **84**
Rushton. *Ches W* 4H **83**
Rushton. *Nptn* 2F **63**
Rushton. *Shrp* 5A **72**
Rushton Spencer. *Staf* 4D **84**
Rushwick. *Worc* 5C **60**
Rushyford. *Dur* 2F **105**
Ruskie. *Stir* 3F **135**
Ruskington. *Linc* 5H **87**
Rusland. *Cumb* 1C **96**
Rusper. *W Sus* 2D **26**
Ruspidge. *Glos* 4B **48**
Russell's Water. *Oxon* 3F **37**
Russel's Green. *Suff* 3E **67**
Russ Hill. *Surr* 1D **26**
Russland. *Orkn* 6C **172**
Rusthall. *Kent* 2G **27**
Rustington. *W Sus* 5B **26**
Ruston. *N Yor* 1D **100**
Ruston Parva. *E Yor* 3E **101**
Ruswarp. *N Yor* 4F **107**
Rutherglen. *S Lan* 3H **127**
Ruthernbridge. *Corn* 2E **6**
Ruthin. *Den* 5D **82**
Ruthin. *V Glam* 4C **32**
Ruthrieston. *Aber* 3G **153**
Ruthven. *Abers* 4C **160**
Ruthven. *Ang* 4B **144**
Ruthven. *High* 5C **158**
(nr. Inverness)
Ruthven. *High* 4B **150**
(nr. Kingussie)
Ruthvoes. *Corn* 2D **6**
Ruthwaite. *Cumb* 1D **102**
Ruthwell. *Dum* 3C **112**
Ruxton Green. *Here* 4A **48**
Ruyton-XI-Towns. *Shrp* 3F **71**
Ryal. *Nmbd* 2D **114**
Ryall. *Dors* 3H **13**
Ryall. *Worc* 1D **48**
Ryarsh. *Kent* 5A **40**
Rychraggan. *High* 5G **157**
Rydal. *Cumb* 4E **103**
Ryde. *IOW* 3D **16**
Rye. *E Sus* 3D **28**
Ryecroft Gate. *Staf* 4D **84**
Ryeford. *Here* 3B **48**
Rye Foreign. *E Sus* 3D **28**
Rye Harbour. *E Sus* 4D **28**
Ryehill. *E Yor* 2F **95**
Rye Street. *Worc* 2C **48**
Ryhall. *Rut* 4H **75**
Ryhill. *W Yor* 3D **93**
Ryhope. *Tyne* 4H **115**
Ryhope Colliery. *Tyne* 4H **115**
Rylands. *Notts* 2C **74**
Rylstone. *N Yor* 4B **98**
Ryme Intrinseca. *Dors* 1A **14**
Ryther. *N Yor* 1F **93**
Ryton. *Glos* 2C **48**
Ryton. *N Yor* 2B **100**
Ryton. *Shrp* 5B **72**
Ryton. *Tyne* 3E **115**
Ryton. *Warw* 2A **62**
Ryton-on-Dunsmore.
Warw 3A **62**
Ryton Woodside. *Tyne* 3E **115**

S

Saasaig. *High* 3E **147**
Sabden. *Lanc* 1F **91**
Sacombe. *Herts* 4D **52**
Sacriston. *Dur* 5F **115**
Sadberge. *Darl* 3A **106**
Saddell. *Arg* 2B **122**
Saddington. *Leics* 1D **62**
Saddle Bow. *Norf* 4F **77**
Saddlescombe. *W Sus* 4D **26**
Saddleworth. *G Man* 4H **91**
Sadgill. *Cumb* 4F **103**
Saffron Walden. *Essx* 2F **53**
Sageston. *Pemb* 4E **43**
Saham Hills. *Norf* 5B **78**
Saham Toney. *Norf* 5A **78**
Saighdinis. *W Isl* 2D **170**
Saighton. *Ches W* 4G **83**
Sain Dunwyd. *V Glam* 5C **32**
Sain Hilari. *V Glam* 4D **32**
St Abbs. *Bord* 3F **131**
St Agnes. *Corn* 3B **6**
St Albans. *Herts* 5B **52**
St Allen. *Corn* 3C **6**
St Andrews. *Fife* 2H **137**
St Andrews Major.
V Glam 4E **33**
St Anne's. *Lanc* 2B **90**
St Ann's. *Dum* 5C **118**
St Ann's Chapel. *Corn* 5E **11**
St Ann's Chapel. *Devn* 4C **8**
St Anthony. *Corn* 5C **6**
St Anthony-in-Meneage.
Corn 4E **5**
St Arvans. *Mon* 2A **34**
St Asaph. *Den* 3C **82**
St Athan. *V Glam* 5D **32**
Sain Tathan. *V Glam* 5D **32**
St Austell. *Corn* 3E **6**
St Bartholomew's Hill.
Wilts 4E **23**
St Bees. *Cumb* 3A **102**
St Blazey. *Corn* 3E **7**
St Blazey Gate. *Corn* 3E **7**
St Boswells. *Bord* 1A **120**
St Breock. *Corn* 1D **6**
St Breward. *Corn* 5A **10**
St Briavels. *Glos* 5A **48**
St Brides. *Pemb* 3B **42**
St Bride's Major. *V Glam* 4B **32**
St Bride's Netherwent.
Mon 3H **33**
St Bride's-super-Ely.
V Glam 4D **32**
St Brides Wentlooge.
Newp 3F **33**
St Budeaux. *Plym* 3A **8**
Saintbury. *Glos* 2G **49**
St Buryan. *Corn* 4B **4**
St Catherine. *Bath* 4C **34**
St Catherines. *Arg* 3A **134**
St Clears. *Carm* 3G **43**
St Cleer. *Corn* 2G **7**
St Clement. *Corn* 4C **6**
St Clether. *Corn* 4C **10**
St Colmac. *Arg* 3B **126**
St Columb Major. *Corn* 2D **6**
St Columb Minor. *Corn* 2C **6**
St Columb Road. *Corn* 3D **6**
St Combs. *Abers* 2H **161**
St Cross. *Hants* 4C **24**
St Cross South Elmham.
Suff 2E **67**
St Cyrus. *Abers* 2G **145**
St Davids. *Pemb* 2B **42**
St David's. *Per* 1B **136**
St Day. *Corn* 4B **6**
St Dennis. *Corn* 3D **6**
St Dogmaels. *Pemb* 1B **44**
St Dominick. *Corn* 2H **7**
St Donat's. *V Glam* 5C **32**
St Edith's Marsh. *Wilts* 5E **35**
St Endellion. *Corn* 1D **6**
St Enoder. *Corn* 3C **6**
St Erme. *Corn* 4C **6**
St Erney. *Corn* 3H **7**
St Erth. *Corn* 3C **4**
St Erth Praze. *Corn* 3C **4**
St Ervan. *Corn* 1C **6**
St Eval. *Corn* 2C **6**
St Ewe. *Corn* 4D **6**
St Fagans. *Card* 4E **32**
St Fergus. *Abers* 3H **161**
Saintfield. *Down* 4J **179**
St Fillans. *Per* 1F **135**
St Florence. *Pemb* 4E **43**
St Gennys. *Corn* 3B **10**
St George. *Cnwy* 3B **82**
St Georges. *N Som* 5G **33**
St Georges. *V Glam* 4D **32**
St George's Hill. *Surr* 4B **38**
St Germans. *Corn* 3H **7**
St Giles in the Wood.
Devn 1F **11**
St Giles on the Heath.
Devn 3D **10**
St Giles's Hill. *Hants* 4C **24**
St Gluvias. *Corn* 5B **6**
St Harmon. *Powy* 3B **58**
St Helena. *Warw* 5G **73**
St Helen Auckland. *Dur* 2E **105**
St Helens. *Cumb* 1B **102**
St Helen's. *E Sus* 4C **28**
St Helens. *IOW* 4E **17**
St Helens. *Mers* 1G **83**
St Hilary. *Corn* 3C **4**
St Hilary. *V Glam* 4D **32**
Saint Hill. *Devn* 2D **12**
Saint Hill. *W Sus* 2E **27**
St Illtyd. *Blae* 5F **47**
St Ippolyts. *Herts* 3B **52**
St Ishmael. *Carm* 5D **44**
St Ishmael's. *Pemb* 4C **42**
St Issey. *Corn* 1D **6**
St Ive. *Corn* 2H **7**
St Ives. *Cambs* 3C **64**
St Ives. *Corn* 2C **4**
St Ives. *Dors* 2G **15**
St James' End. *Nptn* 4E **63**
St James South Elmham.
Suff 2F **67**
St Jidgey. *Corn* 2D **6**
St John. *Corn* 3A **8**
St John's. *IOM* 3B **108**
St Johns. *Worc* 5C **60**
St John's Chapel. *Devn* 4F **19**
St John's Chapel. *Dur* 1B **104**
St John's Fen End. *Norf* 4E **77**
St John's Hall. *Dur* 1D **104**
St John's Town of Dalry.
Dum 1D **110**
St Judes. *IOM* 2C **108**
St Just. *Corn* 5C **6**
(nr. Falmouth)
St Just. *Corn* 3A **4**
(nr. Penzance)
St Just in Roseland. *Corn* 5C **6**
St Katherines. *Abers* 5E **161**
St Keverne. *Corn* 4E **5**
St Kew. *Corn* 5A **10**
St Kew Highway. *Corn* 5A **10**
St Keyne. *Corn* 2G **7**
St Lawrence. *Corn* 2E **7**
St Lawrence. *Essx* 5C **54**
St Lawrence. *IOW* 5D **16**
St Leonards. *Buck* 5H **51**
St Leonards. *Dors* 2G **15**
St Leonards. *E Sus* 5B **28**
St Levan. *Corn* 4A **4**
St Lythans. *V Glam* 4E **32**
St Mabyn. *Corn* 5A **10**
St Madoes. *Per* 1D **136**
St Margarets. *Here* 2G **47**
St Margaret's. *Herts* 4A **52**
(nr. Hemel Hempstead)
St Margarets. *Herts* 4D **53**
(nr. Hoddesdon)
St Margaret's. *Wilts* 5G **35**
St Margaret's at Cliffe.
Kent 1H **29**
St Margaret's Hope.
Orkn 8D **172**
St Margaret South Elmham.
Suff 2F **67**
St Mark's. *IOM* 4B **108**
St Martin. *Corn* 4E **5**
(nr. Helston)
St Martin. *Corn* 3G **7**
(nr. Looe)
St Martins. *Per* 5A **144**
St Martin's. *Shrp* 2F **71**
St Mary Bourne. *Hants* 1C **24**
St Marychurch. *Torb* 2F **9**
St Mary Church. *V Glam* 4D **32**
St Mary Cray. *G Lon* 4F **39**
St Mary Hill. *V Glam* 4C **32**
St Mary Hoo. *Medw* 3C **40**
St Mary in the Marsh.
Kent 3E **29**
St Mary's. *Orkn* 7D **172**
St Mary's Bay. *Kent* 3E **29**
St Maughan's Green.
Mon 4H **47**
St Mawes. *Corn* 5C **6**
St Mawgan. *Corn* 2C **6**
St Mellion. *Corn* 2H **7**
St Mellons. *Card* 3F **33**
St Merryn. *Corn* 1C **6**
St Mewan. *Corn* 3D **6**
St Michael Caerhays. *Corn* 4D **6**
St Michael Penkevil. *Corn* 4C **6**
St Michaels. *Kent* 2C **28**
St Michaels. *Torb* 3E **9**
St Michaels. *Worc* 4H **59**
St Michael's on Wyre.
Lanc 5D **96**
St Michael South Elmham.
Suff 2F **67**
St Minver. *Corn* 1D **6**
St Monans. *Fife* 3H **137**
St Neot. *Corn* 2F **7**
St Neots. *Cambs* 4A **64**
St Newlyn East. *Corn* 3C **6**
St Nicholas. *Pemb* 1D **42**
St Nicholas. *V Glam* 4D **32**
St Nicholas at Wade.
Kent 4G **41**
St Nicholas South Elmham.
Suff 2F **67**
St Ninians. *Stir* 4H **135**
St Olaves. *Norf* 1G **67**
St Osyth. *Essx* 4E **54**
St Osyth Heath. *Essx* 4E **55**
St Owen's Cross. *Here* 3A **48**
St Paul's Cray. *G Lon* 4F **39**
St Paul's Walden. *Herts* 3B **52**
St Peter's. *Kent* 4H **41**
St Peter The Great. *Worc* 5C **60**
St Petrox. *Pemb* 5D **42**
St Pinnock. *Corn* 2G **7**
St Quivox. *S Ayr* 2C **116**
St Ruan. *Corn* 5E **5**
St Stephen. *Corn* 3D **6**
St Stephens. *Corn* 4D **10**
(nr. Launceston)
St Stephens. *Corn* 3A **8**
(nr. Saltash)
St Teath. *Corn* 4A **10**
St Thomas. *Devn* 3C **12**
St Thomas. *Swan* 3F **31**
St Tudy. *Corn* 5A **10**
St Twynnells. *Pemb* 5D **42**
St Veep. *Corn* 3F **7**
St Vigeans. *Ang* 4F **145**
St Wenn. *Corn* 2D **6**
St Weonards. *Here* 3H **47**
St Winnolls. *Corn* 3H **7**
St Winnow. *Corn* 3F **7**
Salcombe. *Devn* 5D **8**
Salcombe Regis. *Devn* 4E **13**
Salcott. *Essx* 4C **54**
Sale. *G Man* 1B **84**
Saleby. *Linc* 3D **88**
Sale Green. *Worc* 5D **60**
Salehurst. *E Sus* 3B **28**
Salem. *Carm* 3G **45**
Salem. *Cdgn* 2F **57**
Salen. *Arg* 4G **139**
Salen. *High* 2A **140**
Salesbury. *Lanc* 1E **91**
Saleway. *Worc* 5D **60**
Salford. *C Beds* 2H **51**
Salford. *G Man*
1C **84** & **Manchester 197**
Salford. *Oxon* 3A **50**
Salford Priors. *Warw* 5E **61**
Salfords. *Surr* 1D **27**
Salhouse. *Norf* 4F **79**
Saligo. *Arg* 3A **124**
Saline. *Fife* 4C **136**
Salisbury. *Wilts* 3G **23** & **201**
Salkeld Dykes. *Cumb* 1G **103**
Sallachan. *High* 2D **141**
Sallachy. *High* 3C **164**
(nr. Lairg)
Sallachy. *High* 5B **156**
(nr. Stromeferry)
Salle. *Norf* 3D **78**
Salmonby. *Linc* 3C **88**
Salmond's Muir. *Ang* 5E **145**
Salperton. *Glos* 3F **49**
Salph End. *Bed* 5H **63**
Salsburgh. *N Lan* 3B **128**
Salt. *Staf* 3D **72**
Salta. *Cumb* 5B **112**
Saltaire. *W Yor* 1B **92**
Saltash. *Corn* 3A **8**
Saltburn. *High* 2B **158**
Saltburn-by-the-Sea.
Red C 2D **106**
Saltby. *Leics* 3F **75**
Saltcoats. *Cumb* 5B **102**
Saltcoats. *N Ayr* 5D **126**
Saltdean. *Brig* 5E **27**
Salt End. *E Yor* 2E **95**
Salter. *Lanc* 3F **97**
Salterforth. *Lanc* 5A **98**
Salters Lode. *Norf* 5E **77**
Salterswall. *Ches W* 4A **84**
Salterton. *Wilts* 3G **23**
Saltfleet. *Linc* 1D **88**
Saltfleetby All Saints.
Linc 1D **88**
Saltfleetby St Clements.
Linc 1D **88**
Saltfleetby St Peter. *Linc* 2D **88**
Saltford. *Bath* 5B **34**
Salthouse. *Norf* 1C **78**
Saltmarshe. *E Yor* 2A **94**
Saltmead. *Card* 4E **33**
Saltness. *Orkn* 9B **172**
Saltness. *Shet* 7D **173**
Saltney. *Flin* 4F **83**
Salton. *N Yor* 2B **100**
Saltrens. *Devn* 4E **19**
Saltwick. *Nmbd* 2E **115**
Saltwood. *Kent* 2F **29**
Salum. *Arg* 4B **138**
Salwarpe. *Worc* 4C **60**
Salwayash. *Dors* 3H **13**
Samalaman. *High* 1A **140**
Sambourne. *Warw* 4E **61**
Sambourne. *Wilts* 2D **22**
Sambrook. *Telf* 3B **72**
Samhia. *W Isl* 2C **170**
Samlesbury. *Lanc* 1D **90**
Samlesbury Bottoms.
Lanc 2E **90**
Sampford Arundel. *Som* 1E **12**
Sampford Brett. *Som* 2D **20**
Sampford Courtenay.
Devn 2G **11**
Sampford Peverell. *Devn* 1D **12**
Sampford Spiney. *Devn* 5F **11**
Samsonslane. *Orkn* 5F **172**
Samuelston. *E Lot* 2A **130**
Sanaigmore. *Arg* 2A **124**
Sancreed. *Corn* 4B **4**
Sancton. *E Yor* 1C **94**
Sand. *High* 4D **162**
Sand. *Shet* 7E **173**
Sand. *Som* 2H **21**
Sandaig. *Arg* 4A **138**
Sandaig. *High* 3F **147**
Sandale. *Cumb* 5D **112**
Sandal Magna. *W Yor* 3D **92**
Sandavore. *High* 5C **146**
Sanday Airport. *Orkn* 3F **172**
Sandbach. *Ches E* 4B **84**
Sandbank. *Arg* 1C **126**
Sandbanks. *Pool* 4F **15**
Sandend. *Abers* 2C **160**
Sanderstead. *G Lon* 4E **39**
Sandfields. *Neat* 3G **31**
Sandford. *Cumb* 3A **104**
Sandford. *Devn* 2B **12**
Sandford. *Dors* 4E **15**
Sandford. *Hants* 2G **15**
Sandford. *IOW* 4D **16**
Sandford. *N Som* 1H **21**
Sandford. *Shrp* 3F **71**
(nr. Oswestry)
Sandford. *Shrp* 2H **71**
(nr. Whitchurch)
Sandford. *S Lan* 5A **128**
Sandfordhill. *Abers* 4H **161**
Sandford-on-Thames.
Oxon 5D **50**
Sandford Orcas. *Dors* 4B **22**
Sandford St Martin. *Oxon* 3C **50**
Sandgate. *Kent* 2F **29**
Sandgreen. *Dum* 4C **110**
Sandhaven. *Abers* 2G **161**
Sandhead. *Dum* 4F **109**
Sandhill. *Cambs* 2E **65**
Sandhills. *Dors* 1B **14**
Sandhills. *Oxon* 5D **50**
Sandhills. *Surr* 2A **26**
Sandhoe. *Nmbd* 3C **114**
Sand Hole. *E Yor* 1B **94**
Sandholes. *Cook* 2B **178**
Sandholme. *E Yor* 1B **94**
Sandholme. *Linc* 2C **76**
Sandhurst. *Brac* 5G **37**
Sandhurst. *Glos* 3D **48**
Sandhurst. *Kent* 3B **28**
Sandhurst Cross. *Kent* 3B **28**
Sandhutton. *N Yor* 1F **99**
(nr. Thirsk)
Sand Hutton. *N Yor* 4A **100**
(nr. York)
Sandiacre. *Derbs* 2B **74**
Sandilands. *Linc* 2E **89**
Sandiway. *Ches W* 3A **84**
Sandleheath. *Hants* 1G **15**
Sandling. *Kent* 5B **40**
Sandlow Green. *Ches E* 4B **84**
Sandness. *Shet* 6C **173**
Sandon. *Essx* 5H **53**
Sandon. *Herts* 2D **52**
Sandon. *Staf* 3D **72**
Sandonbank. *Staf* 3D **72**
Sandown. *IOW* 4D **16**
Sandplace. *Corn* 3G **7**
Sandridge. *Herts* 4B **52**
Sandringham. *Norf* 3F **77**
Sandsend. *N Yor* 3F **107**
Sandside. *Cumb* 2C **96**
Sandsound. *Shet* 7E **173**
Sands, The. *Surr* 2G **25**
Sandtoft. *N Lin* 4H **93**
Sandvoe. *Shet* 2E **173**
Sandway. *Kent* 5C **40**
Sandwich. *Kent* 5H **41**
Sandwick. *Cumb* 3F **103**
Sandwick. *Orkn* 6B **172**
(on Mainland)
Sandwick. *Orkn* 9D **172**
(on South Ronaldsay)
Sandwick. *Shet* 9F **173**
(on Mainland)
Sandwick. *Shet* 5G **173**
(on Whalsay)
Sandwith. *Cumb* 3A **102**
Sandy. *Carm* 5E **45**
Sandy. *C Beds* 1B **52**
Sandy Bank. *Linc* 5B **88**
Sandycroft. *Flin* 4F **83**
Sandy Cross. *Here* 5A **60**
Sandygate. *Devn* 5B **12**
Sandygate. *IOM* 2C **108**
Sandy Haven. *Pemb* 4C **42**
Sandyhills. *Dum* 4F **111**
Sandylands. *Lanc* 3D **96**
Sandylane. *Swan* 4E **31**
Sandy Lane. *Wilts* 5E **35**
Sandystones. *Bord* 2H **119**
Sandyway. *Here* 3H **47**
Sangobeg. *High* 2E **167**
Sangomore. *High* 2E **166**
Sankyn's Green. *Worc* 4B **60**
Sanna. *High* 2F **139**
Sanndabhaig. *W Isl* 4G **171**
(on Isle of Lewis)
Sanndabhaig. *W Isl* 4D **170**
(on South Uist)
Sannox. *N Ayr* 5B **126**
Sanquhar. *Dum* 3G **117**
Santon. *Cumb* 4B **102**
Santon Bridge. *Cumb* 4C **102**
Santon Downham. *Suff* 2H **65**
Sapcote. *Leics* 1B **62**
Sapey Common. *Here* 4B **60**
Sapiston. *Suff* 3B **66**
Sapley. *Cambs* 3B **64**
Sapperton. *Derbs* 2F **73**
Sapperton. *Glos* 5E **49**
Sapperton. *Linc* 2H **75**
Saracen's Head. *Linc* 3C **76**
Sarclet. *High* 4F **169**
Sardis. *Carm* 5F **45**
Sardis. *Pemb* 4D **42**
(nr. Milford Haven)
Sardis. *Pemb* 4F **43**
(nr. Tenby)
Sarisbury. *Hants* 2D **16**
Sarn. *B'end* 3C **32**
Sarn. *Powy* 1E **58**
Sarnau. *Carm* 3E **45**
Sarnau. *Cdgn* 5C **56**
Sarnau. *Gwyn* 2B **70**
Sarnau. *Powy* 2D **46**
(nr. Brecon)
Sarnau. *Powy* 4E **71**
(nr. Welshpool)
Sarn Bach. *Gwyn* 3C **68**
Sarnesfield. *Here* 5F **59**
Sarn Meyllteyrn. *Gwyn* 2B **68**
Saron. *Carm* 4G **45**
(nr. Ammanford)
Saron. *Carm* 2D **45**
(nr. Newcastle Emlyn)
Saron. *Gwyn* 4E **81**
(nr. Bethel)
Saron. *Gwyn* 5D **80**
(nr. Bontnewydd)
Sarratt. *Herts* 1B **38**
Sarre. *Kent* 4G **41**
Sarsden. *Oxon* 3A **50**

Treator—Waringstown

Treator. *Corn* 1D 6
Trebanog. *Rhon* 2D 32
Trebanos. *Neat* 5H 45
Trebarber. *Corn* 2C 6
Trebartha. *Corn* 5C 10
Trebarwith. *Corn* 4A 10
Trebetherick. *Corn* 1D 6
Treborough. *Som* 3D 20
Trebudannon. *Corn* 2C 6
Trebullett. *Corn* 5D 10
Treburley. *Corn* 5D 10
Treburrick. *Corn* 1C 6
Trebyan. *Corn* 2E 7
Trecastle. *Powy* 3B 46
Trecenydd. *Cphy* 3E 33
Trecott. *Devn* 2G 11
Trecwn. *Pemb* 1D 42
Trecynon. *Rhon* 5C 46
Tredaule. *Corn* 4C 10
Tredavoe. *Corn* 4B 4
Tredegar. *Blae* 5E 47
Trederwen. *Powy* 4E 71
Tredington. *Glos* 3E 49
Tredington. *Warw* 1A 50
Tredinnick. *Corn* 2F 7 (nr. Bodmin)
Tredinnick. *Corn* 3G 7 (nr. Looe)
Tredinnick. *Corn* 1D 6 (nr. Padstow)
Tredogan. *V Glam* 5D 32
Tredomen. *Powy* 2E 46
Tredunnock. *Mon* 2G 33
Tredustan. *Powy* 2E 47
Treen. *Corn* 4A 4 (nr. Land's End)
Treen. *Corn* 3B 4 (nr. St Ives)
Treeton. *S Yor* 2B 86
Trefaldwyn. *Powy* 1E 58
Trefasser. *Pemb* 1C 42
Trefdraeth. *IOA* 3D 80
Trefdraeth. *Pemb* 1E 43
Trefecca. *Powy* 2E 47
Trefechan. *Mer T* 5D 46
Trefeglwys. *Powy* 1B 58
Trefenter. *Cdgn* 4F 57
Treffgarne. *Pemb* 2D 42
Treffynnon. *Flin* 3D 82
Treffynnon. *Pemb* 2C 42
Trefil. *Blae* 4E 46
Trefilan. *Cdgn* 5E 57
Trefin. *Pemb* 1C 42
Treflach. *Shrp* 3E 71
Trefnant. *Den* 3C 82
Trefonen. *Shrp* 3E 71
Trefor. *Gwyn* 1C 68
Trefor. *IOA* 2C 80
Treforest. *Rhon* 3D 32
Trefrew. *Corn* 4B 10
Trefriw. *Cnwy* 4G 81
Tref-y-Clawdd. *Powy* 3E 59
Trefynwy. *Mon* 4A 48
Tregada. *Corn* 4D 10
Tregadillett. *Corn* 4D 10
Tregare. *Mon* 4H 47
Tregarne. *Corn* 4E 5
Tregaron. *Cdgn* 5F 57
Tregarth. *Gwyn* 4F 81
Tregear. *Corn* 3C 6
Tregeare. *Corn* 4C 10
Tregeiriog. *Wrex* 2D 70
Tregele. *IOA* 1C 80
Tregeseal. *Corn* 3A 4
Tregiskey. *Corn* 4E 6
Tregole. *Corn* 3B 10
Tregolwyn. *V Glam* 4C 32
Tregonetha. *Corn* 2D 6
Tregonhawke. *Corn* 3A 8
Tregony. *Corn* 4D 6
Tregoodwell. *Corn* 4B 10
Tregorrick. *Corn* 3E 6
Tregoss. *Corn* 2D 6
Tregowris. *Corn* 4E 5
Tregoyd. *Powy* 2E 47
Tregrehan Mills. *Corn* 3E 7
Tre-groes. *Cdgn* 1E 45
Tregullon. *Corn* 2E 7
Tregurrian. *Corn* 2C 6
Tregynon. *Powy* 1C 58
Trehafod. *Rhon* 2D 32
Trehan. *Corn* 3A 8
Treharris. *Mer T* 2E 32
Treherbert. *Rhon* 2C 32
Trehunist. *Corn* 2H 7
Trekenner. *Corn* 5D 10
Trekenning. *Corn* 2D 6
Treknow. *Corn* 4A 10
Trelales. *B'end* 3B 32
Trelan. *Corn* 5E 5
Trelash. *Corn* 3B 10
Trelassick. *Corn* 3C 6
Trelawnyd. *Flin* 3C 82
Trelech. *Carm* 1G 43
Treleddyd-fawr. *Pemb* 2B 42
Trelewis. *Mer T* 2E 32
Treligga. *Corn* 4A 10
Trelights. *Corn* 1D 6
Trelill. *Corn* 5A 10
Trelissick. *Corn* 5C 6
Trellech. *Mon* 5A 48
Trelleck Grange. *Mon* 5H 47
Trelogan. *Flin* 2D 82
Trelystan. *Powy* 5E 71
Tremadog. *Gwyn* 1E 69
Tremail. *Corn* 4B 10
Tremain. *Cdgn* 1C 44
Tremaine. *Corn* 4C 10
Tremar. *Corn* 2G 7
Trematon. *Corn* 3H 7
Tremeirchion. *Den* 3C 82
Tremore. *Corn* 2E 6
Tremorfa. *Card* 4F 33
Trenance. *Corn* 2C 6 (nr. Newquay)
Trenance. *Corn* 1D 6 (nr. Padstow)
Trenarren. *Corn* 4E 7
Trench. *Telf* 4A 72
Trencreek. *Corn* 2C 6
Trendeal. *Corn* 3C 6
Trenear. *Corn* 5A 6
Treneglos. *Corn* 4C 10
Trenewan. *Corn* 3F 7
Trengune. *Corn* 3B 10
Trent. *Dors* 1A 14
Trentham. *Stoke* 1C 72
Trentishoe. *Devn* 2G 19
Trentlock. *Derbs* 2B 74
Treoes. *V Glam* 4C 32
Treorchy. *Rhon* 2C 32
Treorci. *Rhon* 2C 32
Tre'r-ddol. *Cdgn* 1F 57
Tre'r llai. *Powy* 5E 71
Trerulefoot. *Corn* 3H 7
Tresaith. *Cdgn* 5B 56
Trescott. *Staf* 1C 60
Trescowe. *Corn* 3C 4
Tresham. *Glos* 2C 34
Tresigin. *V Glam* 4C 32
Tresillian. *Corn* 4C 6
Tresimwn. *V Glam* 4D 32
Tresinney. *Corn* 4B 10
Treskillard. *Corn* 5A 6
Treskinnick Cross. *Corn* 3C 10
Tresmeer. *Corn* 4C 10
Tresparrett. *Corn* 3B 10
Tresparrett Posts. *Corn* 3B 10
Tressady. *High* 3D 164
Tressait. *Per* 2F 143
Tresta. *Shet* 2H 173 (on Fetlar)
Tresta. *Shet* 6E 173 (on Mainland)
Treswell. *Notts* 3E 87
Treswithian. *Corn* 3D 4
Tre Taliesin. *Cdgn* 1F 57
Trethomas. *Cphy* 3E 33
Trethosa. *Corn* 3D 6
Trethurgy. *Corn* 3E 7
Tretio. *Pemb* 2B 42
Tretire. *Here* 3A 48
Tretower. *Powy* 3E 47
Treuddyn. *Flin* 5E 83
Trevadlock. *Corn* 5C 10
Trevalga. *Corn* 3A 10
Trevalyn. *Wrex* 5F 83
Trevance. *Corn* 1D 6
Trevanger. *Corn* 1D 6
Trevanson. *Corn* 1D 6
Trevarrack. *Corn* 3B 4
Trevarren. *Corn* 2D 6
Trevarrian. *Corn* 2C 6
Trevarrick. *Corn* 4D 6
Tre-vaughan. *Carm* 3E 45 (nr. Carmarthen)
Trevaughan. *Carm* 3F 43 (nr. Whitland)
Treveighan. *Corn* 5A 10
Trevellas. *Corn* 3B 6
Trevelmond. *Corn* 2G 7
Treverva. *Corn* 5B 6
Trevescan. *Corn* 4A 4
Trevethin. *Torf* 5F 47
Trevia. *Corn* 4A 10
Trevigro. *Corn* 2H 7
Trevilley. *Corn* 4A 4
Treviscoe. *Corn* 3D 6
Trevivian. *Corn* 4B 10
Trevone. *Corn* 1C 6
Trevor. *Wrex* 1E 71
Trevor Uchaf. *Den* 1E 71
Trew. *Corn* 4D 4
Trewalder. *Corn* 4A 10
Trewarlett. *Corn* 4D 10
Trewarmett. *Corn* 4A 10
Trewassa. *Corn* 4B 10
Treween. *Corn* 4C 10
Trewellard. *Corn* 3A 4
Trewen. *Corn* 4C 10
Trewennack. *Corn* 4D 5
Trewern. *Powy* 4E 71
Trewetha. *Corn* 5A 10
Trewidland. *Corn* 2G 7
Trewint. *Corn* 3B 10
Trewithian. *Corn* 5C 6
Trewoofe. *Corn* 4B 4
Trewoon. *Corn* 3D 6
Treworthal. *Corn* 5C 6
Trewyddel. *Pemb* 1B 44
Treyarnon. *Corn* 1C 6
Treyford. *W Sus* 1G 17
Triangle. *Staf* 5E 73
Triangle. *W Yor* 2A 92
Trickett's Cross. *Dors* 2F 15
Trillick. *Omag* 7F 176
Trimdon. *Dur* 1A 106
Trimdon Colliery. *Dur* 1A 106
Trimdon Grange. *Dur* 1A 106
Trimingham. *Norf* 2E 79
Trimley Lower Street. *Suff* 2F 55
Trimley St Martin. *Suff* 2F 55
Trimley St Mary. *Suff* 2F 55
Trimpley. *Worc* 3B 60
Trimsaran. *Carm* 5E 45
Trimstone. *Devn* 2F 19
Trinafour. *Per* 2E 142
Trinant. *Cphy* 2F 33
Tring. *Herts* 4H 51
Trinity. *Ang* 2F 145
Trinity. *Edin* 2F 129
Trisant. *Cdgn* 3G 57
Triscombe. *Som* 3E 21
Trislaig. *High* 1E 141
Trispen. *Corn* 3C 6
Tritlington. *Nmbd* 5G 121
Trochry. *Per* 4G 143
Troedrhiwdalar. *Powy* 5B 58
Troedrhiwfuwch. *Cphy* 5E 47
Troedrhiwgwair. *Blae* 5E 47
Troedyraur. *Cdgn* 1D 44
Troedyrhiw. *Mer T* 5D 46
Trondavoe. *Shet* 4E 173
Troon. *Corn* 5A 6
Troon. *S Ayr* 1C 116
Troqueer. *Dum* 2A 112
Troston. *Suff* 3A 66
Trottiscliffe. *Kent* 4H 39
Trotton. *W Sus* 4G 25
Troutbeck. *Cumb* 4F 103 (nr. Ambleside)
Troutbeck. *Cumb* 2E 103 (nr. Penrith)
Troutbeck Bridge. *Cumb* 4F 103
Troway. *Derbs* 3A 86
Trowbridge. *Wilts* 1D 22
Trowell. *Notts* 2B 74
Trowle Common. *Wilts* 1D 22
Trowley Bottom. *Herts* 4A 52
Trowse Newton. *Norf* 5E 79
Trudoxhill. *Som* 2C 22
Trull. *Som* 4F 21
Trumaisgearraidh. *W Isl* 1D 170
Trumpan. *High* 2B 154
Trumpet. *Here* 2B 48
Trumpington. *Cambs* 5D 64
Trumps Green. *Surr* 4A 38
Trunch. *Norf* 2E 79
Trunnah. *Lanc* 5C 96
Truro. *Corn* 4C 6
Trusham. *Devn* 4B 12
Trusley. *Derbs* 2G 73
Trusthorpe. *Linc* 2E 89
Tryfil. *IOA* 2D 80
Trysull. *Staf* 1C 60
Tubney. *Oxon* 2C 36
Tuckenhay. *Devn* 3E 9
Tuckhill. *Staf* 2B 60
Tuckingmill. *Corn* 4A 6
Tuckton. *Bour* 3G 15
Tuddenham. *Suff* 3G 65
Tuddenham St Martin. *Suff* 1E 55
Tudeley. *Kent* 1H 27
Tudhoe. *Dur* 1F 105
Tudhoe Grange. *Dur* 1F 105
Tudorville. *Here* 3A 48
Tudweiliog. *Gwyn* 2B 68
Tuesley. *Surr* 1A 26
Tufton. *Hants* 2C 24
Tufton. *Pemb* 2E 43
Tugby. *Leics* 5E 75
Tugford. *Shrp* 2H 59
Tughall. *Nmbd* 2G 121
Tulchan. *Per* 1B 136
Tullibardine. *Per* 2B 136
Tullibody. *Clac* 4A 136
Tullich. *Arg* 2H 133
Tullich. *High* 4B 156 (nr. Lochcarron)
Tullich. *High* 1C 158 (nr. Tain)
Tullich. *Mor* 4H 159
Tullich Muir. *High* 1B 158
Tulliemet. *Per* 3G 143
Tulloch. *Abers* 5F 161
Tulloch. *High* 4D 164 (nr. Bonar Bridge)
Tulloch. *High* 5F 149 (nr. Fort William)
Tulloch. *High* 2D 151 (nr. Grantown-on-Spey)
Tulloch. *Per* 1C 136
Tullochgorm. *Arg* 4G 133
Tullybeagles Lodge. *Per* 5H 143
Tullyhogue. *Cook* 2C 178
Tullymurdoch. *Per* 3A 144
Tullynessle. *Abers* 2C 152
Tumble. *Carm* 4F 45
Tumbler's Green. *Essx* 3B 54
Tumby. *Linc* 4B 88
Tumby Woodside. *Linc* 5B 88
Tummel Bridge. *Per* 3E 143
Tunbridge Wells, Royal. *Kent* 2G 27
Tunga. *W Isl* 4G 171
Tungate. *Norf* 3E 79
Tunley. *Bath* 1B 22
Tunstall. *E Yor* 1G 95
Tunstall. *Kent* 4C 40
Tunstall. *Lanc* 2F 97
Tunstall. *Norf* 5G 79
Tunstall. *N Yor* 5F 105
Tunstall. *Staf* 3B 72
Tunstall. *Stoke* 5C 84
Tunstall. *Suff* 5F 67
Tunstall. *Tyne* 4G 115
Tunstead. *Derbs* 3F 85
Tunstead. *Norf* 3E 79
Tunstead Milton. *Derbs* 2E 85
Tunworth. *Hants* 2E 25
Tupsley. *Here* 1A 48
Tupton. *Derbs* 4A 86
Turfholm. *S Lan* 1H 117
Turfmoor. *Devn* 2F 13
Turgis Green. *Hants* 1E 25
Turkdean. *Glos* 4G 49
Turkey Island. *Hants* 1D 16
Tur Langton. *Leics* 1E 62
Turleigh. *Wilts* 5D 34
Turlin Moor. *Pool* 3E 15
Turnastone. *Here* 2G 47
Turnberry. *S Ayr* 4B 116
Turnchapel. *Plym* 3A 8
Turnditch. *Derbs* 1G 73
Turners Hill. *W Sus* 2E 27
Turners Puddle. *Dors* 3D 14
Turnford. *Herts* 5D 52
Turnhouse. *Edin* 2E 129
Turnworth. *Dors* 2D 14
Turriff. *Abers* 4E 161
Tursdale. *Dur* 1A 106
Turton Bottoms. *Bkbn* 3F 91
Turtory. *Mor* 4C 160
Turves Green. *W Mid* 3E 61
Turvey. *Bed* 5G 63
Turville. *Buck* 2F 37
Turville Heath. *Buck* 2F 37
Turweston. *Buck* 2E 50
Tushielaw. *Bord* 3F 119
Tutbury. *Staf* 3G 73
Tutnall. *Worc* 3D 61
Tutshill. *Glos* 2A 34
Tuttington. *Norf* 3E 79
Tutts Clump. *W Ber* 4D 36
Tutwell. *Corn* 5D 11
Tuxford. *Notts* 3E 87
Twatt. *Orkn* 5B 172
Twatt. *Shet* 6E 173
Twechar. *E Dun* 2A 128
Tweedale. *Telf* 5B 72
Tweedmouth. *Nmbd* 4F 131
Tweedsmuir. *Bord* 2C 118
Twelveheads. *Corn* 4B 6
Twemlow Green. *Ches E* 4B 84
Twenty. *Linc* 3A 76
Twerton. *Bath* 5C 34
Twickenham. *G Lon* 3C 38
Twigworth. *Glos* 3D 48
Twineham. *W Sus* 3D 26
Twinhoe. *Bath* 1C 22
Twinstead. *Essx* 2B 54
Twinstead Green. *Essx* 2B 54
Twiss Green. *Warr* 1A 84
Twiston. *Lanc* 5H 97
Twitchen. *Devn* 3A 20
Twitchen. *Shrp* 3F 59
Two Bridges. *Devn* 5G 11
Two Bridges. *Glos* 5B 48
Two Dales. *Derbs* 4G 85
Two Gates. *Staf* 5G 73
Two Mile Oak. *Devn* 2E 9
Twycross. *Leics* 5H 73
Twyford. *Buck* 3E 51
Twyford. *Derbs* 3H 73
Twyford. *Dors* 1D 14
Twyford. *Hants* 4C 24
Twyford. *Leics* 4E 75
Twyford. *Norf* 3C 78
Twyford. *Wok* 4F 37
Twyford Common. *Here* 2A 48
Twyncarno. *Cphy* 5E 46
Twynholm. *Dum* 4D 110
Twyning. *Glos* 2D 49
Twyning Green. *Glos* 2E 49
Twynllanan. *Carm* 3A 46
Twyn-y-Sheriff. *Mon* 5H 47
Twywell. *Nptn* 3G 63
Tyberton. *Here* 2G 47
Tyburn. *W Mid* 1F 61
Tyby. *Norf* 3C 78
Tycroes. *Carm* 4G 45
Tycrwyn. *Powy* 4D 70
Tyddewi. *Pemb* 2B 42
Tydd Gote. *Linc* 4D 76
Tydd St Giles. *Cambs* 4D 76
Tydd St Mary. *Linc* 4D 76
Tye. *Hants* 2F 17
Tye Green. *Essx* 3F 53 (nr. Bishop's Stortford)
Tye Green. *Essx* 3A 54 (nr. Braintree)
Tye Green. *Essx* 2F 53 (nr. Saffron Walden)
Tyersal. *W Yor* 1B 92
Ty Issa. *Powy* 3D 70
Tyldesley. *G Man* 4E 91
Tyler Hill. *Kent* 4F 41
Tylers Green. *Buck* 2G 37
Tyler's Green. *Essx* 5F 53
Tylorstown. *Rhon* 2D 32
Tylwch. *Powy* 2B 58
Tynan. *Arm* 5B 178
Ty-nant. *Cnwy* 1B 70
Tyndrum. *Stir* 5H 141
Tyneham. *Dors* 4D 15
Tynehead. *Midl* 4G 129
Tynemouth. *Tyne* 3G 115
Tyneside. *Tyne* 3F 115
Tyne Tunnel. *Tyne* 3G 115
Tynewydd. *Rhon* 2C 32
Tyninghame. *E Lot* 2C 130
Tynron. *Dum* 5H 117
Ty'n-y-bryn. *Rhon* 3D 32
Tyn-y-celyn. *Wrex* 2D 70
Tyn-y-cwm. *Swan* 5G 45
Tyn-y-ffridd. *Powy* 2D 70
Tynygongl. *IOA* 2E 81
Tynygraig. *Cdgn* 4F 57
Tyn-y-groes. *Cnwy* 3G 81
Ty'n-yr-eithin. *Cdgn* 4F 57
Tyn-y-rhyd. *Powy* 4C 70
Tyn-y-wern. *Powy* 3C 70
Tyrie. *Abers* 2G 161
Tyringham. *Mil* 1G 51
Tythecott. *Devn* 1E 11
Tythegston. *B'end* 4B 32
Tytherington. *Ches E* 3D 84
Tytherington. *Som* 2C 22
Tytherington. *S Glo* 3B 34
Tytherington. *Wilts* 2E 23
Tytherleigh. *Devn* 2G 13
Tywardreath. *Corn* 3E 7
Tywardreath Highway. *Corn* 3E 7
Tywyn. *Cnwy* 3G 81
Tywyn. *Gwyn* 5E 69

U

Uachdar. *W Isl* 3D 170
Uags. *High* 5G 155
Ubbeston Green. *Suff* 3F 67
Ubley. *Bath* 1A 22
Uckerby. *N Yor* 4F 105
Uckfield. *E Sus* 3F 27
Uckinghall. *Worc* 2D 48
Uckington. *Glos* 3E 49
Uckington. *Shrp* 5H 71
Uddingston. *S Lan* 3H 127
Uddington. *S Lan* 1A 118
Udimore. *E Sus* 4C 28
Udny Green. *Abers* 1F 153
Udny Station. *Abers* 1G 153
Udston. *S Lan* 4A 128
Udstonhead. *S Lan* 5A 128
Uffcott. *Wilts* 4G 35
Uffculme. *Devn* 1D 12
Uffington. *Linc* 5H 75
Uffington. *Oxon* 3B 36
Uffington. *Shrp* 4H 71
Ufford. *Pet* 5H 75
Ufford. *Suff* 5E 67
Ufton. *Warw* 4A 62
Ufton Nervet. *W Ber* 5E 37
Ugadale. *Arg* 3B 122
Ugborough. *Devn* 3C 8
Ugford. *Wilts* 3F 23
Uggeshall. *Suff* 2G 67
Ugglebarnby. *N Yor* 4F 107
Ugley. *Essx* 3F 53
Ugley Green. *Essx* 3F 53
Ugthorpe. *N Yor* 3E 107
Uidh. *W Isl* 9B 170
Uig. *Arg* 3C 138
Uig. *High* 2C 154 (nr. Balgown)
Uig. *High* 3A 154 (nr. Dunvegan)
Uigshader. *High* 4D 154
Uisken. *Arg* 2A 132
Ulbster. *High* 4F 169
Ulcat Row. *Cumb* 2F 103
Ulceby. *Linc* 3D 88
Ulceby. *N Lin* 3E 94
Ulceby Skitter. *N Lin* 3E 94
Ulcombe. *Kent* 1C 28
Uldale. *Cumb* 1D 102
Uley. *Glos* 2C 34
Ulgham. *Nmbd* 5G 121
Ullapool. *High* 4F 163
Ullenhall. *Warw* 4F 61
Ulleskelf. *N Yor* 1F 93
Ullesthorpe. *Leics* 2C 62
Ulley. *S Yor* 2B 86
Ullingswick. *Here* 1A 48
Ullinish. *High* 5C 154
Ullock. *Cumb* 2B 102
Ulpha. *Cumb* 5C 102
Ulrome. *E Yor* 4F 101
Ulsta. *Shet* 3F 173
Ulting. *Essx* 5B 54
Ulva House. *Arg* 5F 139
Ulverston. *Cumb* 2B 96
Ulwell. *Dors* 4F 15
Umberleigh. *Devn* 4G 19
Unapool. *High* 5C 166
Underbarrow. *Cumb* 5F 103
Undercliffe. *W Yor* 1B 92
Underdale. *Shrp* 4H 71
Underhoull. *Shet* 1G 173
Underriver. *Kent* 5G 39
Under Tofts. *S Yor* 2H 85
Underton. *Shrp* 1A 60
Underwood. *Newp* 3G 33
Underwood. *Notts* 5B 86
Underwood. *Plym* 3B 8
Undley. *Suff* 2F 65
Undy. *Mon* 3H 33
Union Mills. *IOM* 4C 108
Union Street. *E Sus* 2B 28
Unstone. *Derbs* 3A 86
Unstone Green. *Derbs* 3A 86
Unthank. *Cumb* 5E 113 (nr. Carlisle)
Unthank. *Cumb* 5H 113 (nr. Gamblesby)
Unthank. *Cumb* 1F 103 (nr. Penrith)
Unthank End. *Cumb* 1F 103
Upavon. *Wilts* 1G 23
Up Cerne. *Dors* 2B 14
Upchurch. *Kent* 4C 40
Upcott. *Devn* 2F 11
Upcott. *Here* 5F 59
Upend. *Cambs* 5G 65
Up Exe. *Devn* 2C 12
Upgate. *Norf* 4D 78
Upgate Street. *Norf* 1C 66
Uphall. *Dors* 2A 14
Uphall. *W Lot* 2D 128
Uphall Station. *W Lot* 2D 128
Upham. *Devn* 2B 12
Upham. *Hants* 4D 24
Uphampton. *Here* 4F 59
Uphampton. *Worc* 4C 60
Up Hatherley. *Glos* 3E 49
Uphill. *N Som* 1G 21
Up Holland. *Lanc* 4D 90
Uplawmoor. *E Ren* 4F 127
Upleadon. *Glos* 3C 48
Upleatham. *Red C* 3D 106
Uplees. *Kent* 4D 40
Uploders. *Dors* 3A 14
Uplowman. *Devn* 1D 12
Uplyme. *Devn* 3G 13
Up Marden. *W Sus* 1F 17
Upminster. *G Lon* 2G 39
Up Nately. *Hants* 1E 25
Upottery. *Devn* 2F 13
Uppat. *High* 3F 165
Upper Affcot. *Shrp* 2G 59
Upper Arley. *Worc* 2B 60
Upper Armley. *W Yor* 1C 92
Upper Arncott. *Oxon* 4E 50
Upper Astrop. *Nptn* 2D 50
Upper Badcall. *High* 4B 166
Upper Ballinderry. *Lis* 3F 179
Upper Bangor. *Gwyn* 3E 81
Upper Basildon. *W Ber* 4D 36
Upper Batley. *W Yor* 2C 92
Upper Beeding. *W Sus* 4C 26
Upper Benefield. *Nptn* 2G 63
Upper Bentley. *Worc* 4D 61
Upper Bighouse. *High* 3A 168
Upper Boddam. *Abers* 5D 160
Upper Boddington. *Nptn* 5B 62
Upper Bogside. *Mor* 3G 159
Upper Booth. *Derbs* 2F 85
Upper Borth. *Cdgn* 2F 57
Upper Boyndlie. *Abers* 2G 161
Upper Brailes. *Warw* 2B 50
Upper Breinton. *Here* 1H 47
Upper Broadheath. *Worc* 5C 60
Upper Broughton. *Notts* 3D 74
Upper Brynamman. *Carm* 4H 45
Upper Bucklebury. *W Ber* 5D 36
Upper Bullington. *Hants* 2C 24
Upper Burgate. *Hants* 1G 15
Upper Caldecote. *C Beds* 1B 52
Upper Canterton. *Hants* 1A 16
Upper Catesby. *Nptn* 5C 62
Upper Chapel. *Powy* 1D 46
Upper Cheddon. *Som* 4F 21
Upper Chicksgrove. *Wilts* 4E 23
Upper Church Village. *Rhon* 3D 32
Upper Chute. *Wilts* 1A 24
Upper Clatford. *Hants* 2B 24
Upper Coberley. *Glos* 4E 49
Upper Coedcae. *Torf* 5F 47
Upper Cokeham. *W Sus* 5C 26
Upper Common. *Hants* 2E 25
Upper Cound. *Shrp* 5H 71
Upper Cudworth. *S Yor* 4D 93
Upper Cumberworth. *W Yor* 4C 92
Upper Cuttlehill. *Abers* 4B 160
Upper Cwmbran. *Torf* 2F 33
Upper Dallachy. *Mor* 2A 160
Upper Dean. *Bed* 4H 63
Upper Denby. *W Yor* 4C 92
Upper Derraid. *High* 5E 159
Upper Diabaig. *High* 2H 155
Upper Dicker. *E Sus* 5G 27
Upper Dinchope. *Shrp* 2G 59
Upper Dochcarty. *High* 2H 157
Upper Dounreay. *High* 2B 168
Upper Dovercourt. *Essx* 2F 55
Upper Dunsforth. *N Yor* 3G 99
Upper Dunsley. *Herts* 4H 51
Upper Eastern Green. *W Mid* 2G 61
Upper Elkstone. *Staf* 5E 85
Upper Ellastone. *Staf* 1F 73
Upper End. *Derbs* 3E 85
Upper Enham. *Hants* 2B 24
Upper Farmcote. *Shrp* 1B 60
Upper Farringdon. *Hants* 3F 25
Upper Framilode. *Glos* 4C 48
Upper Froyle. *Hants* 2F 25
Upper Gills. *High* 1F 169
Upper Glenfintaig. *High* 5E 149
Upper Godney. *Som* 2H 21
Upper Gravenhurst. *C Beds* 2B 52
Upper Green. *Essx* 2E 53
Upper Green. *W Ber* 5B 36
Upper Green. *W Yor* 2C 92
Upper Grove Common. *Here* 3A 48
Upper Hackney. *Derbs* 4G 85
Upper Hale. *Surr* 2G 25
Upper Halliford. *Surr* 4B 38
Upper Halling. *Medw* 4A 40
Upper Hambleton. *Rut* 5G 75
Upper Hardres Court. *Kent* 5F 41
Upper Hardwick. *Here* 5G 59
Upper Hartfield. *E Sus* 2F 27
Upper Haugh. *S Yor* 1B 86
Upper Hayton. *Shrp* 2H 59
Upper Heath. *Shrp* 2H 59
Upper Hellesdon. *Norf* 4E 79
Upper Helmsley. *N Yor* 4A 100
Upper Hengoed. *Shrp* 2E 71
Upper Hergest. *Here* 5E 59
Upper Heyford. *Nptn* 5D 62
Upper Heyford. *Oxon* 3C 50
Upper Hill. *Here* 5G 59
Upper Hindhope. *Bord* 4B 120
Upper Hopton. *W Yor* 3B 92
Upper Howsell. *Worc* 1C 48
Upper Hulme. *Staf* 4E 85
Upper Inglesham. *Swin* 2H 35
Upper Kilcott. *Glos* 3C 34
Upper Killay. *Swan* 3E 31
Upper Kirkton. *Abers* 5E 161
Upper Kirkton. *N Ayr* 4C 126
Upper Knockando. *Mor* 4F 159
Upper Knockchoilum. *High* 2G 149
Upper Lambourn. *W Ber* 3B 36
Upperlands. *Mag* 6E 174
Upper Langford. *N Som* 1H 21
Upper Langwith. *Derbs* 4C 86
Upper Largo. *Fife* 3G 137
Upper Latheron. *High* 5D 169
Upper Layham. *Suff* 1D 54
Upper Leigh. *Staf* 2E 73
Upper Lenie. *High* 1H 149
Upper Lochton. *Abers* 4E 152
Upper Longdon. *Staf* 4E 73
Upper Longwood. *Shrp* 5A 72
Upper Lybster. *High* 5E 169
Upper Lydbrook. *Glos* 4B 48
Upper Lye. *Here* 4F 59
Upper Maes-coed. *Here* 2G 47
Upper Midway. *Derbs* 3G 73
Uppermill. *G Man* 4H 91
Upper Millichope. *Shrp* 2H 59
Upper Milovaig. *High* 4A 154
Upper Minety. *Wilts* 2F 35
Upper Mitton. *Worc* 3C 60
Upper Nash. *Pemb* 4E 43
Upper Neepaback. *Shet* 3G 173
Upper Netchwood. *Shrp* 1A 60
Upper Nobut. *Staf* 2E 73
Upper North Dean. *Buck* 2G 37
Upper Norwood. *W Sus* 4A 26
Upper Nyland. *Dors* 4C 22
Upper Oddington. *Glos* 3H 49
Upper Ollach. *High* 5E 155
Upper Outwoods. *Staf* 3G 73
Upper Padley. *Derbs* 3G 85
Upper Pennington. *Hants* 3B 16
Upper Poppleton. *York* 4H 99
Upper Quinton. *Warw* 1G 49
Upper Rissington. *Glos* 4H 49
Upper Rochford. *Worc* 4A 60
Upper Rusko. *Dum* 3C 110
Upper Sandaig. *High* 2F 147
Upper Sanday. *Orkn* 7E 172
Upper Sapey. *Here* 4A 60
Upper Seagry. *Wilts* 3E 35
Upper Shelton. *C Beds* 1H 51
Upper Sheringham. *Norf* 1D 78
Upper Skelmorlie. *N Ayr* 3C 126
Upper Slaughter. *Glos* 3G 49
Upper Sonachan. *Arg* 1H 133
Upper Soudley. *Glos* 4B 48
Upper Staploe. *Bed* 5A 64
Upper Stoke. *Norf* 5E 79
Upper Stondon. *C Beds* 2B 52
Upper Stowe. *Nptn* 5D 62
Upper Street. *Hants* 1G 15
Upper Street. *Norf* 4F 79 (nr. Horning)
Upper Street. *Norf* 4F 79 (nr. Hoveton)
Upper Street. *Suff* 2E 55
Upper Strensham. *Worc* 2E 49
Upper Studley. *Wilts* 1D 22
Upper Sundon. *C Beds* 3A 52
Upper Swell. *Glos* 3G 49
Upper Tankersley. *S Yor* 1H 85
Upper Tean. *Staf* 2E 73
Upperthong. *W Yor* 4B 92
Upperthorpe. *N Lin* 4A 94
Upper Thurnham. *Lanc* 4D 96
Upper Tillyrie. *Per* 3D 136
Upperton. *W Sus* 3A 26
Upper Tooting. *G Lon* 3D 38
Uppertown. *Derbs* 4H 85 (nr. Ashover)
Upper Town. *Derbs* 5G 85 (nr. Bonsall)
Upper Town. *Derbs* 5G 85 (nr. Hognaston)
Upper Town. *Here* 1A 48
Uppertown. *High* 1F 169
Upper Town. *N Som* 5A 34
Uppertown. *Nmbd* 2B 114
Uppertown. *Orkn* 8D 172
Upper Tysoe. *Warw* 1B 50
Upper Upham. *Wilts* 4H 35
Upper Upnor. *Medw* 3B 40
Upper Urquhart. *Fife* 3D 136
Upper Wardington. *Oxon* 1C 50
Upper Weald. *Mil* 2G 51
Upper Weedon. *Nptn* 5D 62
Upper Wellingham. *E Sus* 4F 27
Upper Whiston. *S Yor* 2B 86
Upper Wield. *Hants* 3E 25
Upper Winchendon. *Buck* 4F 51
Upperwood. *Derbs* 5G 85
Upper Woodford. *Wilts* 3G 23
Upper Wootton. *Hants* 1D 24
Upper Wraxall. *Wilts* 4D 34
Upper Wyche. *Here* 1C 48
Uppincott. *Devn* 2B 12
Uppingham. *Rut* 1F 63
Uppington. *Shrp* 5H 71
Upsall. *N Yor* 1G 99
Upsettlington. *Bord* 5E 131
Upshire. *Essx* 5E 53
Up Somborne. *Hants* 3B 24
Upstreet. *Kent* 4G 41
Up Sydling. *Dors* 2B 14
Upthorpe. *Suff* 3B 66
Upton. *Buck* 4F 51
Upton. *Cambs* 3A 64
Upton. *Ches W* 4G 83
Upton. *Corn* 2C 10 (nr. Bude)
Upton. *Corn* 5C 10 (nr. Liskeard)
Upton. *Cumb* 1E 102
Upton. *Devn* 2D 12 (nr. Honiton)
Upton. *Devn* 4D 8 (nr. Kingsbridge)
Upton. *Dors* 3E 15 (nr. Poole)
Upton. *Dors* 4C 14 (nr. Weymouth)
Upton. *E Yor* 4F 101
Upton. *Hants* 1B 24 (nr. Andover)
Upton. *Hants* 1B 16 (nr. Southampton)
Upton. *IOW* 3D 16
Upton. *Leics* 1A 62
Upton. *Linc* 2F 87
Upton. *Mers* 2E 83
Upton. *Norf* 4F 79
Upton. *Nptn* 4E 62
Upton. *Notts* 3E 87 (nr. Retford)
Upton. *Notts* 5E 87 (nr. Southwell)
Upton. *Oxon* 3D 36
Upton. *Pemb* 4E 43
Upton. *Pet* 5A 76
Upton. *Slo* 3A 38
Upton. *Som* 4H 21 (nr. Somerton)
Upton. *Som* 4C 20 (nr. Wiveliscombe)
Upton. *Warw* 5F 61
Upton. *W Yor* 3E 93
Upton. *Wilts* 3D 22
Upton Bishop. *Here* 3B 48
Upton Cheyney. *S Glo* 5B 34
Upton Cressett. *Shrp* 1A 60
Upton Crews. *Here* 3B 48
Upton Cross. *Corn* 5C 10
Upton End. *C Beds* 2B 52
Upton Grey. *Hants* 2E 25
Upton Heath. *Ches W* 4G 83
Upton Hellions. *Devn* 2B 12
Upton Lovell. *Wilts* 2E 23
Upton Magna. *Shrp* 4H 71
Upton Noble. *Som* 3C 22
Upton Pyne. *Devn* 3C 12
Upton St Leonards. *Glos* 4D 48
Upton Scudamore. *Wilts* 2D 22
Upton Snodsbury. *Worc* 5D 60
Upton upon Severn. *Worc* 1D 48
Upton Warren. *Worc* 4D 60
Upwaltham. *W Sus* 4A 26
Upware. *Cambs* 3E 65
Upwell. *Cambs* 5D 77
Upwey. *Dors* 4B 14
Upwick Green. *Herts* 3E 53
Upwood. *Cambs* 2B 64
Urafirth. *Shet* 4E 173
Uragaig. *Arg* 4A 132
Urchany. *High* 4C 158
Urchfont. *Wilts* 1F 23
Urdimarsh. *Here* 1A 48
Ure. *Shet* 4D 173
Ure Bank. *N Yor* 2F 99
Urgha. *W Isl* 8D 171
Urlay Nook. *Stoc T* 3B 106
Urmston. *G Man* 1B 84
Urquhart. *Mor* 2G 159
Urra. *N Yor* 4C 106
Urray. *High* 3H 157
Usan. *Ang* 3G 145
Ushaw Moor. *Dur* 5F 115
Usk. *Mon* 5G 47
Usselby. *Linc* 1H 87
Usworth. *Tyne* 4G 115
Utkinton. *Ches W* 4H 83
Uton. *Devn* 3B 12
Utterby. *Linc* 1C 88
Uttoxeter. *Staf* 2E 73
Uwchmynydd. *Gwyn* 3A 68
Uxbridge. *G Lon* 2B 38
Uyeasound. *Shet* 1G 173
Uzmaston. *Pemb* 3D 42

V

Valley. *IOA* 3B 80
Valley End. *Surr* 4A 38
Valley Truckle. *Corn* 4B 10
Valsgarth. *Shet* 1H 173
Valtos. *High* 2E 155
Van. *Powy* 2B 58
Vange. *Essx* 2B 40
Varteg. *Torf* 5F 47
Vatsetter. *Shet* 3G 173
Vatten. *High* 4B 154
Vaul. *Arg* 4B 138
Vauld, The. *Here* 1A 48
Vaynol. *Gwyn* 3E 81
Vaynor. *Mer T* 4D 46
Veensgarth. *Shet* 7F 173
Velindre. *Powy* 2E 47
Vellow. *Som* 3D 20
Velly. *Devn* 4C 18
Veness. *Orkn* 5E 172
Venhay. *Devn* 1A 12
Venn. *Devn* 4D 8
Venngreen. *Devn* 1D 11
Vennington. *Shrp* 5F 71
Venn Ottery. *Devn* 3D 12
Venn's Green. *Here* 1A 48
Venny Tedburn. *Devn* 3B 12
Venterdon. *Corn* 5D 10
Ventnor. *IOW* 5D 16
Vernham Dean. *Hants* 1B 24
Vernham Street. *Hants* 1B 24
Vernolds Common. *Shrp* 2G 59
Verwood. *Dors* 2F 15
Veryan. *Corn* 5D 6
Veryan Green. *Corn* 4D 6
Vicarage. *Devn* 4F 13
Vickerstown. *Cumb* 3A 96
Victoria. *Corn* 2D 6
Victoria Bridge. *Strab* 3F 176
Vidlin. *Shet* 5F 173
Viewpark. *N Lan* 3A 128
Vigo. *W Mid* 5E 73
Vigo Village. *Kent* 4H 39
Vinehall Street. *E Sus* 3B 28
Vine's Cross. *E Sus* 4G 27
Viney Hill. *Glos* 5B 48
Virginia Water. *Surr* 4A 38
Virginstow. *Devn* 3D 11
Vobster. *Som* 2C 22
Voe. *Shet* 5F 173 (nr. Hillside)
Voe. *Shet* 3E 173 (nr. Swinister)
Vole. *Som* 2G 21
Vowchurch. *Here* 2G 47
Voxter. *Shet* 4E 173
Voy. *Orkn* 6B 172
Vulcan Village. *Warr* 1H 83

W

Waberthwaite. *Cumb* 5C 102
Wackerfield. *Dur* 2E 105
Wacton. *Norf* 1D 66
Wadbister. *Shet* 7F 173
Wadborough. *Worc* 1E 49
Wadbrook. *Devn* 2G 13
Waddesdon. *Buck* 4F 51
Waddeton. *Devn* 3E 9
Waddicar. *Mers* 1F 83
Waddingham. *Linc* 1G 87
Waddington. *Lanc* 5G 97
Waddington. *Linc* 4G 87
Waddon. *Devn* 5B 12
Wadebridge. *Corn* 1D 6
Wadeford. *Som* 1G 13
Wadenhoe. *Nptn* 2H 63
Wadesmill. *Herts* 4D 52
Wadhurst. *E Sus* 2H 27
Wadshelf. *Derbs* 3H 85
Wadsley. *S Yor* 1H 85
Wadsley Bridge. *S Yor* 1H 85
Wadswick. *Wilts* 5D 34
Wadwick. *Hants* 1C 24
Wadworth. *S Yor* 1C 86
Waen. *Den* 4D 82 (nr. Llandyrnog)
Waen. *Den* 4B 82 (nr. Nantglyn)
Waen. *Powy* 1B 58
Waen Fach. *Powy* 4E 70
Waen Goleugoed. *Den* 3C 82
Wag. *High* 1H 165
Wainfleet All Saints. *Linc* 5D 89
Wainfleet Bank. *Linc* 5D 88
Wainfleet St Mary. *Linc* 5D 89
Wainhouse Corner. *Corn* 3B 10
Wainscott. *Medw* 3B 40
Wainstalls. *W Yor* 2A 92
Waitby. *Cumb* 4A 104
Waithe. *Linc* 4F 95
Wakefield. *W Yor* 2D 92
Wakerley. *Nptn* 1G 63
Wakes Colne. *Essx* 3B 54
Walberswick. *Suff* 3G 67
Walberton. *W Sus* 5A 26
Walbottle. *Tyne* 3E 115
Walby. *Cumb* 3F 113
Walcombe. *Som* 2A 22
Walcot. *Linc* 2H 75
Walcot. *N Lin* 2B 94
Walcot. *Swin* 3G 35
Walcot. *Telf* 4H 71
Walcot. *Warw* 5F 61
Walcote. *Leics* 2C 62
Walcot Green. *Norf* 2D 66
Walcott. *Linc* 5A 88
Walcott. *Norf* 2F 79
Walden. *N Yor* 1C 98
Walden Head. *N Yor* 1B 98
Walden Stubbs. *N Yor* 3F 93
Walderslade. *Medw* 4B 40
Walderton. *W Sus* 1F 17
Walditch. *Dors* 3H 13
Waldley. *Derbs* 2F 73
Waldridge. *Dur* 4F 115
Waldringfield. *Suff* 1F 55
Waldron. *E Sus* 4G 27
Wales. *S Yor* 2B 86
Walesby. *Linc* 1A 88
Walesby. *Notts* 3D 86
Walford. *Here* 3F 59 (nr. Leintwardine)
Walford. *Here* 3A 48 (nr. Ross-on-Wye)
Walford. *Shrp* 3G 71
Walford. *Staf* 2C 72
Walford Heath. *Shrp* 4G 71
Walgherton. *Ches E* 1A 72
Walgrave. *Nptn* 3F 63
Walhampton. *Hants* 3B 16
Walkden. *G Man* 4F 91
Walker. *Tyne* 3F 115
Walkerburn. *Bord* 1F 119
Walker Fold. *Lanc* 5F 97
Walkeringham. *Notts* 1E 87
Walkerith. *Linc* 1E 87
Walkern. *Herts* 3C 52
Walker's Green. *Here* 1A 48
Walkerton. *Fife* 3E 137
Walkerville. *N Yor* 5F 105
Walkford. *Dors* 3H 15
Walkhampton. *Devn* 2B 8
Walkington. *E Yor* 1C 94
Walkley. *S Yor* 2H 85
Walk Mill. *Lanc* 1G 91
Wall. *Corn* 3D 4
Wall. *Nmbd* 3C 114
Wall. *Staf* 5F 73
Wallaceton. *Dum* 1F 111
Wallacetown. *Shet* 6E 173
Wallacetown. *S Ayr* 2C 116 (nr. Ayr)
Wallacetown. *S Ayr* 4B 116 (nr. Dailly)
Wallands Park. *E Sus* 4F 27
Wallasey. *Mers* 1F 83
Wallaston Green. *Pemb* 4D 42
Wallbrook. *W Mid* 1D 60
Wallcrouch. *E Sus* 2A 28
Wall End. *Cumb* 1B 96
Wallend. *Medw* 3C 40
Wall Heath. *W Mid* 2C 60
Wallingford. *Oxon* 3E 36
Wallington. *G Lon* 4D 39
Wallington. *Hants* 2D 16
Wallington. *Herts* 2C 52
Wallis. *Pemb* 2E 43
Wallisdown. *Pool* 3F 15
Walliswood. *Surr* 2C 26
Wall Nook. *Dur* 5F 115
Walls. *Shet* 7D 173
Wallsend. *Tyne* 3G 115
Wallsworth. *Glos* 3D 48
Wall under Heywood. *Shrp* 1H 59
Wallyford. *E Lot* 2G 129
Walmer. *Kent* 5H 41
Walmer Bridge. *Lanc* 2C 90
Walmersley. *G Man* 3G 91
Walmley. *W Mid* 1F 61
Walnut Grove. *Per* 1D 136
Walpole. *Suff* 3F 67
Walpole Cross Keys. *Norf* 4E 77
Walpole Gate. *Norf* 4E 77
Walpole Highway. *Norf* 4E 77
Walpole Marsh. *Norf* 4D 77
Walpole St Andrew. *Norf* 4E 77
Walpole St Peter. *Norf* 4E 77
Walsall. *W Mid* 1E 61
Walsall Wood. *W Mid* 5E 73
Walsden. *W Yor* 2H 91
Walsgrave on Sowe. *W Mid* 2A 62
Walsham le Willows. *Suff* 3C 66
Walshaw. *G Man* 3F 91
Walshford. *N Yor* 4G 99
Walsoken. *Cambs* 4D 76
Walston. *S Lan* 5D 128
Walsworth. *Herts* 2B 52
Walter's Ash. *Buck* 2G 37
Walterston. *V Glam* 4D 32
Walterstone. *Here* 3G 47
Waltham. *Kent* 1F 29
Waltham. *NE Lin* 4F 95
Waltham Abbey. *Essx* 5D 53
Waltham Chase. *Hants* 1D 16
Waltham Cross. *Herts* 5D 52
Waltham on the Wolds. *Leics* 3F 75
Waltham St Lawrence. *Wind* 4G 37
Waltham's Cross. *Essx* 2G 53
Walthamstow. *G Lon* 2E 39
Walton. *Cumb* 3G 113
Walton. *Derbs* 4A 86
Walton. *Leics* 2C 62
Walton. *Mers* 1F 83
Walton. *Mil* 2G 51
Walton. *Pet* 5A 76
Walton. *Powy* 5E 59
Walton. *Som* 3H 21
Walton. *Staf* 3C 72 (nr. Eccleshall)
Walton. *Staf* 2C 72 (nr. Stone)
Walton. *Suff* 2F 55
Walton. *Telf* 4H 71
Walton. *Warw* 5G 61
Walton. *W Yor* 3D 92 (nr. Wakefield)
Walton. *W Yor* 5G 99 (nr. Wetherby)
Walton Cardiff. *Glos* 2E 49
Walton East. *Pemb* 2E 43
Walton Elm. *Dors* 1C 14
Walton Highway. *Norf* 4D 77
Walton-in-Gordano. *N Som* 4H 33
Walton-le-Dale. *Lanc* 2D 90
Walton-on-Thames. *Surr* 4C 38
Walton-on-the-Hill. *Staf* 3D 72
Walton on the Hill. *Surr* 5D 38
Walton-on-the-Naze. *Essx* 3F 55
Walton on the Wolds. *Leics* 4C 74
Walton-on-Trent. *Derbs* 4G 73
Walton West. *Pemb* 3C 42
Walwick. *Nmbd* 2C 114
Walworth. *Darl* 3F 105
Walworth Gate. *Darl* 2F 105
Walwyn's Castle. *Pemb* 3C 42
Wambrook. *Som* 2F 13
Wampool. *Cumb* 4D 112
Wanborough. *Surr* 1A 26
Wanborough. *Swin* 3H 35
Wandel. *S Lan* 2B 118
Wandsworth. *G Lon* 3D 38
Wangford. *Suff* 2G 65 (nr. Lakenheath)
Wangford. *Suff* 3G 67 (nr. Southwold)
Wanlip. *Leics* 4D 74
Wanlockhead. *Dum* 3A 118
Wannock. *E Sus* 5G 27
Wansford. *E Yor* 4E 101
Wansford. *Pet* 1H 63
Wanshurst Green. *Kent* 1B 28
Wanstead. *G Lon* 2F 39
Wanstrow. *Som* 2C 22
Wanswell. *Glos* 5B 48
Wantage. *Oxon* 3C 36
Wapley. *S Glo* 4C 34
Wappenbury. *Warw* 4A 62
Wappenham. *Nptn* 1E 51
Warbleton. *E Sus* 4H 27
Warblington. *Hants* 2F 17
Warborough. *Oxon* 2D 36
Warboys. *Cambs* 2C 64
Warbreck. *Bkpl* 1B 90
Warbstow. *Corn* 3C 10
Warburton. *G Man* 2A 84
Warcop. *Cumb* 3A 104
Warden. *Kent* 3E 40
Warden. *Nmbd* 3C 114
Ward End. *W Mid* 2F 61
Ward Green. *Suff* 4C 66
Ward Green Cross. *Lanc* 1E 91
Wardhedges. *C Beds* 2A 52
Wardhouse. *Abers* 5C 160
Wardington. *Oxon* 1C 50
Wardle. *Ches E* 5A 84
Wardle. *G Man* 3H 91
Wardley. *Rut* 5F 75
Wardley. *W Sus* 4G 25
Wardlow. *Derbs* 3F 85
Wardsend. *Ches E* 2D 84
Wardy Hill. *Cambs* 2D 64
Ware. *Herts* 4D 52
Ware. *Kent* 4G 41
Wareham. *Dors* 4E 15
Warehorne. *Kent* 2D 28
Warenford. *Nmbd* 2F 121
Waren Mill. *Nmbd* 1F 121
Warenton. *Nmbd* 1F 121
Wareside. *Herts* 4D 53
Waresley. *Cambs* 5B 64
Waresley. *Worc* 4C 60
Warfield. *Brac* 4G 37
Warfleet. *Devn* 3E 9
Wargate. *Linc* 2B 76
Wargrave. *Wok* 4F 37
Warham. *Norf* 1B 78
Waringsford. *Ban* 5G 179
Waringstown. *Cgvn* 4F 178

Wark—Wickhambrook

Wark. Nmbd 1C 120
(nr. Coldstream)
Wark. Nmbd 2B 114
(nr. Hexham)
Warkleigh. Devn 4G 19
Warkton. Nptn 3F 63
Warkworth. Nptn 1C 50
Warkworth. Nmbd 4G 121
Warlaby. N Yor 5A 106
Warland. W Yor 2H 91
Warleggan. Corn 2F 7
Warlingham. Surr 5E 39
Warmanbie. Dum 3C 112
Warmfield. W Yor 2D 93
Warmingham. Ches E 4B 84
Warminghurst. W Sus 4C 26
Warmington. Nptn 1H 63
Warmington. Warw 1C 50
Warminster. Wilts 2D 23
Warmley. S Glo 4B 34
Warmsworth. S Yor 4F 93
Warmwell. Dors 4C 14
Warndon. Worc 5C 60
Warners End. Herts 5A 52
Warnford. Hants 4E 24
Warnham. W Sus 2C 26
Warningcamp. W Sus 5B 26
Warninglid. W Sus 3D 26
Warren. Ches E 3C 84
Warren. Pemb 5D 42
Warrenby. Red C 2C 106
Warren Corner. Hants 2G 25
(nr. Aldershot)
Warren Corner. Hants 4F 25
(nr. Petersfield)
Warrenpoint. New M 8F 178
Warren Row. Wind 3G 37
Warren Street. Kent 5D 40
Warrington. Mil 5F 63
Warrington. Warr 2A 84
Warsash. Hants 2C 16
Warse. High 1F 169
Warslow. Staf 5E 85
Warsop. Notts 4C 86
Warsop Vale. Notts 4C 86
Warter. E Yor 4C 100
Warthermarske. N Yor 2E 98
Warthill. N Yor 4A 100
Wartling. E Sus 5A 28
Wartnaby. Leics 3E 74
Warton. Lanc 2D 97
(nr. Carnforth)
Warton. Lanc 2C 90
(nr. Freckleton)
Warton. Nmbd 4E 121
Warton. Warw 5G 73
Warwick. Warw 4G 61
Warwick Bridge. Cumb 4F 113
Warwick-on-Eden. Cumb 4F 113
Warwick Wold. Surr 5E 39
Wasbister. Orkn 4C 172
Wasdale Head. Cumb 4C 102
Wash. Derbs 2E 85
Washaway. Corn 2E 7
Washbourne. Devn 3E 9
Washbrook. Suff 1E 54
Wash Common. W Ber 5C 36
Washerwall. Staf 1D 72
Washfield. Devn 1C 12
Washfold. N Yor 4D 104
Washford. Som 2D 20
Washford Pyne. Devn 1B 12
Washingborough. Linc 3H 87
Washington. Tyne 4G 115
Washington. W Sus 4C 26
Washington Village. Tyne 4G 115
Waskerley. Dur 5D 114
Wasperton. Warw 5G 61
Wasp Green. Surr 1E 27
Wasps Nest. Linc 4H 87
Wass. N Yor 2H 99
Watchet. Som 2D 20
Watchfield. Oxon 2H 35
Watchgate. Cumb 5G 103
Watchhill. Cumb 5C 112
Watcombe. Torb 2F 9
Watendlath. Cumb 3D 102
Water. Devn 4A 12
Water. Lanc 2G 91
Waterbeach. Cambs 4D 65
Waterbeach. W Sus 2G 17
Waterbeck. Dum 2D 112
Waterditch. Hants 3G 15
Water End. C Beds 2A 52
Water End. E Yor 1A 94
Water End. Essx 1F 53
Water End. Herts 5C 52
(nr. Hatfield)
Water End. Herts 4A 52
(nr. Hemel Hempstead)
Waterfall. Staf 5E 85
Waterfoot. E Ren 4G 127
Waterfoot. Lanc 2G 91
Waterfoot. Moy 4J 175
Waterford. Herts 4D 52
Water Fryston. W Yor 2E 93
Waterhead. Cumb 4E 103
Waterhead. E Ayr 3E 117
Waterhead. S Ayr 5C 116
Waterheads. Bord 4F 129
Waterhouses. Dur 5E 115
Waterhouses. Staf 5E 85
Wateringbury. Kent 5A 40
Waterlane. Glos 5E 49
Waterlip. Som 2B 22
Waterloo. Cphy 3E 33
Waterloo. Corn 5B 10
Waterloo. Here 1G 47
Waterloo. High 1E 147
Waterloo. Mers 1F 83
Waterloo. Norf 4E 78
Waterloo. N Lan 4B 128
Waterloo. Pemb 4D 42
Waterloo. Per 5H 143
Waterloo. Pool 3F 15
Waterloo. Shrp 2G 71
Waterlooville. Hants 2E 17
Watermead. Buck 4G 51
Watermillock. Cumb 2F 103
Water Newton. Cambs 1A 64
Water Orton. Warw 1F 61
Waterperry. Oxon 5E 51
Waterrow. Som 4D 20
Watersfield. W Sus 4B 26
Waterside. Buck 5H 51
Waterside. Cambs 3F 65
Waterside. Cumb 5D 112
Waterside. E Ayr 4D 116
(nr. Ayr)
Waterside. E Ayr 5F 127
(nr. Kilmarnock)
Waterside. E Dun 2H 127
Waterstein. High 4A 154
Waterstock. Oxon 5E 51
Waterston. Pemb 4D 42
Water Stratford. Buck 2E 51
Waters Upton. Telf 4A 72
Water Yeat. Cumb 1B 96
Watford. Herts 1B 38
Watford. Nptn 4D 62
Wath. Cumb 4H 103
Wath. N Yor 3D 98
(nr. Pateley Bridge)
Wath. N Yor 2F 99
(nr. Ripon)
Wath Brow. Cumb 3B 102
Wath upon Dearne. S Yor 1B 86
Watlington. Norf 4F 77
Watlington. Oxon 2E 37
Watten. High 3E 169
Wattisfield. Suff 3C 66
Wattisham. Suff 5C 66
Wattlesborough Heath. Shrp 4F 71
Watton. Dors 3H 13
Watton. E Yor 4E 101
Watton. Norf 5B 78
Watton at Stone. Herts 4C 52
Wattston. N Lan 2A 128
Wattstown. Rhon 2D 32
Wattsville. Cphy 2F 33
Wauldby. E Yor 2C 94
Waulkmill. Abers 4D 152
Waun. Powy 4E 71
Waunarlwydd. Swan 3F 31
Waun Fawr. Cdgn 2F 57
Waunfawr. Gwyn 5E 81
Waungilwen. Carm 1H 43
Waunlwyd. Blae 5E 47
Waun-y-Clyn. Carm 5E 45
Wavendon. Mil 2H 51
Waverbridge. Cumb 5D 112
Waverley. Surr 2G 25
Waverton. Ches W 4G 83
Waverton. Cumb 5D 112
Wavertree. Mers 2F 83
Wawne. E Yor 1D 94
Waxham. Norf 3G 79
Waxholme. E Yor 2G 95
Wayford. Som 2H 13
Way Head. Cambs 2D 65
Waytown. Dors 3H 13
Way Village. Devn 1B 12
Wdig. Pemb 1D 42
Wealdstone. G Lon 2C 38
Weardley. W Yor 5E 99
Weare. Som 1H 21
Weare Giffard. Devn 4E 19
Wearhead. Dur 1B 104
Wearne. Som 4H 21
Weasdale. Cumb 4H 103
Weasenham All Saints. Norf 3H 77
Weasenham St Peter. Norf 3A 78
Weaverham. Ches W 3A 84
Weaverthorpe. N Yor 2D 100
Webheath. Worc 4E 61
Webton. Here 2H 47
Wedderlairs. Abers 5F 161
Weddington. Warw 1A 62
Wedhampton. Wilts 1F 23
Wedmore. Som 2H 21
Wednesbury. W Mid 1D 61
Wednesfield. W Mid 5D 72
Weecar. Notts 4F 87
Weedon. Buck 4G 51
Weedon Bec. Nptn 5D 62
Weedon Lois. Nptn 1E 50
Weeford. Staf 5F 73
Week. Devn 4F 19
(nr. Barnstaple)
Week. Devn 2G 11
(nr. Okehampton)
Week. Devn 1H 11
(nr. South Molton)
Week. Devn 2D 9
(nr. Totnes)
Week. Som 3C 20
Weeke. Devn 2A 12
Weeke. Hants 3C 24
Week Green. Corn 3C 10
Weekley. Nptn 2F 63
Week St Mary. Corn 3C 10
Weel. E Yor 1D 94
Weeley. Essx 3E 55
Weeley Heath. Essx 3E 55
Weem. Per 4F 143
Weeping Cross. Staf 3D 72
Weethly. Warw 5E 61
Weeting. Norf 2G 65
Weeton. E Yor 2G 95
Weeton. Lanc 1B 90
Weeton. N Yor 5E 99
Weetwood Hall. Nmbd 2E 121
Weir. Lanc 2G 91
Welborne. Norf 4C 78
Welbourn. Linc 5G 87
Welburn. N Yor 1A 100
(nr. Kirkbymoorside)
Welburn. N Yor 3B 100
(nr. Malton)
Welbury. N Yor 4A 106
Welby. Linc 2G 75
Welches Dam. Cambs 2D 64
Welcombe. Devn 1C 10
Weld Bank. Lanc 3D 90
Weldon. Nptn 2G 63
Weldon. Nmbd 5F 121
Welford. Nptn 2D 62
Welford. W Ber 4C 36
Welford-on-Avon. Warw 5F 61
Welham. Leics 1E 63
Welham. Notts 2E 87
Welham Green. Herts 5C 52
Well. Hants 2F 25
Well. Linc 3D 88
Well. N Yor 1E 99
Welland. Worc 1C 48
Wellbank. Ang 5D 144
Well Bottom. Dors 1E 15
Welldale. Dum 3C 112
Wellesbourne. Warw 5G 61
Well Hill. Kent 4F 39
Wellhouse. W Ber 4D 36
Welling. G Lon 3F 39
Wellingborough. Nptn 4F 63
Wellingham. Norf 3A 78
Wellingore. Linc 5G 87
Wellington. Cumb 4B 102
Wellington. Here 1H 47
Wellington. Som 4E 21
Wellington. Telf 4A 72
Wellington Heath. Here 1C 48
Wellow. Bath 1C 22
Wellow. IOW 4B 16
Wellow. Notts 4D 86
Wellpond Green. Herts 3E 53
Wells. Som 2A 22
Wellsborough. Leics 5A 74
Wells Green. Ches E 5A 84
Wells-next-the-Sea. Norf 1B 78
Wellswood. Torb 2F 9
Wellwood. Fife 1D 129
Welney. Norf 1E 65
Welsford. Devn 4C 18
Welshampton. Shrp 2G 71
Welsh End. Shrp 2H 71
Welsh Frankton. Shrp 2F 71
Welsh Hook. Pemb 2D 42
Welsh Newton. Here 4H 47
Welsh Newton Common. Here 4A 48
Welshpool. Powy 5E 70
Welsh St Donats. V Glam 4D 32
Welton. Bath 1B 22
Welton. Cumb 5E 113
Welton. E Yor 2C 94
Welton. Linc 2H 87
Welton. Nptn 4C 62
Welton Hill. Linc 2H 87
Welton le Marsh. Linc 4D 88
Welton le Wold. Linc 2B 88
Welwick. E Yor 2G 95
Welwyn. Herts 4C 52
Welwyn Garden City. Herts 4C 52
Wem. Shrp 3H 71
Wembdon. Som 3F 21
Wembley. G Lon 2C 38
Wembury. Devn 4B 8
Wembworthy. Devn 2G 11
Wemyss Bay. Inv 2C 126
Wenallt. Cdgn 3F 57
Wenallt. Gwyn 1B 70
Wendens Ambo. Essx 2F 53
Wendlebury. Oxon 4D 50
Wendling. Norf 4B 78
Wendover. Buck 5G 51
Wendron. Corn 5A 6
Wendy. Cambs 1D 52
Wenfordbridge. Corn 5A 10
Wenhaston. Suff 3G 67
Wennington. Cambs 3B 64
Wennington. G Lon 2G 39
Wennington. Lanc 2F 97
Wensley. Derbs 4G 85
Wensley. N Yor 1C 98
Wentbridge. W Yor 3E 93
Wentnor. Shrp 1F 59
Wentworth. Cambs 3D 65
Wentworth. S Yor 1A 86
Wenvoe. V Glam 4E 32
Weobley. Here 5G 59
Weobley Marsh. Here 5G 59
Wepham. W Sus 5B 26
Wereham. Norf 5F 77
Wergs. W Mid 5C 72
Wern. Gwyn 1E 69
Wern. Powy 4E 46
(nr. Brecon)
Wern. Powy 4E 71
(nr. Guilsfield)
Wern. Powy 4B 70
(nr. Llangadfan)
Wern. Powy 3E 71
(nr. Llanymynech)
Wernffrwd. Swan 3E 31
Wernyrheolydd. Mon 4G 47
Werrington. Corn 4D 10
Werrington. Pet 5A 76
Werrington. Staf 1D 72
Wervin. Ches W 3G 83
Wesham. Lanc 1C 90
Wessington. Derbs 5A 86
West Aberthaw. V Glam 5D 32
West Acre. Norf 4G 77
West Allerdean. Nmbd 5F 131
West Alvington. Devn 4D 8
West Amesbury. Wilts 2G 23
West Anstey. Devn 4B 20
West Appleton. N Yor 5F 105
West Ardsley. W Yor 2C 92
West Arthurlie. E Ren 4F 127
West Ashby. Linc 3B 88
West Ashling. W Sus 2G 17
West Ashton. Wilts 1D 23
West Auckland. Dur 2E 105
West Ayton. N Yor 1D 101
West Bagborough. Som 3E 21
West Bank. Hal 2H 83
West Barkwith. Linc 2A 88
West Barnby. N Yor 3F 107
West Barns. E Lot 2C 130
West Barsham. Norf 2B 78
West Bay. Dors 3H 13
West Beckham. Norf 2D 78
West Bennan. N Ayr 3D 123
Westbere. Kent 4F 41
West Bergholt. Essx 3C 54
West Bexington. Dors 4A 14
West Bilney. Norf 4G 77
West Blackdene. Dur 1B 104
West Blatchington. Brig 5D 27
Westborough. Linc 1F 75
Westbourne. Bour 3F 15
Westbourne. W Sus 2F 17
West Bowling. W Yor 1B 92
West Brabourne. Kent 1E 29
West Bradford. Lanc 5G 97
West Bradley. Som 3A 22
West Bretton. W Yor 3C 92
West Bridgford. Notts 2C 74
West Briggs. Norf 4F 77
West Bromwich. W Mid 1D 61
Westbrook. Here 1F 47
Westbrook. Kent 3H 41
Westbrook. Wilts 5E 35
West Buckland. Devn 3G 19
(nr. Barnstaple)
West Buckland. Devn 4C 8
(nr. Thurlestone)
West Buckland. Som 4E 21
West Burnside. Abers 1G 145
West Burrafirth. Shet 6D 173
West Burton. N Yor 1C 98
West Burton. W Sus 4B 26
Westbury. Buck 2E 50
Westbury. Shrp 5F 71
Westbury. Wilts 1D 22
Westbury Leigh. Wilts 2D 22
Westbury-on-Severn. Glos 4C 48
Westbury on Trym. Bris 4A 34
Westbury-sub-Mendip. Som 2A 22
West Butsfield. Dur 5E 115
West Butterwick. N Lin 4B 94
Westby. Linc 3G 75
West Byfleet. Surr 4B 38
West Caister. Norf 4H 79
West Calder. W Lot 3D 128
West Camel. Som 4A 22
West Carr. N Lin 4H 93
West Chaldon. Dors 4C 14
West Challow. Oxon 3B 36
West Charleton. Devn 4D 8
West Chelborough. Dors 2A 14
West Chevington. Nmbd 5G 121
West Chiltington. W Sus 4B 26
West Chiltington Common. W Sus 4B 26
West Chinnock. Som 1H 13
West Chisenbury. Wilts 1G 23
West Clandon. Surr 5B 38
West Cliffe. Kent 1H 29
Westcliff-on-Sea. S'end 2C 40
West Clyne. High 3F 165
West Coker. Som 1A 14
Westcombe. Som 3B 22
(nr. Evercreech)
Westcombe. Som 4H 21
(nr. Somerton)
West Compton. Dors 3A 14
West Compton. Som 2A 22
West Cornforth. Dur 1A 106
Westcot. Oxon 3B 36
Westcott. Buck 4F 51
Westcott. Devn 2D 12
Westcott. Surr 1C 26
Westcott Barton. Oxon 3C 50
West Cowick. E Yor 2G 93
West Cranmore. Som 2B 22
West Croftmore. High 2D 150
West Cross. Swan 4F 31
West Cullerlie. Abers 3E 153
West Culvennan. Dum 3H 109
West Curry. Corn 3C 10
West Curthwaite. Cumb 5E 113
Westdean. E Sus 5G 27
West Dean. W Sus 1G 17
West Dean. Wilts 4A 24
West Deeping. Linc 5A 76
West Derby. Mers 1F 83
West Dereham. Norf 5F 77
West Down. Devn 2F 19
Westdowns. Corn 4A 10
West Drayton. G Lon 3B 38
West Drayton. Notts 3E 86
West Dunnet. High 1E 169
West Ella. E Yor 2D 94
West End. Bed 5G 63
West End. Cambs 1D 64
West End. Dors 2E 15
West End. E Yor 3E 101
(nr. Kilham)
West End. E Yor 1E 95
(nr. Preston)
West End. E Yor 1C 94
(nr. South Cove)
West End. E Yor 4F 101
(nr. Ulrome)
West End. G Lon 2D 39
West End. Hants 1C 16
West End. Herts 5C 52
West End. Kent 4F 41
West End. Lanc 3D 96
West End. Linc 1C 76
West End. Norf 4G 79
West End. N Som 5H 33
West End. N Yor 4D 98
West End. S Glo 3C 34
West End. S Lan 5C 128
West End. Surr 4A 38
West End. Wilts 4E 23
West End. Wind 4G 37
West End. Worc 2F 49
West End Green. Hants 5E 37
Westenhanger. Kent 2F 29
Wester Aberchalder. High 2H 149
Wester Balgedie. Per 3D 136
Wester Brae. High 2A 158
Wester Culbeuchly. Abers 2D 160
Westerdale. High 3D 168
Westerdale. N Yor 4D 106
Wester Dechmont. W Lot 2D 128
Wester Fearn. High 5D 164
Westerfield. Suff 1E 55
Wester Galcantray. High 4C 158
Westergate. W Sus 5A 26
Wester Gruinards. High 4C 164
Westerham. Kent 5F 39
Westerleigh. S Glo 4B 34
Westerloch. High 3F 169
Wester Mandally. High 3E 149
Wester Quarff. Shet 8F 173
Wester Rarichie. High 1C 158
Wester Shian. Per 5F 143
Wester Skeld. Shet 7D 173
Westerton. Ang 3F 145
Westerton. Dur 1F 105
Westerton. W Sus 2G 17
Westerwick. Shet 7D 173
West Farleigh. Kent 5B 40
West Farndon. Nptn 5C 62
West Felton. Shrp 3F 71
Westfield. Cumb 2A 102
Westfield. E Sus 4C 28
Westfield. High 2C 168
Westfield. Norf 5B 78
Westfield. N Lan 2A 128
Westfield. W Lot 2C 128
Westfields. Dors 2C 14
Westfields of Rattray. Per 4A 144
West Fleetham. Nmbd 2F 121
Westford. Som 1E 13
West Garforth. W Yor 1D 93
Westgate. Dur 1C 104
Westgate. Norf 1B 78
Westgate. N Lin 4A 94
Westgate on Sea. Kent 3H 41
West Ginge. Oxon 3C 36
West Grafton. Wilts 5H 35
West Green. Hants 1F 25
West Grimstead. Wilts 4H 23
West Grinstead. W Sus 3C 26
West Haddlesey. N Yor 2F 93
West Haddon. Nptn 3D 62
West Hagbourne. Oxon 3D 36
West Hagley. Worc 2C 60
Westhall. Suff 2G 67
West Hall. Cumb 3G 113
West Hallam. Derbs 1B 74
Westhall Terrace. Ang 5D 144
West Halton. N Lin 2C 94
Westham. Dors 5B 14
Westham. E Sus 5H 27
West Ham. G Lon 2E 39
Westham. Som 2H 21
Westhampnett. W Sus 2G 17
West Handley. Derbs 3A 86
West Hanney. Oxon 2C 36
West Hanningfield. Essx 1B 40
West Hardwick. W Yor 3E 93
West Harnham. Wilts 4G 23
West Harptree. Bath 1A 22
West Harting. W Sus 4F 25
West Harton. Tyne 3G 115
West Hatch. Som 4F 21
Westhay. Som 2H 21
Westhead. Lanc 4C 90
West Head. Norf 5E 77
West Heath. Hants 1D 24
(nr. Basingstoke)
West Heath. Hants 1G 25
(nr. Farnborough)
West Helmsdale. High 2H 165
West Hendred. Oxon 3C 36
West Heogaland. Shet 4D 173
West Heslerton. N Yor 2D 100
West Hewish. N Som 5G 33
Westhide. Here 1A 48
Westhill. Abers 3F 153
West Hill. Devn 3D 12
West Hill. E Yor 3F 101
West Hill. High 4B 158
West Hill. N Som 4H 33
West Hill. W Sus 2E 27
West Hoathly. W Sus 2E 27
West Holme. Dors 4D 15
Westhope. Here 5G 59
Westhope. Shrp 2G 59
West Horndon. Essx 2H 39
Westhorp. Nptn 5C 62
Westhorpe. Linc 2B 76
Westhorpe. Suff 4C 66
West Horrington. Som 2A 22
West Horsley. Surr 5B 38
West Horton. Nmbd 1E 121
West Hougham. Kent 1G 29
Westhoughton. G Man 4E 91
West Houlland. Shet 6D 173
Westhouse. N Yor 2F 97
Westhouses. Derbs 5B 86
West Howe. Bour 3F 15
Westhumble. Surr 5C 38
West Huntspill. Som 2G 21
West Hyde. Herts 1B 38
West Hynish. Arg 5A 138
West Hythe. Kent 2F 29
West Ilsley. W Ber 3C 36
Westing. Shet 1G 173
West Itchenor. W Sus 2G 17
West Keal. Linc 4C 88
West Kennett. Wilts 5G 35
West Kilbride. N Ayr 5D 126
West Kingsdown. Kent 4G 39
West Kington. Wilts 4D 34
West Kirby. Mers 2E 82
West Knapton. N Yor 2C 100
West Knighton. Dors 4C 14
West Knoyle. Wilts 3D 22
West Kyloe. Nmbd 5G 131
Westlake. Devn 3C 8
West Lambrook. Som 1H 13
West Langdon. Kent 1H 29
West Langwell. High 3D 164
West Lavington. W Sus 4G 25
West Lavington. Wilts 1F 23
West Layton. N Yor 4E 105
West Leake. Notts 3C 74
West Learmouth. Nmbd 1C 120
Westleigh. Devn 4E 19
(nr. Bideford)
Westleigh. Devn 1D 12
(nr. Tiverton)
West Leigh. Devn 2G 11
(nr. Winkleigh)
Westleigh. G Man 4E 91
West Leith. Buck 4H 51
Westleton. Suff 4G 67
West Lexham. Norf 4H 77
Westley. Shrp 5F 71
Westley. Suff 4H 65
Westley Waterless. Cambs 5F 65
West Lilling. N Yor 3A 100
West Lingo. Fife 3G 137
Westlington. Buck 4F 51
Westlinton. Cumb 3E 113
West Linton. Bord 4E 129
West Littleton. S Glo 4C 34
West Looe. Corn 3G 7
West Lulworth. Dors 4D 14
West Lutton. N Yor 3D 100
West Lydford. Som 3A 22
West Lyng. Som 4G 21
West Lynn. Norf 4F 77
West Mains. Per 2B 136
West Malling. Kent 5A 40
West Malvern. Worc 1C 48
Westmancote. Worc 2E 49
West Marden. W Sus 1F 17
West Markham. Notts 3E 86
Westmarsh. Kent 4G 41
West Marsh. NE Lin 4F 95
West Marton. N Yor 4A 98
West Meon. Hants 4E 25
West Mersea. Essx 4D 54
Westmeston. E Sus 4E 27
Westmill. Herts 3D 52
(nr. Buntingford)
Westmill. Herts 2B 52
(nr. Hitchin)
West Milton. Dors 3A 14
Westminster. G Lon 3D 39
West Molesey. Surr 4C 38
West Monkton. Som 4F 21
Westmoor End. Cumb 1B 102
West Moors. Dors 2F 15
West Morden. Dors 3E 15
West Muir. Ang 2E 145
(nr. Brechin)
Westmuir. Ang 3C 144
(nr. Forfar)
West Murkle. High 2D 168
West Ness. N Yor 2A 100
Westness. Orkn 5C 172
Westnewton. Cumb 5C 112
West Newton. E Yor 1E 95
West Newton. Norf 3F 77
Westnewton. Nmbd 1D 120
West Newton. Som 4F 21
West Norwood. G Lon 3E 39
Westoe. Tyne 3G 115
West Ogwell. Devn 2E 9
Weston. Bath 5C 34
Weston. Ches E 5B 84
(nr. Crewe)
Weston. Ches E 3C 84
(nr. Macclesfield)
Weston. Devn 2E 13
(nr. Honiton)
Weston. Devn 4E 13
(nr. Sidmouth)
Weston. Dors 5B 14
(nr. Weymouth)
Weston. Dors 2A 14
(nr. Yeovil)
Weston. Hal 2H 83
Weston. Hants 4F 25
Weston. Here 5F 59
Weston. Herts 2C 52
Weston. Linc 3B 76
Weston. Nptn 1D 50
Weston. Notts 4E 87
Weston. Shrp 1H 59
(nr. Bridgnorth)
Weston. Shrp 3F 71
(nr. Knighton)
Weston. Shrp 3H 71
(nr. Wem)
Weston. S Lan 5D 128
Weston. Staf 3D 73
Weston. Suff 2G 67
Weston. W Ber 4B 36
Weston Bampfylde. Som 4B 22
Weston Beggard. Here 1A 48
Westonbirt. Glos 3D 34
Weston by Welland. Nptn 1E 63
Weston Colville. Cambs 5F 65
Westoncommon. Shrp 3G 71
Weston Coyney. Stoke 1D 72
Weston Ditch. Suff 3F 65
Weston Favell. Nptn 4E 63
Weston Green. Cambs 5F 65
Weston Green. Norf 4D 78
Weston Heath. Shrp 4B 72
Weston Hills. Linc 4B 76
Weston in Arden. Warw 2A 62
Westoning. C Beds 2A 52
Weston-in-Gordano. N Som 4H 33
Weston Jones. Staf 3B 72
Weston Longville. Norf 4D 78
Weston Lullingfields. Shrp 3G 71
Weston-on-Avon. Warw 5F 61
Weston-on-the-Green. Oxon 4D 50
Weston-on-Trent. Derbs 3B 74
Weston Patrick. Hants 2E 25
Weston Rhyn. Shrp 2E 71
Weston-sub-Edge. Glos 1G 49
Weston-super-Mare. N Som 5G 33
Weston Town. Som 2C 22
Weston Turville. Buck 4G 51
Weston under Lizard. Staf 4C 72
Weston under Penyard. Here 3B 48
Weston under Wetherley. Warw 4A 62
Weston Underwood. Derbs 1G 73
Weston Underwood. Mil 5F 63
Westonzoyland. Som 3G 21
West Orchard. Dors 1D 14
West Overton. Wilts 5G 35
Westow. N Yor 3B 100
Westown. Per 1E 137
West Panson. Devn 3D 10
West Park. Hart 1B 106
West Parley. Dors 3F 15
West Peckham. Kent 5H 39
West Pelton. Dur 4F 115
West Pennard. Som 3A 22
West Pentire. Corn 2B 6
West Perry. Cambs 4A 64
West Pitcorthie. Fife 3H 137
West Plean. Stir 1B 128
West Poringland. Norf 5E 79
West Porlock. Som 2B 20
Westport. Som 1G 13
West Putford. Devn 1D 10
West Quantoxhead. Som 2E 20
Westra. V Glam 4E 33
West Rainton. Dur 5G 115
West Rasen. Linc 2H 87
West Ravendale. NE Lin 1B 88
Westray Airport. Orkn 2D 172
West Raynham. Norf 3A 78
Westrigg. W Lot 3C 128
West Rounton. N Yor 4B 106
West Row. Suff 3F 65
West Rudham. Norf 3H 77
West Runton. Norf 1D 78
Westruther. Bord 4C 130
Westry. Cambs 1C 64
West Saltoun. E Lot 3A 130
West Sandford. Devn 2B 12
West Sandwick. Shet 3F 173
West Scrafton. N Yor 1C 98
Westside. Orkn 5C 172
West Sleekburn. Nmbd 1F 115
West Somerton. Norf 4G 79
West Stafford. Dors 4C 14
West Stockwith. Notts 1E 87
West Stoke. W Sus 2G 17
West Stonesdale. N Yor 4B 104
West Stoughton. Som 2H 21
West Stour. Dors 4C 22
West Stourmouth. Kent 4G 41
West Stow. Suff 3H 65
West Stowell. Wilts 5G 35
West Strathan. High 2F 167
West Stratton. Hants 2D 24
West Street. Kent 5D 40
West Tanfield. N Yor 2E 99
West Taphouse. Corn 2F 7
West Tarbert. Arg 3G 125
West Thirston. Nmbd 4F 121
West Thorney. W Sus 2F 17
West Thurrock. Thur 3G 39
West Tilbury. Thur 3A 40
West Tisted. Hants 4E 25
West Tofts. Norf 1H 65
West Torrington. Linc 2A 88
West Town. Bath 5A 34
West Town. Hants 3F 17
West Town. N Som 5H 33
West Tytherley. Hants 4A 24
West Tytherton. Wilts 4E 35
West View. Hart 1C 106
Westville. Notts 1C 74
West Walton. Norf 4D 76
Westward. Cumb 5D 112
Westward Ho!. Devn 4E 19
Westwell. Kent 1D 28
Westwell. Oxon 5H 49
Westwell Leacon. Kent 1D 28
West Wellow. Hants 1A 16
West Wemyss. Fife 4F 137
Westwick. Cambs 4D 64
Westwick. Dur 3D 104
Westwick. Norf 3E 79
West Wick. N Som 5G 33
West Wickham. Cambs 1G 53
West Wickham. G Lon 4E 39
West Williamston. Pemb 4E 43
West Willoughby. Linc 1G 75
West Winch. Norf 4F 77
West Winterslow. Wilts 3H 23
West Wittering. W Sus 3F 17
West Witton. N Yor 1C 98
Westwood. Devn 3D 12
Westwood. Kent 4H 41
Westwood. Pet 1A 64
Westwood. S Lan 4H 127
Westwood. Wilts 1D 22
West Woodburn. Nmbd 1B 114
West Woodhay. W Ber 5B 36
West Woodlands. Som 2C 22
Westwoodside. N Lin 4H 93
West Worldham. Hants 3F 25
West Worlington. Devn 1A 12
West Worthing. W Sus 5C 26
West Wratting. Cambs 5F 65
West Wycombe. Buck 2G 37
West Wylam. Nmbd 3E 115
West Yatton. Wilts 4D 34
West Yell. Shet 3F 173
West Youlstone. Corn 1C 10
Wetheral. Cumb 4F 113
Wetherby. W Yor 5G 99
Wetherden. Suff 4C 66
Wetheringsett. Suff 4D 66
Wethersfield. Essx 2H 53
Wethersta. Shet 5E 173
Wetherup Street. Suff 4D 66
Wetley Rocks. Staf 1D 72
Wettenhall. Ches E 4A 84
Wetton. Staf 5F 85
Wetwang. E Yor 4D 100
Wetwood. Staf 2B 72
Wexcombe. Wilts 1A 24
Wexham Street. Buck 2A 38
Weybourne. Norf 1D 78
Weybourne. Surr 2G 25
Weybread. Suff 2E 67
Weybridge. Surr 4B 38
Weycroft. Devn 3G 13
Weydale. High 2D 168
Weyhill. Hants 2B 24
Weymouth. Dors 5B 14 & 204
Weythel. Powy 5E 59
Whaddon. Buck 2G 51
Whaddon. Cambs 1D 52
Whaddon. Glos 4D 48
Whaddon. Wilts 4G 23
Whale. Cumb 2G 103
Whaley. Derbs 3C 86
Whaley Bridge. Derbs 2E 85
Whaley Thorns. Derbs 3C 86
Whalley. Lanc 1F 91
Whalton. Nmbd 1E 115
Wham. N Yor 3G 97
Whaplode. Linc 3C 76
Whaplode Drove. Linc 4C 76
Whaplode St Catherine. Linc 3C 76
Wharfe. N Yor 3G 97
Wharles. Lanc 1C 90
Wharley End. C Beds 1H 51
Wharncliffe Side. S Yor 1G 85
Wharram-le-Street. N Yor 3C 100
Wharton. Ches W 4A 84
Wharton. Here 5H 59
Whashton. N Yor 4E 105
Whasset. Cumb 1E 97
Whatcote. Warw 1A 50
Whateley. Warw 1G 61
Whatfield. Suff 1D 54
Whatley. Som 2G 13
(nr. Chard)
Whatley. Som 2C 22
(nr. Frome)
Whatlington. E Sus 4B 28
Whatmore. Shrp 3A 60
Whatstandwell. Derbs 5H 85
Whatton. Notts 2E 75
Whauphill. Dum 5B 110
Whaw. N Yor 4C 104
Wheatacre. Norf 1G 67
Wheatcroft. Derbs 5A 86
Wheathampstead. Herts 4B 52
Wheathill. Shrp 2A 60
Wheatley. Devn 3B 12
Wheatley. Hants 2F 25
Wheatley. Oxon 5D 50
Wheatley. S Yor 4F 93
Wheatley. W Yor 2A 92
Wheatley Hill. Dur 1A 106
Wheatley Lane. Lanc 1G 91
Wheatley Park. S Yor 4F 93
Wheaton Aston. Staf 4C 72
Wheatstone Park. Staf 5C 72
Wheddon Cross. Som 3C 20
Wheelerstreet. Surr 1A 26
Wheelock. Ches E 5B 84
Wheelock Heath. Ches E 5B 84
Wheelton. Lanc 2E 90
Wheldrake. York 5A 100
Whelford. Glos 2G 35
Whelpley Hill. Buck 5H 51
Whelpo. Cumb 1E 102
Whelston. Flin 3E 82
Whenby. N Yor 3A 100
Whepstead. Suff 5H 65
Wherstead. Suff 1E 55
Wherwell. Hants 2B 24
Wheston. Derbs 3F 85
Whetsted. Kent 1A 28
Whetstone. G Lon 1D 38
Whetstone. Leics 1C 62
Whicham. Cumb 1A 96
Whichford. Warw 2B 50
Whickham. Tyne 3F 115
Whiddon. Devn 2E 11
Whiddon Down. Devn 3G 11
Whigstreet. Ang 4D 145
Whilton. Nptn 4D 62
Whimble. Devn 2D 10
Whimple. Devn 3D 12
Whimpwell Green. Norf 3F 79
Whinburgh. Norf 5C 78
Whin Lane End. Lanc 5C 96
Whinnyfold. Abers 5H 161
Whinny Hill. Stoc T 3A 106
Whippingham. IOW 3D 16
Whipsnade. C Beds 4A 52
Whipton. Devn 3C 12
Whirlow. S Yor 2H 85
Whisby. Linc 4G 87
Whissendine. Rut 4F 75
Whissonsett. Norf 3B 78
Whisterfield. Ches E 3C 84
Whistley Green. Wok 4F 37
Whiston. Mers 1G 83
Whiston. Nptn 4F 63
Whiston. S Yor 1B 86
Whiston. Staf 1E 73
(nr. Cheadle)
Whiston. Staf 4C 72
(nr. Penkridge)
Whiston Cross. Shrp 5B 72
Whiston Eaves. Staf 1E 73
Whitacre Heath. Warw 1G 61
Whitbeck. Cumb 1A 96
Whitbourne. Here 5B 60
Whitburn. Tyne 3H 115
Whitburn. W Lot 3C 128
Whitburn Colliery. Tyne 3H 115
Whitby. Ches W 3F 83
Whitby. N Yor 3F 107
Whitbyheath. Ches W 3F 83
Whitchester. Bord 4D 130
Whitchurch. Bath 5B 34
Whitchurch. Buck 3G 51
Whitchurch. Card 4E 33
Whitchurch. Devn 5E 11
Whitchurch. Hants 2C 24
Whitchurch. Here 4A 48
Whitchurch. Pemb 2C 42
Whitchurch. Shrp 1H 71
Whitchurch Canonicorum. Dors 3G 13
Whitchurch Hill. Oxon 4E 37
Whitchurch-on-Thames. Oxon 4E 37
Whitcombe. Dors 4C 14
Whitcot. Shrp 1F 59
Whitcott Keysett. Shrp 2E 59
Whiteabbey. Newt 1H 179
Whiteash Green. Essx 2A 54
Whitebog. High 2B 158
Whitebridge. High 2G 149
Whitebrook. Mon 5A 48
Whitecairns. Abers 2G 153
White Chapel. Lanc 5E 97
Whitechurch. Pemb 1F 43
White Colne. Essx 3B 54
White Coppice. Lanc 3E 90
White Corries. High 3G 141
Whitecraig. E Lot 2G 129
Whitecroft. Glos 5B 48
White Cross. Corn 4D 5
(nr. Mullion)
Whitecross. Corn 1D 6
(nr. Wadebridge)
Whitecross. Falk 2C 128
Whitecross. New M 6D 178
White End. Worc 2C 48
Whiteface. High 5E 164
Whitefarland. N Ayr 5G 125
Whitefaulds. S Ayr 4B 116
Whitefield. Dors 3E 15
Whitefield. G Man 4G 91
Whitefield. Som 4D 20
Whiteford. Abers 1E 152
Whitegate. Ches W 4A 84
Whitehall. Devn 1E 13
Whitehall. Hants 1F 25
Whitehall. Orkn 5F 172
Whitehall. W Sus 3C 26
Whitehaven. Cumb 3A 102
Whitehaven. Shrp 3E 71
Whitehead. Carr 7L 175
Whitehill. Hants 3F 25
Whitehill. N Ayr 4D 126
Whitehills. Abers 2D 160
Whitehills. Ang 3D 144
White Horse Common. Norf 3F 79
Whitehough. Derbs 2E 85
Whitehouse. Abers 2D 152
Whitehouse. Arg 3G 125
Whiteinch. Glas 3G 127
Whitekirk. E Lot 1B 130
White Kirkley. Dur 1D 104
White Lackington. Dors 3C 14
Whitelackington. Som 1G 13
White Ladies Aston. Worc 5D 60
White Lee. W Yor 2C 92
Whiteley. Hants 2D 16
Whiteley Bank. IOW 4D 16
Whiteley Village. Surr 4B 38
Whitemans Green. W Sus 3E 27
White Mill. Carm 3E 45
Whitemire. Mor 3D 159
Whitemoor. Corn 3D 6
Whitenap. Hants 4B 24
Whiteness. Shet 7F 173
White Notley. Essx 4A 54
Whiteoak Green. Oxon 4B 50
Whiteparish. Wilts 4H 23
White Pit. Linc 3C 88
Whiterashes. Abers 1F 153
Whiterock. Ards 3K 179
White Rocks. Here 3H 47
White Roding. Essx 4F 53
Whiterow. High 4F 169
Whiterow. Mor 3E 159
Whiteshill. Glos 5D 48
Whiteside. Nmbd 3A 114
Whiteside. W Lot 3C 128
Whitesmith. E Sus 4G 27
Whitestaunton. Som 1F 13
Whitestone. Abers 4D 152
Whitestone. Devn 3B 12
White Stone. Here 1A 48
Whitestones. Abers 3F 161
Whitestreet Green. Suff 2C 54
Whitewall Corner. N Yor 2B 100
White Waltham. Wind 4G 37
Whiteway. Glos 4E 49
Whitewell. Lanc 5F 97
Whitewell Bottom. Lanc 2G 91
Whiteworks. Devn 5G 11
Whitewreath. Mor 3G 159
Whitfield. D'dee 5D 144
Whitfield. Kent 1H 29
Whitfield. Nptn 2E 50
Whitfield. Nmbd 4A 114
Whitfield. S Glo 2B 34
Whitford. Devn 3F 13
Whitford. Flin 3D 82
Whitgift. E Yor 2B 94
Whitgreave. Staf 3C 72
Whithorn. Dum 5B 110
Whiting Bay. N Ayr 3E 123
Whitington. Norf 1G 65
Whitkirk. W Yor 1D 92
Whitland. Carm 3G 43
Whitleigh. Plym 3A 8
Whitletts. S Ayr 2C 116
Whitley. Wilts 5D 35
Whitley Bay. Tyne 2G 115
Whitley Chapel. Nmbd 4C 114
Whitley Heath. Staf 3C 72
Whitley Lower. W Yor 3C 92
Whitley Thorpe. N Yor 2F 93
Whitlock's End. W Mid 3F 61
Whitminster. Glos 5C 48
Whitmore. Dors 2F 15
Whitmore. Staf 1C 72
Whitnage. Devn 1D 12
Whitnash. Warw 4H 61
Whitney. Here 1F 47
Whitrigg. Cumb 4D 112
(nr. Kirkbride)
Whitrigg. Cumb 1D 102
(nr. Torpenhow)
Whitsbury. Hants 1G 15
Whitsome. Bord 4E 131
Whitson. Newp 3G 33
Whitstable. Kent 4F 41
Whitstone. Corn 3C 10
Whittingham. Nmbd 3E 121
Whittingslow. Shrp 2G 59
Whittington. Derbs 3B 86
Whittington. Glos 3F 49
Whittington. Lanc 2F 97
Whittington. Norf 1G 65
Whittington. Shrp 2F 71
Whittington. Staf 2C 60
(nr. Kinver)
Whittington. Staf 5F 73
(nr. Lichfield)
Whittington. Warw 1G 61
Whittington. Worc 5C 60
Whittington Barracks. Staf 5F 73
Whittlebury. Nptn 1E 51
Whittleford. Warw 1H 61
Whittle-le-Woods. Lanc 2D 90
Whittlesey. Cambs 1B 64
Whittlesford. Cambs 1E 53
Whittlestone Head. Bkbn 3F 91
Whitton. N Lin 2C 94
Whitton. Nmbd 4E 121
Whitton. Powy 4E 59
Whitton. Bord 2B 120
Whitton. Shrp 3H 59
Whitton. Stoc T 2A 106
Whittonditch. Wilts 4A 36
Whittonstall. Nmbd 4D 114
Whitway. Hants 1C 24
Whitwell. Derbs 3C 86
Whitwell. Herts 3B 52
Whitwell. IOW 5D 16
Whitwell. N Yor 5F 105
Whitwell. Rut 5G 75
Whitwell-on-the-Hill. N Yor 3B 100
Whitwick. Leics 4B 74
Whitwood. W Yor 2E 93
Whitworth. Lanc 3G 91
Whixall. Shrp 2H 71
Whixley. N Yor 4G 99
Whoberley. W Mid 3G 61
Whorlton. Dur 3E 105
Whorlton. N Yor 4B 106
Whygate. Nmbd 2A 114
Whyle. Here 4H 59
Whyteleafe. Surr 5E 39
Wibdon. Glos 2A 34
Wibtoft. Warw 2B 62
Wichenford. Worc 4B 60
Wichling. Kent 5D 40
Wick. Bour 3G 15
Wick. Devn 2E 13
Wick. High 3F 169
Wick. Shet 8F 173
(on Mainland)
Wick. Shet 1G 173
(on Unst)
Wick. Som 2F 21
(nr. Bridgwater)
Wick. Som 1G 21
(nr. Burnham-on-Sea)
Wick. Som 4H 21
(nr. Somerton)
Wick. S Glo 4C 34
Wick. V Glam 4C 32
Wick. W Sus 5B 26
Wick. Wilts 4G 23
Wick. Worc 1E 49
Wick Airport. High 3F 169
Wicken. Cambs 3E 65
Wicken. Nptn 2F 51
Wicken Bonhunt. Essx 2E 53
Wickenby. Linc 2H 87
Wicken Green Village. Norf 2H 77
Wickersley. S Yor 1B 86
Wicker Street Green. Suff 1C 54
Wickford. Essx 1B 40
Wickham. Hants 1D 16
Wickham. W Ber 4B 36
Wickham Bishops. Essx 4B 54
Wickhambreaux. Kent 5G 41
Wickhambrook. Suff 5G 65

Wickhamford—Zouch

Wickhamford. *Worc* 1F **49**
Wickham Green. *Suff* 4C **66**
Wickham Heath. *W Ber* 5C **36**
Wickham Market. *Suff* 5F **67**
Wickhampton. *Norf* 5G **79**
Wickham St Paul. *Essx* 2B **54**
Wickham Skeith. *Suff* 4C **66**
Wickham Street. *Suff* 4C **66**
Wick Hill. *Wok* 5F **37**
Wicklewood. *Norf* 5C **78**
Wickmere. *Norf* 2D **78**
Wick St Lawrence.
N Som 5G **33**
Wickwar. *S Glo* 3C **34**
Widdington. *Essx* 2F **53**
Widdrington. *Nmbd* 5G **121**
Widdrington Station.
Nmbd 5G **121**
Widecombe in the Moor.
Devn 5H **11**
Widegates. *Corn* 3G **7**
Widemouth Bay. *Corn* 2C **10**
Wide Open. *Tyne* 2F **115**
Widewall. *Orkn* 8D **172**
Widford. *Essx* 5G **53**
Widford. *Herts* 4E **53**
Widham. *Wilts* 3F **35**
Widmer End. *Buck* 2G **37**
Widmerpool. *Notts* 3D **74**
Widnes. *Hal* 2H **83**
Widworthy. *Devn* 3F **13**
Wigan. *G Man* 4D **90**
Wigbeth. *Dors* 2F **15**
Wigborough. *Som* 1H **13**
Wiggaton. *Devn* 3E **12**
Wiggenhall St Germans.
Norf 4E **77**
Wiggenhall St Mary Magdalen.
Norf 4E **77**
Wiggenhall St Mary the Virgin.
Norf 4E **77**
Wiggenhall St Peter. *Norf* 4F **77**
Wiggens Green. *Essx* 1G **53**
Wigginton. *Herts* 4H **51**
Wigginton. *Oxon* 2B **50**
Wigginton. *Staf* 5G **73**
Wigginton. *York* 4H **99**
Wigglesworth. *N Yor* 4H **97**
Wiggonby. *Cumb* 4D **112**
Wiggonholt. *W Sus* 4B **26**
Wighill. *N Yor* 5G **99**
Wighton. *Norf* 1B **78**
Wightwick. *Staf* 1C **60**
Wigley. *Hants* 1B **16**
Wigmore. *Here* 4G **59**
Wigmore. *Medw* 4C **40**
Wigsley. *Notts* 3F **87**
Wigsthorpe. *Nptn* 2H **63**
Wigston. *Leics* 1D **62**
Wigtoft. *Linc* 2B **76**
Wigton. *Cumb* 5D **112**
Wigtown. *Dum* 4B **110**
Wigtwizzle. *S Yor* 1G **85**
Wike. *W Yor* 5F **99**
Wilbarston. *Nptn* 2F **63**
Wilberfoss. *E Yor* 4B **100**
Wilburton. *Cambs* 3D **65**
Wilby. *Norf* 2C **66**
Wilby. *Nptn* 4F **63**
Wilby. *Suff* 3E **67**
Wilcot. *Wilts* 5G **35**
Wilcott. *Shrp* 4F **71**
Wilcove. *Corn* 3A **8**
Wildboarclough. *Ches E* 4D **85**
Wilden. *Bed* 5H **63**
Wilden. *Worc* 3C **60**
Wildern. *Hants* 1C **16**
Wilderspool. *Warr* 2A **84**
Wilde Street. *Suff* 3G **65**
Wildhern. *Hants* 1B **24**
Wildmanbridge. *S Lan* 4B **128**
Wildmoor. *Worc* 3D **60**
Wildsworth. *Linc* 1F **87**
Wildwood. *Staf* 3D **72**
Wilford. *Nott* 2C **74**
Wilkesley. *Ches E* 1A **72**
Wilkhaven. *High* 5G **165**
Wilkieston. *W Lot* 3E **129**
Wilksby. *Linc* 4B **88**
Willand. *Devn* 1D **12**
Willaston. *Ches E* 5A **84**
Willaston. *Ches W* 3F **83**
Willaston. *IOM* 4C **108**
Willen. *Mil* 1G **51**
Willenhall. *W Mid* 3A **62**
(nr. Coventry)
Willenhall. *W Mid* 1D **60**
(nr. Wolverhampton)
Willerby. *E Yor* 1D **94**
Willerby. *N Yor* 2E **101**
Willersey. *Glos* 2G **49**
Willersley. *Here* 1G **47**
Willesborough. *Kent* 1E **28**
Willesborough Lees. *Kent* 1E **29**
Willesden. *G Lon* 2D **38**
Willesley. *Wilts* 3D **34**
Willett. *Som* 3E **20**
Willey. *Shrp* 1A **60**
Willey. *Warw* 2B **62**
Willey Green. *Surr* 5A **38**
Williamscot. *Oxon* 1C **50**
Williamsetter. *Shet* 9E **173**
Willian. *Herts* 2C **52**
Willingale. *Essx* 5F **53**
Willingdon. *E Sus* 5G **27**
Willingham. *Cambs* 3D **64**
Willingham by Stow. *Linc* 2F **87**
Willingham Green. *Cambs* 5F **65**
Willington. *Bed* 1B **52**
Willington. *Derbs* 3G **73**
Willington. *Dur* 1E **105**
Willington. *Tyne* 3G **115**
Willington. *Warw* 2A **50**
Willington Corner.
Ches W 4H **83**
Willisham Tye. *Suff* 5C **66**
Willitoft. *E Yor* 1H **93**
Williton. *Som* 2D **20**
Willoughbridge. *Staf* 1B **72**
Willoughby. *Linc* 3D **88**
Willoughby. *Warw* 4C **62**
Willoughby-on-the-Wolds.
Notts 3D **74**
Willoughby Waterleys.
Leics 1C **62**
Willoughton. *Linc* 1G **87**
Willow Green. *Worc* 5B **60**
Willows Green. *Essx* 4H **53**
Willsbridge. *S Glo* 4B **34**
Willslock. *Staf* 2E **73**
Wilmcote. *Warw* 5F **61**
Wilmington. *Bath* 5B **34**
Wilmington. *Devn* 3F **13**
Wilmington. *E Sus* 5G **27**
Wilmington. *Kent* 3G **39**
Wilmslow. *Ches E* 2C **84**
Wilnecote. *Staf* 5G **73**
Wilney Green. *Norf* 2C **66**
Wilpshire. *Lanc* 1E **91**
Wilsden. *W Yor* 1A **92**
Wilsford. *Linc* 1H **75**
Wilsford. *Wilts* 3G **23**
(nr. Amesbury)
Wilsford. *Wilts* 1G **23**
(nr. Devizes)
Wilsill. *N Yor* 3D **98**
Wilsley Green. *Kent* 2B **28**
Wilson. *Here* 3A **48**
Wilson. *Leics* 3B **74**
Wilsontown. *S Lan* 4C **128**
Wilstead. *Bed* 1A **52**
Wilsthorpe. *E Yor* 3F **101**
Wilsthorpe. *Linc* 4H **75**
Wilstone. *Herts* 4H **51**
Wilton. *Cumb* 3B **102**
Wilton. *N Yor* 1C **100**
Wilton. *Red C* 3C **106**
Wilton. *Bord* 3H **119**
Wilton. *Wilts* 5A **36**
(nr. Marlborough)
Wilton. *Wilts* 3F **23**
(nr. Salisbury)
Wimbish. *Essx* 2F **53**
Wimbish Green. *Essx* 2G **53**
Wimblebury. *Staf* 4E **73**
Wimbledon. *G Lon* 3D **38**
Wimblington. *Cambs* 1D **64**
Wimboldsley. *Ches W* 4A **84**
Wimborne Minster.
Dors 2F **15**
Wimborne St Giles. *Dors* 1F **15**
Wimbotsham. *Norf* 5F **77**
Wimpole. *Cambs* 1D **52**
Wimpstone. *Warw* 1H **49**
Wincanton. *Som* 4C **22**
Winceby. *Linc* 4C **88**
Wincham. *Ches W* 3A **84**
Winchburgh. *W Lot* 2D **129**
Winchcombe. *Glos* 3F **49**
Winchelsea. *E Sus* 4D **28**
Winchelsea Beach. *E Sus* 4D **28**
Winchester. *Hants* 4C **24** & **203**
Winchet Hill. *Kent* 1B **28**
Winchfield. *Hants* 1F **25**
Winchmore Hill. *Buck* 1A **38**
Winchmore Hill. *G Lon* 1E **39**
Wincle. *Ches E* 4D **84**
Windermere. *Cumb* 5F **103**
Winderton. *Warw* 1B **50**
Windhill. *High* 4H **157**
Windle Hill. *Ches W* 3F **83**
Windlesham. *Surr* 4A **38**
Windley. *Derbs* 1H **73**
Windmill. *Derbs* 3F **85**
Windmill Hill. *E Sus* 4H **27**
Windmill Hill. *Som* 1G **13**
Windrush. *Glos* 4G **49**
Windsor. *Wind* 3A **38** & **203**
Windsor Green. *Suff* 5A **66**
Windyedge. *Abers* 4G **153**
Windygates. *Fife* 3F **137**
Windyharbour. *Ches E* 3C **84**
Windyknowe. *W Lot* 3C **128**
Wineham. *W Sus* 3D **26**
Winestead. *E Yor* 2G **95**
Winfarthing. *Norf* 2D **66**
Winford. *IOW* 4D **16**
Winford. *N Som* 5A **34**
Winforton. *Here* 1F **47**
Winfrith Newburgh. *Dors* 4D **14**
Wing. *Buck* 3G **51**
Wing. *Rut* 5F **75**
Wingate. *Dur* 1A **106**
Wingates. *G Man* 4E **91**
Wingates. *Nmbd* 5F **121**
Wingerworth. *Derbs* 4A **86**
Wingfield. *C Beds* 3A **52**
Wingfield. *Suff* 3E **67**
Wingfield. *Wilts* 1D **22**
Wingfield Park. *Derbs* 5A **86**
Wingham. *Kent* 5G **41**
Wingmore. *Kent* 1F **29**
Wingrave. *Buck* 4G **51**
Winkburn. *Notts* 5E **86**
Winkfield. *Brac* 3A **38**
Winkfield Row. *Brac* 4G **37**
Winkhill. *Staf* 5E **85**
Winklebury. *Hants* 1E **24**
Winkleigh. *Devn* 2G **11**
Winksley. *N Yor* 2E **99**
Winkton. *Dors* 3G **15**
Winlaton. *Tyne* 3E **115**
Winlaton Mill. *Tyne* 3E **115**
Winless. *High* 3F **169**
Winmarleigh. *Lanc* 5D **96**
Winnal Common. *Here* 2H **47**
Winnard's Perch. *Corn* 2D **6**
Winnersh. *Wok* 4F **37**
Winnington. *Ches W* 3A **84**
Winnington. *Staf* 2B **72**
Winnothdale. *Staf* 1E **73**
Winscales. *Cumb* 2B **102**
Winscombe. *N Som* 1H **21**
Winsford. *Ches W* 4A **84**
Winsford. *Som* 3C **20**
Winsham. *Devn* 3F **19**
Winsham. *Som* 2G **13**
Winshill. *Staf* 3G **73**
Winsh-wen. *Swan* 3F **31**
Winskill. *Cumb* 1G **103**
Winslade. *Hants* 2E **25**
Winsley. *Wilts* 5C **34**
Winslow. *Buck* 3F **51**
Winson. *Glos* 5F **49**
Winson Green. *W Mid* 2E **61**
Winsor. *Hants* 1B **16**
Winster. *Cumb* 5F **103**
Winster. *Derbs* 4G **85**
Winston. *Dur* 3E **105**
Winston. *Suff* 4D **66**
Winstone. *Glos* 5E **49**
Winswell. *Devn* 1E **11**
Winterborne Clenston.
Dors 2D **14**
Winterborne Herringston.
Dors 4B **14**
Winterborne Houghton.
Dors 2D **14**
Winterborne Kingston.
Dors 3D **14**
Winterborne Monkton.
Dors 4B **14**
Winterborne St Martin.
Dors 4B **14**
Winterborne Stickland.
Dors 2D **14**
Winterborne Whitechurch.
Dors 2D **14**
Winterborne Zelston.
Dors 3E **15**
Winterbourne. *S Glo* 3B **34**
Winterbourne. *W Ber* 4C **36**
Winterbourne Abbas.
Dors 3B **14**
Winterbourne Bassett.
Wilts 4G **35**
Winterbourne Dauntsey.
Wilts 3G **23**
Winterbourne Earls. *Wilts* 3G **23**
Winterbourne Gunner.
Wilts 3G **23**
Winterbourne Monkton.
Wilts 4F **35**
Winterbourne Steepleton.
Dors 4B **14**
Winterbourne Stoke.
Wilts 2F **23**
Winterbrook. *Oxon* 3E **36**
Winterburn. *N Yor* 4B **98**
Winter Gardens. *Essx* 2B **40**
Winterhay Green. *Som* 1G **13**
Winteringham. *N Lin* 2C **94**
Winterley. *Ches E* 5B **84**
Wintersett. *W Yor* 3D **93**
Winterton. *N Lin* 3C **94**
Winterton-on-Sea. *Norf* 4G **79**
Winthorpe. *Linc* 4E **89**
Winthorpe. *Notts* 5F **87**
Winton. *Bour* 3F **15**
Winton. *Cumb* 3A **104**
Winton. *E Sus* 5G **27**
Wintringham. *N Yor* 2C **100**
Winwick. *Cambs* 2A **64**
Winwick. *Nptn* 3D **62**
Winwick. *Warr* 1A **84**
Wirksworth. *Derbs* 5G **85**
Wirswall. *Ches E* 1H **71**
Wisbech. *Cambs* 4D **76**
Wisbech St Mary. *Cambs* 5D **76**
Wisborough Green.
W Sus 3B **26**
Wiseton. *Notts* 2E **86**
Wishaw. *N Lan* 4B **128**
Wishaw. *Warw* 1F **61**
Wisley. *Surr* 5B **38**
Wispington. *Linc* 3B **88**
Wissenden. *Kent* 1D **28**
Wissett. *Suff* 3F **67**
Wistanstow. *Shrp* 2G **59**
Wistanswick. *Shrp* 3A **72**
Wistaston. *Ches E* 5A **84**
Wiston. *Pemb* 3E **43**
Wiston. *S Lan* 1B **118**
Wiston. *W Sus* 4C **26**
Wistow. *Cambs* 2B **64**
Wistow. *N Yor* 1F **93**
Wiswell. *Lanc* 1F **91**
Witcham. *Cambs* 2D **64**
Witchampton. *Dors* 2E **15**
Witchford. *Cambs* 3E **65**
Witham. *Essx* 4B **54**
Witham Friary. *Som* 2C **22**
Witham on the Hill. *Linc* 4H **75**
Witham St Hughs. *Linc* 4F **87**
Withcall. *Linc* 2B **88**
Witherenden Hill. *E Sus* 3H **27**
Withergate. *Norf* 3E **79**
Witheridge. *Devn* 1B **12**
Witheridge Hill. *Oxon* 3E **37**
Witherley. *Leics* 1H **61**
Withermarsh Green. *Suff* 2D **54**
Withern. *Linc* 2D **88**
Withernsea. *E Yor* 2G **95**
Withernwick. *E Yor* 5F **101**
Withersdale Street. *Suff* 2E **67**
Withersfield. *Suff* 1G **53**
Witherslack. *Cumb* 1D **96**
Withiel. *Corn* 2D **6**
Withiel Florey. *Som* 3C **20**
Withington. *Glos* 4F **49**
Withington. *G Man* 1C **84**
Withington. *Here* 1A **48**
Withington. *Shrp* 4H **71**
Withington. *Staf* 2E **73**
Withington Green. *Ches E* 3C **84**
Withington Marsh. *Here* 1A **48**
Withleigh. *Devn* 1C **12**
Withnell. *Lanc* 2E **91**
Withnell Fold. *Lanc* 2E **90**
Withybrook. *Warw* 2B **62**
Withycombe. *Som* 2D **20**
Withycombe Raleigh.
Devn 4D **12**
Withyham. *E Sus* 2F **27**
Withypool. *Som* 3B **20**
Witley. *Surr* 1A **26**
Witnesham. *Suff* 5D **66**
Witney. *Oxon* 4B **50**
Wittering. *Pet* 5H **75**
Wittersham. *Kent* 3D **28**
Witton. *Norf* 5F **79**
Witton. *Worc* 4D **60**
Witton Bridge. *Norf* 2F **79**
Witton Gilbert. *Dur* 5F **115**
Witton-le-Wear. *Dur* 1E **105**
Witton Park. *Dur* 1E **105**
Wiveliscombe. *Som* 4D **20**
Wivelrod. *Hants* 3E **25**
Wivelsfield. *E Sus* 3E **27**
Wivelsfield Green. *E Sus* 4E **27**
Wivenhoe. *Essx* 3D **54**
Wiveton. *Norf* 1C **78**
Wix. *Essx* 3E **55**
Wixford. *Warw* 5E **61**
Wixhill. *Shrp* 3H **71**
Wixoe. *Suff* 1H **53**
Woburn. *C Beds* 2H **51**
Woburn Sands. *Mil* 2H **51**
Woking. *Surr* 5B **38**
Wokingham. *Wok* 5G **37**
Wolborough. *Devn* 5B **12**
Woldingham. *Surr* 5E **39**
Wold Newton. *E Yor* 2E **101**
Wold Newton. *NE Lin* 1B **88**
Wolferlow. *Here* 4A **60**
Wolferton. *Norf* 3F **77**
Wolfhill. *Per* 5A **144**
Wolf's Castle. *Pemb* 2D **42**
Wolfsdale. *Pemb* 2D **42**
Wolgarston. *Staf* 4D **72**
Wollaston. *Nptn* 4G **63**
Wollaston. *Shrp* 4F **71**
Wollaston. *W Mid* 2C **60**
Wollaton. *Nott* 1C **74**
Wollerton. *Shrp* 2A **72**
Wollescote. *W Mid* 2D **60**
Wolseley Bridge. *Staf* 3E **73**
Wolsingham. *Dur* 1D **105**
Wolstanton. *Staf* 1C **72**
Wolston. *Warw* 3B **62**
Wolsty. *Cumb* 4C **112**
Wolterton. *Norf* 2D **78**
Wolvercote. *Oxon* 5C **50**
Wolverhampton.
W Mid 1D **60** & **203**
Wolverley. *Shrp* 2G **71**
Wolverley. *Worc* 3C **60**
Wolverton. *Hants* 1D **24**
Wolverton. *Mil* 1G **51**
Wolverton. *Warw* 4G **61**
Wolverton. *Wilts* 3C **22**
Wolverton Common.
Hants 1D **24**
Wolvesnewton. *Mon* 2H **33**
Wolvey. *Warw* 2B **62**
Wolvey Heath. *Warw* 2B **62**
Wolviston. *Stoc T* 2B **106**
Womaston. *Powy* 4E **59**
Wombleton. *N Yor* 1A **100**
Wombourne. *Staf* 1C **60**
Wombwell. *S Yor* 4D **93**
Womenswold. *Kent* 5G **41**
Womersley. *N Yor* 3F **93**
Wonersh. *Surr* 1B **26**
Wonson. *Devn* 4G **11**
Wonston. *Dors* 2C **14**
Wonston. *Hants* 3C **24**
Wooburn. *Buck* 2A **38**
Wooburn Green. *Buck* 2A **38**
Wood. *Pemb* 2C **42**
Woodacott. *Devn* 2D **11**
Woodale. *N Yor* 2C **98**
Woodall. *S Yor* 2B **86**
Woodbank. *Ches W* 3F **83**
Woodbastwick. *Norf* 4F **79**
Woodbeck. *Notts* 3E **87**
Woodborough. *Notts* 1D **74**
Woodborough. *Wilts* 1G **23**
Woodbridge. *Devn* 3E **13**
Woodbridge. *Dors* 1C **14**
Woodbridge. *Suff* 1F **55**
Wood Burcote. *Nptn* 1E **51**
Woodbury. *Devn* 4D **12**
Woodbury Salterton.
Devn 4D **12**
Woodchester. *Glos* 5D **48**
Woodchurch. *Kent* 2D **28**
Woodchurch. *Mers* 2E **83**
Woodcock Heath. *Staf* 3E **73**
Woodcombe. *Som* 2C **20**
Woodcote. *Oxon* 3E **37**
Woodcote Green. *Worc* 3D **60**
Woodcott. *Hants* 1C **24**
Woodcroft. *Glos* 2A **34**
Woodcutts. *Dors* 1E **15**
Wood Dalling. *Norf* 3C **78**
Woodditton. *Cambs* 5F **65**
Woodeaton. *Oxon* 4D **50**
Wood Eaton. *Staf* 4C **72**
Wood End. *Bed* 4H **63**
Woodend. *Cumb* 5C **102**
Wood End. *Herts* 3D **52**
Woodend. *Nptn* 1E **50**
Woodend. *Staf* 3F **73**
Wood End. *Warw* 2G **61**
(nr. Bedworth)
Wood End. *Warw* 1G **61**
(nr. Dordon)
Wood End. *Warw* 3F **61**
(nr. Tanworth-in-Arden)
Woodend. *W Sus* 2G **17**
Wood Enderby. *Linc* 4B **88**
Woodend Green. *Essx* 3F **53**
Woodfalls. *Wilts* 4G **23**
Woodfield. *Oxon* 3D **50**
Woodfields. *Lanc* 1E **91**
Woodford. *Corn* 1C **10**
Woodford. *Devn* 3D **9**
Woodford. *Glos* 2B **34**
Woodford. *G Lon* 1E **39**
Woodford. *G Man* 2C **84**
Woodford. *Nptn* 3G **63**
Woodford. *Plym* 3B **8**
Woodford Green. *G Lon* 1F **39**
Woodford Halse. *Nptn* 5C **62**
Woodgate. *Norf* 4C **78**
Woodgate. *W Mid* 2D **61**
Woodgate. *W Sus* 5A **26**
Woodgate. *Worc* 4D **60**
Wood Green. *G Lon* 1D **39**
Woodgreen. *Hants* 1G **15**
Woodgreen. *Oxon* 4B **50**
Woodhall. *Inv* 2E **127**
Woodhall. *Linc* 4B **88**
Woodhall. *N Yor* 5C **104**
Woodhall Spa. *Linc* 4A **88**
Woodham. *Surr* 4B **38**
Woodham Ferrers. *Essx* 1B **40**
Woodham Mortimer.
Essx 5B **54**
Woodham Walter. *Essx* 5B **54**
Woodhaven. *Fife* 1G **137**
Wood Hayes. *W Mid* 5D **72**
Woodhead. *Abers* 2G **161**
(nr. Fraserburgh)
Woodhead. *Abers* 5E **161**
(nr. Fyvie)
Woodhill. *N Som* 4H **33**
Woodhill. *Shrp* 2B **60**
Woodhill. *Som* 4G **21**
Woodhorn. *Nmbd* 1G **115**
Woodhouse. *Leics* 4C **74**
Woodhouse. *S Yor* 2B **86**
Woodhouse. *W Yor* 1C **92**
(nr. Leeds)
Woodhouse. *W Yor* 2D **93**
(nr. Normanton)
Woodhouse Eaves. *Leics* 4C **74**
Woodhouses. *Ches W* 3H **83**
Woodhouses. *G Man* 4H **91**
(nr. Failsworth)
Woodhouses. *G Man* 1B **84**
(nr. Sale)
Woodhouses. *Staf* 4F **73**
Woodhuish. *Devn* 3F **9**
Woodhurst. *Cambs* 3C **64**
Woodingdean. *Brig* 5E **27**
Woodland. *Devn* 2D **9**
Woodland. *Dur* 2D **104**
Woodland Head. *Devn* 3A **12**
Woodlands. *Abers* 4E **153**
Woodlands. *Dors* 2F **15**
Woodlands. *Hants* 1B **16**
Woodlands. *Kent* 4G **39**
Woodlands. *N Yor* 4F **99**
Woodlands. *S Yor* 4F **93**
Woodlands Park. *Wind* 4G **37**
Woodlands St Mary.
W Ber 4B **36**
Woodlane. *Shrp* 3A **72**
Woodlane. *Staf* 3F **73**
Woodleigh. *Devn* 4D **8**
Woodlesford. *W Yor* 2D **92**
Woodley. *G Man* 1D **84**
Woodley. *Wok* 4F **37**
Woodmancote. *Glos* 3E **49**
(nr. Cheltenham)
Woodmancote. *Glos* 5F **49**
(nr. Cirencester)
Woodmancote. *W Sus* 2F **17**
(nr. Chichester)
Woodmancote. *W Sus* 4D **26**
(nr. Henfield)
Woodmancote. *Worc* 1E **49**
Woodmancott. *Hants* 2D **24**
Woodmansey. *E Yor* 1D **94**
Woodmansgreen. *W Sus* 4G **25**
Woodmansterne. *Surr* 5D **39**
Woodmanton. *Devn* 4D **12**
Woodmill. *Staf* 3F **73**
Woodminton. *Wilts* 4F **23**
Woodnesborough. *Kent* 5H **41**
Woodnewton. *Nptn* 1H **63**
Woodnook. *Linc* 2G **75**
Wood Norton. *Norf* 3C **78**
Woodplumpton. *Lanc* 1D **90**
Woodrising. *Norf* 5B **78**
Woodrow. *Cumb* 5D **112**
Woodrow. *Dors* 1C **14**
(nr. Fifehead Neville)
Woodrow. *Dors* 2C **14**
(nr. Hazelbury Bryan)
Wood Row. *W Yor* 2D **93**
Woods Eaves. *Here* 1F **47**
Woodseaves. *Shrp* 2A **72**
Woodseaves. *Staf* 3B **72**
Woodsend. *Wilts* 4H **35**
Woodsetts. *S Yor* 2C **86**
Woodsford. *Dors* 3C **14**
Wood's Green. *E Sus* 2H **27**
Woodshaw. *Wilts* 3F **35**
Woodside. *Aber* 3G **153**
Woodside. *Brac* 3A **38**
Woodside. *Derbs* 1A **74**
Woodside. *Dum* 2B **112**
Woodside. *Dur* 2E **105**
Woodside. *Fife* 3G **137**
Woodside. *Herts* 5C **52**
Woodside. *Per* 5B **144**
Wood Stanway. *Glos* 2F **49**
Woodstock. *Oxon* 4C **50**
Woodstock Slop. *Pemb* 2E **43**
Woodston. *Pet* 1A **64**
Wood Street. *Norf* 3F **79**
Wood Street Village. *Surr* 5A **38**
Woodthorpe. *Derbs* 3B **86**
Woodthorpe. *Leics* 4C **74**
Woodthorpe. *Linc* 2D **88**
Woodthorpe. *Notts* 1C **74**
Woodthorpe. *York* 5H **99**
Woodton. *Norf* 1E **67**
Woodtown. *Devn* 4E **19**
(nr. Bideford)
Woodtown. *Devn* 4E **19**
(nr. Littleham)
Woodvale. *Mers* 3B **90**
Woodville. *Derbs* 4H **73**
Woodwalton. *Cambs* 2B **64**
Woodwick. *Orkn* 5C **172**
Woodyates. *Dors* 1F **15**
Woody Bay. *Devn* 2G **19**
Woofferton. *Shrp* 4H **59**
Wookey. *Som* 2A **22**
Wookey Hole. *Som* 2A **22**
Wool. *Dors* 4D **14**
Woolacombe. *Devn* 2E **19**
Woolage Green. *Kent* 1G **29**
Woolage Village. *Kent* 5G **41**
Woolaston. *Glos* 2A **34**
Woolavington. *Som* 2G **21**
Woolbeding. *W Sus* 4G **25**
Woolcotts. *Som* 3C **20**
Wooldale. *W Yor* 4B **92**
Wooler. *Nmbd* 2D **121**
Woolfardisworthy. *Devn* 4D **18**
(nr. Bideford)
Woolfardisworthy. *Devn* 2B **12**
(nr. Crediton)
Woolfords. *S Lan* 4D **128**
Woolgarston. *Dors* 4E **15**
Woolhampton. *W Ber* 5D **36**
Woolhope. *Here* 2B **48**
Woolland. *Dors* 2C **14**
Woollard. *Bath* 5B **34**
Woolley. *Bath* 5C **34**
Woolley. *Cambs* 3A **64**
Woolley. *Corn* 1C **10**
Woolley. *Derbs* 4A **86**
Woolley. *W Yor* 3D **92**
Woolley Green. *Wilts* 5D **34**
Woolmere Green. *Worc* 4D **60**
Woolmer Green. *Herts* 4C **52**
Woolminstone. *Som* 2H **13**
Woolpit. *Suff* 4B **66**
Woolridge. *Glos* 3D **48**
Woolscott. *Warw* 4B **62**
Woolsery. *Devn* 4D **18**
Woolsington. *Tyne* 3E **115**
Woolstaston. *Shrp* 1G **59**
Woolsthorpe By Belvoir.
Linc 2F **75**
Woolsthorpe-by-Colsterworth.
Linc 3G **75**
Woolston. *Devn* 4D **8**
Woolston. *Shrp* 2G **59**
(nr. Church Stretton)
Woolston. *Shrp* 3F **71**
(nr. Oswestry)
Woolston. *Som* 4B **22**
Woolston. *Sotn* 1C **16**
Woolston. *Warr* 1A **84**
Woolstone. *Glos* 2E **49**
Woolstone. *Oxon* 3A **36**
Woolston Green.
Devn 2D **9**
Woolton. *Mers* 2G **83**
Woolton Hill. *Hants* 5C **36**
Woolverstone. *Suff* 2E **55**
Woolverton. *Som* 1C **22**
Woolwell. *Devn* 2B **8**
Woolwich. *G Lon* 3F **39**
Woonton. *Here* 5F **59**
(nr. Kington)
Woonton. *Here* 4H **59**
(nr. Leominster)
Wooperton. *Nmbd* 2E **121**
Woore. *Shrp* 1B **72**
Wooth. *Dors* 3H **13**
Wooton. *Shrp* 2B **60**
Wootton. *Bed* 1A **52**
Wootton. *Hants* 3H **15**
Wootton. *IOW* 3D **16**
Wootton. *Kent* 1G **29**
Wootton. *Nptn* 5E **63**
Wootton. *N Lin* 3D **94**
Wootton. *Oxon* 5C **50**
(nr. Abingdon)
Wootton. *Oxon* 4C **50**
(nr. Woodstock)
Wootton. *Shrp* 3G **59**
(nr. Ludlow)
Wootton. *Shrp* 3F **71**
(nr. Oswestry)
Wootton. *Staf* 3C **72**
(nr. Eccleshall)
Wootton. *Staf* 1F **73**
(nr. Ellastone)
Wootton Bridge. *IOW* 3D **16**
Wootton Common. *IOW* 3D **16**
Wootton Courtenay.
Som 2C **20**
Wootton Fitzpaine. *Dors* 3G **13**
Wootton Rivers. *Wilts* 5G **35**
Wootton St Lawrence.
Hants 1D **24**
Wootton Wawen. *Warw* 4F **61**
Worcester. *Worc* 5C **60** & **203**
Worcester Park. *G Lon* 4D **38**
Wordsley. *W Mid* 2C **60**
Worfield. *Shrp* 1B **60**
Work. *Orkn* 6D **172**
Workhouse Green. *Suff* 2C **54**
Workington. *Cumb* 2A **102**
Worksop. *Notts* 3C **86**
Worlaby. *N Lin* 3D **94**
Worlds End. *Hants* 1E **17**
Worldsend. *Shrp* 1G **59**
World's End. *W Ber* 4C **36**
Worlds End. *W Mid* 2F **61**
World's End. *W Sus* 4E **27**
Worle. *N Som* 5G **33**
Worleston. *Ches E* 5A **84**
Worlingham. *Suff* 2G **67**
Worlington. *Suff* 3F **65**
Worlingworth. *Suff* 4E **67**
Wormbridge. *Here* 2H **47**
Wormegay. *Norf* 4F **77**
Wormelow Tump. *Here* 2H **47**
Wormhill. *Derbs* 3F **85**
Wormingford. *Essx* 2C **54**
Worminghall. *Buck* 5E **51**
Wormington. *Glos* 2F **49**
Worminster. *Som* 2A **22**
Wormit. *Fife* 1F **137**
Wormleighton. *Warw* 5B **62**
Wormley. *Herts* 5D **52**
Wormley. *Surr* 2A **26**
Wormshill. *Kent* 5C **40**
Wormsley. *Here* 1H **47**
Worplesdon. *Surr* 5A **38**
Worrall. *S Yor* 1H **85**
Worsbrough. *S Yor* 4D **92**
Worsley. *G Man* 4F **91**
Worstead. *Norf* 3F **79**
Worsthorne. *Lanc* 1G **91**
Worston. *Lanc* 5G **97**
Worth. *Kent* 5H **41**
Worth. *W Sus* 2E **27**
Wortham. *Suff* 3C **66**
Worthen. *Shrp* 5F **71**
Worthenbury. *Wrex* 1G **71**
Worthing. *Norf* 4B **78**
Worthing. *W Sus* 5C **26**
Worthington. *Leics* 3B **74**
Worth Matravers. *Dors* 5E **15**
Worting. *Hants* 1E **24**
Wortley. *Glos* 2C **34**
Wortley. *S Yor* 1H **85**
Wortley. *W Yor* 1C **92**
Worton. *N Yor* 5C **104**
Worton. *Wilts* 1E **23**
Wortwell. *Norf* 2E **67**
Wotherton. *Shrp* 5E **71**
Wothorpe. *Nptn* 5H **75**
Wotter. *Devn* 2B **8**
Wotton. *Glos* 4D **48**
Wotton. *Surr* 1C **26**
Wotton-under-Edge. *Glos* 2C **34**
Wotton Underwood. *Buck* 4E **51**
Wouldham. *Kent* 4B **40**
Wrabness. *Essx* 2E **55**
Wrafton. *Devn* 3E **19**
Wragby. *Linc* 3A **88**
Wragby. *W Yor* 3E **93**
Wramplingham. *Norf* 5D **78**
Wrangbrook. *W Yor* 3E **93**
Wrangle. *Linc* 5D **88**
Wrangle Lowgate. *Linc* 5D **88**
Wrangway. *Som* 1E **13**
Wrantage. *Som* 4G **21**
Wrawby. *N Lin* 4D **94**
Wraxall. *N Som* 4H **33**
Wraxall. *Som* 3B **22**
Wray. *Lanc* 3F **97**
Wraysbury. *Wind* 3B **38**
Wrayton. *Lanc* 2F **97**
Wrea Green. *Lanc* 1B **90**
Wreay. *Cumb* 5F **113**
(nr. Carlisle)
Wreay. *Cumb* 2F **103**
(nr. Penrith)
Wrecclesham. *Surr* 2G **25**
Wrecsam. *Wrex* 5F **83**
Wrekenton. *Tyne* 4F **115**
Wrelton. *N Yor* 1B **100**
Wrenbury. *Ches E* 1H **71**
Wreningham. *Norf* 1D **66**
Wrentham. *Suff* 2G **67**
Wrenthorpe. *W Yor* 2D **92**
Wrentnall. *Shrp* 5G **71**
Wressle. *E Yor* 1H **93**
Wressle. *N Lin* 4C **94**
Wrestlingworth. *C Beds* 1C **52**
Wretton. *Norf* 1F **65**
Wrexham. *Wrex* 5F **83**
Wreyland. *Devn* 4A **12**
Wrickton. *Shrp* 2A **60**
Wrightington Bar. *Lanc* 3D **90**
Wright's Green. *Essx* 4F **53**
Wrinehill. *Staf* 1B **72**
Wrington. *N Som* 5H **33**
Writtle. *Essx* 5G **53**
Wrockwardine. *Telf* 4A **72**
Wroot. *N Lin* 4H **93**
Wrotham. *Kent* 5H **39**
Wrotham Heath. *Kent* 5H **39**
Wroughton. *Swin* 3G **35**
Wroxall. *IOW* 4D **16**
Wroxall. *Warw* 3G **61**
Wroxeter. *Shrp* 5H **71**
Wroxham. *Norf* 4F **79**
Wroxton. *Oxon* 1C **50**
Wyaston. *Derbs* 1F **73**
Wyatt's Green. *Essx* 1G **39**
Wybers Wood. *NE Lin* 4F **95**
Wyberton. *Linc* 1C **76**
Wyboston. *Bed* 5A **64**
Wybunbury. *Ches E* 1A **72**
Wychbold. *Worc* 4D **60**
Wych Cross. *E Sus* 2F **27**
Wychnor. *Staf* 4F **73**
Wychnor Bridges. *Staf* 4F **73**
Wyck. *Hants* 3F **25**
Wyck Hill. *Glos* 3G **49**
Wyck Rissington. *Glos* 3G **49**
Wycliffe. *Dur* 3E **105**
Wycombe Marsh. *Buck* 2G **37**
Wyddial. *Herts* 2D **52**
Wye. *Kent* 1E **29**
Wyesham. *Mon* 4A **48**
Wyfold Grange. *Oxon* 3E **37**
Wyfordby. *Leics* 4E **75**
Wyke. *Devn* 3B **12**
Wyke. *Dors* 4C **22**
Wyke. *Shrp* 5A **72**
Wyke. *Surr* 5A **38**
Wyke. *W Yor* 2B **92**
Wyke Champflower. *Som* 3B **22**
Wykeham. *Linc* 3B **76**
Wykeham. *N Yor* 2C **100**
(nr. Malton)
Wykeham. *N Yor* 1D **100**
(nr. Scarborough)
Wyken. *Shrp* 1B **60**
Wyken. *W Mid* 2A **62**
Wyke Regis. *Dors* 5B **14**
Wyke, The. *Shrp* 5B **72**
Wykey. *Shrp* 3F **71**
Wykin. *Leics* 1B **62**
Wylam. *Nmbd* 3E **115**
Wylde Green. *W Mid* 1F **61**
Wylye. *Wilts* 3F **23**
Wymering. *Port* 2E **17**
Wymeswold. *Leics* 3D **74**
Wymington. *Bed* 4G **63**
Wymondham. *Leics* 4F **75**
Wymondham. *Norf* 5D **78**
Wyndham. *B'end* 2C **32**
Wynford Eagle. *Dors* 3A **14**
Wyng. *Orkn* 8C **172**
Wynyard Village. *Stoc T* 2B **106**
Wyre Piddle. *Worc* 1E **49**
Wysall. *Notts* 3D **74**
Wyson. *Here* 4H **59**
Wythall. *Worc* 3E **61**
Wytham. *Oxon* 5C **50**
Wythenshawe. *G Man* 2C **84**
Wythop Mill. *Cumb* 2C **102**
Wyton. *Cambs* 3B **64**
Wyton. *E Yor* 1E **95**
Wyverstone. *Suff* 4C **66**
Wyverstone Street. *Suff* 4C **66**
Wyville. *Linc* 3F **75**
Wyvis Lodge. *High* 1G **157**

Y

Yaddlethorpe. *N Lin* 4B **94**
Yafford. *IOW* 4C **16**
Yafforth. *N Yor* 5A **106**
Yalding. *Kent* 5A **40**
Yanley. *N Som* 5A **34**
Yanwath. *Cumb* 2G **103**
Yanworth. *Glos* 4F **49**
Yapham. *E Yor* 4B **100**
Yapton. *W Sus* 5A **26**
Yarburgh. *Linc* 1C **88**
Yarcombe. *Devn* 2F **13**
Yarde. *Som* 3D **20**
Yardley. *W Mid* 2F **61**
Yardley Gobion. *Nptn* 1F **51**
Yardley Hastings. *Nptn* 5F **63**
Yardley Wood. *W Mid* 2F **61**
Yardro. *Powy* 5E **58**
Yarhampton. *Worc* 4B **60**
Yarkhill. *Here* 1B **48**
Yarlet. *Staf* 3D **72**
Yarley. *Som* 2A **22**
Yarlington. *Som* 4B **22**
Yarm. *Stoc T* 3B **106**
Yarmouth. *IOW* 4B **16**
Yarnbrook. *Wilts* 1D **22**
Yarnfield. *Staf* 2C **72**
Yarnscombe. *Devn* 4F **19**
Yarnton. *Oxon* 4C **50**
Yarpole. *Here* 4G **59**
Yarrow. *Nmbd* 1A **114**
Yarrow. *Bord* 2F **119**
Yarrow. *Som* 2G **21**
Yarrow Feus. *Bord* 2F **119**
Yarrow Ford. *Bord* 1G **119**
Yarsop. *Here* 1H **47**
Yarwell. *Nptn* 1H **63**
Yate. *S Glo* 3C **34**
Yateley. *Hants* 5G **37**
Yatesbury. *Wilts* 4F **35**
Yattendon. *W Ber* 4D **36**
Yatton. *Here* 4G **59**
(nr. Leominster)
Yatton. *Here* 2B **48**
(nr. Ross-on-Wye)
Yatton. *N Som* 5H **33**
Yatton Keynell. *Wilts* 4D **34**
Yaverland. *IOW* 4E **16**
Yawl. *Devn* 3G **13**
Yaxham. *Norf* 4C **78**
Yaxley. *Cambs* 1A **64**
Yaxley. *Suff* 3D **66**
Yazor. *Here* 1H **47**
Y Bala. *Gwyn* 2B **70**
Y Bont-Faen. *V Glam* 4C **32**
Y Clun. *Neat* 5B **46**
Y Dref. *Gwyn* 2D **69**
Y Drenewydd. *Powy* 1D **58**
Yeading. *G Lon* 2C **38**
Yeadon. *W Yor* 5E **98**
Yealand Conyers. *Lanc* 2E **97**
Yealand Redmayne.
Lanc 2E **97**
Yealand Storrs. *Lanc* 2D **97**
Yealmpton. *Devn* 3B **8**
Yearby. *Red C* 2D **106**
Yearngill. *Cumb* 5C **112**
Yearsett. *Here* 5B **60**
Yearsley. *N Yor* 2H **99**
Yeaton. *Shrp* 4G **71**
Yeaveley. *Derbs* 1F **73**
Yeavering. *Nmbd* 1D **120**
Yedingham. *N Yor* 2C **100**
Yeldersley Hollies.
Derbs 1G **73**
Yelford. *Oxon* 5B **50**
Yelland. *Devn* 3E **19**
Yelling. *Cambs* 4B **64**
Yelsted. *Kent* 4C **40**
Yelvertoft. *Nptn* 3C **62**
Yelverton. *Devn* 2B **8**
Yelverton. *Norf* 5E **79**
Yenston. *Som* 4C **22**
Yeoford. *Devn* 3A **12**
Yeolmbridge. *Corn* 4D **10**
Yeo Mill. *Devn* 4B **20**
Yeovil. *Som* 1A **14**
Yeovil Marsh. *Som* 1A **14**
Yeovilton. *Som* 4A **22**
Yerbeston. *Pemb* 4E **43**
Yesnaby. *Orkn* 6B **172**
Yetlington. *Nmbd* 4E **121**
Yetminster. *Dors* 1A **14**
Yett. *N Lan* 4A **128**
Yett. *S Ayr* 2D **116**
Yettington. *Devn* 4D **12**
Yetts o' Muckhart.
Clac 3C **136**
Y Fali. *IOA* 3B **80**
Y Felinheli. *Gwyn* 4E **81**
Y Fenni. *Mon* 4G **47**
Y Ferwig. *Cdgn* 1B **44**
Y Fflint. *Flin* 3E **83**
Y Ffor. *Gwyn* 2C **68**
Y Fron. *Gwyn* 5E **81**
Y Gelli Gandryll. *Powy* 1F **47**
Yielden. *Bed* 4H **63**
Yieldshields. *S Lan* 4B **128**
Yiewsley. *G Lon* 2B **38**
Yinstay. *Orkn* 6E **172**
Ynysboeth. *Rhon* 2D **32**
Ynysddu. *Cphy* 2E **33**
Ynysforgan. *Swan* 3F **31**
Ynyshir. *Rhon* 2D **32**
Ynyslas. *Cdgn* 1F **57**
Ynysmaerdy. *Rhon* 3D **32**
Ynysmeudwy. *Neat* 5H **45**
Ynystawe. *Swan* 5G **45**
Ynyswen. *Powy* 4B **46**
Ynyswen. *Rhon* 2C **32**
Ynys y Barri. *V Glam* 5E **32**
Ynysybwl. *Rhon* 2D **32**
Ynysymaerdy. *Neat* 3G **31**
Yockenthwaite. *N Yor* 2B **98**
Yockleton. *Shrp* 4F **71**
Yokefleet. *E Yor* 2B **94**
Yoker. *Glas* 3G **127**
Yonder Bognie. *Abers* 4C **160**
Yonderton. *Abers* 5G **161**
York. *York* 4A **100** & **203**
Yorkletts. *Kent* 4E **41**
Yorkley. *Glos* 5B **48**
Yorkshire Dales. *N Yor* 2H **97**
Yorton. *Shrp* 3H **71**
Yorton Heath. *Shrp* 3H **71**
Youlgreave.
Derbs 4G **85**
Youlthorpe. *E Yor* 4B **100**
Youlton. *N Yor* 3G **99**
Young's End. *Essx* 4H **53**
Young Wood. *Linc* 3A **88**
Yoxall. *Staf* 4F **73**
Yoxford. *Suff* 4F **67**
Yr Hob. *Flin* 5F **83**
Y Rhws. *V Glam* 5D **32**
Yr Wyddgrug. *Flin* 4E **83**
Ysbyty Cynfyn. *Cdgn* 3G **57**
Ysbyty Ifan. *Cnwy* 1H **69**
Ysbyty Ystwyth.
Cdgn 3G **57**
Ysceifiog. *Flin* 3D **82**
Yspitty. *Carm* 3E **31**
Ystalyfera. *Neat* 5A **46**
Ystrad. *Rhon* 2C **32**
Ystrad Aeron. *Cdgn* 5E **57**
Ystradfellte. *Powy* 4C **46**
Ystradffin. *Carm* 1A **46**
Ystradgynlais. *Powy* 4A **46**
Ystradmeurig. *Cdgn* 4G **57**
Ystrad Mynach.
Cphy 2E **33**
Ystradowen. *Carm* 4A **46**
Ystradowen. *V Glam* 4D **32**
Ystumtuen. *Cdgn* 3G **57**
Ythanbank. *Abers* 5G **161**
Ythanwells. *Abers* 5D **160**
Y Trallwng. *Powy* 5E **70**
Y Tymbl. *Carm* 4F **45**
Y Waun. *Wrex* 2E **71**

Z

Zeal Monachorum. *Devn* 2H **11**
Zeals. *Wilts* 3C **22**
Zelah. *Corn* 3C **6**
Zennor. *Corn* 3B **4**
Zouch. *Notts* 3C **74**

INDEX TO SELECTED PLACES OF INTEREST

(1) A strict alphabetical order is used e.g. Benmore Botanic Gdn. follows Ben Macdui but precedes Ben Nevis.

(2) Entries shown without a main map index reference have the name of the appropriate Town Plan and its page number;
e.g. Ashmolean Mus. of Art & Archaeology (OX1 2PH) . . . . **Oxford 200**
The Town Plan title is not given when this is included in the name of the Place of Interest.

(3) Entries in italics are not named on the map but are shown with a symbol only.
Entries in italics and enclosed in (brackets) are not shown on the map.
Where this occurs the nearest town or village may also be given, unless that name is already included in the name of the
Place of Interest.

SAT NAV POSTCODES

Postcodes (in brackets) are included as a navigation aid to assist Sat Nav users and are supplied on this basis.
It should be noted that postcodes have been selected by their proximity to the Place of Interest and that they may not form part of the
actual postal address. Drivers should follow the Tourist Brown Signs when available.

ABBREVIATIONS USED IN THIS INDEX

Garden : Gdn.   Museum : Mus.   Park : Pk.
Gardens : Gdns.   National : Nat

INDEX

A-Z Great Britain Road Atlas 233

Limited Interchange Motorway Junctions are shown on the mapping pages by red junction indicators **2**

Junction M1

2	Northbound	No exit, access from A1 only
	Southbound	No access, exit to A1 only
4	Northbound	No exit, access from A41 only
	Southbound	No access, exit to A41 only
6a	Northbound	No exit, access from M25 only
	Southbound	No access, exit to M25 only
17	Northbound	No access, exit to M45 only
	Southbound	No exit, access from M45 only
19	Northbound	Exit to M6 only, access from A14 only
	Southbound	Access from M6 only, exit to A14 only
21a	Northbound	No access, exit to A46 only
	Southbound	No exit, access from A46 only
24a	Northbound	Access from A50 only
	Southbound	Exit to A50 only
35a	Northbound	No access, exit to A616 only
	Southbound	No exit, access from A616 only
43	Northbound	Exit to M621 only
	Southbound	Access from M621 only
48	Eastbound	Exit to A1(M) northbound only
	Westbound	Access from A1(M) southbound only

Junction M2

1	Eastbound	Access from A2 eastbound only
	Westbound	Exit to A2 westbound only

Junction M3

8	Eastbound	No exit, access from A303 only
	Westbound	No access, exit to A303 only
10	Northbound	No access from A31
	Southbound	No exit to A31
13	Southbound	No access from A335 to M3 leading to M27 Eastbound

Junction M4

1	Eastbound	Exit to A4 eastbound only
	Westbound	Access from A4 westbound only
21	Eastbound	No exit to M48
	Westbound	No access from M48
23	Eastbound	No access from M48
	Westbound	No exit to M48
25	Eastbound	No exit
	Westbound	No access
25a	Eastbound	No exit
	Westbound	No access
29	Eastbound	No exit, access from A48(M) only
	Westbound	No access, exit to A48(M) only
38	Westbound	No access, exit to A48 only
39	Eastbound	No access or exit
	Westbound	No exit, access from A48 only
42	Eastbound	No access from A48
	Westbound	No exit to A48

Junction M5

10	Northbound	No exit, access from A4019 only
	Southbound	No access, exit to A4019 only
11a	Southbound	No exit to A417 westbound
18a	Northbound	No access from M49
	Southbound	No exit to M49

Junction M6

3a	Eastbound	No exit to M6 Toll
	Westbound	No access from M6 Toll
4	Northbound	No exit to M42 northbound
		No access from M42 southbound
	Southbound	No exit to M42
		No access from M42 northbound
4a	Northbound	No exit, access from M42 southbound only
	Southbound	No access, exit to M42 only
5	Northbound	No access, exit to A452 only
	Southbound	No exit, access from A452 only
10a	Northbound	No access, exit to M54 only
	Southbound	No exit, access from M54 only
11a	Northbound	No exit to M6 Toll
	Southbound	No access from M6 Toll
20	Northbound	No exit to M56 eastbound
	Southbound	No access from M56 westbound
24	Northbound	No exit, access from A58 only
	Southbound	No access, exit to A58 only
25	Northbound	No access, exit to A49 only
	Southbound	No exit, access from A49 only
30	Northbound	No exit, access from M61 northbound only
	Southbound	No access, exit to M61 southbound only
31a	Northbound	No access, exit to B6242 only
	Southbound	No exit, access from B6242 only
45	Northbound	No access onto A74(M)
	Southbound	No exit from A74(M)

Junction M6 Toll

T1	Northbound	No exit
	Southbound	No access
T2	Northbound	No access or exit
	Southbound	No access
T5	Northbound	No exit
	Southbound	No access
T7	Northbound	No access from A5
	Southbound	No exit
T8	Northbound	No access from A460 northbound
	Southbound	No exit

Junction M8

8	Eastbound	No exit to M73 northbound
	Westbound	No access from M73 southbound
9	Eastbound	No exit, access only
	Westbound	No exit, access only
13	Eastbound	No access from M80 southbound
	Westbound	No exit to M80 northbound
14	Eastbound	No exit, access only
	Westbound	No exit, access only
16	Eastbound	No exit, access only
	Westbound	No exit, access only
17	Eastbound	No exit, access from A82 only
	Westbound	No access, exit to A82 only
18	Westbound	No exit, access only
19	Eastbound	No exit to A814 eastbound
	Westbound	No access from A814 westbound
20	Eastbound	No exit, access only
	Westbound	No exit, access only
21	Eastbound	No exit, access only
	Westbound	No exit, access only
22	Eastbound	No exit, access from M77 only
	Westbound	No access, exit to M77 only
23	Eastbound	No exit, access from B768 only
	Westbound	No access, exit to B768 only
25	Eastbound &	Access from A739 southbound only
	Westbound	Exit to A739 northbound only
25a	Eastbound	Access only
	Westbound	Exit only
28	Eastbound	No exit, access from airport only
	Westbound	No access, exit to airport only

Junction M9

2	Northbound	No exit, access from B8046 only
	Southbound	No access, exit to B8046 only
3	Northbound	No access, exit to A803 only
	Southbound	No exit, access from A803 only
6	Northbound	No access only
	Southbound	No access, exit to A905 only
8	Northbound	No access, exit to M876 only
	Southbound	No exit, access from M876 only
Junction with A90	Northbound	Exit onto A90 westbound only
	Southbound	Access from A90 eastbound only

Junction M11

4	Northbound	No exit, access from A406 eastbound only
	Southbound	No access, exit to A406 westbound only
5	Northbound	No access, exit to A1168 only
	Southbound	No exit, access from A1168 only
8a	Northbound	No access, exit only
	Southbound	No exit, access only
9	Northbound	No exit, access only
	Southbound	No exit, access only
13	Northbound	No access, exit only
	Southbound	No exit, access only
14	Northbound	No access from A428 eastbound
		No exit to A428 westbound
	Southbound	No exit, access from A428 eastbound only

Junction M20

2	Eastbound	No access, exit to A20 only (access via M26 Junction 2a)
	Westbound	No exit, access only (exit via M26 Jun.2a)
3	Eastbound	No exit, access from M26 eastbound only
	Westbound	No access, exit to M26 westbound only
11a	Eastbound	No access from Channel Tunnel
	Westbound	No exit to Channel Tunnel

Junction M23

7	Northbound	No exit to A23 southbound
	Southbound	No access from A23 northbound

Junction M25

5	Clockwise	No exit to M26 eastbound
	Anti-clockwise	No access from M26 westbound
Spur to A21	Northbound	No access from M26 eastbound
	Southbound	No exit to M26 westbound
19	Clockwise	No exit, access only
	Anti-clockwise	No exit, access only
21	Clockwise &	No exit to M1 southbound
	Anti-clockwise	No access from M1 northbound
31	Northbound	No access, exit only (access via Jun.30)
	Southbound	No exit, access only (exit via Jun.30)

M26

Junction with M25 (M25 Jun.5)

Eastbound	No access from M25 clockwise or spur from A21 northbound
Westbound	No exit to M25 anti-clockwise or spur to A21 southbound

Junction with M20 (M20 Jun.3)

Eastbound	No exit to M20 westbound
Westbound	No access from M20 eastbound

Junction M27

4	Eastbound &	No exit to A33 southbound (Southampton)
	Westbound	No access from A33 northbound
10	Eastbound	No exit, access from A32 only
	Westbound	No access, exit to A32 only

M40 continued

7	N.W bound	No access, exit only
	S.E bound	No exit, access only
13	N.W bound	No exit, access only
	S.E bound	No access, exit only
14	N.W bound	No exit, access only
	S.E bound	No access, exit only
16	N.W bound	No access, exit only
	S.E bound	No exit, access only

Junction M42

1	Eastbound	No exit
	Westbound	No access
7	Northbound	No access, exit to M6 only
	Southbound	No exit, access from M6 northbound only
8	Northbound	No exit, access from M6 southbound only
	Southbound	Exit to M6 northbound only
		Access from M6 southbound only

M45

Junction with M1 (M1 Jun.17)

Eastbound	No access to M1 northbound
Westbound	No access from M1 southbound

Junction with A45 east of Dunchurch

Eastbound	No access, exit to A45 only
Westbound	No exit, access from A45 northbound only

M48

Junction with M4 (M4 Jun.21)

Eastbound	No exit to M4 westbound
Westbound	No access from M4 eastbound

Junction with M4 (M4 Jun.23)

Eastbound	No access from M4 westbound
Westbound	No exit to M4 eastbound

Junction M53

11	Northbound & Southbound	No access from M56 eastbound, no exit to M56 westbound

Junction M56

1	Eastbound	No exit to M60 N.W bound
		No exit to A34 southbound
	S.E bound	No access from A34 northbound
	Westbound	No access from M60
2	Eastbound	No exit, access from A560 only
	Westbound	No access, exit to A560 only
3	Eastbound	No access, exit only
	Westbound	No exit, access only
4	Eastbound	No exit, access only
	Westbound	No access, exit only
7	Westbound	No exit, access only
8	Eastbound	No access or exit
	Westbound	No access from A556 only
9	Eastbound	No access from M6 northbound
	Westbound	No exit to M60 southbound
10a	Northbound	No access, exit only
	Southbound	No exit, access only
15	Eastbound	No exit to M53
	Westbound	No access from M53

Junction M57

3	Northbound	No access, exit only
	Southbound	No exit, access only
5	Northbound	No exit, access from A580 westbound only
	Southbound	No access, exit to A580 eastbound only

Junction M58

1	Eastbound	No exit, access from A506 only
	Westbound	No access, exit to A506 only

Junction M60

2	N.E bound	No access, exit to A560 only
	S.W bound	No exit, access from A560 only
3	Eastbound	No access from A34 southbound
	Westbound	No exit to A34 northbound
4	Eastbound	No exit to M56 S.W bound
		No exit to A34 northbound
	Westbound	No access from A34 southbound
		No access from M56 eastbound
5	N.W bound	No access from or exit to A5103 southbound
	S.E bound	No access from or exit to A5103 northbound
14	Eastbound	No exit to A580
		No access from A580 westbound
	Westbound	No exit to A580 eastbound
		No access from A580
16	Eastbound	No exit, access from A666 only
	Westbound	No access, exit to A666 only
20	Eastbound	No access from A664
	Westbound	No exit to A664
22	Westbound	No access from A62
25	S.W bound	No access from A560 / A6017
26	N.E bound	No access or exit
27	N.E bound	No access, exit only
	S.W bound	No exit, access only

Junction M61

2&3	N.W bound	No access from A580 eastbound
	S.E bound	No exit to A580 westbound

Junction with M6 (M6 Jun.30)

N.W bound	No exit to M6 southbound
S.E bound	No access from M6 northbound

Junction M62

23	Eastbound	No access, exit to A640 only
	Westbound	No exit, access from A640 only

Junction M65

9	N.E bound	No access, exit to A679 only
	S.W bound	No exit, access from A679 only
11	N.E bound	No access, exit only
	S.W bound	No exit, access only

Junction M66

1	Northbound	No access, exit to A56 only
	Southbound	No exit, access from A56 only

Junction M67

1	Eastbound	Access from A57 eastbound only
	Westbound	Exit to A57 westbound only
1a	Eastbound	No access, exit to A6017 only
	Westbound	No exit, access from A6017 only
2	Eastbound	No exit, access from A57 only
	Westbound	No access, exit to A57 only

Junction M69

2	N.E bound	No exit, access from B4669 only
	S.W bound	No access, exit to B4669 only

Junction M73

1	Southbound	No exit to A721 eastbound
2	Northbound	No access from M8 eastbound
		No exit to A89 eastbound
	Southbound	No exit to M8 eastbound
		No access from A89 westbound
3	Northbound	No exit to A80 S.W bound
	Southbound	No access from A80 N.E bound

Junction M74

1	Eastbound	No access from M8 Westbound
	Westbound	No exit to M8 Westbound
3	Eastbound	No exit
	Westbound	No access
3a	Eastbound	No access
	Westbound	No exit
7	Northbound	No exit, access from A72 only
	Southbound	No access, exit to A72 only
9	Northbound	No access or exit
	Southbound	No access from B7078 only
10	Southbound	No access from B7078 only
11	Northbound	No exit, access from B7078 only
	Southbound	No access, exit to B7078 only
12	Northbound	No access, exit to A70 only
	Southbound	No exit, access from A70 only

Junction M77

Junction with M8 (M8 Jun.22)

	Northbound	No exit to M8 westbound
	Southbound	No access from M8 eastbound
4	Northbound	No exit
	Southbound	No access
6	Northbound	No exit to A77
	Southbound	No access from A77
7	Northbound	No access from A77
		No exit to A77

Junction M80

1	Northbound	No access from M8 westbound
	Southbound	No exit to M8 eastbound
4a	Northbound	No access
	Southbound	No exit
6a	Northbound	No exit
	Southbound	No access
8	Northbound	No access from M876
	Southbound	No exit to M876

Junction M90

2a	Northbound	No access, exit to A92 only
	Southbound	No exit, access from A92 only
7	Northbound	No exit, access from A91 only
	Southbound	No access, exit to A91 only
8	Northbound	No access, exit to A91 only
	Southbound	No exit, access from A91 only
10	Northbound	No access from A912
		Exit to A912 northbound only
	Southbound	No exit to A912
		Access from A912 southbound only

Junction M180

1	Eastbound	No access, exit only
	Westbound	No exit, access from A18 only

Junction M606

2	Northbound	No access, exit only

Junction M621

2a	Eastbound	No exit, access only
	Westbound	No access, exit only
4	Southbound	No exit
5	Northbound	No access, exit to A61 only
	Southbound	No exit, access from A61 only
6	Northbound	No exit, access only
	Southbound	No access, exit only
7	Eastbound	No access, exit only
	Westbound	No exit, access only
8	Eastbound	No access, exit only
	Westbound	No exit, access only

Junction M876

Junction with M80 (M80 Jun.5)

N.E bound	No access from M80 southbound
S.W bound	No exit to M80 northbound

Junction with M9 (M9 Jun.8)

N.E bound	No exit to M9 northbound
S.W bound	No access from M9 southbound

Junction A1(M)

Hertfordshire Section

2	Northbound	No access, exit only
	Southbound	No access from A1001 only
3	Northbound	No access, exit only
	Southbound	No access, exit only
5	Northbound	No exit, access only
	Southbound	No access or exit

Cambridgeshire Section

14	Northbound	No exit, access only
	Southbound	No access, exit only

Leeds Section

40	Southbound	Exit to A1 southbound only

43	Northbound	Access from M1 eastbound only
	Southbound	Exit to M1 westbound only

Durham Section

57	Northbound	No access, exit to A66(M)
	Southbound	No exit, access from A66(M)
65	Northbound	Exit to A1 N.W bound and to A194(M) only
	Southbound	Access from A1 S.E bound and from A194(M) only

Junction A3(M)

4	Northbound	No exit, access only
	Southbound	No exit, access only

Aston Expressway A38(M)

Junction with Victoria Road, Aston

Northbound	No access, exit only
Southbound	No exit, access only

Junction A48(M)

Junction with M4 (M4 Jun.29)

N.E bound	Exit to M4 eastbound only
S.W bound	Access from M4 westbound only

29a	N.E bound	Access from A48 eastbound only
	S.W bound	Exit to A48 westbound only

Mancunian Way A57(M)

Junction with A34 Brook Street, Manchester

Eastbound	No access, exit to A34 Brook Street, southbound only
Westbound	No exit, access only

Leeds Inner Ring Road A58(M)

Junction with Park Lane / Westgate

Southbound	No access, exit only

Leeds Inner Ring Road A64(M) (continuation of A58(M))

Junction with A58 Clay Pit Lane

Eastbound	No access, exit only
Westbound	No exit

A66(M)

Junction with A1(M) (A1(M) Jun.57)

N.E bound	Access from A1(M) northbound only
S.W bound	Exit to A1(M) southbound only

Junction A74(M)

18	Northbound	No access
	Southbound	No exit

Newcastle Central Motorway A167(M)

Junction with Camden Street

Northbound	No exit, access only
Southbound	No access or exit

A194(M)

Junction with A1(M) (A1(M) Jun.65) and A1 Gateshead Western By-Pass

Northbound	Access from A1(M) only
Southbound	Exit to A1(M) only

Northern Ireland

Junction M1

3	Northbound	No access, exit only
	Southbound	No access, exit only
7	Westbound	No access, exit only

Junction M2

2	Eastbound	No access to M5 northbound
	Westbound	No exit to M5 southbound

Junction M5

2	Northbound	No access from M2 eastbound
	Southbound	No exit to M2 westbound